The
GOOD HOUSEKEEPING
ALL COLOUR
COOK BOOK

The
GOOD HOUSEKEEPING
ALL COLOUR
COOK BOOK

OVER 300 RECIPES STEP BY STEP

EBURY PRESS LONDON

Published by Ebury Press
Division of The National Magazine Company Ltd
Colquhoun House
27–37 Broadwick Street
London W1V 1FR

First impression 1989

The Good Housekeeping Institute is the food and consumer research centre of
Good Housekeeping magazine.

ISBN 0 85223 788 X

Photography by Jan Baldwin, Martin Brigdale, Laurie Evans, John Heseltine,
James Jackson, David Johnson, Paul Kemp

Cover photograph by Tim Hill, with styling by Zoe Hill, shows
Mozzarella, Avocado and Tomato Salad (page 372), Crown Roast of Lamb (page 143) and
Glazed Fruit Tarts (page 431)

Drawings by Kate Simunek, John Woodcock, Bill le Fever

Printed and bound in Italy by New Interlitho S.p.a., Milan

CONTENTS

COOKERY NOTES

Follow either metric or imperial measures for the recipes in this book as they are not inter-changeable. Sets of spoon measures are available in both metric and imperial size to give accurate measurement of small quantities. All spoon measures are level unless otherwise stated. When measuring milk we have used the exact conversion of 568 ml (1 pint).

* Size 4 eggs should be used except when otherwise stated.
† Granulated sugar is used un-less otherwise stated.
● Plain flour is used unless otherwise stated.

OVEN TEMPERATURE CHART

°C	°F	Gas mark
110	225	$\frac{1}{4}$
130	250	$\frac{1}{2}$
140	275	1
150	300	2
170	325	3
180	350	4
190	375	5
200	400	6
220	425	7
230	450	8
240	475	9

KEY TO SYMBOLS

$\boxed{1.00*}$ Indicates minimum preparation and cooking times in hours and minutes. They do not include prepared items in the list of ingredients; calcu-lated times apply only to the method. An asterisk * indicates extra time should be allowed, so check the note below symbols.

⌂ Chef's hats indicate degree of difficulty of a recipe: no hat means it is straightforward; one hat slightly more complicated; two hats indicates that it is for more advanced cooks.

＊ Indicates that a recipe will freeze. If there is no symbol, the recipe is unsuitable for freezing. An asterisk * indicates special freezer instructions so check the note immediately below the symbols.

$\boxed{309\ cals}$ Indicates calories per serving, including any sugges-tions (e.g. cream, to serve) given in the ingredients.

METRIC CONVERSION SCALE

LIQUID

Imperial	Exact conversion	Recommended ml
$\frac{1}{4}$ pint	142 ml	150 ml
$\frac{1}{2}$ pint	284 ml	300 ml
1 pint	568 ml	600 ml
$1\frac{1}{2}$ pints	851 ml	900 ml
$1\frac{3}{4}$ pints	992 ml	1 litre

For quantities of $1\frac{3}{4}$ pints and over, litres and fractions of a litre have been used.

SOLID

Imperial	Exact conversion	Recommended g
1 oz	28.35 g	25 g
2 oz	56.7 g	50 g
4 oz	113.4 g	100 g
8 oz	226.8 g	225 g
12 oz	340.2 g	350 g
14 oz	397.0 g	400 g
16 oz (1 lb)	453.6 g	450 g

1 kilogram (kg) equals 2.2 lb.

INTRODUCTION

This bumper cookbook is packed with imaginative dishes that all the family will enjoy. In addition to recipes for everyday meals there are recipes for all those special family occasions. Every possible mealtime is covered—from snacks and suppers to main courses, desserts and barbecues.

Every one of the 335 recipes in the main section of the book is illustrated with a colour photograph so that you can see at a glance the finished dishes. There are also helpful step-by-step illustrations to guide you smoothly through the method, ensuring that all the recipes are simple to follow. Special symbols indicate how long each recipe takes to make, the degree of difficulty involved, whether it will freeze and the calorie count. What's more, all the recipes have been double-tested so you can be absolutely sure of achieving successful results every time.

At the back of the book you will find page after page of helpful information and basic recipes. Cooking techniques, methods and equipment are all explained, in addition to advice on choosing ingredients, how to get the best out of your freezer, plus handy hints and tricks of the trade to enable you to give a professional touch to all your cooking.

We hope very much that you enjoy these recipes and feel sure that they will become all-time family favourites.

Soups

AVGOLEMONO

0.35	🥛	98 cals

Serves 4

1.5 litres (2½ pints) homemade
  chicken stock
50 g (2 oz) long grain rice
2 egg yolks
100 ml (4 fl oz) freshly squeezed
  lemon juice
salt and freshly ground pepper
lemon slices and coriander sprigs,
  to garnish

1 Bring the stock to the boil in a
large saucepan. Add the rice
and simmer uncovered for 20
minutes until the rice is cooked.

2 Put the egg yolks and lemon
juice in a bowl and whisk in a
few tablespoonfuls of the hot
chicken stock.

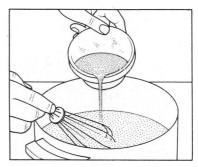

3 Pour the mixture gradually
into the pan of stock, whisking
all the time. Simmer gently without boiling for a few minutes, then
add salt and pepper to taste.

4 Pour into warmed individual
bowls and garnish each one
with a lemon slice and a sprig of
coriander. Serve hot.

Menu Suggestion
Serve this tangy, lemon–flavoured
soup with hot pitta bread before a
main course of chicken or lamb.

CHINESE-STYLE HOT AND SOUR SOUP

| 0.30 🍴 | ✳ 136 cals |

Serves 4

225 g (8 oz) button mushrooms
100 ml (4 fl oz) medium dry sherry
75 ml (5 tbsp) soy sauce
30 ml (2 tbsp) chopped fresh
  coriander
225 g (8 oz) cooked chicken or pork
125 g (4 oz) spring onions
125 g (4.4 oz) jar whole baby
  sweetcorn
75 ml (5 tbsp) white wine vinegar
freshly ground pepper

1 Slice the mushrooms thinly. Place in a large saucepan with the sherry, soy sauce, coriander and 1.1 litres (2 pints) water. Bring to the boil. Simmer, uncovered, for 15 minutes.

2 Thinly shred the chicken (or finely dice the pork) and spring onions. Thinly slice the sweetcorn.

3 Stir the prepared meat and vegetables into the mushroom mixture, with the wine vinegar and season to taste with pepper. Simmer for a further 5 minutes. Serve hot.

Menu Suggestion
Serve with prawn crackers for a Chinese-style meal. Follow with spareribs or a stir-fried dish of meat and vegetables.

GOULASH SOUP WITH CARAWAY DUMPLINGS

2.45 | ✳* | 515–772 cals

* freeze without dumplings

Serves 4–6

700 g (1½ lb) silverside or lean chuck
    steak

salt and freshly ground pepper

25 g (1 oz) butter

2 onions, skinned and chopped

1 small green pepper, seeded and
    chopped

4 tomatoes, skinned and quartered

141-g (5-oz) can tomato paste

600 ml (1 pint) rich beef stock

15 ml (1 tbsp) paprika

450 g (1 lb) potatoes, peeled

100 g (4 oz) self-raising flour

50 g (2 oz) shredded suet

5 ml (1 tsp) caraway seeds

chopped fresh parsley, to garnish

142 ml (5 fl oz) soured cream

1 Remove any excess fat or
gristle from the silverside or
chuck steak and cut the meat into
small pieces. Season well.

2 Melt the butter in a large
saucepan, add the onions and
green pepper and sauté for 10
minutes until tender.

3 Add the meat pieces, tomatoes,
tomato paste, stock and
paprika. Stir well and bring to the
boil. Reduce the heat, cover and
simmer for 2½ hours, stirring
occasionally.

4 Half an hour before the end of
cooking, cut the potatoes into
bite-sized pieces, bring to the boil
in salted water and simmer until
cooked. Drain well and add to the
soup while it is simmering.

5 Make the dumplings. Put the
flour, suet, caraway seeds and
seasoning in a bowl and add
enough cold water to form a firm
mixture. Roll into about sixteen
small dumplings.

6 Twenty minutes before end of
cooking, drop dumplings into
the soup, cover and simmer until
the dumplings are cooked.

7 Garnish with chopped parsley
and serve the soured cream
separately, for each person to
spoon into their soup.

Menu Suggestion
Serve with fresh French bread and
butter and a tossed green salad.

GOULASH

Goulash soup is simply a more
liquid version of goulash, with a
similar base of meat and potatoes
for easy eating. Both are popular
in Austria and Hungary—no-one
is quite sure in which country
the recipe first originated.

Austrian goulash is usually a
simple dish made with beef and
potatoes, while Hungarian
goulash is often made with veal
and far more ingredients—
usually red and green peppers
and mushrooms, sometimes
sauerkraut and smoked pork
sausage as well. Four ingredients
which are common to all goulash
recipes are caraway seeds, onions,
paprika and tomatoes—the latter
giving the dish its characteristic
bright red colour. Dumplings
and soured cream are optional
extras.

WATERCRESS SOUP

0.25	✳	325 cals

Serves 4

100 g (4 oz) butter or margarine

1 medium onion, skinned and chopped

2 bunches watercress

50 g (2 oz) plain flour

750 ml (1¼ pints) chicken or veal stock

300 ml (½ pint) milk

salt and freshly ground pepper

1 Melt the butter in a saucepan, add the onion and cook gently for 10 minutes until soft but not coloured.

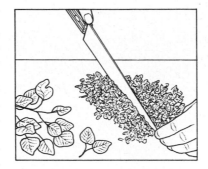

2 Meanwhile, wash and trim the watercress, leaving some of the stem, then chop roughly.

3 Add the chopped watercress to the onion, cover the pan with a lid and cook gently for a further 4 minutes.

4 Add the flour and cook gently, stirring, for 1–2 minutes. Remove from the heat and gradually blend in the stock and milk. Bring to the boil, stirring constantly then, simmer for 3 minutes. Season to taste.

5 Sieve or purée the soup in a blender or food processor. Return to the rinsed-out pan and reheat gently, without boiling. Taste and adjust seasoning, if necessary. Serve hot.

Menu Suggestion
Watercress soup makes a delicious starter for a winter dinner party. Follow it with roast game and end with fruity dessert.

CREAM OF CARROT WITH ORANGE SOUP

0.55	🏺	✳	73–110 cals

Serves 4–6

25 g (1 oz) butter or margarine

700 g (1½ lb) carrots, peeled and sliced

225 g (8 oz) onion, skinned and sliced

1 litre (1¾ pints) chicken or ham stock

salt and freshly ground pepper

1 orange

1 Melt the butter in a saucepan, add the vegetables and cook gently for 10 minutes until softened slightly.

2 Add the stock and bring to the boil. Lower the heat, cover and simmer for about 40 minutes, or until the vegetables are tender.

3 Sieve or purée the vegetables with half of the stock in a blender or food processor. Add this mixture to the stock remaining in the pan.

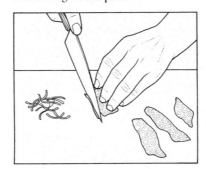

4 Meanwhile, pare half of the orange rind thinly, using a potato peeler, then cut it into shreds. Cook the shreds in gently boiling water until tender.

5 Finely grate the remaining orange rind into the soup. Stir well to combine with the ingredients in the pan.

6 Squeeze the juice of the orange into the pan. Reheat the soup gently, then taste and adjust seasoning. Drain the shreds of orange rind and use to garnish the soup just before serving. Serve hot.

Menu Suggestion
This is an everyday soup made from basic ingredients, but the orange rind and juice give a delicious 'kick' to the flavour. Serve for an informal family meal.

FRENCH ONION SOUP

1.15	🍶	✳	388 cals

Serves 4

50 g (2 oz) butter

15 ml (1 tbsp) vegetable oil

450 g (1 lb) onions, skinned and finely sliced

2.5 ml (½ tsp) sugar

salt and freshly ground pepper

15 ml (1 tbsp) plain flour

1 litre (1¾ pints) beef stock

150 ml (¼ pint) dry white wine

75 g (3 oz) Gruyère, grated

4 slices French bread, toasted on both sides

45 ml (3 tbsp) brandy

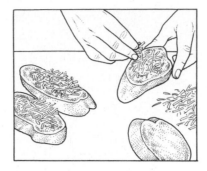

1 Melt the butter with the oil in a large, heavy-based saucepan. Add the onions, stir well, cover and cook gently, stirring occasionally, for 20 minutes.

2 When the onions are completely soft, add the sugar and a pinch of salt and increase the heat to high. Cook for about 2 minutes until the onions caramelise slightly. Stir in the flour and cook for 1 minute until light brown.

3 Stir in the stock and wine, add pepper to taste and bring to the boil. Lower the heat, half cover with a lid and simmer for 40 minutes.

4 Pile a little grated Gruyère onto each round of toasted bread and brown lightly under a preheated grill.

5 Add the brandy to the soup. Stir well, then taste and adjust seasoning. Pour into warmed soup bowls and float the pieces of toasted bread on top. Serve immediately.

Menu Suggestion

French Onion Soup is very filling, so serve before a light French main course such as lamb cutlets grilled with rosemary and herb butter. Alternatively, serve the soup on its own as a supper or lunchtime dish, with crusty fresh French bread.

FRENCH ONION SOUP

Soupe à l'oignon gratinée, as the French call this soup, was made famous in Les Halles, the fruit and vegetable market that used to be in the centre of Paris. In the days when Les Halles was a bustling, lively market, the traders would finish their night's work by calling into one of the numerous cafés or bars and having a bowl of onion soup to revive them. Although onion soup is not exactly the sort of dish you would normally think of eating in the early hours of the morning, it is certainly very sustaining, especially in cold wintry weather. Now that Les Halles no longer exists as a market, Parisian bistros have made the soup their own speciality, and if you visit Paris you will see it on restaurant menus everywhere.

CRÈME DUBARRY

| 0.55 | ✳ | 210 cals |

Serves 4

1 firm cauliflower
40 g (1½ oz) butter or margarine
45 ml (3 tbsp) plain flour
900 ml (1½ pints) chicken or veal
  stock
salt and freshly ground white
  pepper
150 ml (¼ pint) single cream
pinch of grated nutmeg

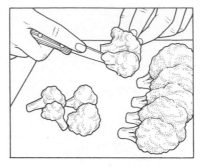

1 Divide the cauliflower into
small sprigs, discarding the
green leaves. Wash thoroughly.

2 Melt the butter in a saucepan,
add the flour and cook gently
for 1–2 minutes. Remove from the
heat and gradually blend in the
stock. Bring to the boil, stirring
constantly, then simmer for 3
minutes until thick and smooth.

3 Add the cauliflower to the pan,
reserving about 12 well-shaped
tiny sprigs. Add salt and pepper to
taste, cover and simmer for about
30 minutes.

4 Meanwhile, cook the reserved
cauliflower sprigs in boiling
salted water for about 10 minutes,
until tender but not broken. Drain
thoroughly.

5 Sieve or purée the soup in a
blender or food processor.
Return to the rinsed-out pan, stir
in the cream and nutmeg and
reheat gently, without boiling.
Taste and adjust seasoning. Serve
hot, garnished with the
cauliflower sprigs.

Menu Suggestion
This creamy cauliflower soup is a
French classic. Serve for a party
before a main course of lamb.

CURRIED POTATO AND APPLE SOUP

0.50	✳*	267 cals

* freeze at step 3, after puréeing

Serves 4

50 g (2 oz) butter or margarine

4 medium old potatoes, peeled and diced

2 eating apples, peeled, cored and diced

10 ml (2 tsp) curry powder

1.2 litres (2 pints) vegetable stock or water

salt and freshly ground pepper

150 ml (¼ pint) natural yogurt, at room temperature

1 Melt the butter or margarine in a large saucepan. Add the potatoes and apples and fry gently for about 10 minutes until lightly coloured, shaking the pan and stirring frequently.

2 Add the curry powder and fry gently for 1–2 minutes, stirring. Pour in the stock or water and bring to the boil. Add salt and pepper to taste. Lower the heat, cover the pan and simmer for 20–25 minutes or until the potatoes and apples are really soft.

3 Sieve or purée the soup in a blender or food processor, then return to the rinsed-out pan.

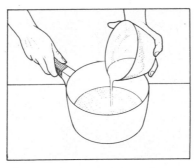

4 Stir the yogurt until smooth, then pour half into the soup. Heat through, stirring constantly, then taste and adjust seasoning.

5 Pour the hot soup into warmed individual bowls and swirl in the remaining yogurt. Serve immediately.

Menu Suggestion

This soup is delicately spiced, with a sweet flavour of apples. Serve with crisp poppadoms and chilled lager for an informal supper or lunch.

CURRIED POTATO AND APPLE SOUP

It is important to fry the curry powder in step 2 of the recipe, or the spices will taste raw in the finished soup. Natural yogurt has a tendency to curdle when stirred into very hot liquids. This problem can be overcome if the yogurt is brought to room temperature and stirred well before use.

CHICKEN AND SWEETCORN CHOWDER

| 1.45 | ✳* | 331 cals |

* freeze after step 4

Serves 6

1.6 kg (3½ lb) chicken

1 litre (1¾ pints) water

salt and freshly ground pepper

1 stick of celery, roughly chopped

1 parsley sprig

1 medium onion, skinned and roughly chopped

1 bay leaf

10 peppercorns

two 335-g (11.8-oz) cans sweetcorn, drained

6 hard-boiled eggs

45 ml (3 tbsp) chopped fresh parsley

150 ml (5 fl oz) single cream, to serve

1 Place the chicken in a large saucepan with the water, salt, celery, parsley sprig, onion, bay leaf and peppercorns.

2 Bring to the boil and simmer gently for 1–1½ hours until the chicken is completely tender.

3 When cooked, remove the chicken from the pan and cut the meat into large bite-size pieces. Discard skin and bones.

4 Strain the chicken stock, return it to the saucepan and add the chicken flesh and sweetcorn and simmer for about 5 minutes.

5 Chop the hard-boiled eggs. Add to the soup with the chopped parsley and salt and pepper to taste. Heat through gently, then pour into warmed individual bowls.

6 Swirl cream into each portion and serve the chicken and sweetcorn chowder immediately.

Menu Suggestion
This is a substantial meal-in-itself soup. Serve for a warming supper with garlic bread or French bread and butter, and a sharp, hard cheese such as Farmhouse Cheddar.

CHICKEN AND SWEETCORN CHOWDER

Chowder is a traditional American dish, which originally described thick and chunky fish soups. Nowadays the term is used more loosely and a chowder can be made from a variety of ingredients as long as the finished dish is a cross between a soup and a stew. Juicy, yellow sweetcorn is a common addition to many chowders.

If time is short, you can make a quick chicken chowder by using ready-cooked chicken, skinned, boned and cut into pieces. Simmer them in 900 ml (1½ pints) stock (made from a cube if necessary), with the vegetables and seasonings in the recipe above for 20 minutes. Drain, discarding the vegetables and seasonings and simmer the chicken pieces and stock with the sweetcorn for 5 minutes, then follow the recipe exactly as from step 5.

WINTER VEGETABLE SOUP

1.45	✳	446 cals

Serves 4

10 ml (2 tsp) lemon juice

225 g (8 oz) Jerusalem artichokes

½ small cabbage, washed

450 g (1 lb) carrots, peeled

225 g (8 oz) turnips, peeled

2 onions, skinned, or 2 leeks, trimmed and washed

2–3 celery sticks, trimmed

1 rasher of bacon, rinded and chopped

75 g (3 oz) dripping or butter

100 g (4 oz) haricot beans, soaked in cold water overnight and drained

bouquet garni

brown stock or water

salt and freshly ground pepper

chopped parsley and grated cheese, to serve

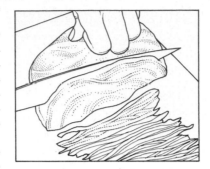

1 Fill a bowl with cold water and pour the lemon juice into it to acidulate it. Peel the artichokes, slice them and then cut them into strips. Drop them into the acidulated water as you work, to prevent them from discoloring.

2 Shred the cabbage coarsely, discarding all thick or woody stalks. Cut the remaining vegetables into fairly small pieces.

3 In a large saucepan, dry fry the bacon lightly. Add the dripping and heat gently until melted, then add all the vegetables (except the cabbage and beans) and fry for about 10 minutes, stirring, until soft but not coloured. Add the beans, bouquet garni and enough stock or water to cover. Add plenty of pepper and bring to the boil, then lower the heat, cover with a lid and simmer for 45 minutes to 1 hour.

4 Add the cabbage and salt to taste. Cook for a further 20–30 minutes, adding more liquid as required. When all the ingredients are soft, discard the bouquet garni and taste and adjust seasoning.

5 Serve the soup hot, sprinkled with freshly chopped parsley and grated cheese handed separately.

Menu Suggestion
This is a really substantial soup, best served as a meal in itself, with crusty French bread or crisp bread rolls. If you like, you can serve it with wedges of cheese as well. A sharp farmhouse Cheddar would hold its own against the definite flavours in the soup —so too would Stilton, if you prefer a blue cheese.

SPICED LENTIL AND CARROT SOUP

0.35	✳	171 cals

Serves 4

50 g (2 oz) butter or margarine
200 g (7 oz) carrots, peeled and grated
1 medium onion, skinned and finely sliced
10 whole green cardamoms
50 g (2 oz) lentils
1.2 litres (2 pints) chicken stock
salt and freshly ground pepper
parsley sprigs, to garnish

1 Melt the butter in a heavy-based saucepan, add the carrots and onion and cook gently for 4–5 minutes.

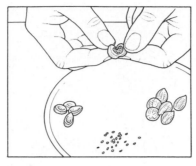

2 Meanwhile, split each cardamom and remove the black seeds. Crush the seeds in a pestle and mortar, or use the end of a rolling pin on a wooden board.

3 Add the crushed cardamom seeds to the vegetables with the lentils. Cook, stirring, for a further 1–2 minutes.

4 Add the chicken stock and bring to the boil. Lower the heat, cover the pan with a lid and simmer gently for about 20 minutes, or until the lentils are just tender. Season to taste with salt and freshly ground pepper. Serve hot garnished with parsley sprigs.

Menu Suggestion
This is a substantial soup for cold, wintry days. Serve for a family supper, with melted cheese on toast.

——— VARIATION ———

Use **ham stock** instead of chicken and add a **ham bone** with the stock, removing it before serving. Scrape the ham off the bone and return to the soup.

SPLIT PEA AND HAM SOUP

2.00	✳	332 cals

Serves 4

2 pig's trotters, split (optional)
1 ham bone
225 g (8 oz) dried green split peas, soaked overnight in 900 ml (1½ pints) water
225 g (8 oz) potatoes, peeled and sliced
3 whole leeks, trimmed, sliced and washed
3 celery sticks, sliced, with leaves reserved
salt and freshly ground pepper
30 ml (2 tbsp) chopped fresh parsley
about 175 g (6 oz) cooked ham, diced

1 Place the pig's trotters (if using) and the ham bone in a large saucepan. Cover with 900 ml (1½ pints) water and bring to the boil. Skim off any scum with a slotted spoon, then lower the heat and simmer for 1 hour.

2 Add the peas and their soaking water. Continue to cook for about 20 minutes.

3 Add the sliced potatoes, leeks (including green parts) and celery and continue cooking for another 40 minutes until the peas are soft. Season to taste with salt and freshly ground pepper.

4 Remove the ham bone and trotters from the pan. Scrape the meat from the bones, discarding fat and gristle. Return the meat to the soup.

5 Thin the soup, if necessary, with a little extra liquid. Chop most of the reserved celery leaves and add to the soup with the parsley and diced ham. Heat through, then taste and adjust seasoning. Serve hot garnished with the celery leaves.

Menu Suggestion
An old-fashioned soup, which is both nutritious and warming. Serve it for a winter lunch or early evening supper, with fresh wholemeal or granary bread rolls.

SPLIT PEA AND HAM SOUP
Pig's trotters are an old-fashioned ingredient which are not always easy to come by. Traditional butchers may sell them, but you may have to order in advance. Although not essential to the soup, they do make a wonderfully tasty and gelatinous stock.

CHICKEN AND PASTA BROTH

| 0.55 | 131–197 cals |

Serves 4–6

two 275 g (10 oz) chicken portions

1–2 small leeks, trimmed, sliced and washed

2 carrots, peeled and thinly sliced

900 ml (1½ pints) chicken stock

1 bouquet garni

salt and freshly ground pepper

50 g (2 oz) small pasta shapes

60 ml (4 tbsp) chopped fresh parsley, to garnish

1 Put the chicken portions in a large pan. Add the leeks and carrots, then pour in the stock and 900 ml (1½ pints) water. Bring to the boil.

2 Add the bouquet garni and salt and pepper to taste, then lower the heat, cover the pan and simmer for 30 minutes until the chicken is tender. Remove the chicken from the liquid and leave until cool enough to handle.

3 Meanwhile, add the pasta to the pan, bring back to the boil and simmer for 15 minutes, stirring occasionally, until tender.

4 Remove the chicken from the bones and cut the flesh into bite-sized pieces, discarding all skin. Return to the pan and heat through. Discard the bouquet garni and taste and adjust seasoning. Serve hot in warmed soup bowls, each one sprinkled with 15 ml (1 tbsp) parsley.

Menu Suggestion

With meat, vegetables and pasta in one dish, this soup makes a hearty first course or even a meal in itself. If serving it as a first course, be sure to follow with something light such as fish.

SMOKED FISH CHOWDER

0.40	✳	261 cals

Serves 4 as a main meal

1 large onion, skinned

225 g (8 oz) potato, peeled

125 g (4 oz) celery, trimmed and finely chopped

450 g (1 lb) smoked haddock fillet, skinned

568 ml (1 pint) milk

salt and freshly ground pepper

15 ml (1 tbsp) lemon juice

paprika, to garnish

3 Using a slotted spoon, lift the fish out of the pan. Discard the fish bones and flake the flesh.

4 Return the flaked fish to the pan. Add the lemon juice, check the seasoning and heat through gently. Serve hot, sprinkled with paprika.

Menu Suggestion

Serve this substantial American-style soup as a supper or lunch dish with crusty French bread. If liked, pour the soup into individual heatproof bowls, grate Cheddar cheese thickly on top and pop under the grill until bubbling and golden.

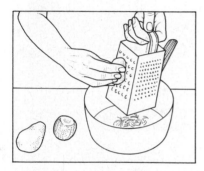

1 Grate the onion and potato into a saucepan. Add the celery and 600 ml (1 pint) water and bring to the boil. Lower the heat, cover the pan with a lid and simmer for 10 minutes.

2 Add the fish and milk and bring back to the boil. Lower the heat, add salt and pepper to taste, then cover the pan with a lid and simmer for 15 minutes until the fish is tender.

SMOKED FISH CHOWDER

A chowder is an American soup usually made with fish, potatoes and milk. American cookbooks have many different recipes for chowders, but the most famous of them all is undoubtedly New England Clam Chowder, made with raw shucked (shelled) clams and salt pork, onion, potatoes and milk. If you would like to make clam chowder, simply follow the recipe above, sub-stituting bottled or canned clams for the smoked haddock. To serve 4 people as a main meal you will need two 170 g (6 oz) jars or cans of clams in brine or natural juices. Use the liquid from the jar or can for added flavour, adding it to the onion and potato instead of some of the measured water in step 1. Cook the clams for only 5 minutes in step 2.

CHILLED PEA AND MINT SOUP

1.30*	✳	224 cals

* plus 2–3 hours chilling

Serves 6

900 g (2 lb) fresh peas

50 g (2 oz) butter or margarine

1 onion, skinned and roughly
    chopped

568 ml (1 pint) milk

600 ml (1 pint) chicken stock

2 large sprigs of fresh mint and
    mint sprigs to garnish

pinch of caster sugar

salt and freshly ground pepper

150 ml (5 fl oz) single cream

3 Cover and simmer gently for about 30 minutes, until the peas are really tender. Cool slightly, reserving about 45 ml (3 tbsp) peas to garnish and rub the remaining peas through a sieve or place in a blender or food processor and blend to form a smooth purée.

4 Pour into a large bowl. Adjust seasoning, cool. Stir in the fresh cream and chill for 2–3 hours before serving. To serve, garnish with the reserved boiled peas and sprigs of mint.

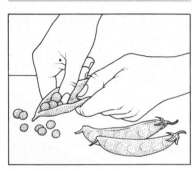

1 Shell the peas. Then melt the butter in a saucepan, add the onion, cover and cook gently for about 15 minutes until it is soft but not brown.

2 Remove from the heat and stir in the milk, stock, peas, the two mint sprigs, sugar and seasoning. Bring to the boil, stirring.

USING FRESH PEAS

This recipe for Chilled Pea and Mint Soup uses fresh peas – perfect for early summer when you can pick fresh peas from the garden or buy them easily at local farms and markets. There is nothing like the sweet, fragrant flavour of freshly picked peas in summer, so it is a good idea to make at least a double quantity of this soup and freeze some to remind you of the summer. If you want to make this soup at other times of year, it can also be made with frozen peas, in which case you will need half the weight specified in the recipe for fresh. There is no need to defrost them – just add them straight from the packet after adding the milk and stock in step 2 and cook as fresh peas.

ICED, TOMATO AND HERB SOUP

| 0.20* | ✳ | 133 cals |

* plus 2 hours chilling

Serves 4

450 g (1 lb) ripe tomatoes

1 small onion, skinned and sliced

20 ml (4 tsp) tomato purée

411 g (14½ oz) can chicken consommé

30 ml (2 tbsp) chopped fresh herbs e.g. basil, coriander, parsley

salt and freshly ground pepper

25 g (1 oz) fresh white breadcrumbs

150 ml (¼ pint) soured cream

fresh basil leaves, to garnish

1 Roughly chop the tomatoes and process them with the onion, tomato purée, consommé and herbs until smooth.

2 Rub the tomato mixture through a nylon sieve into a saucepan. Heat gently to remove the frothy texture, then add plenty of salt and pepper.

3 Pour the soup into a large serving bowl and stir in the breadcrumbs. Chill in the refrigerator for at least 2 hours.

4 Stir the soured cream until smooth, then swirl in. Float the fresh basil leaves on top.

Menu Suggestion
Serve this elegant soup for a summer dinner party starter. Follow with barbecued lamb kebabs and a rice pilaf.

COLD CUCUMBER SOUP

0.20*	267 cals

* plus 8 hours chilling

Serves 4

2 medium cucumbers, peeled

100 g (4 oz) walnuts, chopped

30 ml (2 tbsp) olive oil or a mixture
   of walnut and olive oil

300 ml (½ pint) chicken stock,
   skimmed

1 garlic clove, skinned and crushed

30 ml (2 tbsp) chopped fresh dill or
   10 ml (2 tsp) dried dill

salt and freshly ground pepper

300 ml (½ pint) natural yogurt or
   soured cream

sprigs of fresh dill, to garnish

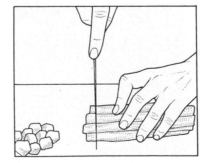

1 Cut the cucumbers into small dice and place in a bowl. Add the walnuts, oil, stock, garlic and chopped dill and season to taste with salt and pepper.

2 Stir the soup well, cover the bowl with cling film and chill in the refrigerator for at least 8 hours, or overnight.

3 To serve, uncover and whisk in the yogurt or soured cream. Ladle into individual soup bowls surrounded by crushed ice and garnish with the sprigs of dill.

Menu Suggestion

Cool, creamy and refreshing, this cucumber soup is best served with crisp Melba toast and chilled dry white wine.

VICHYSOISSE

| 0.50* | ✳ | 296 cals |

* plus 2 hours chilling

Serves 4

50 g (2 oz) butter

4 leeks, trimmed, sliced and washed

1 onion, skinned and sliced

1 litre (1¾ pints) chicken stock

2 potatoes, peeled and thinly sliced

salt and freshly ground pepper

200 ml (7 fl oz) single cream

snipped chives, to garnish

1 Melt the butter in a heavy-based saucepan, add the leeks and onion and cook gently for about 10 minutes, until soft but not coloured. Add the stock and potatoes and bring to the boil.

2 Lower the heat, add salt and pepper to taste and cover the pan with a lid. Simmer for about 30 minutes until the vegetables are completely soft.

3 Sieve or purée the soup in a blender or food processor. Pour into a large serving bowl and stir in the cream. Taste and adjust seasoning if necessary. Chill for at least 4 hours in the refrigerator. Sprinkle with chives just before serving.

Menu Suggestion

Nothing could make a more sophisticated starter to a summer meal than this chilled leek and potato soup. Serve with Melba toast and butter curls, and follow with a main course of chicken, veal or duck to continue the elegant theme of the meal.

Iced Avocado and Chicken Soup

| 0.10* | 293 cals |

* plus 2 hours chilling

Serves 6

2 ripe avocados

1 small onion, skinned and chopped

finely grated rind and juice of 1 lemon

142 ml (5 fl oz) natural yogurt

142 ml (5 fl oz) soured cream

600 ml (1 pint) cold chicken stock

175 g (6 oz) cooked chicken, diced

salt and freshly ground pepper

snipped chives, to garnish

1 Halve the avocados and discard the stones. Scoop out the flesh with a teaspoon.

2 Purée together the avocado flesh, onion, lemon rind and juice, yogurt and soured cream in a blender or food processor.

3 Turn out into a large serving bowl or tureen, gradually whisk in the stock, then add the chicken and seasoning to taste. Cover tightly and chill for at least 2 hours.

4 As a garnish, snip chives over the surface of the soup just before serving.

Menu Suggestion

The perfect soup for a summer dinner party or barbecue. Rich and creamy, yet icy cool, serve with crispbreads or wholemeal crackers and chilled white wine.

ICED AVOCADO AND CHICKEN SOUP

Avocado pears are often sold when still hard and unripe. To help them ripen, wrap in newspaper and put in a warm place. After 3–4 days they will be ready. To test for ripeness, apply gentle pressure with your thumb to the tapered end—the skin and flesh should yield slightly.

When choosing avocados, look for the roundish, dark green ones with uneven skins. These often seem to have more flavour than the more egg-shaped, paler green kind with smooth skins.

Avocado flesh discolours quickly on contact with the air, so don't cut open the pears until just before you are ready to make the soup.

MEDITERRANEAN SUMMER SOUP

0.45*	✳*	149 cals

* plus at least 1 hour chilling; freeze
after step 4

Serves 4

2 very large Marmande or
   Beefsteak tomatoes

1 medium Spanish onion, skinned

1 green pepper, cored and seeded

450 g (1 lb) can potatoes, drained

4 garlic cloves, skinned

60 ml (4 tbsp) wine vinegar

1 litre (1¾ pints) water

30 ml (2 tbsp) olive oil

2.5 ml (½ tsp) paprika

salt and freshly ground pepper

a few ice cubes and fresh mint
   sprigs, to serve

1 Chop all the vegetables and
the garlic roughly and then put
half of them in a blender or food
processor with the vinegar and
about 150 ml (¼ pint) of the
measured water. Work to a
smooth purée.

2 Sieve the purée to remove the
tomato skins, working it into a
large soup tureen or bowl.

3 Repeat the puréeing and
sieving with the remaining
vegetables and another 150 ml
(¼ pint) of the water. Add to the
purée in the tureen or bowl.

4 Pour the remaining water into
the soup and add the oil,
paprika and seasoning to taste.
Stir well to mix, cover and chill in
the refrigerator for at least 1 hour
before serving.

5 To serve, taste and adjust the
seasoning, then stir in the ice
cubes. Float mint sprigs on top.

Menu Suggestion
Serve as a starter for a summer
luncheon or barbecue party, with
bowls of garnish such as tiny
bread croûtons (fried or toasted),
diced red and green pepper, diced
cucumber and finely chopped
hard-boiled eggs.

MEDITERRANEAN SUMMER SOUP

To make croûtons for floating on
top of this soup: remove the
crusts from 3 slices of stale white
bread. Cut the bread into dice,
then deep-fry in hot oil until
golden brown and crisp. Remove
with a slotted spoon and drain on
absorbent kitchen paper. For
toasted croûtons, toast the crustless bread first, then cut into
dice. Croûtons can be successfully frozen.

   For a professional touch, try
cutting the bread or toast into
different shapes with tiny aspic
jelly cutters, available from
specialist kitchen shops and
catering suppliers.

Starters

ARTICHOKE HEARTS À LA GRÈCQUE

0.30	103 cals

Serves 6

75 ml (5 tbsp) olive oil

15 ml (1 tbsp) white wine vinegar

10 ml (2 tsp) tomato purée

1 large garlic clove, skinned and crushed

7.5 ml (1½ tsp) chopped fresh thyme or basil

salt and freshly ground pepper

175 g (6 oz) button onions, skinned

5 ml (1 tsp) caster sugar

225 g (8 oz) small button mushrooms, wiped

two 400-g (14-oz) cans artichoke hearts

1 Make the dressing. Place 45 ml (3 tbsp) oil, vinegar, tomato purée, garlic, thyme and seasoning in a bowl and whisk together.

2 Blanch onions in boiling water for 5 minutes; drain well. Heat remaining oil; add onions and sugar and cook for 2 minutes.

3 Add mushrooms and toss over a high heat for a few seconds. Tip contents of pan into dressing. Drain artichoke hearts, rinse and dry. Add hearts to dressing and toss together. Cover and chill.

CRUDITÉS WITH AÏOLI

0.45	464–698 cals

Serves 4–6

4 garlic cloves, skinned

1 egg yolk

300 ml ($\frac{1}{2}$ pint) olive oil

lemon juice, to taste

salt and freshly ground pepper

6 celery sticks, trimmed

4 carrots, peeled

$\frac{1}{2}$ cucumber

1 large red pepper, washed, cored, seeded and cut into strips

1 large green pepper, washed, cored, seeded and cut into strips

175 g (6 oz) button mushrooms, wiped

1 small cauliflower, cut into florets

1 bunch radishes, trimmed

6 spring onions, trimmed

1 First make the aïoli. Pound the garlic in a mortar and pestle. Stir in the egg yolk. Add the oil a drop at a time, beating until the mixture begins to thicken. This may happen quite suddenly.

2 Continue adding the oil in a thin, steady stream to make a smooth, thick mayonnaise. Stir in lemon juice and salt and pepper to taste. Turn into a bowl, cover and keep in a cool place.

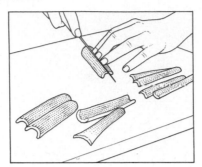

3 Meanwhile, prepare the vegetables. Cut the celery in half crossways, then cut into sticks lengthways. Cut the carrot and cucumber into thin sticks.

4 Lay the mushrooms down with the stalks uppermost, and, using a sharp knife, slice downwards into 'T' shapes.

5 To serve, arrange all the vegetables on one large or two small serving dishes. Serve with the dip.

CRUDITÉS

Crudités – French for raw vegetables – does not have to include all the vegetables suggested in the recipe on this page. The choice depends simply on personal taste and seasonal availability. Make sure, however, that they are all as crisp and fresh as possible.

If you want to make this starter ahead of time, the aïoli – garlic mayonnaise – will keep in a covered container for several days in the refrigerator. The vegetables can be prepared 1–2 hours ahead of time and kept in a bowl of iced water in the refrigerator.

LEEKS À LA VINAIGRETTE

0.30* | 467–600 cals

* plus 30 minutes chilling

Serves 4–6

12 small leeks
salt and freshly ground pepper
150 ml ($\frac{1}{4}$ pint) olive oil
60 ml (4 tbsp) red wine vinegar
15 ml (1 tbsp) tomato purée
15 ml (1 tbsp) coriander seeds,
   lightly crushed
2.5 ml ($\frac{1}{2}$ tsp) sugar
coriander sprigs, to garnish
hot garlic bread, to serve

1 Trim the root ends of the leeks and cut off the damaged tops. Then slit each leek lengthways in two or three places.

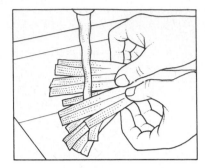

2 Hold under cold running water and wash away any grit caught between the leaves. Cook the leeks in boiling salted water for 6–8 minutes until just tender. Drain, refresh under cold running water, then leave to drain and dry on absorbent kitchen paper.

3 Make the dressing. Put the oil and vinegar in a bowl with the tomato purée, coriander seeds, sugar and salt and pepper to taste. Whisk vigorously with a fork until thick.

4 Arrange the cold leeks in a shallow serving dish and pour the dressing over them. Chill in the refrigerator for at least 30 minutes before serving. Garnish with sprigs of coriander and serve with hot garlic bread.

STUFFED COURGETTES WITH WALNUTS AND SAGE

1.20	🍳	422 cals

Serves 4

4 large courgettes, total weight about 700 g (1½ lb)

1 onion, skinned and chopped

90 g (3½ oz) butter or margarine

50 g (2 oz) walnut pieces, chopped

50 g (2 oz) fresh white breadcrumbs

10 ml (2 tsp) chopped fresh sage

15 ml (1 tbsp) tomato purée

1 egg, beaten

salt and freshly ground pepper

30 ml (2 tbsp) plain flour

300 ml (½ pint) chicken stock

30 ml (2 tbsp) chopped parsley

walnut halves and fresh sage sprigs, to garnish

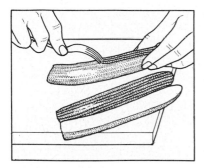

1 Wipe the courgettes. Using a fork, score down skin at 1-cm (½-inch) intervals, then halve each one lengthwise.

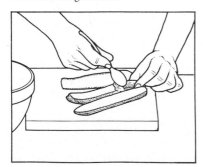

2 Hollow out the centres of the courgettes using a teaspoon. Blanch in boiling water for 4 minutes, drain, then hold under cold tap. Cool for 15–20 minutes.

3 Make the stuffing. Fry the onion in 25 g (1 oz) butter for 5–10 minutes until golden. Remove from heat and stir in half the walnuts, breadcrumbs, half the sage, the tomato purée, beaten egg and plenty of seasoning. Sandwich the courgettes with the stuffing.

4 Place in a buttered ovenproof dish and dot with a little more butter. Cover the courgettes and bake in the oven at 190°C (375°F) mark 5 for about 30 minutes.

5 Meanwhile, make the sauce. Melt 50 g (2 oz) butter in a pan, stir in the flour and cook gently for 1 minute, stirring.

6 Remove from the heat and gradually stir in the stock. Bring to the boil and continue to cook, stirring until the sauce thickens. Stir in the parsley, seasoning and remaining sage and walnuts. Remove from heat and cover the sauce.

7 To serve, reheat the sauce. Pour some over the courgettes and serve the rest separately. Garnish with walnut halves and sage sprigs.

BANG BANG CHICKEN

| 2.00* | 🍶 | 252–378 cals |

* plus cooling and overnight marinating

Serves 4–6

15 ml (1 tbsp) finely chopped fresh root ginger

1.4 kg (3 lb) chicken

salt and freshly ground pepper

60 ml (4 tbsp) soy sauce

3 carrots, peeled and very thinly sliced

75 g (3 oz) beansprouts

60 ml (4 tbsp) vegetable oil

30 ml (2 tbsp) sesame oil

30 ml (2 tbsp) sesame seeds

10 ml (2 tsp) crushed dried red chillies

5 ml (1 tsp) soft brown sugar

45 ml (3 tbsp) dry sherry

lettuce, to serve

spring onion tassels, to garnish

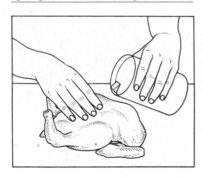

1 Put the ginger inside the cavity of the chicken, then rub the outside of the bird with salt and pepper. Place the bird in a large saucepan and sprinkle over half of the soy sauce. Leave to stand for 30 minutes.

2 Pour enough water into the pan to just cover the chicken. Bring to the boil, then lower the heat, cover and simmer for about 1 hour until the chicken is tender. Leave to cool in the cooking liquid, then remove.

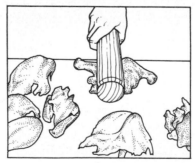

3 Separate the legs and wings from the carcass, then cut the carcass into four. Bang the pieces several times with a rolling pin to loosen the meat from the bones.

4 Cut the meat into neat slices (not too small) or strips. Discard the bones and skin. Combine with carrots and beansprouts.

5 Heat the oils in a heavy-based pan, add the sesame seeds and chillies and fry over brisk heat for a few minutes, stirring until lightly coloured. Remove from the heat and stir in the remaining soy sauce with the sugar and sherry.

6 Pour over the chicken and vegetables, cover and marinate in the refrigerator overnight.

7 To serve, put the chicken and vegetables into a shallow serving dish, lined with lettuce leaves. Pour over any remaining marinade and garnish with spring onion tassels. Serve cold.

Menu Suggestion
A refreshing starter for the first course of a Chinese meal. Serve with a dry white wine.

CRISPY CHICKEN PARCELS

| 0.45* | 🥡 🥡 | ❄* |

| 803–857 cals |

* plus 30 minutes chilling; freeze after step 5

Serves 4

25 g (1 oz) butter or margarine

50 g (2 oz) flour

300 ml (½ pint) milk

225 g (8 oz) cooked chicken, diced

15 ml (1 tbsp) chopped fresh tarragon or 10 ml (2 tsp) dried tarragon

75 g (3 oz) Gruyère cheese, grated

good pinch of ground mace

salt and freshly ground pepper

15 ml (1 tbsp) vegetable oil

8–12 cannelloni tubes

180 ml (12 tbsp) dried breadcrumbs

180 ml (12 tbsp) grated Parmesan cheese

1 egg, beaten

oil, for deep-frying

1 Melt the fat in a heavy-based saucepan, sprinkle in the flour and cook for 2 minutes, stirring.

2 Remove from the heat and gradually stir in the milk, then bring to the boil, stirring all the time until very thick. Add the chicken, tarragon, Gruyère, mace and salt and pepper to taste. Stir to mix.

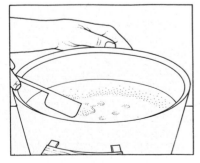

3 Bring a large pan of salted water to the boil, then swirl in the oil. Drop in the cannelloni. Simmer for 5 minutes, drain.

4 Using a teaspoon, or a piping bag fitted with a large plain nozzle, fill each cannelloni tube with the chicken mixture. Pinch the edges to seal.

5 Mix the breadcrumbs and Parmesan in a shallow bowl. Dip the cannelloni tubes first in the beaten egg, then in the breadcrumbs mixed with the Parmesan, making sure they are evenly coated. Chill in the refrigerator for 30 minutes.

6 Heat the oil in a deep-fryer to 180°C (350°F). Deep-fry the parcels a few at a time until golden brown and crisp. Drain on absorbent kitchen paper while frying the remainder. Serve hot.

Menu Suggestion

A substantial, hot starter which needs no accompaniment other than a dry white wine. Can also be served for a tasty lunchtime snack, with a mixed salad.

MARINATED KIPPERS

| 0.20* | 395 cals |

* plus at least 8 hours marinating
Serves 4

4 boneless kipper fillets
150 ml ($\frac{1}{4}$ pint) olive oil
75 ml (5 tbsp) lemon juice
1.25 ml ($\frac{1}{4}$ tsp) mustard powder
1 small onion, skinned and very finely chopped
1–2 garlic cloves, skinned and crushed
freshly ground pepper
a few raw onion rings, parsley sprigs and paprika, to garnish

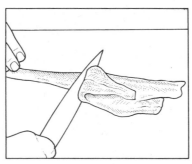

1 Skin the kipper fillets. Place them skin side down on a board, grip each one at the tail end and work the flesh away from the skin with a sharp knife, using a sawing motion.

2 In a jug, whisk together the remaining ingredients, except the garnish, adding pepper to taste.

3 Put the kippers in a shallow dish and pour over the marinade. Cover and chill in the refrigerator for at least 8 hours. Turn the kippers in the marinade occasionally during this time.

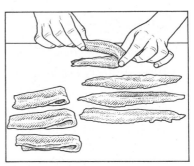

4 To serve, remove the kippers from the marinade and cut each one in half lengthways. Fold each half over crossways, then place in a single layer in a dish.

5 Pour the marinade over the kippers and garnish the top with onion rings, parsley sprigs and a sprinkling of paprika.

Menu Suggestion
Serve this chilled starter with granary bread or rolls and butter, and a bottle of dry white wine.

MARINATED KIPPERS
Kippers are herrings which are split and gutted, soaked in brine, then smoked. The best kippers are said to come from Loch Fyne in Scotland, although those from the Isle of Man are also considered to be very good. The choice of kippers is quite confusing—at fishmongers they are sold whole, boned, and as fillets, whereas in supermarkets they are available frozen as fillets and in vacuum 'boil-in-the-bag' packs. For this recipe you can use fresh or frozen fillets. Avoid buying those which are a deep, chestnut-brown colour as they have probably been dyed.

COARSE LIVER PÂTÉ

3.20* ✱ 454 cals

* plus cooling and overnight chilling

Serves 8

225 g (8 oz) unsmoked rashers of streaky bacon, rinded

300 ml (½ pint) milk

slices of onion, bay leaf, peppercorns and 1 or 2 cloves, for flavouring

25 g (1 oz) butter or margarine

20 g (¾ oz) plain flour

450 g (1 lb) belly of pork, rinded

450 g (1 lb) pig's liver

1 small onion, skinned and quartered

2 garlic cloves, skinned and crushed

30 ml (2 tbsp) medium dry sherry

salt and freshly ground pepper

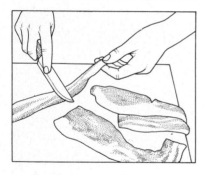

1 Put the bacon rashers on a board and stretch using the back of a knife. Use to line the base and sides of a 1.4 litre (2½ pint) dish or terrine.

2 Pour the milk into a saucepan, add the flavouring ingredients and bring slowly to the boil. Remove from the heat, cover and leave to infuse for 15 minutes.

3 Strain the milk and reserve. Melt the butter in the rinsed-out pan, add the flour and cook gently, stirring, for 1–2 minutes. Remove from the heat and gradually blend in the milk. Bring to the boil, stirring constantly, then simmer for 3 minutes until thick and smooth. Cover and leave to cool slightly.

4 Cut the pork and liver into small pieces. Pass the meats and onion through a mincer, fitted with the coarsest blade. Alternatively, chop in a food processor.

5 Put the minced mixture into a bowl, add the garlic, then stir in the sherry and plenty of salt and pepper. Gradually beat in the cooled sauce and continue beating until well mixed. The mixture may seem a little sloppy, but it will firm up on cooking.

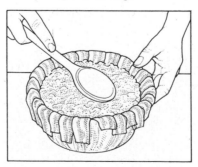

6 Spoon the mixture into the prepared dish and press down with the back of the spoon. Fold over any overlapping bacon. Cover the dish tightly with foil.

7 Place the dish in a roasting tin and half fill with boiling water. Bake in the oven at 180°C (350°F) mark 4 for about 2¼ hours until firm to the touch and the juices run clear when the centre of the pâté is pierced with a fine skewer.

8 Remove the dish from the roasting tin and replace the foil with a fresh piece. Place a plate or dish, small enough just to fit inside the dish, on top of the pâté. Top with heavy weights.

9 Leave the pâté to cool for 1 hour, then chill overnight. To serve, dip the dish into hot water for about 30 seconds then invert the pâté on to a plate.

Menu Suggestion

Coarse Liver Pâté makes a substantial starter for an informal supper party, served with salad, French bread and a full-bodied red wine such as a Côtes du Rhône. Alternatively, cut the pâté into thick slices and use for packed lunches and picnics, with a selection of salads.

CHICKEN LIVER PÂTÉ

| 0.20* | ✳ | 232 cals |

* plus 20 minutes cooling and 2 hours chilling

Serves 8

100 g (4 oz) butter

1 medium onion, skinned and chopped

1 garlic clove, skinned and crushed

450 g (1 lb) chicken livers, cleaned and dried

75 ml (5 tbsp) double cream

15 ml (1 tbsp) tomato purée

15 ml (1 tbsp) brandy

salt and freshly ground pepper

pink peppercorns and fresh bay leaves, to garnish

1 Melt half of the butter in a saucepan, add the onion and garlic and fry gently for 5 minutes. Add the chicken livers and cook for 5 minutes.

2 Cool slightly, then add the cream, tomato purée, brandy and plenty of salt and pepper.

3 Purée the mixture in a blender or food processor, then spoon into a serving dish.

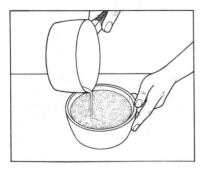

4 Melt the remaining butter gently. Pour the butter over the pâté and leave to cool. Chill for at least 2 hours. Garnish with peppercorns and bay leaves.

Menu Suggestion
Serve this rich, creamy pâté with Melba toast and a dry red wine.

POTTED CHICKEN WITH TARRAGON

2.00*	✳	205–274 cals

* plus at least 4 hours chilling
and 30 minutes to come to room
temperature

Serves 6–8

1.4 kg (3 lb) oven-ready chicken

45 ml (3 tbsp) dry sherry

15 ml (1 tbsp) fresh chopped
    tarragon or 5 ml (1 tsp) dried

50 g (2 oz) butter

1 onion, skinned and chopped

1 carrot, peeled and chopped

salt and freshly ground pepper

fresh tarragon sprigs, to garnish

1 Place the chicken in a flameproof casserole with the
sherry, tarragon, butter,
vegetables and salt and pepper.
Cover tightly and cook in the oven
at 180°C (350°F) mark 4 for about
1½ hours.

2 Lift the chicken out of the
casserole, cut off all the flesh,
reserving the skin and bones.
Coarsely mince the chicken meat
in a food processor or mincer.

3 Return the skin and broken up
bones to the casserole. Boil
the contents rapidly until the
liquid has reduced to 225 ml
(8 fl oz). Strain, reserving the
juices.

4 Mix the minced chicken and
juices together, then check the
seasoning. Pack into small dishes,
cover with cling film and chill in
the refrigerator for at least
4 hours.

5 Leave at cool room
temperature for 30 minutes
before serving. Garnish with fresh
tarragon sprigs.

Menu Suggestion
Serve this subtly flavoured starter
with Melba toast and chilled dry
white wine or French dry cider.

SMOKED MACKEREL MOUSSE

| 0.50* | ✳ | 220 cals |

* plus 20 minutes cooling and 2 hours chilling

Serves 6

| 300 ml ($\frac{1}{2}$ pint) milk |
| a few slices of onion and carrot |
| 1 bay leaf |
| 25 g (1 oz) butter or margarine |
| 30 ml (2 tbsp) plain flour |
| 10 ml (2 tsp) gelatine |
| 275 g (10 oz) smoked mackerel fillet |
| 50 g (2 oz) onion, skinned and chopped |
| 15 ml (1 tbsp) creamed horseradish |
| 150 ml ($\frac{1}{4}$ pint) natural yogurt |
| 15 ml (1 tbsp) lemon juice |
| salt and freshly ground pepper |
| 2 egg whites |
| lamb's lettuce or watercress sprigs and lemon twists, to garnish |

1 Pour the milk into a saucepan, add the flavourings and bring slowly to the boil. Remove from the heat, cover and leave to infuse for 30 minutes.

2 Strain the infused milk into a jug. Discard the flavourings. Melt the butter in the rinsed–out pan, add the flour and cook gently, stirring, for 1–2 minutes. Remove from the heat and gradually blend in the infused milk. Bring to the boil, stirring constantly, then simmer for 3 minutes until thick and smooth.

3 Remove the pan from the heat and sprinkle in the gelatine. Stir briskly until dissolved. Pour into a bowl and leave to cool for 20 minutes.

4 Meanwhile, flake the smoked mackerel fillet, discarding the skin and bones.

5 Work the cooled sauce, mackerel, onion and horseradish in a blender or food processor until smooth. Pour into a bowl and stir in the yogurt, lemon juice and salt and pepper to taste.

6 Whisk the egg whites until they stand in soft peaks, then fold gently through the fish mixture.

7 Spoon the mousse into 6 individual ramekins or soufflé dishes and chill in the refrigerator for at least 2 hours until set. Serve chilled, garnished with lamb's lettuce or watercress sprigs and lemon twists.

Menu Suggestion

For an informal supper party or a buffet party, serve with fingers of wholemeal toast and butter. Follow with a meaty main course such as a casserole, and finish the meal with a glazed open fruit tart.

FRESH HADDOCK MOUSSE

0.40* 🥄	359 cals

* plus 30 minutes cooling, 2 hours chilling and 30 minutes to come to room temperature

Serves 6

350 g (12 oz) fresh haddock fillet

200 ml (7 fl oz) milk

1 bay leaf

6 peppercorns

salt and freshly ground pepper

25 g (1 oz) butter or margarine

30 ml (2 tbsp) plain flour

7.5 ml (1½ tsp) gelatine

15 ml (1 tbsp) Dijon mustard

5 ml (1 tsp) tomato purée

5 ml (1 tsp) Worcestershire sauce

90 ml (6 tbsp) double cream

150 ml (¼ pint) mayonnaise

15 ml (1 tbsp) lemon juice

cucumber, to garnish

1 Place the haddock in a sauté or frying pan. Pour in the milk and add the bay leaf, peppercorns and a good pinch of salt. Bring slowly to the boil, cover and simmer for 5–10 minutes, or until the fish flakes easily when tested with a fork.

2 Strain the cooking liquid from the fish and reserve. Skin and flake the flesh, discarding any bones.

3 Melt the butter in a saucepan, add the flour and cook gently, stirring for 1–2 minutes. Remove from the heat and gradually blend in the strained cooked liquid. Bring to the boil, stirring constantly, then simmer for 3 minutes until thick and smooth. Remove the pan from the heat and sprinkle in the gelatine. Stir briskly until dissolved.

4 Work the sauce in a blender or food processor with the fish, mustard, tomato purée, Worcestershire sauce and salt and pepper to taste. Transfer to a bowl and leave to cool for 30 minutes.

5 Lightly whip the cream and stir it into the fish mixture with the mayonnaise and lemon juice. Check the seasoning.

6 Spoon the mousse into 6 individual ramekins or soufflé dishes and chill in the refrigerator for at least 2 hours until set. Leave at cool room temperature for 30 minutes before serving, garnished with cucumber.

Menu Suggestion
This mousse is light and delicate in flavour. Serve for a dinner party starter with Melba toast; followed by a main course of chicken or veal, then a fresh, fruity dessert.

INDONESIAN PORK SATÉ

0.40*	468 cals

* plus 30 minutes marinating

Serves 4

450 g (1 lb) pork fillet

30 ml (2 tbsp) dark soy sauce

45 ml (3 tbsp) lemon juice

7.5 ml (1½ tsp) ground ginger

125 g (4 oz) unsalted peanuts

30 ml (2 tbsp) oil

1 garlic clove, skinned and crushed

2.5 ml (½ tsp) ground coriander

1.25 ml (¼ tsp) chilli powder

1.25 ml (¼ tsp) salt

450 ml (¾ pint) coconut milk

5 ml (1 tsp) soft brown sugar

freshly ground pepper

½ cucumber

1 Cut the pork fillet into small cubes. Thread on to 8 long saté sticks, or metal skewers.

2 Mix together the soy sauce, lemon juice and 5 ml (1 tsp) of the ginger. Pour over the pork skewers and leave to marinate for at least 30 minutes, turning occasionally.

3 Meanwhile, finely chop the peanuts or grind them in a nut mill. Heat the oil in a saucepan. Add the peanuts, garlic, coriander, chilli powder, remaining ginger and salt and fry for about 4–5 minutes until browned, stirring.

4 Stir in the milk and sugar. Bring to the boil and simmer for about 15 minutes or until the sauce thickens. Check the seasoning, adding pepper to taste.

5 Grill the pork skewers for about 6 minutes, or until the meat is tender, turning occasionally.

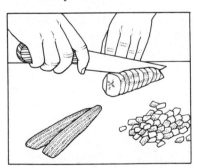

6 Meanwhile, shred the cucumber finely Serve the saté hot, with the shredded cucumber, and the peanut sauce for dipping.

Menu Suggestion
These kebabs come with their own sauce for dipping, and so need no accompaniment. Follow with an Indonesian-style main course of whole steamed or baked fish, or a fish curry.

SPICY SPARERIBS

0.20*	274 cals

* plus 2 hours marinating
Serves 4

1.8 kg (4 lb) pork spareribs
1 onion, skinned and sliced
350 ml (12 fl oz) tomato juice
45 ml (3 tbsp) cider vinegar
30 ml (2 tbsp) clear honey
10 ml (2 tsp) salt
5 ml (1 tsp) paprika
3.75 ml ($\frac{3}{4}$ tsp) chilli powder

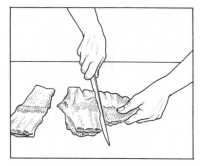

1 Separate the spareribs into sections of 2–3 ribs. Place in a shallow dish. Mix all the remaining ingredients together and pour over the ribs. Cover and marinate in the refrigerator for 2 hours.

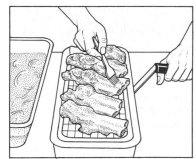

2 Place the spareribs on a pre-heated grill. Brush with the marinade. Grill for 20 minutes, brushing occasionally with the marinade and turning. Heat the marinade and serve as a sauce.

Menu Suggestion
Serve as a first course for a Chinese-style supper party.

CREAMY HAM AND MUSHROOM PUFFS

1.00*	✳*	430–645 cals

* plus cooling; freeze at the end of step 5

Serves 4–6

75 g (3 oz) button mushrooms
1 small onion, skinned
40 g (1½ oz) butter or margarine
30 ml (2 tbsp) plain flour
100 ml (3½ fl oz) milk
100 ml (3½ fl oz) double cream
75 g (3 oz) boiled ham, finely diced
10 ml (2 tsp) chopped fresh tarragon or 5 ml (1 tsp) dried
salt and freshly ground pepper
350 g (12 oz) packet frozen puff pastry, thawed
1 egg, beaten, to glaze

1 Chop the mushrooms and onion very finely. Melt half of the butter in a pan, add them to it and fry over moderate heat for 2–3 minutes. Remove and drain.

2 Melt the remaining butter in the pan, add the flour and cook gently, stirring, for 1–2 minutes. Remove from the heat and gradually blend in the milk. Bring to the boil, stirring constantly. Add the cream and simmer for 3 minutes until thick. Off the heat, fold in the mushroom mixture, ham and seasonings.

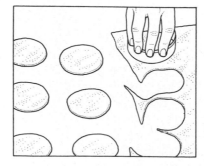

3 Roll out the pastry on a lightly floured surface and cut out 12 rounds using a 10 cm (4 inch) plain round cutter.

4 Put spoonfuls of the ham and mushroom filling on one half of each pastry round.

5 Brush the edges of the pastry rounds with beaten egg, then fold the plain half of the pastry over the filling. Seal the edges and crimp with the prongs of a fork.

6 Place the turnovers on a dampened baking sheet. Brush with beaten egg to glaze, then bake in the oven at 220°C (425°F) mark 7 for 15–20 minutes until puffed up and golden. Serve hot.

Menu Suggestion
These puff pastry turnovers are rich and filling. Follow with a light main course such as grilled or barbecued fish kebabs. A tangy lemon or orange soufflé or mousse would make the ideal dessert.

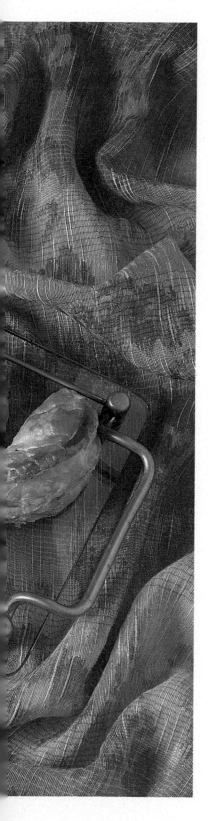

MUSHROOMS IN SOURED CREAM

0.35*	207 cals

* plus cooling and chilling

Serves 4

450 g (1 lb) button mushrooms

1 bunch of spring onions

4 cardamom pods

25 g (1 oz) butter

30 ml (2 tbsp) olive oil

2 garlic cloves, crushed

juice of 1 lemon

150 ml (¼ pint) soured cream

30 ml (2 tbsp) chopped fresh coriander

salt and freshly ground pepper

coriander and paprika, to garnish

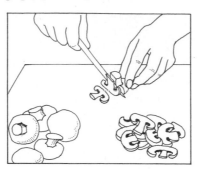

1 Wipe the mushrooms. Slice them thickly and evenly into 'T' shapes. Trim the spring onions and slice finely.

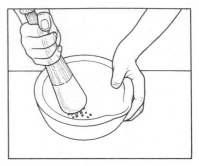

2 Split open the cardamom pods with your fingernails to release the seeds. Crush the seeds with a mortar and pestle or the end of a rolling pin.

3 Melt the butter with the oil in a large frying pan. Add the spring onions and garlic and fry gently for 5 minutes until the onions soften slightly.

4 Add the crushed cardamom seeds to the pan and fry for 1–2 minutes, then increase the heat and add the mushrooms. Cook the mushrooms for a few minutes only until tender, stirring frequently and shaking the pan to ensure even cooking.

5 Transfer the mushrooms and cooking juices to a bowl. Leave to cool then stir in the lemon juice, soured cream and coriander with salt and pepper to taste. Chill in the refrigerator until serving time. Stir well and garnish with coriander and paprika just before serving.

Menu Suggestion
Serve this rich, creamy starter with fresh wholemeal or poppy-seed rolls. Any light main course such as chicken or fish would be suitable to follow, with a tangy, fresh fruit dessert to finish.

INDIVIDUAL MUSHROOM SOUFFLÉS

0.50	330 cals

Serves 6

75 g (3 oz) butter

100 g (4 oz) flat mushrooms, wiped and roughly chopped

20 ml (4 tsp) anchovy essence

squeeze of lemon juice

40 g (1½ oz) plain flour

225 ml (9 fl oz) milk

salt and freshly ground pepper

4 eggs, size 2, separated

freshly grated Parmesan

1 Brush the insides of 6 150 ml (¼ pint) individual soufflé dishes liberally with 15 g (½ oz) butter and set aside.

2 Melt 25 g (1 oz) butter in a saucepan, add the mushrooms, anchovy essence and lemon juice and stir fry over high heat for 2–3 minutes. Transfer the mushrooms with a slotted spoon to a large bowl.

3 Melt the remaining butter in the pan, add the flour and cook gently, stirring, for 1–2 minutes. Remove from the heat and gradually blend in the milk. Bring to the boil, stirring constantly, then simmer for 3 minutes until thick and smooth.

4 Remove the pan from the heat and add the sauce to the mushrooms. Stir well to mix, adding salt and pepper to taste. Beat in the egg yolks one at a time.

5 Whisk the egg whites until stiff, then fold into the soufflé mixture until evenly incorporated. Divide equally between the 6 prepared dishes and sprinkle with Parmesan. Bake immediately in the oven at 200°C (400°F) mark 6 for 15 minutes or until well risen. Serve immediately.

Menu Suggestion
Individual soufflés make an impressive dinner party dessert. Serve with hot garlic or herb bread and follow with a main course such as the French fish stew *bouillabaisse*. A chilled lemon cheesecake would make a suitably refreshing dessert.

HUMMUS
(MIDDLE EASTERN CHICK PEA AND TAHINI DIP)

1.20*	✳*	277–416 cals

* plus overnight soaking and a few hours chilling; freeze without the garnish

Serves 4–6

175 g (6 oz) chick peas, soaked in cold water overnight

about 150 ml ($\frac{1}{4}$ pint) lemon juice

150 ml ($\frac{1}{4}$ pint) tahini paste

3 garlic cloves, skinned and crushed

salt

30 ml (2 tbsp) olive oil

5 ml (1 tsp) paprika

crudités, to serve (see box)

1 Drain the soaked chick peas and rinse well under cold running water. Put the chick peas in a large saucepan and cover with plenty of cold water.

2 Bring slowly to the boil, then skim off any scum with a slotted spoon. Half cover the pan with a lid and simmer gently for about 1 hour, until the chick peas are very tender.

3 Drain the chick peas, reserving 60 ml (4 tbsp) of the cooking liquid. Set a few whole chick peas aside for the garnish, then put the remainder in a blender or food processor. Add the reserved cooking liquid and half of the lemon juice and work to a smooth purée.

4 Add the tahini paste, garlic and 5 ml (1 tsp) salt and work again. Taste and add more lemon juice until the dip is to your liking, then blend in 30 ml (2 tbsp) hot water.

5 Turn into a serving bowl and cover with cling film. Chill in the refrigerator until serving time. Before serving, mix the oil with the paprika and drizzle over the Hummus. Arrange the reserved whole chick peas on top.

PAPA GHANOOYE
(ARABIC AUBERGINE DIP)

0.50*	✳*	322–483 cals

* plus a few hours chilling; freeze without the garnish

Serves 4–6

2 large aubergines

salt

2–3 garlic cloves, skinned and roughly chopped

10 ml (2 tsp) cumin seeds

100 ml (4 fl oz) olive oil

150 ml ($\frac{1}{4}$ pint) tahini paste

about 100 ml (4 fl oz) lemon juice

thin tomato slices, to garnish

crudités, to serve (see box)

1 Slice the aubergines, then place in a colander, sprinkling each layer with salt. Cover with a plate, put heavy weights on top and leave to dégorge for 30 minutes.

2 Meanwhile, crush the garlic and cumin seeds with a pestle and mortar. Add 5 ml (1 tsp) salt and mix well.

3 Rinse the aubergines under cold running water, then pat dry with absorbent kitchen paper. Heat the oil in a large, heavy-based frying pan until very hot. Add the aubergine slices in batches and fry until golden on both sides, turning once. Remove from the pan with a slotted spoon and drain again on kitchen paper.

4 Put the aubergine slices in a blender or food processor with the garlic mixture, the tahini paste and about two-thirds of the lemon juice. Work to a smooth purée, then taste and add more lemon juice and salt if liked.

5 Turn into a serving bowl, cover with cling film and chill in the refrigerator until serving time. Serve chilled, garnished with tomato slices.

SKORDALIA
(GREEK GARLIC DIP)

0.30*	381–572 cals

* plus a few hours chilling

Serves 4–6

75 g (3 oz) crustless white bread

60 ml (4 tbsp) milk

6 garlic cloves

250 ml (8 fl oz) olive oil

about 50 ml (2 fl oz) lemon juice

salt and freshly ground pepper

black olives and finely chopped parsley, to garnish

crudités, to serve (see box)

1 Tear the bread into small pieces into a bowl. Add the milk, mix and soak for 5 minutes.

2 Skin the cloves of garlic, chop roughly, then crush with a pestle and mortar.

3 Squeeze the bread with your fingers, then mix with the crushed garlic. Add the olive oil a drop at a time to form a paste.

4 When the mixture thickens, add a few drops of lemon juice, then continue with the olive oil. Add more lemon juice and salt and pepper. Turn into a bowl and cover with cling film. Chill in the refrigerator and garnish with olives and parsley before serving.

VEGETABLE DIPS
Dips make good starters for informal supper parties, or to serve at a drinks party. Crudités (raw vegetables) are ideal for dipping and dunking. To serve 4–6 people: 4 carrots, peeled and cut into thin sticks, 1 small cauliflower, divided into florets, 4–6 celery sticks, halved, $\frac{1}{2}$ cucumber, seeds removed and cut into sticks, 1 red and 1 green pepper, cored seeded and sliced, 1 bunch of radishes, trimmed. Fingers of hot pitta bread can also be served.

STUFFED PLAICE FILLETS

| 0.45 | 🍴 | 251 cals |

Serves 6

3 large double plaice fillets

75 g (3 oz) butter

5 ml (1 tsp) lemon juice

125 g (4 oz) mushrooms, wiped

175 g (6 oz) leeks, trimmed and washed

50 g (2 oz) long grain rice, cooked and drained

30 ml (2 tbsp) chopped fresh tarragon or 10 ml (2 tsp) dried

salt and freshly ground pepper

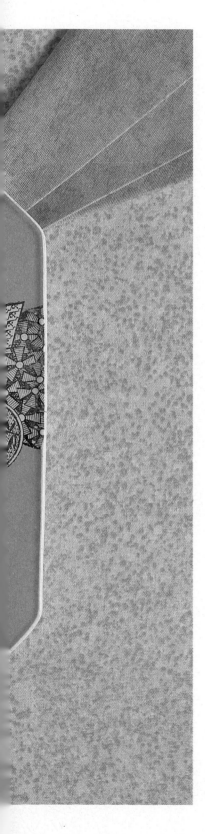

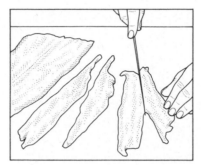

1 Skin the plaice, then cut each into 2 long fillets.

2 Place 1 fillet, skinned side out, round the inside of each of 6 buttered ramekins or individual soufflé dishes.

3 Make the lemon butter. Beat together 50 g (2 oz) of the butter and the lemon juice. Wrap in greaseproof paper and chill in the refrigerator for at least 30 minutes.

4 Meanwhile, finely chop the mushrooms and leeks. Melt remaining butter in a frying pan, add the vegetables and cook gently until softened. Remove from the heat and stir in the rice and tarragon. Season to taste.

5 Spoon the vegetable mixture into the centre of each ramekin, pressing down well.

6 Cover the ramekins with buttered foil, place in a bain marie (page 59) and bake in the oven at 190°C (375°F) mark 5 for about 25 minutes.

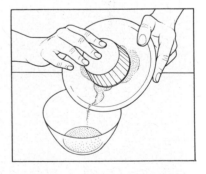

7 To serve, invert the ramekins on to serving plates. With the dishes still in place, pour off any excess liquid. Remove the dishes and serve hot, with a knob of lemon butter on top.

Menu Suggestion

Serve for a special dinner party starter with warm bread rolls and butter. Serve lamb chops or steaks en croûte with seasonal vegetables for the main course, and a fresh fruit pavlova for dessert.

SALADES RÂPÉES CRUES
(GRATED RAW VEGETABLES WITH GARLIC DRESSING)

0.20	240 cals

Serves 4

175 g (6 oz) carrot, peeled

175 g (6 oz) courgettes

175 g (6 oz) celeriac

15 ml (1 tbsp) lemon juice

175 g (6 oz) raw beetroot

90 ml (6 tbsp) olive or vegetable oil

30 ml (2 tbsp) wine vinegar

2.5 ml (½ tsp) sugar

2.5 ml (½ tsp) mustard

1 garlic clove, skinned and crushed

salt and freshly ground black
    pepper

chopped fresh parsley, to garnish

3 Put the oil, vinegar, sugar, mustard and garlic in a screw-top jar with salt and pepper to taste. Shake the jar until the dressing is emulsified.

4 Pour the dressing over the vegetables and toss lightly just to coat. Serve immediately, garnished with chopped parsley.

Menu Suggestion
Serve this French starter as part of a bistro-style meal with hot garlic bread. Follow with a casserole such as boeuf bourguignon, and a selection of French cheeses and fresh fruit to finish.

1 Grate the carrot avoiding the central core. Grate the courgettes and mix with the carrots.

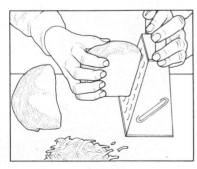

2 Peel and grate the celeriac, toss immediately in the lemon juice and add to the carrot and courgette mixture. Lastly, peel and grate the beetroot and add to the mixture.

ARABIC AUBERGINE CREAM

1.10*	201–301 cals

* plus 1 hour chilling

Serves 4–6

2 large aubergines

salt and freshly ground pepper

100 ml (4 fl oz) olive oil

10 ml (2 tsp) ground cumin

150 ml (¼ pint) natural yogurt

juice of ½ lemon

2 garlic cloves, crushed

chopped fresh coriander and oil,
    to garnish

1 Slice the aubergines thinly, then place in a colander, sprinkling each layer lightly with salt. Cover with a plate, place heavy weights on top, then leave to drain for 30 minutes.

2 Rinse the aubergine slices under cold running water, then pat thoroughly dry.

3 Heat some of the oil in a frying pan and fry the aubergines in batches until golden.

4 Blend or process the aubergines until smooth. Add the remaining ingredients, except garnish, and work again. Season.

5 Turn the cream into a bowl, rough up the surface with a fork and sprinkle with chopped coriander and oil. Chill.

Menu Suggestion
Serve with fingers of hot pitta bread and raw vegetables.

IMAM BAYILDI
(COLD STUFFED BAKED AUBERGINE)

1.40*	372 cals

* plus 1 hour cooling and 2 hours chilling

Serves 6

6 long, small aubergines

salt and freshly ground pepper

200 ml (7 fl oz) olive oil

450 g (1 lb) onions, skinned and finely sliced

3 garlic cloves, skinned and crushed

397 g (14 oz) can tomatoes, drained or 450 g (1 lb) tomatoes, skinned, seeded and chopped

60 ml (4 tbsp) chopped fresh parsley, plus extra to garnish

3.75 ml ($\frac{3}{4}$ tsp) ground allspice

5 ml (1 tsp) sugar

30 ml (2 tbsp) lemon juice

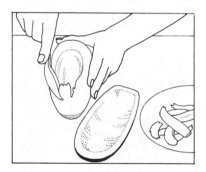

1 Halve the aubergines lengthways. Scoop out the flesh and reserve. Leave a substantial shell so they do not disintegrate.

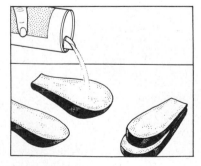

2 Sprinkle the insides of the aubergine shells with salt and invert on a plate for 30 minutes to drain any bitter juices.

3 Heat 45 ml (3 tbsp) olive oil in a saucepan, add the onion and garlic and fry gently for about 15 minutes until soft but not coloured. Add the tomatoes, reserved aubergine flesh, parsley, allspice and salt and pepper to taste. Simmer gently for about 20 minutes until the mixture has reduced and thickened.

4 Rinse the aubergines and pat dry with absorbent kitchen paper. Spoon the filling into each half and place them side by side in a shallow ovenproof dish. They should fit quite closely together.

5 Mix the remaining oil with 150 ml ($\frac{1}{4}$ pint) water, the sugar, lemon juice and salt and pepper to taste. Pour around the aubergines, cover and bake in the oven at 150°C (300°F) mark 2 for at least 1 hour until completely tender.

6 When cooked, remove from the oven, uncover and leave to cool for 1 hour. Chill in the refrigerator for at least 2 hours before serving garnished with lots of chopped parsley.

Menu Suggestion

Imam Bayildi is a Turkish dish, eaten with bread as a first course. Hot pitta bread or crusty French bread are both suitable. Follow with a lamb casserole or kebabs, if you want to continue the Turkish theme.

TARAMASALATA

1.15*	283 cals

* includes 1 hour chilling

Serves 6

225 g (8 oz) smoked cod's roe
1 garlic clove, skinned and crushed
50 g (2 oz) fresh white breadcrumbs
1 small onion, skinned and finely chopped
finely grated rind and juice of 1 lemon
150 ml (¼ pint) olive oil
freshly ground pepper
lemon wedges and pitta or French bread or toast, to serve

1 Skin the smoked cod's roe and break it up into pieces. Place in a blender or food processor with the garlic, breadcrumbs, onion, lemon rind and juice and blend to form a purée.

2 Gradually add the oil and blend well after each addition until smooth. Blend in 90 ml (6 tbsp) hot water with pepper to taste.

3 Spoon into a serving dish and chill in the refrigerator for at least 1 hour. To serve, garnish with lemon slices. Serve with pitta, French bread or toast, if liked.

Menu Suggestion
Taramasalata is always popular as a starter for an informal supper party, served with hot white or wholemeal pitta bread. A dry white Retsina wine makes the perfect accompaniment. To continue the Greek theme of the meal, lamb and aubergine moussaka or lamb kebabs make ideal main courses, or you could try the more unusual pork and coriander stew called *afelia*. As a side dish, serve a Greek salad of shredded white cabbage, tomato, onion and black olives dressed with olive oil and lemon juice. Fresh fruit makes a good ending to the meal.

RAMEKINS OF BAKED CRAB

0.45	166 cals

Serves 6

25 g (1 oz) butter or margarine

50 g (2 oz) onion

225 g (8 oz) white crab meat or
   white and brown mixed

50 g (2 oz) fresh brown
   breadcrumbs

10 ml (2 tsp) French mustard

150 ml ($\frac{1}{4}$ pint) natural yogurt

45 ml (3 tbsp) single cream or milk

cayenne

salt

about 40 g ($1\frac{1}{2}$ oz) Cheddar

lime slices and parsley sprigs,
   to garnish (optional)

1 Melt the butter in a saucepan. Skin and finely chop the onion and fry it gently in the butter until golden brown.

2 Flake the crab meat, taking care to remove any membranes or shell particles. Mix it into the cooked onions and add the bread-crumbs. Mix well together. Stir in the mustard, yogurt and cream. Sprinkle generously with cayenne, then add salt to taste.

3 Spoon the mixture into 6 individual ramekins or individual soufflé dishes. Grate the cheese thinly over the surface of each dish. Stand the dishes on a baking sheet. Place on the top shelf in the oven and cook at 170°C (325°F) mark 3 for 25–30 minutes, or until really hot. Garnish with lime slices and parsley, if liked.

Menu Suggestion
Serve with triangles of crisp hot granary toast for an informal dinner party starter, or for a tasty lunch·or supper snack.

VEGETABLE TARTS

| 1.30 | 🍳 | ✳ | 677 cals |

Makes 4

125 g (5 oz) plain flour
salt and freshly ground pepper
150 g (6 oz) butter or margarine
1 egg yolk
1 small onion, skinned and finely
    chopped
2 medium courgettes, sliced
a little lightly beaten egg white
142 g (5 oz) full fat soft cheese with
    herbs and garlic
2 eggs, beaten
20 ml (4 tsp) chopped fresh basil or
    10 ml (2 tsp) dried
fresh basil sprigs, to garnish
    (optional)

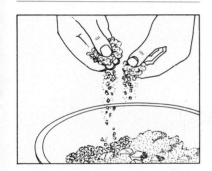

1 Make the pastry cases. Sift the flour into a bowl with a pinch of salt. Add 100 g (4 oz) of the butter in pieces and work into the flour with your fingertips.

2 Add the egg yolk and 5–10 ml (1–2 tsp) cold water and work with a palette knife until the dough draws together.

3 Gather the dough into a ball with one hand, then wrap in cling film or foil. Chill in the refrigerator while making the filling.

4 Melt the remaining butter in a heavy-based frying pan, add the onion and fry gently for about 5 minutes until soft and lightly coloured. Add the courgettes and fry over moderate heat for a few minutes, turning them frequently until they are light golden on all sides. Turn into a bowl and leave until cold.

5 Meanwhile, roll out the dough on a lightly floured surface and cut out 4 circles large enough to line 4 individual loose-bottomed 10 cm (4 inch) quiche or tartlet tins.

6 Place the pastry in the tins, prick the bases with a fork, then line with foil and beans. Bake 'blind' in the oven at 190°C (375°F) mark 5 for 10 minutes.

7 Remove the foil and beans, brush the pastry with the egg white and return to the oven for a further 5 minutes.

8 Put the cream cheese mixture in a bowl and beat with a wooden spoon until soft. Add the eggs and beat well to mix, then the courgettes, basil and salt and pepper to taste.

9 Divide the filling equally between the pastry cases, then return to the oven for a further 10–15 minutes, until the filling is set. Leave to stand for at least 15 minutes before serving. Serve warm, garnished with basil sprigs, if liked.

Menu Suggestion
Individual quiches make a most unusual and attractive dinner party starter. They are quite substantial, and need no accompaniment other than a chilled dry white wine such as a French Muscadet.

Served cold, the tarts make excellent cold luncheon or picnic fare, with a selection of crisp, crunchy salads, fresh granary bread or a French stick, and chilled French dry cider.

PROSCIUTTO CON MELONE
(PARMA HAM WITH MELON)

0.20	104 cals

Serves 4

900 g (2 lb) Cantaloupe melon
8 thin slices of Parma ham
freshly ground black pepper

1 Cut the melon in half length-ways. Scoop out the seeds from the centre.

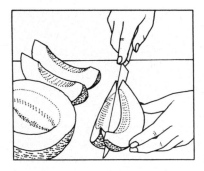

2 Cut each of the melon halves into four even-sized wedge shapes.

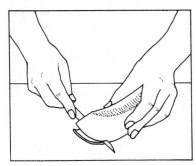

3 With a sharp, pointed knife and using a sawing action, separate the flesh from the skin, keeping it in position on the skin.

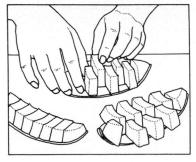

4 Cut the flesh across into bite-sized slices, then push each slice in opposite directions.

5 Carefully roll up each of the eight slices of Parma ham. Place two wedges of melon and two rolls of ham on each plate. Grind pepper over the ham before serving.

VARIATION

Instead of the melon, use fresh figs in season to make Prosciutto Con Fichi. Only use very fresh, ripe figs in peak condition. In Italy, figs are often served whole and unpeeled, but to help guests who are not used to eating figs as much as the Italians are, it is best to peel them first, then cut them in half. For four people, 8–12 figs is sufficient. Arrange them cut-side up on individual serving plates next to the Parma ham, which may or may not be rolled up, according to how you like it.

BAGNA CAUDA
(HOT ANCHOVY DIP)

0.45	🖙	396 cals

Serves 6

225 g (8 oz) asparagus, washed,
    trimmed and freshly cooked

3 globe artichokes, trimmed and
    freshly cooked

1 small cauliflower

1 large red pepper

1 large green pepper

4 carrots, peeled

6 celery sticks, trimmed

3 courgettes, trimmed

1 bunch radishes

150 ml ($\frac{1}{4}$ pint) olive oil

75 g (3 oz) butter

2 garlic cloves, skinned and finely
    chopped

two 50 g (2 oz) cans anchovy fillets,
    drained and finely chopped

1 While the asparagus and artichokes are cooling, prepare the
remaining vegetables. Cut the
cauliflower into florets, discarding
any tough stalks.

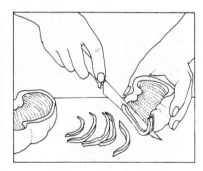

2 Cut the peppers in half lengthways and remove the cores and
seeds. Wash the peppers inside
and out, dry and cut into strips.

3 Cut the carrots, celery and
courgettes into finger-sized
sticks. Trim the radishes.

4 Heat the oil and butter in a
saucepan until just melted, but
not foaming. Add the garlic and
cook gently for 2 minutes. Do not
allow it to colour.

5 Add the anchovies and cook
very gently, stirring all the
time, for 10 minutes or until the
anchovies dissolve into a paste.

6 To serve. Transfer the dip to
an earthenware dish and keep
warm over a fondue burner or
spirit lamp at the table. Each guest
dips the vegetables in the hot
anchovy sauce.

TONNO E FAGIOLI
(TUNA FISH WITH BEANS)

2.30*	316 cals

* plus overnight soaking

Serves 4

175 g (6 oz) dried white haricot or cannellini beans, soaked in cold water overnight

45 ml (3 tbsp) olive oil

15 ml (1 tbsp) wine vinegar

salt and freshly ground pepper

1 small onion, skinned and finely sliced

200 g (7 oz) can tuna fish in oil, drained and flaked into large chunks

chopped fresh parsley, to garnish

1 Drain the beans, rinse under cold running water, then tip into a large saucepan and cover with fresh cold water. Bring to the boil, then lower the heat and simmer gently for 1½–2 hours or until beans are tender. Drain.

2 Whisk together the oil, vinegar, salt and pepper and mix with the hot beans. Cool for 15 minutes.

3 Mix in the onion, then the tuna fish, being careful not to break it up too much.

4 To serve. Taste and adjust seasoning, then transfer to a serving dish. Sprinkle liberally with chopped fresh parsley just before serving.

TONNO E FAGIOLI

Both dried white haricot beans and cannellini are used extensively in Italian cooking—mostly in salads and soups. Soaking is essential with dried beans, but if you forget to soak them overnight, there is an emergency soaking procedure which works just as well. Put the beans in a large saucepan of cold water (never add salt before cooking beans as this causes their skins to toughen) and bring to the boil. Boil steadily for at least 10 minutes, then remove from the heat, cover and leave for about 1 hour or until the water has gone cold. Proceed with the recipe from step 1.

SMOKED TROUT WITH TOMATOES AND MUSHROOMS.

| 0.20* | 189 cals |

* plus 30 minutes to dégorge cucumber

Serves 8 as a starter

700 g (1½ lb) smoked trout
225 g (8 oz) cucumber, skinned
salt and freshly ground pepper
175 g (6 oz) mushrooms, wiped
45 ml (3 tbsp) creamed horseradish
30 ml (2 tbsp) lemon juice
60 ml (4 tbsp) natural yogurt
4 very large Marmande or
   Beefsteak tomatoes, about 350 g
   (12 oz) each
spring onion tops, to garnish

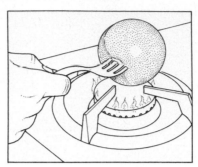

1 Flake the trout flesh, discarding the skin and bones.

2 Finely chop the cucumber, sprinkle with salt and leave for 30 minutes to dégorge. Rinse and drain well, then dry thoroughly with absorbent kitchen paper.

3 Finely chop the mushrooms, combine with the cucumber, horseradish, lemon juice and yogurt. Fold in the trout, then add seasoning to taste.

4 Skin the tomatoes. Pierce each one with a fork in the stalk end and then hold in the flame of a gas hob. Turn the tomato until the skin blisters and bursts, leave until cool enough to handle, then peel off the skin with your fingers.

5 Slice the tomatoes thickly, then sandwich in pairs with the trout mixture.

6 Arrange the tomato 'sandwiches' in a shallow serving dish. Garnish with snipped spring onion tops and chill in the refrigerator until ready to serve.

SMOKED TROUT WITH TOMATOES AND MUSHROOMS

For this recipe, it is important to buy the very large continental-type tomatoes. In the summer months these are widely available, some home-grown as well as the imported types from the Mediterranean. Look for them under the names 'Continental', 'Marmande' and 'Beefsteak'— any of these are suitable, as long as they are not too misshapen or they will not sandwich together. These types of tomatoes are also excellent stuffed.

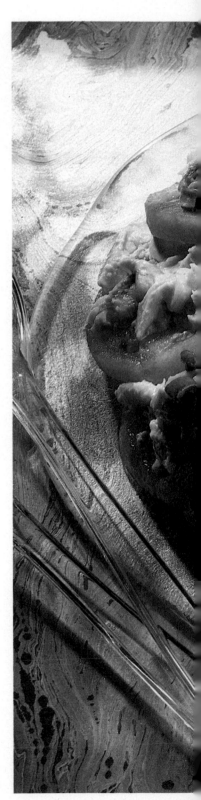

Snacks and
Suppers

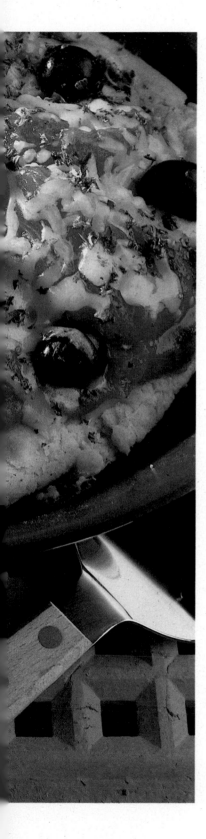

PIZZA-IN-THE-PAN

0.25	1150 cals

Serves 2

225 g (8 oz) self-raising flour
salt and freshly ground pepper
60 ml (4 tbsp) vegetable oil
60 ml (4 tbsp) water
75 ml (5 tbsp) tomato purée
397 g (14 oz) can tomatoes, drained
   and chopped
175 g (6 oz) Cheddar cheese, grated
chopped fresh herbs
a few black olives

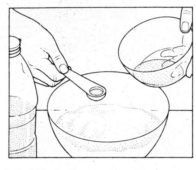

1 Sift the flour and seasoning into a bowl. Make a well in the centre and pour in 30 ml (2 tbsp) of the oil and 60 ml (4 tbsp) of the water. Mix to a soft dough—you will find that it binds together very quickly, although you may need to add a little more water.

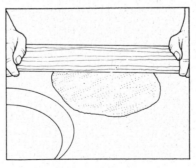

2 Knead the dough lightly on a floured surface, then roll out to a circle that will fit a medium-sized frying pan.

3 Heat half the remaining oil in the pan. Add the circle of dough and fry gently for about 5 minutes until the base is cooked and lightly browned.

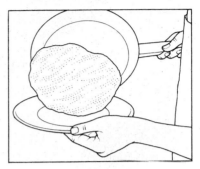

4 Turn the dough out onto a plate and flip it over.

5 Heat the remaining oil in the pan, then slide the dough back into the pan, browned side uppermost. Spread with the tomato purée, then top with the tomatoes and sprinkle over grated cheese, herbs and black olives.

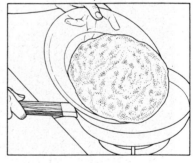

6 Cook for a further 5 minutes until the underside is done, then slide the pan under a preheated grill. Cook for 3–4 minutes until the cheese melts. Serve immediately.

Menu Suggestion
Serve with a mixed salad and an Italian red wine such as Chianti Classico or Valpolicella.

COCOTTE EGGS

| 0.35 | 310 cals |

Serves 4

25 g (1 oz) butter

1 small onion, skinned and finely
chopped

4 rashers of lean back bacon,
rinded and finely chopped

100 g (4 oz) button mushrooms,
finely chopped

10 ml (2 tsp) tomato purée

10 ml (2 tsp) chopped fresh
tarragon or 5 ml (1 tsp) dried
tarragon

salt and freshly ground pepper

4 eggs, size 2

120 ml (8 tbsp) double cream

chopped fresh tarragon,
to garnish

1 Melt the butter in a small
saucepan, add the onion and
fry gently until soft. Add the
bacon and fry until beginning to
change colour, then add the
mushrooms and tomato purée.
Continue frying for 2–3 minutes
until the juices run, stirring
constantly.

2 Remove from the heat and stir
in the tarragon and seasoning
to taste. Divide the mixture
equally between 4 cocottes,
ramekins or individual soufflé
dishes. Make a slight identation
in the centre of each one.

3 Break an egg into each dish, on
top of the mushroom and
bacon mixture, then slowly pour
30 ml (2 tbsp) cream over each
one. Sprinkle with salt and freshly
ground pepper to taste.

4 Place the cocottes on a baking
tray and bake in the oven at
180°C (350°F) mark 4 for 10–12
minutes until the eggs are set.
Serve immediately.

Menu Suggestion
Serve for breakfast, brunch, lunch
or supper, with triangles of wholemeal or granary toast and butter.

COCOTTE EGGS

As an alternative to the
mushrooms in this recipe, you
can use fresh tomatoes. At the
end of the summer when they
are often overripe, they are best
used for cooking rather than in
salads, and this baked egg dish is
a good way to use them up. Skin
them first if you have time as this
will make the finished dish more
palatable. A quick way to skin a
few tomatoes is to pierce one at a
time with a fork in the stalk end
and then hold in the flame of a
gas hob. Turn the tomato until
the skin blisters and bursts, leave
until cool enough to handle, then
peel off the skin with your
fingers. To replace the
mushrooms, use 4 medium
tomatoes, chopped, and substitute basil for the tarragon, if
available.

STUFFED BAKED POTATOES

2.00	362 cals

Serves 4

4 medium potatoes, about 250 g
(8 oz) each

1 medium onion, skinned

25 g (1 oz) butter or margarine

60 ml (4 tbsp) milk

125 g (4 oz) Cheddar cheese, grated

dash of Worcestershire sauce

salt and freshly ground pepper

snipped fresh chives, to garnish

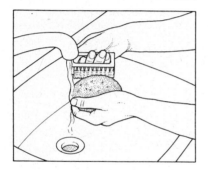

1 Scrub the potatoes with a stiff vegetable brush under cold running water. Pat dry with absorbent kitchen paper and then wrap individually in foil. Bake in the oven at 200°C (400°F) mark 6 for about 1¼–1½ hours, or until just tender. Remove the potatoes from the oven, leaving the oven turned on at the same temperature.

2 Cut the potatoes in half lengthways. Scoop out most of the flesh from the insides, leaving a good rim around the edge of each potato shell. Mash the scooped-out potato in a bowl until free of lumps.

3 Finely chop the onion. Melt the fat in a small saucepan. Add the onion and fry gently until lightly browned. Add the milk and heat gently.

4 Beat this mixture into the mashed potato with half of the grated cheese, the Worcestershire sauce and seasoning to taste.

5 Spoon the potato back into the shells (or pipe with a large, star vegetable nozzle). Sprinkle over the remaining grated cheese.

6 Return to the oven for about 20 minutes, or until golden. Serve immediately, sprinkled with chives.

Menu Suggestion

Serve Stuffed Baked Potatoes on their own for a tasty snack at lunch or supper time. For a more substantial meal, serve with sausages or frankfurters.

——— VARIATIONS ———

Instead of the onion, cheese and Worcestershire sauce, add the following ingredients to the scooped-out mashed potato: 75 g (3 oz) **bacon**, roughly chopped and fried, a little **milk**, **salt** and **freshly ground pepper**; or 75 g (3 oz) **smoked haddock**, cooked and mashed, 5 ml (1 tsp) **chopped fresh parsley**, 5 ml (1 tsp) **lemon juice**, a little **milk**, **salt**, **freshly ground pepper** and **grated nutmeg**, or 30–45 ml (2–3 tbsp) **cream**, 10 ml (2 tsp) **snipped chives**, **salt**.

Pile back into potato skins and serve immediately without returning to the oven.

STUFFED BAKED POTATOES

Baked potatoes, warm and filling, are one of winter's most popular foods—and one of the easiest to cook.

For the best results, buy the varieties recommended for baking. These include Desirée, Kerrs Pink, King Edward, Majestic, Pentland Crown, Pentland Dell and Pentland Ivory. Check before buying that the potatoes are free from disease, mechanical damage and growth shoots, because many people like to eat the skin of jacket-baked potatoes, the most nutritious part. (Potatoes are a rich source of vitamin C, iron, thiamin, riboflavin and nicotinic acid, and the skins also provide dietary fibre.) Also check that the skins are not tinged with green, which is caused by exposure to light and makes the potatoes unpleasant to eat. All potatoes should be stored in the dark to prevent this problem occurring.

MEXICAN BEEF TACOS

| 0.40 | ✳* | 515 cals |

* freeze chilli beef mixture after step 2

Serves 4

30 ml (2 tbsp) vegetable oil

1 onion, skinned and finely
   chopped

1–2 garlic cloves, skinned and
   crushed

5–10 ml (1–2 tsp) chilli powder,
   according to taste

350 g (12 oz) lean minced beef

225 g (8 oz) can tomatoes

15 ml (1 tbsp) tomato purée

2.5 ml ($\frac{1}{2}$ tsp) sugar

salt and freshly ground pepper

283 g (10 oz) can red kidney beans,
   drained and rinsed

8 taco shells

shredded lettuce and grated
   Cheddar cheese, to serve

1 Heat the oil in a pan, add the
onion, garlic and chilli powder
and fry gently until soft. Add the
minced beef and fry until
browned, stirring and pressing
with a wooden spoon to remove
any lumps.

2 Stir in the tomatoes with their
juice and the tomato purée.
Crush the tomatoes well with the
spoon, then bring to the boil, stirring. Lower the heat, add the
sugar and seasoning to taste, then
simmer, uncovered, for 20
minutes until thick and reduced.
Stir occasionally during this time
to combine the ingredients and
prevent them from sticking.

3 Add the kidney beans to the
pan and heat through for 5
minutes. Meanwhile, heat the taco
shells in the oven according to the
instructions on the packet.

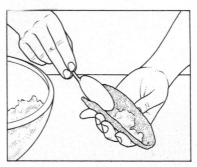

4 To serve, divide the meat
mixture equally between the
taco shells, then top with grated
cheese and shredded lettuce. Eat
immediately, before the taco shells
soften with the heat of the beef.

Menu Suggestion

Crisp taco shells filled with spicy
hot beef chilli are perfect for an
impromptu snack—teenagers love
them. Place warm taco shells on
the table with bowls of chilli beef,
cheese and lettuce and let everyone make their own. Serve with
ice-cold drinks such as cola, root
beer or lager.

MEXICAN BEEF TACOS

Take care when adding chilli
powder, because strengths vary
considerably from one brand to
another. Always add the smallest
amount specified, then taste
before adding more. If you
prefer a mild chilli flavour, buy
'chilli seasoning', which is available in small glass bottles at most
supermarkets. A blend of chilli
powder and other spices, it has
less 'fire' than real chilli powder,
and can be used in larger
amounts.

Mexican taco shells are
available in boxes at most large
supermarkets. Some packs come
with a ready-mixed sauce in a
sachet, so make sure it is only
the taco shells you are buying.

SAUSAGE BURGERS

| 0.50 | 390 cals |

Makes 8

450 g (1 lb) pork sausagemeat

125 g (4 oz) fresh white breadcrumbs

1 medium onion, skinned and finely chopped

60 ml (4 tbsp) chopped fresh parsley

1 egg, size 2, beaten

salt and freshly ground pepper

60 ml (4 tbsp) flour

vegetable oil for frying

1 In a bowl or food processor, mix together the sausagemeat, breadcrumbs, onion, parsley, egg and seasoning to taste.

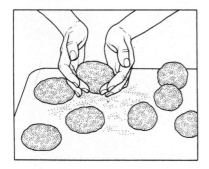

2 Divide the mixture into eight on a floured board. With well-floured hands, shape into rounds about 1 cm (½ inch) thick.

3 Place the burgers on a lightly floured plate and chill in the refrigerator for at least 30 minutes.

4 Heat a little oil in a frying pan, add half of the burgers and fry for 8–10 minutes a side, turning once only. Drain on absorbent kitchen paper and keep hot while frying the remainder.

Menu Suggestion

Serve fresh Sausage Burgers hot in warmed burger baps with a selection of pickles and ketchup. Accompany with a mixed salad of lettuce, tomato and cucumber.

WHOLEWHEAT, APRICOT AND NUT SALAD

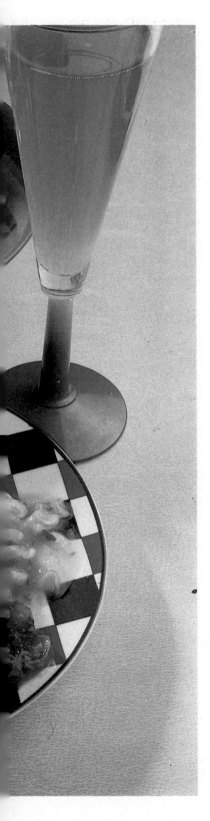

0.35*	325–433 cals

* plus overnight soaking and 2 hours chilling

Serves 6–8

225 g (8 oz) wholewheat grain

3 celery sticks, washed and trimmed

125 g (4 oz) dried apricots

100 g (4 oz) Brazil nuts, roughly chopped

50 g (2 oz) unsalted peanuts

60 ml (4 tbsp) olive oil

30 ml (2 tbsp) lemon juice

salt and freshly ground pepper

chopped fresh parsley and cucumber slices, to garnish

1 Soak the wholewheat grain overnight in plenty of cold water. Drain, then tip into a large saucepan of boiling water. Simmer gently for 25 minutes or until the grains have a little bite left.

2 Drain the wholewheat into a colander and rinse under cold running water. Tip into a large serving bowl and set aside.

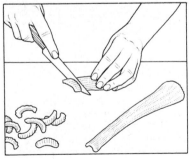

3 Cut the celery into small diagonal pieces with a sharp knife. Stir into the wholewheat.

4 Using kitchen scissors, snip the apricots into small pieces over the wholewheat. Add the nuts and stir well to mix.

5 Mix the oil and lemon juice together with plenty of seasoning, pour over the salad and toss well. Chill in the refrigerator for 2 hours, then toss again and adjust seasoning just before serving.

Menu Suggestion
Serve for a healthy lunch dish with hot granary or wholemeal rolls and a green salad.

WHOLEWHEAT, APRICOT AND NUT SALAD
You can buy the wholewheat grain for this recipe in any good health food shop. Sometimes it is referred to as 'kibbled' wheat, because the grains are cracked in a machine called a 'kibbler', which breaks the grain into little pieces. Do not confuse wholewheat grain with cracked wheat (sometimes also called bulghar or burghul), which is cooked wheat which has been dried and cracked, used extensively in the cooking of the Middle East. Although different, the two kinds of wheat can be used interchangeably in most recipes.

SURPRISE SOUFFLÉ

1.15	474 cals

Serves 4

75 g (3 oz) butter

50 g (2 oz) flour

300 ml ($\frac{1}{2}$ pint) milk

100 g (4 oz) Gruyère cheese, grated

1.25 ml ($\frac{1}{4}$ tsp) ground mace

salt and freshly ground pepper

5 eggs, separated

225 g (8 oz) button mushrooms, finely sliced

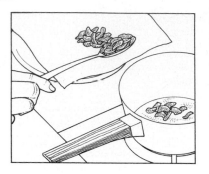

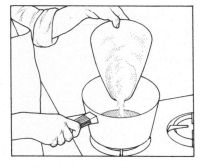

1 Melt 50 g (2 oz) of the butter in a saucepan, sprinkle in the flour and cook for 1–2 minutes, stirring constantly.

2 Remove from the heat and gradually add the milk, beating constantly after each addition. Return to the heat and bring to the boil, stirring, then lower the heat and add the cheese, mace and seasoning to taste. Simmer for about 5 minutes until the cheese melts and the sauce is very thick.

3 Remove from the heat and leave to cool for 5 minutes, then stir in the egg yolks one at a time. Set aside.

4 Melt the remaining butter in a separate pan, add the mushrooms and fry over a high heat for 2 minutes only. Remove from the pan with a slotted spoon; drain on absorbent kitchen paper.

5 Whisk the egg whites until stiff, then fold into the cheese sauce. Spoon three-quarters into a well-buttered 1.5 litre (3 pint) soufflé dish.

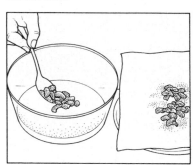

6 Make a well in the centre of the sauce, and spoon in the mushrooms. Cover with the remaining sauce. Bake in the oven at 200°C (400°F) mark 6 for 25–30 minutes until puffed up and golden on top. Serve immediately.

Menu Suggestion
Serve for a supper dish with fresh French bread and a mixed salad tossed in a vinaigrette dressing.

TUNA AND PASTA IN SOURED CREAM

0.25	780 cals

Serves 4

225 g (8 oz) pasta spirals or shells
salt and freshly ground pepper
5 ml (1 tsp) vegetable oil
198 g (7 oz) can tuna, drained
4 eggs, hard-boiled and shelled
25 g (1 oz) butter
150 ml ($\frac{1}{4}$ pint) soured cream
5 ml (1 tsp) anchovy essence
30 ml (2 tbsp) malt vinegar
60 ml (4 tbsp) chopped fresh
   parsley

1 Cook the pasta in plenty of boiling salted water to which the oil has been added, for about 15 minutes until *al dente* (tender but firm to the bite). Drain well.

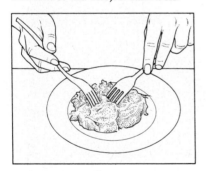

2 Meanwhile, flake the tuna fish with 2 forks. Chop the hard-boiled eggs finely.

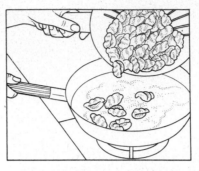

3 Melt the butter in a deep frying pan and toss in the pasta. Stir in the soured cream, anchovy essence and vinegar.

4 Add the tuna and egg to the pan with the parsley. Season well and warm through over low heat, stirring occasionally. Serve immediately.

Menu Suggestion
This rich and filling pasta dish needs a contrasting accompaniment. Serve with a crisp and crunchy green salad of chopped celery, fennel, cucumber and green pepper.

TUNA AND PASTA IN SOURED CREAM

The type of pasta you use for this dish is really a matter of personal taste, although spirals and shells are specified in the ingredients list. As long as the shapes are small *(pasta corta)*, the sauce will cling to them and not slide off—Italians serve short cut pasta with fairly heavy sauces like this one which have chunks of fish or meat in them. Long pasta *(pasta lunga)* such as spaghetti and tagliatelle are best served with smoother sauces. Italian pasta in the shape of shells are called *conchiglie*, and there are many different sizes to choose from. *Farfalle* are shaped like small bow-ties; *fusilli* are spirals, so too are *spirale ricciolo*; *rotelle* are shaped like wheels. There are also many different types of short pasta shaped like macaroni—*penne* are hollow and shaped like quills with angled ends, *rigatoni* have ridges.

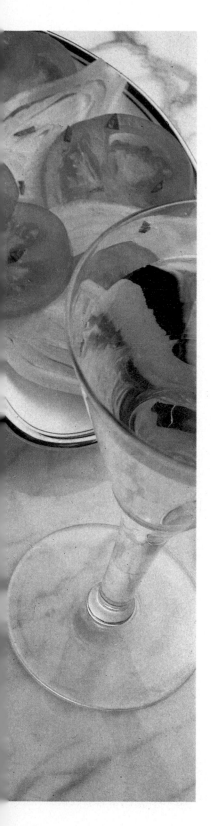

NOODLES IN WALNUT SAUCE

0.20	730 cals

Serves 4

100 g (4 oz) walnut pieces

75 g (3 oz) butter, softened

1 small garlic clove, skinned and roughly chopped

30 ml (2 tbsp) flour

300 ml (½ pint) milk

275 g (10 oz) green tagliatelle

5 ml (1 tsp) vegetable oil

salt and freshly ground pepper

100 g (4 oz) Cheddar cheese, grated

freshly grated nutmeg

1 In a blender or food processor, mix together the walnuts, 50 g (2 oz) of the butter and the garlic. Turn into a bowl.

2 Put the remaining 25 g (1 oz) of butter in the blender or food processor. Add the flour and milk and work until evenly mixed.

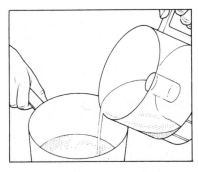

3 Turn the mixture into a saucepan and bring slowly to the boil, stirring. Simmer 6 minutes.

4 Meanwhile, cook the tagliatelle in plenty of boiling salted water, adding the oil to the water (this prevents the pasta from sticking together).

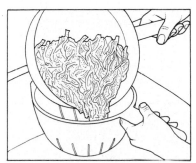

5 For the timing, follow the pack instructions and cook until *al dente* (tender, but firm to the bite). Drain the pasta thoroughly, then return to the pan. Add the nut butter and heat through gently, stirring all the time.

6 Divide the pasta mixture equally between 4 large, individual gratin-type dishes. Add seasoning to the white sauce, then use to coat the pasta.

7 Scatter the grated cheese on top, sprinkle with the nutmeg, then grill for 5–10 minutes until brown and bubbling. Serve immediately.

Menu Suggestion

Serve for a supper dish followed by a tomato and fennel salad dressed with olive oil, lemon juice and chopped fresh basil.

NOODLES IN WALNUT SAUCE

Making velvety smooth sauces is not the easiest of culinary tasks, and most cooks seem to have problems with them at some time or another. Even French chefs have been known to sieve their sauces before serving, to remove lumps! The French method of cooking a roux of butter and flour, then gradually adding milk, requires a certain amount of skill and judgement, whereas the all-in-one method in this recipe is quick and easy to do if you have a blender or food processor — and just about foolproof!

CELERIAC AU GRATIN

1.00	351–527 cals

Serves 4–6

15 ml (1 tbsp) lemon juice

2 heads of celeriac, total weight about 900 g (2 lb)

salt and freshly ground pepper

100 g (4 oz) butter or margarine

150 ml (¼ pint) dry white wine

175 g (6 oz) Gruyère, grated

75 g (3 oz) Parmesan, freshly grated

1 Fill a bowl with cold water and add the lemon juice. Peel the celeriac, then cut into chunky pieces. Place the pieces in the bowl of acidulated water as you prepare them, to prevent discoloration.

2 Drain the celeriac, then plunge quickly into a large pan of boiling salted water. Return to the boil and blanch for 10 minutes. Drain thoroughly.

3 Melt the butter in a flame-proof gratin dish. Add the celeriac and turn to coat in the butter. Stir in the wine. Mix together the Gruyère and Parmesan cheeses and sprinkle over the top of the celeriac, with salt and pepper to taste. Bake in the oven at 190°C (375°F) mark 5 for 30 minutes until the celeriac is tender when pierced with a skewer and the topping is golden brown.

Menu Suggestion
Serve for a vegetarian supper dish, with a colourful tomato or red pepper salad, and hot garlic or herb bread.

CELERIAC AU GRATIN

Make the most of celeriac in the winter months; it is a seasonal vegetable which is rarely seen in the shops at other times of year. From the same family as celery, which it resembles in flavour, it is an unusual, quite ugly-looking vegetable, sometimes called "turnip-rooted celery", which is an apt description. Only buy small celeriac, very large specimens tend to be woody and lacking in flavour—and difficult to deal with. This recipe for Celeriac au Gratin has a definite "European" flavour. The French, Swiss and Italians have always used celeriac a lot in their cooking, and on the continent you will come across many different ways of serving it. Steamed or boiled celeriac is usually served as a vegetable accompaniment, simply tossed in melted butter and chopped fresh herbs, or coated in a béchamel or Hollandaise sauce; lightly blanched fingers of celeriac are coated in a vinaigrette dressing while still warm and served as a first course; and grated raw celeriac is served with mayonnaise to make *céléri-rave rémoulade*, a popular French hors d'oeuvre.

The recipe on this page makes a tasty light supper dish, and would make an excellent main course if you are entertaining vegetarians. If you would like to make it more substantial by adding meat, mix 175–225 g (6–8 oz) chopped cooked bacon or ham with the celeriac, before topping with the cheeses.

TURKEY TERRINE

2.00*	✳	311–415 cals

* plus 2 hours cooling and overnight chilling

Serves 6–8

225 g (8 oz) cooked turkey meat

225 g (8 oz) turkey or pig's liver

175 g (6 oz) thinly sliced streaky bacon rashers, rinded

1 medium onion

225 g (8 oz) sausagemeat

1 garlic clove, skinned and crushed

15 ml (1 tbsp) chopped fresh sage or 5 ml (1 tsp) dried

45 ml (3 tbsp) double cream

30 ml (2 tbsp) brandy

1 egg

salt and freshly ground pepper

bay leaf

1 Mince the turkey, liver, 50 g (2 oz) of the bacon and the onion. (Alternatively, work in a food processor.)

2 Put the minced mixture in a bowl. Add the sausagemeat, garlic, sage, cream, brandy, egg and salt and pepper to taste. Mix with a spoon until all the ingredients are evenly combined.

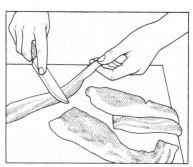

3 Stretch the remaining bacon rashers with the flat side of a blade of a large cook's knife.

4 Use the bacon rashers to line a 1.1 litre (2 pint) terrine or loaf tin, making sure there are no gaps.

5 Spoon the meat mixture into the container and place a bay leaf on top. Cover tightly with foil or a lid, then stand the container in a roasting tin.

6 Pour 3.5 cm ($1\frac{1}{2}$ inches) hot water into the roasting tin, then bake in the oven at 170°C (325°F) mark 3 for about $1\frac{1}{2}$ hours. Remove from the water bath and leave to cool for 2 hours. Place heavy weights on top of the terrine and chill in the refrigerator overnight.

7 To serve, turn the terrine out of the container onto a plate and cut into slices.

TURKEY TERRINE

The method of baking a terrine in a roasting tin with hot water, called a *bain marie* or water bath, is essential if the mixture is to cook properly—the hot water distributes the oven heat evenly through the mixture and gives a moist result. Special water baths can be bought at kitchen equipment shops, but an ordinary roasting tin does the job just as well, and can be used in the oven or on top of the cooker according to individual recipe instructions. Always cover the mixture tightly with foil when cooking in a water bath, or the top of the terrine will form an unpleasant hard crust.

FALAFEL
(ISRAELI CHICK PEA PATTIES)

| 1.40* | 🍴 | 186–279 cals |

* plus overnight soaking and at least 1
hour chilling

Serves 4–6

225 g (8 oz) chick peas, soaked in
    cold water overnight

1 medium onion, skinned and
    roughly chopped

1 garlic clove, skinned and roughly
    chopped

10 ml (2 tsp) ground cumin

30 ml (2 tbsp) chopped fresh
    coriander or 5 ml (1 tsp) dried

1.25 ml ($\frac{1}{4}$ tsp) chilli powder

5 ml (1 tsp) salt

plain flour, for coating

1 egg, beaten

vegetable oil, for deep frying

1 Drain the chick peas and rinse
well under cold running water.
Put in a large saucepan, cover with
plenty of fresh cold water and
bring slowly to the boil. Skim off
any scum with a slotted spoon,
then half cover with a lid and
simmer for 1 hour, or until the
chick peas are tender.

2 Drain the chick peas
thoroughly and place in a
blender or food processor. Add
the onion, garlic, cumin,
coriander, chilli powder and salt.
Work the mixture until smooth.
(Alternatively, work the chick
peas, onion and garlic in a mincer
or vegetable mill, then mix in the
other ingredients.)

3 With floured hands, shape the
mixture into 16–18 small flat
cakes. Dip them 1 at a time in
the beaten egg, then coat them in
more flour seasoned with salt and
pepper. Chill in the refrigerator
for at least 1 hour.

4 Pour enough oil into a deep
frying pan to come about
2.5 cm (1 inch) up the sides. Heat
until very hot, then fry the falafel
in batches for about 3 minutes on
each side until golden, turning
once. Drain on absorbent kitchen
paper while frying the remainder.
Serve hot or cold.

Menu Suggestion
Falafel are sold as a snack in
Israel, usually eaten stuffed into
pockets of pitta bread, with salad.

MEAT LOAF

1.35*	✳	494–659 cals

* plus cooling and overnight chilling

Serves 6–8

900 g (2 lb) boneless leg or shoulder of pork, minced

225 g (8 oz) mushrooms, finely chopped

225 g (8 oz) streaky bacon, rinded and minced

2 medium onions, skinned and finely chopped

1 large garlic clove, skinned and crushed

125 g (4 oz) fresh breadcrumbs

150 ml ($\frac{1}{4}$ pint) soured cream

45 ml (3 tbsp) dry white wine

5 ml (1 tsp) dried mixed herbs

2.5 ml ($\frac{1}{2}$ tsp) ground allspice

1.25 ml ($\frac{1}{4}$ tsp) grated nutmeg

salt and freshly ground pepper

1 In a large bowl, mix all the ingredients together until evenly combined.

2 Pack the mixture into a 1.4 litre (2$\frac{1}{2}$ pint) loaf tin and cover with foil.

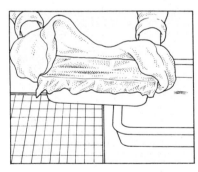

3 Half fill a roasting tin with water and place the loaf tin in the water bath. Cook in the oven at 190°C (375°F) mark 5 for 1 hour.

4 Uncover the tin, increase the oven temperature to 200°C (400°F) mark 6 and cook the meat loaf for a further 30 minutes.

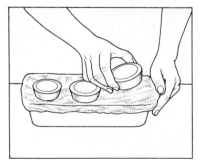

5 Remove the tin from the water bath and leave to cool for 30 minutes. Cover with foil and place heavy weights on top. Chill in the refrigerator overnight.

6 To serve, turn the meat loaf out of the tin and cut into slices for serving.

Menu Suggestion
Thickly sliced Meat Loaf is similar to a pâté or terrine. Serve as a lunch dish with a potato or rice salad, and sprigs of watercress.

SPICY SCOTCH EGGS

0.40*	927 cals

*plus 30 minutes chilling

Makes 4

30 ml (2 tbsp) vegetable oil

1 onion, skinned and very finely chopped

10 ml (2 tsp) medium-hot curry powder

450 g (1 lb) pork sausagemeat

100 g (4 oz) mature Cheddar cheese, finely grated

salt and freshly ground pepper

4 eggs, hard-boiled

plain flour, for coating

1 egg, beaten

100–175 g (4–6 oz) dried breadcrumbs

vegetable oil, for deep-frying

1 Heat the 30 ml (2 tbsp) oil in a small pan, add the onion and curry powder and fry gently for 5 minutes until soft.

2 Put the sausagemeat and cheese in a bowl, add the onion and salt and pepper to taste. Mix with your hands to combine the ingredients well together.

3 Divide the mixture into 4 equal portions and flatten out on a floured board or work surface.

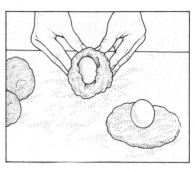

4 Place an egg in the centre of each piece. With floured hands, shape and mould the sausagemeat around the eggs. Coat · lightly with more flour.

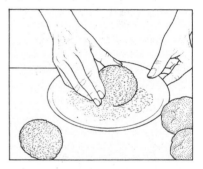

5 Brush each Scotch egg with beaten egg, then roll in the breadcrumbs until evenly coated. Chill for 30 minutes.

6 Heat the oil in a deep-fat fryer to 170°C (325°F). Carefully lower the Scotch eggs into the oil with a slotted spoon and deep-fry for 10 minutes, turning them occasionally until golden brown on all sides. Drain and cool on absorbent kitchen paper.

Menu Suggestion

Home-made Scotch eggs are quite delicious, with far more flavour than the commercial varieties. Serve them cut in halves or quarters with a mixed salad for lunch, or wrap them individually in cling film or foil and pack them for a picnic or packed lunch — they are easy to eat with the fingers. Scotch eggs can also be served hot for a family meal.

MEAT LOAF

The method of cooking meat loaves, pâtés and terrines in a roasting tin half filled with water is called '*au bain marie*' in French. It is a very simple method, but an essential one if the finished meat mixture is to be moist in texture. If the loaf tin is placed directly on the oven shelf, the mixture will dry out and the top will form a hard, unpleasant crust. A *bain marie* creates steam in the oven, which gives a moist heat. Special tins called water baths can be bought at kitchen shops for cooking '*au bain marie*', but an ordinary roasting tin does the job just as well.

FETA CHEESE PUFFS WITH BASIL

| 0.25 | ✳* | 274 cals |

* freeze after stage 4

Makes 8

225 g (8 oz) Feta cheese, grated

142 g (5 oz) natural yogurt

30 ml (2 tbsp) chopped fresh basil or 5 ml (1 tsp) dried

freshly ground pepper

397-g (14-oz) packet frozen puff pastry, thawed

beaten egg

fresh basil leaves, to garnish

1 Mix the grated cheese with the yogurt, basil and pepper. (Don't add salt as the cheese adds sufficient.)

2 Roll out the pastry *thinly* and cut out sixteen 10-cm (4-inch) rounds. Fold and reroll the pastry as necessary.

3 Place half the rounds on two baking sheets. Spoon the cheese mixture into the centre of each one.

4 Brush the pastry edges with egg. Cover with remaining rounds, knocking up and pressing the pastry edges together to seal. Make a small slit in the top of each pastry puff.

5 Glaze with beaten egg. Bake in the oven at 220°C (425°F) mark 7 for about 15 minutes or until well browned and crisp. Serve warm, garnished with fresh basil leaves.

FETA CHEESE

Greek Feta cheese can be made from either sheep's or goat's milk. Vacuum packs, which tend to be rather salty, are available at some large supermarkets and good delicatessens, but the best Feta (sold loose in brine) is found in Greek and Middle Eastern stores.

BLUE CHEESE CROQUETTES

| 1.00* | 🄴 | ✳* | 416–623 cals |

* plus 2–3 hours chilling; freeze after stage 5

Serves 4–6

100 g (4 oz) celery

75 g (3 oz) butter or margarine

75 g (3 oz) plain flour, plus a little extra for coating

225 ml (8 fl oz) milk

175 g (6 oz) Blue Stilton cheese, grated

30 ml (2 tbsp) snipped fresh chives or 15 ml (1 tbsp) dried

2 eggs

freshly ground pepper

65 g (2½ oz) dried white breadcrumbs

vegetable oil, for deep frying

1 Finely chop the celery; sauté in the butter or margarine for 5–10 minutes until beginning to become brown.

2 Stir in the flour; cook for 1 minute. Off the heat stir in the milk. Bring to the boil, stirring, then cook for 1 minute—the mixture will be *very* thick.

3 Remove from the heat and stir in the grated cheese, chives, one egg and pepper (the cheese will add sufficient salt).

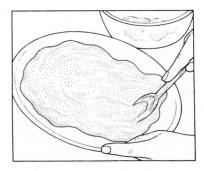

4 Spread the mixture out in a shallow dish, cover with damp greaseproof paper and cool for 30 minutes. Refrigerate for 2–3 hours to firm up.

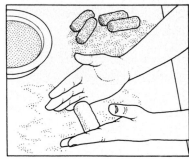

5 Shape the mixture into twelve croquettes then coat lightly in flour, beaten egg and breadcrumbs.

6 Deep fry the croquettes at 180°C (350°F), a few at a time, for 3–4 minutes until golden brown. Serve hot.

KIBBEH

(MIDDLE EASTERN LAMB AND CRACKED WHEAT PATTIES)

| 1.30 | 🍳 🍳 ✳* | 449–748 cals |

* freeze before deep-frying

Serves 4–6

700 g (1½ lb) minced lamb

1 onion, skinned and roughly chopped

225 g (8 oz) cracked wheat (burghul)

salt and freshly ground pepper

vegetable oil, for deep-frying

25 g (1 oz) pine nuts

30 ml (2 tbsp) chopped fresh parsley

1.25 ml (¼ tsp) ground allspice

lemon wedges, to serve

1 Put 550 g (1¼ lb) of the lamb in a blender or food processor with the onion. Work to a smooth, paste-like consistency. (Or work several times through a mincer, fitted with the finest blade.)

2 Put the cracked wheat in a sieve and rinse under cold running water. Turn on to a clean tea towel and wring out as much moisture as possible.

3 Add the wheat to the meat mixture and work again in the machine (or mincer). Add salt and pepper to taste and set aside.

4 Make the filling. Heat 30 ml (2 tbsp) of the oil in a saucepan. Add the pine nuts and fry until browned, shaking the pan and tossing the nuts constantly. Remove with a slotted spoon. Add remaining minced lamb to the pan and fry until browned. Cook gently for 15 minutes, stirring frequently. Remove from the heat and stir in the pine nuts, parsley, allspice and salt and pepper.

5 With wet hands, take a small piece of the wheat and meat mixture, about the size of an egg. Hold it in one hand and, with the index finger of the other, make an indent in the centre.

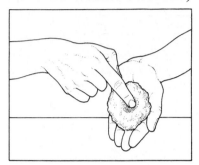

6 Work the kibbeh round in your hand, pressing down with the index finger until the hole in the centre is quite large and the kibbeh is oval or 'torpedo' shaped.

7 Put about 5 ml (1 tsp) of the filling in the centre of the kibbeh, then close the kibbeh around it, wetting the mixture to seal. Roll the kibbeh between wetted palms to ensure a smooth shape, sealing any cracks with water. Repeat with the remaining wheat and meat mixture and the filling until all are used up.

8 Heat the oil in a deep-fat fryer to 190°C (375°F). Deep-fry the kibbeh in batches for about 5 minutes until golden brown on all sides. Drain on absorbent kitchen paper. Serve hot or cold, with lemon for squeezing.

Menu Suggestion

In the Middle East, Kibbeh are traditionally served with a salad. A typical Arabic salad for serving with Kibbeh consists of radishes, green pepper, tomatoes and raw onion. Toss the salad in a dressing made with 60 ml (4 tbsp) tahini paste, the juice of 1 lemon, 150 ml (¼ pint) water, 45 ml (3 tbsp) olive oil and garlic, mint and salt and pepper to taste.

COLD BEEF IN SOURED CREAM

0.30*	318 cals

* plus 2–3 hours chilling

Serves 6

1 large onion, skinned

350 g (12 oz) button mushrooms

700 g (1½ lb) lean rump steak in a thin slice

45 ml (3 tbsp) vegetable oil

salt and freshly ground pepper

7.5 ml (1½ tsp) Dijon mustard

7.5 ml (1½ tsp) chopped fresh thyme or 5 ml (1 tsp) dried

1 large green eating apple

284 ml (10 fl oz) soured cream

15 ml (1 tbsp) lemon juice

crisp lettuce and freshly toasted French bread, to serve

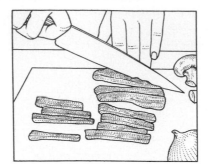

1 Using a sharp knife, finely chop the onion and finely slice the mushrooms. Slice the rump steak into thin strips.

2 Heat the oil in a large frying pan. Quickly brown the steak in a shallow layer, turning occasionally. Don't crowd the pan; cook the meat in two batches if necessary. The beef should remain pink in the centre.

3 Transfer the meat to a bowl using a slotted spoon. Season with salt and pepper.

4 Reheat the fat remaining in the pan. Fry the onion for 5 minutes until golden brown. Add the mushrooms, mustard and thyme. Cook over high heat for 1 minute. Add to beef; allow to cool; refrigerate for 2–3 hours.

5 Quarter and core the apple; slice thinly. Combine with the soured cream and lemon juice.

6 Line a shallow dish with lettuce. Combine the beef and apple mixtures and season. Pile into the centre of the lettuce. Serve with toasted French bread.

SMOKED FISH TIMBALE

0.40*	292 cals

* plus 2–3 hours chilling

Serves 6

350 g (12 oz) long grain rice

15 ml (1 tbsp) ground turmeric

7.5 ml (1½ tsp) salt

350 g (12 oz) smoked haddock or cod fillet

1 small bunch spring onions, washed

2 eggs, hard boiled and shelled

salt and freshly ground pepper

watercress sprigs and fresh prawns, to garnish

1 Cook the rice with the turmeric and salt in a saucepan of water for 10–15 minutes. Drain well and cool.

2 Poach the fish in a little water to just cover for 12–15 minutes. Drain. Flake the fish.

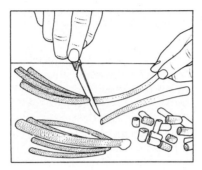

3 Trim the spring onions, then roughly chop them with the hard-boiled eggs, mix with the cold rice and fish, seasoning well.

4 Spoon the mixture into an oiled 1.1-litre (2-pint) ring mould. Press down well, cover and chill for 2–3 hours.

5 To serve, unmould the fish ring on to a plate, and garnish with watercress sprigs and prawns.

HERBY BRIE QUICHE

1.25	✳	473–709 cals

Serves 4–6

150 g (5 oz) plain flour

5 ml (1 tsp) dried mixed herbs

salt

50 g (2 oz) butter

25 g (1 oz) lard

1 egg yolk

a little beaten egg white

225 g (8 oz) ripe Brie

150 ml (5 fl oz) double cream

3 eggs, lightly beaten

30 ml (2 tbsp) chopped fresh mixed
   herbs (e.g. thyme, marjoram,
   parsley, chives)

freshly ground pepper

1 Make the pastry. Sift the flour into a bowl with the herbs and a pinch of salt. Add the butter and lard in small pieces and cut into the flour with a knife.

2 Rub the fat into the flour until the mixture resembles fine breadcrumbs, then stir in the egg yolk. Gather the mixture into a ball of dough, then knead lightly until smooth.

3 Roll out on a floured surface. Use to line a 20-cm (8-inch) plain flan ring set on a baking sheet. Refrigerate for 20 minutes.

4 Prick the base of the dough lightly with a fork, then line with foil and weight down with baking beans. Bake blind in the oven at 200°C (400°F) mark 6 for 10 minutes.

5 Remove the foil and the beans, brush the inside of the pastry case with the beaten egg white, then return to the oven and bake for a further 5 minutes.

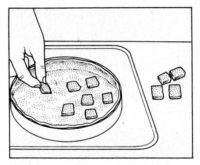

6 Remove the rind from the cheese, cut into squares and place in the base of the pastry case. Soften the cheese with a fork and gradually work in the cream to make a smooth mixture. Whisk in the beaten eggs, then the herbs and salt and pepper to taste.

7 Pour the filling into the pastry case. Bake in the oven at 180°C (350°F) mark 4 for 30 minutes until the filling is just set and the rind from the cheese has formed a golden crust on top. Leave to stand at room temperature for 15 minutes before serving.

BRIE CHEESE

This soft, creamy cheese originated in the province of La Brie in Ile de France, but is now made in factories in other countries besides France—Germany and Denmark, for example, have thriving Brie industries.

Brie is much esteemed by the French, who have called it *roi de fromages*—'the king of cheeses'—since the year 1815 when it was the winner of an international cheese competition in Vienna.

Genuine French Bries often bear the name of their exact place of origin, but this practice is dying out and most simply state the country where they were made. When buying fresh Brie cheese, it is best to buy it freshly cut from a large flat round or wheel at a specialist cheese shop or delicatessen—this is the only way to ensure the cheese is in perfect condition. A ripened cow's milk cheese, a perfect Brie should have a soft, downy rind and a creamy, supple paste. Avoid cheese which has a hard rind or which is either strong-smelling and runny in the centre, or which has a chalky line running through it.

Ripe Brie does not keep well and should be used on the day of purchase. If you need to store it for a few hours, wrap it loosely in foil and place in the least cold part of the refrigerator. Allow to come to room temperature (unwrapped) for 1 hour before required.

SMOKED SALMON QUICHE

1.00*	✳*	336–420 cals

* plus 30 minutes chilling; freeze
for 1 month only

Serves 8–10

225 g (8 oz) plain flour

salt and freshly ground pepper

115 g (4 oz) butter or margarine

1 egg yolk

10 ml (2 tsp) lemon juice

about 30 ml (2 tbsp) cold water

175 g (6 oz) full-fat soft cheese

300 ml (½ pint) single or double
cream

3 eggs

175 g (6 oz) smoked salmon pieces

finely grated rind of 1 lemon

5 ml (1 tsp) paprika

1 Sift the flour and a pinch of
salt together into a bowl. Cut
the butter into small pieces and
add to the flour.

2 Lightly rub in the butter with
your fingertips until the
mixture resembles fine
breadcrumbs.

3 Add the egg yolk and half of
the lemon juice, then add
enough water to bind the mixture
together in large lumps.

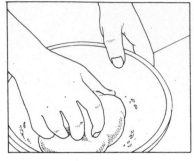

4 With 1 hand, collect the
mixture together to form a
ball. Knead lightly for a few
seconds to give a firm, smooth
dough. Do not overhandle.

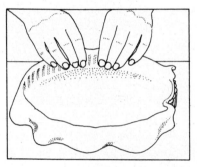

5 Roll out the dough on a
floured surface and use to line
a 25.5 cm (10 inch) loose-bottomed
metal flan tin. Chill in the
refrigerator for 30 minutes.

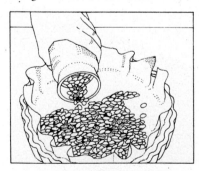

6 Prick the pastry base and then
line with foil and fill with
baking beans. Bake blind on a
preheated baking sheet in the oven
at 200°C (400°F) mark 6 for 10
minutes. Remove the foil and
beans and return to the oven for a
further 5 minutes.

7 Prepare the filling. Put the
cheese in a bowl and gradually
whisk in the cream. When well
mixed and smooth, add the eggs
and beat well to mix.

8 Add the salmon, grated lemon
rind and remaining lemon
juice. Season with a little salt and
plenty of pepper, then add half of
the paprika and beat well to mix.

9 Pour the filling into the baked
flan case and bake in the oven
at 190°C (375°F) mark 5 for 25–30
minutes until set. Sprinkle with
the remaining paprika while very
hot. Serve warm or cold.

WATERCRESS AND RICOTTA QUICHE

1.00*	✳	402–536 cals

* plus 30 minutes chilling

Serves 6–8

pastry made with 225 g (8 oz)
    flour (see left)

50 g (2 oz) butter or margarine

1 bunch of spring onions, trimmed
    and finely chopped

2 bunches of watercress

100 g (4 oz) Ricotta or curd cheese

300 ml ($\frac{1}{2}$ pint) single or double
    cream (or whipping)

3 eggs, beaten

2.5 ml ($\frac{1}{2}$ tsp) grated nutmeg

salt and freshly ground pepper

1 Line a 25.5 cm (10 inch) loose-
bottomed metal flan tin with
the pastry. Bake blind on a preheated baking sheet (see left).

2 Prepare the filling. Melt the
butter in a saucepan, add the
spring onions and fry gently for
about 5 minutes until softened.
Add the watercress and fry for a
few minutes more, stirring
frequently.

3 Transfer the contents of the
pan to a blender or food processor. Add the next 4 ingredients
with salt and pepper to taste and
work until smooth and evenly
blended.

4 Pour the filling into the baked
flan case and bake in the oven
at 190°C (375°F) mark 5 for 25–30
minutes until set. Serve warm or
leave until cold.

COURGETTE QUICHE

2.00* ✳ 732 cals

* includes 45 minutes chilling and 15
  minutes standing time

Serves 4

175 g (6 oz) plain flour
salt
125 g (4 oz) butter or margarine
125 g (4 oz) grated Cheddar cheese
1 egg yolk, beaten
350 g (12 oz) courgettes
3 eggs
150 ml (5 fl oz) double cream
10 ml (2 tsp) chopped fresh basil
finely grated rind of 1 lime (optional)
freshly ground pepper
a little egg white

1 Make the pastry. Sift the flour into a bowl with a pinch of salt. Add the butter in pieces and rub in thoroughly with the finger-tips until the mixture resembles fine breadcrumbs.

2 Stir in the cheese, then the egg yolk. Gather the mixture together with your fingers to make a smooth ball of dough. Wrap and chill the dough in the refrigerator for about 30 minutes.

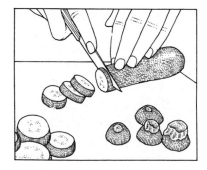

3 Meanwhile, prepare the filling. Trim the ends off the cour-gettes, then cut the courgettes into 2-cm (¾-inch) chunks.

4 Plunge the courgette pieces in-to boiling salted water, bring back to the boil, then simmer for 3 minutes. Drain and set aside.

5 Put the eggs in a jug and beat lightly together with the cream. Stir in the basil, lime rind if using, and season to taste. Set aside.

6 Roll out the chilled dough on a floured surface and use to line a loose-bottomed 23-cm (9-inch) flan tin. Refrigerate for 15 minutes.

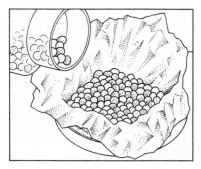

7 Prick the base of the dough with a fork, then line with foil and baking beans. Stand the tin on a preheated baking sheet and bake blind in the oven at 200°C (400°F) mark 6 for 10 minutes.

8 Remove the foil and beans and brush the inside of the pastry case with the egg white to seal. Return to the oven for 5 minutes.

9 Stand the courgette chunks up-right in pastry case; slowly pour in egg and cream mixture. Return to oven for 20 minutes.

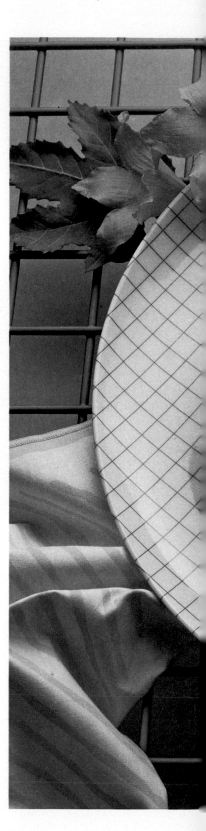

PÂTÉ DE CAMPAGNE WITH BLACK OLIVES

2.20*	475 cals

* plus 2–3 hours chilling and 30 minutes standing time; prepare a day ahead

Serves 8

275 g (10 oz) streaky bacon

75 g (3 oz) black olives

450 g (1 lb) belly pork

275 g (10 oz) pie veal

175 g (6 oz) lamb's liver

2 onions, skinned

1 garlic clove, skinned and crushed

7.5 ml (1½ tsp) salt

freshly ground pepper

5 ml (1 tsp) dried rubbed sage

30 ml (2 tbsp) olive oil

15 ml (1 tbsp) lemon juice

30 ml (2 tbsp) brandy

bay leaves or parsley and black olives, to garnish

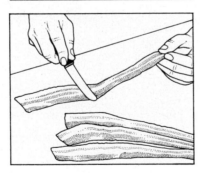

1 Using a sharp knife, cut the rind off the streaky bacon. Stretch the rashers with the back of the knife.

2 Halve, stone and roughly chop the olives. Then pass the belly pork, veal, liver and onions twice through the finest blades of a mincer or food processor. Add the remaining ingredients, except the bacon: mix well.

3 Layer the bacon and minced ingredients in a 1.1-litre (2-pint) terrine, topping with the streaky bacon rashers.

4 Cover tightly with foil and lid, if any, and place in a roasting tin, half filled with boiling water. Cook in the oven at 170°C (325°F) mark 3 for about 2 hours until the pâté is firm.

5 Remove the lid and foil. Pour off juices and reserve in the refrigerator. Weight down the pâté and refrigerate overnight.

6 Skim the fat off the jellied juices. Gently warm the juices. Garnish with herbs and black olives, then spoon over the juices. Refrigerate for 2–3 hours to set. Leave to stand at room temperature for 30 minutes.

TURKEY ROQUEFORT SALAD

| 0.15* | 375 cals |

* plus 30 minutes chilling

Serves 4

150 ml ($\frac{1}{4}$ pint) soured cream

100 g (4 oz) Roquefort or any other
   blue cheese, crumbled

salt and freshly ground pepper

450 g (1 lb) cold cooked turkey,
   skinned and cut into pieces

lettuce or endive leaves, washed
   and trimmed

snipped chives, to garnish

1 Mix the soured cream and
Roquefort together to make a
dressing. Season to taste. Add the
turkey and coat well in it. Cover
and chill in the refrigerator for 30
minutes.

2 To serve, arrange the lettuce
or endive leaves in a serving
bowl. Spoon the turkey mixture in
the centre and sprinkle with
chives. Serve chilled.

Menu Suggestion
Serve for a summer luncheon with
fresh French bread or rolls and a
bottle of dry sparkling white wine.

HAM AND CHEESE SALAD WITH AVOCADO

0.15	502 cals

Serves 4

2 ripe avocados

60 ml (4 tbsp) natural yogurt

1 garlic clove, skinned and crushed

a few drops of Tabasco sauce

salt and freshly ground pepper

225 g (8 oz) lean cooked ham, cubed

225 g (8 oz) Emmenthal or Gruyère cheese, cubed

1 red pepper, cored, seeded and diced

1 Halve the avocados and remove the stones, then peel and mash the flesh. Mix quickly with the yogurt, garlic and Tabasco, seasoning to taste.

2 Fold the ham, cheese and red pepper (reserving some pepper to garnish) into this dressing and pile into a salad bowl. Serve immediately, or the avocado flesh may discolour the dressing. Sprinkle with the reserved red pepper.

Menu Suggestion
This salad is incredibly quick to prepare. Serve it for a healthy lunch, with granary bread rolls.

RED FLANNEL HASH

| 0.45 | 380 cals |

Serves 4

450 g (1 lb) potatoes, scrubbed

salt and freshly ground pepper

225 g (8 oz) salt beef or corned beef, chopped

1 medium onion, skinned and finely chopped

5 ml (1 tsp) garlic salt

225 g (8 oz) cooked beetroot, diced

30 ml (2 tbsp) chopped fresh parsley

50 g (2 oz) beef dripping or lard

1 Cook the potatoes in their skins in lightly salted boiling water for about 20 minutes or until tender when pierced with a fork.

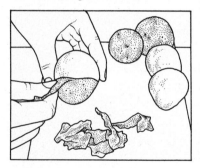

2 Drain the potatoes, leave until cool enough to handle, then peel off the skins with your fingers. Dice the flesh.

3 Put the diced potatoes into a large bowl, add the beef, onion, garlic salt, beetroot and parsley and toss to combine. Add pepper to taste.

4 Heat the dripping or lard in a heavy-based skillet or frying pan until smoking hot. Add the hash mixture and spread evenly with a fish slice or spatula.

5 Lower the heat to moderate and cook the hash, uncovered, for 10–15 minutes. Break up and turn frequently with the slice or spatula, so that the hash becomes evenly browned. Serve hot.

Menu Suggestion

Red Flannel Hash is a traditional dish from New England. Serve it American-style, topped with fried or poached eggs, for a quick evening meal or snack.

SIZZLING STEAK SANDWICHES

0.15	605 cals

Serves 2

2 'flash-fry' steaks, about 75 g (3 oz) each

15 ml (1 tbsp) vegetable oil

salt and freshly ground pepper

4 slices of granary or wholemeal bread, from a large loaf

butter or margarine, for spreading

30 ml (2 tbsp) mayonnaise

about 4 small lettuce leaves, shredded

1 tomato, skinned and sliced

10 ml (2 tsp) Dijon-style mustard

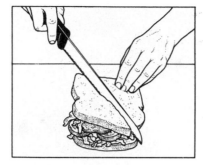

Menu Suggestion
Steak sandwiches make a protein-packed hot snack at any time of day; they make an especially good quick lunch with glasses of beer, lager or cider.

4 Cut each sandwich in half with a serrated knife to make 2 triangles and place on individual plates. Serve immediately.

1 Brush the steaks on one side with half of the oil and sprinkle with pepper to taste. Grill under a preheated hot grill for 3 minutes, then turn them over, brush with the remaining oil, sprinkle with more pepper and grill for a further 3 minutes, or until done to your liking.

2 Meanwhile, toast the bread on both sides, removing the crusts if wished. Spread one side of each slice with butter, then with the mayonnaise. Top 2 slices of toast with the shredded lettuce and sliced tomato and sprinkle with salt and pepper to taste.

3 Place the steaks on top of the salad and spread evenly with the mustard. Cover with the remaining 2 slices of toast.

KEBABS WITH CUMIN

0.30*	✳*	280 cals

* plus overnight chilling; freeze after shaping in step 3

Serves 4

350 g (12 oz) finely minced veal or beef
finely grated rind of 1 small lemon
15 ml (1 tbsp) lemon juice
1 garlic clove, skinned and crushed
5 ml (1 tsp) ground cumin
2.5 ml (½ tsp) salt
2.5 ml (½ tsp) freshly ground pepper
1 small onion, skinned
vegetable oil, for grilling
lemon wedges, to serve

1 Put the minced meat in a bowl with the lemon rind and juice, the garlic, cumin and salt and pepper. Mix well together, preferably by hand.

2 Grate in the onion and mix again. (The longer the mixture is stirred, the drier it becomes and the easier it is to handle.) Cover the bowl and chill in the refrigerator, preferably overnight.

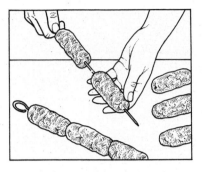

3 Divide the mixture into 12 pieces and form into small sausage shapes. Chill again if possible, then thread on to 4 oiled kebab skewers.

4 Place on a baking sheet. Brush with oil and grill evenly for 10–12 minutes, turning frequently until browned. Serve hot, with lemon wedges.

Menu Suggestion
Serve on a bed of rice or pilaf, or serve in pockets of warm pitta bread with salad.

FRIKADELLER *(DANISH MEAT PATTIES)*

0.30	243 cals

Serves 6

1 egg
300 ml (½ pint) milk
350 g (12 oz) minced veal
100 g (4 oz) minced pork
1 small onion, skinned and finely chopped
100 g (4 oz) plain flour
15 ml (1 tbsp) chopped fresh thyme or 5 ml (½ tsp) dried
2.5 ml (½ tsp) grated nutmeg
salt and freshly ground pepper
45 ml (3 tbsp) vegetable oil

1 Break the egg into a small bowl, add the milk and beat lightly with a fork.

2 Put the minced veal and pork in a separate bowl. Add the onion, flour, thyme, nutmeg and salt and pepper to taste. Mix well together with a wooden spoon.

3 Gradually stir the egg and milk into the meat mixture, then beat well until smooth.

4 Heat the oil in a heavy-based frying pan. Fry heaped tablespoonfuls of the mixture for 5 minutes on each side, or until brown.

5 Remove with a slotted spoon and drain on absorbent kitchen paper. Keep hot while cooking the remainder.

Menu Suggestion
Frikadeller are traditionally served with boiled potatoes.

LAMB AND PEPPER KEBABS

1.00*	✳*	404 cals

* plus 4 hours or overnight
marinating; freeze in the marinade

Serves 4

700 g (1½ lb) lamb fillet, trimmed
   of fat

100 ml (4 fl oz) dry white wine

100 ml (4 fl oz) corn oil

50 ml (2 fl oz) lemon juice

2 celery sticks, trimmed and very
   finely chopped

1 small onion, skinned and grated

2 garlic cloves, skinned and
   crushed

1 large tomato, skinned and finely
   chopped

20 ml (4 tsp) chopped fresh thyme
   or 10 ml (2 tsp) dried thyme

salt and freshly ground pepper

1 medium red pepper

1 medium green pepper

few bay leaves

1 Cut the lamb into cubes and
place in a bowl. In a jug, whisk
together the wine, oil, lemon juice,
celery, onion, garlic, tomato,
thyme and salt and freshly ground
pepper to taste.

2 Pour the marinade over the
lamb and turn the meat until
well coated. Cover the bowl and
marinate in the refrigerator for
4 hours, preferably overnight.

3 When ready to cook, cut the
tops off the peppers and
remove the cores and seeds. Cut
the flesh into squares.

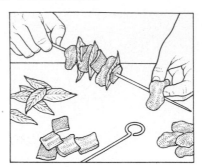

4 Remove the meat from the
marinade (reserving the
marinade) and thread on to 8 oiled
kebab skewers, alternating with the
squares of pepper and bay leaves.

5 Cook over charcoal or under a
preheated moderate grill for
20–25 minutes until the lamb is
tender. Turn the skewers
frequently during cooking and
brush with the reserved marinade.
Serve hot.

Menu Suggestion
For a really quick 'help-yourself'
type of meal, serve these kebabs in
pockets of hot pitta bread, and
accompany with bowls of
shredded lettuce or cabbage, sliced
tomato and cucumber.

**LAMB AND PEPPER
KEBABS**

Lamb fillet is from the neck of
the animal. It is an excellent cut
for cutting into cubes for kebabs,
casseroles and curries, because it
is tender without being dry. Leg
of lamb can be boned and cubed,
but it is such a lean cut that it
tends to dry out on cooking.
Shoulder of lamb is also
sometimes boned and cubed, but
this tends to be more fatty and
sinewy. Many large
supermarkets sell lamb fillet, but
if you are buying it from a
butcher, you may have to order
in advance.

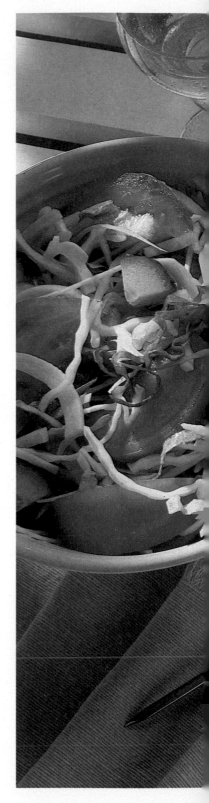

TORTILLA ESPAGNOLA
(SPANISH OMELETTE)

1.00 🍳	376 cals

Serves 4

500 ml (17½ fl oz) vegetable or olive oil, for frying

150 g (5 oz) Spanish onion, skinned and thinly sliced

salt and freshly ground pepper

4 medium potatoes, about 500 g (1 lb) total weight, peeled

4 eggs, size 2

1 Heat 60 ml (4 tbsp) of the oil in a large, heavy-based frying pan or omelette pan. Add the sliced onion and a pinch of salt and fry gently, stirring frequently for 10–15 minutes until soft and a light golden brown. Remove with a slotted spoon and drain on absorbent kitchen paper.

2 Cut the potatoes into small wedges. Dry well with a clean tea-towel. Pour the remaining oil into a deep-fat frier and heat to 190°C (375°F). Fry the potatoes in batches for 5 minutes in the hot oil, covering the pan so that they become soft. Remove with a slotted spoon, place on absorbent kitchen paper, sprinkle with salt and leave to drain.

3 Beat the eggs lightly in a large bowl with salt and pepper to taste. Stir in the onion and potatoes.

4 Reheat the oil remaining in the frying pan until smoking. Pour all but 30 ml (2 tbsp) of the egg and potato mixture into the frying pan. Turn the heat down to low and let the mixture run to the sides. Cook for 3–5 minutes until the underneath is just set.

5 Turn the omelette out upside down on to a plate. Heat 15 ml (1 tbsp) of the deep-frying oil in the frying pan.

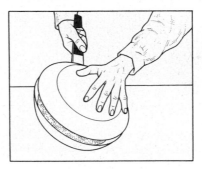

6 Pour the reserved egg mixture into the pan and tip and tilt the pan so that the egg covers the base and forms a protective layer on which to finish cooking the omelette.

7 Immediately slide in the omelette, set side uppermost. Make the edges neat with a palette knife or spatula and fry for 3–5 minutes until set underneath. Slide on to a serving plate and cut into wedges to serve.

Menu Suggestion
Tortilla Espagnola can be served hot or cold as a main course with a tomato or green salad. It is also delicious cold as an appetiser with drinks before a meal, in which case it should be sliced into thin fingers.

STUFFED AUBERGINES

1.30	524 cals

Serves 4

2 medium aubergines

salt and freshly ground pepper

75 ml (5 tbsp) olive oil

1 medium onion, skinned and finely chopped

1–2 garlic cloves, skinned and crushed

1 red or green pepper, cored, seeded and finely diced

175 g (6 oz) button mushrooms, wiped and finely chopped

4 ripe tomatoes, skinned and finely chopped

15 ml (1 tbsp) tomato purée

100 g (4 oz) long grain rice

50 g (2 oz) chopped mixed nuts

30 ml (2 tbsp) chopped fresh parsley

100 g (4 oz) Cheddar cheese, grated

75 g (3 oz) fresh wholemeal breadcrumbs

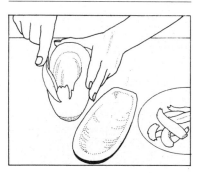

1 Slice the aubergines in half lengthways. Scoop out and reserve the flesh, leaving a narrow margin inside the skin so that the aubergines will hold their shape.

2 Sprinkle the insides of the aubergine shells with salt and stand upside down to drain for 30 minutes.

3 Dice the scooped-out aubergine flesh, then place in a colander, sprinkling each layer with salt. Cover with a plate, place heavy weights on top and leave to dégorge for 30 minutes.

4 Meanwhile, heat 60 ml (4 tbsp) of the oil in a heavy-based saucepan. Add the onion and garlic; fry gently for 5 minutes until soft. Add the diced pepper to the pan and fry gently for 5 minutes.

5 Rinse the diced aubergine under cold running water, then pat dry with absorbent kitchen paper. Add to the pan with the mushrooms, tomatoes and tomato purée. Simmer for about 5 minutes, then add the rice, nuts, parsley and salt and pepper.

6 Rinse the aubergine cases and pat dry with absorbent kitchen paper. Brush a baking dish with the remaining oil, then stand the aubergine cases in the dish. Fill with the stuffing mixture.

7 Mix the grated cheese and breadcrumbs together, then sprinkle evenly over the top of the aubergines. Bake uncovered in the oven at 180°C (350°F) mark 4 for 45 minutes. Serve hot.

Menu Suggestion

Aubergines stuffed with rice and vegetables make a most nutritious main course dish for a family supper or an informal party.

SWISS STUFFED POTATOES

| 1.30 | 346 cals |

Serves 4

4 medium baking potatoes

50 g (2 oz) butter or margarine

1 small onion, skinned and finely
    chopped

450 g (1 lb) fresh spinach,
    cooked, drained and chopped,
    or 225 g (8 oz) frozen chopped
    spinach

100 g (4 oz) full fat soft cheese

1.25 ml ($\frac{1}{4}$ tsp) freshly grated
    nutmeg

salt and freshly ground pepper

50 g (2 oz) Gruyère or Emmental
    cheese, grated

pinch of paprika or cayenne

1 Scrub the potatoes under cold
    running water, then pat dry
with absorbent kitchen paper.

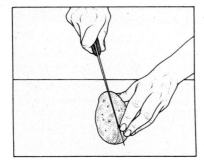

2 With a sharp, pointed knife,
    score a line in the skin around
the middle of each potato.

3 Place the potatoes directly on
    the oven shelf and bake at
200°C (400°F) mark 6 for $1\frac{1}{4}$ hours
or until tender.

4 About 15 minutes before the
    end of the cooking time, melt
the butter in a heavy-based saucepan, add the onion and fry gently
for about 5 minutes until soft and
lightly coloured. Add the fresh
spinach and cook gently for 2–3
minutes, stirring frequently. (If
using frozen spinach, cook for 7–
10 minutes until thawed.) Remove
from the heat.

5 When the potatoes are cooked,
    slice in half lengthways. Scoop
out the flesh into a bowl and add
the spinach mixture, the soft
cheese, nutmeg and salt and
pepper to taste. Mix well.

6 Spoon the mixture into the
    potato shells, mounding it up
in the centre. Stand the stuffed
potatoes on a baking sheet.
Sprinkle over the cheese and
finally the paprika or cayenne.
Return to the oven for 10–15
minutes, until the cheese topping
is bubbling and golden. Serve hot.

MEXICAN BAKED POTATOES

1.25	367 cals.

Serves 4

4 medium baking potatoes

30 ml (2 tbsp) vegetable oil

1 medium onion, skinned and finely chopped

1 garlic clove, skinned and crushed

397 g (14 oz) can tomatoes

10 ml (2 tsp) tomato purée

2.5 ml ($\frac{1}{2}$ tsp) chilli powder

pinch of granulated sugar

salt and freshly ground pepper

432 g (15.25 oz) can red kidney beans, drained

30 ml (2 tbsp) chopped fresh parsley

50 g (2 oz) mature or farmhouse Cheddar cheese, coarsely grated

1 Scrub the potatoes under cold running water, then pat dry. Brush with a little vegetable oil, prick all over with a skewer or fork. Bake at 200°C (400°F) mark 6 for 1$\frac{1}{4}$ hours or until tender.

2 Meanwhile, make the stuffing. Heat the remaining oil in a saucepan, add the onion and garlic and fry gently until soft.

3 Add tomatoes with their juice and stir to break up with a wooden spoon. Add the tomato purée, chilli powder, sugar and salt and pepper to taste and bring to the boil, stirring. Simmer, uncovered, for about 20 minutes, stirring occasionally. Add beans and parsley and heat through.

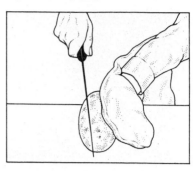

4 When the potatoes are cooked, slice off the top third of each one and reserve for lids. Scoop out some of the potato from the bottom third of each one and add to the tomato sauce.

5 Place 1 potato on each serving plate and spoon the chilli bean mixture into each one, letting it spill out on to the plate. Sprinkle grated cheese on top, then replace the lids at an angle. Serve immediately.

Menu Suggestion

This vegetarian dish is hot, spicy and substantial. Serve for a hearty supper, accompanied by a crisp green salad and glasses of chilled beer or lager.

JACKET BAKED POTATOES

The best potatoes to use for baking are Maris Piper, Desirée and Pentland Squire, although King Edward and Pentland Crown are almost as good. Slightly different methods of baking are used in these 2 recipes. Scoring a line around the middle before baking, as in Swiss Stuffed Potatoes (facing page), makes them easier to cut for stuffing; brushing them with oil, as in Mexican Baked Potatoes (above), gives a crisper skin.

QUICK CHICKEN AND MUSSEL PAELLA

0.50	520–780 cals

Serves 4–6

60 ml (4 tbsp) olive oil

about 450 g (1 lb) boneless chicken meat, skinned and cut into bite-sized cubes

1 onion, skinned and chopped

2 garlic cloves, skinned and crushed

1 large red pepper, cored, seeded and sliced into thin strips

3 tomatoes, skinned and chopped

400 g (14 oz) Valencia or risotto rice

1.2 litres (2¼ pints) boiling chicken stock

5 ml (1 tsp) paprika

2.5 ml (½ tsp) saffron powder

salt and freshly ground pepper

two 150 g (5 oz) jars mussels, drained

lemon wedges, peeled prawns and fresh mussels (optional), to serve

1 Heat the oil in a large, deep frying pan, add the cubes of chicken and fry over moderate heat until golden brown on all sides. Remove from the pan with a slotted spoon and set aside.

2 Add the onion, garlic and red pepper to the pan and fry gently for 5 minutes until softened. Add the tomatoes and fry for a few more minutes until the juices run, then add the rice and stir to combine with the oil and vegetables.

3 Pour in 1 litre (1¾ pints) of the boiling stock (it will bubble furiously), then add half the paprika, the saffron powder and seasoning to taste. Stir well, lower the heat and add the chicken.

4 Simmer, uncovered, for 30 minutes until the chicken is cooked through, stirring frequently during this time to prevent the rice from sticking. When the mixture becomes dry, stir in a few tablespoons of boiling stock. Repeat as often as necessary to keep the paella moist until the end of the cooking time.

5 To serve, fold in the mussels and heat through. Taste and adjust seasoning, then garnish with lemon wedges, mussels in their shells and a sprinkling of the remaining paprika.

Menu Suggestion
Serve for a substantial supper dish with fresh crusty bread and a mixed green salad.

QUICK CHICKEN AND MUSSEL PAELLA

Spain's most famous dish, paella, gets its name from the pan in which it is traditionally cooked — *paellera*. The pan is usually made of a heavy metal such as cast iron, with sloping sides and two flat handles on either side. The *paellera* is not only the best utensil for cooking paella, it is also the most attractive way to serve it, so if you like to make paella fairly frequently it is well worth investing in one — they are obtainable from specialist kitchen shops and some large hardware stores.

CABBAGE AND HAZELNUT CROQUETTES

1.00*		✳	141 cals

* plus 2 hours chilling

Makes 16

450 g (1 lb) potatoes, peeled

salt and freshly ground pepper

900 g (2 lb) cabbage, roughly chopped

45 ml (3 tbsp) milk

50 g (2 oz) butter or margarine

50 g (2 oz) plain flour

50 g (2 oz) hazelnuts, chopped and toasted

2 eggs, beaten

100 g (4 oz) dry white breadcrumbs

vegetable oil, for deep frying

lemon wedges, to serve

1 Boil the potatoes in salted water for about 20 minutes until tender. Drain them well and mash without adding any liquid.

2 Cook the cabbage in boiling salted water for 5–10 minutes or until just tender. Drain well. Purée in a blender or food processor, adding the milk if required—you should have 450 ml (¾ pint) purée.

3 Melt the butter in a saucepan, add the flour and cook gently, stirring, for 1–2 minutes. Gradually blend in the cabbage purée and milk. Bring to the boil, then simmer for 5 minutes.

4 Stir the mashed potatoes and hazelnuts into the sauce, add salt and pepper to taste and mix well. Transfer to a bowl, cool, cover and chill in the refrigerator for at least 1½ hours or until firm.

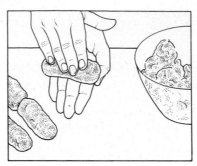

5 With dampened hands, shape the mixture into 16 croquettes. Place on a greased baking sheet and chill again for at least 20 minutes.

6 Coat the croquettes in the beaten eggs and breadcrumbs. Heat the oil to 180°C (350°F) in a deep-fat frier. Deep fry the croquettes in batches for about 4 minutes until crisp and golden. Remove with a slotted spoon and drain on absorbent kitchen paper while frying the remainder. Serve hot, with lemon wedges.

CABBAGE AND HAZELNUT CROQUETTES

Hazelnuts get their name from the Anglo-Saxon word 'haesil', meaning head-dress. This is an apt description, for the outer covering fits over the nut itself. Other names for hazelnuts are filberts and cob nuts, depending on the part of the world in which they are grown. These three nuts are not exactly the same, but they are all close relations of the Corylus family, and are interchangeable in recipes.

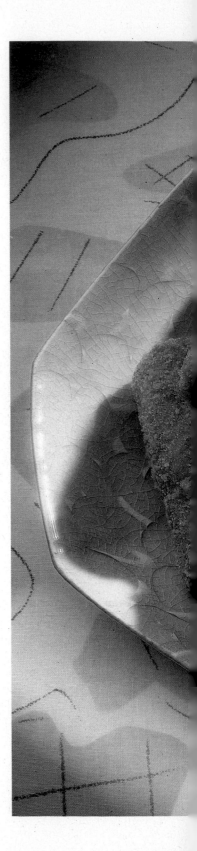

CEVICHE

0.30*	✳*	307 cals

24 hours refrigeration; freeze after step 4. Defrost in refrigerator overnight, then continue from step 5

Serves 4

500 g (1 lb) haddock fillets

5 ml (1 tsp) coriander seeds

5 ml (1 tsp) black peppercorns

juice of 6 limes

5 ml (1 tsp) salt

30 ml (2 tbsp) olive oil

bunch of spring onions, washed, trimmed and sliced

4 tomatoes, skinned and chopped

dash of Tabasco, or to taste

30 ml (2 tbsp) chopped fresh coriander

1 avocado, to finish

lime slices and fresh coriander, to garnish

1 Skin the haddock fillets. Put the fillets skin-side down on a board and grip the tail end of the skin with fingers dipped in salt. Using a sharp knife, work away from you with a sawing action.

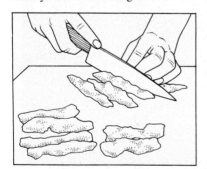

2 Wash the fillets, then pat them dry with absorbent kitchen paper. Cut the fish fillets diagonally into thin, even strips and place in a bowl.

3 Crush the coriander seeds and peppercorns to a fine powder in a mortar and pestle. Mix with the lime juice and salt, then pour over the fish. Cover and chill in the refrigerator for 24 hours, turning the fish occasionally.

4 The next day, heat the oil in a pan, add the spring onions and fry gently for 5 minutes. Add the tomatoes and Tabasco to taste and toss together over brisk heat for 1–2 minutes. Remove from the heat and leave to cool for 20–30 minutes.

5 To serve. Drain the fish from the marinade, discarding the marinade. Combine the fish with the spring onion and tomatoes and the chopped coriander. Taste and adjust seasoning, if necessary.

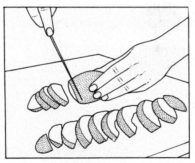

6 Halve the avocado, peel and remove the stone. Slice the flesh crossways. Arrange the slices around the inside of a serving bowl and pile the ceviche in the centre. Garnish with lime slices and coriander leaves. Serve chilled.

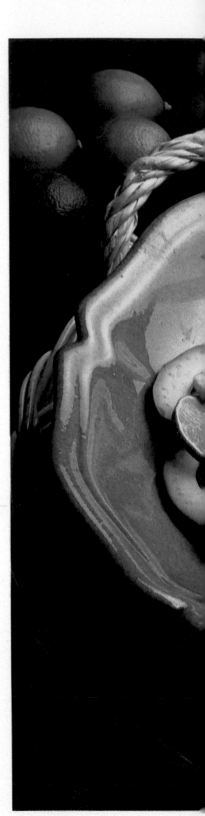

ZUCCHINI ALLA PARMIGIANA
(ITALIAN COURGETTE, PARMESAN AND TOMATO BAKE)

1.00	✳	517 cals

Serves 4

700 g (1½ lb) courgettes

salt and freshly ground pepper

about 150 ml (¼ pint) vegetable oil

1 medium onion, skinned and finely chopped

450 g (1 lb) tomatoes, skinned and chopped

1 large garlic clove, skinned and crushed

30 ml (2 tbsp) tomato purée

15 ml (1 tbsp) chopped fresh marjoram or 5 ml (1 tsp) dried

two 170 g (6 oz) packets Mozzarella cheese, thinly sliced

75 g (3 oz) freshly grated Parmesan cheese

1 Cut the courgettes into 0.5 cm (¼ inch) thick slices. Sprinkle with salt and leave to dégorge for at least 20 minutes.

2 Heat 30 ml (2 tbsp) of the oil in a saucepan, add the onion and fry for about 5 minutes until just beginning to brown.

3 Stir in the tomatoes, garlic, tomato purée and salt and pepper. Simmer for about 10 minutes, stirring with a wooden spoon to break down the tomatoes. Stir in the marjoram and remove from the heat.

4 Rinse the courgettes and pat dry with absorbent kitchen paper. Heat half of the remaining oil in a frying pan, add half of the courgettes and fry until golden brown. Drain well on kitchen paper while frying the remaining courgettes in the remaining oil.

5 Layer the courgettes, tomato sauce and Mozzarella cheese in a shallow ovenproof dish, finishing with a layer of Mozzarella. Sprinkle with the Parmesan cheese.

6 Bake in the oven at 180°C (350°F) mark 4 for about 40 minutes or until brown and bubbling. Serve hot, straight from the dish.

JERUSALEM ARTICHOKE GRATIN

| 1.20 | ✳* | 725 cals |

* freeze before baking at end of step 10

Serves 4

900 g (2 lb) Jerusalem artichokes

salt and freshly ground black pepper

225 g (8 oz) small button or pickling onions

3 medium leeks, trimmed

75 g (3 oz) butter or margarine

15 ml (1 tbsp) olive oil

2 garlic cloves, skinned and crushed

150 ml ($\frac{1}{4}$ pint) dry white wine or vegetable stock, or a mixture of both

1.25 ml ($\frac{1}{4}$ tsp) freshly grated nutmeg

225 g (8 oz) fresh or frozen peas

150 ml ($\frac{1}{4}$ pint) double cream

75 g (3 oz) Gruyère cheese, grated

75 g (3 oz) Cheddar cheese, grated

50 g (2 oz) dried wholemeal breadcrumbs

1 Parboil the Jerusalem artichokes in salted water for 10 minutes. Remove with a slotted spoon and leave until cool enough to handle.

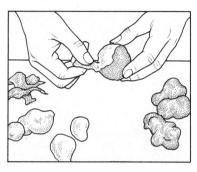

2 Peel the skins off the Jerusalem artichokes and slice the flesh thickly. Set aside.

3 Add the button onions to the water and boil for 2 minutes, then remove with a slotted spoon. Peel off the skins, leaving the root ends intact so that the onions remain whole.

4 Slice the leeks thickly, then wash well under cold running water to remove any grit.

5 Heat 50 g (2 oz) of the butter with the oil in a heavy-based saucepan, add the onions and garlic and toss over moderate heat until the onions are well coated in the butter and oil.

6 Pour in the wine and 150 ml ($\frac{1}{4}$ pint) water and bring to the boil. Add the nutmeg, cover and simmer for 10 minutes.

7 Add the artichokes, leeks and peas and continue simmering for 5 minutes or until all the vegetables are tender. With a slotted spoon, transfer vegetables to a flameproof gratin dish.

8 Boil the cooking liquid rapidly until reduced to about half of its original volume. Lower the heat and stir in the cream.

9 Mix the 2 cheeses together. Stir half of this mixture into the sauce. Add salt and pepper to taste and stir until the cheeses have melted.

10 Pour the cheese sauce over the vegetables in the dish. Mix the remaining cheese with the breadcrumbs, then sprinkle evenly over the top.

11 Dot the remaining butter over the gratin, then bake in the oven at 220°C (425°F) mark 7 for 10 minutes, until the topping is golden brown. Serve hot, straight from the dish.

AVOCADO AND LEMON SALAD WITH OMELETTE RINGS

0.30*	412–618 cals

Serves 4–6

4 eggs

50 g (2 oz) Cheddar cheese, grated

salt and freshly ground pepper

25 g (1 oz) butter or margarine

5 ml (1 tsp) whole black
   peppercorns

5 ml (1 tsp) whole coriander seeds

90 ml (6 tbsp) olive or vegetable oil

45 ml (3 tbsp) lemon juice

2 ripe avocados

parsley sprigs, to garnish
   (optional)

1 Put the eggs in a bowl with
the cheese, 15 ml (1 tbsp)
water and salt and pepper to taste.
Whisk together.

2 Melt a quarter of the butter in
an omelette pan or small non-
stick frying pan. When foaming,
pour in a quarter of the egg
mixture. After a few seconds, push
the set egg mixture into the centre
of the pan to allow the uncooked
egg to run to the edges. Cook until
just set.

3 Brown the omelette under a
preheated hot grill. Turn out
on to a plate. Repeat with the
remaining egg mixture to make
another 3 omelettes.

4 While the omelettes are still
warm, roll them up loosely.
Wrap in greaseproof paper and
leave to cool.

5 Meanwhile, crush the peppercorns and coriander seeds
coarsely with a pestle and mortar,
or with the end of a rolling pin in
a sturdy bowl.

6 In a bowl, whisk together the
oil, lemon juice, crushed spices
and salt and pepper to taste.
Halve, stone and peel the
avocados, then slice thickly into
the dressing. Toss gently to coat
completely.

7 Slice the omelettes thinly.
Arrange the omelette rings and
avocado slices on individual
serving plates. Spoon over the
dressing and garnish with sprigs of
parsley, if liked. Serve
immediately.

Menu Suggestion

Omelette rings and avocado slices
combine together to make this a
substantial and nutritious salad.
Serve for a main course at lunchtime, with wholemeal French-style
bread, or as a light supper.

Meat

CROWN ROAST OF LAMB

| 2.15 | 🍴🍴 | 427–640 cals |

Serves 4–6

| 2 best end necks of lamb, chined, each with 6–8 cutlets |
| 75 g (3 oz) long grain rice |
| salt and freshly ground pepper |
| 25 g (1 oz) butter or margarine |
| 1 small onion, skinned and finely chopped |
| 3 celery sticks, trimmed and finely chopped |
| 1 eating apple, peeled, cored and finely chopped |
| 1 small garlic clove, skinned and crushed |
| 10 ml (2 tsp) curry powder |
| 225 g (8 oz) fresh breadcrumbs, toasted |
| 30 ml (2 tbsp) chopped fresh parsley |
| 1 egg |
| 50 g (2 oz) lard |
| 30 ml (2 tbsp) plain flour |
| 450 ml (¾ pint) beef stock |

1 With a sharp, pointed knife, trim each cutlet bone to a depth of 2.5 cm (1 inch).

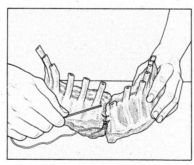

2 Bend the joints around, fat side inwards, and sew together using strong cotton or fine string to form a crown. Cover the exposed bones with foil.

3 Put the rice in a large saucepan of boiling salted water and cook for 12–15 minutes or until tender. Drain, then rinse well under cold running water.

4 Melt the butter in a saucepan, add the onion, celery, apple, garlic and curry powder and cook gently until the vegetables are softened.

5 Remove from the heat and stir in the breadcrumbs, parsley, cooked rice, egg and salt and pepper to taste. Allow to cool, then spoon into the centre of the crown roast. Weigh the joint and calculate the cooking time, allowing 25 minutes per 450 g (1 lb) plus an extra 25 minutes.

6 Melt the lard in a roasting tin then stand the lamb joint in the tin. Roast in the oven at 180°C (350°F) mark 4 for the calculated cooking time, basting occasionally. Cover the joint lightly with foil if the stuffing becomes too brown during roasting.

7 Transfer the crown roast to a warmed serving dish and keep hot. Pour off all but 30 ml (2 tbsp) of the fat from the roasting tin, place the tin on top of the cooker and sprinkle in the flour. Blend well with a wooden spoon, then cook for 2–3 minutes, stirring continuously until golden brown. Gradually stir in the stock and bring to the boil. Simmer for 2–3 minutes, then add salt and pepper to taste. Pour into a gravy boat or jug and serve hot with the joint.

Menu Suggestion
Serve Crown Roast of Lamb for a special occasion meal. With its mildly curried stuffing, it goes well with a medley of courgettes and button onions, or an exotic vegetable such as aubergines or peppers stuffed with a mixture of spiced rice, nuts and raisins.

LAMB WITH ROSEMARY AND GARLIC

3.15*	✳*	305 cals

* plus 12 hours standing; freeze after stage 3

Serves 6

2-kg (4¼-lb) leg of lamb
2 large garlic cloves, skinned
50 g (2 oz) butter, softened
15 ml (1 tbsp) chopped fresh
   rosemary or 5 ml (1 tsp) dried
salt and freshly ground pepper
30 ml (2 tbsp) plain flour
450 ml (¾ pint) chicken stock
fresh rosemary sprigs, to garnish

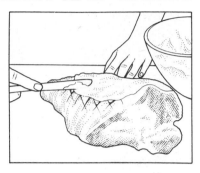

3 Mix the butter with the rosemary and seasoning and then spread all over the lamb. Place the joint in a shallow dish, cover tightly with cling film and refrigerate for at least 12 hours.

4 Uncover the lamb and transfer it to a medium roasting tin. Place in the oven and cook at 180°C (350°F) mark 4 for about 2¼ hours, basting occasionally as the fat begins to run. Pierce the joint with a fine skewer; when done the juices should run clear at first, then with a hint of red.

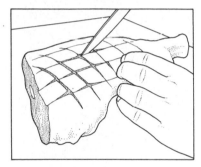

1 Using a sharp knife, score the surface of the lamb into a diamond pattern to the depth of about 12 mm (½ inch).

5 Place the joint on a serving plate, cover loosely and keep warm in a low oven. Pour all excess fat out of the roasting tin leaving about 45 ml (3 tbsp) fat with the meat juices. Sprinkle the flour into the roasting tin and stir until evenly mixed. Cook over a gentle heat for 2–3 minutes until well browned, stirring frequently.

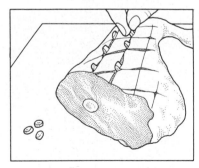

2 Cut the cloves of garlic into wafer thin slices. Push the slices into the scored surface of the lamb with your fingers.

6 Add the stock and seasoning and bring to the boil, stirring. Simmer for 3–4 minutes, adjust the seasoning. To serve, garnish the lamb with rosemary and serve the gravy separately.

LAMB KORMA

| 2.15 | ✳ | 348 cals |

Serves 4

2 onions, skinned and chopped

2.5 cm (1 inch) piece fresh root ginger, peeled

40 g (1½ oz) blanched almonds

2 garlic cloves, skinned

90 ml (6 tbsp) water

5 ml (1 tsp) ground cardamom

5 ml (1 tsp) ground cloves

5 ml (1 tsp) ground cinnamon

5 ml (1 tsp) ground cumin

5 ml (1 tsp) ground coriander

1.25 ml (¼ tsp) cayenne pepper

45 ml (3 tbsp) vegetable oil or ghee

900 g (2 lb) boned tender lamb, cubed

300 ml (½ pint) natural yogurt

salt and freshly ground pepper

cucumber and lime slices, to garnish

1 Put the onions, ginger, almonds and garlic in a blender or food processor with the water and blend to a smooth paste. Add the spices and mix well.

2 Heat the oil or ghee in a heavy-based saucepan and fry the lamb for 5 minutes until browned on all sides.

3 Add the paste mixture and fry for about 10 minutes, stirring, until the mixture is lightly browned. Stir in the yogurt 15 ml (1 tbsp) at a time and season.

4 Cover with a tight-fitting lid, reduce the heat and simmer for 1¼–1½ hours or until the meat is really tender.

5 Transfer to a warmed serving dish and serve garnished with cucumber and lime slices.

Menu Suggestion

Serve with plain boiled or pilau rice, poppadoms, cucumber and yogurt raita, and a sag aloo (spinach and potato curry).

LAMB KORMA

Mild in flavour, creamy in texture, the Indian korma is a very special dish, which was originally only served on special occasions such as feast days and holidays. Our version is relatively simple compared with some of the korma recipes which were devised for celebrations. These often contained such luxurious ingredients as saffron (the most expensive spice in the world), cashew nuts and double cream. If you want to make a richer korma for a dinner party main course, then add powdered saffron or infused saffron liquid with the ground spices in step 1, and stir in 50 g (2 oz) chopped unsalted cashew nuts just before serving. Substitute double cream for the yogurt and swirl more cream over the top of the korma before garnishing.

LAMB CUTLETS EN CROÛTE

| 1.00* | 🥄 🥄 | ✳ | 890 cals |

* freeze after cooking only if serving cold

Serves 6

25 g (1 oz) butter

1 onion, skinned and chopped

25 g (1 oz) fresh white breadcrumbs

1 egg, beaten

30 ml (2 tbsp) chopped fresh mint

salt and freshly ground pepper

squeeze of lemon juice

12 lamb cutlets, trimmed

450 g (1 lb) puff pastry or two 368-g (13-oz) packets frozen puff pastry, thawed

beaten egg, to glaze

sprig of fresh mint, to garnish

1 Make the stuffing. Melt the butter in a pan and fry the onion for about 5 minutes until soft but not brown. Remove from the heat. Stir in the breadcrumbs and bind with the beaten egg. Mix in the mint, salt, freshly ground pepper and lemon juice.

2 Grill or fry the cutlet for 3 minutes on both sides. They should be browned, but pink inside. Leave to cool.

3 Roll out each piece of pastry thinly and cut each one into six squares.

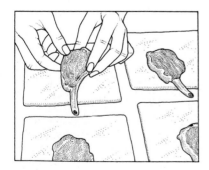

4 Place each of the lamb cutlets on a square of pastry so that the bone extends over the edge of the pastry.

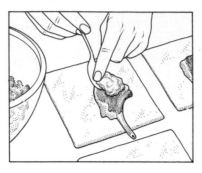

5 Press even amounts of stuffing on the eye of each cutlet. Dampen the pastry edges, wrap the pastry over the cutlets and seal.

6 Place on a dampened baking tray, folded sides underneath. Use any pastry trimmings to decorate the cutlets. Brush with a little beaten egg.

7 Bake in the oven at 220°C (425°F) mark 7 for 15–20 minutes, then reduce the oven temperature to 190°C (375°F) mark 5 and bake for a further 15 minutes until the pastry is golden. Serve hot or cold, garnished with a sprig of fresh mint, if wished.

TANGY CHOPS

0.45	526 cals

Serves 4

30 ml (2 tbsp) vegetable oil

4 lamb chump chops

salt and freshly ground pepper

finely grated rind and juice of 1
   lemon

30 ml (2 tbsp) chopped fresh
   parsley or 10 ml (2 tsp)
   dried parsley

15 ml (1 tbsp) chopped fresh mint
   or 5 ml (1 tsp) dried mint

5 ml (1 tsp) sugar

150 ml ($\frac{1}{4}$ pint) beef or chicken stock

1 Heat the oil in a sauté pan or
frying pan, add the chops and
fry over brisk heat until browned
on both sides. Lower the heat and
season the chops with salt and
pepper to taste.

2 Mix the remaining ingredients
together. Spoon this mixture
over the chops and pour in the
stock. Cover the pan tightly and
simmer gently for 30 minutes or
until the meat is tender. Serve hot
on a warmed dish, with the juices
poured over.

Menu Suggestion
Serve for an informal family meal
with grilled or oven-baked
tomatoes, potatoes and a seasonal
green vegetable.

SPICED LENTIL BAKE

2.30	630 cals

Serves 4

45 ml (3 tbsp) vegetable oil

8 middle neck lamb chops, total weight about 1.1 kg (2½ lb), trimmed of excess fat

2 medium onions, skinned and thinly sliced

15 ml (1 tbsp) turmeric

5 ml (1 tsp) paprika

5 ml (1 tsp) ground cinnamon

75 g (3 oz) red lentils

salt and freshly ground pepper

450 g (1 lb) potatoes, peeled and thinly sliced

450 g (1 lb) swede, peeled and thinly sliced

300 ml (½ pint) lamb or chicken stock

1 Heat the oil in a large sauté or frying pan, add the chops and brown well on both sides. Remove from the pan with a slotted spoon.

2 Add the onions to the pan with the turmeric, paprika, cinnamon and lentils. Fry for 2–3 minutes. Add plenty of salt and pepper and spoon into a shallow 2 litre (3½ pint) ovenproof dish.

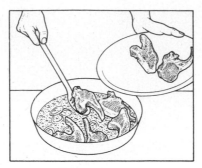

3 Place the chops on top of the onion and lentil mixture. Arrange the vegetable slices on top of the chops, then season and pour over the stock.

4 Cover the dish tightly and cook in the oven at 180°C (350°F) mark 4 for about 1½ hours, or until the chops are tender. Uncover and cook for a further 30 minutes, or until lightly browned on top. Serve hot, straight from the dish.

Menu Suggestion
Spiced Lentil Bake is a complete meal in itself, with lamb chops, lentils, potatoes and swede baked together in one dish. Serve with a crisp green salad or a seasonal green vegetable.

SPICED LENTIL BAKE
The different kinds of lentils available can be confusing, especially in health food shops where there is always such a large selection. The red lentils used in this recipe are the most common kind, sometimes also described as 'split red lentils' or even 'Egyptian lentils'. They do not need soaking and are quick-cooking, but they tend to lose their shape. 'Continental lentils' are green, brown or reddish-brown in colour, and are whole rather than split. These varieties keep their shape and have a nuttier texture than red lentils, but take longer to cook.

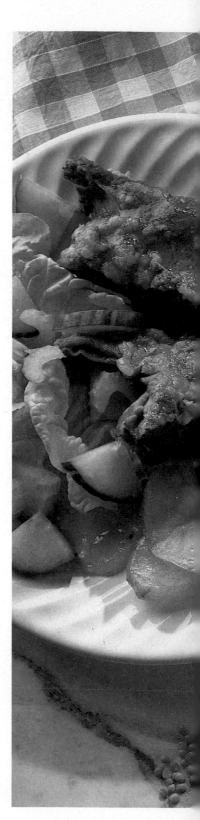

Oriental Lamb

1.00	493 cals

Serves 4

1.4 kg (3 lb) lean shoulder of lamb
450 g (1 lb) small new potatoes
225 g (8 oz) small pickling onions
30 ml (2 tbsp) vegetable oil
25 g (1 oz) butter or margarine
15 ml (1 tbsp) flour
5 ml (1 tsp) ground ginger
300 ml ($\frac{1}{2}$ pint) chicken stock
15 ml (1 tbsp) Worcestershire sauce
30 ml (2 tbsp) soy sauce
salt and freshly ground pepper
2 caps canned pimento, diced

1 Slice all the meat off the bone, discarding any excess fat, and cut into 2.5 cm (1 inch) pieces about 5 mm ($\frac{1}{4}$ inch) thick.

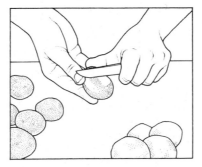

2 Wash the new potatoes and scrub them with a vegetable brush, or scrape with a knife.

3 Skin the onions. Put them in a bowl and pour in enough boiling water to cover. Leave to stand for 2 minutes, then drain and plunge into a bowl of cold water. Peel off the skin with your fingers.

4 Heat the oil and fat in a large sauté pan and brown the meat in it a few pieces at a time. Remove from the pan with a slotted spoon.

5 Add the potatoes and onions to the residual fat in the pan and fry them until lightly browned, turning frequently.

6 Return the meat to the pan, sprinkle in the flour and ginger and stir well. Cook gently, stirring, for 2 minutes.

7 Add the stock, Worcestershire sauce, soy sauce and seasoning to taste. Bring to the boil, stirring, then cover and simmer for 30 minutes or until the meat is tender.

8 Add the pimentos and stir over low heat to bring to serving temperature. Taste and adjust seasoning, then transfer to a warmed serving dish. Serve hot.

Menu Suggestion
This casserole has its own vegetables included with the meat. Serve with a simple green salad, or a seasonal green vegetable such as courgettes, if liked.

LAMB NOISETTES WITH RED WINE SAUCE

1.00	617 cals

Serves 6

12 lamb noisettes

flour, for coating

25 g (1 oz) butter

60 ml (4 tbsp) vegetable oil

2 large onions, skinned and sliced

1 garlic clove, skinned and finely chopped

225 g (8 oz) button mushrooms, wiped

300 ml ($\frac{1}{2}$ pint) red wine

150 ml ($\frac{1}{4}$ pint) chicken stock

15 ml (1 tbsp) tomato purée

2 bay leaves

salt and freshly ground pepper

1 Lightly coat the lamb noisettes with flour. Heat the butter and oil in a large flameproof casserole. Add the noisettes, a few at a time, and brown quickly on both sides. Remove from the casserole with a slotted spoon and set aside.

2 Add the onion and garlic to the casserole and fry for about 5 minutes until golden. Add the mushrooms and fry for a further 2–3 minutes. Stir in the red wine, stock, tomato purée and bay leaves. Season well with salt and freshly ground pepper.

3 Replace the noisettes and bring to the boil, then cover and simmer gently for about 40 minutes until tender, turning the meat once during this time.

4 Lift the noisettes out of the sauce and remove the string. Place the noisettes on a warmed serving dish and keep warm. Boil the remaining liquid rapidly for 5–10 minutes to reduce the sauce. Taste and adjust the seasoning, then pour over the noisettes. Serve immediately.

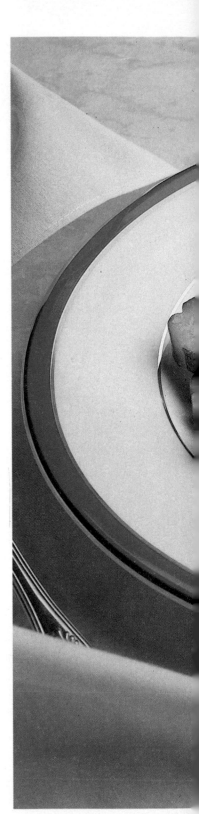

LAMB NOISETTES WITH RED WINE SAUCE

Lamb noisettes are a very special cut of meat. You can buy them ready-prepared at some large supermarkets, or ask your butcher to prepare them for you as they are a little tricky to do yourself. Lamb noisettes are cut from the best end of neck. This is the same cut which is used for making Guard of Honour, except that the bones are removed from the whole rack, then the meat is rolled up and tied at intervals according to how many cutlets there were in the rack—usually six or eight.

ROLLED STUFFED BREASTS OF LAMB

| 1.55 | ✳* | 925 cals |

* freeze at end of step 4

Serves 4

25 g (1 oz) butter or margarine

1 medium onion, skinned and
   chopped

25 g (1 oz) streaky bacon, rinded
   and chopped

226 g (8 oz) packet frozen leaf
   spinach, thawed

75 g (3 oz) fresh breadcrumbs

45 ml (3 tbsp) chopped fresh
   parsley

finely grated rind of $\frac{1}{2}$ lemon

15 ml (1 tbsp) lemon juice

pinch of grated nutmeg

1 egg, beaten

salt and freshly ground pepper

2 large breasts of lamb, boned and
   trimmed, total weight about
   1.1 kg (2$\frac{1}{2}$ lb)

45 ml (3 tbsp) vegetable oil

watercress, to garnish

1 Melt the butter in a saucepan,
   add the onion and bacon and
fry for about 5 minutes until
lightly browned.

2 Drain the spinach and chop
   roughly. Place in a bowl with
the onion and bacon, breadcrumbs, parsley, lemon rind and
juice, nutmeg and egg. Mix
together well, adding salt and
pepper to taste.

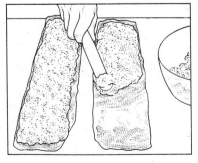

3 Lay the breasts of lamb fat
   side down on a work surface
and spread the stuffing evenly
over them with a palette knife.

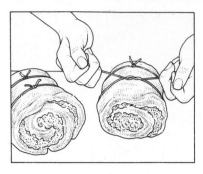

4 Roll up the lamb breasts
   loosely and tie in several places
with string to hold their shape.

5 Weigh each joint and calculate
   the cooking time, allowing 25
minutes per 450 g (1 lb) plus 25
minutes for each joint. Heat the oil
in a roasting tin and place the
joints in the tin. Roast in the oven
at 180°C (350°F) mark 4 for the
calculated cooking time, basting
occasionally. Serve hot, garnished
with watercress.

Menu Suggestion

Breast of lamb makes an
economical midweek roast. This
recipe has a spinach stuffing,
therefore only one or two
additional vegetables is necessary.
New potatoes tossed in mint
butter would go well, with glazed
carrots.

**ROLLED STUFFED
BREASTS OF LAMB**

Breast of lamb is one of the
fattier cuts, but it is excellent
cooked in this way with a tasty
and substantial stuffing. When
buying breasts of lamb, look for
the leanest ones possible—not all
lamb breasts are very fatty. Any
visible fat should be white and
dry, whereas the meat should be
pink and moist. Most lambs are
aged between 3 and 6 months at
the time of slaughtering, after
this time the meat darkens in
colour and becomes more
coarsely grained.

LANCASHIRE HOT POT

2.40	✳	427 cals

Serves 4

8 middle neck lamb chops

2 lamb's kidneys

8 shelled oysters (optional—see box)

2 medium onions, skinned and sliced

125 g (4 oz) mushrooms, sliced

5 ml (1 tsp) dried thyme

salt and freshly ground pepper

450 g (1 lb) potatoes, peeled and thinly sliced

450 ml (¾ pint) lamb or beef stock

25 g (1 oz) lard or dripping

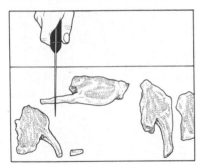

1 Remove any excess fat from the lamb. Select a large, deep casserole. If it is not deep enough to hold the meat, chop the ends off the bones.

2 Skin, halve and core the kidneys and divide each half into 3–4 pieces.

3 Layer the meat in the casserole with the oysters, if using, the kidneys, onions and mushrooms. Sprinkle each layer with thyme and salt and pepper to taste. If the casserole has a narrow top, add some of the potatoes at this stage. Pour in the stock.

4 Arrange a layer of overlapping potato slices on top. Melt the lard and brush over the potatoes. Cover and cook in the oven at 170°C (325°F) mark 3 for 2 hours, or until both the meat and the potatoes are tender when tested with a skewer.

5 Remove the lid carefully, increase the oven temperature to 220°C (425°F) mark 7 and continue cooking for about 20 minutes, or until the potatoes are golden brown and crisp.
Serve hot.

Menu Suggestion

Lancashire Hot Pot makes a filling family meal. It is especially good in cold weather, with a nourishing vegetable dish like 'mushy' peas or mashed root vegetables. Pickled red cabbage was the traditional accompaniment, but ordinary red cabbage tastes just as good.

LANCASHIRE HOT POT

One of the best known of Lancashire dishes, the hot pot takes its name from the tall earthenware dish in which it was traditionally cooked. The long boned chops from the Pennine sheep could be stood vertically around the pot and the centre filled with vegetables, kidneys, mushrooms and, in the days when they were cheap, oysters. A thatch of sliced potatoes completed the dish.

MOUSSAKA

| 1.40* | ⬚ | ✳* | 632–948 cals |

* plus 30 minutes to dégorge the aubergines and 15 minutes standing; freeze before baking at step 8

Serves 4–6

2 medium aubergines

salt and freshly ground pepper

about 150 ml ($\frac{1}{4}$ pint) olive or vegetable oil, or a mixture of both

1 large onion, skinned and roughly chopped

1–2 garlic cloves, skinned and crushed

450 g (1 lb) minced lamb

227 g (8 oz) can tomatoes

30 ml (2 tbsp) tomato purée

10 ml (2 tsp) dried oregano

5 ml (1 tsp) ground allspice

2 bay leaves

410 g (14$\frac{1}{2}$ oz) can evaporated milk

40 g (1$\frac{1}{2}$ oz) cornflour

25 g (1 oz) butter or margarine

25 g (1 oz) plain flour

pinch of grated nutmeg

1 egg, beaten

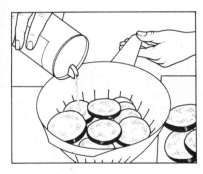

1 Slice the aubergines thinly and place in a colander, sprinkling each layer with salt. Cover with a plate, place heavy weights on top and leave the aubergines to dégorge for 30 minutes.

2 Meanwhile, heat 30 ml (2 tbsp) of the oil in a heavy-based saucepan, add the onion and garlic and fry gently for 5 minutes until soft and lightly coloured. Add the minced lamb and fry until well browned, stirring and pressing with a wooden spoon to break up any lumps.

3 Add the tomatoes with their juice, the tomato purée, oregano, allspice and salt and pepper to taste, then add the bay leaves. Cover and simmer for about 20 minutes, stirring occasionally to break up the tomatoes.

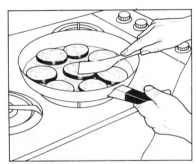

4 Meanwhile, rinse the aubergines under cold running water, then pat dry with absorbent kitchen paper. Pour enough oil into a heavy-based frying pan to just cover the base. Heat until very hot, then add a layer of aubergine slices. Fry until golden on both sides, turning once, then remove with a spatula and drain on absorbent kitchen paper. Continue frying and draining all the aubergine slices in this way, adding more oil to the pan as necessary.

5 Make the sauce for the topping. Dilute the evaporated milk with water to make up to 1 litre (1$\frac{3}{4}$ pints) as directed on the can. In a jug, mix the cornflour to a smooth paste with a few spoonfuls of the milk.

6 Melt the butter in a saucepan, add the flour and cook gently, stirring, for 1–2 minutes. Remove from the heat and gradually blend in the milk. Bring to the boil, stirring constantly, then simmer for 3 minutes.

7 Stir in the cornflour paste and continue simmering and stirring until the sauce is thick. Remove the pan from the heat, add the nutmeg and salt and pepper to taste, then stir in the beaten egg.

8 Arrange the meat and aubergines in layers in a baking dish, then pour over the sauce. Bake, uncovered, in the oven at 180°C (350°F) mark 4 for 40 minutes. Leave to stand at room temperature for at least 15 minutes before serving.

Menu Suggestion

Greek Moussaka is an extremely filling dish. Serve for a family meal, or even for an informal supper party, with Greek sesame seed bread and a mixed salad. Retsina wine is the ideal drink to accompany Greek food.

GREEK LAMB

| 2.20 | ✳ | 673–1011 cals |

Serves 4–6

60 ml (4 tbsp) olive oil

900 g (2 lb) small new potatoes, scraped, or old potatoes, peeled and cut into cubes

1.1 kg (2½ lb) boned lean shoulder of lamb, trimmed of fat and cubed

2 large onions, skinned and sliced

15 ml (1 tbsp) plain flour

300 ml (½ pint) dry white wine

350 g (12 oz) tomatoes, skinned and chopped

30 ml (2 tbsp) wine vinegar

2 cinnamon sticks

2 bay leaves

10 ml (2 tsp) chopped fresh thyme or 5 ml (1 tsp) dried

salt and freshly ground pepper

thyme sprigs, to garnish

1 Heat 30 ml (2 tbsp) of the oil in a large flameproof casserole. Pierce each potato (or potato cube) with a sharp knife, add to the casserole and fry over moderate heat until golden on all sides. Remove from the oil with a slotted spoon and drain on absorbent kitchen paper.

2 Heat the remaining oil in the casserole, add the lamb and onions in batches and fry over moderate heat until browned on all sides. Sprinkle in the flour and fry 1 further minute, stirring until it is absorbed.

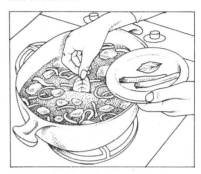

3 Pour the wine into the casserole and add the tomatoes and wine vinegar. Bring slowly to boiling point, then lower the heat and add the cinnamon, bay leaves, thyme and seasoning to taste. Cover and simmer gently for 1 hour, stirring occasionally.

4 Add the fried potatoes to the casserole and continue simmering for 1 further hour or until the lamb and potatoes are tender. Remove the cinnamon sticks and bay leaves, then taste and adjust seasoning. Garnish with thyme sprigs and serve the casserole immediately.

Menu Suggestion
Serve with a Greek-style salad of tomato, shredded white cabbage, raw onion, black olives and chopped fresh coriander.

GREEK LAMB

A rich and pungent dish, Greek Lamb is given its authentic flavour with the combination of olive oil, white wine, tomatoes, cinnamon and fresh thyme. Greek olive oil from the first cold pressing of the olives is thick and green, often with flecks of olives floating in it. Look for it in Greek and Cypriot food shops—its superb flavour and texture make it good for salads as well as cooking.

LAMB IN TOMATO SAUCE WITH HERB BREAD

2.40	✳*	747 cals

* freeze lamb in tomato sauce only, without French bread

Serves 4

30 ml (2 tbsp) vegetable oil

1 kg (2¼ lb) boned lean shoulder of lamb, trimmed of fat and cubed

1 medium onion, skinned and sliced

20 ml (4 tsp) plain flour

397 g (14 oz) and 227 g (8 oz) can tomatoes

30 ml (2 tbsp) tomato purée

pinch of granulated sugar

2.5 ml (½ tsp) dried rosemary

60 ml (4 tbsp) red wine (optional)

salt and freshly ground pepper

lamb or beef stock, if necessary

40 g (1½ oz) butter

15 ml (1 tbsp) snipped fresh chives

eight 1 cm (½ inch) slices of French bread

1 Heat the oil in a flameproof casserole, add the lamb and fry over high heat until browned on all sides. Remove from the casserole with a slotted spoon and set aside.

2 Add the onion to the pan and fry for 5 minutes until soft. Stir in the flour and cook for 1 minute. Add the tomatoes with their juice, the tomato purée, sugar, rosemary and wine, if using. Bring to the boil, stirring all the time.

3 Return the meat to the pan and add salt and pepper to taste. Add a little stock, if necessary, to cover the meat. Cover the casserole and cook in the oven at 170°C (325°F) mark 3 for about 1¼ hours.

4 Meanwhile, make the herb butter. Beat the butter until smooth, then beat in the chives and salt and pepper to taste.

5 Spread the butter on to the slices of French bread. Uncover the casserole and place the bread, butter side up, on top. Cook for 1 further hour, or until the meat is tender. Serve hot.

Menu Suggestion
With its garnish of herb bread, this lamb casserole is quite a substantial dish. Serve simply, with a seasonal green vegetable.

LAMB IN TOMATO SAUCE WITH HERB BREAD
Shoulder of lamb is an excellent cut for casseroles such as this one, because it is so economical. It can be fatty, however, especially if the lamb is not an early-season, young animal. Check with your butcher before buying. An alternative cut of lamb which tends to be less fatty is the fillet. This cut comes from the middle neck and scrag; it is quite lean and tender, yet it does not become dry in casseroles as with the more expensive leg of lamb, which is too lean.

SAG GOSHT
(INDIAN LAMB AND SPINACH CURRY)

2.00	✱	589 cals

Serves 4

1–2 garlic cloves, skinned and roughly chopped

2.5 cm (1 inch) piece of fresh root ginger, peeled and roughly chopped

15 ml (1 tbsp) mustard seeds

15 ml (1 tbsp) coriander seeds

5 ml (1 tsp) turmeric

2.5 ml ($\frac{1}{2}$ tsp) chilli powder or to taste

salt

65 g (2$\frac{1}{2}$ oz) ghee or butter

3 medium onions, skinned and thinly sliced

900 g (2 lb) boneless lamb fillet, trimmed of fat and cut into cubes

300 ml ($\frac{1}{2}$ pint) natural yogurt

450 g (1 lb) fresh spinach, trimmed and washed, or 225 g (8 oz) frozen leaf spinach, thawed

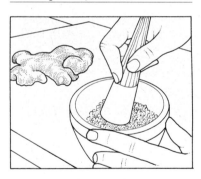

1 Put the garlic and ginger in a mortar and pestle with the mustard seeds and coriander. Pound until well crushed, then mix in the turmeric, chilli powder and 5 ml (1 tsp) salt.

2 Melt 50 g (2 oz) of the ghee in a flameproof casserole, add two-thirds of the onions and fry gently for about 10 minutes until softened and lightly coloured.

3 Add the crushed spice mixture and fry gently, stirring, for a few minutes. Add the lamb in batches, increase the heat and fry until well browned on all sides.

4 Return all the lamb to the casserole. Add the yogurt to the meat, 15 ml (1 tbsp) at a time. Stir-fry after each addition to mix with the meat, then cover and cook gently for 1 hour or until the lamb is tender.

5 Add the spinach to the casserole, stir well to mix with the meat and continue cooking for a further 5 minutes.

6 Meanwhile, melt the remaining ghee in a small frying pan, add the remaining sliced onion and fry, stirring constantly, over moderate heat until the onion is softened and golden.

7 Taste the curry and add more salt, if necessary. Turn into a warmed serving dish and sprinkle the golden onion slices over the top. Serve hot.

Menu Suggestion
The rich combination of spinach and lamb needs a plain accompaniment. Serve with boiled basmati rice, a yogurt and cucumber or onion raita, crispy poppadoms and chutneys.

RAAN
(INDIAN SPICED LAMB)

4.00*		685 cals

* plus 2–3 days marinating and 1 hour coming to room temperature

Serves 6

1.8 kg (4 lb) leg of lamb, skin and H-bone removed

6 large garlic cloves, skinned and roughly chopped

1 large piece of fresh root ginger, weighing about 50 g (2 oz), peeled and roughly chopped

300 ml ($\frac{1}{2}$ pint) natural yogurt

thinly pared rind and juice of 1 lemon

15 ml (1 tbsp) cumin seeds

seeds of 6 cardamom pods

6 whole cloves

150 g (5 oz) blanched almonds

10 ml (2 tsp) salt

5 ml (1 tsp) turmeric

5–10 ml (1–2 tsp) chilli powder, according to taste

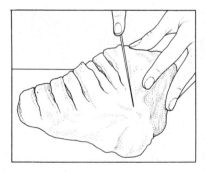

1 Make deep slashes all over the leg of lamb with a sharp, pointed knife. Set aside while making the marinade.

2 Put the garlic and ginger in a blender or food processor with 60 ml (4 tbsp) of the yogurt, the lemon rind and juice, the cumin seeds, cardamom pods and cloves. Work to a paste.

3 Roughly chop 100 g (4 oz) of the almonds, then add to the machine with a few more spoonfuls of yogurt. Work again, then add the remaining yogurt with the salt, turmeric and chilli powder. Work until all the ingredients are thoroughly combined.

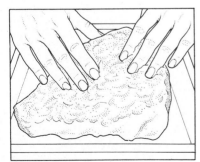

4 Put the leg of lamb in a roasting tin and spread all over with the spiced yogurt paste. Work the paste into the cuts in the meat as much as possible. Cover the lamb loosely with foil and marinate in the refrigerator for 2–3 days.

5 When ready to cook, uncover the lamb and allow the meat to come to room temperature for about 1 hour. Roast in the oven at 220°C (425°F) mark 7 for 30 minutes.

6 Lower the oven temperature to 180°C (350°F) mark 4 and roast for a further 1 hour, then lower the temperature to 170°C (325°F) mark 3 and roast for a further 2 hours, or until the meat is very tender and almost falling off the bone.

7 Remove the lamb from the roasting tin and place on a warmed serving platter. Cover loosely with foil and keep warm in a low oven.

8 Pour off the excess fat from the roasting tin, then place the tin on top of the cooker. Boil the sediment and juices to reduce, stirring and scraping the pan with a wooden spoon.

9 Uncover the lamb and pour over the pan juices. Arrange the remaining almonds over the lamb in a decorative 'flower' pattern. Serve hot.

Menu Suggestion
Raan is quite a spectacular dish to serve, either for a dinner party or for a special Sunday roast. Saffron rice looks good as an accompaniment, and *sag bhaji* (curried spinach) complements the flavour of the lamb well. Alternatively, serve with *sag aloo* (spinach and potato curry) instead of separate dishes of rice and spinach.

169

LAMB AND SPINACH LASAGNE

| 1.45 | 🍶 | ✳* | 799 cals |

* freeze at the end of step 6

Serves 6

450 g (1 lb) fresh spinach, washed

30 ml (2 tbsp) vegetable oil

1 medium onion, skinned and
   chopped

450 g (1 lb) minced lamb

227 g (8 oz) can tomatoes

1 garlic clove, skinned and crushed

30 ml (2 tbsp) chopped fresh mint

5 ml (1 tsp) ground cinnamon

freshly grated nutmeg

salt and freshly ground pepper

50 g (2 oz) butter or margarine

50 g (2 oz) plain flour

900 ml (1½ pints) milk

150 ml (¼ pint) natural yogurt

12–15 sheets oven-ready lasagne

175 g (6 oz) Feta or Cheddar cheese,
   grated

1 Put the spinach in a saucepan
with only the water that clings
to the leaves and cook gently for
about 4 minutes. Drain well and
chop finely.

2 Heat the oil in a large saucepan, add the onion and fry
gently for 5 minutes until
softened. Add the lamb and brown
well, then drain off all the fat.

3 Stir in the spinach with the
tomatoes and their juice, the
garlic, mint and cinnamon. Season
with nutmeg, salt and pepper to
taste. Bring to the boil and simmer,
uncovered, for about 30 minutes.
Leave to cool while making the
white sauce.

4 Melt the butter in a saucepan,
add the flour and cook gently,
stirring, for 1–2 minutes. Remove
from the heat and gradually blend
in the milk. Bring to the boil,
stirring constantly, then simmer
for 3 minutes until thick and
smooth. Add the yogurt and salt
and pepper to taste.

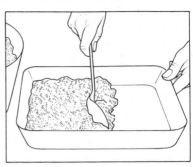

5 Spoon one-third of the meat
mixture over the base of a
rectangular baking dish.

6 Cover with 4–5 sheets of
lasagne and spread over one-
third of the white sauce. Repeat
these layers twice more, finishing
with the sauce, which should completely cover the lasagne. Sprinkle
the cheese on top.

7 Stand the dish on a baking
sheet. Bake in the oven at
180°C (350°F) mark 4 for 45–50
minutes, or until the top is well
browned and bubbling. Serve hot.

Menu Suggestion

Lamb and Spinach Lasagne is rich
and filling. Serve with a tomato
salad dressed with oil, lemon juice
and raw onion rings, chopped
spring onion or snipped fresh
chives.

STEAK AND MUSHROOM PIE

`3.00*` 🥧 `562 cals`

*plus 1 hour cooling
Serves 4

700 g (1½ lb) stewing steak, cut into 2.5 cm (1 inch) cubes
30 ml (2 tbsp) plain flour
1 medium onion, skinned and sliced
450 ml (¾ pint) beef stock
100 g (4 oz) button mushrooms
212 g (7½ oz) packet frozen puff pastry, thawed
beaten egg, to glaze

1 Coat the meat with the flour, then put in a heavy-based saucepan with the sliced onion. Pour in the beef stock.

2 Bring to the boil, then lower the heat and simmer for 1½–2 hours, until the meat is tender. (Alternatively, the meat can be cooked in a covered casserole in the oven at 170°C (325°F) mark 3 for 2 hours.) Leave for about 1 hour, until cold.

3 Using a slotted spoon, transfer the meat to a 1 litre (2 pint) pie dish. Mix in the mushrooms.

4 Slowly pour in enough of the cold cooking liquid to half fill the pie dish.

5 Roll out the pastry 2.5 cm (1 inch) larger than the top of the dish. Cut off a 1 cm (½ inch) strip from round the edge of the pastry and put this strip round the dampened rim of the dish.

6 Dampen the edges of the pastry with water and put on the top of the pie, without stretching the pastry; trim if necessary and knock up the edges. Use the trimmings to make decorations, if wished. Brush the top of the pie with beaten egg to glaze the pastry.

7 Bake the pie in the oven at 220°C (425°F) mark 7 for 20 minutes. Reduce the heat to 180°C (350°F) mark 4 and cook for a further 20 minutes. Serve hot, straight from the dish.

Menu Suggestion
Steak and Mushroom Pie is a traditional English dish. Serve with boiled or creamed potatoes and seasonal vegetables for a substantial family meal.

STEAK AND MUSHROOM PIE

There are lots of ways in which you can vary this pie. For everyday family meals, it can be made more colourful with the addition of 2–3 carrots, peeled and sliced, which should be cooked with the beef in steps 1 and 2. Parsnips could also be used to add bulk; they taste really good with beef and also add a touch of sweetness to the gravy. For those who like them, 100 g (4 oz) lambs' kidneys can be added, which will increase the nutritional value of the dish — kidneys are rich in iron and vitamin B. Steak and Mushroom Pie also makes a delicious main course for a dinner party with a traditional English theme. Make it more special by using half red wine and half beef stock, and by including a few fresh or smoked oysters or fresh scallops.

BRAISED BEEF

3.00	703 cals

Serves 6

1.4 kg (3 lb) piece of silverside
2 medium carrots, peeled
2 medium parsnips, peeled
3 celery sticks
2 small turnips, peeled
2 medium onions, skinned
30 ml (2 tbsp) vegetable oil or dripping
75 g (3 oz) streaky bacon rashers, rinded and chopped
1 bay leaf
salt and freshly ground pepper
150 ml ($\frac{1}{4}$ pint) beef stock
150 ml ($\frac{1}{4}$ pint) cider
15 ml (1 tbsp) arrowroot
chopped fresh parsley, to garnish

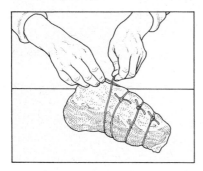

1 Tie up the meat to form a neat joint. Cut the carrots and parsnips into slices about 1 cm ($\frac{1}{2}$ inch) thick, halving them if large. Cut the celery and turnip into similar-sized pieces. Cut the onions in half and slice thickly.

2 Heat the oil in a deep 3.4 litre (6 pint) flameproof casserole. Add the bacon and fry until beginning to brown. Remove with a slotted spoon and reserve.

3 Reheat the oil in the casserole for a few seconds. Add the meat and fry until browned all over, then remove from the casserole and set aside.

4 Add the vegetables to the casserole and fry over high heat. Return the bacon to the casserole, add the bay leaf and plenty of salt and pepper.

5 Place the joint in the centre of the bed of vegetables. Pour in the stock and cider and bring to the boil.

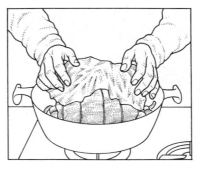

6 Fit a piece of foil over the meat and vegetables to form a 'tent', then cover with a close-fitting lid.

7 Cook the joint in the oven at 160–170°C (300–325°F) mark 2–3 for 2–2$\frac{1}{2}$ hours. Halfway through the cooking time, turn the joint over and re-cover firmly. Test the meat after 2 hours; if it is done, a fine skewer will glide easily and smoothly into the joint.

8 Lift the joint on to a board and cut into slices no more than 0.5 cm ($\frac{1}{4}$ inch) thick. Remove the vegetables from the casserole with a slotted spoon and place on a shallow serving dish. Arrange the meat over the vegetables, cover with foil and place in a low oven.

9 Mix the arrowroot to a smooth paste with 45 ml (3 tbsp) water. Skim off the excess fat from the cooking juices, then stir in the arrowroot.

10 Place the casserole on top of the cooker and bring slowly to the boil, stirring. Boil for 1 minute, then taste and adjust seasoning. Spoon a little gravy over the meat and sprinkle with parsley. Serve the remaining gravy separately in a sauceboat.

Menu Suggestion
With its own vegetables and gravy, this joint of braised silverside needs no accompaniment other than creamed or boiled potatoes.

BRAISED BEEF

Braising is the perfect cooking method for a joint of silverside. The long, slow cooking breaks down tough fibres and ensures tender meat, and the simmering in vegetables and liquid gives both flavour and succulence. With braising, it is important to choose a casserole dish which fits the joint snugly, and to keep it tightly covered during cooking. This is so that none of the juices can escape and the flavours of the different vegetables and liquid can concentrate as much as possible. Frying the meat and vegetables first also helps accentuate flavour.

BEEF WITH STOUT

2.30	✳ 509 cals

Serves 4

700 g (1½ lb) stewing beef

30 ml (2 tbsp) vegetable oil

2 large onions, skinned and sliced

15 ml (1 tbsp) flour

275 ml (9.68 fl oz) can stout

200 ml (7 fl oz) beef stock

30 ml (2 tbsp) tomato purée

100 g (4 oz) stoned prunes

225 g (8 oz) carrots, peeled and sliced

salt and freshly ground pepper

croûtons, to garnish

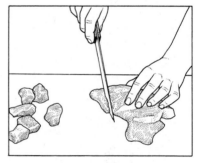

1 Cut the meat into 4 cm (1½ inch) cubes, trimming off all fat. Heat the oil in a flameproof casserole, add the meat and fry until well browned on all sides. Remove with a slotted spoon.

2 Add the onions to the remaining oil in the pan and fry gently until lightly browned. Stir in the flour and cook for 1 minute. Stir in the stout, stock, tomato purée, prunes and carrots. Bring to the boil and season well.

3 Replace the meat, cover and cook in the oven at 170°C (325°F) mark 3 for 1½–2 hours until tender. Adjust seasoning. Serve garnished with croûtons.

BOEUF STROGANOFF
(BEEF WITH MUSHROOMS AND SOURED CREAM)

0.25	538 cals

Serves 4

700 g (1½ lb) rump steak, thinly
    sliced

45 ml (3 tbsp) flour

salt and freshly ground pepper

50 g (2 oz) butter

1 onion, skinned and thinly sliced

225 g (8 oz) mushrooms, wiped and
    sliced

150 ml (¼ pint) soured cream

10 ml (2 tsp) tomato purée
    (optional)

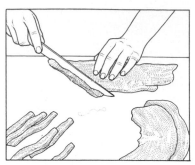

2 Trim the fat off the steak and discard. Cut the meat across the grain into thin strips.

3 Coat the strips of steak in the flour seasoned with salt and pepper. Melt half the butter in a sauté pan, add the meat and fry for 5–7 minutes, tossing constantly until golden brown.

4 Add the remaining butter, the onion and mushrooms and fry, stirring, for 3–4 minutes. Stir in the soured cream and tomato purée (if liked), and season well, using plenty of pepper. Heat through gently, without boiling. Transfer to a warmed serving dish and serve immediately.

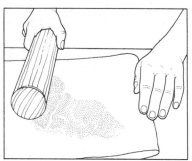

1 Beat the steak with a meat mallet or rolling pin between two sheets of greaseproof paper.

BOEUF STROGANOFF

The story goes that this dish was created in the nineteenth century by a French chef for a Russian nobleman called Count Stroganoff. The chef worked for the Count, who was something of a gourmet. In the freezing temperatures of the Russian winter, there were always problems cutting meat, which was more or less permanently frozen. On one occasion when the Count ordered beef, the chef hit upon the idea of cutting it into wafer-thin slices—this way it was easier to cut and it also cooked more quickly. The result of this experiment has since become a famous, classic dish, so it must have met with the Count's approval!

GOULASH
(BEEF STEW WITH PAPRIKA)

3.10	✳	354 cals

Serves 8

1.4 kg (3 lb) stewing veal or braising
   steak

75 g (3 oz) butter or margarine

700 g (1½ lb) onions, skinned and
   thinly sliced

450 g (1 lb) carrots, peeled and
   thinly sliced

45–60 ml (3–4 tbsp) paprika

30 ml (2 tbsp) plain flour

900 ml (1½ pints) chicken stock

60 ml (4 tbsp) dry white wine

salt and freshly ground pepper

142 ml (5 fl oz) soured cream

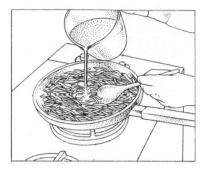

1 Cut the meat into 4 cm (1½
inch) pieces. Melt the fat in a
frying pan and fry the meat, a
little at a time, until browned.
Drain and place in a shallow ovenproof dish.

2 Fry the onions and carrots in
the fat remaining in the pan
for about 5 minutes until lightly
browned. Add the paprika and
flour and fry for 2 minutes.
Gradually stir in the stock, wine
and seasoning. Bring to the boil
and pour over the meat.

3 Cover tightly and cook in the
oven at 150°C (300°F) mark 2
for 2¾ hours until tender. When
cooked, pour the soured cream
over the goulash and serve.

Menu Suggestion
Goulash is traditionally served
with dumplings or noodles. An
unusual alternative to these
accompaniments is a dish of boiled
new potatoes and sautéed button
mushrooms, tossed together with
chopped fresh herbs and some
melted butter.

GOULASH

This recipe for goulash is
simple and straightforward —
typical of the kind of goulash to
be found in Austria. Hearty
and warming, it is the ideal dish
to serve in cold weather, especially in the depths of winter when
snow is on the ground — the
Austrians frequently eat goulash
or bowls of goulash soup to keep
them warm at lunchtime after a
morning's skiing. Goulash is also
very popular in Hungary, where
it is often made with extra
ingredients such as red and green
peppers, mushrooms and
tomatoes, resulting in a more
flamboyant-looking dish with a
stronger flavour. When buying
paprika to make goulash, look for
the variety in the silver sachet
from Hungary which is labelled
süss (sweet).

SUSSEX STEW

| 3.00 | ✳ | 533 cals |

Serves 4

30 ml (2 tbsp) plain flour

5 ml (1 tsp) dried thyme

salt and freshly ground pepper

900 g (2 lb) stewing steak, in one
    piece

30 ml (2 tbsp) beef dripping or lard

1 large onion, skinned and sliced

300 ml (½ pint) sweet stout

30 ml (2 tbsp) mushroom ketchup

thyme sprigs, to garnish

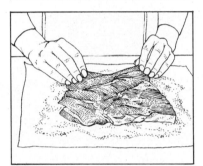

1 Mix the flour with the thyme
and salt and pepper and spread
out on a large flat plate or sheet of
greaseproof paper. Coat the meat
in the flour.

2 Melt the dripping or lard in a
flameproof casserole. Add the
onion slices and fry gently for 5
minutes until soft but not
coloured. Remove with a slotted
spoon and set aside. Add the beef
to the casserole, increase the heat
and fry quickly until browned on
both sides.

3 Return the onion slices to the
casserole, then pour in the
stout mixed with the mushroom
ketchup. Bring slowly to boiling
point, then cover with a lid and
cook in the oven at 150°C (300°F)
mark 2 for 2–2½ hours until
tender. Taste and adjust seasoning. Serve the casserole garnished
with thyme sprigs.

Menu Suggestion

Sussex Stew has plenty of thick,
rich gravy. Accompanied by
creamed potatoes and carrots
tossed in chopped fresh herbs, it
makes a perfectly balanced
family meal.

SUSSEX STEW

Sussex Stew is an old, traditional
English dish, in which stewing
beef is slowly braised in sweet
stout and mushroom ketchup
until wonderfully succulent and
full of flavour. Although an
everyday family dish, take care
with your choice of ingredients
for best results. Sweet stout
rather than ordinary stout or ale
is essential for the richness of the
gravy, and mushroom ketchup
gives it a special tang, which
helps offset the sweetness of the
stout. Mushroom ketchup is easy
to find in large supermarkets and
delicatessens; sold in bottles, it
keeps indefinitely, so is well
worth buying as it can be used
in other dishes.

COTTAGE PIE

| 1.45 | ✳✳ | 592 cals |

* freeze before cooking in step 4
Serves 4

900 g (2 lb) potatoes, peeled
salt and freshly ground pepper
45 ml (3 tbsp) milk
knob of butter or margarine
15 ml (1 tbsp) vegetable oil
1 large onion, skinned and
   chopped
450 g (1 lb) minced beef
30 ml (2 tbsp) plain flour
300 ml (½ pint) beef stock
30 ml (2 tbsp) chopped fresh
   parsley or 10 ml (2 tsp) dried
   mixed herbs

1 Cook the potatoes in boiling salted water for 15–20 minutes, then drain and mash with the milk, butter and salt and pepper to taste.

2 Heat the oil in a frying pan, add the onion and fry for about 5 minutes until browned. Stir in the minced beef and fry for a further 5–10 minutes until browned, stirring occasionally.

3 Add the flour and cook for 2 minutes, then stir in the stock, parsley and salt and pepper to taste. Bring to the boil and simmer for 30 minutes.

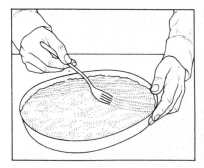

4 Spoon into an ovenproof dish and cover with mashed potato. Bake in the oven at 190°C (375°F) mark 5 for 25–30 minutes.

Menu Suggestion
Serve with seasonal vegetables, and gravy for those who like it.

BEEF AND RED BEAN GRATIN

1.30	✳*	436 cals

* freeze before baking

Serves 4

100 g (4 oz) dried red kidney beans, soaked in cold water overnight

75 g (3 oz) butter or margarine

1 small onion, skinned and thinly sliced

225 g (8 oz) minced beef

65 g (2½ oz) plain flour

200 ml (7 fl oz) beef stock

cayenne pepper

salt and freshly ground pepper

225 g (8 oz) tomatoes, skinned and chopped

15 ml (1 tbsp) tomato purée

5 ml (1 tsp) chopped fresh mixed herbs or 2.5 ml (½ tsp) dried

250 ml (9 fl oz) milk

50 g (2 oz) Cheddar cheese, grated

1.25 ml (¼ tsp) made English mustard

1 Drain the beans and put them into a large saucepan. Cover with fresh cold water and bring to the boil. Boil rapidly for a full 10 minutes, then lower the heat and boil gently for about 45 minutes or until tender. Drain.

2 Melt 25 g (1 oz) of the butter in a heavy-based saucepan, add the onion and minced beef and brown over high heat, stirring.

3 Stir in 40 g (1½ oz) of the flour, the stock and cayenne, salt and pepper to taste. Bring to the boil and cook for 2–3 minutes until very thick. Transfer to a deep 1.7 litre (3 pint) ovenproof dish.

4 Melt another 25 g (1 oz) of the butter in the saucepan, add the tomatoes and cook for about 10 minutes until they are soft and broken up. Stir in the beans, tomato purée and herbs and simmer until reduced and thickened. Spread over the meat.

5 Melt the remaining butter in a clean saucepan and add the remaining flour. Cook, stirring, for 2 minutes. Remove from the heat and gradually blend in the milk, stirring after each addition to prevent lumps forming. Bring to the boil slowly and continue to cook, stirring all the time, until the sauce comes to the boil and thickens.

6 Stir in half of the cheese, the mustard and salt and pepper to taste. Pour the sauce over the bean layer and sprinkle the remaining cheese on top. Bake in the oven at 200°C (400°F) mark 6 for about 25 minutes until golden brown on top. Serve hot.

Menu Suggestion
This dish is very substantial and therefore needs only a light accompaniment such as a mixed or green salad.

MEAT LOAF WITH ONION SAUCE

2.00	511 cals

Serves 4

50 g (2 oz) butter or margarine

2 medium onions, skinned and finely chopped

5 ml (1 tsp) paprika

450 g (1 lb) minced beef

65 g (2½ oz) fresh breadcrumbs

1 garlic clove, skinned and crushed

60 ml (4 tbsp) tomato purée

15 ml (1 tbsp) chopped fresh mixed herbs or 5 ml (1 tsp) dried

salt and freshly ground pepper

1 egg, beaten

15 g (½ oz) plain flour

300 ml (½ pint) milk

1 Grease a 450 g (1 lb) loaf tin, then line the base with greased greaseproof paper. Set aside.

2 Melt 25 g (1 oz) of the butter in a frying pan, add half of the onions and cook until softened. Add the paprika and cook for 1 minute, stirring, then turn the mixture into a large bowl.

3 Add the beef, breadcrumbs, garlic, tomato purée, herbs and salt and pepper to taste. Stir thoroughly until evenly mixed, then bind with the beaten egg.

4 Spoon the mixture into the loaf tin, level the surface and cover tightly with foil. Stand the tin in a roasting tin and pour in water to a depth of 2.5 cm (1 inch). Bake in the oven at 180°C (350°F) mark 4 for 1½ hours.

5 Meanwhile, melt the remaining butter in a saucepan. Add the rest of the onion and cook over low heat, stirring occasionally, for 10 minutes until soft but not coloured. Add the flour and cook over low heat, stirring, for 2 minutes.

6 Remove the pan from the heat and gradually blend in the milk, stirring after each addition to prevent lumps forming.

7 Bring to the boil slowly and continue to cook, stirring all the time, until the sauce comes to the boil and thickens. Simmer very gently for a further 2–3 minutes, then add salt and pepper to taste.

8 To serve, turn out the meat loaf on to a warmed serving plate and peel off the lining paper. Serve immediately, with the hot onion sauce.

Menu Suggestion

Serve for a family supper with creamed potatoes and a cucumber and dill salad.

MEAT LOAF

Meat Loaf is a traditional Jewish dish called Klops, and just about every Jewish family have their own favourite version. Some cooks include matzo meal amongst the ingredients, to bind the mixture and help 'stretch' the meat in the same way as breadcrumbs. Onion sauce is traditional with Meat Loaf, and sometimes mushrooms are added. For this quantity of sauce, use 100 g (4 oz) button mushrooms, sliced, and add them to the sauce at the end of step 7.

BEEF KEBABS WITH HORSERADISH DIP

0.45	501 cals

Serves 4

75 ml (3 fl oz) whipping cream

150 ml ($\frac{1}{4}$ pint) soured cream

30 ml (2 tbsp) grated fresh
   horseradish

5 ml (1 tsp) white wine vinegar

2.5 ml ($\frac{1}{2}$ tsp) sugar

salt and freshly ground pepper

450 g (1 lb) minced beef

1 small onion, skinned

25 g (1 oz) fresh white or brown
   breadcrumbs

30 ml (2 tbsp) chopped fresh
   coriander or parsley

10 ml (2 tsp) ground cumin

1.25 ml ($\frac{1}{4}$ tsp) cayenne pepper

5 ml (1 tsp) salt

1 egg, beaten

8 cherry tomatoes or 2 tomatoes,
   quartered

12 bay leaves

vegetable oil, for brushing

chopped coriander leaves, to
   garnish

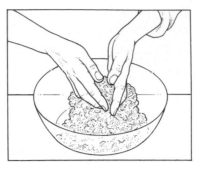

1 First make the dip. Whip the creams together, then fold in the horseradish, vinegar and sugar. Add salt and pepper to taste, then spoon into a serving bowl and chill in the refrigerator.

2 Put the minced beef in a bowl. Grate in the onion, then add the breadcrumbs, coriander, cumin, cayenne and the salt.

3 Mix the ingredients well with your hands until evenly combined. Bind with the egg.

4 With wetted hands, form the mixture into 16 balls. Thread 4 balls on each of 4 oiled kebab skewers, alternating with tomatoes and bay leaves.

5 Brush the kebabs with oil, then grill under a preheated moderate grill for 10 minutes, turning them frequently and brushing with more oil so that they cook evenly.

6 Serve the beef kebabs hot on individual plates, garnish with coriander leaves and serve the horseradish dip separately.

Menu Suggestion
These spicy kebabs and creamy dip make an interesting family supper dish. Serve on a bed of long grain rice. A crunchy mixed salad is the only other accompaniment needed.

ITALIAN-STYLE MEATBALLS

1.00	⚱	✳	557 cals

Serves 4

30 ml (2 tbsp) olive oil

1 large onion, skinned and finely
   chopped

2 garlic cloves, skinned and
   crushed

397 g (14 oz) can chopped
   tomatoes

10 ml (2 tsp) dried mixed herbs

10 ml (2 tsp) dried oregano

salt and freshly ground pepper

450 g (1 lb) minced beef

50 g (2 oz) fresh white
   breadcrumbs

50 g (2 oz) Parmesan cheese,
   freshly grated

1 egg, beaten

20 small black olives, stoned

vegetable oil, for deep frying

100 ml (4 fl oz) red or white dry
   Italian wine

1 Heat the oil in a heavy-based
saucepan, add the onion and
half of the crushed garlic and fry
gently for about 5 minutes until
soft and lightly coloured.

2 Add the tomatoes, half of the
herbs and salt and pepper to
taste. Bring to the boil, stirring,
then lower the heat, cover and
simmer for about 20 minutes.

3 Meanwhile, make the
meatballs. Put the minced beef
in a bowl with the breadcrumbs,
Parmesan, remaining garlic and
herbs. Mix well with your hands,
then add salt and pepper to taste
and bind with the beaten egg.

4 Pick up a small amount of the
mixture about the size of a
walnut. Press 1 olive in the centre,
then shape the mixture around it.
Repeat with the remaining olives
and meat to make 20 meatballs
altogether.

5 Heat the oil in a deep-fat fryer
to 190°C (375°F). Deep-fry
the meatballs in batches for
2–3 minutes until lightly browned,
then drain thoroughly on
absorbent kitchen paper.

6 Stir the wine into the tomato
sauce, then add 300 ml (½ pint)
water and the meatballs. Shake the
pan to coat the balls in the sauce,
adding more water if necessary.
Cover and simmer for a further
15 minutes, then taste and adjust
seasoning. Serve hot.

Menu Suggestion
Serve for a family supper with
tagliatelle or spaghetti, and hand
round a bowl of freshly grated
Parmesan for sprinkling on top.

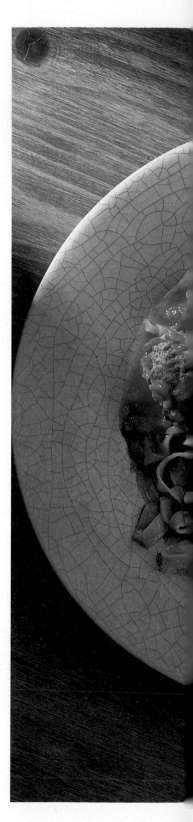

PASTITSIO

1.00	447–671 cals

Serves 4–6

30 ml (2 tbsp) olive oil

1 medium onion, skinned and
   finely chopped

1 garlic clove, skinned and crushed

450 g (1 lb) minced beef

397 g (14 oz) can tomatoes

10 ml (2 tsp) chopped fresh
   marjoram or 5 ml (1 tsp) dried

5 ml (1 tsp) ground allspice

salt and freshly ground pepper

225 g (8 oz) macaroni

2 eggs

300 ml (½ pint) natural yogurt

1 Heat the oil in a heavy-based saucepan, add the onion and garlic and fry gently for about 5 minutes until soft and lightly coloured.

2 Add the minced beef in batches and fry until browned, pressing the meat with the back of a wooden spoon to remove any lumps.

3 Add the tomatoes, marjoram, half of the allspice and salt and pepper to taste. Bring to the boil, stirring, then lower the heat, cover and simmer for 20 minutes.

4 Meanwhile, bring a large pan of salted water to the boil. Add the macaroni and boil for 10 minutes. Drain well.

5 Put the macaroni and minced beef mixture in an ovenproof dish. Mix well together, then taste and adjust seasoning.

6 In a bowl, beat the eggs with the yogurt and remaining allspice. Pour over the beef and macaroni. Bake in the oven at 190°C (375°F) mark 5 for 30 minutes. Serve hot.

Menu Suggestion
This Greek dish goes well with a salad of unpeeled cucumber cut into chunks, stoned black olives dressed with olive oil and lemon juice, and chopped fresh mint.

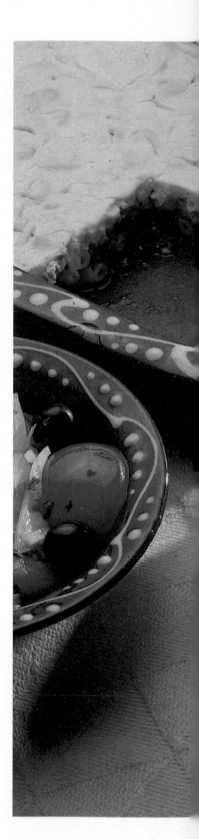

PASTITSIO

There are many variations of this Greek dish, which is immensely popular throughout mainland Greece as well as on the islands—if you have visited Greece on holiday you are sure to have eaten Pastitsio in one form or another. In many ways it bears a close resemblance to that other, more famous, Greek dish, moussaka, in that it has the same flavourings of tomatoes and allspice, and a similar thick topping made from natural yogurt and eggs. In Greece, this type of dish is almost always served lukewarm. The custard topping sets on standing, and the dish is them cut into slices or wedges like a cake.

VEAL IN TOMATO AND WINE SAUCE

2.30	✳	414 cals

Serves 4

25 g (1 oz) butter

30 ml (2 tbsp) olive oil

3 onions, skinned and chopped

2 carrots, peeled and chopped

1–2 celery stalks, trimmed and chopped

1 garlic clove, skinned and crushed

4 pieces shin of veal, 900 g (2 lb) total weight

plain flour, for coating

salt and freshly ground pepper

300 ml ($\frac{1}{2}$ pint) dry white wine

350 g (12 oz) tomatoes, skinned and chopped, or 396 g (14 oz) can tomatoes

150 ml ($\frac{1}{4}$ pint) chicken stock

2 strips of lemon peel

1 bay leaf

15 ml (1 tbsp) chopped fresh parsley

2.5 ml ($\frac{1}{2}$ tsp) dried basil

1.25 ml ($\frac{1}{4}$ tsp) dried thyme

1 Melt the butter with the oil in a large frying pan. Add the chopped vegetables and the garlic and fry gently for 5 minutes until lightly coloured.

2 With a slotted spoon, transfer the vegetables to a large flame-proof casserole which will hold the pieces of veal in one layer.

3 Coat the pieces of veal in flour seasoned with salt and pepper. Add to the frying pan and fry over moderate heat until browned on all sides.

4 Place the pieces of browned veal on top of the vegetables in the casserole.

5 Pour the wine into the frying pan and bring to boiling point. Stir constantly with a wooden spoon, scraping base and sides of pan to dislodge any sediment.

6 Add the remaining ingredients and simmer, stirring, until the tomatoes are broken down. Add seasoning to taste, then pour over the veal in the casserole.

7 Cover and cook in the oven at 180°C (350°F) mark 4 for about 2 hours or until the veal is tender. Taste and adjust seasoning before serving.

Menu Suggestion
Serve with Italian risotto for a dinner party main course with a difference. A chilled dry Italian white wine such as Orvieto, Frascati or Soave would be an ideal drink.

195

VEAL IN CREAM SAUCE

| 1.45 | 🍶 | 469 cals |

Serves 6

900 g (2 lb) stewing veal or braising
   steak, cubed

450 g (1 lb) carrots, peeled and cut
   into fingers

225 g (8 oz) button onions, skinned

bouquet garni

150 ml (¼ pint) white wine

900 ml (1½ pints) water

salt and freshly ground pepper

chicken stock, if necessary

50 g (2 oz) butter

50 g (2 oz) plain flour

300 ml (½ pint) single cream

lemon slices and grilled bacon
   rolls, to garnish

1 Cover the meat with cold
   water, bring to the boil and
boil for 1 minute. Strain in a
colander and rinse under cold
running water to remove all scum.
Place the meat in a flameproof
casserole.

2 Add the carrots and onions to
   the casserole with the bouquet
garni, wine, water and plenty of
seasoning. Bring slowly to the
boil, cover and simmer gently for
about 1¼ hours or until the meat
is tender.

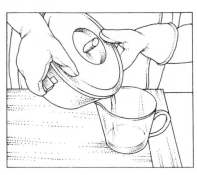

3 Strain off the cooking liquor,
   make up to 750 ml (1¼ pints)
with stock if necessary, reserve.
Keep the meat and vegetables
warm in a covered serving dish.

4 Melt the butter in a saucepan
   and stir in the flour, cook
gently for 1 minute. Remove from
the heat and stir in the strained
cooking liquor; season well. Bring
to the boil, stirring all the time,
and cook gently for 5 minutes.

5 Take the sauce off the heat
   and stir in the cream. Warm
very gently, without boiling, until
the sauce thickens slightly. Adjust
the seasoning. Pour the sauce over
the meat. Garnish with lemon
slices and bacon rolls.

Menu Suggestion
Veal in Cream Sauce is a very rich
dinner party dish. Serve with
plain boiled rice and a green salad
tossed in a vinaigrette dressing.

SWEDISH VEAL MEATBALLS

492 cals

*plus 1 hour chilling; freeze after step 5

Serves 4

450 g (1 lb) lean veal, pork or beef (or a mixture of these)

100 g (4 oz) smoked streaky bacon, rinded

½ small onion, skinned

50 g (2 oz) stale brown bread

2.5 ml (½ tsp) ground allspice

salt and freshly ground pepper

75 g (3 oz) unsalted butter

450 ml (¾ pint) chicken stock

juice of ½ lemon

10 ml (2 tsp) chopped fresh dill or 5 ml (1 tsp) dried

142 ml (5 fl oz) soured cream

dill sprigs, to garnish (optional)

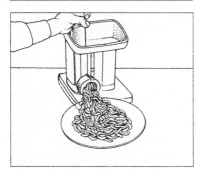

1 Put the meat, bacon, onion and bread through the blades of a mincer twice so that they are minced very fine. (Or work them in a food processor.)

2 Add the allspice to the mixture with seasoning to taste, then mix in with the fingertips to bind the mixture. (Pick up a handful and press firmly in the hand—it should cling together, but not be too wet.) Chill in the refrigerator for 1 hour.

3 Melt the butter gently in a large flameproof casserole. Dip a tablespoon in the butter, then use to shape a spoonful of the minced mixture.

4 Add the meatball to the casserole and then continue dipping the spoon in the butter and shaping meatballs until there are 12–14 altogether.

5 Fry the meatballs half at a time, if necessary, over moderate heat until they are browned on all sides. Return all the meatballs to the casserole, pour in the stock and lemon juice and bring slowly to boiling point. Lower the heat, add the dill and seasoning to taste, then cover the casserole and simmer gently for 30 minutes.

6 Stir the soured cream into the casserole and mix gently to combine evenly with the meatballs and cooking liquid. Taste and adjust the seasoning of the sauce and then garnish with dill sprigs, if liked. Serve hot.

Menu Suggestion
In Sweden and other parts of Scandinavia, these meatballs are traditionally served with boiled potatoes and creamed spinach.

SWEDISH VEAL MEATBALLS

Egg-shaped meatballs like these are popular all over Scandinavia, where they are served for the evening meal with hot vegetables. Our version are casseroled, but they are often served simply fried in butter, with a gravy made from the pan juices. In Denmark, these are known as frikadeller, and are immensely popular. The Danes use minced pork to make them, and sometimes they add a little smoked bacon to the mixture, for extra flavour. Some Scandinavian cooks stir a little soda water into the meat mixture before it is shaped. If you have soda water to hand, you can add up to 45 ml (3 tbsp) for a lighter result.

PORK ESCALOPES WITH SAGE

0.20	✳*	444 cals

* freeze at the end of stage 3

Serves 4

450 g (1 lb) pork fillet

1 egg, beaten

100 g (4 oz) fresh brown
   breadcrumbs

30 ml (2 tbsp) fresh sage or 10 ml
   (2 tsp) dried

grated rind of 1 lemon

75 g (3 oz) butter, melted

lemon wedges, to serve

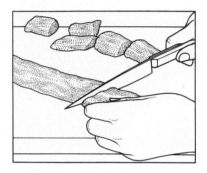

1 Using a sharp knife, trim any
   excess fat from the pork fillet
and cut the meat into 5-mm ($\frac{1}{4}$-
inch) slices.

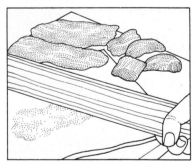

2 Beat out into even thinner
   slices between two sheets of
greaseproof paper, using a meat
cleaver or a wooden rolling pin.

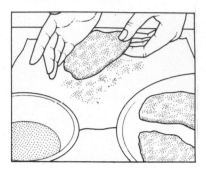

3 Coat the escalopes with the
   beaten egg. Then mix together
the breadcrumbs, sage and grated
lemon rind and coat the pork
escalopes.

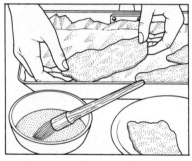

4 Lay in the base of a grill pan
   lined with foil (this quantity
will need to be grilled in two
batches). Brush with melted
butter. Grill for about 3 minutes
each side. Serve with lemon
wedges.

PORK CHOPS IN ORANGE JUICE

| 1.00 | ✳* | 395 cals |

* freeze after step 5

Serves 4

30 ml (2 tbsp) plain flour, for
   coating

2.5 ml (½ tsp) ground mixed spice

salt and freshly ground pepper

4 loin pork chops, trimmed of rind
   and fat

15 g (½ oz) butter

30 ml (2 tbsp) vegetable oil

1 medium onion, skinned and
   chopped

half 170 ml (6 fl oz) can frozen
   concentrated orange juice

Tabasco sauce, to taste

1 bay leaf

30–45 ml (2–3 tbsp) shredded
   orange rind, to garnish

1 Place the flour in a bowl. Add
the spice and seasoning. Dip
the chops in the seasoned flour,
ensuring that they are evenly
coated on both sides.

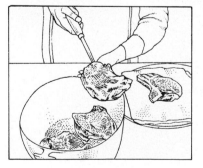

2 Melt the butter with the oil in
a large flameproof casserole.
Add the chops and fry over
moderate heat until browned on
all sides. Remove from the
casserole with a slotted spoon and
drain on absorbent kitchen paper.

3 Add the onion to the casserole
with any flour remaining from
the chops and fry gently for 5
minutes until onion is soft but
not coloured.

4 Dilute the orange juice with
200 ml (7 fl oz) water, then
pour into the casserole and stir to
combine with the onion.

5 Return the chops to the casserole and bring slowly to boiling point. Lower heat, add bay leaf and Tabasco to taste. Cover and simmer for 45 minutes until the chops are tender. Baste occasionally during this time.

6 A few minutes before the end of the cooking time, blanch the orange rind for 1 minute in boiling water. Drain, rinse under cold running water (to preserve a good colour), then dry on absorbent kitchen paper.

7 Transfer the chops to a warmed serving dish, then remove the bay leaf and taste and adjust the seasoning of the orange sauce. Pour the sauce over the chops, sprinkle with the blanched orange rind and serve at once.

Menu Suggestion
A colourful, fruity main course for a dinner party. Serve with buttered noodles and a crisp green salad or seasonal green vegetable.

STIR-FRIED PORK AND VEGETABLES

| 0.50 | 433 cals |

Serves 4

700 g (1½ lb) pork fillet or
   tenderloin, trimmed of fat

60 ml (4 tbsp) dry sherry

45 ml (3 tbsp) soy sauce

10 ml (2 tsp) ground ginger

salt and freshly ground pepper

1 medium cucumber

30 ml (2 tbsp) vegetable oil

1 bunch of spring onions, trimmed
   and finely chopped

1–2 garlic cloves, skinned and
   crushed (optional)

30 ml (2 tbsp) cornflour

300 ml (½ pint) chicken stock

175 g (6 oz) beansprouts

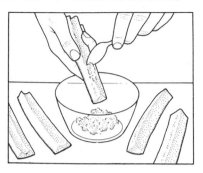

3 Using a sharp-edged teaspoon, scoop out the seeds and discard. Cut the cucumber quarters lengthways again, then slice across into strips about 2.5 cm (1 inch) long.

4 Heat the oil in a wok or large, heavy-based frying pan, add the spring onions and garlic, if using, and fry gently for about 5 minutes until softened.

5 Add the pork to the pan, increase the heat and stir-fry for 2–3 minutes until lightly coloured, tossing constantly so that it cooks evenly.

6 Mix the cornflour with the cold chicken stock and set aside.

7 Add the cucumber, spring onions and beansprouts to the pork, with the cornflour and stock. Stir-fry until the juices thicken and the ingredients are well combined. Taste and adjust seasoning, then turn into a warmed serving dish. Serve immediately.

Menu Suggestion
Both meat and vegetables are cooked together in this Chinese-style dish. For a simple meal, serve on a bed of egg noodles or plain boiled rice.

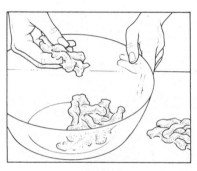

1 Cut the pork in thin strips and place in a bowl. Add the sherry, soy sauce, ginger and salt and pepper to taste, then stir well to mix. Set aside.

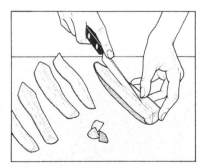

2 Prepare the cucumber sticks. Cut the cucumber in half, then cut into quarters lengthways, discarding the rounded ends. Leave the skin on, to add colour.

CIDER PORK SAUTÉ

1.45	536 cals

Serves 4

450 g (1 lb) green dessert apples
450 g (1 lb) floury old potatoes
   (eg King Edwards)
salt and freshly ground pepper
50 g (2 oz) butter
450 g (1 lb) pork escalope
15 ml (1 tbsp) vegetable oil
1 small onion, skinned and finely
   chopped
15 ml (1 tbsp) plain flour
300 ml (½ pint) dry cider
30 ml (2 tbsp) capers
beaten egg, to glaze

1 Peel half of the apples. Halve, core and slice thickly. Peel the potatoes, then cut them into small chunks.

2 Cook the prepared apples and potatoes together in a saucepan of salted water for 20 minutes or until the potatoes are tender. Drain well.

3 Press the apples and potatoes through a sieve into a bowl. Beat in 25 g (1 oz) of the butter, then add salt and pepper to taste.

4 Spoon or pipe the mixture down both ends of a 1.4 litre (2½ pint) shallow ovenproof dish.

5 Meanwhile, cut the pork escalope into fine strips. Quarter and core the remaining apples (but do not peel them). Slice them thickly into a bowl of cold water.

6 Heat the remaining butter and the oil in a large frying pan, add the pork strips, a few at a time, and fry until browned. Remove with a slotted spoon.

7 Add the onion to the pan and fry for 2–3 minutes. Return all the pork strips and stir in the flour. Cook, stirring, for 1–2 minutes, then blend in the cider and bring to the boil.

8 Drain the apple slices and stir into the pork. Simmer gently for 4–5 minutes, or until the pork is tender but the apple still holds its shape. Stir in the capers, with salt and pepper to taste.

9 Spoon the mixture into the centre of the dish. Brush the potato with beaten egg. Bake in the oven at 200°C (400°F) mark 6 for 25–30 minutes until golden. Serve hot, straight from the dish.

Menu Suggestion
Cider Pork Sauté is ideal for mid-week entertaining. Potatoes are included, so all you need is a seasonal vegetable like creamed spinach or a purée of sprouts.

CHINESE PORK AND GINGER CASSEROLE

| 1.25 | ✳* | 448 cals |

* freeze after step 4

Serves 4

30 ml (2 tbsp) vegetable oil

1 small onion, skinned and finely chopped

2.5 cm (1 inch) piece fresh root ginger

700 g (1½ lb) boneless lean pork (e.g. shoulder or sparerib), cubed

30 ml (2 tbsp) dry sherry

15 ml (1 tbsp) soy sauce

300 ml (½ pint) dry or American ginger ale

2.5 ml (½ tsp) five-spice powder

salt and freshly ground pepper

50 g (2 oz) stem ginger, sliced

½ red pepper, cored, seeded and sliced

½ yellow pepper, cored, seeded and sliced

1 Heat the oil in a flameproof casserole, add the onion and fry gently for 5 minutes until soft but not coloured.

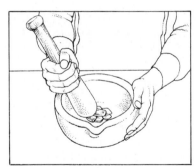

2 Meanwhile, skin the root ginger and then crush the flesh with a mortar and pestle.

3 Add the crushed ginger to the casserole with the pork, increase the heat and fry until the meat is browned on all sides.

4 Stir in the sherry and soy sauce, then the ginger ale, five-spice powder and seasoning to taste. Bring slowly to boiling point, stirring, then lower the heat, cover and simmer for about 1 hour until the pork is just tender.

5 Add the stem ginger and pepper slices to the casserole and continue cooking for a further 10 minutes. Serve hot.

Menu Suggestion

An informal supper party dish. Serve with Chinese egg noodles and stir-fried vegetables such as grated carrots, finely sliced celery, green pepper and beansprouts.

SWEET AND SOUR SPARE RIB CHOPS

1.15*	✳*	372 cals

* plus 4 hours marinating; freeze in
the marinade before cooking

Serves 4

30 ml (2 tbsp) wine vinegar
30 ml (2 tbsp) soy sauce
30 ml (2 tbsp) soft brown sugar
15 ml (1 tbsp) Worcestershire sauce
5 ml (1 tsp) garlic salt
1.25 ml ($\frac{1}{4}$ tsp) chilli powder
4 spare rib pork chops (see box)
45 ml (3 tbsp) vegetable oil
300 ml ($\frac{1}{2}$ pint) chicken stock or water
1 small bunch of spring onions, to finish

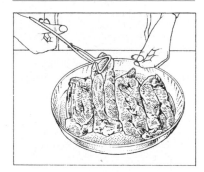

1 Make the marinade. Mix the
first six ingredients together in
a shallow dish. Add the chops and
turn to coat, then cover and leave
to marinate for 4 hours. Turn the
chops in the marinade occasionally
during this time.

2 Remove the chops from the
marinade. Heat 30 ml (2 tbsp)
of the oil in a flameproof casserole,
which is large enough to hold the
chops in a single layer. Add the
chops and fry over brisk heat until
browned on all sides.

3 Mix the marinade with the
stock or water, then pour over
the chops. Bring slowly to boiling
point, then lower the heat, cover
and simmer gently for 45 minutes
or until the chops are tender.

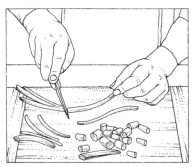

4 Ten minutes before serving,
chop the spring onions, reserving the tops for the garnish.
Heat the remaining oil in a small
pan, add the chopped onions and
fry gently for a few minutes until
softened. Sprinkle over the dish
just before serving and garnish
with the reserved tops.

Menu Suggestion

Serve these spare rib chops for an
informal supper party with a
medley of fried rice, diced pepper
and spring onions. Follow with a
mixed salad.

**SWEET AND SOUR SPARE
RIB CHOPS**

Take care to buy the right cut
of pork for this recipe. Spare
rib chops are from the neck end
of the pig; thick and meaty, they
become succulent and tender
when casseroled, and yet they are
inexpensive to buy compared
with the leaner loin chops, that
are better suited to a quick-
cooking method such as grilling.
Do not confuse spare rib chops
with spare ribs, which are cut
from inside the thick end of the
belly—these are the kind used in
Chinese cookery, most often
served in a sweet and sour sauce.

CHILLI PORK AND BEANS

3.30*	465–698 cals

* plus overnight soaking

Serves 4–6

30 ml (2 tbsp) vegetable oil

900 g (2 lb) boneless pork shoulder, trimmed of fat and cut into cubes

1 large onion, skinned and roughly chopped

2 celery sticks, trimmed and sliced

1–2 garlic cloves, skinned and crushed

175 g (6 oz) red kidney beans, soaked in cold water overnight

15 ml (1 tbsp) black treacle

15 ml (1 tbsp) French mustard

5 ml (1 tsp) chilli powder

salt and freshly ground pepper

1 Heat 15 ml (1 tbsp) of the oil in a flameproof casserole, add the pork in batches and fry over high heat until coloured on all sides. Remove with a slotted spoon and drain on absorbent kitchen paper.

2 Lower the heat, then add the remaining oil to the pan with the onion, celery and garlic. Fry gently for 10 minutes until softened.

3 Drain the kidney beans and add to the pan with 1.1 litres (2 pints) water. Bring to the boil, stirring, then boil rapidly for 10 minutes to destroy any toxins in the beans.

4 Lower the heat, return the pork to the pan and add the black treacle, mustard, chilli powder and pepper to taste. Stir well to mix.

5 Cover the casserole and cook in the oven at 150°C (300°F) mark 2 for 3 hours. Stir the pork and beans occasionally during the cooking time and add more water if dry. Add 5 ml (1 tsp) salt half-way through, then taste and adjust seasoning before serving, adding more chilli powder if a hotter flavour is liked.

Menu Suggestion

Serve this hot Mexican-style dish for a family supper, with plain boiled rice and a salad of sliced avocado and tomato dressed with oil and lemon juice. A bowl of natural yogurt can also be served, to cool and refresh the palate.

PORK PAPRIKASH

2.30	✳✳	653 cals

* freeze at the end of step 3

Serves 4

50 g (2 oz) butter or margarine

30 ml (2 tbsp) olive oil

900 g (2 lb) boneless pork sparerib, trimmed of excess fat and cut into cubes

450 g (1 lb) Spanish onions, skinned and thinly sliced

2 garlic cloves, skinned and crushed (optional)

15 ml (1 tbsp) paprika

10 ml (2 tsp) caraway seeds

450 ml ($\frac{3}{4}$ pint) chicken stock

salt and freshly ground pepper

about 150 ml ($\frac{1}{4}$ pint) soured cream and snipped chives, to finish

1 Heat half of the butter with the oil in a flameproof casserole, add the cubes of pork and fry over high heat for about 5 minutes until coloured on all sides. Remove with a slotted spoon to a plate.

2 Reduce the heat to very low and melt the remaining butter in the pan. Add the onions and garlic, if using, and fry very gently for about 30 minutes until very soft and golden, stirring frequently to prevent catching and burning.

3 Stir the paprika and caraway seeds into the onions, then add the pork and juices and mix well. Pour in the stock, add salt and pepper to taste and bring slowly to the boil, stirring. Cover and cook gently for about 1$\frac{1}{2}$ hours until the pork is tender.

4 Before serving, taste and adjust seasoning. Drizzle over soured cream and sprinkle with chives. Serve hot.

Menu Suggestion

Pork Paprikash is best served on a bed of noodles or rice. Accompany with a green vegetable such as broccoli, courgettes or French beans, or follow with a colourful mixed salad of shredded lettuce or endive, red and green pepper rings and sliced cucumber.

CHINESE RED-COOKED PORK

2.30	887–1330 cals

Serves 4–6

1.8 kg (4 lb) rolled neck end of pork
  with skin

450 ml (¾ pint) chicken stock or
  water

200 ml (⅓ pint) soy sauce

4 garlic cloves, skinned and sliced

5 cm (2 inch) piece of fresh root
  ginger, peeled and sliced

10 ml (2 tsp) Chinese five-spice
  powder (see box)

60 ml (4 tbsp) sugar

150 ml (¼ pint) dry sherry

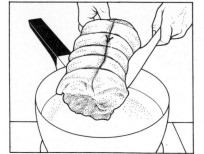

1 Bring a large saucepan of
water to the boil. Add the pork
and remove immediately, to scald
it. Drain and pat dry.

2 Pour the stock into a large
flameproof casserole. Add the
soy sauce, garlic, ginger, five-spice
powder and sugar. Bring to the
boil, then lower the heat and
simmer for 5 minutes.

3 Add the pork, skin side down,
to the casserole and baste well.
Cover and cook in the oven at 180°C
(350°F) mark 4 for 1½ hours.

4 Remove the lid of the
casserole, turn the meat skin
side up and baste well with the
juices. Return to the oven,
uncovered, for another 30 minutes
or until the pork is very tender,
basting regularly.

5 Transfer the casserole to the
top of the cooker. Add the
dry sherry and then bring the
juices to the boil.

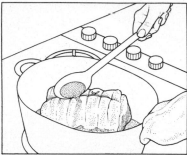

6 Boil rapidly for about 15
minutes, continually basting
the meat until glazed. Take care
that the meat does not catch or
burn. Serve the meat sliced, hot or
cold, with any remaining sauce.

Menu Suggestion
Red-Cooked Pork is rich and
spicy. Serve with a contrasting
plain accompaniment such as
boiled rice, and follow with stir-
fried crisp spring vegetables.

SWEET AND SOUR PORK

0.30	447 cals

Serves 4

700 g (1½ lb) boneless leg or
  shoulder of pork

20 ml (4 tsp) cornflour

salt and freshly ground pepper

vegetable oil for deep-frying,
  plus 15 ml (1 tbsp)

1 green pepper, cored, seeded
  and thinly sliced

30 ml (2 tbsp) sugar

30 ml (2 tbsp) white wine vinegar

30 ml (2 tbsp) tomato purée

30 ml (2 tbsp) pineapple juice

30 ml (2 tbsp) soy sauce

2 fresh or canned pineapple rings,
  finely chopped

1 Trim the fat off the pork, then
cut the meat into 2.5 cm
(1 inch) cubes. Coat in the cornflour, reserving 5 ml (1 tsp) for the
sauce. Add salt to taste.

2 Heat the vegetable oil in a
deep-fat fryer to 180°C
(350°F). Add half of the pork and
deep-fry for 8–9 minutes or until
tender. Remove with a slotted
spoon and drain on absorbent
kitchen paper. Keep hot while
frying the remaining pork.

3 Make the sauce. Heat the 15 ml (1 tbsp) vegetable oil in a wok or frying pan, add the green pepper and stir-fry for 1 minute. Stir in the remaining ingredients with the reserved cornflour. Stir-fry for 1–2 minutes.

4 Add the pork and stir-fry for 1 minute. Taste and adjust seasoning, then turn into a warmed serving bowl. Serve hot.

Menu Suggestion
For a Chinese-style meal, serve Sweet and Sour Pork with white rice. Boil the rice, drain, then toss in a little sesame oil for an authentic flavour. Follow with a salad of raw beansprouts, grated carrot, shredded Chinese leaves and strips of cucumber. Toss the salad in an oil and vinegar dressing flavoured with soy sauce.

CHINESE RED-COOKED PORK
Five-spice powder is so called because it is a mixture of five different spices. Cinnamon, cloves, fennel, star anise and Szechuan peppercorns is the usual combination, but the blend can vary from one brand to another, so that not all five-spice powder tastes the same. Look for it in packets and small jars in Chinese specialist shops, and in some large supermarkets and delicatessens. It is not absolutely essential for this dish if you are unable to obtain it, ground mixed spice can be used instead.

215

HUNTINGDON FIDGET PIE

1.15*	686 cals

* plus 30 minutes chilling

Serves 4

250 g (9 oz) plain flour

100 g (4 oz) butter or margarine

salt and freshly ground pepper

225 g (8 oz) streaky bacon, rinded
  and roughly chopped

1 medium onion, skinned and
  roughly chopped

225 g (8 oz) cooking apples, peeled,
  cored and roughly chopped

15 ml (1 tbsp) chopped parsley

150 ml ($\frac{1}{4}$ pint) medium cider

beaten egg, to glaze

1 Make the pastry. Sift 225 g (8 oz) of the flour and a pinch of salt into a bowl. Cut the butter into small pieces and rub into the flour until the mixture resembles breadcrumbs. Add enough water to mix to a firm dough.

2 Gather the dough into a ball and knead lightly. Wrap in foil and chill for 30 minutes.

3 Meanwhile, combine the bacon, onion and apples in a 600 ml (1 pint) pie dish. Add the parsley and salt and pepper.

4 Blend the remaining flour with the cider, a little at a time, and pour into the pie dish.

5 Roll out the pastry. Cut out a thin strip long enough to go around the rim of the pie dish. Moisten the rim with water and place the pastry strip on the rim.

6 Roll out the remaining pastry for a lid, moisten the strip of pastry, then place the lid on top and press to seal. Knock up and flute the edge.

7 Make a diagonal cross in the centre almost to the edges of the dish, then fold back to reveal the filling.

8 Brush the pastry with the beaten egg. Bake in the oven at 190°C (375°F) mark 5 for about 45 minutes, or until the pastry is golden and the filling is cooked.

Menu Suggestion
Serve with seasonal vegetables for an economical, yet tasty family supper. Tankards of beer, lager or cider make ideal drinks.

HUNTINGDON FIDGET PIE

Fidget or Fitchett Pie was traditionally made at harvest time to feed the hungry workers. Potatoes can be added to the filling.

BACON IN CIDER WITH SAGE AND ONION DUMPLINGS

2.30	858 cals

Serves 6

1.1 kg (2½ lb) smoked collar of bacon
4 cloves
300 ml (½ pint) dry cider
1 bay leaf
125 g (4 oz) fresh white
    breadcrumbs
175 g (6 oz) self raising flour
50 g (2 oz) shredded suet
5 ml (1 tsp) rubbed sage
25 g (1 oz) butter or margarine
2 medium onions, skinned
salt and freshly ground pepper
parsley sprigs, to garnish

1 Place the bacon in a saucepan and cover with cold water. Bring slowly to the boil. Drain off the water. Pat the bacon dry.

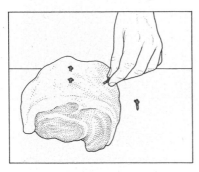

2 Slice off the rind if it is not cooked enough to peel away. Stud the fat with cloves.

3 Put the bacon in a shallow casserole with the cider and bay leaf. Cover tightly and cook in the oven at 180°C (350°F) mark 4 for 2¼ hours.

4 Meanwhile, mix the breadcrumbs, flour, suet and sage together in a bowl. Rub in the butter with your fingertips.

5 Coarsely grate in the onions. Bind to a soft dough with water, then add a little salt and freshly ground pepper.

6 Shape the dough into 12 dumplings. Forty-five minutes before the end of the cooking time, add the dumplings to the juices surrounding the bacon. Cover again and finish cooking. Serve the bacon sliced, with a little of the cooking liquid spooned over, surrounded by the dumplings. Garnish with parsley sprigs.

Menu Suggestion
With its sage and onion dumplings, this bacon dish is very substantial—ideal for a winter family supper. Serve with a seasonal green vegetable such as Brussels sprouts or spinach.

PEANUT GLAZED BACON HOCK

2.45	518 cals

Serves 6

1.1 kg (2½ lb) bacon hock

1 medium carrot, peeled and sliced

1 medium onion, skinned and quartered

1 bay leaf

30 ml (2 tbsp) lemon marmalade

30 ml (2 tbsp) demerara sugar

10 ml (2 tsp) lemon juice

dash of Worcestershire sauce

25 g (1 oz) salted peanuts, chopped

1 Put the bacon in a casserole with the carrot, onion and bay leaf. Pour in enough water to come half-way up the joint. Cover and cook in the oven at 180°C (350°F) mark 4 for about 2¼ hours.

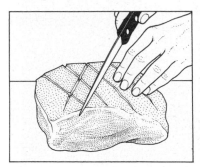

2 Remove the bacon from the casserole, carefully cut off and discard the rind, then score the fat with a sharp knife.

3 Put the marmalade, sugar, lemon juice and Worcestershire sauce in a bowl and mix well together with a wooden spoon.

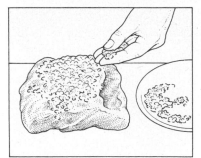

4 Spread the mixture over the surface of the joint. Sprinkle on the chopped peanuts.

5 Place the joint in a roasting tin. Increase the oven temperature to 220°C (425°F) mark 7 and return the joint to the oven for 15 minutes to glaze. Serve sliced.

Menu Suggestion

Glazed bacon is good for a family meal, served hot with seasonal vegetables. Alternatively, serve it sliced cold for a buffet party, with a selection of salads.

POT ROAST OF PORK AND RED CABBAGE

2.15	531 cals

Serves 4

45 ml (3 tbsp) red wine vinegar

450 g (1 lb) red cabbage

225 g (8 oz) cooking apple

15 ml (1 tbsp) demerara sugar

15 ml (1 tbsp) plain flour

salt and freshly ground pepper

700 g (1½ lb) boneless pork shoulder, rinded

coriander sprigs, to garnish

1 Bring a large saucepan of water to the boil, to which 15 ml (1 tbsp) of the vinegar has been added.

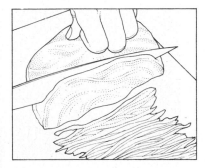

2 Meanwhile, shred the red cabbage. When the water is boiling, add the cabbage, bring back to the boil, then drain well.

3 Peel, core and slice the apple and place with the cabbage in a casserole just wide enough to take the pork joint.

4 Add the sugar, the remaining vinegar, the flour and salt and pepper to taste. Stir well together.

5 Slash the fat side of the joint several times and sprinkle with plenty of salt and pepper. Place on top of the cabbage and cover the casserole.

6 Cook in the oven at 190°C (375°F) mark 5 for about 1¾ hours, or until pork is tender. Serve the pork sliced on a warmed serving platter, surrounded by cabbage. Garnish with coriander and serve the remaining cabbage in a serving dish.

Menu Suggestion
This tasty dish is good served for an everyday evening meal, with a plain accompaniment such as creamed potatoes.

GLAZED GAMMON STEAKS

0.25	753 cals

Serves 4

15 ml (1 tbsp) soy sauce

2.5 ml ($\frac{1}{2}$ tsp) dry mustard

15 ml (1 tbsp) golden syrup

1.25 ml ($\frac{1}{4}$ tsp) ground ginger

90 ml (6 tbsp) orange juice

garlic salt

freshly ground black pepper

15 ml (1 tbsp) cornflour

15 ml (1 tbsp) lemon juice

8 bacon chops or 4 gammon steaks

1 In a small saucepan, combine the first five ingredients, with garlic salt and pepper to taste.

2 Blend the cornflour with the lemon juice, stir in a little of the mixture from the pan and then return it all to the pan. Bring to the boil, stirring all the time, until the mixture has thickened to a glaze. Remove from the heat.

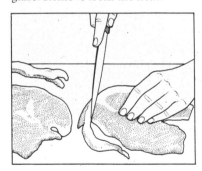

3 Cut most of the fat from the bacon chops or gammon steaks and then brush half of the glaze on one side.

4 Grill under moderate heat for 15 minutes, until the meat is cooked right through, brown and bubbling. Turn several times and brush with the remaining glaze during cooking. Serve hot.

Menu Suggestion

Serve with sauté potatoes and a medley of frozen vegetables such as peas, sweetcorn and peppers. Frozen stir-fried vegetables (available in packets from most supermarkets) make a good standby accompaniment when you are preparing a last-minute meal such as this one.

GLAZED GAMMON STEAKS

For everyday family meals and informal entertaining, bacon chops and gammon steaks are a good buy because they cook so quickly. They are also economical in that they have very little wastage in the form of fat or bone. For this recipe, a small amount of fat around the edges of the meat will help keep the meat moist during grilling. If you are using gammon steaks, it is a good idea to cut the fat at regular intervals to help prevent curling. Simply snip through the fat with sharp kitchen scissors, allowing about 5 mm ($\frac{1}{4}$ inch) between cuts. This will give the finished dish an attractive professional touch, as well as helping the meat to cook more evenly.

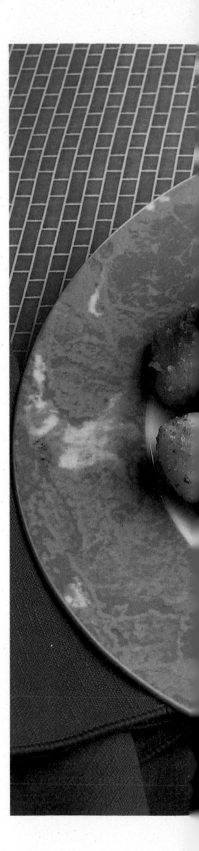

BRAISED OXTAIL

4.30	✳	256 cals

Serves 4

2 small oxtails cut up, about 1.4 kg (3 lb) total weight

30 ml (2 tbsp) plain flour

salt and freshly ground pepper

40 g (1½ oz) lard

350 g (12 oz) onions, skinned and sliced

900 ml (1½ pints) beef stock

150 ml (¼ pint) red wine

15 ml (1 tbsp) tomato purée

pared rind of ½ lemon

2 bay leaves

225 g (8 oz) carrots, peeled and thickly sliced

450 g (1 lb) parsnips, peeled and cut into chunks

chopped fresh parsley, to garnish

1 Coat the oxtails in the flour seasoned with salt and pepper. Heat the lard in a large flameproof casserole and brown the oxtail pieces, a few at a time. Remove from the casserole.

2 Fry the onions in the casserole for 5 minutes until lightly browned. Stir in any remaining flour, the stock, wine, tomato purée, lemon rind, bay leaves and season well. Bring to the boil and replace the meat.

3 Cover the pan with a tight-fitting lid and simmer the contents for 2 hours; skim well to remove any excess fat.

4 Stir the carrots and parsnips into the casserole. Cover and simmer for a further 2 hours or until the meat is tender.

5 Skim all fat off the surface of the casserole, adjust the seasoning and garnish with chopped parsley.

Menu Suggestion
Braised oxtail is a rich, satisfying dish for a midweek meal in winter. Serve with plain boiled or mashed potatoes and crisply cooked winter cabbage.

BRAISED OXTAIL

Oxtail is an inexpensive cut of beef with an excellent 'meaty' flavour and wonderfully succulent texture if cooked slowly as in this recipe. The main problem with oxtail, however, is its fattiness, which many people find off-putting, and yet there is a simple solution. Cook the casserole the day before required and leave it until completely cold. Chill it in the refrigerator overnight, at the end of which time the fat will have risen to the surface and formed a solid layer. Simply lift off this layer and you will find a thick, gelatinous gravy underneath, which becomes rich and flavoursome on reheating.

LIVER GOUJONS WITH ORANGE SAUCE

0.40	607 cals

Serves 4

350 g (12 oz) lamb's liver, sliced

75 ml (5 tbsp) plain flour

salt and freshly ground pepper

1 egg, beaten

125 g (4 oz) medium oatmeal

50 g (2 oz) butter or margarine

1 medium onion, sliced

300 ml ($\frac{1}{2}$ pint) lamb or beef stock

finely grated rind and juice of 1 medium orange

5 ml (1 tsp) dried sage

few drops of gravy browning

60 ml (4 tbsp) vegetable oil

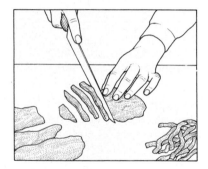

1 Cut the liver into 5 cm (2 inch) pencil-thin strips. Coat evenly in 45 ml (3 tbsp) of the flour, liberally seasoned with salt and freshly ground pepper.

2 Dip the liver in the beaten egg, then roll in the oatmeal to coat. Chill in the refrigerator while preparing the sauce.

3 Melt 25 g (1 oz) of the butter in a saucepan, add the onion and fry gently until golden brown. Add the remaining flour and cook gently, stirring, for 1–2 minutes.

4 Gradually blend in the stock, orange rind and juice, sage and salt and pepper to taste. Bring to the boil, stirring constantly, then simmer for 10–15 minutes. Add the gravy browning and taste and adjust seasoning.

5 Heat the remaining butter and the oil in a frying pan, add the liver goujons and fry gently for 1–2 minutes until tender.

6 Arrange the goujons on a warmed serving platter and pour over a little of the sauce. Hand the remaining sauce separately in a sauceboat or jug.

Menu Suggestion

Serve on a bed of tagliatelle or Chinese noodles, and accompany with a green vegetable, or crunchy salad of raw beansprouts, celery and finely chopped walnuts, unsalted peanuts or cashews.

LIVER GOUJONS

The French word *goujon* is used in cooking to describe small strips or thin slivers of food; fish is often cut into goujons, then coated in egg and breadcrumbs before deep-frying. In this recipe, goujons of liver are coated in egg and oatmeal, which gives a nutty crunch to the coating, contrasting well with the soft texture of the liver inside.

Orange is a popular flavour with liver in France, so too is vermouth. To give the dish an added 'kick', add a splash of dry vermouth with the orange juice in step 4.

LIVER AND BACON WITH POTATO PANCAKES

1.00	662 cals

Serves 4

2 large potatoes, peeled

1 egg, beaten

60 ml (4 tbsp) self raising flour

salt and freshly ground pepper

vegetable oil and butter (optional), for frying

450 g (1 lb) lamb's liver, cut thickly

25 g (1 oz) plain flour

8 rashers of back bacon

2 medium onions, skinned and finely sliced

10 ml (2 tsp) wine vinegar

30 ml (2 tbsp) chopped fresh parsley, to garnish

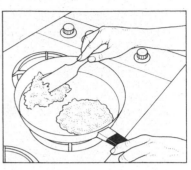

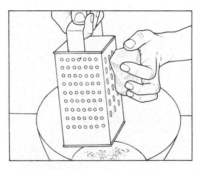

1 Grate the potatoes finely. Place in a sieve and rinse under cold water. Leave to drain for about 15 minutes. Wrap the potato in a clean tea towel and squeeze out any excess moisture.

2 Put the grated potatoes in a bowl. Add the egg, self raising flour and salt and pepper to taste, then mix well together.

3 Heat enough oil in a frying pan to come 0.5 cm (¼ inch) up the sides. When hot, add large spoonfuls of potato mixture, pressing them into flat pancakes with a spatula or fish slice.

4 Cook the pancakes for about 5 minutes on each side until golden brown. Remove from the pan and drain on absorbent kitchen paper. Keep hot in the oven while cooking the liver.

5 Remove any ducts from the liver and discard. Dip the liver in the plain flour seasoned with salt and pepper. Heat a little oil or butter in a frying pan, add the liver and fry for 3–4 minutes on each side (it should still be slightly pink inside). Cover and keep hot.

6 Add the bacon to the pan and fry over brisk heat until crisp. Keep hot, but do not cover as it will become soggy.

7 Add the onions to the pan and cook for 5 minutes until just beginning to brown. Remove from the pan and arrange on a serving dish. Top with the liver and bacon and keep warm.

8 Add the vinegar and 45 ml (3 tbsp) water to the frying pan. Bring to the boil, scraping up any sediment from the bottom of the pan. Pour over the liver and bacon, then garnish with chopped parsley. Serve with the pancakes.

Menu Suggestion

This dish of fried liver, bacon and onions has its own accompaniment in the potato pancakes. Serve with colourful vegetables such as grilled tomatoes and peas.

PAN-FRIED LIVER AND TOMATO

0.15*	290 cals

* plus several hours marinating

Serves 4

450 g (1 lb) lamb's liver, sliced

30 ml (2 tbsp) Marsala or sweet sherry

salt and freshly ground pepper

225 g (8 oz) tomatoes, skinned

30 ml (2 tbsp) vegetable oil

2 medium onions, skinned and finely sliced

pinch of ground ginger

150 ml (¼ pint) chicken stock

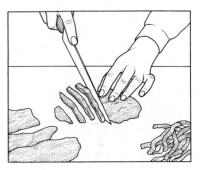

1 Using a very sharp knife, cut the liver into wafer-thin strips. Place in a shallow bowl with the Marsala or sweet sherry. Sprinkle with freshly ground pepper to taste. Cover and leave to marinate for several hours.

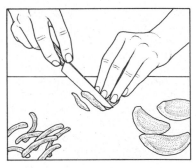

2 Cut the tomatoes into quarters and remove the seeds, reserving the juices. Slice the flesh into fine strips and set aside.

3 Heat the oil in a sauté pan or non-stick frying pan. When very hot, add the liver strips, a few at a time. Shake the pan briskly for about 30 seconds until pearls of blood appear.

4 Turn the slices and cook for a further 30 seconds only (liver hardens if it is overcooked). Remove from the pan with a slotted spoon and keep warm while cooking the remaining batches.

5 Add the onions and ginger to the residual oil in the pan and cook, uncovered, for about 5 minutes. Add the stock and seasoning to taste, return the liver to the pan and add the tomatoes and their juice. Bring just to the boil, then turn into a warmed serving dish and serve immediately.

Menu Suggestion

Serve with Chinese egg noodles and a stir-fried vegetable dish of onion, ginger, beansprouts and carrots.

PAN-FRIED LIVER AND TOMATO

The Marsala used in this recipe is an Italian fortified white wine, available at good off licences and some large super-markets with good wine depart-ments. The wine is named after the town of Marsala, in the western part of the island of Sicily in the Mediterranean, where it has been made for over two hundred years. It was first introduced into Britain by a Liverpool merchant, John Woodhouse, who set up a thriving business importing Marsala from Sicily—he even supplied Lord Nelson's fleet with it! There are different types of Marsala, from very dry to sweet. For this recipe, use one of the dry varieties.

LIVER AND BACON ROULADES

0.25*	226–301 cals

*plus 1 hour marinating

Serves 3–4

4 rashers streaky bacon, about 100 g (4 oz) total weight

225 g (8 oz) lamb's liver

60 ml (4 tbsp) orange juice

30 ml (2 tbsp) brandy

15 ml (1 tbsp) chopped fresh marjoram or oregano or 5 ml (1 tsp) dried

salt and freshly ground pepper

1 Cut the rind off each rasher and stretch the rashers with a blunt-edged knife. Cut each rasher across into three pieces.

2 Divide the liver into twelve even-sized pieces, removing any skin and ducts.

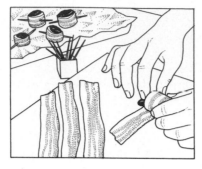

3 Roll a piece of bacon around each piece of liver and secure with a cocktail stick. Place in the base of a foil-lined grill pan.

4 Mix the orange juice, brandy, herbs and seasoning together and spoon over the bacon rolls. Leave to marinate in a cool place for 1 hour or longer.

5 Cook under a moderate grill for 12–15 minutes, turning and basting occasionally. Remove cocktail sticks before serving, replacing them with fresh ones if liked. Serve hot.

LIVER AND BACON ROULADES

The French word *roulade* means a roll or a rolled slice in culinary terms, and here it is used to describe the way in which bacon is rolled around pieces of lamb's liver. The method of marinating meat in a mixture of alcohol, fruit juice, herbs and seasonings is a very common one in French cookery—the purpose of a marinade is to tenderize the meat and make it flavoursome.

Some meats are left to marinate for as long as 2–3 days, but most marinades are left for an hour or so, overnight at the most. The combination of alcohol and an acid liquid such as juice from citrus fruit helps break down any tough fibres and sinews in meat, so it is a process which is well worth doing if it is specified in a recipe, especially if the meat is one of the inexpensive, tougher cuts. Any alcohol can be used, but red or white wine and brandy are popular.

Wine vinegar and lemon juice are the usual acid ingredients, although orange juice as specified in this recipe has much the same effect. Fresh pineapple juice is another popular marinade ingredient; it contains an enzyme which breaks down tough fibres in tough cuts of meat.

KIDNEYS AND MUSHROOMS IN RED WINE

0.30	294–392 cals

Serves 3–4

50 g (2 oz) butter
2 onions, skinned and chopped
10 lamb's kidneys
45 ml (3 tbsp) plain flour
150 ml (¼ pint) red wine
150 ml (¼ pint) beef stock
bouquet garni
30 ml (2 tbsp) tomato purée
salt and freshly ground pepper
100 g (4 oz) mushrooms, sliced
chopped fresh parsley, to garnish

1 Melt the butter in a saucepan or a frying pan and fry the onions for about 5 minutes until golden brown.

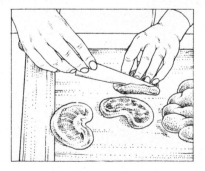

2 Wash, skin and core the kidneys and cut them into halves lengthways. Add to the pan and cook for 5 minutes, stirring occasionally.

3 Stir in the flour, pour in the wine and stock and bring slowly to the boil. Stir in the bouquet garni, tomato purée, seasoning and mushrooms. Cover and simmer for about 15 minutes until the kidneys are tender.

4 Remove the bouquet garni and adjust the seasoning. Serve sprinkled with chopped parsley.

Menu Suggestion
Serve for an informal supper party with boiled long-grain rice and a mixed salad tossed in plenty of vinaigrette dressing.

SAUSAGE AND BEAN RAGOUT

| 2.30* | ✳ | 710 cals |

* plus overnight soaking

Serves 4

125 g (4 oz) haricot beans, soaked
   overnight

125 g (4 oz) red kidney beans,
   soaked overnight

30 ml (2 tbsp) vegetable oil

450 g (1 lb) pork sausages

175 g (6 oz) onions, skinned and
   sliced

227 g (8 oz) can tomatoes

15 ml (1 tbsp) cornflour

15 ml (1 tbsp) chilli seasoning

30 ml (2 tbsp) tomato purée

350 ml (12 fl oz) dry cider

salt and freshly ground pepper

1 Drain the haricot and kidney beans and place in a saucepan. Cover with cold water, bring to the boil and boil rapidly for 10 minutes, then drain again.

2 Heat the oil in a large flame-proof casserole and fry the sausages for about 5 minutes until browned. Remove from the casserole and cut each sausage in half crossways.

3 Add the onions to the casserole and fry for 5 minutes until golden brown. Return the sausages to the casserole together with the beans and tomatoes.

4 Blend the cornflour, chilli seasoning and tomato purée with a little cider until smooth, then stir in the rest of the cider. Pour into the casserole, mix well and add pepper to taste.

5 Cover tightly and cook in the oven at 170°C (325°F) mark 3 for about 2 hours or until beans are tender. Add salt before serving the ragout.

Menu Suggestion
A filling midweek family meal, Sausage and Bean Ragout may be served with fresh French bread, boiled rice or creamed potatoes. Follow with a green salad and fresh fruit to complete the meal.

TOAD IN THE HOLE

0.45	483–643 cals

Serves 3–4

450 g (1 lb) pork sausages
25 g (1 oz) lard or dripping
225 ml (8 fl oz) milk
100 g (4 oz) plain flour
pinch of salt
1 egg

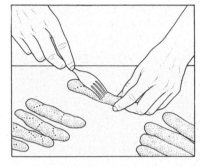

1 Prick the sausages all over with a fork. Put the lard in a Yorkshire pudding tin or small roasting tin and add the sausages.

2 Bake in the oven at 220°C (425°F) mark 7 for 10 minutes until the lard is hot.

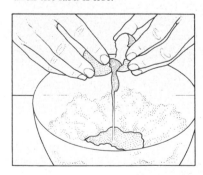

3 Meanwhile, make the batter. Mix the milk and 50 ml (2 fl oz) water together in a jug. Put the flour and salt in a bowl. Make a hollow in the centre and break the egg into it.

4 Mix the flour and egg together gradually, then add the milk and water, a little at a time, and beat until the mixture is smooth.

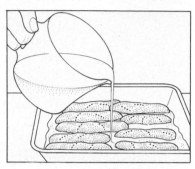

5 Pour the batter into the tin. Bake for about 30 minutes, or until golden brown and well risen. Do not open the oven door during baking or the batter might sink. Serve at once.

Menu Suggestion
Serve for an everyday family supper, with a crisply cooked green vegetable. Children will probably like Toad in the Hole with baked beans, which are just as nutritious as green vegetables.

TOAD IN THE HOLE
One of northern England's most famous dishes, Toad in the Hole is simply a Yorkshire pudding batter cooked with pork sausages. Years ago in Victorian times, when larger quantities of meat were eaten than they are today, Toad in the Hole was made with rump steak. Some cooks even added oysters and mushrooms to the steak, and there is even a recipe for Toad in the Hole made with a boned, stuffed chicken! Kidneys were also a favourite ingredient in those days and, if you like their flavour, they make a good combination with the sausages. You will need about 3 lamb's kidneys, which should be sliced and cooked with the sausages before pouring in the batter.

BAKED STUFFED LAMB'S HEARTS

3.20–3.50	425 cals

Serves 4

4 small lamb's hearts, total weight about 550 g (1¼ lb)

2 large onions, skinned

60 ml (4 tbsp) vegetable oil

50 g (2 oz) streaky bacon, rinded and chopped

50 g (2 oz) button mushrooms, chopped

50 g (2 oz) fresh breadcrumbs

finely grated rind of ½ lemon

15 ml (1 tbsp) lemon juice

30 ml (2 tbsp) chopped fresh parsley

salt and freshly ground pepper

2 carrots, peeled and sliced

300 ml (½ pint) lamb or chicken stock

15 ml (1 tbsp) tomato purée

chopped parsley and blanched julienne of lemon zest, to garnish

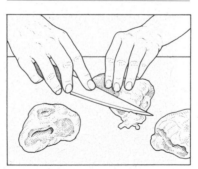

1 Wash the hearts thoroughly under cold running water. Trim them and remove any ducts.

2 Cut 1 of the onions in half and chop 1 half finely. Heat half of the oil in a frying pan, add the chopped onion, bacon and mushrooms and fry for about 5 minutes until the onion is softened. Turn into a bowl, add the breadcrumbs, lemon rind and juice, parsley and salt and pepper to taste. Mix well together. Leave to cool for 10 minutes.

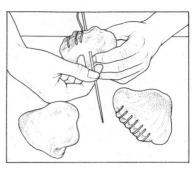

3 Use the stuffing to fill the hearts and sew up neatly to hold in the stuffing.

4 Chop the remaining onions roughly. Heat the remaining oil in a flameproof casserole, add the hearts, carrot and chopped onion and fry for about 5 minutes until lightly browned.

5 Stir in the stock, tomato purée, and salt and pepper. Bring to the boil. Cover tightly and cook in the oven at 170°C (325°F) mark 3 for 2½–3 hours, or until tender. Serve the hearts whole or sliced and pour the skimmed juices over. Garnish with chopped parsley and blanched julienne of lemon zest.

Menu Suggestion

Economical and filling, these stuffed lamb's hearts make a deliciously different family meal. Serve with a colourful vegetable macédoine and creamed potatoes.

BAKED STUFFED LAMB'S HEARTS

Lamb's hearts vary in size quite considerably, depending on the time of year. Very young lamb's hearts are small, weighing only about 75 g (3 oz) each, whereas the more mature hearts can weigh as much as double this. For this recipe, look for hearts weighing around 150 g (5 oz) each. Alternatively, if only the small hearts are available, buy 6 and slice them before serving.

Poultry
and Game

CHICKEN WITH GARLIC

2.15	208 cals

Serves 6

60 ml (4 tbsp) olive or corn oil

1.8 kg (4 lb) chicken

1 sprig each of rosemary, thyme, savory and basil or 2.5 ml (½ tsp) dried

1 bay leaf

40 garlic cloves

salt and freshly ground pepper

grated nutmeg

300 ml (½ pint) hot water

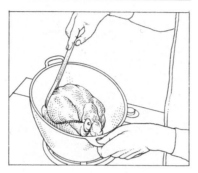

1 Heat the oil in a flameproof casserole and fry the chicken for about 8 minutes until browned on all sides. Remove chicken from the casserole.

2 Place the herbs in the base of the casserole. Arrange the garlic, unpeeled, in one layer over them. Place the chicken on top and season well with salt, pepper and nutmeg.

3 Cover and cook over a very low heat for 1¼–1¾ hours until tender, adding a little hot water if necessary.

4 When cooked, remove the chicken and place on a warmed serving dish. Set aside and keep hot until required.

5 Strain the sauce into a bowl, pushing the garlic cloves through the sieve, using the back of a wooden spoon.

6 Add the hot water to the casserole and stir to lift the sediment. Return the sauce, taste and adjust seasoning, and simmer for 2 minutes or until hot. Transfer to a warm sauceboat and serve with the chicken.

Menu Suggestion
This French main course dish is traditionally served with rounds of French bread. A crisp green salad is usually served afterwards, to refresh the palate.

CHICKEN WITH GARLIC

In France, Poulet aux Quarantes Gousses d'Ail, is a popular recipe, and it's surprising how such a large number of garlic cloves tastes so mild. Any garlic residue can be used in the classic French potato dish Gratin Dauphinois, or another favourite French way of serving it is to spread it on slices of toasted baguette (French stick). This garlic-spread bread is then offered as an accompaniment to the chicken dish, and is considered a great delicacy by the French.

CHICKEN TERIYAKI

0.30*	✳*	220 cals

* plus overnight marinating; freeze after step 2

Serves 4

4 boneless chicken breasts, skinned

90 ml (6 tbsp) soy sauce, preferably *shoyu* (Japanese light soy sauce)

90 ml (6 tbsp) *sake* (Japanese rice wine) or dry sherry

25 g (1 oz) sugar

2 garlic cloves, skinned and crushed

2.5-cm (1-inch) piece of fresh root ginger, peeled and crushed

salt and freshly ground pepper

15–30 ml (1–2 tbsp) vegetable oil

1 Cut the chicken breasts into bite-size pieces. Place the pieces in a shallow bowl.

2 Mix together half the soy sauce, *sake* and sugar, then add half the garlic and ginger with salt and pepper to taste. Pour over the chicken, cover and leave to marinate overnight.

3 Turn the chicken pieces in the marinade occasionally during the marinating time.

4 Thread the cubes of chicken on to oiled kebab skewers. Brush with oil. Barbecue or grill under moderate heat for about 10 minutes until the chicken is tender. Baste the chicken with the marinade and turn frequently during cooking.

5 While the chicken is cooking, put the remaining soy sauce, *sake* and sugar in a small pan with the remaining garlic and ginger. Add salt and pepper to taste and heat through.

6 Serve the chicken hot, with the warmed soy sauce mixture poured over to moisten.

Menu Suggestion

Spicy and sweet, this Japanese skewered chicken looks good on a bed of saffron rice. For an exotic touch, follow with a mixed salad of oriental vegetables such as beansprouts, bamboo shoots, spring onions and fresh root ginger.

CHICKEN TERIYAKI

This is a classic Japanese dish in which pieces of chicken are marinated overnight to tenderise and flavour them, then threaded onto skewers, grilled and served with a hot spicy sauce.

The marinade contains the Japanese rice wine, known as *sake*, which is sold in oriental stores. For a really authentic touch, try using bamboo skewers instead of metal ones—they will need soaking in hot water for about 15 minutes before use.

Pork fillet can be used in place of the chicken.

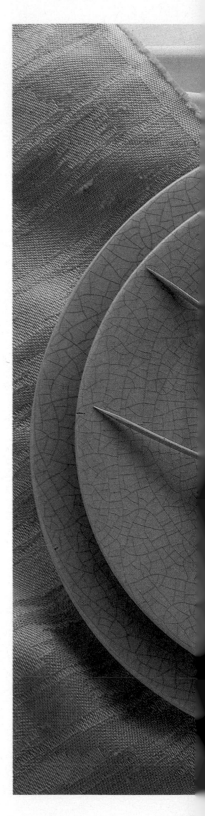

GINGERED JAPANESE CHICKEN

1.00	🍴	361 cals

Serves 4

1.4-kg (3-lb) oven-ready chicken
15 ml (1 tbsp) plain flour
15 ml (1 tbsp) ground ginger
60 ml (4 tbsp) vegetable oil
1 onion, skinned and sliced
283-g (10-oz) can bamboo shoots
1 red pepper, halved, seeded and
   sliced
150 ml (¼ pint) chicken stock
45 ml (3 tbsp) soy sauce
45 ml (3 tbsp) medium dry sherry
salt and freshly ground pepper
100 g (4 oz) mushrooms, sliced

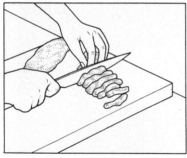

1 Cut all the flesh off the chicken and slice into chunky 'fingers', discarding the skin.

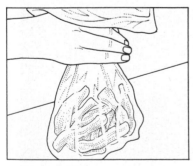

2 Mix the flour and ginger together in a polythene bag and toss the chicken in it to coat.

3 Heat the oil in a very large sauté or deep frying pan and fry the chicken and sliced onion together for 10–15 minutes until they are both golden.

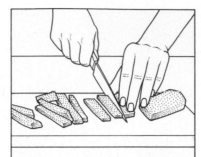

4 Cut up the canned bamboo shoots into 1-cm (½-inch) strips; add to the pan, together with the sliced pepper. Then stir in stock, soy sauce, sherry and seasoning. Bring to boil, cover, simmer 15 minutes.

5 Add the sliced mushrooms, cover again with lid and cook for a further 5–10 minutes, or until the chicken is tender.

BAMBOO SHOOTS

These are used extensively in oriental cooking, although the Chinese and Japanese use fresh shoots rather than the canned ones specified in this recipe. If fresh bamboo shoots are not obtainable, buy canned ones which are available at oriental specialist stores, large supermarkets and delicatessens. These make a very convenient substitute—they are pre-cooked, so all they need is draining and heating through.

The flavour of bamboo shoots is very difficult to describe. Some say they taste like mild asparagus, although asparagus afficionadoes would probably disagree! Look for those canned in water rather than those canned in vinegar—they will have a milder flavour.

CHICKEN WITH SAFFRON

| 1.15 | 🍳 | 316 cals |

Serves 6

6 chicken breasts about 175 g (6 oz)
   each
30 ml (2 tbsp) plain flour
salt and freshly ground pepper
40 g (1½ oz) butter
200 ml (⅓ pint) chicken stock
30 ml (2 tbsp) dry white wine
large pinch of saffron strands
2 egg yolks
60 ml (4 tbsp) single cream
vegetable julienne, to garnish

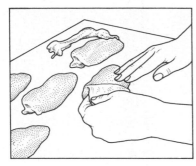

1 Skin the chicken breasts and remove any fat. Lightly coat the chicken in the flour, seasoned with salt and pepper.

2 Melt the butter in a medium flameproof casserole. Fry the chicken pieces, half at a time, for 5–10 minutes until golden brown.

3 Return all the chicken pieces to the pan with any remaining flour and pour in the chicken stock and white wine.

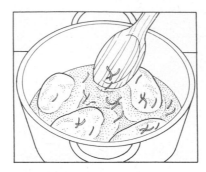

4 Sprinkle in the saffron, pushing it down under the liquid. Bring up to the boil, cover tightly, and bake in the oven at 180°C (350°F) mark 4 for about 50 minutes until cooked.

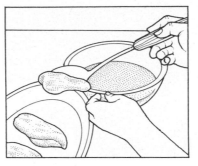

5 Lift the chicken out of the juices and place in an edged serving dish. Cover and keep warm in a low oven.

6 Strain the cooking juices into a small saucepan. Mix the egg yolks and cream together and off the heat stir into the cooking juices until evenly mixed.

7 Cook gently, stirring all the time until the juices thicken slightly. Do not boil. To serve, adjust seasoning, spoon over the chicken and garnish with vegetable julienne. Serve immediately.

NORMANDY CHICKEN

1.20	622 cals

Serves 4

30 ml (2 tbsp) vegetable oil

40 g (1½ oz) butter

4 chicken portions

6 eating apples

salt and freshly ground pepper

300 ml (½ pint) dry cider

60 ml (4 tbsp) Calvados

60 ml (4 tbsp) double cream
   (optional)

1 Heat the oil with 25 g (1 oz) of the butter in a large flame-proof casserole. Add the chicken portions and fry over moderate heat until golden brown on all sides. Remove from the pan and drain on absorbent kitchen paper.

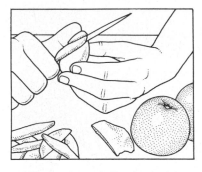

2 Peel, core and slice four of the apples. Add to the pan and fry gently, tossing constantly, until lightly coloured.

3 Return the chicken portions to the pan, placing them on top of the apples. Sprinkle with salt and pepper to taste, then pour in the cider. Bring to the boil, then cover and cook in the oven at 180°C (350°F) mark 4 for 45 minutes or until the chicken portions are tender.

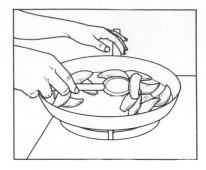

4 Meanwhile, peel, core and slice the remaining apples. Melt the 15 g (½ oz) butter in a frying pan, add the apple slices and toss to coat in the fat. Fry until lightly coloured, then spoon over chicken.

5 Warm the Calvados gently in a ladle or small pan, then ignite and pour over the chicken and apples. Serve as soon as the flames have died down, drizzled with cream, if liked.

Menu Suggestion

Calvados and cider combine together to make this main course dish quite heady. Serve with plain boiled potatoes sprinkled with melted butter and chopped fresh herbs, with a green salad tossed in a sharp vinaigrette dressing to follow. French dry cider would make an unusual drink to serve instead of wine.

CHICKEN PUFF PIE

2.15*	✳*	409–613 cals

* plus about 30 minutes cooling;
freeze after step 8

Serves 4–6

900 g (2 lb) chicken

1 bay leaf

2 sprigs of fresh rosemary or marjoram, or 10 ml (2 tsp) dried

salt and freshly ground pepper

4 leeks, trimmed, washed and cut into 2-cm (¾-inch) lengths

2 large carrots, peeled and thickly sliced

100 g (4 oz) boiled ham, cut into bite-size pieces

25 g (1 oz) butter or margarine

1 medium onion, skinned and chopped

45 ml (3 tbsp) flour

150 ml (¼ pint) milk

60 ml (4 tbsp) double cream

225 g (8 oz) frozen puff pastry, defrosted

1 egg, beaten, to glaze

1 Put the chicken in a large saucepan with the herbs and salt and pepper to taste. Cover with water and bring to the boil, then cover with a lid and simmer for 45–60 minutes until the chicken is tender.

2 Remove the chicken from the liquid and leave to cool slightly. Meanwhile, add the leeks and carrots to the liquid, bring to the boil and simmer for about 7 minutes until tender but still crunchy. Remove from the pan with a slotted spoon.

3 Remove the chicken meat from the bones, discarding the skin. Cut into bite-size chunks.

4 Mix the chicken with the ham and cooked leeks and carrots in a 1.1-litre (2-pint) pie dish.

5 Melt the fat in a clean saucepan, add the onion and fry gently until soft. Sprinkle in the flour and cook for 1–2 minutes, stirring, then gradually add 600 ml (1 pint) of the cooking liquid (discarding the bay leaf and herb sprigs, if used). Bring to the boil and simmer, stirring, until thick, then stir in the milk and cream with salt and pepper to taste. Pour into the pie dish and leave for about 30 minutes until cold.

6 Roll out the pastry on a floured work surface until about 2.5 cm (1 inch) larger all round than the pie dish.

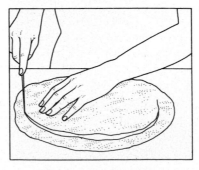

7 Cut off a strip from all round the edge of the pastry. Place the strip on the moistened rim of the pie dish, moisten the strip, then place the pastry lid on top.

8 Press the edge firmly to seal, then knock up and flute. Make a hole in the centre of the pie and use the pastry trimmings to make decorations, sticking them in place with water.

9 Brush the pastry with beaten egg, then bake in the oven at 190°C (375°F) mark 5 for 30 minutes until puffed up and golden brown. Serve hot.

Menu Suggestion
Ideal for a midweek family meal, this filling chicken pie needs no further accompaniment other than a freshly cooked green vegetable such as French beans or spinach.

--- VARIATIONS ---

Replace the leeks with **6 sticks of celery**, cleaned and cut in the same way. Add them to the pan 3 minutes after adding the carrots.

Replace all of the leeks with **8 Jerusalem artichokes**, peeled and thickly sliced.

Replace one of the carrots with **1 medium turnip**, peeled and roughly cubed.

Replace the carrots with **1 medium celeriac**, peeled and cubed.

Replace the puff pastry with the same weight of shortcrust pastry.

Add **100 g (4 oz) thickly sliced mushrooms** and **5 ml (1 teaspoon) celery seeds** at step 5 when frying the onion.

STIR-FRIED CHICKEN WITH WALNUTS

0.20*	358 cals

* plus at least 1 hour marinating

Serves 4

4 boneless chicken breasts,
**   skinned and cut into thin strips**

5-cm (2-inch) piece of fresh root
**   ginger, peeled and thinly sliced**

60 ml (4 tbsp) soy sauce

60 ml (4 tbsp) dry sherry

5 ml (1 tsp) five-spice powder

45 ml (3 tbsp) sesame or vegetable
**   oil**

30 ml (2 tbsp) cornflour

150 ml ($\frac{1}{4}$ pint) chicken stock

salt and freshly ground pepper

75 g (3 oz) walnut pieces

$\frac{1}{4}$ cucumber, cut into chunks

spring onion tassels, to garnish

1 Put the chicken in a bowl with the ginger, soy sauce, sherry and five-spice powder. Stir well to mix, then cover and marinate for at least 1 hour.

2 Remove the chicken and ginger from the marinade with a slotted spoon. Reserve marinade.

3 Heat 30 ml (2 tbsp) of the oil in a wok or large heavy-based frying pan. Add the chicken and stir-fry over brisk heat for 5 minutes until well browned.

4 Mix the marinade with the cornflour then stir in the stock. Pour into the pan and bring to the boil, then add salt and pepper to taste and stir-fry for a further 5 minutes or until the chicken strips are tender.

5 Heat the remaining oil in a separate small pan, add the walnuts and cucumber and stir-fry briefly to heat through.

6 Transfer the chicken mixture to a warmed serving dish and top with the walnuts and cucumber. Garnish with spring onion tassels and serve.

Menu Suggestion
Serve with Chinese egg noodles, followed by a mixed salad of beansprouts, grated carrot, chopped celery and onion tossed in a dressing of oil, lemon juice and soy sauce.

CHICKEN FLORENTINE

1.00	527 cals

Serves 4

450 g (1 lb) fresh spinach

salt and freshly ground pepper

4 boneless chicken breasts, skinned

75 g (3 oz) butter or margarine

15 ml (1 tbsp) vegetable oil

1.25 ml ($\frac{1}{4}$ tsp) freshly grated
    nutmeg

25 g (1 oz) flour

450 ml ($\frac{3}{4}$ pint) milk

100 g (4 oz) Cheddar or Double
    Gloucester cheese, grated

pinch of ground mace

a little paprika

1 Wash the spinach, put into a pan with a pinch of salt. Cook over low heat for 7 minutes until just tender. Drain well.

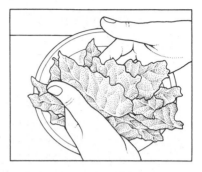

2 Meanwhile, cut each chicken breast in two horizontally. Melt 25 g (1 oz) of the fat in a frying pan with the oil. Fry the chicken for 3 minutes on each side.

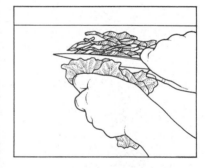

3 Chop the drained spinach. Mix with half of the remaining fat, the nutmeg and salt and pepper to taste. Put the spinach in the base of an ovenproof dish, then arrange the chicken on top.

4 Melt the remaining fat in a pan. Add the flour and stir for 2 minutes. Gradually add the milk, then the cheese, mace and seasoning. Simmer until thick.

5 Pour over the chicken, then sprinkle with the remaining cheese and a little paprika. Bake at 190°C (375°F) mark 5 for 30 minutes.

Menu Suggestion
Serve with mashed potatoes.

CHICKEN CROQUETTES

0.20*	✳*	642 cals

* plus 30 minutes cooling and at least
2–3 hours chilling; freeze after step 3

Serves 2

50 g (2 oz) butter or margarine
60 ml (4 tbsp) flour
200 ml ($\frac{1}{3}$ pint) milk
$\frac{1}{2}$ lemon
15 ml (1 tbsp) capers, chopped
175 g (6 oz) cooked chicken, minced
15 ml (1 tbsp) chopped fresh parsley
salt and freshly ground pepper
1 egg, beaten
50 g (2 oz) dry white breadcrumbs
vegetable oil, for frying
lemon wedges, to garnish

1 Melt the fat in a saucepan. Add the flour and cook gently, stirring, for 3 minutes. Remove from the heat and gradually stir in the milk. Bring to the boil and cook for about 5 minutes, stirring all the time, until the sauce is smooth and thick.

2 Grate in the lemon rind. Add the capers and chicken with the parsley and seasoning. Mix well together. Cool for 30 minutes, then chill in the refrigerator for 2–3 hours or preferably overnight.

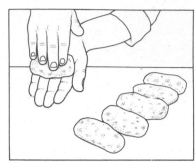

3 Shape the mixture into six even-sized croquettes. Dip in the beaten egg, then roll in the breadcrumbs to coat.

4 Deep-fry at 180°C (350°F) or shallow fry in hot oil for about 10 minutes or until golden brown. Serve hot, with lemon wedges.

Menu Suggestion
Serve Chicken Croquettes hot with French fries and a colourful medley of mixed vegetables such as peas, sweetcorn and red peppers, or a tomato salad.

CHICKEN CROQUETTES

Croquettes come in all shapes and sizes. Although they are most often made into sausage shapes as here, you can also try making them into rectangles, balls, egg shapes or flat cakes. Traditionally, they were often served as an entrée, or made very small and used as a garnish for roast meat or game.

The basic mixture can be varied by replacing the sauce with egg-enriched rice or potato purée, seasoned and mixed with any variety of flavourings and finely chopped or minced meat, fish or vegetable. Croquettes can also be made from thin pancakes stuffed and rolled up, then sliced, dipped in egg and bread-crumbs and deep-fried.

CHICKEN CORDON BLEU

| 0.45* | 🍴 | ✳* | 452 cals |

* plus 30 minutes chilling; freeze after step 5

Serves 4

4 boneless chicken breasts, skinned

4 thin slices of boiled ham

4 thin slices of Gruyère cheese

salt and freshly ground pepper

about 25 g (1 oz) flour

1 egg, beaten

75 g (3 oz) dried white breadcrumbs

60 ml (4 tbsp) vegetable oil

50 g (2 oz) butter

lemon twists and sprigs of fresh herbs, to garnish

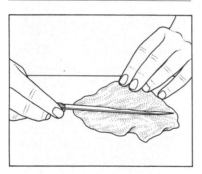

1 Slit along one long edge of each chicken breast, then carefully work knife to the opposite edge, using a sawing action.

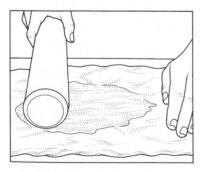

2 Open out the chicken breast, place between two sheets of damp greaseproof paper or cling film and beat with a meat bat or rolling pin to flatten slightly.

3 Place a slice of ham on top of each piece of chicken, then a slice of cheese. Fold the chicken over to enclose ham and cheese.

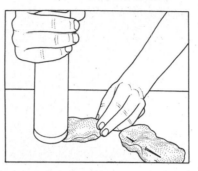

4 Pound the open edge of the parcels so that they stay together, then secure with wooden cocktail sticks.

5 Sprinkle the chicken parcels with salt and pepper to taste, then coat lightly in flour. Dip in the beaten egg, then in the breadcrumbs. Press the breadcrumbs on firmly so that they adhere evenly and completely coat the chicken. Refrigerate for about 30 minutes.

6 Heat the oil and butter together in a large heavy-based frying pan (you may need to use two if the chicken parcels are large), then fry the chicken for 10 minutes on each side until crisp and golden. Drain on absorbent paper, remove the cocktail sticks, then arrange the chicken on a warmed serving platter and garnish with lemon and herbs.

Menu Suggestion
Crunchy on the outside, meltingly delicious on the inside, Chicken Cordon Bleu goes well with vegetables such as mushrooms, or French beans, spinach, courgettes and mange-touts. Sauté potatoes can also be served, for hungry guests!

CIRCASSIAN CHICKEN

| 1.30 | 366–549 cals |

Serves 4–6

1.8 kg (4 lb) chicken

1 medium onion, skinned and sliced

2 sticks of celery, roughly chopped

1 carrot, peeled and roughly chopped

few sprigs of parsley

salt and freshly ground pepper

100 g (4 oz) shelled walnuts

40 g ($1\frac{1}{2}$ oz) butter

45 ml (3 tbsp) vegetable oil

1.25 ml ($\frac{1}{4}$ tsp) ground cinnamon

1.25 ml ($\frac{1}{4}$ tsp) ground cloves

5 ml (1 tsp) paprika

1 Put the chicken in a large saucepan with the vegetables, parsley, 5 ml (1 tsp) salt and pepper to taste. Cover the chicken with water and bring to the boil. Lower heat, half cover pan with a lid and simmer for 40 minutes.

2 Remove the chicken from the pan, strain the cooking liquid and set aside. Cut the chicken into serving pieces, discarding the skin.

3 Pound the walnuts with a pestle in a mortar until very fine, or grind them in an electric grinder or food processor.

4 Melt the butter with 15 ml (1 tbsp) oil in a large frying pan. Add the chicken pieces and fry over moderate heat for 3–4 minutes until well coloured.

5 Add 450 ml ($\frac{3}{4}$ pint) of the cooking liquid, the walnuts, cinnamon and cloves. Stir well to mix, then simmer uncovered for about 20 minutes or until the chicken is tender and the sauce thickly coats the chicken. Stir the chicken and sauce frequently during this time.

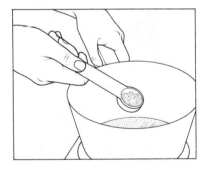

6 Just before serving, heat the remaining oil in a separate small pan. Sprinkle in the paprika, stirring to combine with the oil.

7 Taste and adjust the seasoning of the walnut sauce. Arrange the chicken and sauce on a warmed serving platter and drizzle with the paprika oil. Serve at once.

Menu Suggestion
For a Middle-Eastern style meal, serve the chicken and walnut sauce in a ring of saffron rice. Follow with a tomato, onion and black olive salad sprinkled with olive oil and lemon juice.

KOTOPOULO KAPANICI

1.00	✳	416 cals

Serves 4

4 chicken portions, skinned

salt and freshly ground pepper

45 ml (3 tbsp) olive oil

15 g (½ oz) butter

1 small onion, skinned and chopped

3 garlic cloves, skinned and crushed

100 ml (4 fl oz) dry white wine

450 g (1 lb) ripe tomatoes, skinned, seeded and chopped

15 ml (1 tbsp) tomato purée

1 cinnamon stick

4 cloves

6 allspice berries

150 ml (¼ pint) water

175-g (6-oz) can or jar artichoke hearts, drained (optional)

15–30 ml (1–2 tbsp) chopped fresh parsley or coriander

1 Sprinkle the chicken liberally with salt and pepper. Heat the oil with the butter in a large flame-proof casserole, add the chicken and fry over moderate heat for about 5 minutes until well coloured on all sides. Remove from the pan with a slotted spoon and set aside.

2 Add the onion and garlic to the pan and fry gently for about 5 minutes until soft.

3 Return the chicken to the pan, pour in the wine, then add the tomatoes and tomato purée and mix well. Let the mixture bubble for a few minutes.

4 Meanwhile, pound the spices with a pestle in a mortar. Add to the casserole with the water and stir well to mix. Cover the pan and simmer for about 45–60 minutes until the chicken is tender

5 Add the artichokes (if using) about 10 minutes before the end of cooking time, to heat through. Taste and adjust seasoning, stir in the parsley or coriander and serve immediately.

Menu Suggestion

This Greek chicken casserole with its spicy tomato sauce goes well with plain boiled rice or a Greek potato dish made by tossing new potatoes in their skins in a mixture of olive oil, white wine and crushed coriander seeds. Follow with a salad of raw shredded white cabbage and lettuce, sliced onion, black olives and crumbled Feta cheese tossed in an olive oil and lemon juice dressing.

KOTOPOULO KAPANICI

This spicy chicken casserole comes from Greece. The Greeks would choose a boiling fowl rather than a young chicken, which would be reserved for grilling, or any other quick method of cooking. The chicken is simmered gently in a rich tomato and wine mixture until very tender and juicy. What makes it different from other chicken casseroles is the addition of cinnamon, cloves and allspice which give the finished dish a distinctive warm and spicy flavour. Although all these spices are available ground, the flavour is far superior if you buy them whole and grind your own just before using.

Cinnamon is the aromatic bark of a type of laurel tree, native to India, while allspice 'berries' are the dried fruit of the pimento tree, native to the West Indies. Cloves are the dried flower buds of the clove tree, most often associated with baking.

SPANISH CHICKEN

| 1.15 | ✳ | 513 cals |

Serves 4

60 ml (4 tbsp) olive oil

1 onion, skinned and chopped

2 garlic cloves, skinned and crushed

4 chicken portions

60 ml (4 tbsp) brandy

2 small peppers (1 red and 1 green or yellow), cored, seeded and sliced

4 large tomatoes, skinned and chopped

150 ml (¼ pint) dry white wine

150 ml (¼ pint) chicken stock or water

10 ml (2 tsp) chopped fresh rosemary or 5 ml (1 tsp) dried

salt and freshly ground pepper

1 Heat the oil in a flameproof casserole, add the onion and garlic and fry gently for 5 minutes until soft but not coloured.

2 Add the chicken portions and fry for a few minutes more, turning the chicken constantly so that the pieces become browned on all sides.

3 Warm the brandy gently in a small pan or ladle. Remove the casserole from the heat, pour the brandy over the chicken and set it alight with a match.

4 When the flames have died down, return the casserole to the heat and add the peppers and tomatoes. Fry over moderate heat for about 10 minutes, mashing the tomatoes down to a purée with a wooden spoon.

5 Pour in the wine and stock and bring slowly to boiling point. Lower the heat, add the rosemary and seasoning to taste, then cover and simmer for 30 minutes or until the chicken is tender when pierced with a skewer. Taste and adjust seasoning before serving.

Menu Suggestion

A quick-to-make main course for an informal dinner party, Spanish Chicken is best served with saffron rice or hot herb bread. Follow with a salad of shredded lettuce and finely chopped onion tossed in olive oil, lemon juice and salt and freshly ground pepper.

SPANISH CHICKEN

Olive oil, onion, garlic, peppers and tomatoes are all ingredients which conjure up a vivid image of colourful Spanish cookery. Wine and spirits also play quite a large part in the cuisine of Spain, although this is less well known than with French cookery, for example.

Don't worry about the high alcohol content of this recipe, which combines both brandy and wine together—a popular Spanish combination. The actual alcohol content is burnt off by the flaming of the brandy, and evaporated by the heating of the wine, as long as the cooking time is at least 20 minutes, which it is in the case of the recipe above. If the alcohol were not eliminated in this way, the flavour of the finished dish would be raw and harsh. In this recipe the alcohol gives body and richness to the sauce.

CHICKEN DHANSAK

1.15	✳	568 cals

Serves 4

40 g (1½ oz) ghee or clarified butter

1 onion, skinned and chopped

2.5 cm (1 inch) piece fresh root ginger, skinned and crushed

1–2 garlic cloves, skinned and crushed

4 chicken portions

5 ml (1 tsp) ground coriander

2.5 ml (½ tsp) chilli powder

2.5 ml (½ tsp) ground turmeric

1.25 ml (¼ tsp) ground cinnamon

salt

225 g (8 oz) red lentils, rinsed and drained

juice of 1 lime or lemon

fresh lime slices and coriander leaves, to garnish

1 Melt the ghee or butter in a flameproof casserole, add the onion, ginger and garlic and fry gently for 5 minutes until soft but not coloured.

2 Add the chicken portions and spices and fry for a few minutes more, turning the chicken constantly so that the pieces become coloured on all sides.

3 Pour enough water into the casserole to just cover the chicken. Add salt to taste, then the red lentils.

4 Bring slowly to boiling point, stirring, then lower the heat and cover the casserole. Simmer for 40 minutes or until the chicken is tender when pierced with a skewer. During cooking, turn the chicken in the sauce occasionally, and check that the lentils have not absorbed all the water and become too dry—add water if necessary.

5 Remove the chicken from the casserole and leave until cool enough to handle. Take the meat off the bones, discarding the skin. Cut the meat into bite-sized pieces, return to the casserole and heat through thoroughly. Stir in the lime or lemon juice; taste and add more salt if necessary. Garnish with fresh lime slices and coriander leaves before serving.

Menu Suggestion
Serve this hot Indian curry with boiled or fried basmati rice and a yogurt and cucumber salad (raita) for a cooling effect. Indian bread such as paratha or puri (packet mixes are now widely available) can also be served as an appetising accompaniment.

CHICKEN DHANSAK
Ghee or clarified butter is used frequently in Asian cookery. To make it, simmer melted butter in a heavy pan until a thick froth forms on top. Lower the heat and continue simmering until froth starts to separate and sediment settles at the bottom. Cool slightly, then strain through a metal sieve lined with muslin or a clean tea-towel. Discard sediment. Store ghee in refrigerator.

CARIBBEAN CHICKEN

0.50* | 447 cals

* plus overnight marinating

Serves 4

4 boneless chicken breasts, skinned

15 ml (1 tbsp) vinegar

425 g (15 oz) can pineapple slices in natural juice

10 ml (2 tsp) soft brown sugar

salt and freshly ground pepper

45 ml (3 tbsp) vegetable oil

175 g (6 oz) long grain rice

1½ green, red or yellow peppers, cored, seeded and sliced

Tabasco sauce, to taste

60 ml (4 tbsp) dark rum

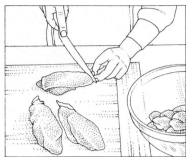

1 Cut the chicken into bite-sized pieces and place in a bowl. Make the marinade. Mix together the vinegar, pineapple juice, sugar, 10 ml (2 tsp) salt and pepper to taste. Pour over the chicken, cover and leave to marinate overnight. Turn the chicken in the marinade occasionally during this time.

2 Drain the chicken and reserve the marinade. Make the marinade up to 600 ml (1 pint) with water and set aside.

3 Heat the oil in a flameproof casserole, add the chicken and fry over moderate heat until turning colour on all sides. Add the rice and most of the pepper and fry for 5 minutes, stirring.

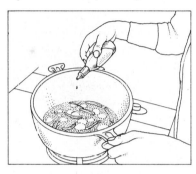

4 Pour in the marinade and bring slowly to the boil. Stir once, then shake in Tabasco sauce to taste and lower the heat. Cover and simmer for 20 minutes or until the chicken and rice are tender and most of the liquid has been absorbed.

5 Chop the pineapple and add to the casserole with the rum. Fold in gently and heat through. Taste and adjust seasoning before serving. Garnish with remaining pepper slices.

Menu Suggestion
Caribbean Chicken combines meat, vegetables and rice in one dish. Serve with hot French bread and follow with a green salad, for an informal meal.

STOVED CHICKEN

2.15	586 cals

Serves 4

50 g (2 oz) butter

1.4 kg (3 lb) chicken, jointed

100 g (4 oz) streaky bacon, rinded and chopped

1.1 kg (2½ lb) floury potatoes such as King Edwards

2 large onions, skinned and sliced

salt and freshly ground pepper

10 ml (2 tsp) chopped fresh thyme or 2.5 ml (½ tsp) dried

600 ml (1 pint) chicken stock

snipped chives, to garnish

1 Melt 25 g (1 oz) of the butter in a frying pan and fry the chicken and bacon for 5 minutes until lightly browned.

2 Peel the potatoes and cut into 5 mm (¼ inch) slices. Place a thick layer of potato slices, then sliced onion, in the base of a casserole. Season well, add the thyme and dot with butter.

3 Add the chicken, season and dot with butter. Cover with the remaining onions and finally a layer of potatoes. Season and dot with butter. Pour over the stock.

4 Cover and cook in the oven at 150°C (300°F) mark 2 for about 2 hours until the chicken is tender and the potatoes are cooked, adding a little more hot stock if necessary.

5 Just before serving sprinkle snipped chives over the top of the dish.

Menu Suggestion

Chicken and potatoes are cooked together in this casserole recipe. A seasonal vegetable such as carrots, peas or green beans is all that is needed for a family meal.

STOVED CHICKEN

This hearty dish made with simple, everyday ingredients would originally have been made with a boiling fowl, but nowadays these are not so easy to obtain, so an oven-ready or roasting chicken is used instead. The recipe originated in Scotland, where it is also sometimes called 'stovies', from the French verb 'étouffer', meaning to cook in an enclosed pot. During the alliance between the Scottish and the French in the 17th century, there were many words such as this one with a French derivation. Stoved Chicken or Stovies used to be served at rural weddings in the Highlands, but this custom has died out now and the dish has become traditional family fare.

GOLDEN BAKED CHICKEN

| 1.15 | 324 cals |

Serves 4

4 chicken portions

1 small onion, skinned and finely chopped

salt and freshly ground pepper

50 g (2 oz) fresh white breadcrumbs

15 ml (1 tbsp) chopped fresh parsley and thyme or 5 ml (1 tsp) dried mixed herbs

50 g (2 oz) butter or margarine, melted

1 Wipe the chicken portions and season well with salt and freshly ground pepper.

2 Mix the breadcrumbs with the onion and herbs.

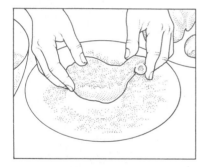

3 Brush the chicken joints all over with the butter or margarine; toss them in the herbed breadcrumbs and place in a buttered ovenproof dish.

4 Bake in the oven at 190°C (375°F) mark 5, for about 1 hour or until golden. Baste occasionally during cooking. Serve hot, straight from the dish.

Menu Suggestion
Serve with jacket-baked potatoes cooked in the oven at the same time, and a salad of tomato and raw onion with a lemony vinaigrette dressing.

FRENCH-STYLE ROAST CHICKEN

1.00	349–465 cals

Serves 3–4

1–1.4 kg (2¼–3 lb) oven ready chicken

5–6 sprigs fresh tarragon or parsley or 5 ml (1 tsp) dried tarragon or parsley

100 g (4 oz) butter, softened

salt and freshly ground pepper

150 ml (¼ pint) chicken stock

watercress, to garnish

1 Wipe the inside of the chicken, then put the tarragon or parsley inside it, with 15 g (½ oz) of the butter and some pepper.

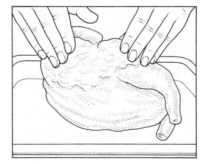

2 Place on one side in a roasting tin, smear all over with one third of the remaining butter and roast in the oven at 220°C (425°F) mark 7 for 15 minutes.

3 Turn the chicken onto the other side, smear with half the remaining butter and return to the oven. Roast for another 15 minutes.

4 Turn the chicken breast side up, smear with the rest of the butter, return to the oven and roast at 190°C (375°F) mark 5 for 20–30 minutes, or until tender.

5 Place the chicken on a serving dish and keep warm while making the gravy.

6 To make the gravy, place the roasting tin on top of the cooker and scrape any sediment sticking to the bottom. Add the stock and bring to the boil, then simmer for 2–3 minutes, stirring. Add seasoning to taste and pour into a warmed gravy boat. Garnish the chicken with watercress and serve immediately, with the gravy handed separately.

Menu Suggestion

Serve with the French potato dish *gratin dauphinois*—thinly sliced potatoes baked in a gratin dish with onion, cream and Gruyère cheese. Follow with a simple green salad tossed in vinaigrette dressing.

FRENCH-STYLE ROAST CHICKEN

The French have a unique way of cooking chicken which gives a wonderfully moist and succulent flesh. The secret lies in smearing the bird with plenty of butter and turning it over at regular intervals during roasting. Tarragon has a natural affinity with chicken, and is the most popular herb to cook with it in France, so try to use it if you want an authentic 'French' flavour—it grows very easily in the garden in summer.

HINDLE WAKES

3.15*	281–421 cals

* plus overnight soaking

Serves 4–6

1.6 kg (3½ lb) boiling chicken with giblets, trussed
600 ml (1 pint) water
salt and freshly ground pepper
50 g (2 oz) butter or margarine
450 g (1 lb) leeks, sliced and washed
6 carrots, peeled and thickly sliced
225 g (8 oz) prunes, soaked overnight and stoned
25 g (1 oz) plain flour

1 Place the giblets in a saucepan with the water and 5 ml (1 tsp) salt. Bring to the boil, then cover and simmer for 30 minutes.

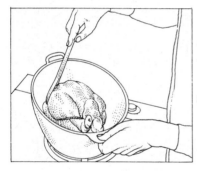

2 Meanwhile, melt 25 g (1 oz) of the fat in a large flame-proof casserole and fry the chicken for about 8 minutes until browned all over. Remove from casserole.

3 Fry the leeks and carrots for 3 minutes. Return the chicken and add the drained prunes. Strain in the giblet stock and season with pepper.

4 Cover and cook in the oven at 170°C (325°F) mark 3 for about 2–2½ hours or until tender.

5 Arrange the chicken, vegetables and prunes on a large warmed platter. Keep hot.

6 Skim any fat off the sauce. Blend together the remaining fat and the flour to form a paste. Add to the sauce, a little at a time, and stir over a gentle heat until thickened. Do not boil. Adjust the seasoning to taste and serve the sauce separately.

Menu Suggestion

Serve this old English dish with jacket baked potatoes or creamed potatoes and a green vegetable.

TURKEY PAPRIKA WITH PASTA

| 0.40 | 385 cals |

Serves 4

30 ml (2 tbsp) vegetable oil

75 g (3 oz) onion, skinned and sliced

450 g (1 lb) turkey breasts

10 ml (2 tsp) paprika

450 ml ($\frac{3}{4}$ pint) chicken stock

salt and freshly ground pepper

1 green pepper, cored, seeded and sliced

100 g (4 oz) small pasta shapes

142 ml (5 fl oz) soured cream

paprika, to garnish

1 Heat the oil in a large sauté pan and fry the onion for 5 minutes until golden brown.

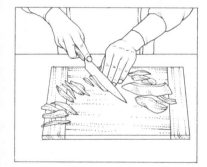

2 Skin the turkey breasts, discard any bone and cut flesh into small finger-sized pieces.

3 Add the turkey and paprika to the pan and toss over a moderate heat for 2 minutes.

4 Stir in the stock and seasoning and bring to the boil. Add the green pepper and pasta, cover and simmer gently for 15–20 minutes until turkey and pasta are tender.

5 Stir in the soured cream and adjust the seasoning. To serve, garnish with a little paprika.

Menu Suggestion
Quick and easy to make, this casserole needs no accompaniment other than a crisp green salad.

TRADITIONAL ROAST TURKEY

5.30–6.30	668–834 cals

Serves 8–10

50 g (2 oz) butter

3 medium onions, skinned and finely chopped

225 g (8 oz) lean veal, minced

175 g (6 oz) lean bacon, rinded and minced

175 g (6 oz) fresh white breadcrumbs

2 large mushrooms, chopped

15 ml (1 tbsp) chopped fresh parsley or 5 ml (1 tsp) dried

2.5 ml ($\frac{1}{2}$ tsp) mace

1.25 ml ($\frac{1}{4}$ tsp) cayenne

salt and freshly ground pepper

1 egg, beaten

100 g (4 oz) suet or 60 ml (4 tbsp) beef dripping

225 g (8 oz) medium oatmeal

4.5–5.5 kg (10–12 lb) turkey

melted dripping or butter, for brushing

1 Make the veal forcemeat stuffing. Melt the butter in a small frying pan, add 1 of the onions and fry gently for 5 minutes.

2 Meanwhile, put the veal and bacon in a bowl and beat well.

3 Stir in the fried onions, breadcrumbs, mushrooms, parsley, mace, cayenne and salt and pepper to taste. Bind with the beaten egg; if the mixture is too stiff, add a little milk. Cool for 20 minutes.

4 Make the oatmeal stuffing. Melt the suet or dripping in a frying pan, add the remaining onions and fry gently for 5 minutes until soft but not coloured. Stir in the oatmeal and cook over a gentle heat, stirring, until the mixture is thick and thoroughly cooked. Add plenty of salt and pepper to taste. Turn into a greased 600 ml (1 pint) pudding basin. Cover with greaseproof paper and foil.

5 Remove the giblets and wash the bird. Drain well and pat dry with absorbent kitchen paper.

6 Stuff the neck end of the turkey with the veal stuffing, taking care not to pack it too tightly. Cover the stuffing smoothly with the neck skin.

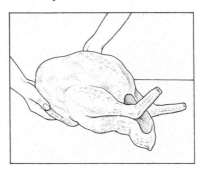

7 With the bird breast side up, fold the wing tips neatly under the body, catching in the neck skin.

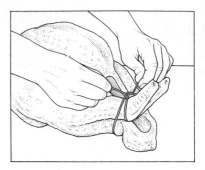

8 Truss the bird and tie the legs together. Make the body as plump and even in shape as possible.

9 Weigh the bird and calculate the cooking time, allowing 20 minutes per 450 g (1 lb) plus 20 minutes. Put the bird breast side up on a rack in a roasting tin. Brush with melted dripping and sprinkle with plenty of salt and pepper.

10 Cover the bird loosely with foil. Roast in the oven at 180°C (350°F) mark 4 for the calculated cooking time until tender, removing the foil and basting the turkey 30 minutes before the end of cooking time. Turn off the oven and leave the turkey to rest for up to 30 minutes before carving. One hour before the end of cooking the turkey; put the oatmeal stuffing to steam.

TRADITIONAL ROAST TURKEY

Turkey has been the traditional meat for Christmas in Britain since the 16th century. Turkeys were in fact brought to England from the New World by a Yorkshireman, William Strickland, and in his home town of Boynton-on-the-Wold, near Bridlington, there is a wooden turkey lectern in his honour in the local church.

In early days, the turkeys were walked to market at Christmastime, sometimes hundreds of miles. To protect their feet during the long journey, they wore leather 'boots', or their feet were painted with tar!

TURKEY IN SPICED YOGURT

| 1.30* | 328 cals |

* plus overnight marinating

Serves 6

turkey leg on the bone, about 1.1 kg (2½ lb) in weight

7.5 ml (1½ tsp) ground cumin

7.5 ml (1½ tsp) ground coriander

2.5 ml (½ tsp) ground turmeric

2.5 ml (½ tsp) ground ginger

salt and freshly ground pepper

284 g (10 oz) natural yogurt

30 ml (2 tbsp) lemon juice

45 ml (3 tbsp) vegetable oil

225 g (8 oz) onions, skinned and sliced

45 ml (3 tbsp) desiccated coconut

30 ml (2 tbsp) plain flour

150 ml (¼ pint) chicken stock or water

chopped fresh parsley, to garnish

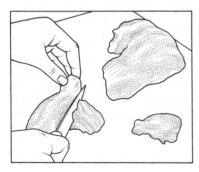

1 Cut the turkey meat off the bone into large fork-sized pieces, discarding the skin (there should be about 900 g [2 lb] meat).

2 Make the marinade. In a large bowl mix the spices with the seasoning, yogurt and lemon juice. Stir well until evenly blended. Fold through the turkey meat until coated with the yogurt mixture. Cover tightly with cling film and refrigerate overnight.

3 Heat the oil in a medium flameproof casserole, add the onion and fry for about 5 minutes until lightly brown. Add the coconut and flour and fry gently, stirring for about 1 minute.

4 Off the heat stir in the turkey with its marinade, and the stock. Return to the heat and bring slowly to the boil, stirring all the time to prevent sticking.

5 Cover tightly and cook in the oven at 170°C (325°F) mark 3 for 1–1¼ hours or until the turkey is tender when tested with a fork. To serve, adjust the seasoning and serve garnished with parsley.

YOGURT

Plain unsweetened yogurt is used extensively in Indian and Middle Eastern cooking for many reasons. It is often used as a marinade as in this recipe, because it has the effect of tenderizing meat—it contains certain live bacteria which help break down tough fibres and sinews, making the meat more succulent and juicy when cooked.

Plain yogurt is also used to offset the hotness of chillies and the rawness of spices. For this reason it can be combined with the other ingredients as here, although it is often served as a side dish for people to help themselves whenever they feel a dish is too hot for their liking. It is for this same reason that Indians often drink yogurt when eating curry—to counteract the heat of the food, refresh the palate and aid digestion. Called *lassi*, this yogurt drink is made by diluting yogurt with water then whisking it until frothy.

BAKED TURKEY ESCALOPES WITH CRANBERRY AND COCONUT

| 0.50 | 🗋 | ✳* | 391 cals |

* freeze after step 2

Serves 4

450 g (1 lb) boneless turkey breast

salt and freshly ground pepper

20 ml (4 tsp) Dijon mustard

60 ml (4 tbsp) cranberry sauce

15 g ($\frac{1}{2}$ oz) flour

1 egg, beaten

15 g ($\frac{1}{2}$ oz) desiccated coconut

40 g (1$\frac{1}{2}$ oz) fresh breadcrumbs

50 g (2 oz) butter or margarine

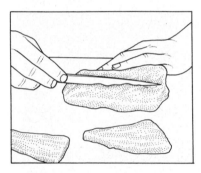

1 Thinly slice the turkey breast to give four portions.

2 Bat out the escalopes between two sheets of damp grease-proof paper or cling film. Season, then spread each portion with mustard and cranberry sauce.

3 Roll up, starting from the thin end, and secure with a cocktail stick or toothpick. Dust each portion with flour, then brush with egg. Combine the coconut and breadcrumbs then coat the turkey with the mixture.

4 Melt the fat in a frying pan, add the turkey portions, and fry until brown on both sides. Transfer to a baking tin just large enough to take the turkey in a single layer and baste with more fat. Bake in the oven at 180°C (350°F) mark 4 for about 40 minutes until tender.

Menu Suggestion

Serve these scrumptiously crisp escalopes with a salad of chopped and grated raw vegetables (e.g. celery, peppers, white cabbage, carrot and onion) tossed in a mayonnaise, soured cream or yogurt dressing. Alternatively, serve with a simple green salad.

BAKED TURKEY ESCALOPES WITH CRANBERRY AND COCONUT

Cranberries are a distinctively sharp-tasting fruit which make a delicious sauce, used here to add zest to turkey meat. The fresh fruit have a limited season, but they can also be bought frozen or canned throughout the year. Cultivated mainly in America, the ruby red berries grow on vines in flooded marshy soil. To harvest them, the water is whipped up by a machine. This dislodges the fruit which floats to the surface and is separated off from the leaves and other debris. The sorting process includes a special machine which bounces the berries over a barrier seven times—if the berries don't bounce they are rejected as unsound!

Cranberry sauce is good mixed with fresh orange juice and poured over vanilla ice-cream, sweet pancakes or waffles, and whole berries are good in beef and pork casseroles.

TURKEY GROUNDNUT STEW

| 1.15 | 465–698 cals |

Serves 4–6

30 ml (2 tbsp) vegetable oil

2 onions, skinned and chopped

1 garlic clove, skinned and crushed

1 large green pepper, cored, seeded and chopped

900 g (2 lb) boneless turkey, cut into cubes

175 g (6 oz) shelled peanuts

600 ml (1 pint) chicken stock

salt and freshly ground pepper

60 ml (4 tbsp) crunchy peanut butter

10 ml (2 tsp) tomato purée

225 g (8 oz) tomatoes, skinned and roughly chopped

2.5–5 ml ($\frac{1}{2}$–1 tsp) cayenne pepper

few drops of Tabasco sauce

chopped green pepper, to garnish

1 Heat the oil in a flameproof casserole, add the onion, garlic and green pepper and fry gently for 5 minutes until they are soft but not coloured.

2 Add the turkey and fry for a few minutes more, turning constantly until well browned on all sides.

3 Add the peanuts, stock and salt and pepper to taste and bring slowly to boiling point. Lower the heat, cover and simmer for 45 minutes or until the turkey is tender.

4 Remove the turkey from the cooking liquid with a slotted spoon and set aside. Leave the cooking liquid to cool for about 5 minutes.

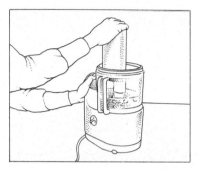

5 Work the cooking liquid and nuts in an electric blender or food processor, half at a time, until quite smooth. Return to the pan with the remaining ingredients, add the turkey and reheat. Taste and adjust seasoning before serving, adding more cayenne if a hot flavour is liked. Garnish with chopped green pepper.

Menu Suggestion

Groundnut stews are traditionally served in the Caribbean with plain boiled rice and a dish of root vegetables such as turnip, swede or parsnip. If liked, hot pepper sauce can also be offered as an additional accompaniment.

TURKEY GROUNDNUT STEW

Groundnut stews originated in West Africa, where groundnuts (or peanuts as we call them) grow in profusion. The cook would buy fresh peanut paste from the market to make groundnut stew, which was a popular Sunday lunch dish — served with ice-cold beer and garnished with fried bananas. Due to the slave trade, groundnut stews spread to the West Indies, becoming an integral part of the local cuisine.

Recipes for groundnut stew vary enormously, some using beef, others chicken, turkey or rabbit. Some recipes use only peanut butter, others like this one, a combination of whole peanuts and peanut butter, which is more authentic. If you like, you can toast or roast the peanuts after shelling, for a darker colour.

STUFFED TURKEY LEGS

2.00	459 cals

Serves 6

2 turkey legs (drumsticks), at least 900 g (2 lb) total weight

225 g (8 oz) pork sausagemeat

15 ml (1 tbsp) chopped fresh tarragon or 2.5 ml ($\frac{1}{2}$ tsp) dried tarragon

10 ml (2 tsp) chopped fresh parsley

salt and freshly ground pepper

50 g (2 oz) button mushrooms, sliced

25 g (1 oz) flour

1 egg white, beaten

175 g (6 oz) fresh white breadcrumbs

100 g (4 oz) butter or margarine, softened

15 ml (1 tbsp) French mustard

watercress, to garnish

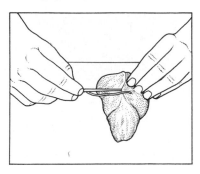

3 Reshape the stuffed turkey legs, then sew them up neatly, using fine string.

4 Dip the legs in flour, brush with beaten egg white and place seam side down in a greased roasting tin.

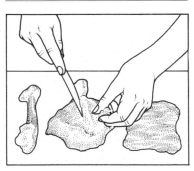

1 Skin the turkey legs, slit the flesh and carefully ease out the bone and large sinews.

2 Mix the sausagemeat, herbs and seasoning, and spread one quarter of the mixture over each boned leg. Cover with a layer of sliced mushrooms, then top with more sausagemeat stuffing.

5 Beat together the breadcrumbs, butter and mustard. Spread over the tops and sides only of the legs.

6 Bake in the oven at 190°C • (375°F) mark 5 for about 1 hour 40 minutes, until tender with a crisp, golden crust. Remove the string, slice, and serve with gravy made from the pan juices. Garnish with a sprig of watercress.

Menu Suggestion

Serve these roasted turkey legs sliced, as an unusual alternative to the traditional Sunday roast, with vegetables, roast potatoes and gravy made from the turkey's cooking juices.

TURKEY SAUTÉ WITH LEMON AND WALNUTS

| 0.20 | 383 cals |

Serves 4

450 g (1 lb) turkey breast steaks
30 ml (2 tbsp) cornflour
1 green pepper
30 ml (2 tbsp) vegetable oil
40 g (1½ oz) walnut halves or pieces
25 g (1 oz) butter or margarine
60 ml (4 tbsp) chicken stock
30 ml (2 tbsp) lemon juice
45 ml (3 tbsp) lemon marmalade
5 ml (1 tsp) white wine vinegar
1.25 ml (¼ tsp) soy sauce
salt and freshly ground pepper

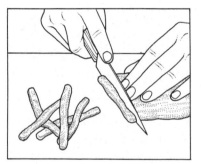

1 Cut up the turkey flesh into 5-cm (2-inch) pencil thin strips. Toss in the cornflour.

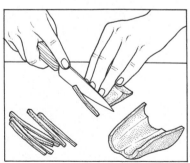

2 Slice the green pepper into fine strips, discarding the core and all the seeds.

3 Heat the oil in a large sauté or deep frying pan, add the walnuts and pepper strips and fry for 2–3 minutes. Remove from the pan with a slotted spoon.

4 Melt the fat in the residual oil and fry the turkey strips for 10 minutes until golden. Stir in the stock and lemon juice, stirring well to remove any sediment at the bottom of the pan. Add the lemon marmalade, vinegar, soy sauce and some salt and pepper.

5 Return the walnuts and green pepper to the pan. Cook gently for a further 5 minutes, until the turkey is tender. Taste and adjust seasoning and serve immediately.

Menu Suggestion

The subtle sweetness of this simple-to-make sauté dish gives it a most unusual flavour. Serve with a plain accompaniment such as boiled rice or Chinese egg noodles, so your guests can appreciate its flavour to the full.

TURKEY SAUTÉ

The French word sauté (literally 'to jump') has been adopted into the English language, and this method of quick cooking is now very popular.

Whatever food you choose to cook, the principles of sautéing are always the same—the meat is cut into fairly small pieces and tossed quickly in hot fat or oil. It is then cooked for the minimum amount of time with the other chosen ingredients and a dash of liquid to moisten the pan until the food is just tender. The whole process is easy, and it's a conveniently quick and tasty way of cooking.

TURKEY STROGANOFF

| 0.15 | 🖙 | 310 cals |

Serves 4

450 g (1 lb) turkey fillet

15 ml (1 tbsp) vegetable oil

50 g (2 oz) butter

30 ml (2 tbsp) brandy

1 garlic clove, skinned and crushed

salt and freshly ground pepper

225 g (8 oz) button mushrooms, sliced

1 green pepper, cored, seeded and sliced

60 ml (4 tbsp) soured cream

1 Slice the piece of turkey fillet into pencil-thin strips, using a sharp knife.

2 Heat the oil and butter in a large sauté pan and brown the turkey strips. Remove from the heat. Heat the brandy in a small pan, ignite and pour over the turkey. Return to the heat then add the garlic and seasoning.

3 Cover the pan and simmer for about 4–5 minutes or until the turkey is just tender.

4 Increase the heat, add the mushrooms and pepper and cook for 3–4 minutes, turning occasionally, until just softened.

5 Reduce the heat, stir in the soured cream, taste and adjust seasoning. Serve immediately.

Menu Suggestion
Serve on a bed of boiled white rice or buttered noodles, with a crisp green salad to follow.

TURKEY AND BACON KEBABS

| 0.45* | ✳* | 551 cals |

* plus at least 4 hours marinating; freeze in the marinade

Serves 4

30 ml (2 tbsp) cranberry sauce

90 ml (6 tbsp) vegetable oil

45 ml (3 tbsp) freshly squeezed orange juice

1 garlic clove, skinned and crushed

2.5 ml ($\frac{1}{2}$ tsp) ground allspice

salt and freshly ground pepper

700 g (1$\frac{1}{2}$ lb) boneless turkey escalopes

1 small onion, skinned

1 large red pepper, cored, seeded and cut into chunks

6 streaky bacon rashers, rinded and halved

1 Put the cranberry sauce, oil and orange juice in a shallow dish with the garlic, allspice and seasoning to taste. Whisk with a fork until well combined.

2 Cut the turkey into bite-sized pieces and place in the dish. Stir to coat in the oil and orange juice mixture, then cover and leave to marinate for at least 4 hours. Stir the meat in the marinade occasionally during this time.

3 When ready to cook, cut the onion into squares or even-sized chunks.

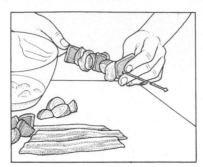

4 Thread the turkey, onion and red pepper on to oiled skewers with the bacon, dividing the ingredients as evenly as possible.

5 Grill under a preheated moderate grill for about 20 minutes, turning the skewers frequently and basting with the remaining marinade. Serve hot.

Menu Suggestion

Make a quick, hot sauce to pour over the kebabs by heating together bottled cranberry sauce with orange juice to taste. Serve on a bed of saffron rice with a chicory, orange and walnut salad tossed in a sharp oil and vinegar dressing.

TURKEY AND BACON KEBABS

Turkey is lean and flavoursome, but it has little natural fat, so it can be dry if not prepared and cooked in the correct way. The marinade of oil and orange juice in this recipe is an excellent way of adding moisture to the flesh, and the acid content of the orange helps break down any tough connective tissue. Don't be tempted to omit the marinating time if you are in a hurry; the longer the turkey is marinated the better. If it is more convenient, the turkey can be marinated in the refrigerator overnight, but allow it to come to room temperature before grilling.

ROAST DUCK WITH APPLE STUFFING

2.30–3.00*	610 cals

* plus 15 minutes cooling

Serves 4

15 g (½ oz) butter
1 celery stick, trimmed and finely chopped
2 small onions, skinned and chopped
100 g (4 oz) fresh white breadcrumbs
1 small eating apple, peeled, cored and grated
15 ml (1 tbsp) chopped fresh sage or 5 ml (1 tsp) dried
salt and freshly ground pepper
1 egg, beaten
2 kg (4 lb) oven-ready duck (with giblets)
1 bay leaf
15 ml (1 tbsp) plain flour
watercress, to garnish

1 Melt the butter in a saucepan, add the celery and half of the chopped onions and fry gently until soft but not brown.

2 Put the breadcrumbs, apple and sage into a bowl and add the softened celery and onion. Mix very well together, add salt and pepper to taste, then bind with the beaten egg. Cool for 15 minutes.

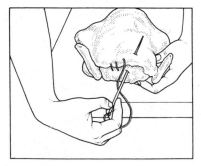

3 Stuff the neck cavity of the duck with this mixture, then sew or truss it together to keep in the stuffing. (If there is too much stuffing for the duck, make the rest into small balls.)

4 Weigh the stuffed duck and calculate the cooking time, allowing 30–35 minutes per 450 g (1 lb). Put the duck on a wire rack in a roasting tin—duck is very fatty and this stops it cooking in its own fat.

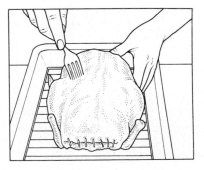

5 Prick the skin of the duck all over to let the fat escape and sprinkle the breast with salt and pepper. Roast in the oven at 180°C (350°F) mark 4 for the calculated cooking time. Cook the stuffing balls in a separate tin on the oven shelf below the duck for the last 30 minutes.

6 While the bird is cooking, make the gravy. Put the giblets in a saucepan with the remaining chopped onion, 600 ml (1 pint) water, the bay leaf and salt and pepper. Simmer for 1 hour; strain.

7 When the duck is cooked, remove from the tin and keep warm in a low oven. Pour off any excess fat from the tin, leaving behind the sediment and about 30 ml (2 tbsp) fat. Transfer to the top of the cooker and blend in the flour. Cook until browned, stirring continuously and scraping any sediment from the bottom of the tin. Slowly stir in the giblet stock and bring to the boil, stirring. Taste and adjust seasoning.

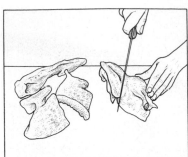

8 To serve, joint the duck into 4 portions, arrange on a warmed serving dish, with the stuffing balls if there are any. Pour the gravy round and garnish with sprigs of watercress. Serve immediately.

Menu Suggestion

Serve roast duck for the Christmas Day meal as an alternative to turkey. It is the traditional bird to serve for a small gathering. The usual trimmings for turkey can be served with duck—roast potatoes, bacon rolls and chipolatas, and Brussels sprouts with chestnuts.

ROAST DUCK WITH APPLE STUFFING

It was the Chinese who first discovered how delicious ducks were to eat, and who first bred the white, or Peking, duck for the table. Now ducks are farmed all over the world, and the duck breeding industry is enormous. Of all the duck breeds, it is the English Aylesbury duck which is the most famous. The Aylesbury duck is believed to be a strain of the original Peking duck, taking its name from the Vale of Aylesbury in Buckinghamshire, where it was originally bred. If you see Aylesbury duckling for sale, then you can be sure of buying a good-quality, meaty bird; the flesh will be tender, and the flavour superb.

PEKING DUCK WITH THIN PANCAKES

4.00* 🥛 🥛   **768 cals**

* plus chilling during the previous day and overnight

Serves 4

2.3 kg (5 lb) duck

4.5 litres (8 pints) boiling water

15 ml (1 tbsp) salt

15 ml (1 tbsp) dry sherry

thin pancakes (see below)

60 ml (4 tbsp) maple-flavoured syrup

100 ml (4 fl oz) hoisin sauce

4 spring onions, cut into 5-cm (2-inch) pieces

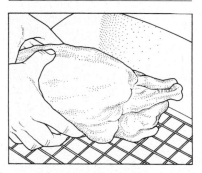

1 Early on the day before serving the duck, rinse the bird and drain on a rack in the sink. Pour the boiling water slowly over the duck until the skin whitens. Drain well.

2 Gently pat dry the skin and body cavity with absorbent kitchen paper. Rub the body cavity with the salt and sherry.

3 Put the duck, breast side down, on a rack in a roasting tin and refrigerate until the evening. Do not cover. Meanwhile, make the thin pancakes.

4 Early that evening, brush the duck all over with maple syrup. Leave on rack, breast side up, and refrigerate uncovered overnight.

5 About 3 hours before serving, put the duck breast down on its rack in the tin, and cook in the oven at 190°C (375°F) mark 5 for 1½ hours. Turn, and cook for 1–1½ hours more until the skin is crisp and golden.

6 To serve, slice the duck thinly into pieces about 5 × 2.5 cm (2 × 1 inch) and arrange on a warmed plate. Put the hoisin sauce in a small bowl and the spring onions on a small plate.

7 Each person assembles their own portion. Put one or two slices of duck in the centre of a pancake, add a dab of hoisin sauce and some spring onion. Roll up, and eat with your hands.

THIN PANCAKES

275 g (10 oz) flour

2.5 ml (½ tsp) salt

225 g (8 fl oz) boiling water

vegetable oil, for brushing

1 Sift the flour and salt into a large bowl. Gradually blend in the boiling water with a fork.

2 Press the dough into a ball, place on a floured surface and knead for about 5 minutes.

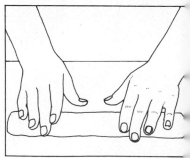

3 Shape the dough into a roll measuring about 40 cm (16 inches) long.

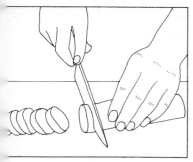

4 Slice crossways into sixteen pieces. Cover with a damp cloth. Take two pieces of dough at a time and put them on a lightly floured surface.

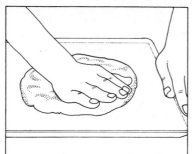

5 Flatten into 10 cm (4-inch) circles. Brush with oil. Place the circles one on top of another, oiled surfaces together. With a lightly floured rolling pin, roll from the centre to form a 20-cm (8-inch) circle.

6 Heat an ungreased frying pan. Add the circle of dough and cook each side for 2–3 minutes or until light brown. Remove to an ovenproof plate and separate the two layers. Stack the pancakes, browned side up, and cover with foil. Repeat to make 16 pancakes.

7 To reheat, put the plate of pancakes over a pan of boiling water and cover with foil. Reduce the heat and simmer until hot.

Menu Suggestion
Serve as part of a Chinese feast — after a first course of soup or pancake rolls and before a stir-fried main course.

CHRISTMAS ROAST GOOSE

2.35	🖐	744 cals

Serves 6

3.2–3.6 kg (7–8 lb) goose
½ lemon
salt and freshly ground pepper
350 g (12 oz) cooking apples, cored and roughly chopped
450 g (1 lb) prunes, soaked, stoned and chopped
25 g (1 oz) butter or margarine
40 g (1½ oz) flour
60 ml (4 tbsp) redcurrant jelly (optional)

For the garnish

175 g (6 oz) sugar
300 ml (½ pint) water
4 even-sized eating apples, peeled, cored and halved
225 g (8 oz) prunes
port, sherry or Madeira
whole blanched almonds (optional)

1 Remove the neck, giblets and fat from the body cavity and reserve the neck and giblets for making the gravy.

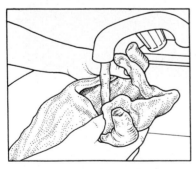

2 Rinse the goose under cold running water (letting the water run through the body cavity). Dry inside and out with absorbent kitchen paper.

3 Rub the cavity inside and out with the lemon and season with salt and pepper. Mix together the chopped apples and prunes and stuff the cavity.

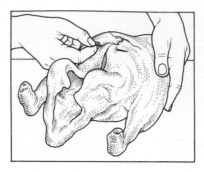

4 Sew or skewer the opening, to contain the stuffing, then weigh the bird.

5 Prick the bird all over with a sharp skewer or fork to let the fat run during cooking. Rub the skin with salt, and place the bird on a trivet or rack in a roasting tin containing 1 cm (½ inch) water. Place the neck and giblets (except the liver) in the water.

6 Roast in the oven at 220°C (425°F) mark 7 for 20 minutes. Cover the breast with greased paper and reduce the heat to 180°C (350°F) mark 4 and roast for 13–15 minutes per 450 g (1 lb). About 20 minutes before the end of the cooking time, uncover the breast and pour off the liquid from the tin. Reserve for gravy.

7 Meanwhile, prepare the garnish. In a shallow pan, dissolve 125 g (4 oz) of the sugar in the water. Boil for 3 minutes, then lower the heat to a gentle simmer. Add the apple halves and simmer for about 10–15 minutes until just tender. Lift out the apples with a slotted spoon and keep warm.

8 In a different saucepan, cover the prunes with water and bring to the boil. Drain, return the prunes to the pan and add the remaining 50 g (2 oz) sugar and enough port, sherry or madeira to cover the prunes. Simmer for 15–20 minutes. Cool for 15 minutes then drain, reserving the wine.

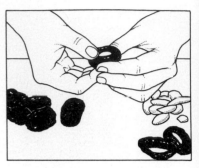

9 Remove the stones from the prunes carefully and, if liked, replace each stone with a blanched almond. Place a prune in each apple hollow and keep warm.

10 Skim the fat off the reserved roasting juices and strain the liquid to remove the neck and giblets. Add enough water to make up to 450 ml (¾ pint) and transfer to a saucepan. Bring to the boil. Cream together the fat and flour and gradually whisk into the liquid. As the butter melts, the gravy will thicken.

11 Simmer for 5 minutes and finally stir in the redcurrant jelly (if using) with the reserved wine. Simmer again for 5 minutes and check seasoning, adding more water if gravy is too thick.

12 Serve the goose surrounded by the stuffed apple halves and hand the gravy separately.

Menu Suggestion
Serve with roast potatoes and Brussels sprouts. A beetroot salad with horseradish dressing would offset the richness of the goose.

RABBIT CASSEROLE WITH CIDER AND MUSTARD

| 2.30 | 445 cals |

Serves 4

50 g (2 oz) butter or margarine

100 g (4 oz) streaky bacon, rinded and diced

12–18 small button onions, skinned

1 rabbit, jointed

25 g (1 oz) plain flour

salt and freshly ground pepper

10 ml (2 tsp) French mustard

300 ml (½ pint) dry cider

450 ml (¾ pint) chicken stock

1 Melt the fat in a frying pan and fry the bacon and onions for 5 minutes until lightly browned. Remove to a casserole with a slotted spoon.

2 Coat the rabbit in a little flour seasoned with salt and pepper and fry in the pan for about 8 minutes until golden brown. Arrange in the casserole.

3 Stir the remaining flour and the French mustard into the pan. Gradually add the cider and stock. Season, bring to the boil and pour over the rabbit.

4 Cover and cook in the oven at 170°C (325°F) mark 3 for about 2 hours or until the rabbit is tender. Adjust the seasoning before serving.

Menu Suggestion

A delicious main course dish for a winter dinner party, Rabbit Casserole with Cider and Mustard tastes good with ribbon noodles tossed in butter and chopped fresh parsley. Finish with a crisp green salad in a vinaigrette dressing.

PIGEON AND CABBAGE CASSEROLE

| 2.00 | 547 cals |

Serves 4

1 green, white or red cabbage, quartered

salt and freshly ground pepper

25 g (1 oz) bacon fat or butter

2–4 pigeons, depending on size

8 chipolatas

2 onions, skinned and chopped

6 streaky bacon rashers, rinded and chopped

2.5 ml ($\frac{1}{2}$ tsp) ground cloves

300 ml ($\frac{1}{2}$ pint) red wine or wine and stock

1 Blanch the cabbage for 5 minutes in boiling salted water. Drain.

2 Melt the bacon fat or butter in a large frying pan and fry the pigeons and chipolatas for about 8 minutes until browned all over. Remove from the pan. Fry the onions in the fat remaining in the pan for 5 minutes until golden. Sprinkle the chopped bacon over the base of a casserole.

3 Shred the cabbage and mix with the onions and ground cloves. Spread half the cabbage mixture over the bacon, season with pepper and place the pigeons and chipolatas on top. Cover with the remaining cabbage, season with more pepper and pour over the wine.

4 Cover and cook in the oven at 170°C (325°F) mark 3 for about 1$\frac{1}{2}$ hours or until the birds are tender. Serve hot.

Menu Suggestion
Simple homely fare, this pigeon casserole is best served with mashed or creamed potatoes and a seasonal vegetable such as carrots or broccoli.

PIGEON AND CABBAGE CASSEROLE

For this recipe, an older pigeon can be used because of the long, slow cooking. Young pigeons and squabs (pigeons under 5 weeks old) are best reserved for roasting and grilling. Although classed as game birds, pigeons do not have a closed season and are therefore available all year round. Wood pigeons, which weigh around 700 g (1$\frac{1}{2}$ lb) each, are the ones to look for in your local poulterer or game dealer, especially in the spring and summer months, when they are said to be at their best. For those who find the flavour of game, rather strong, and their smell too 'high', pigeons are ideal. They are not hung like other game birds and are therefore quite mild in flavour, like poultry.

JUGGED HARE

| 3.30 | ✳ | 469 cals |

Serves 6

1.6 kg (3½ lb) hare, jointed, with its blood

75 ml (5 tbsp) seasoned plain flour

5 ml (1 tsp) red wine vinegar

125 g (4 oz) streaky bacon, rinded and chopped

50 g (2 oz) butter

900 ml (1½ pints) beef stock

150 ml (¼ pint) port

5 ml (1 tsp) dried marjoram

45 ml (3 tbsp) redcurrant jelly

2 onions, skinned

12 whole cloves

salt and freshly ground pepper

parsley sprigs, to garnish

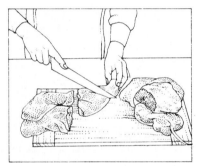

1 Wipe the hare and divide into smaller pieces if necessary. Toss in the seasoned flour.

2 Mix the blood with the vinegar (to keep it fresh), cover and refrigerate until required.

3 Meanwhile, fry the bacon in its own fat in a large flame-proof casserole for about 5 minutes until browned. Remove from the pan. Add the butter to the pan and fry the hare joints for 5 minutes until they are lightly browned.

4 Add the stock, port, marjoram and redcurrant jelly with the onions studded with the cloves. Replace bacon and season well.

5 Bring to the boil, cover and cook in the oven at 170°C (325°F) mark 3 for 3 hours until tender. Remove hare to a serving dish and keep warm. Discard the onions.

6 Mix the blood with some cooking juices until smooth. Add to the pan and heat. Adjust seasoning and pour over hare. Garnish with parsley sprigs.

OLD ENGLISH GAME STEW

| 3.00 | ✳* | 542 cals |

* freeze after step 4

Serves 6

225 g (8 oz) chuck steak
700 g (1½ lb) stewing venison
75 g (3 oz) butter
4 large celery sticks, trimmed and roughly sliced
2 onions, skinned and finely sliced
45 ml (3 tbsp) plain flour
150 ml (¼ pint) port
450 ml (¾ pint) chicken stock
salt and freshly ground pepper

100 g (4 oz) streaky bacon
1 small onion, skinned and finely chopped
125 g (4 oz) fresh white breadcrumbs
1.25 ml (¼ tsp) dried thyme
1 egg, beaten
celery leaves, to garnish

1 Cut the steak and venison into cubes 2.5 cm (1 inch) square, discarding excess fat and sinew.

2 Melt 50 g (2 oz) of the butter in a large flameproof casserole and fry the steak pieces for about 5 minutes until browned. Remove from the pan and drain. Add the venison to the pan and fry for about 8 minutes until browned. Remove from the pan.

3 Add the celery and sliced onions to the pan and lightly brown for about 5 minutes. Stir in the flour, port, stock and seasoning and bring to the boil.

4 Return the steak and venison to the casserole. Cover tightly and cook in the oven at 180°C (350°F) mark 4 for 1½–2 hours or until the meats are almost tender.

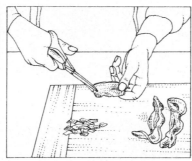

5 Meanwhile make the forcemeat balls. Grill the bacon until crisp and, removing rind, snip into small pieces.

6 Melt the remaining butter in a saucepan and fry the chopped onion for about 5 minutes until golden. Stir into the breadcrumbs together with the bacon, thyme and seasoning.

7 Bind the mixture with beaten egg and shape into 6 even-sized balls.

8 Place them between the meat in the casserole and cover. Increase the oven temperature to 190°C (375°F) mark 5 and return the casserole to the bottom of the oven for a further 30 minutes. Adjust the seasoning and garnish with celery leaves.

Menu Suggestion
Serve this rich stew for a winter dinner party with creamed or jacket baked potatoes and a selection of seasonal vegetables.

GAME PIE

| 2.45 | 🍴 | ✳* | 602–903 cals |

* freeze after stage 5

Serves 4–6

450 g (1 lb) boned game (e.g. pigeon, venison, partridge, hare or pheasant)
30 ml (2 tbsp) plain flour, for coating
10 ml (2 tsp) dried thyme
2.5 ml (½ tsp) ground cinnamon
salt and freshly ground pepper
45 ml (3 tbsp) vegetable oil
300 ml (½ pint) red wine
6 juniper berries, lightly crushed
350 g (12 oz) pork sausagemeat
225 g (8 oz) packet frozen puff pastry, thawed
1 beaten egg, to glaze

1 Cut the meat into even-sized cubes, then toss in the flour mixed with the thyme, cinnamon and seasoning.

2 Heat the oil in a flameproof casserole, add the meat and fry over moderate heat for 5 minutes until browned on all sides. Pour in the wine, add the juniper berries, then cover and simmer gently for 1–1½ hours until tender. Leave until cold, preferably overnight.

3 Put half the sausagemeat in the bottom of an ovenproof pie dish. Put the game mixture on top, then cover with the remaining sausagemeat and level the surface.

4 Roll out the dough on a floured surface and cut a thin strip long enough to go around the rim of the pie dish. Moisten the rim with water, then place the strip on the rim.

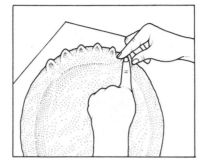

5 Roll out the remaining dough for a lid, moisten the strip of dough, then place the lid on top and press to seal. Knock up and flute the edge, and use pastry trimmings to make decorations for the top of the pie, sticking them on with water.

6 Brush the pastry with beaten egg, then bake in the oven at 200°C (400°F) mark 6 for 30 minutes until golden brown and crisp. Leave to stand for 15 minutes before serving, or serve cold.

GAME

When buying game for a casserole or pie such as this one, it is not necessary to buy young, small birds (these are best reserved for roasting). Ask your dealer for an older bird, which should be less expensive.

Fresh venison is excellent meat for casseroles and pies, since certain cuts such as shoulder benefit from long, slow cooking, and they are not too expensive. It is only in season for a short time, but some supermarkets sell frozen venison out of season which is ready cut up. This—and cubed hare and rabbit (which is not strictly speaking game)—is usually a good buy for pies and casseroles.

All game bought from a licensed dealer will have been hung for the appropriate length of time (to tenderize the flesh and intensify the 'gamey' flavour), so you will not have to worry about this—or plucking and drawing. Carefully remove the raw flesh from the carcass, then cut into bite-sized pieces. You will need approximately 4 pigeons, 2–3 partridges or 1–2 pheasants to obtain 450 g (1 lb) boneless meat for the game pie recipe on this page. Venison can be simply cut up like stewing steak; hare and rabbit joints should be boned and cut up as for chicken portions. If using frozen game, it should be defrosted before cooking—allow a full 24 hours in the refrigerator.

SCALLOPS IN CREAMY BASIL SAUCE

0.25		457 cals

Serves 4

900 g (2 lb) shelled scallops, defrosted if frozen

30 ml (2 tbsp) vegetable oil

15 g ($\frac{1}{2}$ oz) butter

1 small onion, skinned and finely chopped

2 garlic cloves, skinned and crushed

150 ml ($\frac{1}{4}$ pint) dry white wine

20 ml (4 tsp) chopped fresh basil

salt and freshly ground pepper

150 ml (5 fl oz) double cream

few fresh basil sprigs, to garnish

5 Remove the scallops from the liquid with a slotted spoon and set aside on a plate. Boil the liquid until reduced by about half, then stir in the cream a little at a time and simmer until the sauce is thick.

6 Return the scallops to the pan and heat gently. To serve, taste and adjust the seasoning, and serve garnished with basil sprigs.

1 Cut the scallops (including the coral) into fairly thick slices. Pat dry with absorbent kitchen paper and set aside.

2 Heat the oil and butter in a large frying pan, add the onion and garlic and fry gently for 5 minutes until soft and lightly coloured.

3 Add the scallops to the pan and toss to coat in the oil and butter. Stir in the wine, basil and salt and pepper to taste.

4 Fry the scallops over moderate heat for 10 minutes until they are tender, turning them constantly so that they cook evenly on all sides. Do not overcook or they will become tough and rubbery.

SCALLOPS

One of the prettiest of shellfish, fresh scallops are sold in their delicately-coloured, fan-shaped shells. Frozen scallops, now available at high-class fish-mongers, are sold off the shell, but your fishmonger will let you have shells for serving if you ask him. Scald them in boiling water and scrub them before use.

Scallops are amongst the most expensive of shellfish, but their rich creaminess means a small amount goes a long way. The beautiful dark pink coral is considered a great delicacy. If you still feel they are extravagant, use half the quantity specified in this recipe and make up the weight with white button mushrooms.

HADDOCK AND CARAWAY CHEESE SOUFFLÉ

1.20	466 cals

Serves 4

450 g (1 lb) floury potatoes

450 g (1 lb) fresh haddock fillets

100 g (4 oz) button mushrooms, wiped and thinly sliced

300 ml ($\frac{1}{2}$ pint) milk

1 bay leaf

25 g (1 oz) butter

25 g (1 oz) plain flour

2.5 ml ($\frac{1}{2}$ tsp) caraway seeds

125 g (4 oz) mature Cheddar cheese, grated

2 eggs, separated

salt and freshly ground pepper

1 Scrub the potatoes, boil until tender. Drain and peel, then mash three-quarters of the potatoes. Grate the remaining quarter into a bowl and set aside.

2 Meanwhile, place the haddock, mushrooms, milk and bay leaf in a small saucepan. Cover and poach for 15–20 minutes until tender. Drain, reserving milk and mushrooms. Flake fish, discarding skin and bay leaf.

3 Make the sauce. Melt the butter in a pan, stir in the flour and cook gently for 1 minute, stirring. Remove from the heat, add the caraway seeds and gradually stir in the milk. Bring to the boil, stirring, and simmer for 2–3 minutes until thickened and smooth.

4 Stir the mashed potato into the sauce with 75 g (3 oz) cheese, the egg yolks, fish and mushrooms. Season well.

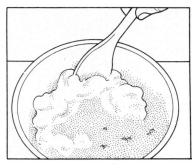

5 Stiffly whisk the egg whites. Fold into the fish mixture. Turn into a 1.6-litre (2$\frac{3}{4}$-pint) buttered soufflé dish.

6 Sprinkle over the reserved grated potato and remaining grated cheese. Bake in the oven at 190°C (375°F) mark 5 for about 1 hour or until just set and golden brown.

TIPS FOR MAKING HOT SOUFFLÉS

- Always make sure to use the exact size of soufflé dish specified in the recipe.
- Check your oven temperature carefully and don't be tempted to bake a soufflé at a different temperature from the one specified.
- Preheat oven and baking sheet to required temperature well before baking.
- Fold egg whites in with a large metal spoon in a figure of eight motion so that the maximum amount of air is incorporated.
- Don't open the oven door during baking.
- Serve *immediately*—have your guests seated at the table well before the soufflé is due to come out of the oven.

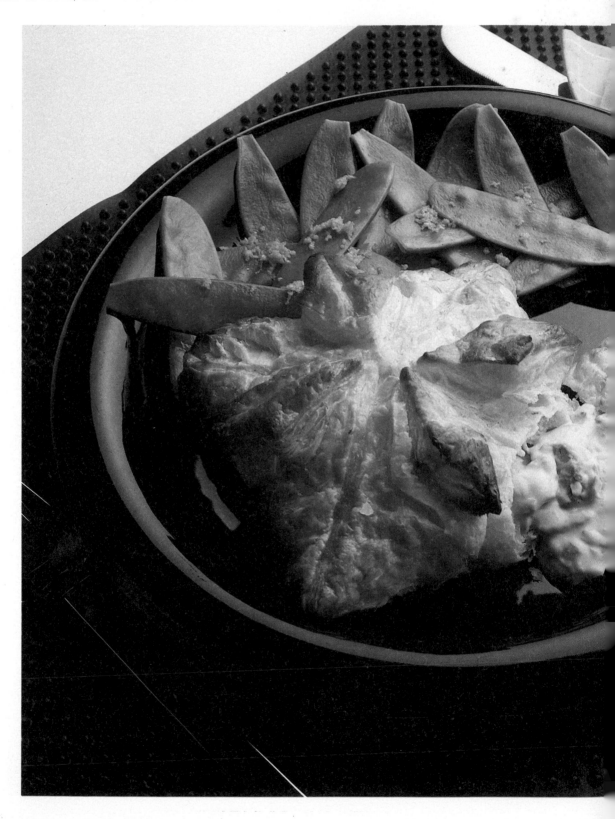

HADDOCK AND MUSHROOM PUFFS

| 0.40* | ✳ | 791 cals |

* plus 30 minutes chilling

Serves 4

397 g (14 oz) packet puff pastry,
  thawed if frozen
450 g (1 lb) haddock fillet, skinned
213 g (7½ oz) can creamed
  mushrooms
5 ml (1 tsp) lemon juice
20 ml (4 tsp) capers, chopped
15 ml (1 tbsp) snipped fresh chives
  or 5 ml (1 tsp) dried
salt and freshly ground pepper
1 egg

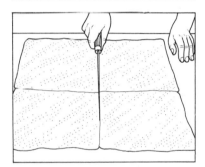

1 Roll out the pastry on a
floured surface into a 40.5 cm
(16 inch) square. Using a sharp
knife, cut into four squares, trim
the edges and reserve the
trimmings of pastry.

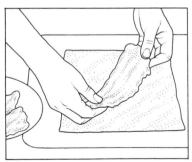

2 Place the squares on dampened
baking sheets. Divide the fish
into four and place diagonally
across the pastry squares.

3 Combine the creamed mushrooms with the lemon juice,
capers, chives and seasoning to
taste. Mix well, then spoon over
the pieces of haddock fillet.

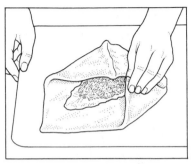

4 Brush the edges of each square
lightly with water. Bring the
four points of each square together
and seal the edges to form an
envelope-shaped parcel.

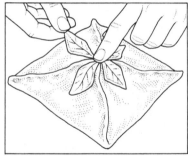

5 Decorate with pastry trimmings and make a small hole
in the centre of each parcel. Chill
in the refrigerator for 30 minutes.

6 Beat the egg with a pinch of
salt and use to glaze the pastry.
Bake in the oven at 220°C (425°F)
mark 7 for about 20 minutes or
until the pastry is golden brown
and well risen. Serve hot.

Menu Suggestion
Serve for a substantial supper dish
with a seasonal green vegetable
such as French beans.

STUFFED PLAICE WITH LEMON SAUCE

| 0.50 | 🍴🍴 | 232 cals |

Serves 4

4 small whole plaice, cleaned

65 g (2½ oz) butter

100 g (4 oz) button mushrooms, finely chopped

100 g (4 oz) white breadcrumbs

90 ml (6 tbsp) chopped parsley

45 ml (3 tbsp) green peppercorns, crushed

finely grated rind and juice of 2 lemons

1.25 ml (¼ tsp) mustard powder

salt and freshly ground pepper

1 egg, beaten

150 ml (¼ pint) dry white wine

25 g (1 oz) plain flour

150 ml (¼ pint) water

60 ml (4 tbsp) single cream

lemon slices and parsley sprigs, to garnish

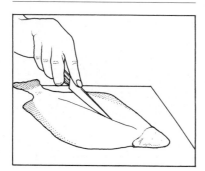

1 With the white skin uppermost, cut down the backbone of each of the four plaice.

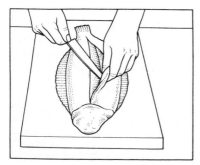

2 Carefully make a pocket on each side of the backbone by easing white flesh from bone.

3 Make the stuffing. Beat 15 g (½ oz) butter until softened then add the mushrooms, breadcrumbs, parsley, 30 ml (2 tbsp) peppercorns, lemon rind, mustard and salt and pepper to taste. Mix well and moisten with the egg and a little of the lemon juice.

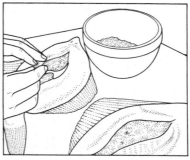

4 Spoon the stuffing carefully into the pockets in the fish. Then place the fish in a single layer in a buttered ovenproof dish. Pour the wine around the fish and cover loosely with foil. Cook in the oven at 190°C (375°F) mark 5 for 30 minutes.

5 Remove the fish from the dish and place on a warmed serving dish. Cover and keep warm in the oven turned to its lowest setting.

6 Make the sauce. Melt the remaining butter in a pan, add flour and stir over low heat for 1–2 minutes. Gradually stir in the fish cooking juices, the water and the remaining lemon juice. Bring to the boil, stirring, then lower the heat and stir in the remaining peppercorns and the cream.

7 To serve, taste and adjust the seasoning, then pour into a warmed sauceboat. Garnish the fish and serve at once, with the sauce handed separately.

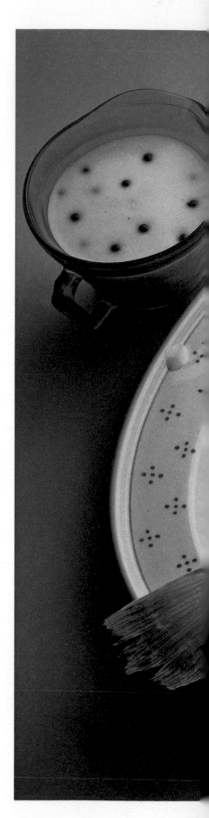

FRICASSÉE OF MONKFISH WITH CORIANDER

0.40	288 cals

Serves 6

700 g (1½ lb) monkfish fillets

450 g (1 lb) halibut cutlets

150 ml (¼ pint) dry vermouth

300 ml (½ pint) water

1 small onion, skinned and sliced

salt and freshly ground pepper

125 g (4 oz) small button
    mushrooms, wiped

40 g (1½ oz) butter

45 ml (3 tbsp) plain flour

30 ml (2 tbsp) chopped fresh
    coriander and sprigs to garnish

60 ml (4 tbsp) single cream

1 Cut the monkfish and halibut
into large, fork-sized pieces,
discarding skin and bone.

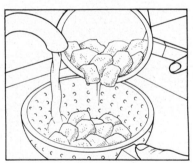

2 Place the fish in a medium
saucepan, cover with cold
water and bring slowly to the boil.
Strain fish in a colander and then
rinse off any scum.

3 Return the fish to the clean
pan and pour over the vermouth with the 300 ml (½ pint)
water. Add the onion with seasoning and bring to the boil. Cover
the pan, reduce heat, and simmer
gently for 8–10 minutes or until
the fish is just tender and beginning to flake.

4 Add the mushrooms after 6
minutes of the cooking time.
Strain off the cooking liquor and
reserve for the sauce.

5 Melt the butter in a separate
saucepan and stir in the flour
followed by the cooking liquor.
Bring slowly to the boil, stirring
all the time, and bubble for 2
minutes until thickened and
smooth.

6 Stir in the coriander, cream,
mushrooms, onion and fish
and adjust seasoning. Warm
through gently, being careful not
to break up the fish. Serve hot,
garnished with sprigs of coriander.

MONKFISH

Most good fishmongers stock
monkfish nowadays, although it
hasn't always been a popular fish
because of its ugly appearance
when whole. For this reason it is
almost always displayed without
the head, which is its ugliest part,
and many fishmongers also skin
and fillet it before offering it for
sale. Monkfish fillets and steaks
taste very like lobster and scampi,
however, at a fraction of the
price.

Monkfish has always been
popular in Mediterranean countries, particularly Spain where it
is called *rape* and France where
it is known as *lotte de mer* or
baudroie. The Spanish like to
serve it cold in the same way as
lobster, or hot with potatoes and
tomatoes; the French braise it in
white wine or serve it *en bro-
chette* (on skewers).

SEAFOOD SAFFRON RISOTTO

0.45		488–732 cals

Serves 4–6

good pinch of saffron strands

150 ml ($\frac{1}{4}$ pint) boiling water

45 ml (3 tbsp) olive oil

30 ml (2 tbsp) butter or margarine

1 onion, skinned and chopped

2 garlic cloves, skinned and crushed

$\frac{1}{2}$ green pepper, finely chopped

$\frac{1}{2}$ red pepper, finely chopped

400 g (14 oz) Italian risotto rice

about 600 ml (1 pint) hot fish or chicken stock

120 ml (8 tbsp) dry white wine

1 bay leaf

salt and freshly ground pepper

350–450 g ($\frac{3}{4}$–1 lb) frozen shelled scampi or jumbo prawns, thawed and thoroughly drained and dried

24 cooked mussels, shelled

a few mussels in shells, to garnish

freshly grated Parmesan cheese, to serve

1 Prepare the saffron water. Soak the saffron strands in the 150 ml ($\frac{1}{4}$ pint) boiling water for at least 30 minutes.

2 Meanwhile, heat the oil and half the butter in a heavy-based pan, add the onion, garlic and peppers and fry gently for 5 minutes until soft.

3 Add the rice and stir until coated in the oil and butter. Pour in a few spoonfuls of the stock and the wine, then add the saffron liquid.

4 Add the bay leaf and salt and pepper to taste and simmer gently, stirring frequently, until all the liquid is absorbed by the rice.

5 Add a few more spoonfuls of stock and simmer again until it is absorbed. Continue adding stock in this way for about 15 minutes, stirring frequently until the rice is *al dente* (tender but firm to the bite).

6 Melt the remaining butter in a separate pan, add the scampi and toss gently for about 5 minutes until they change colour.

7 Remove the bay leaf from the risotto, then stir in the scampi and juices and the mussels. Warm through, taste and adjust seasoning. Turn into a warmed serving dish. Top with whole mussels and serve at once with grated Parmesan cheese handed separately.

HOW TO MAKE AN AUTHENTIC RISOTTO

An Italian risotto is quite unlike any other rice dish in consistency —it is creamy and moist (the Italians call this *all'onda*) and the grains of rice tend to stick together unlike the fluffy individual grains of an Indian pilau, for example. The reasons for this are the type of rice used, and the method of incorporating the liquid, both of which are incredibly important if the risotto is to look and taste authentic.

Italian risotto rice has a rounded grain (but not so rounded as pudding rice); it is available in supermarkets in boxes labelled 'Italian risotto rice', but the best risotto rice to buy are *avorio* and *arborio*, both of which are available loose at Italian delicatessens.

When making a risotto, follow the instructions in the method carefully, adding the liquid a little at a time as in this recipe. The rice should absorb each amount of liquid before you add the next, therefore it is really a case of standing over it and stirring and adding liquid almost constantly until the correct consistency is obtained. Don't worry if you do not need to add all the liquid specified in a recipe—this will depend on the type of rice used, the quantity of other ingredients and the cooking temperature.

In Italy, risotto is always served on its own before the main course of fish or meat, but it can of course be served as a meal in itself, accompanied by fresh crusty bread, a salad and a bottle of chilled white wine—a dry Soave or Frascati would go well with the seafood in this risotto.

TARRAGON STUFFED TROUT

1.30		320 cals

Serves 6

25 g (1 oz) long-grain rice

100 g (4 oz) peeled prawns

225 g (8 oz) button mushrooms, wiped

100 g (4 oz) onion, skinned

50 g (2 oz) butter

5 ml (1 tsp) chopped fresh tarragon or 1.25 ml (¼ tsp) dried

salt and freshly ground pepper

30 ml (2 tbsp) lemon juice

6 whole trout, about 225 g (8 oz) each, cleaned

tarragon sprigs, to garnish

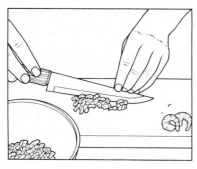

1 Make the stuffing. Cut up each of the peeled prawns into two or three pieces. Boil the rice until tender; drain.

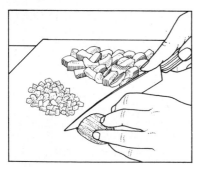

2 Roughly chop the mushrooms and finely chop the onion. Melt the butter in a large frying pan, add the onion and fry for 5 minutes until golden brown.

3 Add the mushrooms with the tarragon and seasoning and cook over high heat for 5–10 minutes until all excess moisture has evaporated. Cool for about 30 minutes.

4 Mix the prawns, rice, lemon juice and mushroom mixture together and season with salt and freshly ground pepper to taste.

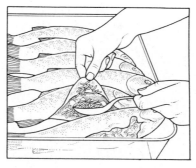

5 Place the fish side by side in a lightly buttered oven-proof dish and stuff with the mixture. Cover and cook in the oven at 180°C (350°F) mark 4 for about 30 minutes. To serve, garnish the fish with sprigs of tarragon.

TYPES OF TROUT

When buying the fish for this recipe, choose between salmon trout and rainbow trout—both are available in suitable sizes for stuffing, although salmon trout can be as large as true salmon, so check carefully with your fishmonger first. Both are members of the salmon family, although the salmon trout, also called the sea trout because it spends the major part of its life at sea, is the closest to the salmon or 'king of the river'.

Fresh salmon trout are in season from early to mid summer, but frozen fish can be bought at other times of year. The flesh of salmon trout is a pretty, delicate shade of pink when cooked—similar to that of true salmon. Because it is less expensive than salmon it is a popular substitute in recipes calling for salmon.

For this recipe, rainbow trout is ideal. A freshwater fish, rainbow trout is now reared in large quantities on trout farms, and so is available all year round—fresh at fishmongers, chilled or frozen from supermarkets.

It is easily recognisable by its attractive silver skin and the shimmer of pink running down the centre of the fish from head to tail. The flesh of rainbow trout is pale and creamy in colour when cooked, the texture is soft and smooth, and the flavour very delicate.

Other kinds of trout which can be used for this recipe include grilse (a salmon which has only spent one year at sea before returning to spawn in fresh water) or brown or red trout.

SEAFOOD CURRY

0.30	361 cals

Serves 4

1 fresh green chilli

45 ml (3 tbsp) vegetable oil

2 onions, skinned and sliced into rings

25 g (1 oz) desiccated coconut

15 ml (1 tbsp) plain flour

5 ml (1 tsp) ground coriander

450 g (1 lb) fresh haddock fillet, skinned and cut into chunks

150 ml (¼ pint) white wine

25 g (1 oz) salted peanuts

125 g (4 oz) frozen prawns, thawed, drained and thoroughly dried

salt and freshly ground pepper

coriander sprigs and shredded coconut, toasted, to garnish

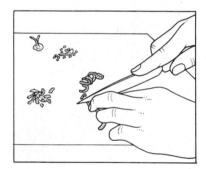

1 Halve the chilli, remove seeds and finely chop the flesh. Heat the oil in a large sauté pan, and brown the onion rings.

2 Mix coconut, flour and coriander and toss with the haddock and chopped chilli. Add to pan and fry gently for 5–10 minutes until golden, stirring.

3 Pour in wine, bring to boil and add peanuts, prawns and seasoning. Cover tightly and simmer for 5–10 minutes or until fish is tender. To serve, garnish with coriander and coconut.

Skate with Capers and Black Butter

| 0.20 | 290 cals |

Serves 4

700–900 g (1½–2 lb) wing of skate

salt

50 g (2 oz) butter

15 ml (1 tbsp) white wine vinegar

10 ml (2 tsp) capers

10 ml (2 tsp) chopped fresh parsley,
   to garnish

1 Simmer the fish in salted
water for 10–15 minutes until
tender, drain and keep warm.

2 Heat the butter in a pan until
lightly browned. Add the
vinegar and capers, cook for a
further 2–3 minutes and pour it
over the fish. Serve at once, garnished with the parsley.

SPECIAL PARSLEY FISH PIE

1.00	683 cals

Serves 4

450 g (1 lb) haddock fillets

300 ml ($\frac{1}{2}$ pint) milk, plus 90 ml (6 tbsp)

1 bay leaf

6 peppercorns

1 onion, skinned and sliced

salt

65 g (2$\frac{1}{2}$ oz) butter or margarine

45 ml (3 tbsp) plain flour

freshly ground pepper

2 eggs, hard-boiled and chopped

150 ml (5 fl oz) single cream

30 ml (2 tbsp) chopped fresh parsley

100 g (4 oz) cooked prawns

900 g (2 lb) potatoes, peeled

1 egg, beaten, to glaze

1 Rinse and drain the fish. Place in a pan and pour over 300 ml ($\frac{1}{2}$ pint) of milk; add the bay leaf, peppercorns, onion and a pinch of salt. Bring to the boil and simmer for 10 minutes until just tender.

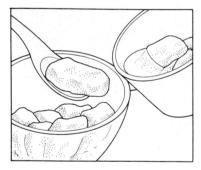

2 Lift from the pan, flake the flesh and remove the skin and bones. Strain the cooking liquid and reserve.

3 Make the sauce. Melt 40 g (1$\frac{1}{2}$ oz) of the butter in a pan, stir in the flour and cook gently for 1 minute, stirring. Remove the pan from the heat and gradually stir in the reserved cooking liquid. Bring to the boil, stirring, until sauce thickens, then cook for a further 2–3 minutes. Season to taste.

4 Add the eggs to the sauce with the fresh cream, fish, parsley and prawns. Check the seasoning, and spoon the mixture into a 1.1-litre (2-pint) pie dish.

5 Meanwhile, boil the potatoes, drain and mash without any liquid. Heat the remaining 90 ml (6 tbsp) of milk and remaining 25 g (1 oz) butter and beat into the potatoes; season.

6 Spoon the potatoes into a piping bag and pipe across the fish mixture. Alternatively, spoon the potato over the fish and roughen the surface with a fork.

7 Bake in the oven at 200°C (400°F) mark 6 for 10–15 minutes, until the potato is set. Brush the beaten egg over the pie. Return to oven for a further 15 minutes, until golden brown.

ITALIAN FISH STEW

1.00	🍴	481 cals

Serves 4

good pinch of saffron strands

about 900 g (2 lb) mixed fish fillets (e.g. red mullet, bream, bass, brill, monkfish, plaice or cod)

10–12 whole prawns, cooked

60 ml (4 tbsp) olive oil

1 large onion, skinned and finely chopped

3 garlic cloves, skinned and crushed

2 slices of drained canned pimiento, sliced

450 g (1 lb) tomatoes, skinned, seeded and chopped

2 canned anchovy fillets, drained

150 ml ($\frac{1}{4}$ pint) dry white wine

150 ml ($\frac{1}{4}$ pint) water

2 bay leaves

45 ml (3 tbsp) chopped fresh basil

salt and freshly ground pepper

10–12 mussels, in their shells

4 slices of hot toast, to serve

1 Prepare the saffron water. Soak the saffron strands in a little boiling water for 30 minutes.

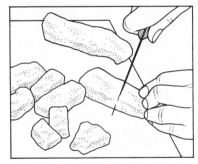

2 Meanwhile, skin the fish and cut into chunky bite-sized pieces. Shell the prawns.

3 Heat the oil in a large heavy-based pan, add the onion, garlic and pimiento and fry gently for 5 minutes until soft.

4 Add the tomatoes and anchovies and stir with a wooden spoon to break them up. Pour in the wine and the water and bring to the boil, then lower the heat and add the bay leaves and half the basil. Simmer uncovered for 20 minutes, stirring occasionally.

5 Add the firm fish to the tomato mixture, then strain in the saffron water and add salt and pepper to taste. Cook for 10 minutes, then add the delicate-textured fish and cook for a further 5 minutes or until tender.

6 Add the prawns and mussels and cook, covered, for 5 minutes or until the mussels open. Remove the bay leaves and discard.

7 To serve, put one slice of toast in each of four individual soup bowls. Spoon over the soup, sprinkle with the remaining basil and serve at once.

ITALIAN FISH STEW

This type of fish stew is popular in coastal regions, especially in the regions around the Adriatic Sea and in the southern part of Italy around Sicily.

There are numerous different versions of fish stew or soup, called *zuppa di pesce* in Italian, with recipes varying from one village and one cook to another—there are no hard and fast rules. *Burrida* is the famous fish and tomato stew from Genoa; it contains many unusual fish which are not available outside local waters, but it can be made successfully outside the region with monkfish, octopus and squid, together with clams, mussels and shrimps.

Around the Adriatic Sea, fish soup is called *brodetto*—the ones from Venice, Rimini and Ravenna being the most famous. These fish soups use similar fish to the Genoese *burrida*, but they do not contain tomatoes and they are traditionally served with bread fried or baked in oil—called *casada*. Another well-known Italian fish soup is *caciuccio Livornese*, a main course dish flavoured strongly with tomatoes and hot red peppers, and served with *casada*.

Don't worry if you can't find the authentic fish when making an Italian fish stew or soup. The recipe on this page suggests substitutes which are readily available outside Italy and which will taste equally good—as long as you use a good variety and make sure they are as fresh as possible. Try to include at least some red or grey mullet; monkfish is also a good buy—it has a strong flavour and dense texture, and does not break up easily during cooking.

SPANISH COD WITH PEPPERS, TOMATOES AND GARLIC

1.30		324 cals

Serves 4

700 g (1½ lb) cod fillets

1.1 litres (1¾ pints) mussels or about 450 g (1 lb) weight

30 ml (2 tbsp) vegetable oil

2 onions, skinned and sliced

1 red pepper, cored, seeded and sliced

1 green pepper, cored, seeded and sliced

1–2 garlic cloves, skinned and crushed

450 g (1 lb) tomatoes, skinned and chopped

300 ml (½ pint) white wine

2.5 ml (½ tsp) Tabasco sauce

1 bay leaf

salt and freshly ground pepper

1 Using a sharp knife, skin the cod and cut it into chunks.

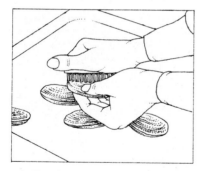

2 Scrub the mussels, discarding any which are open. Place in a pan, cover and cook over a high heat for about 8 minutes or until mussels have opened.

3 Shell all but four mussels. Heat the oil in a frying pan and cook the onions, peppers and garlic for about 5 minutes until starting to soften. Add the tomatoes and wine, bring to the boil and simmer for 5 minutes, then add the Tabasco.

4 Layer the fish and vegetables in a casserole and add the bay leaf and seasoning. Pour over the wine. Push the four mussels in shells into the top layer. Cover and cook in the oven at 180°C (350°F) mark 4 for 1 hour. Serve hot.

Menu Suggestion
Serve with hot French bread, followed by a crisp green salad tossed in an olive oil and lemon juice dressing.

SPANISH COD WITH PEPPERS, TOMATOES AND GARLIC

As soon as you get fresh mussels home from the fishmonger, immerse them in a bowl of cold water until you are ready to start dealing with them. If you add 15 ml (1 tbsp) oatmeal to the water, the live mussels will feed on it and this will help 'flush them out' so that you can be sure they are thoroughly clean inside. If the water becomes very murky during this time, replace it with fresh water and more oatmeal. Before preparation in step 2 of the recipe, tap any open mussels against the bowl or work surface—if they do not close they should be thrown away.

CREAMY FISH CASSEROLE

1.30	379–569 cals

Serves 4–6

700 g (1½ lb) cod steaks, skinned and cut into bite-sized pieces

30 ml (2 tbsp) plain flour

salt and freshly ground pepper

40 g (1½ oz) butter

15 ml (1 tbsp) vegetable oil

600 ml (1 pint) dry cider

2 bay leaves, crumbled

900 g (2 lb) old floury potatoes, scrubbed

150 ml (5 fl oz) single cream

30 ml (2 tbsp) chopped fresh parsley

1 Coat the pieces of cod in the flour seasoned with salt and pepper to taste.

2 Melt 25 g (1 oz) of the butter with the oil in a frying pan, add the pieces of cod and fry gently until golden on all sides. Remove from the pan with a slotted spoon and set aside.

3 Pour the cider into the frying pan and stir to dislodge the sediment from the bottom and sides of the pan. Add the bay leaves and salt and pepper to taste. Bring to the boil and simmer for a few minutes, then pour into a jug.

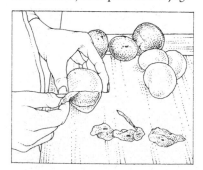

4 Blanch the potatoes in their skins in boiling salted water for 10 minutes. Drain, leave until cool enough to handle, then peel off the skins and slice.

5 Put half the fish in the bottom of a shallow casserole. Stir the cream into the cider mixture, then pour half over the fish.

6 Cover with half the potato slices, overlapping them so that they cover the fish completely. Sprinkle with half the parsley. Put the remaining fish on top of the potatoes, then pour over the remaining cider and cream.

7 Cover with the remaining potato slices as before, then dot with the remaining butter. Cook in the oven at 190°C (375°F) mark 5 for 45 minutes. Sprinkle the remaining parsley over the top before serving.

Menu Suggestion

Serve for a family supper accompanied by a seasonal green vegetable such as courgettes or French beans. Ice-cold dry cider is the ideal drink with this casserole.

SMOKED HADDOCK WITH CREAM AND PERNOD

| 0.40 | 382 cals |

Serves 4

4 smoked haddock fillets, about 700 g (1½ lb) total weight

300 ml (½ pint) milk

few slices of onion

2 bay leaves

few black peppercorns

2.5 ml (½ tsp) crushed fennel seeds

150 ml (5 fl oz) double cream

15 g (½ oz) butter

60 ml (4 tbsp) Pernod

salt and freshly ground pepper

fennel sprigs, to garnish

1 Put the smoked haddock fillets in a large flameproof casserole. Pour in the milk and add the onion slices, bay leaves, peppercorns and fennel seeds. Pour in a little water if the liquid does not completely cover the smoked haddock.

2 Bring slowly to boiling point, then lower the heat, cover and simmer gently for 15 minutes or until the fish flakes easily when tested with a fork.

3 Remove the fish fillets from the cooking liquid and then flake into chunky pieces. Discard all skin and any bones.

4 Strain the cooking liquid and return to the rinsed-out pan. Boil to reduce slightly, then add the cream, butter and Pernod and boil again until the sauce thickens.

5 Return the fish to the liquid and heat through. Add salt and pepper to taste (taking care not to add too much salt as the fish is salty), then transfer to a warmed serving dish. Garnish with fennel sprigs and serve immediately.

Menu Suggestion

A rich and filling dinner party main course, best served with a plain accompaniment such as boiled rice or duchesse potatoes. If liked, the quantities may be halved and the dish served as a first course, with hot French bread.

SMOKED HADDOCK WITH CREAM AND PERNOD

As a starter this dish is most unusual, with its subtle flavouring of fennel and aniseed. Serve it for a special dinner party when you want to surprise your guests with something just that little bit different, but be sure to serve something quite plain as the main course.

The choice of smoked haddock at the fishmonger can sometimes be confusing. The bright yellow fish sold as 'golden cutlets' is in fact smoked cod. Thicker than smoked haddock, it is an excellent fish for dishes like this one where the fish needs to be flaked into chunky pieces.

INDONESIAN FISH CURRY

0.40	287 cals

Serves 4

1 small onion, skinned and
    chopped

1 garlic clove, skinned and chopped

2.5 cm (1 inch) piece fresh root
    ginger, skinned and chopped

5 ml (1 tsp) ground turmeric

2.5 ml ($\frac{1}{2}$ tsp) laos powder (see box)

1.25 ml ($\frac{1}{4}$ tsp) chilli powder

30 ml (2 tbsp) vegetable oil

salt

700 g (1$\frac{1}{2}$ lb) haddock fillets, skinned
    and cut into bite-sized pieces

225 g (8 oz) peeled prawns

300 ml ($\frac{1}{2}$ pint) coconut milk (see
    box)

juice of 1 lime

shredded coconut and lime
    wedges, to garnish

1 Work the first seven ingredients in an electric blender or
processor with 2.5 ml ($\frac{1}{2}$ tsp) salt.

2 Transfer the mixture to a
flameproof casserole and fry
gently, stirring, for 5 minutes.
Add the haddock pieces and
prawns and fry for a few minutes
more, tossing fish to coat with the
spice mixture.

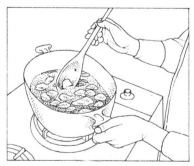

3 Pour in the coconut milk,
shake the pan and turn the fish
gently in the liquid. (Take care not
to break up the pieces of fish.)
Bring slowly to boiling point, then
lower the heat, cover and simmer
for 10 minutes until tender.

4 Add the lime juice, taste and
adjust seasoning, then transfer
to a warmed serving dish and
sprinkle with coconut. Serve hot,
garnished with lime wedges.

Menu Suggestion
Serve with plain boiled rice,
prawn crackers and lime pickle.

INDONESIAN FISH CURRY
Laos powder is used extensively
in the cooking of Southeast Asia;
it comes from a root rather like
ginger and has a peppery hot
taste. Look for it in specialist
delicatessens in small bottles,
sometimes labelled galangal or
galingale. To make 300 ml
($\frac{1}{2}$ pint) coconut milk, break
100 g (4 oz) block creamed
coconut into a measuring jug,
pour in boiling hot water up to
the 300 ml ($\frac{1}{2}$ pint) mark and stir
to dissolve. Strain before using.

MONKFISH WITH LIME AND PRAWNS

0.45	294 cals

Serves 4

550 g (1¼ lb) monkfish

salt and freshly ground pepper

15 ml (1 tbsp) plain flour

30 ml (2 tbsp) vegetable oil

1 small onion, skinned and
    chopped

1 garlic clove, skinned and chopped

225 g (8 oz) tomatoes, skinned and
    chopped

150 ml (¼ pint) dry white wine

finely grated rind and juice of 1
    lime

pinch of sugar

100 g (4 oz) peeled prawns

lime slices, to garnish

1 Using a sharp knife, skin the
fish, if necessary, then cut fish
into 5 cm (1 inch) chunks and
toss in seasoned flour.

2 Heat the oil in a flameproof
casserole and gently fry the
onion and garlic for 5 minutes.
Add fish and fry until golden.

3 Stir in the tomatoes, wine,
rind and juice of the lime,
sugar and seasoning. Bring to
the boil.

4 Cover and cook in the oven at
180°C (350°F) mark 4 for 15
minutes. Add the prawns and continue to cook for a further 15
minutes until the monkfish is
tender. Garnish with lime slices.

Menu Suggestion
Served in a ring of saffron rice,
this Monkfish Casserole with
Lime and Prawns makes an
exceptionally pretty main course
dish for a dinner party.

TROUT POACHED IN WINE

0.45	357 cals

Serves 4

4 small trout, with heads on

salt and freshly ground pepper

50 g (2 oz) butter

1 large onion, skinned and sliced

2 celery sticks, trimmed and
   sliced

2 carrots, peeled and very thinly
   sliced

300 ml (½ pint) dry white wine

bouquet garni

15 ml (1 tbsp) plain flour

lemon wedges and chopped fresh
   parsley, to garnish

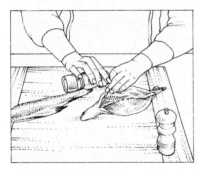

1 Wash the trout under cold
   running water and drain.
Pat dry and season the insides.

2 Melt 25 g (1 oz) of the butter
   in a small saucepan, add the
onion, celery and carrots and stir
well to cover with butter. Cover
and sweat for 5 minutes.

3 Lay the vegetables in a greased
   casserole and arrange the fish
on top. Pour over the wine and
add the bouquet garni.

4 Cover tightly and cook in the
   oven at 180°C (350°F) mark 4
for about 25 minutes until the
trout are cooked.

5 Transfer the trout and vegetables to a warmed serving
dish and keep hot.

6 Pour the cooking juices into a
   small pan, discarding the
bouquet garni. Blend together the
remaining butter and the flour.
Whisk into the sauce and simmer
gently, stirring, until thickened.
Pour into a sauceboat or jug.
Garnish the trout with lemon
wedges and parsley.

Menu Suggestion
Serve with steamed or boiled new
potatoes and a seasonal green
vegetable or salad.

TROUT POACHED IN WINE

If you are unused to buying
whole fresh fish at the fishmonger, you may find the different types of trout confusing. Sea
trout are the larger of the
species, so called because they
have migrated to the sea from
the rivers. Some fishmongers call
them 'salmon trout', because
their flesh is firm and salmony
pink, and they can be used as
an inexpensive alternative to
fresh salmon.

For this recipe you will need
to buy freshwater trout, i.e.
river, rainbow or lake trout,
which are now becoming
increasingly widely available,
both fresh and frozen, at supermarkets. Look for shiny, slippery
skin and bright eyes—both good
indications of freshness.

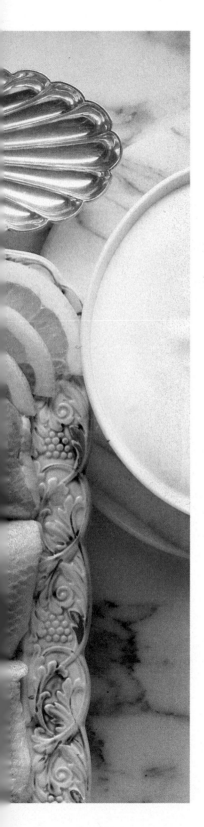

SWEDISH HERRINGS

1.00*	452 cals

* plus 2–3 hours cooling

Serves 4

4 fresh herrings, filleted

salt and freshly ground pepper

4 whole cloves

2 dried chillies

12 peppercorns

1 bay leaf

1 blade of mace

60 ml (4 tbsp) malt vinegar

75 ml (5 tbsp) tarragon vinegar

150 ml ($\frac{1}{4}$ pint) water

1 shallot, skinned and finely chopped

lemon slices, to garnish

142 ml (5 fl oz) soured cream, to serve

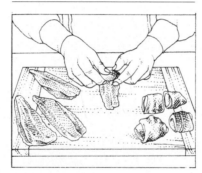

1 Sprinkle the herring fillets with salt and freshly ground pepper and roll up from the head end, skin side outermost.

2 Arrange in a casserole and add the cloves, chillies, peppercorns, bay leaf and mace. Cover with the vinegars and water and sprinkle the shallot on top.

3 Cover and cook in the oven at 170°C (325°F) mark 3 for about 45 minutes or until tender.

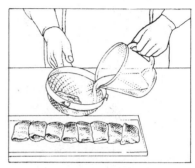

4 Transfer the fish carefully to a serving dish and strain or pour the liquor over. Leave to cool for about 2–3 hours.

5 Garnish the casserole with lemon slices and serve cold with soured cream.

Menu Suggestion

Swedish Herrings make an excellent cold dish for a summer luncheon served with fresh French bread and butter and a selection of salads. Alternatively, halve the quantities given in the recipe and serve for a starter.

SWEDISH HERRINGS

Herrings are inexpensive to buy, yet extremely nutritious. Being oily fish, they are rich in vitamins A and D as well as minerals, and contain almost as much protein as meat. Although they are eaten fresh just as any other oily fish, herrings are immensely popular pickled or soused, especially in northern European and Scandinavian countries where they are a favourite starter. Such herrings are easy to obtain from delicatessens and supermarkets, either loose or in jars (rollmops are a kind of soused herring), but it is so much nicer to make your own using fresh herring fillets as here. For a neat appearance to the finished dish, try to get fillets which are all of an even size and thickness.

SEAFOOD STIR FRY

0.25	288 cals

Serves 4

2 celery sticks, washed and
   trimmed

1 medium carrot, peeled

350 g (12 oz) coley, haddock or cod
   fillet, skinned

350 g (12 oz) Iceberg or Cos lettuce

about 45 ml (3 tbsp) peanut oil

1 garlic clove, skinned and crushed

100 g (4 oz) peeled prawns

425 g (15 oz) can whole baby
   sweetcorn, drained

5 ml (1 tsp) anchovy essence

salt and freshly ground pepper

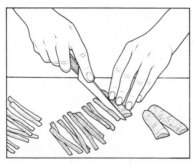

1 Slice the celery and carrot into
   thin matchsticks, 5 cm (2 inch)
long. Cut the fish into 2.5 cm
(1 inch) chunks.

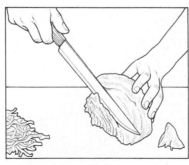

2 Shred the lettuce finely with a
   sharp knife, discarding the
core and any thick stalks.

3 Heat 15 ml (1 tbsp) of the oil
   in a wok or large frying pan
until smoking. Add the lettuce and
fry for about 30 seconds until
lightly cooked. Transfer to a
serving dish with a slotted spoon
and keep warm in a low oven.

4 Heat another 30 ml (2 tbsp) of
   oil in the pan until smoking.
Add the celery, carrot, white fish
and garlic and stir-fry over high
heat for 2–3 minutes, adding
more oil if necessary.

5 Lower the heat, add the
   prawns, baby sweetcorn and
anchovy essence. Toss well
together for 2–3 minutes to heat
through and coat all the ingredients in the sauce (the fish will
flake apart).

6 Add seasoning to taste, spoon
   on top of the lettuce and serve
immediately.

Menu Suggestion
This stir-fried dish has its own
vegetables and therefore needs no
further accompaniment other than
a dish of plain boiled rice.

SEAFOOD STIR FRY

It may seem unusual to stir fry
lettuce, which is usually only
served as a raw salad vegetable,
but it is a method often used in
Chinese cookery. As long as you
use the crisp varieties suggested
here—Iceberg or Cos—you will
find it gives a fresh, crunchy
texture to the dish which
contrasts well with the softness
of the fish. Avoid using round or
cabbage lettuces, which would
become limp on cooking, and
make sure to time the cooking
accurately.

ITALIAN MARINATED TROUT

0.15*	221 cals

* plus at least 8 hours marinating

Serves 4

30 ml (2 tbsp) olive oil

4 whole trout, about 225 g (8 oz) each, cleaned

30 ml (2 tbsp) flour

1 small bulb Florence fennel, trimmed and finely sliced

1 onion, skinned and finely sliced

300 ml ($\frac{1}{2}$ pint) dry white Italian wine

finely grated rind and juice of 1 orange

salt and freshly ground pepper

orange slices and chopped fennel tops, to garnish

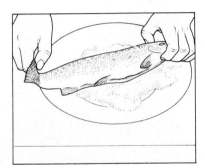

1 Heat the olive oil in a frying pan. Dip the trout in the flour and fry gently for 4 minutes on each side. With a fish slice, transfer the fish to a shallow dish.

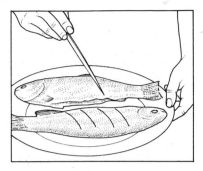

2 With a sharp knife, score the skin diagonally, being careful not to cut too deeply into the flesh. Set aside.

3 Add the fennel and onion to the frying pan and fry for 5 minutes. Add the wine, orange rind and juice, and seasoning to taste. Bring to the boil. Boil rapidly for 1 minute, add the chopped fennel tops and pour immediately over the fish. Cool.

4 Marinate in the refrigerator for at least 8 hours, but no more than 3 days.

5 Serve at room temperature, garnished with orange slices and the chopped fennel tops.

Menu Suggestion

Serve for a cold summer supper party with hot garlic or herb bread and a mixed salad.

ITALIAN MARINATED TROUT

The bulb vegetable Florence fennel looks rather like a squat version of celery with feathery leaves. The flavour of fennel is like aniseed; for the most subtle taste of aniseed, buy white or pale green fennel, for a stronger flavour, choose vegetables which are dark green in colour. In this recipe, fennel is fried with onion and used in a marinade for fish, with which it has a particular affinity. Other more usual uses for fennel are sliced or chopped raw in salads (fennel and tomato are particularly good together), and braised in the oven with stock or a white or cheese sauce. As its name suggests, Florence fennel comes from Italy, where it is used extensively in cooking.

Vegetables

HOT POTATOES WITH DILL

0.35	174 cals

Serves 6

900 g (2 lb) potatoes

salt

4 spring onions, washed and finely chopped

15 ml (1 tbsp) chopped fresh dill and a sprig, to garnish

freshly ground pepper

142 ml (5 fl oz) soured cream

1 Place the potatoes in cold, salted water, bring to the boil and cook for 12–15 minutes until tender.

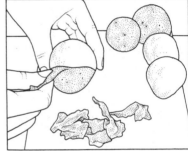

2 Drain the potatoes, leave until just cool enough to handle, then remove the skins.

3 Cut the potatoes into small dice and place in a bowl. Add the chopped onions to the potatoes with the dill and salt and pepper to taste.

4 Thin the soured cream, if necessary, with a little boiling water or milk, stir it into the potatoes and toss gently.

5 Leave to stand for a few minutes so that the flavours can blend. To serve, garnish with a sprig of dill.

HERBY COURGETTE FINGERS WITH CREAM

0.30*	147–196 cals

* plus 1 hour to dégorge

Serves 6–8

900 g (2 lb) small or medium courgettes

salt and freshly ground pepper

50 g (2 oz) butter

1–2 garlic cloves, skinned and crushed

150 ml (¼ pint) vegetable stock or water

20 ml (4 tsp) chopped fresh basil or 10 ml (2 tsp) dried

150 ml (¼ pint) double cream

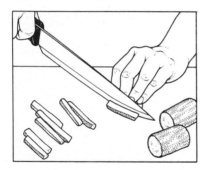

1 Trim the courgettes, then cut them into neat strips about 5 cm (2 inches) long and 0.5 cm (¼ inch) wide.

2 Put the courgette strips in a colander, sprinkling each layer with salt. Cover with a plate, place heavy weights on top and leave to dégorge for 1 hour.

3 Rinse the courgette strips thoroughly under cold running water, then pat dry in a clean tea towel.

4 Melt half of the butter in a heavy-based saucepan, add the courgettes and garlic and toss over moderate heat for a few minutes.

5 Pour in the stock, then add half of the basil with salt and pepper to taste. Cover the pan and simmer gently for 5 minutes or until the courgettes are tender but still with some crunch. Transfer the courgettes to a warmed serving dish with a slotted spoon, cover and keep hot.

6 Increase the heat and boil the liquid to reduce slightly. Add the cream and the remaining butter and basil. Simmer until the sauce is of a coating consistency. Taste and adjust seasoning, then pour over the courgettes. Serve immediately.

Menu Suggestion
Serve this creamy vegetable dish in summer when courgettes are plentiful; it goes especially well with lamb and chicken dishes.

HERBY COURGETTE FINGERS WITH CREAM

Courgettes are members of the same cucurbit family as pumpkins, gourds, marrows, squashes and cucumbers. They are believed to have been eaten originally by the American Indians, who ground down the seeds of gourds rather than eating the flesh. Marrows were known in Roman times, and courgettes were cultivated from them.

It is a good idea to dégorge courgettes before cooking, as in this recipe. They are a watery vegetable, and can dilute sauces such as this creamy one if they are not dégorged beforehand. Older courgettes can also be bitter, another reason for extracting the juice before cooking. Always rinse them thoroughly after dégorging, or the finished dish may be salty.

FRENCH BEANS IN SOURED CREAM WITH PAPRIKA

0.25	141 cals

Serves 4

700 g (1½ lb) French beans

25 g (1 oz) butter or margarine

1 small onion, skinned and chopped

5 ml (1 tsp) paprika

salt and freshly ground pepper

150 ml (¼ pint) chicken stock

142 ml (5 fl oz) soured cream

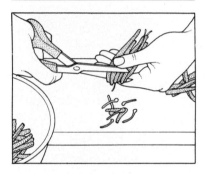

1 Using kitchen scissors, top and tail the French beans and cut them into 2.5-cm (1-inch) lengths. Melt the butter in a pan, add the onion and cook gently for 5 minutes until soft and golden, but do not brown.

2 Stir in 2.5 ml (½ tsp) paprika, beans, seasoning and stock. Bring to the boil, cover and simmer for 5–10 minutes until the French beans are tender.

3 Stir the cream into the pan and reheat without boiling. Turn into a heated serving dish and dust the top with the remaining paprika.

NEW POTATOES WITH TARRAGON CREAM

0.15	204 cals

Serves 4

15 g (½ oz) butter or margarine

4 spring onions, washed, trimmed and chopped

142 ml (5 fl oz) soured cream

salt and freshly ground pepper

3 sprigs of fresh tarragon

700 g (1½ lb) cooked new potatoes, drained and kept hot

1 Melt the butter in a pan, add the onions and cook for 5 minutes until soft. Stir in the cream, seasoning, and two tarragon sprigs and heat without boiling.

2 Add the cooked potatoes to the creamy onion and tarragon mixture in the pan. Reheat gently, do not boil.

3 Turn the potatoes and the sauce into a warm serving dish and serve garnished with a sprig of fresh tarragon.

SPINACH TIMBALE

1.20	257 cals

Serves 6

25 g (1 oz) butter or margarine

1 onion, skinned and finely chopped

900 g (2 lb) fresh spinach, washed, trimmed and roughly chopped

150 ml ($\frac{1}{4}$ pint) milk

150 ml (5 fl oz) single cream

4 eggs

50 g (2 oz) Gruyère cheese, grated

50 g (2 oz) fresh white breadcrumbs

pinch of grated nutmeg

salt and freshly ground pepper

thin tomato strips and fresh coriander, to garnish

tomato sauce, (right)

1 Melt the butter in a saucepan, stir in the onion and cook gently for about 5 minutes until soft. Stir in the spinach and cook for a further 5 minutes until soft, stirring occasionally. Stir in the milk and cream and heat gently.

2 Beat the eggs in a bowl and stir in the spinach mixture, cheese, breadcrumbs, nutmeg and salt and pepper.

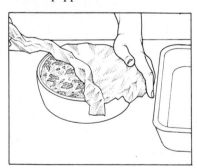

3 Turn the mixture into a greased 1.1-litre (2-pint) ring mould, cover with foil and place the dish in a roasting tin, half filled with hot water. Bake in the oven at 180°C (350°F) mark 4 for 1$\frac{1}{4}$ hours until firm to the touch and a knife, inserted in the centre, comes out clean. Meanwhile, prepare the tomato sauce.

4 Remove the dish from the water and leave for 5 minutes. Loosen the timbale from the sides of the dish with a knife.

5 Turn the timbale out on to a warmed flat serving dish. Garnish with thin tomato strips and coriander. If liked, serve with a tomato sauce.

TIMBALES

The French word *timbale* is used to describe a container, usually silver or gold, which has a handle on either side and is designed for holding drinks. The word has also taken on a broader meaning in culinary terms, however, and is now generally used to describe a dish which is baked and then turned out of its cooking dish – as in this recipe.

TOMATO SAUCE

Makes about 300 ml ($\frac{1}{2}$ pint)

1 small onion, skinned and chopped

1 small carrot, peeled and chopped

25 g (1 oz) butter

25 ml (1$\frac{1}{2}$ tbsp) flour

450 g (1 lb) tomatoes, quartered, or a 397-g (14-oz) can tomatoes, drained

300 ml ($\frac{1}{2}$ pint) chicken stock

1 bay leaf

1 clove

2.5 ml ($\frac{1}{2}$ tsp) sugar

10 ml (2 tsp) tomato purée

15–60 ml (1–4 tbsp) dry white wine (optional)

salt and freshly ground pepper

1 Lightly fry the onion and carrot in the butter for 5 minutes. Stir in the flour and add the tomatoes, stock, bay leaf, clove, sugar, tomato purée, wine, if used, and salt and pepper.

2 Bring to the boil, cover and simmer for 30–45 minutes, or until the vegetables are cooked. Sieve, reheat and adjust seasoning, if necessary.

——— VARIATION ———

NEAPOLITAN TOMATO SAUCE

450 g (1 lb) tomatoes, skinned or a 397-g (14-oz) can tomatoes, drained

1 garlic clove, skinned and crushed

50 ml (2 fl oz) olive oil

2.5 ml ($\frac{1}{2}$ tsp) sugar

3 basil leaves, torn, or 10 ml (2 tsp) chopped fresh parsley, or 5 ml (1 tsp) oregano

salt and freshly ground pepper

Place all the ingredients in a saucepan and simmer, uncovered, stirring occasionally for about 10 minutes until the oil has separated from the tomatoes.

RATATOUILLE

2.05*	✳	252 cals

* includes 30 minutes standing time

Serves 6

450 g (1 lb) aubergines

salt

450 g (1 lb) courgettes

3 red or green peppers

120 ml (8 tbsp) olive oil

450 g (1 lb) onions, skinned and chopped

1 garlic clove, skinned and crushed

450 g (1 lb) tomatoes, skinned, seeded and chopped, or one 397-g (14-oz) can tomatoes, drained

30 ml (2 tbsp) tomato purée

bouquet garni

freshly ground pepper

1 Cut the aubergines into thin slices. Sprinkle liberally with salt and set aside to drain in a sieve or colander for 30 minutes. Rinse under cold running water and pat dry with absorbent kitchen paper.

2 Meanwhile, wash the courgettes and pat dry with absorbent kitchen paper. Top and tail them and then cut into thin slices.

3 Wash the peppers; pat dry with absorbent kitchen paper. Slice off the stems and remove the seeds. Cut into thin rings.

4 Heat the oil in a large saucepan. Add the onions and garlic and cook gently for about 10 minutes until soft and golden.

5 Add the tomatoes and purée and cook for a few more minutes, then add the aubergines, courgettes, peppers, bouquet garni and salt and pepper. Cover and simmer gently for 1 hour. The vegetables should be soft and well mixed but retain their shape and most of the cooking liquid should have evaporated.

6 To reduce the liquid, remove the lid and cook gently for another 20 minutes. Check the seasoning and serve hot or cold.

SUMMER VEGETABLE FRICASSÉE

0.30	114–171 cals

Serves 4–6

4 courgettes, washed and trimmed

225 g (8 oz) French beans, topped and tailed and cut into 5-cm (2-inch) lengths

salt and freshly ground pepper

45 ml (3 tbsp) olive oil

1 onion, skinned and sliced

2 garlic cloves, skinned and crushed

5 ml (1 tsp) crushed coriander seeds

3 peppers (red, yellow, green), cored, seeded and sliced

150 ml ($\frac{1}{4}$ pint) dry white wine

10 ml (2 tsp) tomato purée

2.5 ml ($\frac{1}{2}$ tsp) sugar

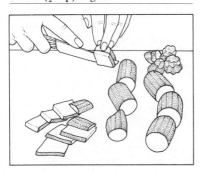

1 Cut the courgettes crossways into thirds, then cut them lengthways into slices about 0.5 cm ($\frac{1}{4}$ inch) thick.

2 Blanch the courgettes and beans in boiling salted water for 5 minutes only. Drain and set aside until required.

3 Heat the oil in a flameproof casserole, add the onion, garlic and coriander seeds and fry gently for 5 minutes until onion is soft.

4 Add the pepper slices and fry gently for a further 5 minutes, stirring constantly. Stir in the wine, tomato purée and sugar, with salt and pepper to taste. Bring to the boil, then simmer for a few minutes, stirring all the time until the liquid begins to reduce.

5 Add the courgettes and beans to the pan and stir gently to combine with the sauce. Heat through, taking care not to overcook the vegetables. Taste and adjust seasoning. Serve hot, straight from the casserole.

CABBAGE WITH CARAWAY

0.15	110 cals

Serves 6

1.4 kg (3 lb) green cabbage

salt

50 g (2 oz) butter or margarine

5 ml (1 tsp) caraway seeds

freshly ground pepper

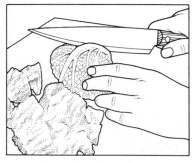

1 Shred the cabbage finely, discarding any core or tough outer leaves. Wash well under cold running water.

2 Cook in a large pan of boiling salted water for 2 minutes only—the cabbage should retain its crispness and texture. Drain well.

3 Melt the butter in the saucepan; add the drained cabbage with the caraway seeds and seasoning. Stir over a moderate heat for 2–3 minutes until the cabbage is really hot. Adjust seasoning and serve immediately.

PEPPERED CARROTS

0.20	157 cals

Serves 4

50 g (2 oz) butter or margarine

5 ml (1 tsp) sugar

450 g (1 lb) carrots, peeled or scrubbed and thinly sliced

3 spring onions, washed and trimmed

1.25 ml ($\frac{1}{4}$ tsp) cayenne pepper or to taste

45 ml (3 tbsp) soured cream

salt and freshly ground pepper

1 Melt the butter with the sugar in a deep sauté pan which has a tightly fitting lid. Put the carrots into the pan, cover tightly and cook gently for 10–15 minutes until tender.

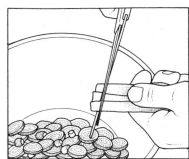

2 Remove the lid from the pan and snip in the spring onions with a pair of sharp kitchen scissors. Transfer carrots and onions with a slotted spoon to a serving dish and keep warm.

3 Stir the cayenne pepper and soured cream into the pan. Taste and adjust seasoning, and warm through for 1–2 minutes. Pour over the carrots and serve.

TURNIPS IN CURRY CREAM SAUCE

0.30	270 cals

Serves 4

700 g (1½ lb) small turnips

salt

50 g (2 oz) butter or margarine

1 onion, skinned and finely chopped

100 g (4 oz) cooking apple

50 g (2 oz) sultanas

5 ml (1 tsp) mild curry powder

5 ml (1 tsp) plain flour

150 ml (¼ pint) dry cider

150 ml (5 fl oz) single cream

10 ml (2 tsp) lemon juice

freshly ground pepper

1 Peel the turnips, boil in salted water for 10–15 minutes until just tender. Meanwhile, make the sauce. Melt the butter, add the onion, cover and cook gently for 10 minutes until soft and tinged with colour. Peel and finely chop the apple and add to the onion, together with the sultanas, curry powder and flour. Cook, stirring constantly, for 3–4 minutes.

2 Pour the cider into the pan, bring to the boil, bubble gently for 2 minutes, stirring. Off the heat stir in the cream, lemon juice and seasoning. Keep warm without boiling.

3 Drain the turnips in a colander. To serve, place in a heated dish and pour over the curry cream sauce. Serve immediately.

HOT BEETROOT WITH HORSERADISH

0.20	53–80 cals

Serves 4–6

450 g (1 lb) cooked beetroot

15 ml (1 tbsp) caster sugar

60 ml (4 tbsp) red wine vinegar

30 ml (2 tbsp) freshly grated
horseradish

salt and freshly ground pepper

15 ml (1 tbsp) cornflour

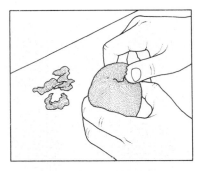

1 Rub the skin off the beetroot carefully, using your
fingers. Slice the beetroot neatly
into rounds.

2 Put the beetroot in a large
heavy-based pan, then sprinkle
with the sugar. Pour in the wine
vinegar and add the horseradish
with salt and pepper to taste.

3 Bring to the boil, without stirring, then lower the heat, cover
and simmer gently for 10 minutes.

4 Transfer the beetroot slices
carefully with a slotted spoon
to a warmed serving dish. Mix the
cornflour to a paste with a little
cold water, then stir into the cooking liquid in the pan. Boil for 1–2
minutes, stirring vigorously until
the liquid thickens. To serve, taste
and adjust seasoning, then pour
over the beetroot. Serve
immediately.

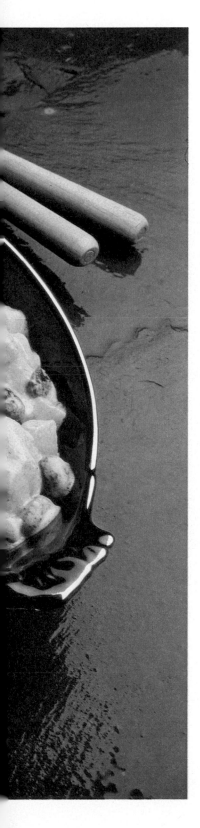

CHINESE VEGETABLE STIR-FRY

0.15	157 cals

Serves 4

1 turnip, peeled

4 small carrots, peeled

4 celery sticks

2 young leeks, washed and trimmed

30 ml (2 tbsp) sesame oil

15 ml (1 tbsp) vegetable oil

100 g (4 oz) beansprouts, washed and drained

10 ml (2 tsp) soy sauce

5 ml (1 tsp) white wine vinegar

5 ml (1 tsp) soft brown sugar

5 ml (1 tsp) five-spice powder

salt

2 Slice the celery and leeks finely. Then heat the oils in a wok, and add the prepared vegetables with the beansprouts. Stir-fry over moderate heat for 3–4 minutes, then sprinkle in the soy sauce, wine vinegar, sugar, five-spice powder and salt to taste. Stir-fry for 1 further minute. Serve at once, while piping hot.

1 Using a sharp knife, cut the turnip and the peeled carrots into matchstick strips.

STIR-FRYING

The beauty of the Chinese stir-frying technique is that it is so quick and easy—perfect for entertaining when you want to be with your guests as much as possible. With stir-frying, everything can be prepared ahead of time so that all you have to do is quickly cook the ingredients at the last moment.

A Chinese wok is best for stir-frying, but not absolutely essential. The reason why a wok is so successful is that the bottom is round and cone-shaped so that the heat is concentrated in the centre—food cooks very fast when it is pushed to the base of the pan. A Chinese wok keeps an intense level of heat throughout cooking, but if you don't have one, a cast iron frying-pan can be used instead.

Traditionally, very long chopsticks are used to push the food around the wok during stir frying, but if you find it easier you can use a wooden spatula or fork.

BARBECUED BEANS

4.20*		213 cals

* plus overnight soaking

Serves 6

350 g (12 oz) red kidney beans, soaked overnight

1.1 litres (2 pints) tomato juice

1 large onion, skinned and sliced

30 ml (2 tbsp) soy sauce

60 ml (4 tbsp) cider vinegar

15 ml (1 tbsp) Worcestershire sauce

15 ml (1 tbsp) mustard powder

15 ml (1 tbsp) honey

2.5 ml ($\frac{1}{2}$ tsp) chilli powder

salt and freshly ground pepper

1 Drain the beans and place in a saucepan. Cover with cold water, bring to the boil and boil rapidly for 10 minutes then drain.

2 Put the tomato juice, onion, soy sauce, vinegar, Worcestershire sauce, mustard, honey and chilli powder in a flameproof casserole. Bring to the boil then add the beans.

3 Cover and cook in the oven at 140°C (275°F) mark 1 for about 4 hours until the beans are tender. Season well with salt and freshly ground pepper.

Menu Suggestion

Serve as a vegetable accompaniment to any roast or grilled meat or poultry.

RED CABBAGE AND APPLE CASSEROLE

3.30	121–182 cals

Serves 4–6

700 g (1½ lb) red cabbage

2 cooking apples

1 large Spanish onion

15 g (½ oz) butter or margarine

50 g (2 oz) raisins

salt and freshly ground pepper

30 ml (2 tbsp) granulated sugar

60 ml (4 tbsp) white wine or wine vinegar

30 ml (2 tbsp) port (optional)

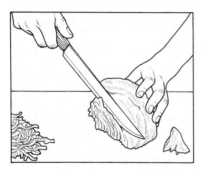

1 Shred the cabbage finely, discarding the thick central stalk. Peel and core the apples and slice them thinly. Skin the onion and slice thinly.

2 Brush the inside of a large ovenproof dish with the butter. Put a layer of shredded cabbage in the bottom and cover with a layer of sliced apple and onion. Sprinkle over a few of the raisins and season with salt and pepper to taste.

3 In a jug, mix the sugar with the wine, and the port if using. Sprinkle a little of this mixture over the ingredients in the dish.

4 Continue layering the ingredients in the dish until they are all used up. Cover the dish and bake in the oven at 150°C (300°F) mark 2 for 3 hours. Taste and adjust seasoning, then turn into a warmed serving dish. Serve the casserole hot.

Menu Suggestion

This vegetable casserole has a tangy fruit flavour, which makes it the ideal accompaniment for rich meats. It is especially good with roast pork, duck, pheasant and partridge, and would also go well with the festive turkey at Christmastime.

RED CABBAGE AND APPLE CASSEROLE

Casseroles of cabbage like this one are popular in northern France, particularly in Ardennes, which borders on Belgium. Both white and red cabbage are used, but with white cabbage dry white wine is usually preferred to the red used here. A spoonful or two of redcurrant jelly is sometimes added to red cabbage casseroles. Substitute this for the port if liked, plus a few crushed juniper berries, which are a favourite flavouring ingredient in northern Europe.

This quantity of cabbage makes enough for 4–6 good helpings; reheat any leftover casserole for another supper as it will have an excellent flavour. If there is any left over, refrigerate it in a covered bowl overnight, then the next day, toss it in a pan with a little butter until hot.

TIAN À LA PROVENÇALE
(AUBERGINE GRATIN)

| 1.15 | 🥄 | ✳* | 428 cals |

* freeze before baking at step 6

Serves 4

450 g (1 lb) aubergines

salt and freshly ground pepper

25 g (1 oz) butter or margarine

25 g (1 oz) plain flour

300 ml ($\frac{1}{2}$ pint) milk

60 ml (4 tbsp) Parmesan cheese, freshly grated

1.25 ml ($\frac{1}{4}$ tsp) freshly grated nutmeg

about 150 ml ($\frac{1}{4}$ pint) olive or vegetable oil

350 g (12 oz) tomatoes, skinned and sliced

2 garlic cloves, skinned and roughly chopped

2 eggs, beaten

1 Slice the aubergines thinly, then place in a colander, sprinkling each layer with salt. Cover with a plate, place heavy weights on top and leave to dégorge for 30 minutes.

2 Meanwhile, melt the butter in a saucepan, add the flour and cook gently, stirring, for 1–2 minutes. Remove from the heat and gradually blend in the milk. Bring to the boil, stirring constantly, then simmer for 3 minutes until thick and smooth. Add half of the cheese, the nutmeg and salt and pepper to taste, stir well to mix, then remove from the heat.

3 Rinse the aubergine slices under cold running water, then pat dry with absorbent kitchen paper.

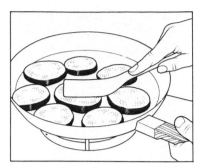

4 Pour enough oil into a heavy-based frying pan to cover the base. Heat until very hot, then add a layer of aubergine slices. Fry over moderate heat until golden brown on both sides, turning once. Remove with a slotted spoon and drain on absorbent kitchen paper. Repeat with more oil and aubergines.

5 Arrange alternate layers of aubergines and tomatoes in an oiled gratin or baking dish. Sprinkle each layer with garlic, a little salt and plenty of pepper.

6 Beat the eggs into the sauce, then pour slowly into the dish. Sprinkle the remaining cheese evenly over the top. Bake in the oven at 200°C (400°F) mark 6 for 20 minutes or until golden brown and bubbling. Serve hot.

Menu Suggestion
This substantial, creamy vegetable dish is excellent served with roast lamb or grilled chops. It also makes a tasty vegetarian dinner with potatoes and a salad.

CELERIAC WITH TOMATO SAUCE

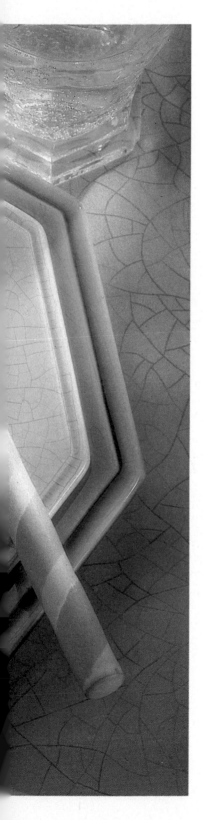

| 1.10 | ✳* | 295 cals |

* freeze before baking at end of step 6

Serves 4

60 ml (4 tbsp) olive oil

1 large onion, skinned and finely chopped

3 garlic cloves, skinned and crushed

350 g (12 oz) ripe tomatoes, skinned and finely chopped

15 ml (1 tbsp) tomato purée

30 ml (2 tbsp) red wine or red wine vinegar

60 ml (4 tbsp) chopped fresh parsley

5 ml (1 tsp) ground cinnamon

1 bay leaf

salt and freshly ground pepper

2 heads of celeriac, total weight about 900 g (2 lb)

5 ml (1 tsp) lemon juice

50 g (2 oz) dried brown or white breadcrumbs

50 g (2 oz) Parmesan cheese, freshly grated

1 Prepare the tomato sauce. Heat the oil in a heavy-based saucepan, add the onion and garlic and fry gently for about 10 minutes until very soft and lightly coloured.

2 Add the tomatoes, tomato purée, wine, parsley, cinnamon, bay leaf and salt and pepper to taste. Add 450 ml ($\frac{3}{4}$ pint) hot water and bring to the boil, stirring with a wooden spoon to break up the tomatoes.

3 Lower the heat, cover and simmer the tomato sauce for 30 minutes, stirring occasionally.

4 Meanwhile, peel the celeriac, then cut into chunky pieces. As you prepare the celeriac, place the pieces in a bowl of water to which the lemon juice has been added, to prevent discoloration.

5 Drain the celeriac, then plunge quickly into a large pan of boiling salted water. Return to the boil and blanch for 10 minutes.

6 Drain the celeriac well, then put in an ovenproof dish. Pour over the tomato sauce (discarding the bay leaf), then sprinkle the breadcrumbs and cheese evenly over the top.

7 Bake the celeriac in the oven at 190°C (375°F) mark 5 for 30 minutes, until the celeriac is tender when pierced with a skewer and the topping is golden brown. Serve hot, straight from the dish.

Menu Suggestion

With its strongly flavoured tomato sauce, this gratin of celeriac tastes good with plain roast or grilled meat and poultry.

COLCANNON
(IRISH MASHED POTATOES WITH KALE AND LEEKS)

0.35	211 cals

Serves 6

450 g (1 lb) potatoes, peeled and
   quartered

salt and freshly ground pepper

450 g (1 lb) kale or cabbage, cored
   and shredded

2 small leeks, sliced and washed

150 ml ($\frac{1}{4}$ pint) milk or double
   cream

50 g (2 oz) butter or margarine

melted butter, to serve

1 Cook the potatoes in boiling salted water for 15–20 minutes until tender. Meanwhile, cook the kale in a separate saucepan of boiling salted water for 5–10 minutes until tender. Drain both potatoes and kale.

2 Put the leeks and milk or cream in a saucepan and simmer gently for 10–15 minutes until soft.

3 Put the leeks in a large bowl, add the potatoes, then the kale, butter and salt and pepper to taste. Beat together over gentle heat until the mixture is thoroughly blended.

4 Mound the mixture on a warmed serving dish and make a hollow in the top. Pour a little melted butter into the hollow, to be mixed in at the last minute.

Menu Suggestion
Serve Colcannon for a mid-week family meal with chops or sausages.

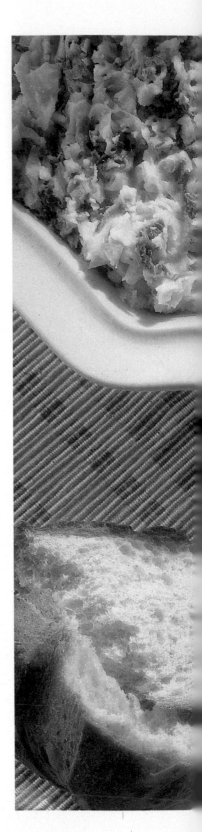

COLCANNON

In Ireland, Colcannon is traditionally eaten on All Hallows' Day, which is Hallowe'en, 31 October. Older recipes were made with kale, which was cooked with bacon to make it really tasty, but nowadays cabbage is often used or a mixture of kale and cabbage. Minced onion can be substituted for the leeks, if leeks are not available. Although Colcannon is essentially a homely dish, the addition of cream and butter makes it quite rich and special. There is a superstition surrounding Colcannon in Ireland, much the same as the one associated with plum pudding in Britain. Years ago, Irish cooks are said to have hidden gold wedding rings in the mixture, and it was believed that the finder would be married within the year. If the cook hid a thimble, however, this would mean the finder would remain unmarried.

GREEK-STYLE NEW POTATOES

| 0.45 | 🥄 | 280 cals |

Serves 4

1 kg (2 lb) small new potatoes, preferably Cyprus

250 ml (8 fl oz) vegetable oil

125 ml (4 fl oz) white or red wine (see box)

60 ml (4 tbsp) chopped fresh coriander, mint or parsley

salt and freshly ground pepper

1 Scrub the potatoes clean, leaving them whole. Pat the potatoes thoroughly dry with a clean tea towel.

2 With a meat mallet, hit each potato once or twice so that the flesh breaks slightly. Heat the oil in a heavy-based deep frying pan, skillet or saucepan until a stale bread cube turns golden in 2–3 seconds.

3 Add the potatoes to the hot oil and fry over moderate heat, turning them frequently, until golden brown on all sides.

4 Pour off the oil, then pour the wine over the potatoes. Add half of the chopped coriander and a liberal sprinkling of salt and pepper. Shake the pan to combine the ingredients, then cover and simmer for about 15 minutes, until the potatoes are tender.

5 Turn the potatoes into a warmed serving dish and sprinkle with the remaining coriander. Serve immediately.

Menu Suggestion

These tasty potatoes are good with plain roast or grilled lamb; they are also excellent with barbecued meat, especially lamb kebabs.

GREEK-STYLE NEW POTATOES

For an authentic flavour to these potatoes, cook them in Greek retsina wine. Most retsina is white, but you can use either white or red, depending on which is easier to obtain. Retsina, or resinated wine, is something of an acquired taste. It has a strong bouquet and flavour of turpentine, which was discovered almost my mistake.

Originally, some hundreds of years ago, the wine jars or amphorae were sealed with a mixture of resin and plaster, and the flavour of the seal naturally made its way into the wine. The Greeks became so fond of the taste, that they began to add pine resin to the must during fermentation, which resulted in a heady wine with a distinctive flavour.

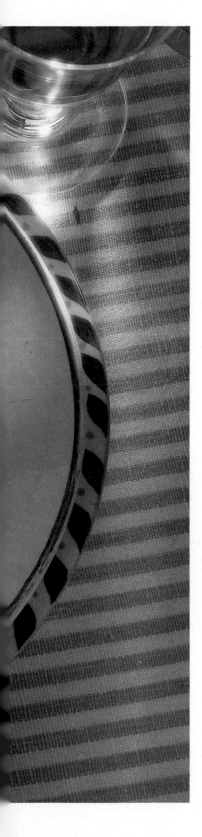

PETITS POIS WITH PARMA HAM

0.25	206 cals

Serves 4

50 g (2 oz) Parma ham

50 g (2 oz) butter or margarine

900 g (2 lb) fresh young peas, shelled

12 spring onions, washed, trimmed and sliced

1 firm-hearted lettuce, washed and shredded

5 ml (1 tsp) sugar

salt and freshly ground pepper

150 ml ($\frac{1}{4}$ pint) chicken stock

sprig of mint, to garnish

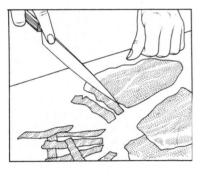

1 Using a sharp knife, cut the ham into small strips. Then melt the butter in a large pan, add the peas, ham and the next 6 ingredients.

2 Bring to the boil, cover and simmer gently for 15–20 minutes. Serve in a warm serving dish with the cooking liquid. Garnish with a sprig of mint.

PETITS POIS

These are small, sweet, tender young peas, much used in continental Europe. The term literally means 'little peas' in French. This recipe, with Parma ham, is claimed by the Italians. The ham can be omitted if liked, or other varieties of ham used. Without the addition of ham it is known as *petits pois à la française*, a traditional, well-known French dish.

This recipe can only be made in spring and summer, when all the vegetables are fresh and young. Fresh young peas should be eaten with their cooking liquid so that their full flavour is appreciated.

It is essential to cook peas as soon as possible after they are picked, as the sugar in them begins to 'die' and turn to starch the moment they leave the parent plant. When you are picking or buying fresh peas, the pods should be crisp, young and well-filled.

If fresh peas are unavailable, good quality frozen varieties are available, and make a good substitute. Ordinary frozen peas, however, cannot be substituted for *petits pois*.

SWISS CHALET POTATOES WITH CREAM AND CHEESE

1.20	529–793 cals

Serves 4–6

1.4 kg (3 lb) even-sized small
   potatoes, peeled

salt and freshly ground pepper

300 ml ($\frac{1}{2}$ pint) double cream

1–2 garlic cloves, skinned and
   crushed

good pinch of freshly grated
   nutmeg

75 g (3 oz) Gruyère or Emmental
   cheese, grated

75 g (3 oz) Parmesan cheese,
   freshly grated

1 Parboil the potatoes in a large
   saucepan of salted water for 10
minutes. Drain well.

2 Stand the potatoes upright in a
   buttered baking dish. Mix the
cream with the garlic, nutmeg and
salt and pepper to taste, then pour
over the potatoes.

3 Mix the 2 cheeses together and
   sprinkle over the potatoes to
cover them completely. Bake,
uncovered, in the oven at 190°C
(375°F) mark 5 for 1 hour, or until
the potatoes feel tender when
pierced with a skewer. Serve hot,
straight from the dish.

Menu Suggestion
This luscious potato dish is very
rich, and therefore best reserved
for special occasions.

SWISS CHALET POTATOES WITH CREAM AND CHEESE

The Swiss cheeses Gruyère and
Emmental are expensive, but
their uniquely sweet and nutty
flavour makes them well worth
the extra cost for a potato dish
such as this one—and you only
need a small amount to
appreciate their special flavour.
   Genuine Gruyère cheese has
the alpenhorn symbol and the
red 'Switzerland' stamp on its
rind; it is full in flavour, which
comes from its long ripening
period of up to 12 months. It is a
moist cheese, with few holes
when cut, and is excellent for
melting, which is why it is the
traditional cheese to use in
fondue.
   Emmental is a relation of
Gruyère and also carries the red
Switzerland stamp on its rind. It
differs from Gruyère in that it is
milder in flavour, with holes the
size of cherries. Both Gruyère and
Emmental are widely available.

MOZZARELLA, AVOCADO AND TOMATO SALAD

0.20	283 cals

Serves 4

2 ripe avocados

120 ml (8 tbsp) basic vinaigrette
(see page 567)

175 g (6 oz) Mozzarella cheese,
thinly sliced

4 medium tomatoes, thinly sliced

chopped fresh parsley and mint,
to garnish

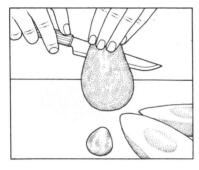

1 Halve the avocados lengthways
and carefully remove the
stones. Then peel and cut the avocados into slices.

2 Pour the vinaigrette over the
avocado slices. Stir to coat the
avocado slices thoroughly and prevent discoloration.

3 Arrange slices of Mozzarella,
tomato and avocado on four
individual serving plates. Spoon
over the dressing and garnish with
chopped parsley and a sprig of
mint.

PREPARING AVOCADOS
To prepare avocados, use a stainless steel knife, cut the avocados in half lengthways, through to the stone. Hold the pear in both hands and gently twist. Open the halves and remove the stone. If necessary, the peel can either be removed with a potato peeler or lightly score the skin once or twice and peel back the skin. Always brush the exposed flesh immediately with lemon juice to prevent discoloration.

BEETROOT SALAD WITH MINT

0.15*	43–64 cals

* plus 2–3 hours or overnight chilling
Serves 4–6

120 ml (8 tbsp) chopped fresh mint
700 g (1½ lb) cooked beetroot
150 ml (¼ pint) malt vinegar
5 ml (1 tsp) granulated sugar
salt and freshly ground pepper
2 medium onions, skinned and
    finely sliced into rings

1 Put 90 ml (6 tbsp) of the mint in a bowl and pour over 150 ml (¼ pint) boiling water. Leave to stand for 2–3 minutes.

2 Peel the beetroot and slice thinly. Place in a large shallow dish. Add the vinegar and sugar to the mint and water with salt and pepper to taste. Pour over the beetroot. Cover and chill in the refrigerator for at least 2–3 hours or overnight.

3 To serve, place alternate layers of beetroot and onion in a serving dish. Pour over the mint dressing and garnish with the remaining chopped fresh mint. Serve chilled.

Menu Suggestion
Beetroot salads go especially well with roast lamb, turkey and duck, and cold meats such as ham and salami.

BEETROOT SALAD WITH MINT

Did you know that the Victorians were extremely fond of beetroots? They not only used them as a salad vegetable, but also dried and ground them with coffee to make the coffee go further, pickled them, made them into wine, candied them as sweets—and made them into a lotion for rinsing hair!

RICE SALAD

0.40*		577 cals

*plus 1 hour cooling

Serves 4

275 g (10 oz) long grain brown rice
salt and freshly ground pepper
1 head of fennel
1 red pepper
175 g (6 oz) beansprouts
75 g (3 oz) cashew nuts
90 ml (6 tbsp) corn or vegetable oil
finely grated rind and juice of
    1 large orange
few orange segments, to garnish

1 Cook the brown rice in plenty of boiling salted water for 30 minutes (or according to packet instructions), until tender but firm to the bite.

2 Meanwhile, prepare the remaining ingredients. Trim the fennel, reserving a few feathery tops for the garnish. Cut the top off the red pepper and remove the core and seeds. Wash the pepper and pat dry with absorbent kitchen paper.

3 Chop the fennel and red pepper finely. Wash the beansprouts and drain well. Chop the cashew nuts roughly.

4 In a jug, whisk the oil, orange rind and juice together, with salt and pepper to taste.

5 Drain the rice thoroughly, then turn into a bowl. Add the dressing while the rice is still hot and toss well to combine. Leave to stand for about 1 hour, or until the rice is cold.

6 Add the prepared vegetables and nuts to the rice and toss well to mix. Taste and adjust seasoning. Turn the salad into a serving bowl and garnish with the reserved fennel tops and the orange segments. Serve at room temperature.

Menu Suggestion
This nutty brown rice salad has a tangy orange dressing, which makes it the perfect accompaniment to rich meat dishes such as pork and duck. Alternatively, it can be served with other vegetable salads for a vegetarian meal—it goes particularly well with green salad ingredients such as chicory, endive, lettuce and watercress.

TOMATO, AVOCADO AND PASTA SALAD

0.20	626 cals

Serves 4

175 g (6 oz) small wholemeal pasta
   shells
salt and freshly ground pepper
105 ml (7 tbsp) olive oil
45 ml (3 tbsp) lemon juice
5 ml (1 tsp) wholegrain mustard
30 ml (2 tbsp) chopped fresh basil
2 ripe avocados
2 red onions
16 black olives
225 g (8 oz) ripe cherry tomatoes,
   if available, or small salad
   tomatoes
fresh basil leaves, to garnish

1 Cook the pasta in plenty of
boiling salted water for about 5
minutes until just tender. Drain in
a colander and rinse under cold
running water to stop the pasta
cooking further. Cool for 20
minutes.

2 Meanwhile, whisk the oil in a
bowl with the lemon juice,
mustard, chopped basil and salt
and pepper to taste.

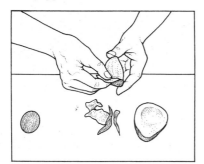

3 Halve and stone the avocados
then peel off the skins. Chop
the avocado flesh into large pieces
and fold gently into the dressing.

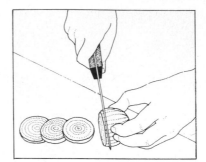

4 Slice the onions thinly into
rings. Stone the olives. Halve
the tomatoes and mix them with
the onion rings, the olives and the
cold pasta shells.

5 Spoon the pasta and tomato on
to 4 individual serving plates.
Spoon over the avocado and dressing and garnish with fresh basil
leaves. Serve immediately.

Menu Suggestion
This pretty salad makes a
delicious summer starter. Serve
with chunky slices of fresh
wholemeal bread and butter, with
a chilled dry white wine to drink.
Alternatively, serve the salad as an
accompaniment to barbecued or
grilled meat.

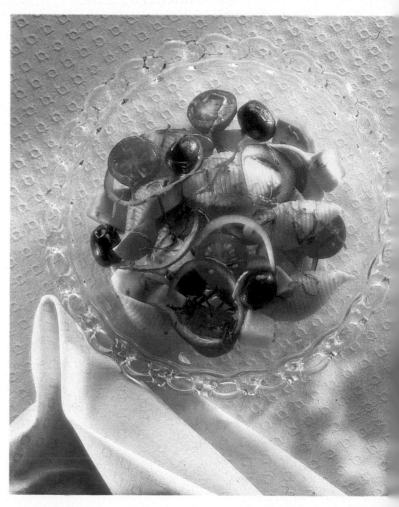

RAW SPINACH AND MUSHROOM SALAD

0.50	402–604 cals

Serves 2–3

225 g (8 oz) young spinach leaves
225 g (8 oz) button mushrooms
2 thick slices of white bread
90 ml (6 tbsp) olive oil
25 g (1 oz) butter or margarine
1 garlic clove, skinned and crushed
30 ml (2 tbsp) tarragon vinegar
5 ml (1 tsp) tarragon mustard
salt and freshly ground pepper

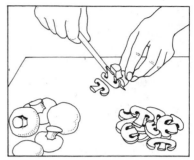

1 Wash the spinach well, discarding any damaged or yellowing leaves. Cut out and discard any thick ribs.

2 Tear the spinach leaves into a large salad bowl, discarding any thick stalks.

3 Wipe the mushrooms but do not peel them. Slice them thinly into neat 'T' shapes.

4 Add the mushrooms to the spinach. Using your hands, toss the 2 ingredients together. Set aside while making the croûtons and dressing.

5 Cut the crusts off the bread and cut the bread into 1 cm ($\frac{1}{2}$ inch) cubes. Heat the oil and butter in a frying pan, add the garlic and the cubes of bread and fry until crisp and golden. Remove the croûtons with a slotted spoon and drain well on absorbent kitchen paper.

6 Add the vinegar to the oil in the pan, with the mustard and salt and pepper to taste. Stir well to combine, then remove the pan from the heat and leave to cool for 5 minutes.

7 Add the croûtons to the salad, then the dressing. Toss well to combine and serve immediately.

Menu Suggestion
This nutritious salad of raw ingredients tossed in a warm oil and vinegar dressing makes an unusual light lunch or supper. Serve with hot crusty rolls.

CELERIAC AND BEAN SALAD

1.10* | **226–339 cals**

* plus overnight soaking, 20 minutes cooling and 1 hour chilling

Serves 4–6

225 g (8 oz) dried flageolet beans, soaked in cold water overnight

1 large green pepper

finely grated rind and juice of 1 lemon

60 ml (4 tbsp) olive or vegetable oil

15 ml (1 tbsp) whole grain mustard

1 garlic clove, skinned and crushed

45 ml (3 tbsp) chopped fresh parsley

salt and freshly ground pepper

225 g (8 oz) celeriac

1 Drain the soaked beans and rinse well under cold running water. Put the beans in a large saucepan and cover with plenty of fresh cold water. Bring slowly to the boil, then skim off any scum with a slotted spoon. Half cover the pan with a lid and simmer gently for about 1 hour, or until the beans are just tender.

2 Meanwhile, halve the pepper and remove the core and seeds. Cut the flesh into strips and then into cubes.

3 In a bowl, whisk together the grated lemon rind, about 30 ml (2 tbsp) lemon juice, the oil, mustard, garlic, parsley and salt and pepper to taste.

4 Just before the beans are ready, peel the celeriac and chop roughly into 2.5 cm (1 inch) cubes. Blanch in boiling salted water for 5 minutes. Drain well.

5 Drain the beans well and place in a bowl. Add the celeriac and toss all the salad ingredients together while the beans and celeriac are still hot. Leave to cool for 20 minutes, then cover and chill in the refrigerator for at least 1 hour before serving. Serve chilled.

Menu Suggestion
Serve this tangy, nutritious salad as a first course with hot garlic or herb bread. It would also make a good side salad to serve with meat and poultry dishes.

WINTER CABBAGE AND CAULIFLOWER SALAD

0.25*	480 cals

* plus about 1 hour chilling

Serves 4

225 g (8 oz) hard white cabbage

225 g (8 oz) cauliflower florets

2 large carrots, peeled

75 g (3 oz) mixed shelled nuts, roughly chopped

50 g (2 oz) raisins

60 ml (4 tbsp) chopped fresh parsley or coriander

90 ml (6 tbsp) mayonnaise

90 ml (6 tbsp) soured cream or natural yogurt

10 ml (2 tsp) French mustard

30 ml (2 tbsp) olive or vegetable oil

juice of $\frac{1}{2}$ lemon

salt and freshly ground pepper

3 red-skinned eating apples

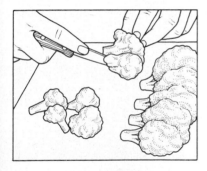

1 Shred the cabbage finely with a sharp knife and place in a large bowl. Divide the cauliflower florets into small sprigs and add to the cabbage. Mix the vegetables gently with your hands.

2 Grate the carrots into the bowl, then add the nuts, raisins and parsley. Mix the vegetables together again until evenly combined.

3 Put the remaining ingredients except the apples in a jug. Whisk well to combine, then pour over the vegetables in the bowl and toss well.

4 Core and chop the apples, but do not peel them. Add to the salad and toss again to combine with the other ingredients. Cover the bowl and chill the salad in the refrigerator for about 1 hour before serving.

Menu Suggestion
This crunchy, colourful salad can be served as an accompaniment to a selection of cold meats for a quick and nutritious lunch. With extra nuts, for vegetarians, it would make a meal in itself, served with cheese and wholemeal or granary bread.

INDONESIAN FRUIT AND VEGETABLE SALAD

0.55* | **260 cals**

* including 30 minutes standing time

Serves 4

1 small fresh pineapple

¼ cucumber

175 g (6 oz) young carrots, peeled

1 crisp green eating apple

100 g (4 oz) beansprouts

30 ml (2 tbsp) crunchy peanut butter

20 ml (4 tsp) soy sauce

60 ml (4 tbsp) olive oil

juice of ½ lemon

salt and freshly ground pepper

1 Cut the top and bottom off the pineapple. Stand the fruit upright on a board. Using a large, sharp knife, slice downwards in sections to remove the skin and 'eyes' of the fruit.

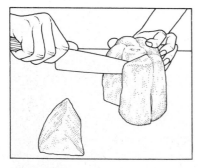

2 Slice off the pineapple flesh, leaving the core. Then discard the core.

3 Cut the pineapple flesh into small cubes, then cut the cucumber and carrots lengthways into thin matchstick shapes. Quarter and core the apple (but do not peel), then chop roughly. Then combine all the fruit and vegetables together in a bowl with the beansprouts.

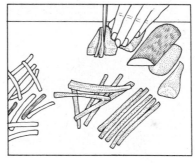

4 Make the dressing. Put the peanut butter in a bowl, then gradually whisk in the remaining ingredients with a fork. Season.

5 Pour the dressing over the salad and toss well to mix. Cover and leave to stand for 30 minutes before serving.

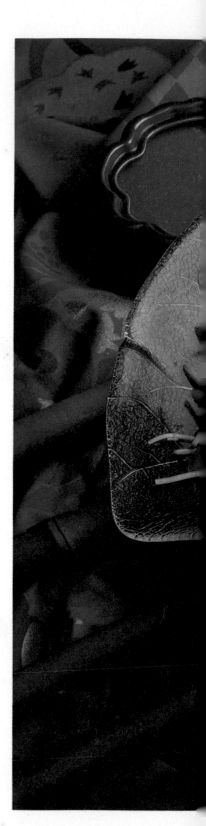

CAESAR SALAD

| 0.45 | 438 cals |

Serves 4

1 large garlic clove, skinned and crushed

150 ml (¼ pint) olive oil

75 g (3 oz) stale white bread

1 lettuce

salt and freshly ground pepper

1 egg

30 ml (2 tbsp) lemon juice

25 g (1 oz) grated Parmesan cheese

8 anchovy fillets, chopped and drained

croûtons, to serve

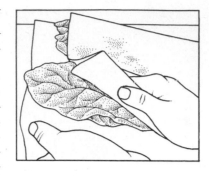

3 Carefully wash the lettuce under cold running water. Drain well and pat dry with absorbent kitchen paper.

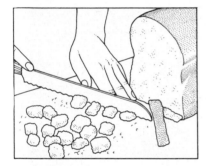

1 Add the garlic to the oil and leave to stand for 30 minutes. Cut the stale white bread into 0.5-cm (¼-inch) dice.

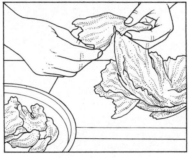

4 Tear into bite-sized pieces and place in a salad bowl. Pour over the remaining garlic oil and toss until the leaves are completely coated. Season well.

5 Add the lemon juice, cheese, anchovies and croûtons and toss well. Boil the egg for 1 minute only, add to the salad and give the salad a final toss. Serve immediately.

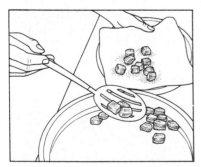

2 Heat a little of the garlic oil in a frying pan and fry the bread until golden brown on all sides. Lift from the pan and drain.

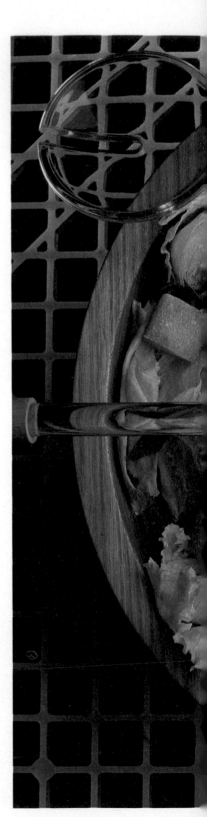

TOMATO AND OKRA VINAIGRETTE

0.15	191 cals

Serves 8

450 g (1 lb) okra

150 ml ($\frac{1}{4}$ pint) vegetable oil

30 ml (2 tbsp) lemon juice

5 ml (1 tsp) tomato purée

pinch of caster sugar

salt and freshly ground pepper

450 g (1 lb) tomatoes, skinned

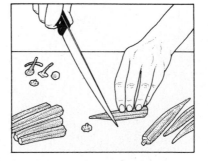

1 Trim off the tops and tails of the okra. Cook in boiling salted water for about 4 minutes or until just tender. Drain well and place in a bowl.

2 In a jug, whisk together the oil, lemon juice, tomato purée, sugar, and salt and pepper to taste. Pour over the warm okra and fold gently to mix.

3 Slice the tomatoes thinly. Arrange in a serving bowl with the okra and vinaigrette. Cover and chill in the refrigerator for at least 30 minutes before serving.

Menu Suggestion
Serve for an unusual and attractive first course, with hot garlic or herb bread. Or serve as a side salad—okra goes particularly well with lamb.

RADICCHIO AND ALFALFA SALAD

0.15	141–212 cals

Serves 4–6

2 heads of radicchio

50–75 g (2–3 oz) alfalfa sprouts

90 ml (6 tbsp) olive or vegetable oil

30 ml (2 tbsp) white wine vinegar

15 ml (1 tbsp) single cream (optional)

1 small garlic clove, skinned and crushed

1.25 ml ($\frac{1}{4}$ tsp) granulated sugar

salt and freshly ground pepper

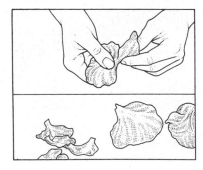

1 Tear the radicchio into bite-sized pieces. Wash, drain and pat dry on absorbent kitchen paper. Wash and dry the alfalfa sprouts.

2 Mix the alfalfa and radicchio together in a serving bowl. In a jug, whisk together the remaining ingredients, with salt and pepper to taste. Just before serving, pour over the radicchio and alfalfa and toss together.

Menu Suggestion

Serve as a side salad whenever a colourful and crunchy accompaniment is required, or serve with a selection of cheeses and wholemeal or granary bread for a nutritious lunch.

CHILLI, AUBERGINE AND RED PEPPER SALAD

1.15*	✳	256 cals

* 30 minutes cooling and 1 hour chilling

Serves 4

2 red peppers

3 medium aubergines, total weight about 700 g (1½ lb)

salt and freshly ground pepper

90 ml (6 tbsp) olive or vegetable oil

2 medium onions, skinned and roughly chopped

15 ml (1 tbsp) chilli seasoning

1.25 ml (¼ tsp) chilli powder

150 ml (¼ pint) dry white wine

30 ml (2 tbsp) tomato purée

15 ml (1 tbsp) lemon juice

15 ml (1 tbsp) wine vinegar

2.5 ml (½ tsp) granulated sugar

chopped fresh parsley, to garnish

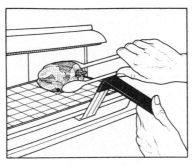

1 Put the red peppers whole under a preheated moderate grill and turn them constantly until their skins are charred all over. Put the peppers in a bowl.

2 Trim the aubergines and cut into 2.5 cm (1 inch) cubes. Place in a colander, sprinkling each layer with salt. Cover with a plate, put heavy weights on top and leave to dégorge for about 30 minutes.

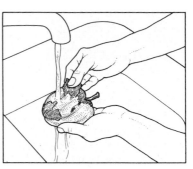

3 Meanwhile, hold the peppers under cold running water and rub the skins off with your fingers. Discard the skins, stems, cores and seeds. Cut the pepper flesh into long, thin shreds and add to the bowl.

4 Rinse the aubergines under cold running water, then pat dry with absorbent kitchen paper. Heat the oil in a heavy-based saucepan. Add the aubergines and onions and fry over moderate heat for 3–4 minutes. Stir in the chilli seasoning and powder. Fry for 1–2 minutes, then add the wine, tomato purée, lemon juice, vinegar, sugar and salt and pepper to taste.

5 Bring to the boil, cover and simmer for 10–12 minutes, or until the aubergine is cooked. Leave to cool for 30 minutes, then turn into a serving bowl.

6 Stir in the red pepper shreds. Cover and chill in the refrigerator for 1 hour. Sprinkle with plenty of chopped parsley before serving.

Menu Suggestion

Serve this smoky flavoured salad with plain roast, barbecued or grilled meat. Or serve for a tasty lunch dish, with hot pitta bread.

CRISP ENDIVE WITH ORANGE AND CROÛTONS

0.20	138 cals

Serves 8

1 large head of curly endive
½ bunch of watercress
2 large oranges
2 thick slices of white bread
vegetable oil, for shallow frying
60 ml (4 tbsp) olive oil
60 ml (4 tbsp) white wine vinegar
2.5 ml (½ tsp) caster sugar
salt and freshly ground pepper

1 Remove and discard any coarse or discoloured leaves from the endive. Tear the endive into pieces, wash and dry thoroughly with a clean tea towel. Wash, trim and dry the watercress.

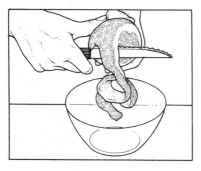

2 With a small serrated knife and working over a bowl to catch the juices, cut away all the skin and pith from the oranges. Reserve the juices.

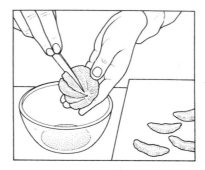

3 Cut the orange flesh into segments, leaving the membrane behind. Remove any pips with the tip of the knife.

4 Arrange the endive, watercress and orange in a serving bowl. Cut the crusts off the bread and cut the bread into 1 cm (½ inch) cubes. Heat the vegetable oil in a frying pan, add the cubes of bread and fry until crisp and golden. Remove the croûtons with a slotted spoon and drain well on absorbent kitchen paper. Sprinkle with salt.

5 In a jug, whisk the reserved orange juice with the olive oil, vinegar, sugar and salt and pepper to taste. Pour over the salad and add the croûtons just before serving.

Menu Suggestion
This colourful winter salad is good with rich meat dishes, especially duck and game.

CRISP ENDIVE WITH ORANGE AND CROÛTONS

Although native to the Mediterranean, curly endive is now grown in other temperate countries throughout the world, and is available virtually all year round. At its best, curly endive is crisp, pale green and frondy, with a mildly bitter flavour. It does not keep well and quickly goes limp and yellow. Most heads of endive are very large, but some greengrocers will split them in halves or quarters. Take care not to confuse curly endive with the torpedo-shaped chicory. In France, chicory is called endive, whereas curly endive is called *chicorée frisée* or 'frizzy chicory'.

FENNEL À LA GRECQUE
(GREEK-STYLE MARINATED FENNEL)

| 1.10* | ✳ | 249 cals |

* plus 30 minutes cooling and 1 hour chilling

Serves 4

90 ml (6 tbsp) olive or vegetable oil

1 large onion, skinned and finely chopped

1 garlic clove, skinned and finely chopped

150 ml ($\frac{1}{4}$ pint) dry white wine

4 ripe tomatoes, skinned and chopped

juice of $\frac{1}{2}$ lemon

10 ml (2 tsp) tomato purée

1 bay leaf

5 ml (1 tsp) coriander seeds, crushed

5 ml (1 tsp) granulated sugar

2.5 ml ($\frac{1}{2}$ tsp) chopped fresh basil

salt and freshly ground pepper

2 medium fennel heads

1 Heat the oil in a large saucepan, add the onion and garlic and fry gently for about 10 minutes or until they are soft but not coloured.

2 Add the wine, tomatoes, lemon juice, tomato purée, bay leaf, crushed coriander, sugar, basil and salt and pepper to taste. Bring to the boil, stirring, then cover and simmer for 20 minutes.

3 Meanwhile, trim the fennel of any green feathery tops and set aside for the garnish.

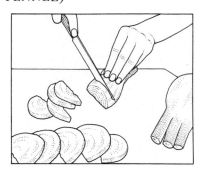

4 Remove and discard any discoloured patches from the fennel, halve the heads and slice them thinly.

5 Bring a large saucepan of salted water to the boil, add the fennel and blanch for 5 minutes. Drain the fennel well, add to the tomato sauce, cover and simmer gently for about 30 minutes.

6 Leave to cool for 30 minutes, then cover with cling film and chill in the refrigerator for at least 1 hour.

7 Before serving, chop the reserved fennel tops finely. Taste and adjust the seasoning of the tomato sauce, then turn into a serving dish and garnish with the chopped fennel. Serve chilled.

Menu Suggestion
The flavour of fennel goes particularly well with lamb and chicken, and the tomato sauce makes this dish most suitable for serving with plain roast or grilled meat. The salad also makes the most delicious first course, served with crusty French bread to mop up the juices.

Barbecues

TURKEY AND HAM PARCELS

| 2.35* | 242 cals |

* includes 2 hours chilling time
Serves 8

700 g (1½ lb) turkey escalopes
8 thin slices of cooked ham
100 g (4 oz) Cotswold cheese
30 ml (2 tbsp) creamed horseradish
salt and freshly ground pepper
20 ml (4 tsp) plain flour
egg, beaten
90 ml (6 tbsp) dried breadcrumbs
vegetable oil
lime slices, to garnish

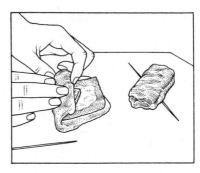

3 Enclose each ham roll in a slice of the turkey meat, securing firmly with wooden cocktail sticks pierced through the centre.

4 Coat the turkey parcels in flour, beaten egg and dried breadcrumbs. Then chill in the refrigerator for at least 2 hours.

5 Brush the turkey and ham parcels with plenty of oil and barbecue or grill them for about 8 minutes on each side. Serve hot, garnished with lime slices.

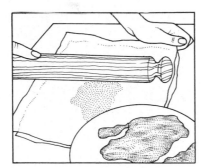

1 Cut the escalopes into sixteen even-sized pieces. Using a rolling pin or meat mallet, bat out thinly between sheets of grease-proof paper.

2 Halve each of the eight slices of ham and cut the cheese into sixteen pieces. Then wrap a piece of cheese, a little creamed horseradish and seasoning in each of the slices of ham.

COTSWOLD CHEESE

The Cotswold cheese specified for the filling of Turkey and Ham Parcels may sound unusual, but it is in fact a variety of Double Gloucester – an English semi-hard cheese which is now widely available in supermarkets and delicatessens. Cotswold is Double Gloucester flavoured with chopped onions and chives; it has a rich, golden colour, a velvety texture and a slightly sharp, tangy flavour. Like Cheddar, all Double Gloucester cheeses are excellent in cooking for their melting qualities.

CHICKEN AND BEEF SATAY WITH PEANUT SAUCE

0.35*	✳	594 cals

*plus 4 hours marinating

Serves 4

2 boneless chicken breast fillets, about 350 g (12 oz) total weight

350 g (12 oz) flash-fry steak

5 ml (1 tsp) coriander seeds

5 ml (1 tsp) cumin seeds

1 onion, skinned and chopped

60 ml (4 tbsp) tamarind liquid (see box, opposite)

30 ml (2 tbsp) soy sauce

2 garlic cloves, skinned and crushed

30 ml (2 tbsp) vegetable oil

5 ml (1 tsp) ground turmeric

5 ml (1 tsp) 5-spice powder

salt

100 g (4 oz) crunchy peanut butter

100 g (4 oz) creamed coconut, crumbled

300 ml (½ pint) boiling water

20 ml (4 tsp) lemon juice

15 ml (1 tbsp) soft brown sugar

2.5–5 ml (½–1 tsp) chilli powder

1 Prepare the satay. Using a sharp knife, cut the chicken and the flash-fry steak into small chunks. Set aside.

2 Heat a small frying pan, add the coriander and cumin and fry over dry heat for 1–2 minutes, stirring constantly. Remove from the heat and pound to a fine powder in a mortar and pestle.

3 Put the pounded spices in a blender or food processor with the onion, tamarind liquid, 15 ml (1 tbsp) soy sauce, garlic, vegetable oil, turmeric, 5-spice powder and a pinch of salt. Work for a few seconds, then pour over the meat. Cover and leave to marinate for 4 hours, turning the meat occasionally during this time.

4 Thread the meat on oiled wooden sticks, keeping the chicken and beef separate if liked. Place on the barbecue and grill for 10–15 minutes, turning frequently and basting with any remaining marinade.

5 Meanwhile, make the peanut sauce. Put the peanut butter, coconut, water, lemon juice, 15 ml (1 tbsp) soy sauce, sugar and chilli powder in a pan and bring slowly to the boil, stirring constantly. Lower the heat and simmer gently for about 5 minutes until the coconut has dissolved and the sauce thickens. Taste and adjust seasoning according to taste.

6 Serve the satay sticks hot on a platter, with a small bowl of peanut sauce for dipping.

SATAY

Satay is a Malaysian dish, which is usually served as a starter on wooden sticks, with the sauce for dipping. Although metal kebab skewers can be used, wooden ones are more authentic; they are available from oriental specialist shops. Remember to soak them in cold water for 2 hours before using – this helps prevent them setting alight on the barbecue!

Tamarind pulp and 5-spice powder are also available at oriental shops. Make tamarind liquid by soaking a 2.5-cm (1-inch) piece of tamarind pulp in about 100 ml (3 fl oz) hot water for a few minutes, then squeezing the pulp to extract as much liquid as possible. Discard the pulp.

In Malaysia, the traditional accompaniments to satay are wedges of unpeeled cucumber, spring onions and cubes of rice cake, which is made by boiling glutinous rice, then pressing it until it can be cut like a cake. Although not authentic, cubes of bean curd (available at health food shops as well as oriental stores) may be served instead of rice cake.

CHILLI CHICKEN

| 0.35* | ✳* | 70 cals |

* plus at least 4 hours marinating;
freeze in marinade, before cooking

Serves 4

8 chicken drumsticks

150 ml (¼ pint) vegetable oil

4 garlic cloves, skinned and
   roughly chopped

½ onion, skinned and chopped

45 ml (3 tbsp) natural yogurt

15 ml (1 tbsp) tomato purée

5 ml (1 tsp) ground turmeric

2.5 ml (½ tsp) chilli powder

2.5 ml (½ tsp) salt

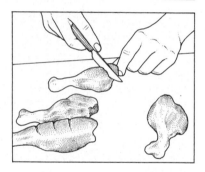

1 Skin the drumsticks, then slash the flesh with a sharp, pointed knife. Make the marinade. Blend the remaining ingredients in a blender or food processor to a smooth purée.

2 Put the drumsticks in a single layer in a shallow container, then pour over the marinade. Cover and leave for at least 4 hours, preferably overnight. Turn drumsticks occasionally and baste with the marinade.

3 Put the drumsticks on the bar-becue and grill for 20 minutes, turning them frequently and basting them with the marinade until nicely charred on all sides. Serve hot or cold.

BARBECUED SPARE RIBS

| 1.35 | 309 cals |

Serves 4

1.8 kg (4 lb) American pork spare ribs

1 onion, skinned and sliced

350 ml (12 fl oz) tomato juice

45 ml (3 tbsp) cider vinegar

30 ml (2 tbsp) clear honey

10 ml (2 tsp) salt

5 ml (1 tsp) paprika

3.75 ml ($\frac{3}{4}$ tsp) chilli powder

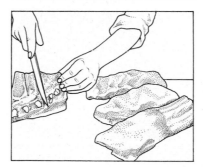

1 Divide the spare ribs into portions of two or three ribs each. Put them all in a large flameproof casserole or saucepan, add the onion and cover with cold water.

2 Bring to the boil, reduce the heat, cover and simmer for 1 hour or until almost tender. Drain and cover until required. Make the sauce. Mix all the remaining ingredients in a bowl together.

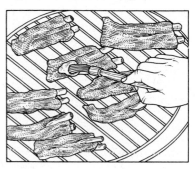

3 Put the spare ribs on the barbecue and brush with sauce. Cook for 20 minutes until tender; brush with sauce and turn occasionally. Heat remaining sauce to serve separately.

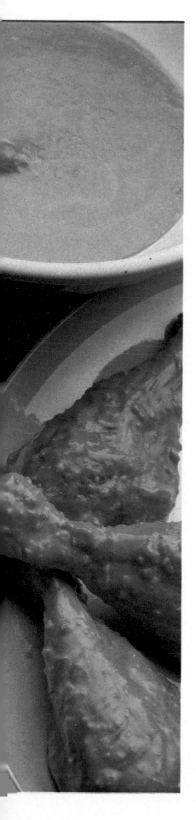

BARBECUED AUBERGINE DIP

0.40*	199 cals

* plus 2–3 hours chilling

Serves 4

2 large aubergines, wiped

3 garlic cloves, skinned

salt

about 150 ml (¼ pint) tahini (paste of finely ground sesame seeds)

juice of about 3 lemons

coriander leaves, black olives and lemon wedges, to garnish

hot pitta bread, to serve

1 Place the aubergines on the barbecue and grill for about 20 minutes until the skin blisters and chars and the flesh feels soft. Turn the aubergines constantly.

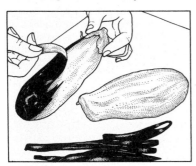

2 Remove from the heat and leave until cool enough to handle. Then carefully peel off the skins and discard them.

3 Put the aubergine flesh in a blender or food processor and blend to form smooth purée. Alternatively, push it through a sieve

4 Crush the garlic with salt, then add to the aubergine flesh. Add half the tahini paste and the juice of 1½ lemons and work again until evenly incorporated.

5 Taste the dip and add a little more tahini paste and lemon juice. Continue adding tahini and lemon gradually until the flavour is to your liking. Add more salt if liked.

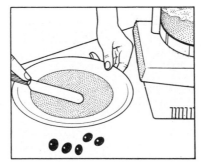

6 Turn the dip into a shallow serving bowl and smooth the surface. Garnish with coriander and olives and refrigerate for 2–3 hours until serving time. Serve with hot pitta bread cooked on the barbecue.

AUBERGINE DIP

A recipe from the Middle East, where it is called *baba ghanoush* or *papa ghanooye*, this Barbecued Aubergine Dip has a wonderfully smoky flavour and creamy texture. In the Middle East it is served as part of the *mezze* at the beginning of a meal, but you can serve it on its own as a starter — with hot pitta bread.

Although cooking the aubergines on the barbecue gives the dip its smoky flavour, this is not absolutely essential – the tahini paste made from finely ground sesame seeds is fairly strong. If you find it more convenient, grill the aubergines until their skins char and blister, taking care to watch them all the time they are under the grill and turning them frequently so they do not burn.

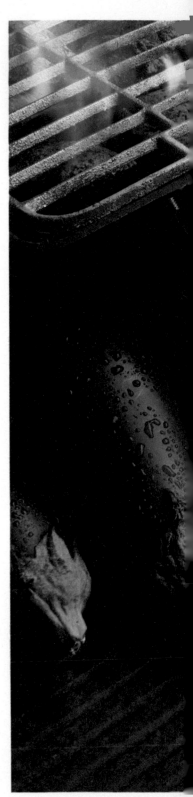

SPICY LAMB KEBABS

0.45* | 516 cals

* plus 2–3 hours marinating
Makes 8

700 g (1½ lb) boned leg of lamb
450 g (1 lb) courgettes
8 tomatoes, halved
1 large corn on the cob
8 shallots
salt
142 g (5 oz) natural yogurt
1 garlic clove, skinned and crushed
2 bay leaves, crumbled
15 ml (1 tbsp) lemon juice
15 ml (1 tbsp) vegetable oil
5 ml (1 tsp) ground allspice
15 ml (1 tbsp) coriander seeds
freshly ground pepper
lemon wedges, to garnish

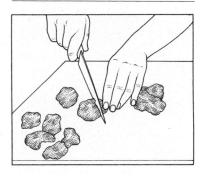

1 Using a sharp knife, cut the lamb into 2.5-cm (1-inch) cubes, making sure to trim off any excess fat from the meat.

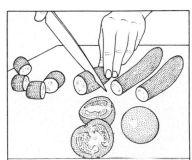

2 Cut the courgettes into 0.5-cm (¼-inch) slices, discarding the tops and tails. Halve the tomatoes.

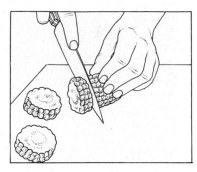

3 Cut the corn into eight slices. Blanch in boiling salted water, drain well and set aside.

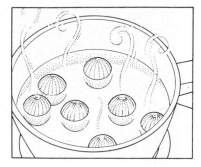

4 Blanch the shallots in boiling, salted water, skin and set aside. Make the marinade. Pour the yogurt into a shallow dish and stir in garlic, bay leaves, lemon juice, oil, allspice, coriander seeds and seasoning.

5 Thread the lamb cubes on to eight skewers with courgettes, tomatoes, corn and shallots. Place in dish, spoon over marinade, cover and leave for 2–3 hours, turning once to ensure even coating.

6 Cook the kebabs for about 15–20 minutes, turning and brushing with the marinade occasionally. To serve, spoon remaining marinade over the kebabs and garnish.

SHASHLIK
(CAUCASIAN LAMB KEBABS)

0.45*	✳*	723 cals

* plus at least 8 hours marinating;
freeze the lamb in the marinade

Serves 4

700–900 g (1½–2 lb) boneless lamb
   (eg fillet or leg), trimmed of fat

75 ml (5 tbsp) red wine vinegar

90 ml (6 tbsp) olive oil

10 ml (2 tsp) grated nutmeg

10 ml (2 tsp) dried marjoram

salt and freshly ground pepper

8 thick rashers of unsmoked fatty
   streaky bacon

4 small onions, skinned

16 bay leaves

extra olive oil, for brushing
   (if necessary)

1 Cut the lamb into large cubes (if you cut the cubes too small the lamb will cook too quickly and not be juicy).

2 Put the wine vinegar, oil, nutmeg and marjoram in a bowl with plenty of pepper. Whisk with a fork until well combined, then add the cubes of lamb and stir to coat in the marinade.

3 Cover the bowl and marinate the lamb in the refrigerator for at least 8 hours, turning occasionally during this time.

4 When ready to cook, cut each bacon rasher into 4–6 pieces, discarding the rind and any small pieces of bone.

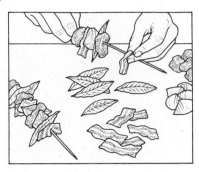

5 Cut the onions into eighths. Thread the lamb, bacon, onions and bay leaves on to 8 oiled kebab skewers. Alternate the ingredients as evenly as possible — divide the meat equally between the skewers, allow 4–6 pieces of bacon per skewer, 4 onion pieces and 2 bay leaves.

6 Cook over a charcoal barbecue or under a preheated grill for about 15 minutes until the lamb is tender but still pink and juicy on the inside. Turn the skewers frequently during cooking and baste with any remaining marinade or olive oil. Sprinkle with salt and pepper to taste before serving.

Menu Suggestion
Serve Shashlik for a summer barbecue meal in the garden. Warm through pitta bread on the barbecue grid for a few moments and stuff the kebabs in the pockets of bread. Accompany with lemon wedges, a green salad and a tomato and onion salad. Alternatively, serve on a bed of rice.

BASS ON THE BARBECUE

1.00*	✳*	478 cals

* plus 2–3 hours chilling time; freeze before cooking

Serves 4

100 g (4 oz) unsalted butter

20 ml (4 tsp) dried dillweed

finely grated rind and juice of 1 lemon

salt and freshly ground pepper

1.5-kg (3-lb) sea bass, cleaned

75 ml (3 fl oz) dry white wine

lemon slices and dill sprigs, to garnish

1 Work the butter with the dill-weed, lemon rind and salt and pepper to taste. Form into a roll, wrap in foil and chill in the refrigerator for 2–3 hours until firm.

2 Cut a sheet of foil large enough to enclose the fish. Place the fish in the centre of the foil.

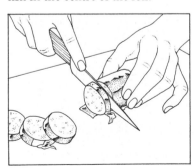

3 Using a sharp knife, cut the flavoured butter into slices. Peel off and discard foil after cutting.

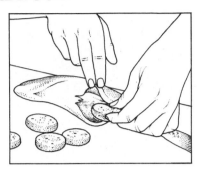

4 Place the butter slices inside the belly of the fish. Sprinkle the outside of the fish with salt and pepper, then slowly pour over the wine and lemon juice.

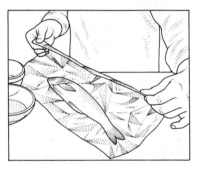

5 Fold the foil over the fish to form a loose package so that the wine and juices do not leak out. Place the foil package on the barbecue and grill for 45 minutes. Serve hot, straight from the foil, garnished with a few lemon slices and fresh dill sprigs.

SAUSAGE KEBABS

0.25* | 294 cals

* plus 1–2 hours marinating
Serves 8

8 rashers streaky bacon
24 cocktail sausages
24 cherry tomatoes or 6 small tomatoes, quartered
24 silverskin onions, well drained
90 ml (6 tbsp) vegetable oil
45 ml (3 tbsp) lemon juice
15 ml (1 tbsp) French mustard
10 ml (2 tsp) Worcestershire sauce
salt and freshly ground pepper

1 Remove the rind from the bacon and cut each rasher into 3 pieces with sharp kitchen scissors.

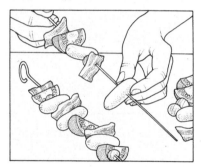

2 Thread 3 pieces of bacon on to each of 8 oiled kebab skewers, with 3 cocktail sausages, 3 tomatoes, or tomato quarters and 3 onions.

3 Make the marinade. Whisk together the oil, lemon juice, mustard and Worcestershire sauce. Add seasoning to taste. Brush over the kebabs.

4 Leave the kebabs to marinate in the refrigerator for 1–2 hours, brushing them with any marinade that collects under them.

5 Cook the kebabs on a preheated barbecue for about 10 minutes until the sausages and bacon are cooked. Turn the skewers often and brush with any remaining marinade. Serve hot.

RICE SALAD RING

0.30* | 160 cals

* plus at least 1 hour chilling
Serves 8

225 g (8 oz) long grain rice
salt and freshly ground pepper
1 green pepper, seeded and diced
3 caps canned pimento, diced
198 g (7 oz) canned sweetcorn, drained
75 ml (5 tbsp) chopped fresh parsley
50 g (2 oz) salted peanuts
45 ml (3 tbsp) lemon juice
celery salt
watercress, to garnish

1 Cook the rice in plenty of boiling salted water for 10–15 minutes until tender, then tip into a sieve and drain.

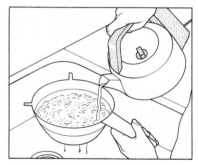

2 Rinse the rice through with hot water from the kettle, then rinse under cold running water and drain thoroughly. Leave to cool completely.

3 Blanch the green pepper in boiling water for 1 minute, drain, rinse under cold running water and drain again.

4 In a large bowl, mix the cold rice, pepper and pimento, sweetcorn, parsley, peanuts and lemon juice, and season well with celery salt and pepper.

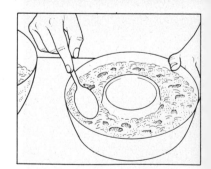

5 Press the salad into a lightly oiled 1.4 litre (2½ pint) ring mould and refrigerate for 1 hour.

6 Turn the rice salad ring out on to a flat serving plate and fill with watercress. Serve chilled.

SPARKLING FRUIT CUP

0.05	230 cals

Makes 3.4 litres (8 pints)

½ bottle (350 ml/12 fl oz) orange-flavoured liqueur

4 × 75 cl (1¼ pint) bottles sparkling cider

ice cubes

350 g (12 oz) fresh or frozen raspberries, defrosted

fresh mint sprigs

1 Make this drink up just as the guests arrive. Pour half of the liqueur into a cold glass bowl. Pour in half the wine and cider and stir quickly with a ladle.

2 Drop a few ice cubes into the bowl, then float half of the raspberries and mint sprigs on the top. Ladle into glasses immediately.

3 Make up more with the remaining ingredients as soon as the bowl needs replenishing.

BARBECUED BANANAS WITH TROPICAL SAUCE

0.20	195 cals

Serves 8

25 g (1 oz) unsalted butter

30 ml (2 tbsp) clear honey

150 ml (¼ pint) dark rum

150 ml (¼ pint) freshly squeezed orange juice

150 ml (¼ pint) pineapple juice

1.25 ml (¼ tsp) ground ginger

1.25 ml (¼ tsp) ground cinnamon

8 firm, ripe bananas

blanched orange shreds, to decorate

pouring cream or scoops of vanilla ice cream, to serve (optional)

1 Make the tropical sauce. Melt the butter in a heavy-based pan, add the honey and stir until melted. Stir in the rum, orange and pineapple juices, then add the spices.

2 Bring to the boil, stirring, then simmer for a few minutes to allow the flavours to mingle. Pour into a heatproof jug and stand on the barbecue grid to keep warm.

3 When the barbecue coals are just dying down, place the bananas (in their skins) on the barbecue grid. Cook for 7 minutes, turning once, until the skins become quite black.

4 To serve, peel off the banana skins and place the bananas in a warmed serving dish. Pour over the sauce and sprinkle with orange shreds. Serve immediately, with cream or vanilla ice cream handed separately, if liked.

FRUIT KEBABS WITH YOGURT AND HONEY DIP

1.15*	298 cals

* includes 30 minutes marinating

Serves 4

1 small pineapple

3 large firm peaches

2 large firm bananas

3 crisp eating apples

1 small bunch large black grapes, seeded

finely grated rind and juice of 1 large orange

60 ml (4 tbsp) brandy, or orange-flavoured liqueur

50 g (2 oz) unsalted butter, melted

200 ml (7 fl oz) natural yogurt

45 ml (3 tbsp) clear honey

few fresh mint sprigs

YOGURT AND HONEY

The combination of natural yogurt and honey is popular all over Greece, Turkey and the Middle East. Served on its own or with fresh fruit as in this sweet kebab recipe, it is most refreshing in hot climates.

When choosing natural yogurt, check the label on the carton carefully: there are many different varieties now available. All are suitable for this dip, choose according to your own personal taste.

Yogurt labelled 'live' means that it contains live bacteria, and that a special culture (or starter) has been used. Bulgarian and Greek 'live' yogurts are noted for being thick and creamy, although they can be tangy in flavour. Yogurt labelled simply 'natural', is always unsweetened; sometimes it is made with whole milk, sometimes it is low-fat — check the small print carefully. Natural set yogurt is very thick, as its name suggests; it is also sometimes called 'thick set' or 'dairy yogurt'. All the thick-set yogurts are made with whole milk.

1 Prepare the fruit. Cut the top and bottom off the pineapple. Stand the fruit upright on a board. Using a large, sharp knife, slice downwards in sections to remove the skin and 'eyes'. Slice off the flesh, leaving the core. Then cut the flesh into small cubes.

2 Skin and halve the peaches and remove the stones. Cut the flesh into chunks.

3 Peel the bananas and then slice them into thick chunks. Quarter and core the apples, but do not skin them.

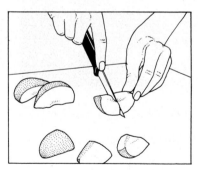

4 Cut each quarter in half cross-ways. Then put all the fruit together in a bowl. Mix together the orange rind and juice and the brandy or liqueur. Pour over the fruit, cover and leave for at least 30 minutes.

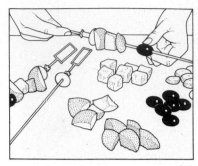

5 Thread the fruit on to kebab skewers, then brush with the melted butter. Place on the barbecue and grill for 10–15 minutes, turning and basting frequently during this time.

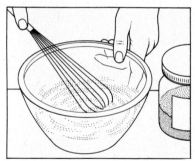

6 Meanwhile, make the dip. Whisk together the yogurt and 30 ml (2 tbsp) of the honey. Pour into a serving bowl and drizzle over the remaining 15 ml (1 tbsp) of honey. Garnish with a few fresh mint sprigs.

7 Serve the fruit kebabs as soon as possible after barbecuing, with the yogurt dip handed separately in a small bowl.

Puddings
and Desserts

TRADITIONAL TRIFLE

1.00*	497–663 cals

* plus 20 minutes infusing, 1 hour cooling and 4–6 hours chilling

Serves 6–8

8 trifle sponges

175 g (6 oz) strawberry jam

100 g (4 oz) macaroons

200 ml (7 fl oz) medium sherry

568 ml (1 pint) milk

1 vanilla pod

2 whole eggs

2 egg yolks

15 ml (1 tbsp) cornflour

30 ml (2 tbsp) caster sugar

450 ml (¾ pint) whipping cream

glacé cherries and angelica, or toasted flaked almonds, to decorate

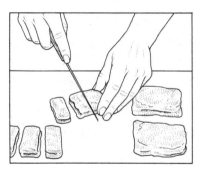

1 Split the trifle sponges in half and spread with the jam. Sandwich together and cut into fingers. Arrange in the bottom of a large, shallow glass serving dish.

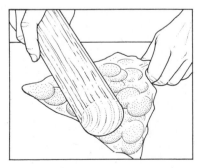

2 Crush the macaroons lightly and sprinkle on top. Spoon over the sherry and leave for 30 minutes to soak.

3 Meanwhile, put the milk and vanilla pod in a saucepan, bring to the boil, then remove from the heat. Cover the pan and leave to infuse for 20 minutes.

4 Put the eggs, egg yolks, cornflour and sugar in a heatproof bowl standing over a saucepan of gently simmering water (or in the top of a double boiler). Add the milk, removing the vanilla pod. Place over gentle heat and cook until the custard is thick enough to coat the back of a wooden spoon, stirring all the time.

5 Pour the custard over the sponges. Leave for 1 hour until cold, then chill in the refrigerator for 3–4 hours.

6 Whip the cream until stiff. Spread half on top of the custard. Pipe the remaining cream on top and decorate with the cherries and angelica, or scatter with almonds. Chill again for 1–2 hours before serving.

Menu Suggestion
Trifle is traditional in England at teatime on Christmas Day, but it can also be served as a dessert at any time during the festive season.

TRADITIONAL TRIFLE
It seems we have to thank the Victorians for giving us the trifle, although they would probably frown upon the elaborate fruit and cream concoctions that call themselves trifles these days. The original Victorian trifle was similar to this recipe, a bottom layer of plain cake sandwiched together with jam, a light sprinkling of crushed macaroons, and a heavy soaking of sherry! This was then topped with a vanilla-flavoured egg custard and then a final layer of whipped cream. Cherries, angelica and almonds were the traditional trifle decoration.

ZUCCOTTO
(FLORENTINE TIPSY CAKE)

0.45*	✳	902 cals

* plus 12 hours chilling

Serves 6

50 g (2 oz) blanched almonds

50 g (2 oz) hazelnuts

45 ml (3 tbsp) brandy

30 ml (2 tbsp) orange-flavoured
liqueur

30 ml (2 tbsp) cherry- or almond-
flavoured liqueur

350 g (12 oz) trifle sponges or
Madeira cake

150 g (5 oz) plain chocolate

450 ml (15 fl oz) double cream

150 g (5 oz) icing sugar

25 g (1 oz) cocoa powder, to
decorate

1 Spread the almonds and hazelnuts out separately on a baking tray and toast in the oven at 200°C (400°F) mark 6 for 5 minutes until golden.

2 Transfer the hazelnuts to a clean tea towel and rub off the skins while still warm. Spread all the nuts out to cool for 5 minutes and then roughly chop.

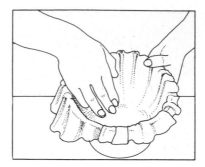

3 Line a 1.4-litre (2½-pint) pudding basin or round-bottomed bowl with damp muslin.

4 In a separate bowl, mix together the brandy and the liqueurs and set aside.

5 Split the trifle sponges in half through the middle (if using Madeira cake, cut into 1 cm (½ inch) slices). Sprinkle with the brandy and liqueurs.

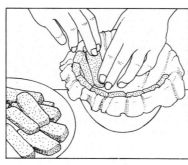

6 Line the basin with the moistened split sponges, reserving enough to cover the top.

7 Using a sharp knife, chop 75 g (3 oz) of the plain chocolate into small pieces, and set aside.

8 In a separate bowl, whip the cream with 125 g (4 oz) icing sugar until stiff and fold in the chopped chocolate and nuts.

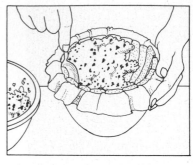

9 Divide this mixture in two and use one half to spread over the sponge lining in an even layer.

10 Melt the remaining chocolate, cool slightly, then fold into the remaining cream mixture. Use this to fill the centre of the pudding.

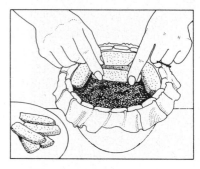

11 Level the top of the zuccotto and cover with the remaining moistened sponge. Trim edges. Cover and refrigerate for at least 12 hours.

12 To serve. Uncover, invert a flat serving plate over basin and turn upside down. Lift off the bowl, and carefully remove the muslin. Serve cold, dusted with the remaining icing sugar and cocoa powder.

Rhubarb and Orange Fool

1.35*	✳	201 cals

* plus 1–2 hours chilling

Serves 6

450 g (1 lb) rhubarb
grated rind and juice of 1 orange
pinch of cinnamon
25–50 g (1–2 oz) sugar
300 ml (10 fl oz) whipping cream
5 ml (1 tsp) orange flower water
shredded orange rind, to decorate
sponge fingers, to serve

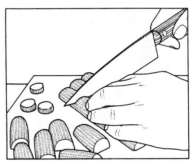

1 Wipe the rhubarb and chop into 2.5-cm (1-inch) pieces, discarding the leaves and the white ends of the stalks.

2 Put the rhubarb, orange rind, juice, cinnamon, and sugar into a pan and cook gently, covered, for about 15 minutes.

3 Remove the lid and boil rapidly for 10 minutes, stirring frequently, until the mixture becomes a thick purée. Cool for 1 hour.

4 When cool, whip the cream until stiff. Fold into the mixture with the orange flower water to taste. Spoon into glasses and chill for 1–2 hours until required. Decorate with orange rind and serve with sponge fingers.

COEURS À LA CRÈME

0.20*	325–487 cals

* plus overnight draining

Serves 4–6

225 g (8 oz) cottage cheese

25 g (1 oz) caster sugar

300 ml (10 fl oz) double cream

5 ml (1 tsp) lemon juice

2 egg whites, stiffly whisked

150 ml (5 fl oz) single cream, and
    fresh raspberries or strawberries,
    to serve

1 Press the cottage cheese
through a nylon sieve into a
bowl. Add sugar and mix well.

2 Whip the cream until stiff
then add the lemon juice. Mix
into the cheese and sugar mixture.

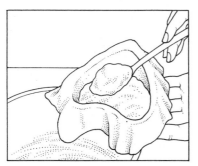

3 Line 4 or 6 small heart–shaped
moulds with muslin (this is un-
necessary if serving in the moulds).
Fold stiffly whisked egg whites
into cheese mixture. Spoon mixture into moulds. Drain overnight
in refrigerator. Serve with cream
and fruit.

DANISH 'PEASANT GIRL IN A VEIL'

0.30*	601 cals

* plus cooling and 2–3 hours chilling

Serves 4

50 g (2 oz) butter or margarine

175 g (6 oz) fresh breadcrumbs

75 g (3 oz) soft brown sugar

700 g (1½ lb) cooking apples

30 ml (2 tbsp) water

juice of ½ a lemon

sugar to taste

150 ml (5 fl oz) double or whipping cream

50 g (2 oz) grated chocolate, to decorate

1 Melt the fat in a frying pan. Mix the crumbs and sugar together and fry in the hot fat until crisp, stirring frequently with a wooden spoon to prevent the crumbs from catching and burning.

2 Peel, core and slice the apples. Put them in a saucepan with the water, lemon juice and some sugar to taste. Cover and cook gently for 10–15 minutes until they form a pulp. Leave to cool, then taste for sweetness.

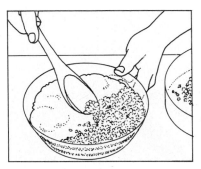

3 Put alternate layers of the fried crumb mixture and the apple pulp into a glass dish, finishing with a layer of crumbs. Refrigerate for 2–3 hours.

4 Whip the cream until stiff. Pipe over the top of the crumb mixture and decorate with grated chocolate. Serve chilled.

DANISH 'PEASANT GIRL IN A VEIL'

This simple but delicious pudding of stewed apples layered with fried breadcrumbs and sugar is very similar to an apple charlotte. In Denmark, where it is called *bondepige med slør*, it takes its name from the fact that the apple and crumbs are 'veiled' or covered with cream. Like apple charlotte, it is a country-style pudding, yet it tastes so good that it would be perfect for any type of special occasion, especially if made in a glass bowl so that the layers can be seen.

You can ring the changes by using different breadcrumbs. White breadcrumbs can of course be used, but wholemeal or granary bread give a more nutty texture. In Denmark, rye bread would be used to make the crumbs, so if you can find a bakery or Jewish delicatessen that sells rye bread, it is well worth trying.

RØDGRØD

0.35*	✱	339–452 cals

* plus 10 minutes cooling and 30
minutes chilling

Serves 6–8

450 g (1 lb) fresh redcurrants or
   425-g (15-oz) can, drained

450 g (1 lb) fresh raspberries or
   425-g (15-oz) can, drained

45 ml (3 tbsp) arrowroot

225–350 g (8–12 oz) caster sugar, if
   using fresh fruit

25 g (1 oz) blanched almonds and
   whipped cream, to decorate

1 Place the fresh fruits in a
saucepan with 60 ml (4 tbsp)
water. Simmer gently for about 20
minutes or until really soft.

2 Purée in a blender or food processor until smooth, then push
through a nylon sieve. If using
canned fruit, push through a sieve.

3 Blend a little of the purée with
the arrowroot, put the rest
into a saucepan and bring slowly
to boiling point. Stir into the
blended mixture, then return it all
to the pan. Bring to the boil again,
cook for 2–3 minutes and sweeten
to taste if using fresh fruit. Leave
to cool for 10 minutes.

4 Shred the almonds into thin
strips with a sharp knife. Toast
them lightly under the grill. Cool
for 5 minutes.

5 Pour the rødgrød into individual tall or shallow glasses and
refrigerate for 30 minutes. Top
with whipped cream and the
shredded almonds just before
serving.

RØDGRØD

Rødgrød is a Danish dessert which
is best described as a fruit soup.
It is always made with fresh soft
summer fruit: redcurrants and
raspberries are used in our
version, although blackcurrants,
blackberries, strawberries,
cherries and even rhubarb can be
used, depending on what is available. The important thing is to
mix at least two of these fruits
together to provide good flavour
and colour.

    Such fruit soups are popular all
over Scandinavia, and are sometimes even eaten as a starter,
either hot or cold. In Finland,
they are called *kiisseli*, and are
often made with more unusual
soft red fruits such as bilberries,
cloudberries and cranberries.

    This recipe for rødgrød is re-
freshingly simple, whereas some
recipes use spices such as cinnamon and the thinly pared zest
of citrus fruit—you can add
these too if you wish. Fresh
whipped cream to serve is traditional, or you can use soured
cream or natural yogurt, in
which case the soup will look
most attractive if the cream or
yogurt is swirled over the top
just before serving.

TEA CREAM

| 0.45* | 🥛 | | 293 cals |

* plus 2–3 hours setting

Serves 4

300 ml (½ pint) milk

15 g (½ oz) Earl Grey tea

2 eggs, separated

30 ml (2 tbsp) caster sugar

45 ml (3 tbsp) water

15 ml (3 tsp) gelatine

150 ml (5 fl oz) double cream

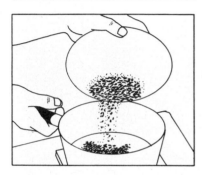

1 Put the milk into a saucepan, add the tea and bring to the boil. Remove from the heat and leave to infuse for 10–15 minutes, or until the milk is well coloured with the tea.

2 Beat the egg yolks with the sugar, then strain on the milk and mix well. Return to the pan and cook gently for 10 minutes, stirring all the time, until the custard thickens slightly and just coats the back of the spoon.

3 Put the water in a small heat-proof bowl and sprinkle in the gelatine. Stand the bowl over a saucepan of hot water and heat gently until dissolved. Mix into the tea mixture, then leave for about 2 hours until beginning to set. Stir the mixture occasionally.

4 Whip the cream until thick but not stiff, then fold into the custard. Finally, whisk the egg whites until stiff and fold into the mixture.

5 Pour the cream mixture into a dampened 600-ml (1-pint) mould and refrigerate for about 2–3 hours until set. Turn out on to a chilled dish to serve.

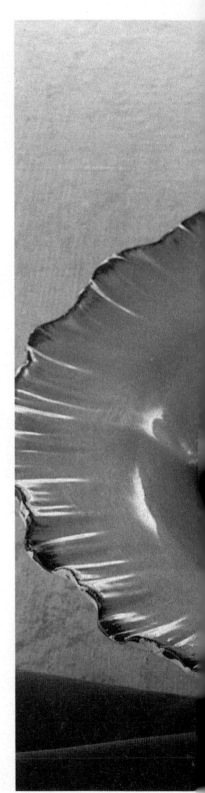

TEA CREAM

Earl Grey tea, a blended black tea flavoured with bergamot oil, gives this unusual tea cream a subtle, perfumed flavour.

It isn't essential to use Earl Grey, however, you can use any of your favourite Ceylon or China teas, although aromatic teas are more flavoursome in cooking. Why not try jasmine tea, lapsang souchong or orange pekoe?

MANDARIN AND LYCHEE MOUSSE

0.45*	✳	292 cals

* plus 30 minutes cooling and at least
2 hours setting

Serves 6

3 eggs, separated

2 egg yolks

75 g (3 oz) caster sugar

298-g (10½-oz) can mandarin
   oranges in natural juice

310-g (11-oz) can lychees in syrup

15 ml (3 tsp) gelatine

150 ml (5 fl oz) double cream

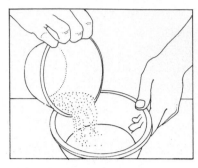

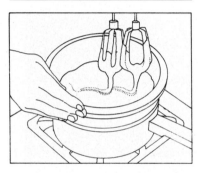

1 Put the 5 egg yolks and sugar
in a large heatproof bowl and
stand over a saucepan of gently
simmering water. Whisk until the
mixture is thick and holds a
ribbon trail, then remove the bowl
from the pan. Leave for 30
minutes, whisking occasionally.

2 Reserve 60 ml (4 tbsp) of the
mandarin juice. Purée half the
oranges and the remaining juice in
a blender or food processor with
the lychees and half the syrup.

3 Put the reserved mandarin
syrup in a heatproof bowl and
sprinkle in the gelatine. Stand the
bowl over a saucepan of hot water
and heat gently until dissolved.
Remove the bowl from the pan
and leave to cool slightly.

4 Stir the mandarin purée into
the cooled egg yolk mixture,
then stir in the gelatine liquid
until evenly mixed.

5 Whip the cream until standing
in soft peaks. Whisk the egg
whites until stiff. Fold first the
cream and then the egg whites into
the mousse until evenly blended.
Turn into a glass serving bowl and
chill for at least 2 hours until set.

6 When the mousse is set serve
decorated with the reserved
mandarin oranges and extra
whipped cream, if liked.

LYCHEES
The tree fruit lychee (lichee or
litchi as it is also known) originated in China, but it is now
grown in tropical countries else-
where in the world. Canned
peeled lychees, with their trans-
lucent white flesh, are readily
available. The skin of a lychee is
a most attractive reddish brown
with a rough almost brittle
texture, but the fresh fruit is
rarely seen outside specialist
markets. The unique perfumed
flavour of lychees, and their
beautifully smooth texture,
makes them an interesting ingredient to include in a mousse
such as the one on this page.

TANGERINE SYLLABUB

1.00* 🍴	335 cals

* plus 2 hours macerating and 2 hours chilling

Serves 6

700 g (1½ lb) tangerines—about 6
30 ml (2 tbsp) lemon juice
30 ml (2 tbsp) orange-flavoured liqueur
50 g (2 oz) dark soft brown sugar
300 ml (½ pint) double cream
sponge fingers, to serve

1 Finely grate the rind from 3 tangerines into a small bowl; use a stiff brush to remove all the rind from the teeth of the grater.

2 Peel these 3 tangerines and pull the segments apart. Remove the membranes from around each segment if tough.

3 Halve and squeeze the remaining tangerines, or liquidise the flesh and strain it.

4 Measure out 120 ml (8 tbsp) juice. Strain over the tangerine rinds. Add the lemon juice and liqueur, then cover and leave to soak for at least 2 hours.

5 Put the sugar in a bowl and strain in the liquid. Mix well until the sugar has dissolved.

6 Whip the cream until stiff, then gradually whisk in the juices, keeping the cream thick.

7 Put the tangerine segments in the base of 6 stemmed glasses, reserving 6 segments for decoration. Divide the cream mixture between the glasses, cover with cling film and chill in the refrigerator for 2 hours.

8 Decorate with tangerine segments and serve with sponge fingers.

TANGERINE SYLLABUB

The syllabub is one of the oldest of English desserts. Originally it was made with very fresh milk—wine was poured into a bowl, then the cow milked straight into it! The idea behind this was that the acid in the wine curdled the warm milk. Early 19th century recipes for syllabub suggested that the milk should be poured from a height onto the alcohol, in the absence of a cow ready for milking. These days, fresh double cream is used, with equal success!

GRAPE SORBET

0.30* 🍴 ✳	221 cals

* plus 6–7 hours freezing

Serves 6

900 g (2 lb) black grapes
125 g (4 oz) granulated sugar
10 ml (2 tsp) lemon juice
1 egg white
45 ml (3 tbsp) kirsch
brandy snaps, to serve

1 Pluck the grapes off the stalks but do not bother to peel or seed them.

2 Put the sugar in a heavy-based saucepan with 450 ml (¾ pint) water and heat gently until the sugar has dissolved. Bring to the boil and bubble for 5 minutes. Remove from the heat, stir in the lemon juice, then cool slightly.

3 Put the grapes and sugar syrup together in a blender or food processor and work to a purée. Sieve to remove the seeds and skin.

4 Pour into a shallow freezer container and freeze for 4–5 hours or until the mixture is beginning to set. Remove the sorbet from the freezer and mash with a fork to break down the ice crystals.

5 Whisk the egg white lightly, then fold the kirsch and egg white into the sorbet. Return to the freezer and freeze for at least a further 2 hours until firm.

6 Serve the grape sorbet straight from the freezer, with brandy snaps handed separately.

ECLAIRS

$1.45*$ 🍴 ✱* 213 cals*

* includes 20–30 minutes cooling;
freeze after stage 3; 201 cals with
plain chocolate

Makes 12

1 quantity choux pastry (see page
647)

300 ml (10 fl oz) double cream

1 quantity chocolate glacé icing
(see page 662) or 30 g (2 oz) plain
chocolate

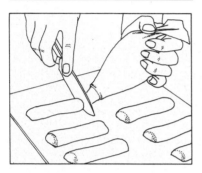

1 Dampen a baking sheet with
water. Put the choux pastry
into a piping bag fitted with a
medium plain nozzle and pipe
fingers, 9 cm (3½ inches) long, on
to the baking sheet, keeping the
lengths even and cutting the pastry
off with a wet knife.

2 Bake in the oven at 200°C
(400°F) mark 6 for about 35
minutes until crisp and golden.

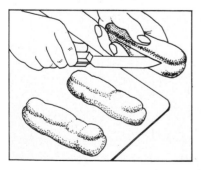

3 Make a slit down the side of
each bun with a sharp, pointed
knife to release the steam then
transfer to a wire rack and leave for
20–30 minutes to cool completely.

4 Just before serving, whip the
double cream until stiff and
use it to fill the éclairs.

5 Ice with chocolate glacé icing
or break the chocolate into a
heatproof bowl and place over
simmering water. Stir until the
chocolate is melted.

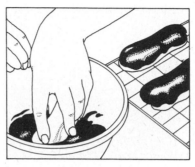

6 Pour into a shallow bowl and
dip in the filled éclairs, drawing each one across the surface of
the chocolate.

--- VARIATIONS ---

For less rich éclairs, replace the
double cream with 300 ml (½ pint)
crème pàtissière (see page 663).
Although chocolate is the
favourite flavour for éclairs,, ring
the changes with coffee glacé icing
(see page 662).

To make savoury éclairs for a
cocktail party, shape the choux
pastry into very small éclairs and
bake for 15–20 minutes. When
cold, fill them with a mixture of
100 g (4 oz) full fat soft cheese
creamed with 50 g (2 oz) butter
and seasoned with 5 ml (1 tsp)
lemon juice and salt and pepper to
taste. Or cream 100 g (4 oz) full fat
soft cheese with 50 g (2 oz) butter,
10 ml (2 tsp) tomato purée, a few
drops of Worcestershire sauce and
salt and pepper to taste. For anchovy éclairs, cream 175–225 g
(6–8 oz) butter with 10 ml (2 tsp)
anchovy essence and pepper to
taste; pipe into the éclairs when
cold.

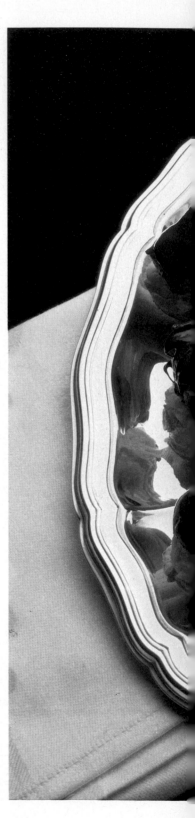

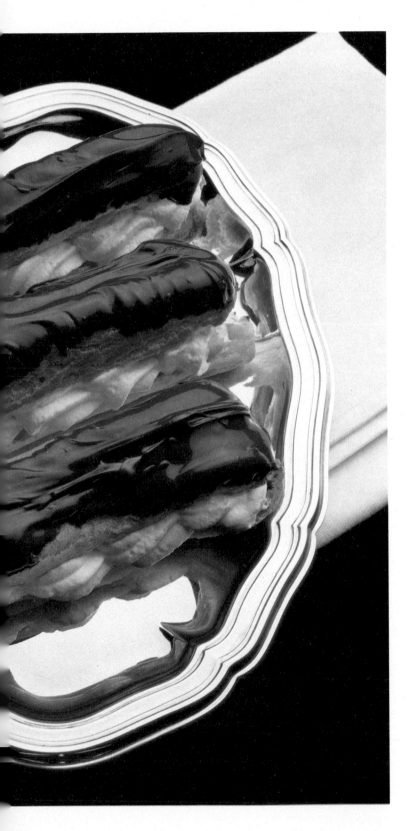

GLAZED FRUIT TARTS

Illustrated on front cover

| 2.00 | 🝙 | ✳* | 377 cals |

* after stage 2

Makes 8

1 quantity pâte sucrée (see page 644)

150 ml (5 fl oz) double cream

50 ml (2 fl oz) single cream

225 g (8 oz) fresh strawberries

60 ml (4 tbsp) redcurrant jelly, to glaze

1 Roll out the pâte sucrée on a lightly floured working surface and use to line eight 9-cm (3½-inch) shallow patty tins.

2 Bake 'blind' in the oven at 190°C (375°F) mark 5 for 15–20 minutes until pale golden. Turn out on to a wire rack and leave for 30 minutes to cool.

3 Whip the double and single creams together until stiff. Spread a layer of cream over the tart bases.

4 Using a sharp knife, slice the strawberries. Arrange on top of the cream in an overlapping circle on each tart.

5 Melt the redcurrant jelly over a very low heat, adding a little water if necessary. Brush over the strawberries to glaze.

GOOSEBERRY MACAROON CRUNCH

| 0.25* | 321 cals |

* plus several hours chilling

Serves 6

450 g (1 lb) gooseberries, topped
   and tailed

30 ml (2 tbsp) water

100 g (4 oz) caster sugar

30 ml (2 tbsp) kirsch

100 g (4 oz) French almond
   macaroons (ratafias), crumbled

150 ml (¼ pint) whipping cream

3 macaroons or 6 ratafias,
   to decorate

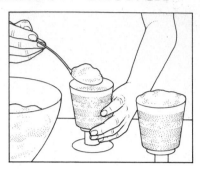

1 Cook the gooseberries with the water and sugar for 10–15 minutes until the fruit is soft and well reduced, then sieve it. Stir in the kirsch. Chill for 30 minutes.

2 Arrange the macaroon crumbs and gooseberry purée in alternate layers in 6 tall glasses. Chill in the refrigerator for several hours for the flavours to mellow.

3 Whip the cream until it barely holds its shape. Spoon some of the soft cream over each glass and top each with a halved macaroon or whole ratafias. Serve immediately.

GOOSEBERRY MACAROON CRUNCH

There are many variations of this pretty dessert. According to seasonal availability, you can use different fruit from the gooseberries and an alternative liqueur to the kirsch. For example, cherries and kirsch would go well together; strawberries or raspberries and an orange-flavoured liqueur (in which case you can use the fruit raw); stewed apples and calvados or brandy; banana with rum; peaches or apricots go well with the Italian almond-flavoured liqueur Amaretto, which would also complement the flavour of the almond macaroons. For a less rich (and less fattening) dessert, natural yogurt can be used instead of the whipping cream or, for those who are not so keen on yogurt, a combination of half cream, half yogurt, which is less sharp in flavour.

SPICED DRIED FRUIT COMPOTE

0.50*	218 cals

* plus 1–2 hours cooling and at least 2 hours chilling

Serves 4

15 ml (1 tbsp) jasmine tea

2.5 ml ($\frac{1}{2}$ tsp) ground cinnamon

1.25 ml ($\frac{1}{4}$ tsp) ground cloves

300 ml ($\frac{1}{2}$ pint) boiling water

100 g (4 oz) dried apricots, soaked overnight, drained

100 g (4 oz) dried prunes, soaked overnight, drained and stoned

100 g (4 oz) dried apple rings

150 ml ($\frac{1}{4}$ pint) dry white wine

50 g (2 oz) sugar

toasted flaked almonds, to decorate

1 Put tea, cinnamon and cloves in a bowl; pour in boiling water. Leave for 20 minutes.

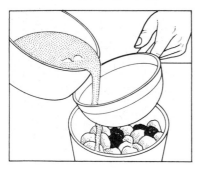

2 Put dried fruit in a saucepan, then strain in tea and spice liquid. Add wine and sugar; heat gently until sugar has dissolved.

3 Simmer for 20 minutes until tender, then cover and leave for 1–2 hours until cold.

4 Turn the compote into a serving bowl and chill for at least 2 hours. Sprinkle with almonds just before serving.

COFFEENUT ICE CREAM

| 0.40* 🔲 | ✳ 669 cals |

* plus at least 6 hours freezing and 30
minutes softening

Serves 4

100 g (4 oz) shelled hazelnuts

**50 ml (2 tbsp plus 4 tsp) coffee-
flavoured liqueur**

**15 ml (1 tbsp) coffee and chicory
essence**

300 ml (10 fl oz) double cream

300 ml (10 fl oz) single cream

75 g (3 oz) icing sugar, sifted

1 Toast the hazelnuts under the
grill for a few minutes, shaking
the grill pan constantly so that the
nuts brown evenly.

2 Tip the nuts into a clean tea-
towel and rub to remove the
skins. Chop finely.

3 Mix 30 ml (2 tbsp) coffee
liqueur and the essence together in a bowl. Stir in the
chopped nuts, reserving a few for
decoration.

4 In a separate bowl, whip the
creams and icing sugar together until thick. Fold in the nut
mixture, then turn into a shallow
freezerproof container. Freeze for
2 hours until ice crystals form
around the edge of the ice cream.

5 Turn the ice cream into a bowl
and beat thoroughly for a few
minutes to break up the ice
crystals. Return to the freezer container, cover and freeze for at least
4 hours, preferably overnight (to
allow enough time for the flavours
to develop).

6 To serve, transfer the ice
cream to the refrigerator for 30
minutes to soften slightly, then
scoop into individual glasses.
Spoon 5 ml (1 tsp) coffee liqueur
over each serving and sprinkle
with the remaining nuts. Serve
immediately.

ICE CREAM MAKERS

It is always satisfying to make
your own ice cream, but sometimes the texture is disappointing because large ice crystals
have formed in the mixture due
to insufficient beating. Electric
ice cream makers help enormously with this problem: they
are not very expensive and are
well worth buying if you like to
make ice cream for occasions
such as dinner parties when
everything needs to be as near
perfect as possible. The mixture
is placed in the machine, which
is then put into the freezer and
switched on (the cable is flat so
that the freezer door can close
safely on it). Paddles churn the
mixture continuously until the
mixture is thick, creamy and
velvety smooth—a consistency
that is almost impossible to
obtain when beating by hand.

ICED TUTTI FRUTTI PUDDING

| 0.30* | 🍴 | ❄ | 624 cals |

* plus 2–3 hours soaking fruit, 6–7 hours freezing and 20 minutes standing before serving

Serves 8

100 g (4 oz) glacé cherries

40 g (1½ oz) angelica

50 g (2 oz) blanched almonds

4 canned pineapple rings, drained

120 ml (8 tbsp) orange-flavoured liqueur

900 ml (1½ pints) whipping cream

130 g (4½ oz) caster sugar

6 eggs, beaten

1 Cut the cherries in half, finely chop the angelica, almonds and roughly chop the pineapple.

2 Pour over the liqueur, cover and leave to macerate for 2–3 hours, stirring occasionally.

3 Meanwhile, put the cream, sugar and eggs in a heatproof bowl standing over a saucepan of gently simmering water (or in the top of a double boiler). Place over gentle heat and cook until the custard is thick enough to coat the back of a wooden spoon, stirring all the time. Do not boil.

4 Pour the custard into a large bowl, cover and leave to cool for about 1 hour. When cold, freeze the custard for about 2 hours until mushy in texture.

5 Mash the frozen mixture with a fork, then freeze again for about 2 hours until slushy.

6 Mash the frozen mixture again and stir in the fruit mixture. Mix well and pack into a 1.4 litre (2½ pint) pudding basin, base-lined with non-stick paper. Return to freezer for 2–3 hours until firm.

7 About 1 hour before serving, remove from the freezer and leave to soften slightly at room temperature. Turn out and serve immediately.

Menu Suggestion
This dessert is like an ice cream version of Christmas pudding. Serve it instead of Christmas pudding for a change—children usually prefer it to the rich and heavy traditional plum pudding.

ICED TUTTI FRUTTI PUDDING
Tutti frutti, which literally translated means 'all fruit' in Italian, was originally an American invention. Assorted fruits such as cherries, currants, raspberries, strawberries, apricots, peaches and pineapple were steeped in brandy in a stone crock for at least 3 months.

RASPBERRY REDCURRANT FREEZE

| 0.30* | ✳ | 284–392 cals |

* plus 1 hour chilling, 4 hours freezing
and 1 hour standing before serving

Serves 4–6

**350 g (12 oz) fresh or frozen
   raspberries**

225 g (8 oz) jar redcurrant jelly

300 ml (½ pint) soured cream

small crisp biscuits, to serve

1 Put the raspberries and jelly in
a saucepan and heat gently,
stirring frequently, until the fruit
is soft. Transfer to a blender or
food processor and work to a
purée. Sieve to remove the seeds.
Chill in the refrigerator for about
1 hour until cold.

2 Whisk in the soured cream,
then pour into a freezer container (not metal) at least 5 cm
(2 inches) deep. Freeze for about 2
hours until firm but not hard.

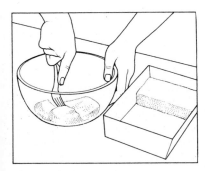

3 Turn the frozen mixture into a
bowl and break into pieces.
Beat until smooth, creamy and
lighter in colour. Return to the
freezer container and freeze for a
further 2 hours until firm.

4 Allow to soften slightly in the
refrigerator for about 1 hour
before serving with biscuits.

Menu Suggestion
Serve for a cool and refreshing
dessert after a rich main course.

STRAWBERRIES WITH RASPBERRY SAUCE

0.20*	91 cals

* plus at least 30 minutes chilling

Serves 6

900 g (2 lb) small strawberries

450 g (1 lb) raspberries

50 g (2 oz) icing sugar

1 Hull the strawberries and place them in individual serving dishes.

2 Purée the raspberries in a blender or food processor until just smooth, then work through a nylon sieve into a bowl to remove the pips.

3 Sift the icing sugar over the bowl of raspberry purée, then whisk in until evenly incorporated. Pour over the strawberries. Chill in the refrigerator for at least 30 minutes before serving.

STRAWBERRIES WITH RASPBERRY SAUCE

Freshly picked raspberries freeze successfully (unlike strawberries which tend to lose texture and shape due to their high water content). If you have raspberries which are slightly overripe or misshapen, the best way to freeze them is as a purée; this takes up less space in the freezer and is immensely useful for making quick desserts and sauces at the last minute. For this recipe, for example, you can freeze the purée up to 12 months in advance, then it will only take a few minutes to put the dessert together after the purée has thawed. The purée can be frozen with or without the icing sugar.

ORANGE SHERBET

0.10*	268 cals

* plus 4–5 hours freezing

Serves 8

178 ml (6¼ oz) carton frozen orange
    juice

175 g (6 oz) caster sugar

45 ml (3 tbsp) golden syrup

45 ml (3 tbsp) lemon juice

568 ml (1 pint) milk

300 ml (½ pint) single cream

shreds of orange rind and sprigs of
    mint, to decorate

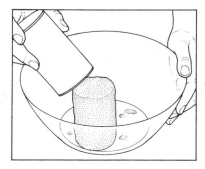

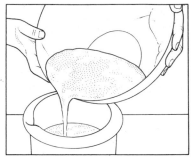

1 Tip the frozen, undiluted
orange juice into a deep bowl.
Leave until beginning to soften,
then add the sugar, golden syrup
and lemon juice. Whisk until
smooth.

2 Combine the orange mixture
with the milk and cream and
pour into a deep, rigid container.
Cover and freeze for 4–5 hours.
There is no need to whisk the
mixture during freezing.

3 Transfer to the refrigerator to
soften 45 minutes–1 hour
before serving. Serve scooped into
individual glasses or orange shells,
decorated with orange shreds and
sprigs of mint.

Menu Suggestion
Make up a batch or two and keep
in the freezer for dinner parties. It
makes a tangy and refreshing end
to a rich meal.

ORANGE SHERBET
There is always some confusion
over the term 'sherbet' when
used to describe a dessert. The
word 'sherbet' is in fact the
American term for a sorbet,
although it is often mistakenly
used to describe a water ice.
Water ices are simple concoctions of sugar syrup and fruit
purée or fruit juice, sometimes
with liqueur or other alcohol
added. Sorbets are a smoother
version of water ices. They are
made in the same way, with
sugar syrup and fruit, but at the
half-frozen stage they have
whisked egg whites or other
ingredients folded into them.

ICED STRAWBERRY MERINGUES

0.20*	✳	344 cals

* plus 1 hour cooling, 6–8 hours open
freezing and 20–30 minutes standing
before serving

Serves 6

225 g (8 oz) strawberries, hulled

25 g (1 oz) caster sugar

30 ml (2 tbsp) water

300 ml (10 fl oz) double cream

18 medium meringue shells, about
150 g (5 oz) total weight

30 ml (2 tbsp) brandy

double cream, to decorate
(optional)

1 Place the strawberries (reserving 3 to decorate) in a small
saucepan with the caster sugar and
water. Cover the pan and heat
gently for about 5 minutes until
mushy, cool slightly.

2 Purée the pan ingredients in a
blender or food processor and
rub through a nylon sieve to remove any pips; allow the purée to
cool for about 1 hour.

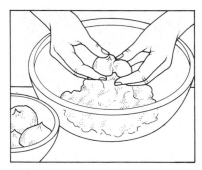

3 Lightly whip the cream in a
large mixing bowl. Break each
meringue shell up into three or
four pieces.

4 Fold the pieces of meringue
shell through the double cream
together with the brandy and the
cold fruit purée.

5 Spoon the mixture into six
individual soufflé or ramekin
dishes. Open freeze for 6–8 hours
or overnight until firm, then wrap
with foil and return to the freezer
until required.

6 20–30 minutes before serving,
transfer to the refrigerator. If
wished, serve decorated with a
whirl of cream and reserved strawberries, halved.

STRAWBERRIES

If you have frozen strawberries
or frozen strawberry purée in the
freezer, this is the ideal dessert to
use them for. You could even
freeze some summer strawberries
away specifically for making this
dessert in wintertime. Whole
strawberries do not retain their
shape in the freezer because they
have too high a water content,
but as this recipe involves
working the fruit to a purée before combining it with the
meringues and cream, this will
not matter – save your perfect
whole strawberries for eating as
they are.

BANANA CHEESECAKE

 0.40* ⬦   ✳*

428–570 cals

* plus 3–4 hours chilling; freeze after
step 5. Defrost in refrigerator
overnight, then continue with step 6.

Serves 6–8

225 g (8 oz) ginger biscuits

100 g (4 oz) unsalted butter, melted
   and cooled

225 g (8 oz) full fat soft cheese

142-ml (5-fl oz) carton soured
   cream

3 bananas

30 ml (2 tbsp) clear honey

15 ml (1 tbsp) chopped preserved
   ginger (with syrup)

15 ml (3 tsp) gelatine

60 ml (4 tbsp) lemon juice

banana slices and preserved ginger
   slices, to decorate

1 Make the biscuit crust. Crush
   the biscuits finely in a bowl
with the end of a rolling pin. Stir
in the melted butter.

2 Press the mixture over the
   base of a 20.5-cm (8-inch)
springform tin or deep cake tin
with a removable base. Chill in
the refrigerator for about 30
minutes.

3 Meanwhile, make the filling.
   Beat the cheese and cream together until well mixed. Peel and
mash the bananas, then beat into
the cheese mixture with the honey
and ginger.

4 Sprinkle the gelatine over the
   lemon juice in a small heatproof bowl. Stand the bowl over a
saucepan of hot water and heat
gently until dissolved.

5 Stir the dissolved gelatine
   slowly into the cheesecake
mixture, then spoon into the
biscuit-lined tin. Chill in the
refrigerator for about 3–4 hours
until the mixture is set.

6 To serve, remove the cheesecake carefully from the tin and
place on a serving plate. Decorate
around the edge with banana and
ginger slices. Serve as soon as possible or the banana will discolour.

——— VARIATION ———

The flavours of banana and ginger
go very well together, but you can
ring the changes by using
chocolate digestive biscuits for the
base of this cheesecake instead of
ginger biscuits, and omitting the
preserved ginger from the filling.
Decorate the top with banana
slices arranged alternately with
chocolate buttons.

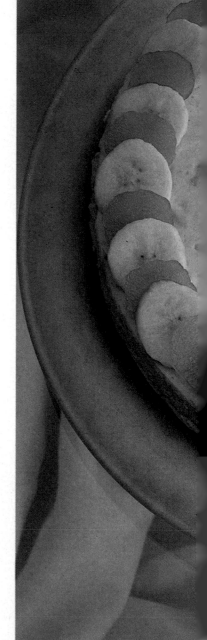

GOOSEBERRY CHEESECAKE

2.30*	☐	✳*	664 cals

* plus 30 minutes cooling and 1–2
hours chilling; freeze after stage 8

Serves 6

450 g (1 lb) gooseberries, topped and tailed
75 ml (5 tbsp) water
125 g (4 oz) caster sugar
75 g (3 oz) shelled hazel nuts
75 g (3 oz) butter
175 g (6 oz) digestive biscuits, finely crushed
125 g (4 oz) cottage cheese
225 g (8 oz) full fat soft cheese
150 ml (5 fl oz) double cream
2 eggs, separated
15 ml (1 tbsp) lemon juice
7.5 ml (1½ tsp) gelatine

1 Put the gooseberries into a pan
with 60 ml (4 tbsp) water and
75 g (3 oz) caster sugar. Cover and
cook slowly for 20 minutes until
the fruit becomes mushy.

2 To remove the pips, push the
fruit through a nylon sieve into
a clean bowl and let the purée cool
for 30 minutes.

3 Roughly chop 50 g (2 oz) hazel
nuts and fry gently in the
butter until golden, stir in the
finely crushed digestive biscuits.

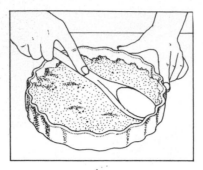

4 Press the digestive biscuit mixture into the base of a 24-cm
(9½-inch) deep fluted flan dish.
Refrigerate for 30 minutes to 1
hour to set.

5 Sieve the cottage cheese into a
large bowl and gradually beat
in the soft cheese followed by the
cream to give a smooth consistency.

6 Whisk the egg yolks and remaining caster sugar until
thick enough to leave a trail on the
surface when the whisk is lifted.
Stir into the cheese mixture.

7 Spoon the lemon juice into a
small bowl with the remaining
water and sprinkle in the gelatine.
Leave to soak for 10 minutes.
Stand the bowl over a pan of gently
simmering water until the gelatine
dissolves then stir into the cheese
mixture with half the fruit purée.

8 Whisk one egg white until stiff
and fold into the mixture then
spoon into the lined flan dish. Refrigerate for 1–2 hours.

9 Meanwhile, brown the remaining nuts: spread them out on a
baking sheet and brown in the
oven at 200°C (400°F) mark 6 for
5–10 minutes. Put into a soft tea
towel and rub off the skins. Chop
and use to decorate. Serve remaining purée separately.

MINI GRAPE CHEESECAKES

`1.30*` ✳* `247 cals`

* plus 30 minutes cooling and 1 hour
chilling; freeze after stage 5

Makes 24

275 g (10 oz) plain flour plus 10 ml
  (2 tsp)

pinch of salt

175 g (6 oz) butter or block
  margarine, cut into pieces

75 g (3 oz) caster sugar

about 60 ml (4 tbsp) water

225 g (8 oz) full fat soft cheese

2 eggs, beaten

finely grated rind and juice of ½
  lemon

175 g (6 oz) black grapes, halved
  and seeded

150 ml (5 fl oz) whipping cream,
  whipped

1 Put 275 g (10 oz) flour and the
salt into a bowl. Rub in the
butter with the fingertips until the
mixture resembles breadcrumbs.
Stir in 50 g (2 oz) sugar, and
water to mix to a smooth dough.

2 Roll out the dough on a lightly
floured surface and cut out
twelve 7.5-cm (3-inch) circles
using a fluted pastry cutter. Use to
line twenty-four deep patty tins.

3 Cook the pastry cases 'blind'
(see page 147) in the oven at
200°C (400°F) mark 6 for 10
minutes, remove the foil and
beans, then return to the oven for
a further 5 minutes.

4 Meanwhile, make the filling.
In a bowl, beat the soft cheese,
eggs, the remaining sugar and flour
and the lemon rind and juice until
evenly mixed.

5 Pour the filling into the pastry
cases. Lower the oven temperature to 150°C (300°F) mark 2
and bake the cheesecakes for 15
minutes until the fillings are set.
Cool on a wire rack for 30
minutes then refrigerate for at
least 1 hour.

6 Just before serving, decorate
the top of each cheesecake
with the grapes and piped whipped
cream.

LEMON CHEESECAKE

`1.00*` 🥛 ✳* `375–500 cals`

* plus 2–3 hours chilling; freeze after
stage 7

Serves 6

1½ packets of lemon jelly

60 ml (4 tbsp) water

2 eggs, separated

300 ml (½ pint) milk

grated rind of 2 lemons

90 ml (6 tbsp) lemon juice

450 g (1 lb) cottage cheese

65 g (2½ oz) caster sugar

150 ml (5 fl oz) double cream

100 g (4 oz) digestive biscuits, finely
  crushed

50 g (2 oz) butter, melted

fresh lemon slices, to decorate

1 Lightly oil a 20-cm (8-inch)
spring-release cake tin fitted
with a tubular base.

2 Put the jelly and water into a
small pan and warm gently
over a low heat, stirring until dissolved. Remove from the heat.

3 Beat together the egg yolks and
milk, pour on to the jelly, stir
and return to the heat for a few
minutes without boiling. Remove
from the heat and add the lemon
rind and juice.

4 Sieve the cottage cheese and
stir into the jelly or put jelly
and cottage cheese into an electric
blender or food processor and
blend to form a smooth purée.
Turn the mixture into a bowl and
leave to cool for 10 minutes.

5 Whisk the egg whites until stiff,
add 15 g (½ oz) sugar and whisk
again until stiff. Fold into the
cooled cheese mixture.

6 Whip the cream until stiff and
fold into the mixture. Turn
into the cake tin.

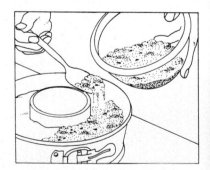

7 Mix together the biscuit
crumbs and remaining sugar
and stir in the melted butter. Use
to cover the cheesecake mixture,
pressing it on lightly. Refrigerate
for 2–3 hours or overnight. To
serve, turn cheesecake out and
decorate with slices of lemon.

HOT CHOCOLATE CHEESECAKE

| 2.45 | 🍴🍴 | 377–471 cals |

Serves 8–10

100 g (4 oz) unsalted butter, melted

225 g (8 oz) chocolate digestive
biscuits, crushed

2 eggs, separated

75 g (3 oz) caster sugar

225 g (8 oz) curd cheese

40 g (1½ oz) ground or very finely
chopped hazel nuts

150 ml (5 fl oz) double cream

25 g (1 oz) cocoa powder

10 ml (2 tsp) dark rum

icing sugar, to finish

2 Whisk the egg yolks and sugar
together until thick enough to
leave a trail on the surface when
the whisk is lifted.

3 Whisk in the cheese, nuts,
cream, cocoa powder and rum
until evenly blended.

4 Whisk the egg whites until
stiff, then fold into the cheese
mixture. Pour into the biscuit base,
then bake in the oven at 170°C
(325°F) mark 3 for 1½–1¾ hours
until risen.

1 Stir the melted butter into the
crushed biscuits and mix well,
then press into the base and 4 cm
(1½ inches) up the sides of a 20-cm
(8-inch) loose-bottomed cake tin.
Refrigerate for 30 minutes.

5 Remove carefully from the tin,
sift the icing sugar over the
top to coat lightly and serve
immediately while still hot.

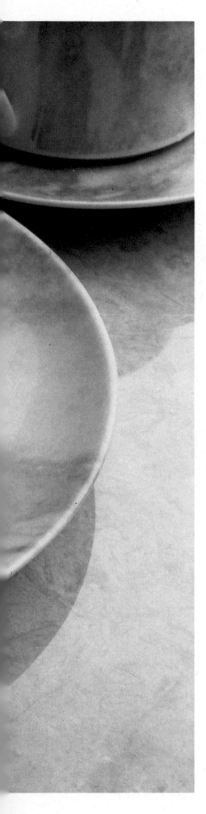

MINCEMEAT TART

| 1.30* | 🍳 | ✳* | 662–993 cals |

* plus chilling and cooling; freeze
before baking at step 7

Serves 4–6

225 g (8 oz) plain flour

pinch of salt

100 g (4 oz) ground almonds

100 g (4 oz) caster sugar

100 g (4 oz) butter

1 egg, beaten

225 g (8 oz) mincemeat

50 g (2 oz) slivered or flaked
almonds, chopped

30 ml (2 tbsp) almond-flavoured
liqueur, rum or brandy

1 medium cooking apple

45–60 ml (3–4 tbsp) apricot jam,
to glaze

single cream or vanilla ice
cream, to serve

1 Make the almond pastry. Sift
the flour and salt onto a
marble slab or other cold surface
and stir in the almonds and sugar.
Make a well in the centre.

2 Cut the butter into small dice
and place in the centre of the
flour. Work with the fingertips,
gradually drawing the flour
mixture into the centre and
rubbing it into the butter. Stir in
the beaten egg.

3 Gather the dough together and
form into a rough ball. (The
dough is rich and quite sticky, so
work as quickly and lightly as
possible, with cold hands.) Wrap
the ball of dough in foil and chill
in the refrigerator for 30 minutes.

4 Reserve a little dough for the
lattice. With your fingertips,
press the remaining dough into a
20.5 cm (8 inch) loose-bottomed
flan tin standing on a baking sheet.
Chill in the refrigerator for a
further 15 minutes.

5 Meanwhile, prepare the filling.
Put the mincemeat in a bowl
with the chopped almonds and
liqueur. Peel and core the apple,
then grate into the bowl. Stir well
to mix, then spoon into the chilled
flan case. Level the surface.

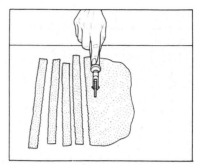

6 Roll out the reserved dough
and cut into strips for the
lattice, using a pastry wheel to give
a pretty edge.

7 Place the strips over the filling
in a lattice pattern, then seal
the edges with water. Bake in the
oven at 190°C (375°F) mark 5 for
35 minutes until the pastry is a
light golden brown.

8 Leave the filling to settle for
10–15 minutes. Heat the
apricot jam gently in a saucepan,
then sieve and brush over the top
of the tart to glaze. Leave for a
further 10–15 minutes and serve
warm or cold, with single cream
or scoops of vanilla ice cream.

Menu Suggestion
Mincemeat Tart makes the most
delicious dessert with cream or ice
cream, but it is just as good served
plain as a teatime cake.

MINCEMEAT TART

As its name suggests, mincemeat
was originally made with minced
meat. The combination of fruit,
spices and a large amount of
alcohol had a preservative effect
on the meat, which was stored in
stone crocks, and always left to
mature from at least the
beginning of December. Beef,
tongue and venison were the
usual meats included in mincemeat, but nowadays only fruit is
used, and shredded beef suet is
added to make up for the lack of
meat. If you can spare the time,
it is much better to make your
own mincemeat for Christmas,
to be sure of knowing exactly
what goes into it. Many
commercial brands have far too
much suet and a watery flavour
and texture, although some of
the more expensive varieties do
contain plump fruit and a fair
amount of alcohol. Read the
label carefully before buying,
and inspect the contents through
the glass jar if possible.

ALMOND AND CHERRY FLAN

1.25	676 cals

Serves 6

225 g (8 oz) plain flour

225 g (8 oz) butter or margarine

2 eggs, separated

30–45 ml (2–3 tbsp) water

350 g (12 oz) fresh ripe black cherries, stoned

50 g (2 oz) caster sugar

125 g (4 oz) ground almonds

5 ml (1 tsp) almond flavouring

15 ml (1 tbsp) almond-flavoured liqueur (optional)

50 g (2 oz) self-raising flour

2.5 ml (½ tsp) baking powder

30 ml (2 tbsp) milk

25 g (1 oz) flaked almonds

thick pouring cream, to serve

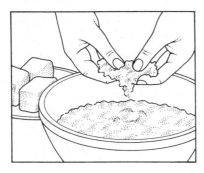

1 Place the plain flour in a large mixing bowl. Cut up and rub in 175 g (6 oz) butter until mixture resembles fine breadcrumbs. Bind to a firm dough with 1 egg yolk mixed with water.

2 Roll out the pastry, and use to line a 24-cm (9½-inch) flan dish. Bake blind in the oven at 200°C (400°F) mark 6 for 15–20 minutes until set but not browned; cool slightly.

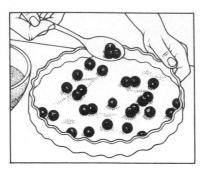

3 Scatter the cherries over the pastry. Then cream the remaining butter and sugar well together and beat in ground almonds with the almond flavouring, liqueur, if using, and the remaining egg yolk. Fold in the self-raising flour and baking powder, sifted together, and lightly stir in the milk.

4 Whisk the two egg whites until they are stiff, and fold them into the creamed ingredients.

5 Spread over the cherries in the flan case and scatter the flaked almonds on top. Bake in the oven at 180°C (350°F) mark 4 for about 30 minutes. Serve warm with cream.

AMARETTO

Almond-flavoured liqueur — *amaretto* — a famous Italian liqueur, which comes from the town of Saronno near Milan in northern Italy, is said to be the best. Look for it in specialist off licences or Italian delicatessens with wine counters, and don't be confused between it and the little almond-flavoured macaroons called *amaretti*. The Italians are so fond of almonds that they even eat *amaretti* with *amaretto* after the coffee at the end of a meal!

BUTTERSCOTCH CREAM PIE

1.15*	⛑	✳	574 cals

* plus 30 minutes chilling and 1 hour cooling

Serves 6

150 g (6 oz) plain flour
1.25 ml ($\frac{1}{4}$ tsp) salt
165 g (5$\frac{1}{2}$ oz) butter or block margarine
10 ml (2 tsp) caster sugar
5 egg yolks and 1 egg white
150 ml ($\frac{1}{4}$ pint) milk
170 g (6 oz) evaporated milk
50 g (2 oz) dark soft brown sugar
15 ml (1 tbsp) cornflour
300 ml (10 fl oz) double cream

1 Put the flour into a bowl with half the salt. Add the 100 g (4 oz) fat in pieces and rub in with the fingertips until the mixture resembles fine breadcrumbs.

2 Stir in the sugar and 1 egg yolk and draw the dough together to form a ball. Add a few drops of cold water if the dough is too dry.

3 Press the dough gently into a 20.5-cm (8-inch) loose-bottomed fluted flan tin or ring placed on a baking sheet. Refrigerate for 30 minutes.

4 Prick the base of the pastry case and bake blind in the oven at 200°C (400°F) mark 6 for 10 minutes. Remove the foil and beans, brush the pastry with the egg white, then return to the oven and bake for a further 10 minutes until crisp and lightly coloured. Leave to cool.

5 Meanwhile, make the filling. Put the milk and evaporated milk in a saucepan and scald by bringing up to boiling point. Put the brown sugar, cornflour, remaining butter, egg yolks and salt in a heavy-based saucepan. Heat gently until the butter has melted and sugar dissolved, then gradually stir in the scalded milks. Stir well until heated through.

6 Cook over gentle heat, whisking constantly until the custard is thick. (Don't worry if the mixture is lumpy at first—keep whisking vigorously with a balloon whisk and it will become smooth.)

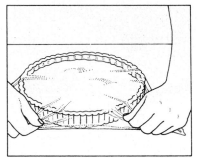

7 Remove from the heat and cool slightly, then pour into the baked pastry case. Cover the surface of the butterscotch cream closely with cling film (to prevent a skin forming) and leave for about 1 hour until completely cold.

8 To serve, whip the cream until stiff, then pipe on top of pie. Chill until serving time.

APPLE AND BANANA FRITTERS

1.00		218–328 cals

Serves 4–6

100 g (4 oz) plain flour
pinch of salt
90 ml (6 tbsp) lukewarm water
20 ml (4 tsp) vegetable oil
2 egg whites
1 large cooking apple
2 bananas
juice of ½ a lemon
vegetable oil, for deep frying
caster sugar, to serve

1 Place the flour and salt into a bowl. Make a well in the centre. Add the water and oil and beat to form a smooth batter.

2 Beat the egg whites in a clean dry bowl until they are stiff; then set aside.

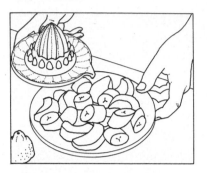

3 Peel, quarter and core the apple. Peel the bananas. Slice the fruit thickly and sprinkle at once with the lemon juice to prevent discoloration.

4 Fold the beaten egg whites into the batter, then immediately dip in the slices of fruit.

5 Deep-fry the fritters a few at a time in hot oil until puffed and light golden. Remove with a slotted spoon and pile on to a serving dish lined with absorbent kitchen paper. Serve immediately, sprinkled with caster sugar.

RUM AND COFFEE JUNKET

0.15*	283 cals

* plus 4 hours setting and 1 hour chilling

Serves 4

568 ml (1 pint) plus 60 ml (4 tbsp) milk —not UHT, long-life or sterilised

30 ml (2 tbsp) caster sugar

10 ml (2 tsp) essence of rennet

10 ml (2 tsp) rum

142 ml (5 fl oz) soured cream

10 ml (2 tsp) coffee and chicory essence

plain and white chocolate, to decorate

1 Put the 568 ml (1 pint) milk in a saucepan and heat until just warm to the finger.

2 Add the sugar, rennet and rum and stir until the sugar has dissolved.

3 Pour the mixture at once into four individual dishes or a 900-ml (1½-pint) shallow, edged serving dish. Put in a warm place, undisturbed, for 4 hours to set.

4 Lightly whisk the soured cream. Gradually add the 60 ml (4 tbsp) milk and the coffee essence, whisking until smooth.

5 Carefully flood the top of the junket with the coffee cream, taking care not to disturb the junket. Decorate with pared or coarsely grated chocolate. Refrigerate for 1 hour.

SPICED APPLE AND PLUM CRUMBLE

| 1.10* | ❄ | 402 cals |

*plus 30 minutes cooling

Serves 6

450 g (1 lb) plums
700 g (1½ lb) cooking apples
100 g (4 oz) butter or margarine
100 g (4 oz) sugar
7.5 ml (1½ tsp) ground mixed spice
175 g (6 oz) plain wholewheat flour
50 g (2 oz) blanched hazelnuts, toasted and chopped

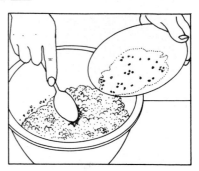

1 Using a sharp knife, cut the plums in half and then carefully remove the stones.

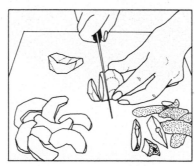

2 Peel, quarter, core and slice the apples. Place in a medium saucepan with 25 g (1 oz) fat, half the sugar and about 5 ml (1 tsp) mixed spice.

3 Cover the pan and cook gently for 15 minutes until the apples begin to soften. Stir in the plums and turn into a 1.1-litre (2-pint) shallow ovenproof dish. Leave to cool for about 30 minutes.

4 Stir the flour and remaining mixed spice well together, then rub in the remaining fat until the mixture resembles fine breadcrumbs. Stir in the rest of the sugar with the chopped hazelnuts.

5 Spoon the crumble mixture over the fruit and bake in the oven at 180°C (350°F) mark 4 for about 40 minutes or until the top is golden, crisp and crumbly.

PLUMS FOR COOKING

All plums can be cooked, but dessert varieties tend to be more expensive, therefore it makes good sense to look for cooking plums. Unfortunately, greengrocers and supermarkets do not always specify the variety of plums on sale, but it is always worth asking. Whether you cook with red or yellow plums is entirely a matter of personal choice, but cooking plums worth looking for are Czars, small red cherry plums, Pershore Yellow Egg, Purple Pershore and Belle de Loutain. The famous Victoria plum is a dual purpose fruit: sweet and juicy, it is equally suitable for cooking and eating. Greengages and damsons come from the same family as the plum, and can be used in any recipe calling for plums, although extra sugar may be required.

BLACKBERRY AND PEAR COBBLER

0.45	✳	424 cals

Serves 4

450 g (1 lb) blackberries

450 g (1 lb) ripe cooking pears (e.g. Conference)

finely grated rind and juice of 1 lemon

2.5 ml ($\frac{1}{2}$ tsp) ground cinnamon

225 g (8 oz) self raising flour

pinch of salt

50 g (2 oz) butter or block margarine

25 g (1 oz) caster sugar

about 150 ml ($\frac{1}{4}$ pint) milk plus extra to glaze

1 Pick over the blackberries and wash them. Peel and core the pears, then slice them thickly.

2 Put the blackberries and pears into a saucepan with the lemon rind and juice and the cinnamon. Poach gently for 15 or 20 minutes until the fruit is juicy and tender.

3 Meanwhile, place the flour and salt into the bowl. Rub in the fat, then stir in the sugar. Gradually add the milk to mix to a fairly soft dough.

4 Roll out the dough on a floured work surface until 1.5 cm ($\frac{1}{2}$ inch) thick. Cut out rounds using a fluted 5-cm (2-inch) pastry cutter.

5 Put the fruit in a pie dish and top with overlapping pastry rounds, leaving a gap in the centre. Brush the top of the pastry rounds with milk. Bake in the oven at 220°C (425°F) mark 7 for 10–15 minutes until pastry is golden brown. Serve hot.

COBBLER

Recipes with the strange-sounding title of 'cobbler' are invariably American in origin, although very little is known for certain about the meaning behind the word in culinary terms. Cobblers can be sweet or savoury; they always have a scone dough topping which is stamped into small rounds — sometimes the whole surface of the dish is covered with these rounds of dough, although often they are simply placed around the outside to reveal the filling in the centre. One theory is that the word cobbler originates from the fact that the rounds of dough look like 'cobbles' or stones.

SUSSEX POND PUDDING

4.30 🥄	649 cals

Serves 6

350 g (12 oz) self raising flour
2.5 ml (½ tsp) salt
175 g (6 oz) shredded suet
about 175 ml (6 fl oz) water
100 g (4 oz) butter, cut into pieces
100 g (4 oz) demerara sugar
1 large lemon

1 Place the flour and salt into a bowl, then stir in the suet and enough cold water to make a light, elastic dough. Knead lightly until it is smooth.

2 Roll out two thirds of the pastry on a floured work surface to a circle, 2.5 cm (1 inch) larger all round than the top of a 1.5-litre (2½-pint) pudding basin.

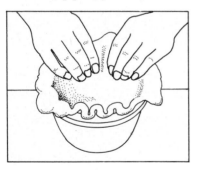

3 Use the rolled-out pastry to line the pudding basin. Put half the butter into the centre with half the sugar.

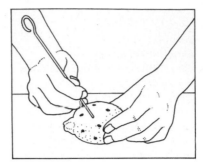

4 Prick the lemon all over with a skewer. Put the whole lemon on top of the butter and sugar. Add the remaining butter and sugar.

5 Roll out the remaining pastry to a circle to fit the top of the pudding. Dampen the edges and seal the lid. Cover with greaseproof paper and foil.

6 Place over a pan of boiling water and steam for about 4 hours, topping up the water as necessary. Remove paper and turn out on to a warm serving dish. During cooking the lemon inside the pudding bursts and produces a delicious lemon sauce. Each serving should have a piece of the lemon, which will be much softened by the cooking.

SUSSEX POND PUDDING

An old-fashioned recipe from the south of England, Sussex Pond Pudding takes its name from the fact that during cooking the whole lemon inside bursts, and the resulting juice combines with the other ingredients of butter and sugar to produce a delicious pool or 'pond' of lemon sauce.

Be sure to prick the fruit thoroughly all over with a skewer before placing it inside the suet pastry case—if you do not do this the lemon will remain whole and spoil the finished effect. This pudding is rich enough to be served on its own, but pouring cream can be handed separately for those who like to indulge themselves!

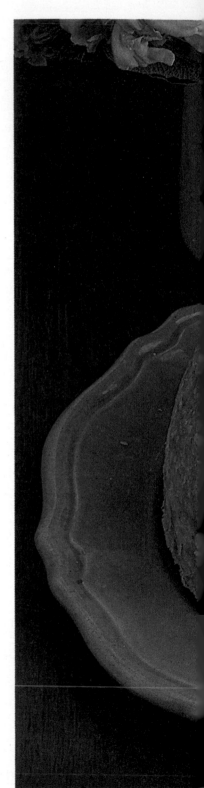

ALMOND EVE'S PUDDING

1.30	784 cals

Serves 4

700 g (1½ lb) cooking apples
5 ml (1 tsp) ground cinnamon
175 g (6 oz) demerara sugar
125 g (4 oz) butter, softened
2 eggs, beaten
125 g (4 oz) self raising flour
25 g (1 oz) ground almonds
2.5 ml (½ tsp) almond flavouring
30 ml (2 tbsp) milk
25 g (1 oz) flaked almonds
icing sugar, to dredge
single cream, to serve

1 Peel, quarter and core the cooking apples, then slice them thickly into a 1.4-litre (2½-pint) ovenproof dish. Combine the cinnamon with 50 g (2 oz) of the demerara sugar and scatter over the apples. Cover tightly with cling film while preparing the topping.

2 Beat the butter and remaining sugar, creaming them together until fluffy. Gradually beat in eggs.

3 Fold in the flour, ground almonds, flavouring and milk. Spread the mixture over the cooking apples.

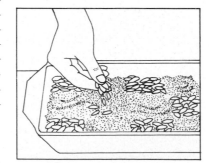

4 Place the flaked almonds on top in six squares to form a chequerboard effect. Bake in the oven at 180°C (350°F) mark 4 for 50–60 minutes until the apples are tender and the sponge risen and golden brown.

5 Dredge icing sugar between the flaked nut squares. Serve with cream.

—— VARIATION ——

If liked, you can add 50 g (2 oz) sultanas, currants or raisins to the apple mixture in the base of this delicious family pudding. Grated orange or lemon zest added to the sponge topping also adds extra flavour—and goes particularly well with the cinnamon-flavoured apples.

LOCKSHEN PUDDING

1.00	356 cals

Serves 4

100 g (4 oz) vermicelli (lockshen)

pinch of salt

1 egg

50 g (2 oz) sugar

1.25 ml ($\frac{1}{4}$ tsp) ground cinnamon

finely grated rind of $\frac{1}{2}$ a lemon

50 g (2 oz) currants

50 g (2 oz) chopped almonds (optional)

25 g (1 oz) margarine

1 Drop the vermicelli into rapidly boiling salted water and cook for about 10 minutes until tender.

2 Drain into a sieve and rinse with plenty of hot water to remove excess starch. Drain well.

3 Whisk the egg and sugar together and stir in the cinnamon, rind, currants and nuts, if using. Then stir in the vermicelli.

4 Melt the margarine in a 5-cm (2-inch) deep, flameproof baking dish until hot but not smoking. Swirl around the dish to coat the sides and pour the excess into the noodle mixture.

5 Stir well and pour the mixture into the baking dish. Bake in the oven at 190°C (375°F) mark 5 for 45 minutes until set, crisp and brown on top. Serve hot.

467

ROLY-POLY WITH HOT JAM SAUCE

2.30	499 cals

Serves 4

175 g (6 oz) self raising flour
1.25 ml ($\frac{1}{4}$ tsp) salt
75 g (3 oz) shredded suet
finely grated rind of 1 orange
45–60 ml (3–4 tbsp) hot water
90 ml (6 tbsp) red jam plus 45 ml
  (3 tbsp)
a little milk
finely grated rind of 1 orange
10 ml (2 tsp) arrowroot
150 ml ($\frac{1}{4}$ pint) fresh orange juice

1 Place the flour and salt into a bowl, then stir in the suet and orange rind. Gradually stir in the hot water until the dough binds together. Form into a ball, turn out on to a floured surface and knead lightly until smooth.

2 Roll out the dough on a floured work surface to a 25 × 20 cm (10 × 8 inch) oblong. Spread the first quantity of jam over the dough to 0.5 cm ($\frac{1}{4}$ inch) of the edges. Brush the edges with milk.

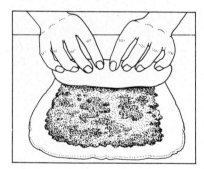

3 Roll up the pastry evenly like a Swiss roll, starting from one short side.

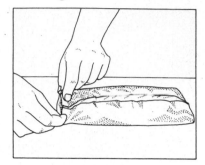

4 Place the roll, seam side down, on a sheet of greased foil measuring at least 35 × 23 cm (12 × 9 inches). Wrap the foil loosely around the roll to allow room for expansion during cooking. Seal well.

5 Place the roly-poly in the top of a steamer over a pan of boiling water and steam for 1$\frac{1}{2}$–2 hours, topping up the water as necessary.

6 Just before serving, make the sauce. Put the remaining jam and orange rind in a heavy-based saucepan. Mix the arrowroot to a paste with a little of the orange juice, then stir the remaining orange juice into the pan. Heat gently until the jam has melted, then stir in the arrowroot paste and bring to the boil. Simmer until thickened, stirring constantly.

7 Unwrap the roly-poly and place on a warmed serving plate. Pour over the hot jam sauce and serve immediately.

SPOTTED DICK

2.30	🥄	604 cals

Serves 4

100 g (4 oz) fresh white
    breadcrumbs
75 g (3 oz) self raising flour
pinch of salt
75 g (3 oz) shredded suet
50 g (2 oz) caster sugar
175 g (6 oz) currants
finely grated rind of ½ a lemon
75–90 ml (5–6 tbsp) milk
custard, to serve

1 Place the breadcrumbs, flour, salt, suet, sugar, currants and lemon rind in a bowl. Stir well until thoroughly mixed.

2 Add enough milk to the dry ingredients to bind together, cutting it through with a palette knife until well mixed. Using one hand only, bring the ingredients together to form a soft, slightly sticky dough.

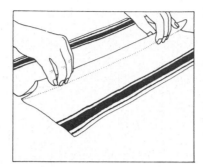

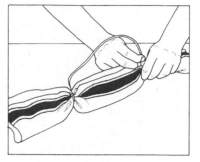

4 Make a 5-cm (2-inch) pleat across a fine-textured, colour-fast teatowel or pudding cloth. Alternatively pleat together sheets of greased, greaseproof paper and strong kitchen foil. Encase the roll in the cloth or foil, pleating the open edges tightly together. Tie the ends securely with string to form a cracker shape. Make a string handle across the top.

5 Lower the suet roll into a large saucepan, two-thirds full of boiling water, curling it if necessary to fit the pan. Cover the pan, lower the heat to a gentle boil and cook for 2 hours. Top up with boiling water at intervals.

6 Lift the spotted dick out of the water. Snip the string and gently roll the pudding on to a serving plate. Decorate with lemon slices if liked and serve immediately, with custard.

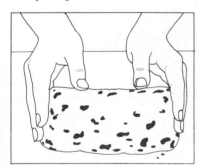

3 Turn the dough out on to a floured work surface. Dust lightly with flour, then knead gently until just smooth. Shape the dough into a neat roll about 15 cm (6 inches) in length.

QUEEN OF PUDDINGS

1.30	306 cals

Serves 4

450 ml (¾ pint) milk

25 g (1 oz) butter or margarine

finely grated rind of ½ a lemon

2 eggs, separated

50 g (2 oz) caster sugar

75 g (3 oz) fresh white
   breadcrumbs

30 ml (2 tbsp) red jam

1 Put the milk, fat and lemon rind in a saucepan and heat gently. Whisk the egg yolks and half of the sugar lightly and pour on the milk, stirring well.

2 Strain the milk over the breadcrumbs. Pour into a greased 1.1-litre (2-pint) ovenproof dish and leave to stand for 15 minutes.

3 Bake in the oven at 180°C (350°F) mark 4 for 25–30 minutes, until lightly set; remove from the oven.

4 Put the jam in a small saucepan. Warm it over low heat, then spread it over the pudding.

5 Whisk the egg whites until stiff and add half the remaining sugar; whisk again and fold in the remaining sugar.

6 Pile the meringue on top of the jam and bake for a further 15–20 minutes, until the meringue is lightly browned.

QUEEN OF PUDDINGS

Queen of Puddings is a traditional English pudding from the nineteenth century. Original recipes for this homely dish (which can be made entirely from store-cupboard ingredients) used red jam and flavoured the pudding with lemon rind, but you can make your own version according to what ingredients you have to hand. Any kind of jam can be used of course, or orange marmalade or ginger marmalade can be used instead of the jam, and grated orange rind or a little finely chopped stem ginger instead of the lemon. Lemon curd makes a delicious

Queen of Puddings, with 25 g (1 oz) desiccated coconut added to the breadcrumb and sugar mixture.

When finishing the pudding with the meringue topping, make absolutely sure that it covers the surface completely and that there are no gaps around the edges for the jam to seep through during baking. After piling the meringue on top, draw it up into peaks with the back of a metal spoon for an attractive effect. Better still, for a neater finish, pipe the meringue on top with a large star nozzle.

CREMA FRITTA

| 1.25* | 🍳 | 314–471 cals |

* plus 2–3 hours cooling

Serves 4–6

3 eggs

50 g (2 oz) caster sugar

50 g (2 oz) plain flour

225 ml (8 fl oz) milk

300 ml (10 fl oz) single cream

finely grated rind of ½ a lemon

100 g (4 oz) dry white breadcrumbs

vegetable oil, for frying

caster sugar, to serve

1 In a large bowl, beat 2 eggs and the sugar together until the mixture is pale.

2 Add the flour, beating all the time, and then, very slowly, beat in the milk and cream. Add the lemon rind.

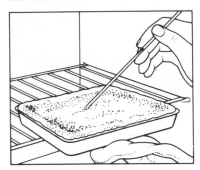

3 Pour the mixture into a buttered shallow 18-cm (7-inch) square cake tin. Bake in the oven at 180°C (350°F) mark 4 for about 1 hour, until a skewer inserted in the middle comes out clean. Leave to cool for 2–3 hours, preferably overnight.

4 When completely cold, cut into sixteen cubes and remove from the cake tin.

5 Beat the remaining egg in a bowl. Dip the cubes in the egg and then in the breadcrumbs until well coated.

6 Heat the oil in a frying pan and when hot, slide in the cubes. Fry for 2–3 minutes until golden brown and a crust is formed. Turn and fry the second side. Drain well on absorbent kitchen paper. Serve immediately, sprinkled with caster sugar.

CREMA FRITTA

Literally translated, this simple Italian dessert means 'fried cream', which is in fact exactly what it is—a thick creamy sauce which is baked, chilled and cut into squares, then fried in oil until crisp and golden.

In Italy, it is traditional to celebrate *Carnevale*—the day before Lent—by eating *crema fritta*. Children and young people invite friends home and everyone eats *crema fritta* in the way that people in other countries eat pancakes. Sprinkled liberally with white sugar, they are always eaten informally—with the fingers.

FLOATING ISLANDS

0.50* | 412 cals

* plus 1 hour chilling

Serves 4

5 egg yolks, beaten

450 ml (¾ pint) milk

50 g (2 oz) caster sugar plus
75 ml (5 tbsp)

2.5 ml (½ tsp) vanilla flavouring

1 egg white

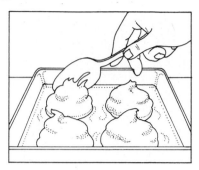

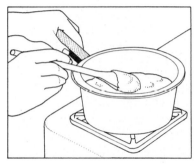

1 Make custard. Put egg yolks, milk and 50 g (2 oz) sugar in the top of a double boiler, or in a heavy-based saucepan over low heat. Cook gently for about 15 minutes, stirring constantly, until the mixture thickens and coats the back of the spoon. Stir in the vanilla flavouring.

2 Divide the custard between four stemmed glasses or dessert dishes. Cover and refrigerate for 1 hour.

3 Meanwhile, whisk the egg white until it will stand in stiff peaks. Add 30 ml (2 tbsp) sugar and whisk again until the sugar is dissolved.

4 Put some cold water into a shallow tin. Bring to a gentle simmer and spoon on the meringue in four even mounds. Poach for about 5 minutes until set, turning once.

5 Remove the meringues with a slotted spoon, drain for a minute on absorbent kitchen paper and spoon on to the custard in the glasses.

6 Put the remaining sugar into a heavy-based saucepan and cook, stirring constantly, for about 3 minutes or until it forms a golden syrup.

7 Remove from the heat and leave for 2 minutes to cool slightly, then drizzle a little of the warm syrup over the top of each meringue. Serve immediately.

Baking

DARK GINGER CAKE

1.45*	✳*	332–442 cals

* plus 2 hours cooling, freeze after
    stage 3

Serves 6–8

75 g (3 oz) black treacle

75 g (3 oz) golden syrup

50 g (2 oz) dark soft brown sugar

75 g (3 oz) butter or block
    margarine

225 g (8 oz) flour

10 ml (2 tsp) ground ginger

5 ml (1 tsp) mixed spice

5 ml (1 tsp) bicarbonate of soda

1 egg, beaten

100 ml (4 fl oz) milk

100 g (4 oz) icing sugar

15 ml (1 tbsp) warm water

50 g (2 oz) stem ginger, drained and
    sliced

1 Base-line and grease an 18-cm
(7-inch) round deep cake tin.
In a saucepan, gently heat the
treacle, syrup, sugar and butter
for 5 minutes until blended.

2 Sift the flour, spices and bicarbonate of soda together into
a bowl. Make a well in the centre
and pour in the treacle mixture
with egg and milk. Beat well with
a wooden spoon until smooth.

3 Pour into the prepared tin and
bake in the oven at 150°C
(300°F) mark 2 for about 1 hour
30 minutes. Turn out on to a wire
rack to cool for at least 2 hours.

4 To make the glacé icing, sift
the icing sugar into a bowl and
gradually add the water. The icing
should be thick enough to coat the
back of a spoon. If necessary add
more water or sugar to adjust the
consistency. Use at once to decorate the cake. Leave for 30 minutes
to set slightly then decorate with
the ginger.

GINGER

This spicy, iced version of old-
fashioned gingerbread contains
two different forms of ginger —
ground ginger in the cake, stem
ginger in the icing. Both come
from the ginger root, a spice
which has origins long before
recorded history, when it was
used as a medicine rather than a
flavouring. Most of the ginger
we buy comes from the Far East,
where it first originated.

Ground ginger is made by
grinding the dried root very
finely. Jamaica ginger is said to
be the finest and most delicate
in flavour, but it is rare that
the type of ginger is specified.

Stem ginger is also called preserved or Chinese ginger. It is
the young tender roots which are
cleaned and peeled then simmered in a heavy syrup. Look for
it in the prettily patterned
Chinese jars, especially around
Christmas time.

GUERNSEY APPLE CAKE

2.00*	✳	337 cals

*plus 1–2 hours cooling

Serves 8

225 g (8 oz) wholewheat flour

10 ml (2 tsp) freshly ground nutmeg

5 ml (1 tsp) ground cinnamon

10 ml (2 tsp) baking powder

225 g (8 oz) cooking apples, peeled, cored and chopped

125 g (4 oz) butter

225 g (8 oz) soft dark brown sugar

2 eggs, beaten

a little milk (optional)

15 ml (1 tbsp) clear honey

15 ml (1 tbsp) demerara sugar

1 Grease an 18-cm (7-inch) deep round cake tin. Line with greaseproof paper and grease the paper.

2 Add the wholewheat flour, nutmeg, cinnamon and baking powder into a bowl. Mix in the chopped cooking apples.

3 Put the butter and sugar into a bowl and beat until pale and fluffy. Add the eggs, a little at a time, and continue to beat.

4 Fold the flour mixture into the creamed mixture with a little milk, if necessary, to give a dropping consistency.

5 Turn the mixture into the prepared tin. Bake in the oven at 170°C (325°F) mark 3 for about 1½ hours. Turn out on to a wire rack to cool for 1–2 hours. Brush with honey and sprinkle with the demerara sugar to decorate. Eat within 1–2 days.

HALF-POUND CAKE

3.00* ✳ 658 cals

* plus 2 hours cooling

Serves 8

225 g (8 oz) butter or margarine

225 g (8 oz) caster sugar

4 eggs, beaten

225 g (8 oz) plain flour

2.5 ml (½ tsp) salt

2.5 ml (½ tsp) mixed spice

225 g (8 oz) seedless raisins

225 g (8 oz) mixed currants and
sultanas

100 g (4 oz) glacé cherries, halved

15 ml (1 tbsp) brandy

a few walnut halves

1 Grease a 20-cm (8-inch) round cake tin. Line with greaseproof paper and grease the paper.

2 Put the fat and sugar into a bowl and beat together until pale and fluffy. Add the egg a little at a time, beating well after each addition.

3 Sift the flour, salt and spice together into a bowl and stir in the raisins, mixed fruit and cherries. Fold the flour and fruit into the creamed mixture with a metal spoon.

4 Add the brandy and mix to a soft dropping consistency. Turn the mixture into the prepared tin, level the surface and arrange the nuts on top.

5 Bake in the oven at 150°C (300°F) mark 2 for about 2½ hours. Leave the cake for 15 minutes to cool slightly in the tin, then turn out on to a wire rack to cool completely for 2 hours.

ORANGE-GLAZED GINGER CAKE

1.45*	✳✳	451 cals

* plus 1 hour setting and 2 hours cooling; freeze after stage 4

Serves 8

125 g (4 oz) lard

125 g (4 oz) caster sugar

1 egg, beaten

275 g (10 oz) plain flour

7.5 ml (1½ tsp) bicarbonate of soda

2.5 ml (½ tsp) salt

5 ml (1 tsp) ground cinnamon

5 ml (1 tsp) ground ginger

100 g (4 oz) golden syrup

100 g (4 oz) black treacle

225 ml (8 fl oz) water

pared rind and juice of 1 orange

1 Grease a 23-cm (9-inch) round cake tin. Line with greaseproof paper and grease the paper.

2 Put the lard and sugar into a bowl and beat together until pale and fluffy. Beat in the egg, then the flour, bicarbonate of soda, salt and spices.

3 Warm together the golden syrup and black treacle in a pan with the water and bring to the boil. Stir into the lard mixture, beating all the time until completely incorporated.

4 Turn the mixture into the prepared tin. Bake in the oven at 180°C (350°F) mark 4 for about 50 minutes or until a fine warmed skewer inserted in the centre comes out clean. Cool in the tin for about 10 minutes before turning out on to a wire rack to cool completely for 2 hours.

5 Cut the orange rind into strips; put into a pan and cover with water. Boil until tender, about 10 minutes and drain well. Make up 100 g (4 oz) glacé icing (see page 154), using 30 ml (2 tbsp) orange juice.

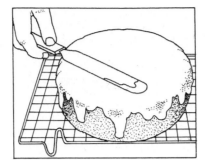

6 Evenly coat the top of the cake and leave to set for 1 hour. Sprinkle the orange strips around the top.

THE GILT ON THE GINGERBREAD

Medieval gingerbread would have been made with honey, not treacle or syrup, but it would have been spiced much the same as this cake. For sale in the markets and fairgrounds it was made in large slabs. Decorative patterns were traditionally made on the bread, sometimes with real gold leaf, and spices such as cloves, of which the heads might be gilded. Our strips of orange rind may seem a poor substitute, but they go well with the spices.

LEMON SWISS ROLL

| 1.00* | ✷* | 376–502 cals |

* plus 1 hour setting and 30 minutes cooling; freeze after stage 4

Serves 6–8

3 eggs, size 2

100 g (4 oz) caster sugar

100 g (4 oz) plain flour

150 ml (5 fl oz) double cream

about 275 g (10 oz) lemon curd

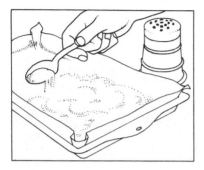

1 Grease a 33 × 23 × 1.5 cm (13 × 9 × ½ inch) Swiss roll tin. Line the base with greaseproof paper and grease the paper. Dust with caster sugar and flour.

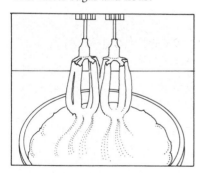

2 Whisk the eggs and sugar in a bowl until thick enough to leave a trail on the surface when the whisk is lifted. Sift in flour and fold gently through the mixture.

3 Turn the mixture into the prepared tin and level the surface. Bake in the oven at 200°C (400°F) mark 6 for 10–12 minutes or until the cake springs back when pressed lightly with a finger and has shrunk away a little from the tin.

4 Sugar a sheet of greaseproof paper and turn the cake out on to it. Roll up with the paper inside. Transfer to a wire rack and leave to cool for 30 minutes.

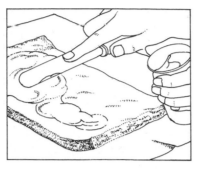

5 Whip the cream until it just holds its shape. Unroll the Swiss roll and spread with three quarters of the lemon curd. Top with cream then roll up again and place on a serving plate.

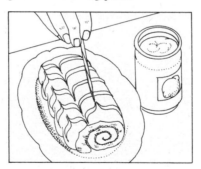

6 Make 100 g (4 oz) glacé icing (see page 154), using 20 ml (4 tsp) water and spoon on to the Swiss roll. Immediately, using the point of a teaspoon, draw rough lines of lemon curd across the icing and pull a skewer through to form a feather pattern. Leave to set, about 1 hour.

RASPBERRY ROULADE

1.00*   ⊟   ✳*   448 cals

* plus 30 minutes cooling; freeze after
rolling the roulade

Serves 6

450 g (1 lb) raspberries, hulled

5 eggs, separated

125 g (4 oz) caster sugar

50 g (2 oz) plain flour

30 ml (2 tbsp) orange-flavoured
  liqueur

300 ml (10 fl oz) double cream

45 ml (3 tbsp) icing sugar

1 Cut out two sheets of greaseproof paper and one of foil,
38 × 40 cm (15 × 16 inches) each.

2 Place the papers on top of each
other with the foil underneath.
Fold up 4 cm (1½ inches) on all
four sides and secure the corners
with paperclips to form a case.

3 Brush the case out with melted
lard, and when set, dust with
caster sugar. Put the case on a
baking sheet.

4 Put half the raspberries into a
blender and work until just
smooth, then press through a nylon
sieve to remove the pips.

5 Whisk the egg yolks in a deep
bowl with the caster sugar
until really thick. Gradually whisk
in the raspberry purée, keeping
the mixture stiff.

6 Sift the flour over the surface
and fold lightly into the egg
and raspberry mixture.

7 Whisk the egg whites until
stiff, and fold them gently
through the raspberry mixture.

8 Turn into the prepared paper
case and smooth the surface.
Bake in the oven at 200°C (400°F)
mark 6 for about 12 minutes or
until the mixture springs back
when pressed lightly with a finger.

9 Cover immediately with a sheet
of greaseproof paper which has
been wrung out under the cold
tap. Lay a clean tea towel over the
top and leave for about 30 minutes
to cool.

10 Meanwhile, reserving six
raspberries for decoration,
sprinkle the rest with the liqueur
and sift over the icing sugar. Whip
the cream until it is just stiff
enough to hold its shape.

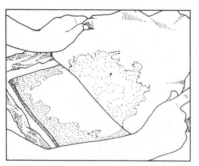

11 Remove the cloth from the
roulade and carefully ease
off the top greaseproof paper. Remove the paperclips. Trim the
edges of the roulade, spread three
quarters of the cream over the top
and scatter with raspberries.

12 Carefully roll up the
roulade, gradually easing off
the paper. Roll on to a large flat
serving plate and decorate with
whirls of cream. Just before
serving, dust with sieved icing
sugar and decorate with the reserved raspberries.

APRICOT CRUNCH

| 1.15* | ✳ | 195 cals |

* plus 1½ hours cooling

Makes 16 wedges

75 g (3 oz) dried apricots

200 ml (⅓ pint) water

100 g (4 oz) butter

100 g (4 oz) demerara sugar

75 ml (5 tbsp) golden syrup

200 g (7 oz) crunchy toasted
    muesli cereal

140 g (5 oz) rolled oats

2.5 ml (½ tsp) mixed spice

10 ml (2 tsp) lemon juice

1 Base-line two 18-cm (7-inch) round sandwich tins with non-stick paper.

2 Simmer the apricots gently in the water for about 10 minutes, or until softened. Blend contents of pan to form a smooth purée. Cool for about 1 hour.

3 Slowly melt the butter, sugar and syrup. Stir in the cereal and oats and continue stirring until thoroughly combined. Add the puréed apricots, mixed spice and lemon juice. Mix well.

4 Divide the mixture between the prepared tins and spread evenly over the base. Press down well to level the surface.

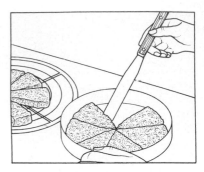

5 Bake in the oven at 180°C (350°F) mark 4 for about 35 minutes. Cut each round into eight wedges. Cool in the tin for 30 minutes until firm. Carefully ease the wedges out of the tin and store in an airtight container when completely cold.

LEMON SEED CAKE

1.35*	✳*	604–806 cals

* plus 1 hour cooling; freeze after
stage 3

Serves 6–8

325 g (11 oz) butter

175 g (6 oz) soft brown sugar

finely grated rind and juice of 2
    large lemons

3 eggs, separated

250 g (9 oz) self-raising flour

10 ml (2 tsp) caraway seeds

175 g (6 oz) icing sugar, plus a little
    extra to decorate

1 Grease and base-line an 18-cm
(7-inch) round cake tin. In a
bowl, cream together 175 g (6 oz)
butter, the brown sugar and the
rind from one lemon, until fluffy.

2 Beat in the egg yolks, then
stir in flour, caraway seeds and
45 ml (3 tbsp) lemon juice.

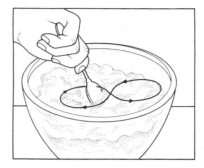

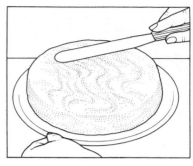

3 Fold in the stiffly whisked egg
whites; turn into tin. Bake in
the oven at 180°C (350°F) mark 4
for 1 hour. Turn out onto a wire
rack and leave to cool for 1 hour.

4 To make the butter icing, cream
remaining butter until fluffy.
Gradually sift in icing sugar until
smooth. Beat in 15 ml (1 tbsp)
lemon juice and the remaining
grated lemon rind.

5 Use the lemon butter icing to
completely coat the cake and
then swirl using a small palette
knife. Dust lightly with sifted icing
sugar. Best eaten the next day.

CARAMEL BANANA TORTE

| 1.45* | 🔲 🔲 ✳* | 403 cals |

* plus 2 hours cooling; freeze after stage 4

Serves 8

175 g (6 oz) self-raising flour

1.25 ml ($\frac{1}{4}$ tsp) baking powder

1.25 ml ($\frac{1}{4}$ tsp) bicarbonate of soda

50 g (2 oz) butter, cut into pieces

150 g (5 oz) caster sugar

350 g (12 oz) ripe bananas

2.5 ml ($\frac{1}{2}$ tsp) freshly grated nutmeg

45 ml (3 tbsp) milk

1 egg, beaten

75 g (3 oz) sugar

175 g (6 oz) full fat soft cheese

30 ml (2 tbsp) lemon juice

30 ml (2 tbsp) icing sugar

50 g (2 oz) flaked almonds, browned

1 Grease a 20-cm (8-inch) round cake tin. Base-line with grease-proof paper and grease the paper.

2 Sift the flour, baking powder and bicarbonate of soda into a bowl. Rub in the butter until the mixture resembles fine bread-crumbs then stir in the caster sugar.

3 Peel half the bananas and mash them in a bowl then beat in the grated nutmeg, milk and egg and stir into the dry ingredients. Turn the mixture into the pre-pared tin and level the surface.

4 Bake in the oven at 180°C (350°F) mark 4 for about 40 minutes or until a warmed fine skewer inserted in the centre comes out clean. Cool in tin for 5 minutes before turning out on to wire rack to cool completely (about 2 hours). Slice the cake in half horizontally.

5 Make the caramel. Put rest of sugar into a small pan. Dissolve, without stirring, over gentle heat, then boil until a rich brown colour.

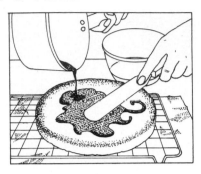

6 When the caramel is ready, immediately pour it over the top surface of the cake. Use an oiled knife to spread the caramel over the cake.

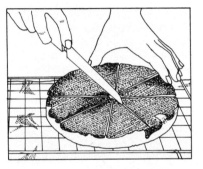

7 Mark the caramel topped cake into eight portions with the point of a knife.

8 Put the soft cheese, lemon juice and icing sugar into a bowl and beat together. Peel and chop the remaining bananas and add to half of the cheese mixture. Use to sandwich the cakes together.

9 Spread a little cheese mixture around the sides and cover with most of the almonds. Decorate top with the remaining cheese mixture and almonds.

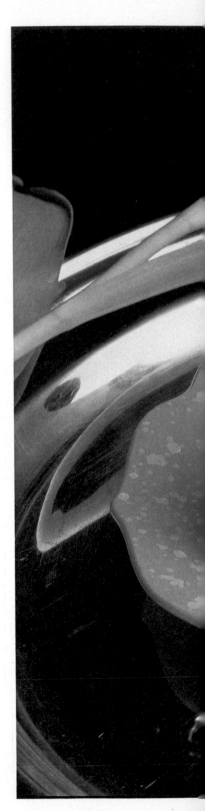

BLACK FOREST GÂTEAU

1.45* 🥧	✳*

516–645 cals

* plus 30 minutes cooling; freeze after stage 5 after cooling

Serves 8–10

100 g (4 oz) butter

6 eggs

225 g (8 oz) caster sugar

75 g (3 oz) plain flour

50 g (2 oz) cocoa powder

2.5 ml ($\frac{1}{2}$ tsp) vanilla flavouring

two 425-g (15-oz) cans stoned black cherries

60 ml (4 tbsp) kirsch

600 ml (20 fl oz) whipping cream

100 g (4 oz) chocolate curls, to decorate (see page 153)

5 ml (1 tsp) arrowroot

1 Grease a 23-cm (9-inch) round cake tin. Line with greaseproof paper and grease the paper. Put the butter into a bowl, stand this over a pan of warm water and beat it until really soft but not melted.

2 Put the eggs and sugar into a large bowl and whisk until thick enough to leave a trail on the surface when the whisk is lifted.

3 Sift the flour and cocoa into the mixture and lightly fold in with a metal spoon. Fold in vanilla flavouring and softened butter.

4 Turn the mixture into the prepared tin, tilt the tin to spread the mixture evenly, and bake in the oven at 180°C (350°F) mark 4 for about 40 minutes until risen and firm to the touch.

5 Turn out of the tin on to a wire rack, covered with greaseproof paper, to cool for 30 minutes. Strain the syrup from the cans of cherries, reserving the cherries, 45 ml (3 tbsp) syrup for the glaze and 75 ml (5 tbsp) syrup for the filling. Add the kirsch to latter syrup.

6 Cut the cake into three horizontally. Place a layer on a flat plate and spoon over 45 ml (3 tbsp) of the kirsch-flavoured syrup.

7 Whip the cream until it holds its shape and spread a little thinly over the soaked sponge. Reserve a quarter of the cherries for decoration and scatter half the remainder over the cream.

8 Repeat the layers of sponge, syrup, cream and cherries. Top with the third cake round and spoon over the remaining kirsch-flavoured syrup.

9 Spread a thin layer of cream around the sides of the cake, reserving a third to decorate. Press on the chocolate curls, reserving a few to decorate the top.

10 Fill a piping bag, fitted with a large star nozzle, with the remaining whipped cream and pipe whirls of cream around the edge of the cake. Top each whirl with a chocolate curl.

11 Fill the centre with the reserved cherries. Blend the arrowroot with the reserved 45 ml (3 tbsp) syrup and boil, stirring. Brush the glaze over the cherries.

DEVIL'S FOOD CAKE

2.00* ☐ ✳* 696 cals

* plus 30 minutes cooling and 1 hour standing time; freeze after stage 8

Serves 8

75 g (3 oz) plain chocolate plus 25 g (1 oz) (optional)

250 g (9 oz) soft light brown sugar

200 ml (⅓ pint) milk

75 g (3 oz) butter or block margarine

2 eggs

175 g (6 oz) plain flour

3.75 ml (¾ tsp) bicarbonate of soda

450 g (1 lb) caster sugar

120 ml (8 tbsp) water

2 egg whites

1 Lightly brush two 19-cm (7½-inch) sandwich tins with melted lard. Base-line with grease-proof paper and grease the paper. Leave for 5 minutes to set, then dust with sugar and flour.

2 Break 75 g (3 oz) of the chocolate in small pieces into a saucepan. Add 75 g (3 oz) of the brown sugar and the milk. Heat very gently, stirring to dissolve the sugar and blend the ingredients, then remove from the heat and leave to cool for 10 minutes.

3 Put the butter into a bowl and beat until pale and soft. Gradually add the remaining brown sugar and beat until pale and fluffy.

4 Lightly whisk the eggs and gradually beat into the creamed mixture. Slowly add the cooled chocolate mixture beating until combined.

5 Sift the flour and bicarbonate of soda into the creamed mixture and gently fold in using a metal spoon. Turn the mixture into prepared tins, then tap gently to level it.

6 Bake in the oven at 180°C (350°F) mark 4 for about 35 minutes. The cakes are cooked when they spring back when pressed lightly with a finger and have shrunk away a little from the sandwich tins.

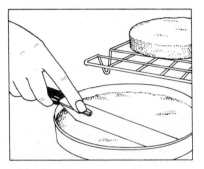

7 Cool in the tins for a couple of minutes before turning out on to a wire rack to cool completely. Ease them away from the tins using a palette knife, taking care not to break the crust.

8 Tap the tins on the work surface to loosen the cakes. Gently pull off the paper and leave to cool.

9 Put the sugar for the frosting in a pan with the water, dissolve over a low heat, then boil rapidly to 115°C (240°F) on a sugar thermometer, or until the mixture reaches the soft ball stage. Check by plunging a teaspoonful into a bowl of iced water. It should form a ball in your fingers.

10 Meanwhile, whisk the egg whites in a large bowl until stiff. Allow the bubbles in the syrup to settle, then slowly pour the hot syrup on to the egg whites, beating constantly. Once all the sugar syrup is added, continue beating until the mixture stands in peaks and just starts to become matt round the edges. (The icing sets quickly, so work rapidly.)

11 Sandwich the cakes together with a little of the frosting. Spread the remaining frosting over the cake with a palette knife. Pull the icing up into peaks all over, then leave the cake for about 30 minutes, to allow the icing to set slightly.

12 Break up the chocolate, if using, and put it in a small bowl over a pan of hot water. Heat gently, stirring, until the chocolate has melted. Dribble the chocolate over the top of the cake with a teaspoon to make a swirl pattern. Leave for 30 minutes before serving.

AMERICAN CAKES

Two classic cakes from America are Angel Food Cake and Devil's Food Cake. The first is an airy vanilla-flavoured sponge. It is very white in colour and light in texture because it is made with flour and egg whites, with no egg yolks. Its opposite number is the rich, moist chocolate cake recipe given here. Generously filled and coated with frosting, Devil's Food Cake is a favourite for serving as a dinnertime dessert, or at coffee parties.

MARBLED CHOCOLATE RING CAKE

2.00* 🍴🍴 ✳*	775 cals

* plus 1¼ hours cooling and 1 hour
setting; freeze after stage 6

Serves 8

250 g (9 oz) plain chocolate
5 ml (1 tsp) vanilla flavouring
45 ml (3 tbsp) water
350 g (12 oz) butter
225 g (8 oz) caster sugar
4 eggs, size 2, beaten
225 g (8 oz) plain flour
10 ml (2 tsp) baking powder
2.5 ml (½ tsp) salt
50 g (2 oz) ground almonds
30 ml (2 tbsp) milk

1 Grease a 1.7-litre (3-pint) ring
mould. Break 50 g (2 oz) chocolate into a heatproof bowl. Add the
vanilla flavouring and 15 ml
(1 tbsp) water and place over simmering water. Stir until the chocolate is melted, then remove from
heat and leave to cool for 10
minutes.

2 Put 225 g (8 oz) butter and the
caster sugar into a bowl and
beat together until pale and fluffy.
Beat in the eggs one at a time.

3 Fold the flour, baking powder
and salt into the creamed mixture with the ground almonds. Stir
in the milk. Spoon half the mixture into base of ring mould.

4 Stir the cooled but still soft
chocolate into the remaining
mixture. Spoon into the tin.

5 Draw a knife through the cake
mixture in a spiral. Level the
surface of the mixture again.

6 Bake in the oven at 180°C
(350°F) mark 4 for about 55
minutes or until a fine warmed
skewer inserted in the centre
comes out clean. Turn out on to a
wire rack to cool for 1 hour.

7 Make the chocolate frosting.
Break 150 g (5 oz) chocolate
into a heatproof bowl with 30 ml
(2 tbsp) water and the remaining
butter. Place over simmering water
and stir until the chocolate is
melted, then pour over the cooled
cake, working quickly to coat top
and sides. Leave to set for 1 hour.

8 Melt the remaining chocolate
over simmering water as before. Spoon into a greaseproof
paper piping bag, snip off the tip
and drizzle chocolate over the cake.

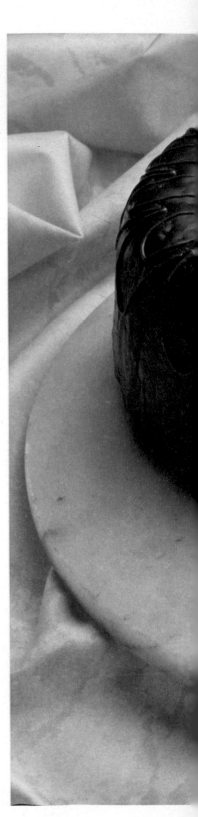

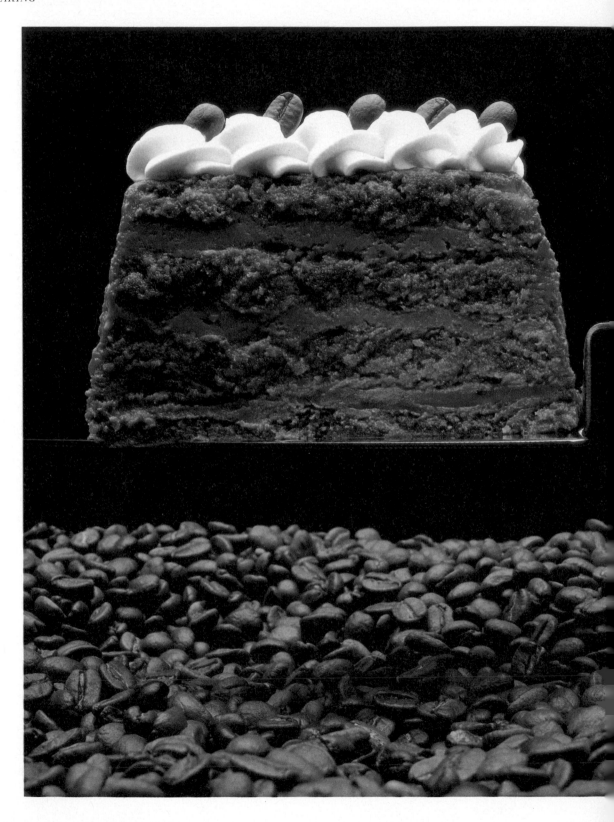

CHOCOLATE COFFEE REFRIGERATOR SLICE

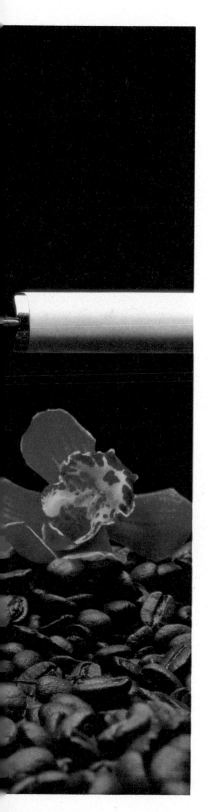

$1.00*$		$**$

752–1129 cals

* plus 3–4 hours chilling; freeze after stage 7

Serves 4–6

| 30 ml (2 tbsp) instant coffee granules |
| 250 ml (7 fl oz) boiling water |
| 45 ml (3 tbsp) brandy |
| 125 g (4 oz) plain chocolate |
| 125 g (4 oz) unsalted butter, softened |
| 50 g (2 oz) icing sugar |
| 2 egg yolks |
| 300 ml (10 fl oz) whipping cream |
| 50 g (2 oz) chopped almonds, toasted |
| about 30 sponge fingers |
| coffee beans, to decorate |

1 Grease a 22×11.5 cm ($8\frac{1}{2} \times 4\frac{1}{2}$ inch) top measurement loaf tin and base-line with greaseproof paper. Grease the paper.

2 Make up the coffee granules with the boiling water and stir in the brandy. Set aside to cool for 15 minutes.

3 Break the chocolate into a small heatproof bowl with 15 ml (1 tbsp) water and place over simmering water. Stir until the chocolate is melted then remove from the heat and allow to cool for about 5 minutes.

4 Sift the icing sugar into a bowl. Add the butter and beat them together until pale and fluffy. Add the egg yolks, beating well.

5 Lightly whip the cream and refrigerate half of it. Stir the remaining cream, the cooled chocolate and the nuts into the butter and egg yolk mixture.

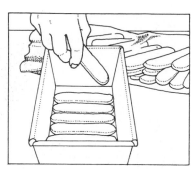

6 Line the bottom of the prepared loaf tin with sponge fingers, cutting to fit if necessary. Spoon over one quarter of the coffee and brandy mixture. Spoon over one third of the chocolate mixture.

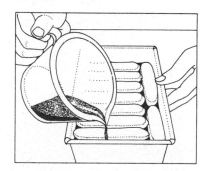

7 Continue layering the chocolate mixture and sponge fingers into the tin, soaking each layer with coffee and ending with soaked sponge fingers. Weight down lightly and refrigerate for 3–4 hours until set.

8 Turn out, remove the paper and decorate with the reserved whipped cream and the coffee beans.

CHOCOLATE MACAROON LOG

| 2.00* | 🍴 | 477 cals |

* plus overnight chilling
Serves 10

3 egg whites, size 6
175 g (6 oz) ground almonds
275 g (10 oz) caster sugar
7.5 ml (1½ tsp) almond flavouring
100 g (4 oz) shelled hazel nuts
100 g (4 oz) plain chocolate
300 ml (10 fl oz) double cream
45 ml (3 tbsp) almond liqueur
icing sugar, cocoa, chocolate
   leaves, to decorate

1 Line two baking sheets with non-stick paper. Whisk the egg whites until stiff then fold in the ground almonds, caster sugar and almond flavouring.

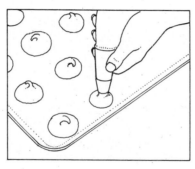

2 Spoon into a piping bag fitted with a 1-cm (½-inch) plain nozzle and pipe 30 small rounds on to the prepared baking sheets, allowing room between each for the mixture to spread.

3 Bake in the oven at 180°C (350°F) mark 4 for about 20 minutes. Transfer to a wire rack for 20 minutes to cool.

4 Spread the nuts out on a baking sheet and brown in the oven at 200°C (400°F) mark 6 for 5–10 minutes. Put into a soft tea towel and rub off the skins. Chop finely, reserving two whole nuts.

5 Break the chocolate in small pieces into a heatproof bowl and place over simmering water until the chocolate is melted, then remove from heat and cool for 5 minutes.

6 Whip the cream until it holds its shape and gradually beat in the cooled chocolate, nuts and liqueur.

7 Use some of the chocolate cream to sandwich the macaroons together.

8 Place side by side on a serving plate to form a double log. Spread chocolate cream on top and add a further layer of macaroons. Spread remaining chocolate cream over the top and sides, refrigerate overnight.

9 Dust with icing sugar and cocoa then decorate with chocolate leaves and the reserved whole hazel nuts. Serve with more whipped cream, if liked.

——————— VARIATION ———————

To make the hazel nut flavour more pronounced in this recipe, substitute ground, unblanched hazel nuts for the almonds when making the macaroons and omit the almond flavouring.

COFFEE PRALINE GATEAU

| 1.30* 🥄 | ❋* | 350 cals |

* plus 2–4 hours cooling; freeze after stage 4

Serves 6

2 eggs, size 2

100 g (4 oz) caster sugar

50 g (2 oz) plain flour

15 ml (1 tbsp) coffee essence

25 g (1 oz) blanched almonds

150 ml (5 fl oz) double cream

30 ml (2 tbsp) coffee-flavoured liqueur

icing sugar, for dusting

25 ml (5 tsp) instant coffee powder

7.5 ml (1½ tsp) arrowroot

170-g (6-oz) can evaporated milk

30 ml (2 tbsp) soft light brown sugar

1 Grease a 20-cm (8-inch) round cake tin. Base-line with grease-proof paper and grease the paper. Dust with caster sugar and flour.

2 Put eggs into a deep bowl with 75 g (3 oz) caster sugar and whisk vigorously until the mixture is very thick and light and leaves a trail. If hand mixing, whisk the mixture over a saucepan of simmering water.

3 Sift the flour evenly over sur-face of the egg mixture and fold in lightly until no traces of flour remain. Lightly fold in the coffee essence.

4 Turn into the prepared tin and bake at once in the oven at 180°C (350°F) mark 4 for about 30 minutes or until the sponge springs back when pressed lightly with a finger and has shrunk away a little from the tin. Turn out on to a wire rack and leave for 1–2 hours.

5 Meanwhile, make the praline. Oil a baking sheet. Put the remaining caster sugar into a small frying pan with the blanched al-monds and heat gently until the sugar dissolves and caramelises.

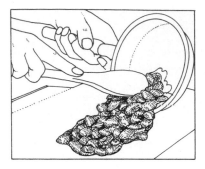

6 Pour the praline on to the pre-pared baking sheet and leave for 10–15 minutes to cool and harden.

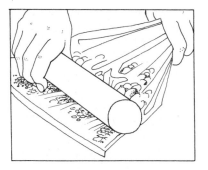

7 When cold, grind or crush with end of a rolling pin in a strong bowl. Whip the cream until it holds its shape then whisk in the liqueur and fold in three-quarters of praline (ground nut mixture).

8 Split the sponge in half and sandwich with the cream. Dust the top with icing sugar and decor-ate with praline. Refrigerate for 1–2 hours.

9 Make the coffee sauce. In a small pan, mix the coffee powder and arrowroot to a smooth paste with a little water then make up to 150 ml (¼ pint) with more water. Add the evaporated milk and brown sugar and bring slowly to the boil, stirring. Bubble for 1 minute. Serve warm.

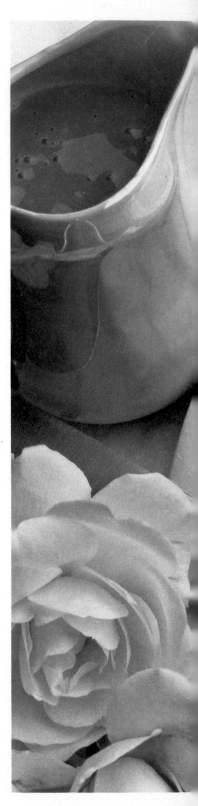

HARVEST CAKE

| **3.45*** 🍰 | ❄** | 605 cals |

* plus 2–3 hours cooling; freeze after stage 7

Serves 10

175 g (6 oz) butter or block margarine

175 g (6 oz) dark soft brown sugar

3 eggs, beaten

225 g (8 oz) plain flour

5 ml (1 tsp) baking powder

5 ml (1 tsp) ground cinnamon

5 ml (1 tsp) freshly grated nutmeg

pinch of salt

225 g (8 oz) sultanas

100 g (4 oz) seedless raisins

100 g (4 oz) dried apricots, chopped

175 g (6 oz) Brazil nuts, chopped

60 ml (4 tbsp) black treacle

finely grated rind and juice of 1 lemon

about 30 ml (2 tbsp) brandy

300 g (11 oz) marzipan

icing sugar

15–30 ml (1–2 tbsp) apricot jam

marzipan fruits (see below)

1 Grease a 20-cm (8-inch) round cake tin. Line with greaseproof paper and grease the paper.

2 Put the butter and sugar into a bowl and beat together until pale and fluffy. Beat in the eggs a little at a time.

3 Sift the flour with the baking powder, spices and salt and fold into the creamed mixture. Stir in the dried fruit and nuts, black treacle, lemon rind and juice until evenly mixed.

4 Add enough brandy to give a soft, dropping consistency. (Add more brandy or a little milk if the mixture is too stiff.)

5 Turn the mixture into the prepared tin and make a slight hollow in the centre with the back of a metal spoon. Bake at 170°C (325°F) mark 3 for 1 hour.

6 Cover with foil and lower the oven to 150°C (300°F) mark 2. Cook for a further 2 hours or until a fine warmed skewer inserted in the centre comes out clean.

7 Leave the cake to cool in the tin for 2–3 hours, then turn out and peel off the lining paper.

8 Knead the marzipan on a surface lightly dusted with icing sugar. Roll out to a circle slightly larger than the diameter of the cake.

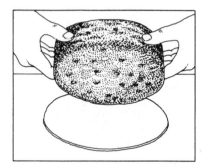

9 Brush the top of the cake with the apricot jam, then press the cake gently on to the marzipan, jam-side down.

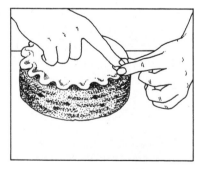

10 Turn the cake the right way up, trim off the excess marzipan with a sharp knife, then crimp the edge and decorate with marzipan fruits.

MARZIPAN FRUITS
Mould marzipan into fruit shapes. Paint with diluted food colouring; use cloves for stalks.

BÛCHE DE NOËL
(FRENCH CHRISTMAS LOG)

  ✳*

759–1012 cals

* plus 35 minutes cooling; freeze after step 8

Serves 6 8

1 egg white

175 g (6 oz) caster sugar, plus a
　little extra for dredging

3 eggs, size 2

75 g (3 oz) plain flour, plus a
　little extra for dredging

30 ml (2 tbsp) cocoa powder

225 g (8 oz) unsalted butter

50 g (2 oz) plain chocolate

500 g (1 lb) icing sugar, plus a
　little extra for decorating

440 g (15½ oz) can sweetened
　chestnut purée

holly sprigs, to decorate

1 Line a baking sheet with non-stick paper. Make meringue mushrooms. Whisk the egg white until stiff, add 25 g (1 oz) of the sugar and whisk again until stiff. Fold in another 25 g (1 oz) sugar.

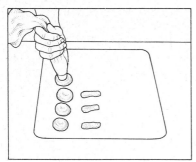

2 Spoon the meringue into a piping bag fitted with a plain nozzle. Pipe the meringue on to the prepared baking sheet to resemble small mushroom caps and stalks. Bake in the oven at 110°C (225°F) mark ¼ for about 1½ hours until dry. Leave to cool for at least 15 minutes.

3 Grease a 33 × 23 cm (13 × 9 inch) Swiss roll tin. Line with greaseproof paper and grease the paper. Dredge with the extra caster sugar then flour, knocking out any excess.

4 Put the eggs and measured caster sugar in a deep bowl which fits snugly inside the rim of a saucepan of simmering water.

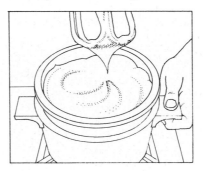

5 Whisk the eggs and sugar until thick enough to leave a trail on the surface when the beaters are lifted. Do not overheat the bowl by letting it come into contact with the simmering water or by having the heat under the saucepan too high.

6 Take the bowl off the saucepan and whisk the mixture for 5 minutes until cool. Sift in the measured flour and cocoa and gently fold through the mixture. Fold in 15 ml (1 tbsp) water.

7 Pour the mixture gently into the prepared tin and lightly level off the surface. Bake in the oven at 200°C (400°F) mark 6 for about 12 minutes until slightly shrunk away from the tin.

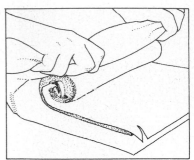

8 Meanwhile, place a sheet of greaseproof paper over a tea towel. Dredge the paper with caster sugar and turn the cake out on to it. Trim off the crusty edges with a sharp knife. Roll up with the paper inside. Transfer to a wire rack, seam side down. Leave to cool for 20 minutes.

9 Put the butter in a bowl and beat until soft. Put the chocolate and 15 ml (1 tbsp) water in a bowl over a pan of hot water. Melt, then leave to cool slightly. Gradually sift and beat the icing sugar into the softened butter, then add the cool chocolate.

10 Unroll the cold Swiss roll and spread the chestnut purée over the surface. Roll up again without the paper inside. Place on a cake board or plate.

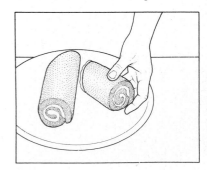

11 Cut a thick diagonal slice off one end of the Swiss roll and attach with butter cream to the side of the roll.

12 Using a piping bag and a large star nozzle, pipe thin lines of butter cream over the log. Pipe 1 or 2 swirls of butter cream to represent knots in the wood. Sandwich the meringues together with a little butter cream to form mushrooms. Decorate the log with the mushrooms and sprigs of holly. Dust lightly with sifted icing sugar. Store in an airtight container for up to 2–3 days.

Menu Suggestion
In France, Bûche de Noël is served on Christmas Eve as a dessert, after the traditional main course of Roast Turkey.

BÛCHE DE NOËL
Bûche de Noël is the traditional cake eaten in France at Christmas time. The tradition of serving this and the English Yule log dates back to the days when a huge log used to be burnt on Christmas Eve.

ALMOND SPONGE CHRISTMAS CAKE WITH GLACÉ FRUIT

2.30* 🍴🍴	477–597 cals

* plus cooling

Serves 8–10

225 g (8 oz) butter or margarine

225 g (8 oz) caster sugar

4 eggs, beaten

125 g (4 oz) self-raising flour, sifted with a pinch of salt

100 g (4 oz) ground almonds

225 g (8 oz) can pineapple slices

about 30 ml (2 tbsp) warm water

30 ml (2 tbsp) apricot jam

50 g (2 oz) glacé cherries

50 g (2 oz) blanched almonds

25–40 g (1–1½ oz) candied angelica

red and green ribbon, to decorate

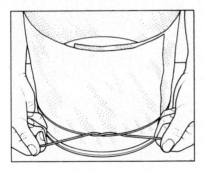

1 Prepare the cake tin. Grease and base line a deep 20.5 cm (8 inch) loose-bottomed round cake tin. Tie a double thickness of brown paper around the outside of the tin, to come about 5 cm (2 inches) above the rim.

2 Put the butter and sugar in a large bowl and beat until light and fluffy. Add the eggs a little at a time and beat until thoroughly combined. Add a little of the flour with the last addition of the egg, to prevent curdling, then beat in the ground almonds and the remaining flour.

3 Drain the pineapple slices and chop roughly. Dry thoroughly with absorbent kitchen paper. Fold into the cake mixture, then add enough warm water to give a soft dropping consistency. Spoon the mixture into the prepared cake tin and level the surface.

4 Bake the cake in the oven at 170°C (325°F) mark 3 for 1½ hours or until cooked through, covering the top with a double thickness of greaseproof paper after 1 hour's cooking time, if necessary, to prevent over-browning. To test if the cake is cooked, insert a warmed fine skewer in the centre—it should come out clean.

5 Leave the cake to settle in the tin for 5–10 minutes, then remove and stand on a wire rack.

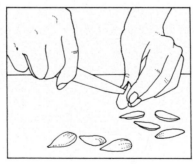

6 Make the decoration for the top of the cake while the cake is still warm. Cut the glacé cherries in half. Split the blanched almonds in half lengthways. Cut the angelica into diamond shapes.

7 Warm half of the jam until melted, then sieve and brush over the top of the warm cake. Press the cherries, nuts and angelica on top of the cake in a decorative design (as in the photograph or use your own design). Melt and sieve the remaining jam, then brush over the design.

8 To serve, tie red and green ribbon around the cake to give it a festive look. Store the cake in an airtight tin for up to 2 weeks.

Menu Suggestion
This cake is equally good served at teatime or with morning coffee.

ALMOND SPONGE CHRISTMAS CAKE WITH GLACÉ FRUIT

For those who do not like the traditional rich fruit cake at Christmas, this cake is the perfect alternative. The cake itself is light and moist, and the decoration looks as festive as a traditional snowscene, or any other design using marzipan and royal icing.

The decoration of glacé cherries, almonds and candied angelica gives a Christmassy look, but you can vary this according to taste; at Christmas-time, many stores and delicatessens stock other glacé fruit such as apricots and pineapples.

FRUIT CRUSTED CIDER CAKE

1.15* 🄼	268–334 cals

* plus 1 hour cooling

Serves 8–10

45 ml (3 tbsp) golden syrup

150 g (5 oz) butter or block margarine

350 g (12 oz) cooking apples, peeled, cored and finely chopped

45 ml (3 tbsp) mincemeat

50 g (2 oz) cornflakes, crushed

125 g (4 oz) caster sugar

2 eggs, beaten

125 g (4 oz) self-raising flour

45 ml (3 tbsp) dry cider

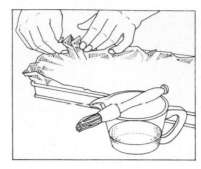

1 Line a 35.5 × 11.5 cm (14 × 4½ inch) shallow rectangular tart frame with foil. Grease the foil. Put the syrup into a pan with 25 g (1 oz) butter and melt. Add apples, mincemeat, cornflakes. Set aside.

2 Put the remaining butter and the sugar into a bowl and beat together until pale and fluffy. Gradually beat in the eggs.

3 Fold the flour into the mixture. Pour in the cider and mix it in. Turn the mixture into the prepared frame and level the surface. Spread the apple mixture evenly over it.

4 Bake in the oven at 170°C (325°F) mark 3 for 45–50 minutes or until firm to the touch. Cool in the metal frame for 1 hour, then cut into bars for serving.

GINGERBREAD SLAB

1.40*	✳	121–145 cals

* plus 1 hour cooling; store for at least 2 days before eating

Makes 20–24 slices

125 g (4 oz) black treacle
125 g (4 oz) golden syrup
50 g (2 oz) butter or block margarine
50 g (2 oz) lard
225 g (8 oz) plain flour
1.25 ml (¼ tsp) bicarbonate of soda
5 ml (1 tsp) mixed spice
5 ml (1 tsp) ground ginger
100 g (4 oz) dark soft brown sugar
150 ml (¼ pint) milk

1 Grease an 18-cm (7-inch) square cake tin. Base-line with greaseproof paper and then grease the paper.

2 Put the black treacle, golden syrup, butter or margarine and lard into a saucepan and heat gently to melt the mixture.

3 Sift the flour, bicarbonate of soda and spices into a bowl and stir in the sugar.

4 Make a well in the centre of the dry ingredients and pour in the milk and the treacle mixture. Beat well until smooth and of a thick pouring consistency.

5 Turn into the prepared tin and bake in the oven at 170°C (325°F) mark 3 for 1–1¼ hours or until a fine warmed skewer inserted in the centre of the cake comes out clean.

6 Cool in the tin for 1 hour. Remove from tin, wrap and store for at least 2 days in an airtight tin before eating. Serve sliced, plain or buttered.

CHERRY AND COCONUT CAKE

2.00*	✳	336–420 cals

* plus 1 hour cooling

Serves 8–10

| 250 g (9 oz) self-raising flour |
| 1.25 ml ($\frac{1}{4}$ tsp) salt |
| 125 g (4 oz) butter or block margarine, cut into pieces |
| 75 g (3 oz) desiccated coconut |
| 125 g (4 oz) caster sugar |
| 125 g (4 oz) glacé cherries, finely chopped |
| 2 eggs, size 6, beaten |
| 225 ml (8 fl oz) milk |
| 25 g (1 oz) shredded coconut |

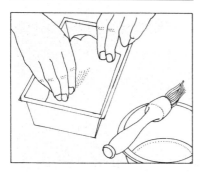

1 Grease a 1.3-litre ($2\frac{1}{4}$-pint) loaf tin. Base-line with grease-proof paper, grease the paper and dust with flour.

2 Put the flour and salt into a bowl and rub in the fat until the mixture resembles fine bread-crumbs. Stir in the coconut, sugar and cherries.

3 Whisk together the eggs and milk and beat into the dry in-gredients. Turn the mixture into the tin, level the surface and scatter over the shredded coconut.

4 Bake in the oven at 180°C (350°F) mark 4 for $1\frac{1}{2}$ hours until a fine warmed skewer in-serted in the centre comes out clean. Check after 40 minutes and cover with greaseproof paper if overbrowning. Turn out on to a wire rack to cool for 1 hour.

PRUNE AND NUT TEABREAD

1.30* ✻ 261–326 cals

* plus 1 hour cooling; wrap and store for 1–2 days before slicing

Serves 8–10

275 g (10 oz) self-raising flour

pinch of salt

7.5 ml (1½ tsp) ground cinnamon

75 g (3 oz) butter or block
   margarine, cut into pieces

75 g (3 oz) demerara sugar

1 egg, beaten

100 ml (4 fl oz) milk

50 g (2 oz) shelled walnuts, chopped

100 g (4 oz) pitted tenderised prunes

15 ml (1 tbsp) clear honey

1 Grease a 2-litre (3½-pint) loaf tin. Base-line the loaf tin with greaseproof paper and grease the paper.

2 Sift the flour and salt into a bowl and add the cinnamon. Rub in the fat until the mixture resembles fine breadcrumbs.

3 Stir in the sugar, and make a well in the centre. Add the egg and milk and gradually draw in the dry ingredients to form a smooth dough.

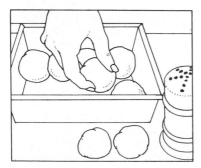

4 Using floured hands shape the mixture into sixteen even-sized rounds. Place eight in the base of the tin. Sprinkle over half the nuts.

5 Snip the prunes and sprinkle on top of the nuts. Place the remaining dough rounds on top and sprinkle over the remaining chopped walnuts.

6 Bake in the oven at 190°C (375°F) mark 5 for about 50 minutes or until firm to the touch. Check near the end of cooking time and cover with greaseproof paper if it is overbrowning.

7 Turn out on to a wire rack to cool for 1 hour. When cold brush with the honey to glaze. Wrap and store for 1–2 days in an airtight tin before slicing and buttering.

TEABREADS

A teabread mixture is usually less rich than cake, but no less delicious for that. Serve it sliced and thickly buttered, like good fresh bread. It is excellent served with afternoon tea or mid-morning coffee, or try it occasionally as a lunchtime pudding. A fruity teabread like this one improves as it matures, the flavour and moisture from the fruit penetrating the cake and mellowing it over a number of days.

In continental Europe it is traditional to serve sweet breads for breakfast, with either butter or cheese. Try thin slices of Edam or Gouda cheese, or spread with curd cheese instead of butter and omit the cheese.

GINGER MARMALADE TEABREAD

1.30*	✳	167–208 cals

* plus 1 hour cooling

Serves 8–10

200 g (7 oz) plain flour

5 ml (1 tsp) ground ginger

5 ml (1 tsp) baking powder

40 g (1½ oz) block margarine

65 g (2½ oz) soft light brown sugar

60 ml (4 tbsp) ginger marmalade

1 egg, beaten

60 ml (4 tbsp) milk

40 g (1½ oz) stem ginger, chopped

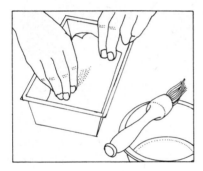

1 Grease a 900-ml (1½-pint) loaf tin with melted lard. Base-line with greaseproof paper and grease the paper.

2 Put the flour, ginger and baking powder into a bowl and rub in fat until mixture resembles fine breadcrumbs. Stir in sugar.

3 Mix together the marmalade, egg and most of the milk. Stir into the dry ingredients and add the rest of the milk, if necessary, to mix to a soft dough.

4 Turn the mixture into the prepared tin, level the surface and press pieces of ginger on top. Bake in the oven at 170°C (325°F) mark 3 for about 1 hour or until golden. Turn out on to a wire rack for 1 hour to cool.

MIXED FRUIT TEABREAD

1.35*	✳	229–287 cals

* plus overnight soaking, 1 hour
cooling and 1–2 days maturing

Serves 8–10

175 g (6 oz) raisins

125 g (4 oz) sultanas

50 g (2 oz) currants

175 g (6 oz) soft brown sugar

300 ml ($\frac{1}{2}$ pint) strained cold tea

1 egg, beaten

225 g (8 oz) plain wholemeal flour

7.5 ml ($1\frac{1}{2}$ tsp) baking powder

2.5 ml ($\frac{1}{2}$ tsp) ground mixed spice

1 Place the dried fruit and the sugar in a large bowl. Pour over the tea, stir well to mix and leave to soak overnight.

2 The next day, add the egg, flour, baking powder and mixed spice to the fruit and tea mixture. Beat thoroughly with a wooden spoon until all the ingredients are evenly combined.

3 Spoon the cake mixture into a greased and base-lined 900 g (2 lb) loaf tin. Level the surface.

4 Bake in the oven at 180°C (350°F) mark 4 for about $1\frac{1}{4}$ hours until the cake is well risen and a skewer inserted in the centre comes out clean.

5 Turn the cake out of the tin and leave on a wire rack until completely cold. Wrap in cling film and store in an airtight container for 1–2 days before slicing and eating.

Menu Suggestion
Serve this moist, fruity teabread sliced and buttered at teatime. Or serve with thin wedges of sharp Cheddar cheese for a snack at any time of day.

POPPY SEED GRANARY ROUND

| 1.15* | 🍳 | ❄ | 280 cals |

* plus 1½ hours rising and proving

Makes 8 rolls

15 g (½ oz) fresh yeast or 7.5 g (¼ oz)
    dried yeast and 2.5 ml (½ tsp)
    sugar

300 ml (½ pint) warm water

450 g (1 lb) granary bread flour

5 ml (1 tsp) salt

50 g (2 oz) butter

50 g (2 oz) Cheddar cheese, grated

25 g (1 oz) poppy seeds

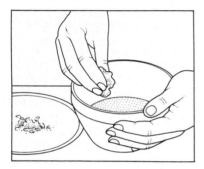

1 Grease a 20.5-cm (8-inch)
sandwich tin. In a bowl,
crumble the fresh yeast into the
water and stir until dissolved. (If
using dried yeast, sprinkle it into
water mixed with the sugar. Leave
in a warm place for 15 minutes
until frothy.)

2 Make the dough. Place the
flour and salt in a large bowl
and rub in the butter. Add the
cheese and the poppy seeds, reserving 5 ml (1 tsp) to garnish. Stir
in the yeast liquid and mix to a
stiff dough.

3 Turn on to a lightly floured
surface and knead for 10 minutes until smooth. Place in a bowl,
cover with a cloth and leave to rise
in a warm place for about 1 hour
until doubled in size.

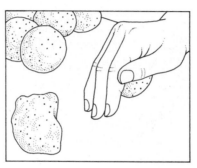

4 Turn on to a lightly floured
surface and knead for 2–3
minutes until smooth.

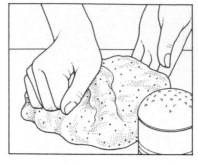

5 Using a sharp knife, divide the
dough into eight equal pieces
and shape into neat, even-sized
rolls with your hands.

6 Arrange in the tin, cover with
a clean cloth and leave to prove
in a warm place for about 30
minutes until doubled in size.

7 Sprinkle with the reserved
poppy seeds. Bake in the oven
at 200°C (400°F) mark 6 for about
25 minutes until golden brown and
sounds hollow when the bottom of
the bread is tapped.

HERBY CHEESE LOAF

1.00*		1458 cals

* plus 1 hour cooling

Makes one 450-g (1-lb loaf)

225 g (8 oz) self-raising flour

7.5 ml (1½ tsp) salt

5 ml (1 tsp) mustard powder

5 ml (1 tsp) snipped fresh chives

15 ml (1 tbsp) chopped fresh parsley

75 g (3 oz) mature Cheddar cheese, grated

1 egg, beaten

150 ml (¼ pint) water

25 g (1 oz) butter or block margarine, melted

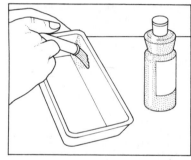

1 Grease a 450-g (1-lb) loaf tin. Sift the flour, salt and mustard into a bowl and stir in the herbs and cheese. Add the egg, water and melted fat and stir until well blended with a wooden spoon.

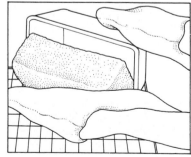

2 Spoon into the loaf tin and bake in the oven at 190°C (375°F) mark 5 for about 45 minutes. Turn out and cool on a wire rack for about 1 hour. Serve sliced and buttered while warm.

BROWN SODA BREAD

0.20*	3650 cals

* plus 30 minutes cooling

Serves 6

600 g (1¼ lb) plain wholewheat flour
350 g (12 oz) plain white flour
10 ml (2 tsp) bicarbonate of soda
20 ml (4 tsp) cream of tartar
10 ml (2 tsp) salt
10 ml (2 tsp) sugar (optional)
900 ml (1½ pints) milk and water, mixed

1 Sift the flours, bicarbonate of soda, cream of tartar and salt into a bowl. Stir in the bran (from the wholewheat flour) left in the bottom of the sieve, then the sugar. Add enough milk and water to mix to a soft dough.

2 Turn the dough onto a floured surface and knead lightly until smooth and soft.

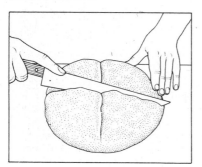

3 Shape the dough into a round. Score into quarters with a sharp knife and place on a greased baking sheet or tray.

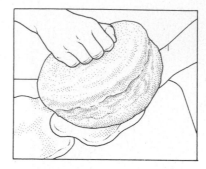

4 Bake in the oven at 220°C (425°F) mark 7 for 25–30 minutes until the bottom of the bread sounds hollow when tapped with the knuckles of your hand. Cool on a wire rack before serving.

Menu Suggestion
Soda bread is best eaten really fresh—on the day of baking. Serve with a mature Farmhouse Cheddar, tomatoes and spring onions for a homemade 'ploughman's lunch'.

BROWN SODA BREAD

Soda bread is the ideal bread to make when you are short of time for baking. The raising agent in soda bread is bicarbonate of soda mixed with an acid, which releases the carbon dioxide necessary to make the bread light. In this recipe, fresh milk is made sour (acid) with cream of tartar, but you can use bicarbonate of soda on its own with sour milk or buttermilk, which will provide enough acid without the cream of tartar. The end result is much the same whichever ingredients you use, although bread made with buttermilk does tend to have a softer texture.

CINNAMON CHERRY BARS

2.15* 🍴 170 cals

* plus 1 hour cooling

Makes 24

125 g (4 oz) ground almonds

1 egg, beaten

225 g (8 oz) plain flour

225 g (8 oz) caster sugar

175 g (6 oz) soft tub margarine

5 ml (1 tsp) ground cinnamon

grated rind of 1 lemon

125 g (4 oz) black cherry jam

icing sugar, to dredge

1 Lightly grease a 28 × 18 cm (11 × 7 inch) shallow tin. Put the first seven ingredients into a large bowl and beat well.

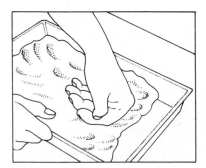

2 Knead lightly. Cover and refrigerate for at least 30 minutes. Press half the dough evenly into the prepared tin. Spread the jam over the surface.

3 On a lightly floured work surface, lightly knead the remaining dough. With well floured hands, roll into pencil-thin strips. Arrange over the jam to form a close lattice pattern. Refrigerate for 30 minutes.

LAMINGTONS

1.30* 🍶🍶 ✳*	340 cals

* plus 30 minutes cooling and 30 minutes setting; freeze after stage 6

Makes 12

50 g (2 oz) butter
65 g (2½ oz) plain flour
15 ml (1 tbsp) cornflour
3 eggs, size 2
75 g (3 oz) caster sugar
450 g (1 lb) icing sugar
75 g (3 oz) cocoa
100 ml (4 fl oz) milk
75 g (3 oz) desiccated coconut

1 Grease a 28 × 18 cm (11 × 7 inch) cake tin. Line the tin with greaseproof paper and grease the paper.

2 Melt 40 g (1½ oz) butter and let it stand for a few minutes for the salt and any sediment to settle. Sift the flour and cornflour.

3 Put the eggs and sugar into a large bowl and whisk until light and creamy—the mixture should be thick enough to leave a trail on the surface for a few seconds when the whisk is lifted. If whisking by hand, place the bowl over simmering water, then remove from the heat and whisk for 5–10 minutes until cool.

4 Re-sift the flours and fold half into the egg mixture with a metal spoon.

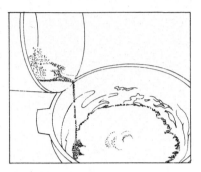

5 Pour the cooled but still flowing butter round the edge of the mixture, taking care not to let the salt and sediment run in.

6 Fold the butter very lightly into the mixture, alternating with the rest of the flour.

7 Turn the mixture into the tin. Bake in the oven at 190°C (375°F) mark 5 until firm to the touch, 20–25 minutes. Turn out on to a wire rack and leave to cool.

8 Meanwhile, for the icing: sift the icing sugar and cocoa into the top part of a double boiler or into a heatproof bowl placed over simmering water.

9 Add the remaining butter and the milk and stir over a gentle heat to a coating consistency.

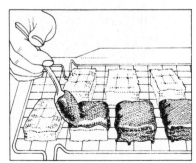

10 Cut the cake into twelve even-sized pieces. Place on a wire cooling rack. Spoon the icing over each cake to cover. Sprinkle the tops of each with coconut. Leave for 30 minutes until set.

4 Bake at 180°C (350°F) mark 4 for 40 minutes. Cool for 1 hour; dredge with icing sugar. Cut into 24 bars and ease out of the tin. Wrap and store in an airtight tin for up to 1 week.

ENGLISH MADELEINES

| 1.20 | ⬦ | ✳* | 239 cals |

* freeze after stage 3

Makes 10

100 g (4 oz) butter or block
    margarine

100 g (4 oz) caster sugar

2 eggs, beaten

100 g (4 oz) self-raising flour

30 ml (2 tbsp) red jam, sieved and
    melted

50 g (2 oz) desiccated coconut

5 glacé cherries, halved, and
    angelica pieces, to decorate

1 Grease ten dariole moulds. Put the butter and sugar into a bowl and beat together until pale and fluffy. Add the eggs a little at a time, beating well after each addition. Fold in half the flour, using a tablespoon. Fold in rest.

2 Turn the mixture into the moulds, filling them three-quarters full. Bake in the oven at 180°C (350°F) mark 4 for about 20 minutes until well risen and firm to the touch. Turn out on to a wire rack to cool for 20 minutes.

3 When the cakes are almost cold, trim the bases so they stand firmly and are about the same height.

4 Spread the coconut out on a large plate. Spear each cake on a skewer, brush with melted jam, then roll in the coconut to coat.

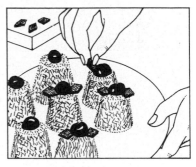

5 Top each madeleine with half a glacé cherry and small pieces of angelica.

FRENCH MADELEINES

The continental cousin of the English madeleine is confusingly different. Made either from pastry or a firm, butter-rich cake mixture such as Genoese sponge, French madeleines are baked in shallow, shell-shaped moulds. They are served undecorated or lightly dusted with icing sugar.

French madeleines are a speciality of the town of Commercy, in Lorraine. Their history is said to go back to the early 18th century and the days of Stanislas Leszinski, a king of Poland who became Duke of Lorraine when ousted from his homeland.

STRAWBERRY SHORTCAKES

| 1.30 | ✳* | 611 cals |

* after stage 6

Serves 6

275 g (10 oz) self-raising flour

7.5 ml (1½ tsp) baking powder

good pinch of salt

75 g (3 oz) butter, cut into nut-size pieces

50 g (2 oz) caster sugar

1 egg, beaten

few drops vanilla flavouring

75–90 ml (5–6 tbsp) milk

450 g (1 lb) fresh strawberries, 6 set aside, the remainder hulled

30 ml (2 tbsp) orange-flavoured liqueur

30 ml (2 tbsp) icing sugar

300 ml (10 fl oz) double or whipping cream

45 ml (3 tbsp) redcurrant jelly

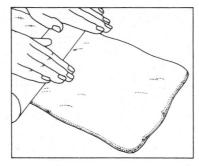

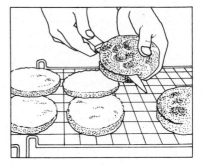

1 Brush a little melted lard over a large flat baking sheet; leave to cool for about 5 minutes. Dust the surface lightly with flour.

2 Sift the flour, baking powder and salt into a bowl. Rub in the butter until the mixture resembles breadcrumbs. Stir in the caster sugar.

3 Make a well in the centre of the dry ingredients and add the egg, vanilla flavouring and milk. Using a palette knife, cut through the dry ingredients until evenly blended, then quickly and lightly bring the mixture together using the fingertips of one hand.

4 Turn the dough out on to a lightly floured surface and knead gently until just smooth. Roll out to a thickness of 1 cm (½ inch) and cut out six 9-cm (3½-inch) fluted rounds.

5 Gather up the scraps, knead lightly and roll out again. Place on the prepared baking sheet.

6 Brush the tops of the rounds with milk—don't let it trickle down the sides. Bake in the oven at 230°C (450°F) mark 8 for about 11 minutes or until the shortcakes are well risen and golden brown. Remove from the oven and keep warm.

7 Thickly slice half the strawberries. Put into a bowl and add the liqueur. Sieve in half the icing sugar.

8 With a fork, lightly crush the remaining strawberries and sieve in the rest of the icing sugar. Whip the cream until it just holds its shape and stir in the crushed strawberries.

9 Cut the shortcakes in half while they are still warm. Carefully run the point of a sharp knife from the side of the shortcake into the centre.

10 Rotate the shortcake and saw with the sharp knife until the cake is cut in two.

11 Spoon half the cream on to the shortcake bases and cover with the sliced strawberries. Spoon over the remaining cream and replace the shortcake tops.

12 Put the redcurrant jelly into a small pan and heat gently until liquid. Cool for 5–10 minutes, then brush over the shortcakes. Decorate with whole strawberries.

—— VARIATION ——

Any other soft fruits such as raspberries, loganberries, blackberries, bilberries or redcurrants can be used as an alternative filling for these delicious shortcakes. Skinned and roughly chopped peaches and nectarines would also be delicious. The tart flavour of berries or currants can be counteracted by adding a little more sugar.

ECCLES CAKES

| 1.00* | ⬛ | ✳ | 167–209 cals |

* plus 30 minutes cooling

Makes 8–10

212-g (7½-oz) packet frozen puff pastry, thawed, or ¼ quantity puff or flaky pastry (see pages 646 and 647)

25 g (1 oz) butter, softened

25 g (1 oz) soft dark brown sugar

25 g (1 oz) finely chopped mixed peel

50 g (2 oz) currants

caster sugar

1 Roll out the pastry on a lightly floured working surface and cut into eight to ten 9-cm (3½-inch) rounds.

2 For the filling: mix the butter, sugar, mixed peel and currants in a bowl.

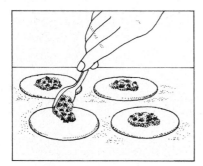

3 Place 5 ml (1 tsp) of the fruit and butter mixture in the centre of each pastry round. Draw up the edges of each pastry round to enclose the filling and then re-shape.

4 Turn each round over and roll lightly until the currants just show through.

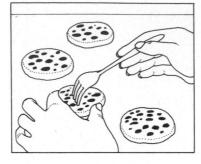

5 Prick the top of each with a fork. Allow the pastry rounds to 'rest' for about 10 minutes in a cool place.

6 Dampen a baking sheet and transfer the rounds to it. Bake in the oven at 230°C (450°F) mark 8 for about 15 minutes until golden. Transfer to a wire rack to cool for 30 minutes. Sprinkle with caster sugar while still warm.

ECCLES CAKES

Dripping with butter and loaded with currants, Eccles cakes are among the nation's favourite regional pastries. It is not just in Lancashire that village bakeries are obliged to produce them in large quantities every morning. Some versions are made with shortcrust pastry, others favour the richer puff or flaky pastries suggested here, either way the pastry must be rolled really thinly, so that the dark fruit shows through. Take care that it does not burst though.

Eccles cakes are at their best very fresh, preferably still slightly warm from the oven. If you want to make them for eating next day do not sprinkle with caster sugar; store them in an airtight tin when cold then reheat the next day and sprinkle with sugar after they come out of the oven.

SPICED WALNUT SCONES

0.25	123 cals

Makes 16

125 g (4 oz) plain wholemeal flour

125 g (4 oz) plain white flour

15 ml (3 tsp) baking powder

2.5 ml ($\frac{1}{2}$ tsp) ground mixed spice

pinch of salt

50 g (2 oz) butter or block
   margarine

15 ml (1 tbsp) caster sugar

75 g (3 oz) walnut pieces, roughly
   chopped

10 ml (2 tsp) lemon juice

200 ml (7 fl oz) milk

honey and chopped walnuts,
   to decorate

1 Sift the flours into a bowl with
the baking powder, mixed
spice and salt. Stir in the bran
(from the wholemeal flour) left in
the bottom of the sieve. Rub in the
fat. Stir in the sugar and two-
thirds of the walnuts.

2 Mix the lemon juice with
170 ml (6 fl oz) of the milk and
stir into the dry ingredients until
evenly mixed.

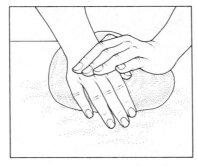

3 Turn the dough onto a floured
surface and knead lightly until
smooth and soft.

4 Roll out the dough to a
20.5 cm (8 inch) square and
place on a baking sheet. Mark the
surface into 16 squares, cutting
the dough through to a depth of
3 mm ($\frac{1}{8}$ inch).

5 Lightly brush the dough with
the remaining milk, then
sprinkle over the remaining
chopped walnut pieces.

6 Bake in the oven at 220°C
(425°F) mark 7 for about 18
minutes or until well risen, golden
brown and firm to the touch.
Cut into squares. Serve warm,
brushed with honey.

Menu Suggestion

Quick to make from store-
cupboard ingredients, these
Spiced Walnut Scones can be
served plain or buttered, whichever you prefer.

——————— VARIATION ———————

For a savoury scone mixture, use
2.5 ml ($\frac{1}{2}$ tsp) chilli powder
instead of the sugar and omit the
mixed spice.

CHEWY CHOCOLATE BROWNIES

0.15*	156 cals

* plus cooling time

Makes 16

75 g (3 oz) plain flour
175 g (6 oz) dark soft brown sugar
25 g (1 oz) cocoa powder
1.25 ml (¼ tsp) salt
100 g (4 oz) butter or margarine
2 eggs, beaten
5 ml (1 tsp) vanilla flavouring
75 g (3 oz) chopped mixed nuts

1 Put all the ingredients in a bowl and beat thoroughly (preferably with an electric whisk) until evenly combined.

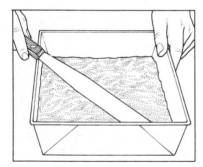

2 Turn the mixture into a greased 20.5 cm (8 inch) square cake tin and level the surface with a palette knife.

3 Bake in the oven at 180°C (350°F) mark 4 for 25 minutes until only just set (the mixture should still wobble slightly in the centre). Stand the cake tin on a wire rack and leave until the cake is completely cold. Cut into 16 squares and put in an airtight tin.

Menu Suggestion
Moist and munchy Chocolate Brownies are a favourite at any time of day. Try them as a fun dessert for children with scoops of vanilla ice cream and chocolate sauce or chopped nuts.

CHOCOLATE CHEQUERBOARDS

2.00		92 cals

Makes 32

200 g (7 oz) soft tub margarine

90 g (3½ oz) caster sugar

290 g (10½ oz) plain flour

15 ml (1 tbsp) cocoa powder

vanilla flavouring

beaten white egg

1 Beat together the margarine, sugar and flour to give a workable dough.

2 Remove two-thirds of the dough to another bowl. Into this, work the cocoa powder mixed to a paste with 15 ml (1 tbsp) water. Knead to an even coloured ball. Halve.

3 Work a few drops of vanilla into the remaining plain dough. On a floured surface, roll the vanilla dough into six 1 × 15 cm (½ × 6 inch) strips. Repeat with one piece of the chocolate dough.

4 Assemble the strips into 2 logs. Lay 3 strips, alternating vanilla and chocolate, side by side. Place another 3 strips on top to make a chequerboard pattern. Brush with a little beaten egg.

5 Halve the remaining chocolate dough. Roll out each piece into a sheet large enough to encase a log. Roll round each log and brush with beaten egg white.

6 Straighten up the logs and chill for about 1 hour until very firm. Cut each log into 1-cm (½-inch) slices. Place on lightly greased baking sheets and bake in the oven at 190°C (375°F) mark 5 for about 15–20 minutes. Turn out and cool on a wire rack for 30 minutes. Store in an airtight container for 2–3 weeks.

CHOCOLATE NUT SNAPS

1.20*	✳	109 cals

* plus 1 hour cooling and setting;
freeze after stage 5

Makes 24

1 egg, separated

100 g (4 oz) caster sugar

125 g (5 oz) plain chocolate

125 g (4 oz) hazel nuts, finely
   chopped

40 g (1½ oz) plain flour

200 g (7 oz) icing sugar

about 30 ml (2 tbsp) water

1 Grease two baking sheets. Whisk the egg white until stiff. Fold in the caster sugar.

2 Coarsely grate 75 g (3 oz) plain chocolate into the mixture and stir in with the hazel nuts, flour and egg yolk.

3 Turn out on a well floured surface and knead lightly. Cover and refrigerate for about 30 minutes.

4 Roll the dough out to 5 mm (¾ inch) thickness. Using a 5-cm (2-inch) plain cutter, cut out 24 shapes. Knead lightly and place on the prepared baking sheets. Cover and refrigerate the biscuits again for 30 minutes.

5 Bake in the oven at 190°C (375°F) mark 5 for about 20 minutes until crisp. Immediately ease off the baking sheet on to a wire rack to cool for 30 minutes.

6 Break the remaining chocolate into a heatproof bowl and place over simmering water. Stir until the chocolate is melted, then remove from heat.

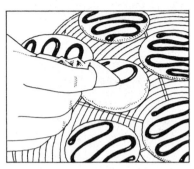

7 Cut the tip off a paper icing bag and spoon in the melted chocolate. Pipe lines of chocolate across the biscuits. Leave to set for 30 minutes. The biscuits can be stored, un-iced, in airtight containers for 2–3 weeks.

ROLLED BISCUITS

Short biscuit doughs are often difficult to roll without breaking. Chilling helps, but you could also try rolling the dough between sheets of cling film. This not only holds the dough together, but eliminates the need for extra flour on the board, which can harden the surface of the baked biscuits.

After rolling, remove the top sheet of film to cut the biscuits, then lift each one on the bottom piece of cling film to transfer it to the baking sheet.

PEANUT CRUNCHIES

1.00*	✳	105 cals

* plus 30 minutes cooling

Makes about 24

125 g (4 oz) butter or margarine
125 g (4 oz) soft light brown sugar
45 ml (3 tbsp) peanut butter
225 g (8 oz) plain flour
2.5 ml ($\frac{1}{2}$ tsp) bicarbonate of soda
2.5 ml ($\frac{1}{2}$ tsp) cream of tartar
30 ml (2 tbsp) water
beaten egg, to glaze
50 g (2 oz) salted peanuts

1 Grease a baking sheet. Put the butter into a bowl and beat until creamy. Add the sugar and peanut butter and beat again until pale and fluffy.

2 Sift in flour, bicarbonate of soda and cream of tartar. Using a fork, work dry ingredients in with water to form a soft mixture. Cover; chill for 20 minutes.

3 Turn out on to a lightly floured surface, knead into a ball and roll out fairly thinly. Cut out about 24 biscuits using a 5-cm (2-inch) cutter. Re-knead trimmings as necessary and roll out again.

4 Place on the prepared baking sheet. Brush with beaten egg and press a few peanuts into the centre of each to decorate. Bake in the oven at 190°C (375°F) mark 5 for 20 minutes until crisp and golden. Turn on to a wire rack to cool for 30 minutes.

BROWN SUGAR WHEATMEALS

1.00*	✳	98 cals

* plus 30 minutes cooling

Makes about 20

175 g (6 oz) plain wheatmeal flour
1.25 ml ($\frac{1}{4}$ tsp) bicarbonate of soda
1.25 ml ($\frac{1}{4}$ tsp) salt
50 g (2 oz) light soft brown sugar
75 g (3 oz) butter or block
    margarine, cut into pieces
125 g (4 oz) currants
50 g (2 oz) oatflakes
1 egg, beaten
about 15 ml (1 tbsp) water

1 Grease two baking sheets. Add the flour, bicarbonate of soda, salt and sugar into a bowl. Rub in the fat until the mixture resembles fine breadcrumbs.

2 Stir in the currants and oat-flakes, then stir in the beaten egg and just enough water to bind the mixture together. Knead in the bowl until smooth. Cover and refrigerate for 20 minutes.

3 On a lightly floured surface, roll the dough out to about 5 mm ($\frac{1}{4}$ inch) thickness. Cut into rounds with a 6.5-cm (2$\frac{1}{2}$-inch) fluted cutter and remove centres with a 2.5-cm (1-inch) cutter.

4 Carefully transfer the rings to the prepared baking sheets. Re-roll trimmings as necessary. Refrigerate for at least 20 minutes.

5 Bake in the oven at 190°C (375°F) mark 5 for about 15 minutes until firm. Transfer to a wire rack to cool for 30 minutes.

Left to right:
Honey Jumbles, Peanut crunchies,
Brown Sugar Wheatmeals

Honey Jumbles

*1.00** 🍴	86 cals

* plus 1½ hours chilling and 30 minutes cooling

Makes 32

150 g (5 oz) soft tub margarine

150 g (5 oz) caster sugar

few drops of vanilla flavouring

finely grated rind of 1 lemon

1 egg, beaten

225 g (8 oz) plain flour

clear honey, to glaze

demerara sugar, to sprinkle

1 Put the margarine and sugar into a bowl and beat until pale and fluffy. Beat in the vanilla flavouring, lemon rind and egg.

2 Stir in the flour, mix to a firm paste. Knead lightly, cover and chill for 30 minutes.

3 Roll the dough into a sausage shape—5 cm (2 inches) in diameter, 20 cm (8 inches) long. Wrap in greaseproof paper. Chill for 30 minutes.

4 Lightly grease two baking sheets. Cut the chilled dough into 5-mm (¼-inch) rounds. Roll into pencil-thin strips 10 cm (4 inches) long. Twist into 'S' shapes and place on the prepared baking sheets. Refrigerate for 30 minutes.

5 Bake in the oven at 190°C (375°F) mark 5 for 12–15 minutes until pale golden.

6 Remove from the oven and while still warm, brush well with honey, sprinkle with demerara sugar and grill for 1–2 minutes until caramelised.

7 Transfer to a wire rack to cool for 30 minutes. Wrap and store in an airtight tin for up to 3 weeks.

GRANDMA'S BISCUITS

0.35*	101 cals

* plus cooling time

Makes 35

100 g (4 oz) butter or margarine
175 g (6 oz) dark soft brown sugar
30 ml (2 tbsp) golden syrup
150 g (5 oz) self-raising flour
2.5 ml (½ tsp) bicarbonate of soda
125 g (4 oz) rolled oats
150 g (5 oz) desiccated coconut
1 egg, beaten

1 Put the fat, sugar and golden syrup in a heavy-based pan and heat gently until melted, stirring occasionally.

2 Meanwhile, put the flour, bicarbonate of soda, oats and coconut in a large mixing bowl and stir well to mix.

3 Pour the melted mixture on to the dry ingredients and stir well to mix. Add the beaten egg and stir again until all of the ingredients are evenly combined.

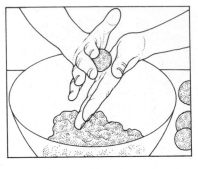

4 With the palms of your hands, shape and roll the mixture into about 35 small, walnut-sized balls.

5 Place the balls slightly apart on greased baking sheets to allow for spreading during baking, then flatten with the back of a fork to make an attractive pattern.

6 Bake in the oven at 180°C (350°F) mark 4 for 12–15 minutes until browned. Leave to settle on the baking sheets for a few minutes, then transfer to a wire rack and leave to cool completely before serving. To keep crisp, store in an airtight tin.

Menu Suggestion
Crisp, crunchy and wholesome, these old-fashioned biscuits are a great hit with children—ideal for packed lunches.

REFRIGERATOR COOKIES

0.35*	37–49 cals

* plus overnight chilling and about 30 minutes cooling; freeze dough at the end of step 3

Makes 50–60

225 g (8 oz) plain flour
5 ml (1 tsp) baking powder
100 g (4 oz) butter or margarine
175 g (6 oz) caster sugar
5 ml (1 tsp) vanilla flavouring
1 egg, beaten

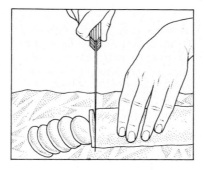

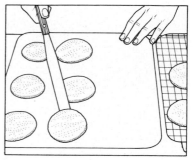

1 Sift the flour and baking powder into a bowl. Rub in the fat until the mixture resembles breadcrumbs, then add the sugar and stir until evenly combined.

2 Add the vanilla flavouring and egg and mix to a smooth dough with a wooden spoon.

4 To shape and bake: slice the roll very thinly into as many cookies as required. (The remainder of the roll can be wrapped again in the foil and returned to the refrigerator for up to 1 week.)

5 Place the cookies well apart on a buttered baking sheet. Bake in the oven at 190°C (375°F) mark 5 for 10–12 minutes until golden.

6 Leave the cookies to settle on the baking sheet for a few minutes, then transfer to a wire rack and leave to cool completely. Store in an airtight tin if not eating immediately.

Menu Suggestion
Serve for children's teas or when unexpected visitors call. Keep a roll of dough in the refrigerator ready to make a batch of cookies at a moment's notice.

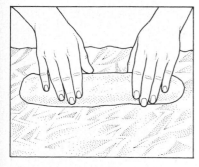

3 Turn the dough onto a large sheet of foil and shape into a long roll about 5 cm (2 inches) in diameter. Wrap in the foil and chill in the refrigerator overnight.

--- VARIATIONS ---

Walnut: add **50 g (2 oz) very finely chopped walnuts** with the sugar in step 1.
Coconut: add **50 g (2 oz) desiccated coconut** with the sugar in step 1.
Sultana: add **50 g (2 oz) very finely chopped sultanas** with the sugar in step 1.
Chocolate: add **50 g (2 oz) very finely grated plain chocolate** with the sugar in step 1.
Spicy: omit the vanilla and sift in **10 ml (2 tsp) ground mixed**

spice with the flour in step 1.
Lemon: omit the vanilla and add the **finely grated rind of 1 lemon** with the sugar in step 1.
Ginger: omit the vanilla and sift in **7.5 ml (1½ tsp) ground ginger** with the flour in step 1.
Cherry: add **50 g (2 oz) very finely chopped glacé cherries** with the sugar in step 1.
Orange: omit the vanilla and add the **finely grated rind of 1 orange** with the sugar in step 1.

MELOMACAROUNA
(CYPRIOT ALMOND AND HONEY COOKIES)

1.30	🍴🍴	214 cals

Makes about 30

125 ml (4 fl oz) vegetable oil

125 ml (4 fl oz) evaporated milk

100 g (4 oz) butter, softened

finely grated rind of 1 orange

50 ml (2 fl oz) orange juice

7.5 ml ($\frac{1}{2}$ tbsp) lemon juice

225 g (8 oz) granulated sugar

pinch of salt

165 g ($5\frac{1}{2}$ oz) fine semolina

375 g (13 oz) plain flour

7.5 ml ($\frac{1}{2}$ tbsp) bicarbonate of soda

125 g (4 oz) ground almonds

2.5 ml ($\frac{1}{2}$ tsp) ground cinnamon

90 ml (6 tbsp) clear honey

1 Put the oil in a bowl with the evaporated milk, butter, orange rind and juice, lemon juice, half of the sugar and the salt. Beat well.

2 Gradually add the semolina and the flour sifted with the bicarbonate of soda, and mix to a stiff dough. Turn onto a floured work surface and knead well.

3 With your hands, form small pieces of the mixture into 30 almond shapes, about 7.5 cm (3 inches) long and 4 cm ($1\frac{1}{2}$ inches) wide. Place on greased baking sheets. spacing them well apart. Bake in 2 batches in the oven at 180°C (350°F) mark 4 for 30 minutes. Transfer to a wire rack and leave to cool slightly.

4 Meanwhile, mix the ground almonds and cinnamon together on a large flat plate. Set aside. Put the remaining sugar in a heavy-based, small saucepan, with the honey and 125 ml (4 fl oz) water. Heat gently until the sugar has dissolved, then simmer for 3–4 minutes. Remove the froth from the surface of the liquid with a slotted spoon.

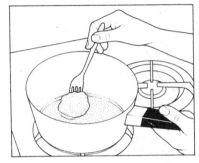

5 Turn the heat down to very low and dip the melomacarouna in the syrup one at a time, turning gently with a fork to ensure even coating.

6 Lift out of the syrup with the fork, transfer to the plate of almonds and cinnamon and coat thoroughly, using your fingertips to pat the mixture on. Return to the wire rack and leave to dry and cool. Store in an airtight tin for up to 2 weeks.

MELOMACAROUNA
Melomacarouna are traditionally eaten in Cyprus during the Christmas period. Their name comes from the Greek words 'melo' meaning honey, and 'macarouna' meaning almond, the two main flavours of these delicious sweetmeats. For speed and ease, make them with an electric mixer.

FRUIT SALAMI

| 0.45* 🍽 | 263–307 cals |

* plus overnight chilling

Makes 12–14 slices

100 g (4 oz) blanched almonds

225 g (8 oz) mixed dried whole fruit
(eg apricots, figs, dates),
unsoaked

100 g (4 oz) dark chocolate

50 g (2 oz) glacé cherries, chopped

100 g (4 oz) dark soft brown sugar

175 g (6 oz) unsalted butter

1 egg, beaten

cocoa powder, for dredging

1 Chop the nuts and dried fruit finely. Discard any stones from the fruit.

2 Break the chocolate in pieces into a heatproof bowl standing over a saucepan of gently simmering water. Add the rum and heat gently until chocolate has melted, stirring only once or twice after the chocolate has started to melt.

3 Add the sugar and butter and stir over gentle heat until the sugar has dissolved, then remove from the heat and beat in the chopped fruit and nuts and the egg. Continue beating until mixture cools.

4 Place the mixture on a sheet of non-stick baking parchment and form into two sausage shapes, about 5 cm (2 inches) thick. Wrap in the paper and chill in the refrigerator overnight.

5 To serve, unwrap and dredge liberally with icing sugar. Cut into diagonal slices while still chilled, then arrange on a serving plate. Allow to come to room temperature for about 30 minutes before serving.

FRUIT SALAMI

This after-dinner sweetmeat is similar to a Christmas speciality from Czechoslovakia, where it is called *ovocný salám*. There are many different versions, some made with all dried fruit and no chocolate, and some with honey rather than butter. This version is very fruity, and is best made with the kind of dried fruits which are sold at health food shops. These fruits are plump, juicy and full of flavour, because they have been dried naturally in the sun. Choose whichever fruits you like best, bearing in mind that the salami will look most attractive when sliced if the fruits contrast well in colour, as they do in the photograph.

FINNISH STAR BISCUITS

| 0.30* | ✳ | 70 cals |

* plus 1 hour chilling and cooling

Makes about 30

75 g (3 oz) black treacle

100 g (4 oz) butter

4 green cardamoms

50 g (2 oz) caster sugar

15 ml (1 tbsp) ground almonds

200 g (7 oz) plain flour

2.5 ml ($\frac{1}{2}$ tsp) bicarbonate of soda

2.5 ml ($\frac{1}{2}$ tsp) ground cinnamon

2.5 ml ($\frac{1}{2}$ tsp) ground ginger

1 egg yolk

coloured ribbon, to decorate

1 Put the treacle and butter in a saucepan and heat gently, stirring occasionally, until melted and blended. Cool slightly for 5 minutes.

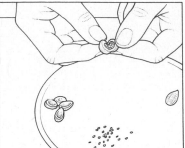

2 Split the cardamom pods open and remove the seeds; crush in a pestle and mortar or in a bowl with the end of a rolling pin.

3 Put all the dry ingredients in a bowl. Make a well in the centre, add the treacle mixture and egg yolk and mix well to form a smooth dough. Wrap in cling film and chill in the refrigerator for at least 30 minutes.

4 Knead the dough on a lightly floured surface, then roll out to just 1 cm ($\frac{1}{2}$ inch) thickness.

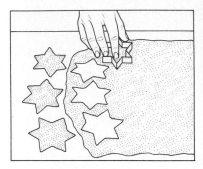

5 Using a 6.5 cm ($2\frac{1}{2}$ inch) star cutter, stamp out about 30 biscuits, re-rolling the dough as necessary.

6 Place the biscuits on baking sheets lined with non-stick baking parchment. Bake in the oven at 190°C (375°F) mark 5 for about 8 minutes.

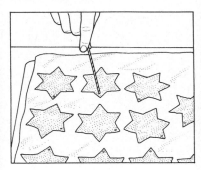

7 Using a skewer, immediately make a small hole near the edge of each star. Transfer to a wire rack and leave to cool for 30 minutes.

8 Thread coloured ribbon through the biscuits to hang on the Christmas tree and to serve. If keeping them for any longer than 8 hours, remove from the tree and pack in an airtight tin.

USEFUL INFORMATION
AND
BASIC RECIPES

Kitchencraft and Cooking Techniques

Busy cooks deserve good tools to work with, and pleasant surroundings in which to work. Often having to conjure up meals in minutes, today's cook can turn to many gadgets and appliances which will make life in the kitchen a lot easier. There is no magic about cooking. There is a simple explanation for everything that happens when a food is cooked. The section on cooking techniques will help you understand why you should cook foods in a certain way in order to prepare them with speed and ease.

KITCHENCRAFT AND COOKING TECHNIQUES

A good cook, like a good crafts-man, needs good tools. This does not mean necessarily buying the most expensive equipment and the latest gadgets. It means working out which utensils will be most useful to your style of cooking and eating and making the most of them to save you both time and effort.

The most sophisticated kitchen equipment is of little use if you do not have a well planned kitchen. Kitchens need to have method in the way in which they are laid out; they should save you time and effort in your daily domestic routine; and they should be pleasing places in which to work.

Ingredients for an easy-to-work-in kitchen

Here are some guidelines for use when planning your kitchen. They are aimed at making your time in the kitchen as pleasant and as efficiently spent as possible.

- Make your kitchen physically comfortable, as well as practical to work in.
- Plan activity centres in your kitchen so that they are well positioned in relation to one another.
- These activity centres need, ideally, to be arranged in the logical order for preparing a meal ie store cupboard, prep-aration area/work surface, and serving/eating area.
- Wherever possible avoid narrow gaps between work surfaces and appliances.
- Store cupboards/larders should allow for the storage of all types of food: dry cupboards for canned and packaged goods; ventilated racks for vegetables and firm fruits. You will also need a refrigerator and a freezer.
- For the work surface choose a durable material, that will with-stand fairly hard wear. There should be a good chopping sur-face, either separate or inset into the work top—wood or some other non-slip surface. Marble and slate are also good as they can serve the dual purpose of chopping surface and a perfect pastry-making surface.
- If possible, keep all large pieces of equipment on the work surface so that they are to hand when you need them. Keep all small preparation equipment and gadgets close to the work surface.
- Storage of saucepans, baking tins etc, depends very much on how your cooking facilities are arranged. If you have a split level cooker, with a hob set into the work surface, then it is advisable to have a cupboard close to the hob; most wall-mounted ovens are set into a housing unit, with drawer space underneath for storing pans and tins.

    With a free-standing cooker, keep all cooking pots and pans, colanders and sieves as close as possible in adjacent cupboards, or hang them on the wall or suspend them from hooks on the ceiling or units.
- Serving and eating areas should, ideally, be close to one another.
- You will also need good lighting, effective ventilation, and a comfortable floor. You need a good source of light directed on all principle work areas. An extractor hood or fan is essential, both to remove excess cooking smells and steam, and to keep the kitchen as cool as possible. The kitchen floor should obviously look nice, but it should also be comfortable to stand on and easy to keep clean. Choose a non-slip surface, which is easy on the feet.

COOKING EQUIPMENT

Choosing the right piece of equipment for a particular job will, in the end, save you time. It pays to invest in good quality equipment as it lasts longer and does the job consistently better than inferior equipment. Here is a guide to the types of equipment you will need to produce delicious food efficiently.

SAUCEPANS

Good pans are usually expensive, but they last; cheap saucepans do not last and often give off toxic metal substances into the food, which is not desirable.

The best pans to use are those made of metals that conduct heat well: copper, cast iron, or good-quality enamelled steel or stainless steel are good choices. Saucepans with a non-stick finish are excellent for boiling milk and making sauces, but they are not such a good choice for some of the 'tougher' cooking jobs. Long term they are a bad buy for the non-stick coating starts to wear off. The heavier the pan the safer it is to use; solid based pans are also less prone to sticking. Handles are another important aspect to be considered when buying pans. If they are riveted they are much more secure than handles which have been screwed on.

Four saucepans of varying sizes, and one good-sized frying pan, is the minimum that you can probably get away with. In addition, most kitchens can make good use of one very large pan, with a handle fixed on either side; it is useful for cooking whole chickens and large pieces of gammon and can double as a preserving pan.

FRYING PANS

Deep frying pans are better than shallow ones; they will hold more food and there is less likelihood of liquids spitting and bubbling over. A lid is essential.

Omelette and pancake pans are by no means musts, but they do make the cooking of both these foods a great deal easier. The sides

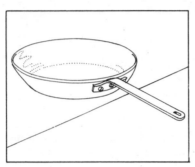
Omelette pan

of an omelette pan are curved and not too high, so that the omelette will roll up readily and fall onto the plate without breaking.

WOKS

A wok is a Chinese cooking utensil which is now very popular in the West as well. It looks like a curve-based large frying pan with two rounded handles and is traditionally made of cast iron though nowadays you can also buy stainless steel and non-stick ones.

Balance it on a metal collar directly over the heat, so that the wok can be moved backwards and forwards to ensure even cooking when stir frying. The wok is a very versatile cooking utensil. Food can be deep fried in it, and then drained on a semi-circular rack which clips on to the rim of the wok; this is very useful when you are frying food in batches. A small circular rack can be positioned in the centre of the wok and used as a steamer with a domed lid fitted neatly over the top.

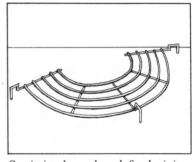
Semi-circular wok rack for draining

FISH KETTLE

A fish kettle is best for poaching whole, large fish. The long oval-shaped pan has handles at either end, and the draining rack that the fish lies on fits neatly inside. The shape of the kettle allows the fish to lie completely flat, without curling; once cooked, the fish can be lifted out easily on the rack, without any danger of it breaking or splitting. If the fish is to be eaten cold it is usually left in the fish kettle in its cooking liquid to cool, and then lifted out.

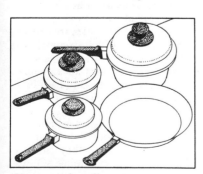
Choose good quality pans

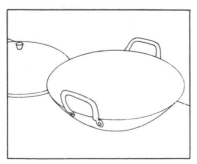
Cast iron wok

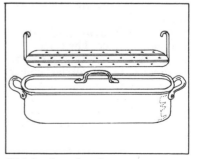
Fish kettle and rack

EGG POACHERS

If you like regular shaped poached eggs, then an egg poacher is the answer. A poacher consists of a base pan (rather like a deep frying pan) which you half fill with water

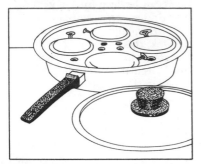

Egg poacher

and a tray containing small poaching cups that sits on top (these are often non-stick). A lid goes over the top of the pan while the eggs are poaching gently in the buttered cups.

BAKING TINS

Baking is a skill; it relies on the precision of the cook, good quality ingredients, and the right shape and size of tin. Even a straight-forward packet cake mix can turn out to be a flop if the wrong tin is used. Most recipes specify a parti-cular size of tin, and this should always be used. Rich mixtures should be baked in strong tins; if the tin is too thin then the mixture will burn.

The greatest worry with baking tins is that of sticking; mixtures that are relatively high in fat are usually fairly safe, but those that contain little fat or are high in sugar, can be very difficult to turn out of a tin.

To line a tin really neatly takes time and patience. The perfect solution is to use baking tins with a non-stick surface; all the familiar shaped tins that are used in every-day baking are available with a non-stick lining. Here is a list of tins you will need for quick, easy baking:

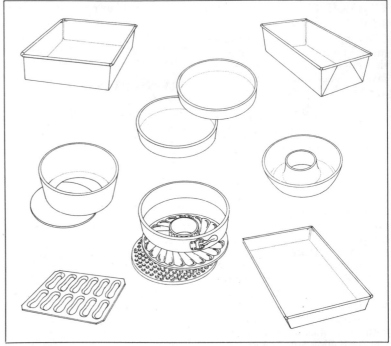

Baking tins: a sandwich tin, loaf tin, round cake tins, madeleine tins and a Swiss roll tin

BASIC TINS

Loaf tins—these come in 450 g (1 lb) and 900 g (2 lb) sizes. Use them for cakes and breadmaking.
Flan rings and tins—use a round tin with plain or fluted sides and a removable base for pastry flans.
Sandwich tins—these come in sizes 18–25.5 cm (7–10 inches) and are shallow, round tins with straight sides for making sandwich and layer cakes. (You can also use spring release tins.)
Swiss roll tins

Lining a deep tin for fruit cake

Standard cake tins—you will need 15-cm (6-inch), 16-cm (7-inch) and 17-cm (8-inch) tins.

KNIVES

Good sharp knives are the cook's most important tools. Knives vary enormously in quality, the best ones have taper ground blades—the blade, bolster and tang is forged from one piece of steel, and the handle is fixed securely in place with rivets.
Cook's knives are the classic knives used by all top chefs and professional cooks. They have strong, broad and very sharp blades, and the handles are firmly riveted to give added strength while chopping. Classic cook's knives have heavy handles, there-fore if they fall they land handle first, avoiding damage to the blade. The larger size cook's knives, those with blades between 15–20 cm (6–8 inches) long, are extremely versatile—they can be used for chopping, cubing, slicing, 'mincing', and crushing. Small

Two useful sizes of cook's knife

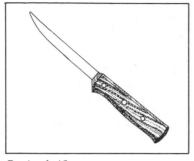

Boning knife

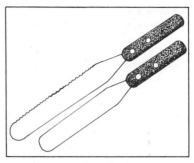

Two types of palette knife

cook's knives, with blades about 10 cm (4 inches) long are very good for paring vegetables and shaping vegetable garnishes.

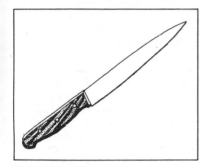

Filleting knife

Filleting knives have a long, slim, pliable blade. Sharpness and flexibility are essential, as the blade has to follow the bones of the fish very closely. These knives are also useful for skinning.

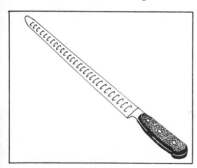

Fishmonger's knife

Fishmonger's knives have a strong, rigid, scalloped blade. These are very heavy knives which make them ideal for cutting through the backbones of fish.

Boning knives have rigid, narrow, broad-backed blades, with very sharp points. They come in different lengths, depending on what they are going to be used to bone. The handles are indented and shaped to prevent your hand from slipping.

Carving knives come in many different styles and sizes. Knives suitable for carving large joints of meat are shaped like an elongated filleting knife; sturdy, but flexible towards the tip of the blade. Serrated knives tend to tear the texture of hot meat, and are best reserved for cutting cold joints.

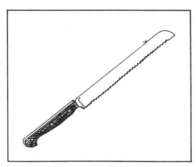

Bread knife with serrated edge

A bread knife should have a fairly rigid blade, but it should be long enough to slice through the largest of loaves—many bread knives have serrated blades, and they tend to cause less crumbs than a plain-edged knife. Serrated knives can also cope with crisp crusts much better.

The palette knife gets its name from its artistic associations; it is the same shape as the knife that painters use to mix paint colour with oil. It has a long evenly-wide blade, which is extremely pliable. A palette knife is used primarily for spreading soft mixtures, such as icings, and for flipping foods such as pancakes.

Serrated palette knives are very useful for slicing sponges and other cakes into layers.

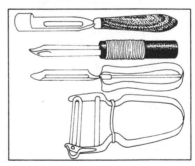

Varieties of potato peeler

Potato peelers are not strictly speaking knives, but they do have a cutting blade and are a must for every kitchen.

CHOPPERS

Choppers have very heavy, deep rectangular blades; they are extremely strong and need to be used with care. They are blade-heavy and tend to drop forward when held. Choppers will cut through most bones, and they are particularly useful for cutting up oxtail. The cleaver is the Chinese equivalent of the chopper, but it is much more versatile; the blade is finer and sharper and can be used for chopping, slicing, 'mincing' and scraping, and for making vegetable garnishes.

SCISSORS

All-purpose kitchen scissors can be used for removing bacon rinds; splitting bread dough decoratively; roughly cutting parsley, chives and other herbs; removing the cores from kidneys.
Fish scissors have serrated blades, with one slightly longer than the other. Use for trimming fins and tails, and cutting through bones.
Poultry shears have a strong spring between the two blades,

which makes them extremely robust. They are excellent for cutting through the bones and carcass of all poultry.

KITCHEN SCALES

There are basically two different types of kitchen scales: balance (the traditional variety) and spring balance. Long term, balance scales are a better buy as there is less that can go wrong; unlike spring balance scales they are not dependent on a spring.

Spring balance scales are extremely easy to use and fairly accurate. However, the needle on the dial occasionally gets knocked out of position, so it should be reset each time the scales are used. Some spring balance scales are designed to sit on the work surface, while others can be mounted on the kitchen wall. Unless you have very smooth and level kitchen walls, it is better to buy free-standing scales for accuracy.

Manual juice extractors

SQUEEZERS

Juice squeezers
Juice squeezers or citrus presses come in different shapes and sizes; some are manual and others are operated electrically. The basic principle behind all of them is exactly the same. A ridged dome of glass or plastic presses into the centre of the halved fruit, thus squeezing out the juice. Some of the juicers are hand held, which means that you hold them over a bowl; others have a container beneath the squeezer which collects the juice. Apart from those squeezers which will take halved grapefruits and oranges, there are also smaller ones.

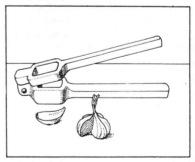
Garlic press

Garlic presses
These are the smallest squeezers of all. They look like small potato ricers, and work in a similar manner. Put the peeled clove of garlic into the press and squeeze down gently—if you squeeze very gently you just get the juice of the garlic—harder, you get the flesh.

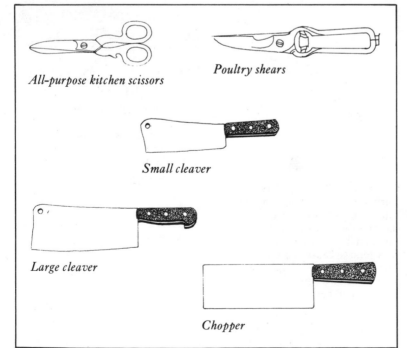
All-purpose kitchen scissors

Poultry shears

Small cleaver

Large cleaver

Chopper

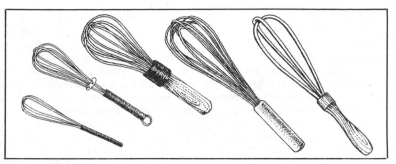

Balloon whisks are available in varying sizes for different tasks

WHISKS

Whisks and beaters cope with a variety of culinary tasks. There are three different kinds of hand whisks: balloon, coiled and rotary. **Balloon whisks** come in different sizes and weights and they are extremely effective. The large, lightweight, very round whisks are the best for egg whites—they are easy to handle and can be used at quite a speed. Slimmer, thicker ridged, and heavier balloon whisks are better for coping with thick sauces, choux pastry or semi-set ice cream mixtures. They will incorporate more air into a mixture than any other type of whisk, and they are extremely easy to clean. **Coiled whisks**, which look just as their name suggests, are cheaper than balloon whisks, but nowhere near as effective. You need to use a lot of effort for not much result. **Rotary whisks** have two four-bladed beaters, which are operated by a small handle. Although you need one hand to steady the whisk and one to turn the handle, it is a speedy and efficient way of whisk-ing slack mixtures such as egg whites and thin sauces.

Electric whisks and whisk attachments

Hand-operated electric whisks, with two beaters like a rotary whisk, are very efficient. The

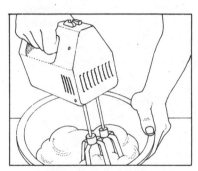

Hand operated electric whisk

beaters can be moved around the inside of a bowl or saucepan (non-stick) with relative ease. This is an advantage when making sauces.

The whisk attachment which goes with several food processors is not that effective; the size of the beaters is relatively small and they cannot move freely through a mix-ture to incorporate a noticeable amount of air. It is reasonably effective with whisked cake mix-tures, but one must not forget that the bowl of most food processors is relatively small. The whisk attachment on large electric mixers is particularly powerful; it is shaped like a squashed balloon whisk and reaches almost every part of the mixing bowl.

BLENDERS

Electric blenders, also called liquidisers, have become very much an integral part of the kitchen gadget scene. They are ex-tremely labour saving. Some

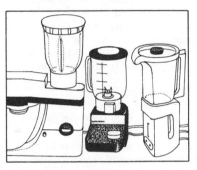

Different types of blender

blenders operate freely as a separ-ate gadget, while others fit onto an electric food mixer. The only way in which they differ tends to be as far as capacity and speed are con-cerned; some are larger and faster than others. The blades in the base of the plastic or glass goblet rotate at a high speed, pulverising the ingredients inside. It is an in-valuable gadget for liquidising soups, sauces, and fruit and vege-table purées, but it can also chop and grind ingredients to varying degrees. There is a hole in the lid of the blender, so ingredients can be dropped through the top while the blades are whirring.

Rotary egg whisk

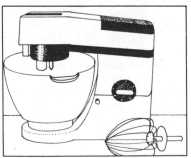

Electric mixer and whisk attachment

ELECTRIC MIXERS AND FOOD PROCESSORS

Electric mixers and food processors can tackle most of the day-to-day culinary tasks, and they are great labour-saving devices for those who are pushed for time and/or have a large family to feed.

The electric mixer

The large size electric mixers, or table mixers as they are often called, have very powerful motors, which can drive a variety of attachments such as: potato peelers, bean shredders and cream makers. The main disadvantage with the table mixer is that it is so bulky, and consequently takes up a lot of space, either on the work surface or in a cupboard. The bowl of the standard table mixer is very capacious, and will hold twice as much as most food processors.

The food processor

The food processor is a compact machine, which is primarily used for chopping, mincing, grinding and blending. It is simple to use, strong, and comparatively quiet. The plastic processor bowl fits over a spindle; the cutting, shredding and whisking attachments in turn fit over the spindle.

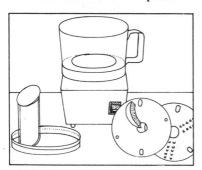

Food processor showing blades

The lid that fits over the bowl has a funnel through which food or liquid can be fed. When the machine is turned on, the cutting blade or other attachments move very fast—vegetables are chopped in 10 seconds, minced in 15 seconds, and puréed in 20 seconds. Food processors have revolutionsed some of our methods of preparation, for example, they are a great help when making pastry and bread doughs, soups, pâtés and terrines.

A word of warning: even though you can buy whisking attachments for food processors, they are not as effective as the beaters on a traditional electric table mixer.

MINCERS

This useful gadget quickly turns cooked or raw meat, fish and vegetables into tiny particles. It is an asset when using up leftover cooked food and is also excellent for preparing your own freshly minced meat at home.

Hand mincers are usually made from cast iron or a strong plastic. They fit firmly onto the work surface, either by means of small rubber suction pads or a screw clamp; the latter is the most secure, and the larger mincers are always fitted with a clamp. The handle on the mincer turns a 'screw' which pushes the food to be minced towards small cutting blades or extruding discs. The size of the perforations in the metal discs dictates the final texture of the minced food, which will either be fine, medium or coarse.

Mincer attachments can also be bought to fit into many table electric mixers.

PRESSURE COOKERS

Pressure cookers can save you a great deal of time. There are many different models available, but basically a pressure cooker looks like a heavy duty saucepan, with a domed lid. It has a weight on it which helps determine the level of pressure at which the food will cook and it also has a safety valve for steam to escape. It works on the principle of increasing the boiling temperature of water and then trapping the resultant steam. (This is achieved by means of added pressure.) Some models of pressure cooker only operate under one pressure; however, the more recent models operate under three; so you can choose which pressure to use according to the type of food you are cooking.

The food is put into the base of the cooker with the appropriate amount of liquid; the lid is then firmly closed and the pan placed over the heat until steam comes through the vents. The necessary pressure weight is then added until a hissing noise is emitted; at this point the heat is turned down for the remainder of the cooking time. (This is always indicated in individual recipes.) After cooking, the pressure has to be released, either slowly or quickly, depending on the food inside. Most recent pressure cookers have an automatic setting on the lid, complete with a timer; this enables you to set both the cooking time and the speed at which pressure should be released.

The pressure cooker is particularly good for cooking the following types of foods:

STOCKS AND SOUPS

Meat—the less expensive, tougher cuts
Poultry and game (especially boiling fowl and casserole game)
Firm textured fish (pressure cooking eliminates the fishy smell)
Root vegetables, such as swedes
Pulses
Grain—brown rice
Steamed puddings—both sweet and savoury

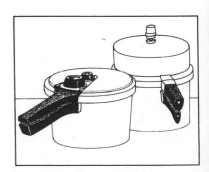

Two types of pressure cooker

Preserves—jams, marmalade, bottled fruits and chutney

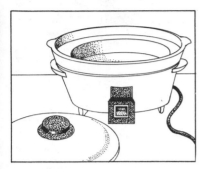

Crockpot or slow cooker

CROCKPOTS

Cooking in a crockpot (or slow-cooker) is an up-dated version of a traditional method of cooking: our great-grandmothers would leave casseroles cooking gently all day in the very coolest part of the kitchen range.

The crockpot consists of an earthenware bowl which sits neatly inside an outer casing. An electric element is fixed between the base of the bowl and the casing, and it operates on two settings—low (75 watts) and high (130 watts). When plugged in it only uses about the same amount of power as a light bulb.

As the name suggests, a crockpot or slow-cooker cooks foods very slowly; so slowly that it can cook food while you are out of the house. It saves time, money and fuel. With most recipes, all the ingredients can be put into the crockpot at once and then left to cook for several hours. The steam which condenses on the crockpot lid returns to the pot, thus keeping the food moist. Subtle, rich flavours develop during long, slow cooking, and it is ideal for the tougher and cheaper cuts of meat. The crockpot heats very gently so there is no risk of burning, sticking or boiling over; consequently it is very easy to clean. Food does not need to be stirred during cooking and it is important to resist the temptation to remove the lid while cooking. If it is removed,

heat is lost from the crockpot and it takes a long time for the original temperature to be regained.

General guidelines
- The crockpot needs pre-heating before food is added.
- Meat has a better appearance and flavour if it is lightly fried before it goes into the crockpot.
- Always bring stock and other liquids to the boil before adding them to the crockpot.
- Most foods should be started off on the High setting, and then reduced to Slow for the remainder of the time; chicken and pork to be 'roasted' should be cooked on High for the whole cooking time.
- Always follow the given quantities of liquid in a recipe accurately; too much liquid can result in overcooking.
- Meats with a high fat content should be trimmed very well before being put into the crockpot; fats do not bake-off as they do in a conventional oven.
- A crockpot should not be used for re-heating any cooked frozen food.
- Leftovers from food that has been cooked in a crockpot must be brought to boiling point in a saucepan before being eaten.

A crockpot is suitable for cooking most foods, as long as recipes are adapted accordingly. It is, however, particularly successful when preparing the following:

Soups
Cooked pâtés
Root vegetables
Meat and poultry—casseroles and 'roasts'
Fish casseroles
Cheese fondue
Steamed puddings
Rice pudding (and other grain puddings)
Lemon curd

COOKING BRICKS

Cooking bricks are simplicity itself to use and always produce delicious-tasting, moist and tender

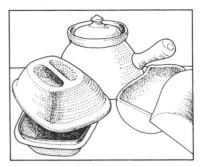

Unglazed, earthenware cooking bricks

food. They come in a variety of shapes and sizes and can be used for cooking most meats, fish and even potatoes, although they always tend to be referred to as 'chicken bricks'. Made of porous, unglazed earthenware, with close-fitting lids, these bricks are very similar in concept to the clay pots used in Greek and Roman times. Before using a brick, always give it a preliminary soaking in cold water each time that you use it in order for it to impart moisture to the food being cooked.

After draining, place the seasoned food into the cooking brick with herbs, chopped vegetables, and any other flavourings or seasonings that you like, and put the lid on top. Put the brick into a cold oven, and then turn it on. As the oven heats up, condensation forms on the lid of the brick, and trickles back onto the food; this acts as a baste and keeps the food moist. All the flavour, juices and aroma of the food are conserved naturally, and the food is far less fatty than it is when cooked by many other more conventional methods, such as roasting or frying.

Cooking bricks should never be washed with detergent as this will taint the food. Just wipe out well with a clean damp cloth or wash in water to which a little vinegar has been added. The bricks do darken with use, but this does not mean that they are dirty, just discoloured.

ELECTRIC DEEP FRYERS

Many people avoid deep frying if they can, because they hate the smell and mess that are associated with it. However careful you are when deep frying food in an open fryer, you cannot prevent the lingering odour. Frying in hot deep fat can also be extremely dangerous. If the temperature of the fat is not regulated very carefully, it can burn; and if moisture gets into the hot fat, it can bubble up and boil over. Electrically operated deep fryers are not only safer, but they also guarantee successful results every time and there is little or no smell. Most electric deep fryers are thermostatically controlled, so that the temperature of the fat or oil is controlled automatically. When the fryer is plugged in and switched on, an indicator light comes on; once the desired temperature of the oil or fat has been reached, the light goes out. The

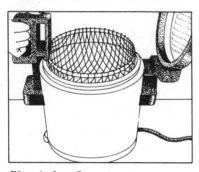

Electric deep fryer

frying basket clips onto the inside of the fryer and can be fixed at various heights. This enables you to put the food that is to be fried into the basket, before the oil or fat is heated—there is no need to lift the lid of the fryer off, as the basket can be lowered into the hot fat from the outside of the fryer. A special filter is fitted into the lid of the fryer which neutralises all the fat and cooking smells. The controlled temperature of the fat ensures that foods are fried to just the right degree.

COOKING TECHNIQUES

When cooking you can use a variety of different techniques from grilling to frying and roasting to poaching. As well as understanding all the techniques you must also bear in mind the type of food that you are going to cook and the time you have to cook it in. Under each technique are given guidelines as to which foods are best suited to this particular method of preparation.

Here are some quick and easy techniques—including grilling and frying—as well as a number of longer cooking methods, like casseroling. Once you have grasped the basics of these you will find them extraordinarily straightforward.

GRILLING

Grilling is one of the simplest and quickest methods of cooking. It simply involves placing the food under the heat source, turning it and then removing it when cooked. Generally, small pieces of food are grilled like chicken portions, sausages or fish fillets, all of which cook relatively quickly.

To perfect the technique always preheat the grill before using it. The high temperature sears the surface of the food, sealing in all the juices, before cooking continues. With thick pieces of food, such as steaks or chops, sear both sides, but you do not need to do this with finer foods such as thin cutlets or fillets of fish, ideal foods when you are in a hurry. To speed up cooking time place foods to be seared near the source of heat, then lower the grill pan for the remainder of the cooking time.

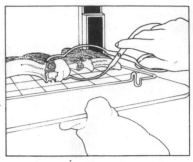

Turning meat under the grill

To make the food taste its best keep it moist throughout grilling; brush it from time to time with oil, melted butter or a marinade. However, do not be tempted to season meat with salt until after it has been cooked as this can toughen it. Test the food while it is cooking to see if it is done.

When grilling chicken and pork, always grill them very thoroughly to ensure that they are cooked through. Steak and lamb, however, can be cooked according to personal preference and to the amount of time available.

Use tongs for turning the food during grilling, and never pierce it with a fork or skewer or you may get hot fat sprayed at you. Always serve grilled foods immediately as they dry out quickly and toughen if kept warm.

Brushing meat with marinade

IDEAL GRILLING FOODS

Beef—steaks (fillet, rump, sirloin, entrecôte and T-bone), sausages and beefburgers
Lamb—chump chops, loin chops, cutlets, leg steaks (cut from fillet end), liver and kidneys
Pork—fillet, spare-rib chops, loin chops, sausages, liver and kidney
Bacon and Gammon—rashers and chops
Veal—fillet (as kebabs), cutlets, loin chops, liver (calf's)
Chicken—breasts, drumsticks, leg and wing joints, split and flattened poussins
Fish—thick fillets, steaks, small whole fish
Mushrooms
Tomatoes

FRYING

Foods can be deep fried, shallow fried or stir fried. It is useful to have all these ways of cooking at your fingertips since they all give quick results and are easy to do once you have mastered the technique. Basically they all depend on two simple principles which are that you use relatively small pieces of food and that you use hot fat to cook them in.

DEEP FRYING

A variety of foods can be successfully deep fried from potatoes to cheese, chicken and fish. Indeed, entire meals can be deep fried.

The technique involves heating a large amount of oil, usually vegetable oil, in a solid-based pan or deep-fat fryer, lowering food into it, letting it cook for a few minutes and then taking it out. Here are some steps on deep frying.

Steps to deep frying
Fill a heavy-based pan no more than two-thirds full of oil. Start heating the oil very gently at first, and then raise the heat. Check the temperature of the oil carefully, either by using a frying thermometer, or test with a cube of stale bread (see below).
● Coat the foods for deep frying

with breadcrumbs or batter, this protects them while being cooked and also prevents

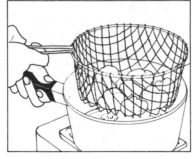
Deep frying small portions

moisture from the food leaking into the oil.
● When cooking small portions or pieces of food, lower them into the fat in a wire frying basket; this makes it easier to remove them from the hot fat.
● Always lower the food into the hot oil slowly.
● Once the food is cooked, remove it carefully using a wire basket or a perforated spoon, and drain on absorbent kitchen paper.
● Remove all crumbs and remnants of fried food with a perforated spoon, otherwise they will burn and taint the flavour of the oil. Do not allow water or other liquids to get into the fat or it will 'spit'.
● Turn the heat off as soon as

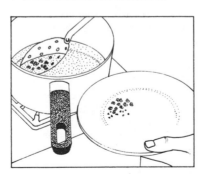
Removing crumbs after frying

you have finished deep frying, and leave the pan to cool without moving it.

Straining cooled oil for storage

● Once the oil is quite cool, strain it thoroughly, and store in a clean bottle for future use.

Deep frying temperatures
The temperature of hot oil for deep frying varies considerably according to the type of food and on whether it is raw or has already been cooked. Raw food is cooked at a lower temperature than cooked. A frying thermometer is the most accurate method of gauging the heat of the oil; alternatively, use a cube of day-old bread.

The bread cube method
● If the bread cube sinks to the bottom of the pan of oil, and does not frizzle at all, then the oil is not yet hot enough.
● If the bread cube frizzles gently, then the oil has reached about 180°C (350°F) and you can fry beignets and do the 'first frying' of chipped potatoes.
● If a light blue haze rises from the oil and the bread cube browns in 1 minute then the oil has reached about 190°C (375°F) and is at the right temperature for frying coated fish fillets, croquettes and fruit fritters.
● If a noticeable blue haze rises from the oil and the bread cube browns in 30 seconds, then the oil has reached about 200°C (400°F) and it is ready for frying small fritters, croûtons, coated cooked foods (such as fish cakes), and the second frying of chipped potatoes.

SHALLOW FRYING

Shallow frying is another quick and easy method of cooking, although not quite as quick as deep frying. It is ideal for cooking chops, steaks, escalopes, liver, sausages, bacon, eggs and fish. All you need to do is fry the food in a shallow amount of hot fat (about 1–2.5 cm/½–1 inch) over a moderate heat. Turn the food once during cooking. You can use a variety of fats from cooking oil, vegetable oil, olive oil, white cooking fat, lard, margarine, butter, or a mixture. If you want to use butter don't use it on its own as it burns at a relatively low temperature. It is advisable to mix it with oil or margarine.

It is best to coat the food before shallow frying it; this helps to protect it from the temperature of the fat, and also prevents fragile items, such as fish fillets, from collapsing.

The guidelines for safe and successful shallow frying are very similar to those for deep fat frying, although there are distinct differences. The fat must be heated gently at all times, even during the actual cooking; there is no need to use a fat thermometer to test the heat of the oil, just drop a small piece of stale bread into the hot fat and it should sizzle steadily without spitting. Lower the coated food into the hot fat gently, and turn it during frying with a per-

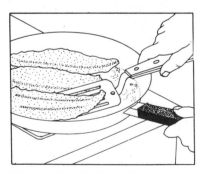

Turning food during frying

forated spoon or fish slice. (Scoop off any crumbs or remnants of food from the surface of the cooking fat so they don't burn.)

Remove the cooked food with a perforated spoon or slice and drain thoroughly.

STIR FRYING

Stir frying is a traditional Chinese method of cooking, which has gained tremendous popularity throughout Europe in recent years. It is a quick and versatile technique that can be used for vegetables, meat, fish, rice and noodles. The secret of the technique lies in cutting up the food into uniformly-sized small pieces and then cooking them very quickly in oil. The beauty of this method of cooking is that the food retains its shape, texture and taste.

A wok, the traditional Chinese cooking utensil, is the best receptacle to use for stir frying. It is a large, deep metal pan, with a completely spherical base and two looped handles.

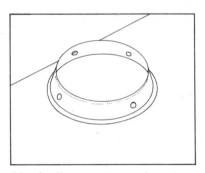

Metal collar to support wok on ring

Place the wok directly on the gas or electric ring. (It works better on gas.) You can buy a metal collar which you fit around your cooking ring, which acts as a support for the wok. This makes it easier to move the wok around as the food is cooking, ensuring that each surface of the wok comes in contact with an even temperature; an all essential fact in stir frying.

When you stir fry foods you'll find that they cook very quickly, so it's important to have everything well prepared in advance. Chop your food up into evenly-sized small pieces and, if using meat or fish, coat it in flour. Place

the wok over the heat, preferably standing on a metal collar, and add a few spoonfuls of oil to it. Once the oil is hot, add the finely cut ingredients, either all in one go or in stages, depending on the recipe. Garlic, root ginger and other highly flavoured ingredients are often used. These should be fried first and then the other ingredients should be added. Tilt the wok backwards and forwards

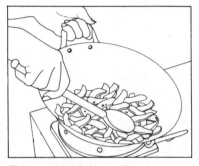

Tilting wok while stir-frying

over the heat, while you stir and turn the ingredients with a long-handled spatula until cooked.

POACHING

This is a subtle cooking technique used for preparing delicate foods which cook quickly. Poaching describes the gentle agitation of a hot liquid by natural movement of the liquid. Odd bubbles occur, but not the steady bubbling that one associates with simmering. The choice of cooking liquid depends

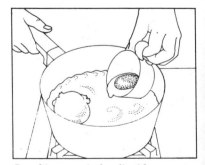

Poaching eggs in hot liquid

to a large extent on what you are poaching; for fish, a court bouillon or wine would be most appropriate; for meat, a vegetable or meat stock or wine; for eggs, water.

When poaching eggs and quenelles, add them to the liquid, once it is hot and 'quivering'. Fish fillets, on the other hand, should be put into the pan with cold liquid and then brought to the correct temperature for poaching. Fish is usually poached covered, but many other foods are poached without a lid.

Suitable poaching foods

Boned and skinned chicken breasts
Meat and fish quenelles
Fish fillets and thin fish cutlets
Shellfish, such as scallops
Eggs
Gnocchi
Soft fruits, such as peaches

STEAMING

This is a quick and nutritious way of cooking food and is generally applied to vegetables. All you need is a simple metal steamer which you place in a saucepan. Pour in

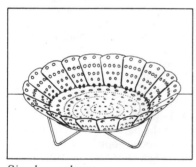

Simple metal steamer

boiling water to just beneath the steamer, add the vegetables and cover with a lid. The vegetables will cook in the steam and, unlike when they are cooked in water, very little nutritious value will be lost. Steaming is also an excellent way of reheating food.

ROASTING

Roasting is certainly a very effortless way of cooking. Once the food is in the oven, you can virtually forget about it, apart from giving it the occasional baste. However, roasting is only suitable for prime, tender cuts of meat, and for poultry and most game.

Roasting is a direct heat method of cooking, and the food needs to be kept moist throughout cooking. Before putting the joint or bird into the oven spread it with fat (duck is the only exception to this rule—it is naturally fatty and should be pricked with a skewer before roasting). With meat, poultry or game that dries out quickly, like chicken, veal, venison, pheasant and grouse, it is advisable to cover it with strips of

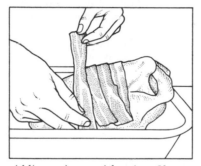

Adding moisture with strips of bacon

streaky bacon. This gives added moisture.

Veal, lamb and pork can be boned, stuffed and rolled before roasting as can poultry and game. Use a well-flavoured stuffing which will moisten and enhance the flavour of the meat during cooking. Stuffing makes the meat go further, but it takes longer to cook.

Another way of keeping the food moist during roasting, is to cover it with cooking foil, dull side uppermost; the foil can be removed either for the first or last part of the cooking time, to allow the food to brown. When using foil, add on an extra few minutes cooking time.

Place your meat, poultry or feathered game on a grid or rack in

a roasting tin. This is important since it makes it easy to baste the food during cooking and to roast vegetables under it.

Roast in a preheated oven for the given time, basting with the

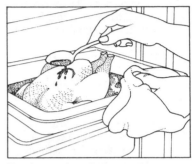

Basting poultry during cooking

juices and fat in the roasting tin from time to time. Test to see whether the meat is done. Push a skewer right into the meat, take it out and feeling it, when it is hot to the touch the meat is done. Beef, lamb and game are often served underdone, but chicken, turkey and pork should always be cooked right through. If you are using a meat thermometer, insert the thermometer in the thickest part of the meat before it goes into the oven, making sure that it does not touch the bone. All roast meats are

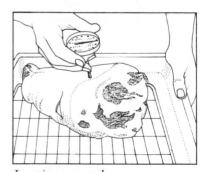

Inserting a meat thermometer

much easier to carve or cut if they are first allowed to 'settle' after cooking. Remove from the oven and keep warm for about 15 minutes until ready to serve.

What to roast
Beef—whole fillet, rump, fore rib, sirloin on the bone, boned sirloin, wing rib, topside, silverside
Lamb—leg, best end of neck, breast, shoulder, loin
Pork—whole fillet, spare rib, hand and spring, belly, loin, blade
Veal—loin, leg, shoulder, breast, best end of neck
Poultry—chicken, poussins, turkey, duck, guinea fowl
Game (young)—wild duck, pheasant, pigeon, grouse, venison.

Roasting times and methods
There are three basic methods of roasting (see chart for methods and timing).

Method A
The meat is first roasted at 230°C (450°F) mark 8, for 15 minutes, and the heat is then reduced to 180°C (350°F) mark 4, for the remainder of the cooking time.

Method B
The meat is roasted at 190°C (375°F) mark 5 for the whole cooking time.

Method C
The meat is roasted at 160°C (325°F) mark 3 for the whole cooking time. This long slow method of roasting is most suitable for large turkeys, and for joints which are not considered prime roasting joints like, for example, silverside of beef, hand and spring of pork and breast of lamb.

Remember to allow extra roasting time if foil and/or stuffing are used, and to weigh joints and birds *after* stuffing in order to calculate accurate cooking time.

	Methods A & B	Method C
Beef (whole fillet, rump, sirloin, ribs, topside, silverside)	15–20 minutes for every 450 g (1 lb) plus 20 minutes	30 minutes for every 450 g (1 lb) plus 30 minutes
Lamb (leg shoulder, loin, best end of neck, breast)	20–25 minutes for every 450 g (1 lb) plus 25 minutes	35–40 minutes for every 450 g (1 lb) plus 40 minutes
Pork (whole fillet, loin, leg, sparerib, hand and spring, belly, loin, blade)	30 minutes for every 450 g (1 lb) plus 30 minutes	40–45 minutes for every 450 g (1 lb) plus 45 minutes
Veal (loin, leg, shoulder, breast, best end of neck)	25–30 minutes for every 450 g (1 lb) plus 30 minutes	35–40 minutes for every 450 g (1 lb) plus 40 minutes
Chicken (whole bird)	20 minutes for every 450 g (1 lb) plus 20 minutes	30 minutes for every 450 g (1 lb) plus 30 minutes
Turkey 2.25–3.5 kg (5–8 lb)	20 minutes for every 450 g (1 lb) plus 20 minutes	30 minutes for every 450 g (1 lb) plus 30 minutes
3.5–6.5 kg (8–14 lb)	—	20 minutes for every 450 g (1 lb) plus 20 minutes
Over 6.5 kg (14 lb)	—	15 minutes for every 450 g (1 lb) plus 15 minutes
Duck	15 minutes for every 450 g (1 lb) plus 15 minutes	20 minutes for every 450 g (1 lb) plus 20 minutes

BARBECUING
Barbecuing is a wonderfully easy way of cooking food out of doors. It lends itself perfectly to entertaining, since you can get delicious results with the minimum of effort.

A barbecue is like an outdoor grill, depending on charcoal for its fuel. The grill needs to be heated first and then the meat or fish which is to be cooked is placed either directly on the grill or first in foil and then on the grill.

Preparing food for barbecuing
- Always use good-quality meat; poor quality meat does not cook very well on a barbecue
- Marinate the food for at least 1 hour before barbecuing it. This enhances its flavour and ensures moistness
- Allow chilled foods to come to room temperature before putting them on the barbecue; chilled foods give off moisture which can cause spitting
- Brush foods with oil to prevent them from sticking to the barbecue grill
- Season meat and poultry with salt after cooking as salt draws off the meat juices
- Watch food carefully once it is on the barbecue, and test from time to time.
- As well as barbecuing directly on the barbecue grill, food can also be wrapped in foil and cooked either on the grill or in the coals

Good foods for barbecues
Beef—lean steaks, good stewing (kebabs)
Lamb—chops, leg steaks, fillet (kebabs)
Pork—chops, spare-ribs, fillet (kebabs)
Bacon and sausages
Veal—chops, leg fillet (kebabs)
Chicken—drumsticks, legs, split poussins
Offal—kidneys
Fish—firm-textured fish such as halibut, monkfish and cod; whole fish such as bass, bream, trout,

mackerel and sardines
Shellfish—split lobster, large prawns and scallops
Vegetables—corn on the cob is particularly good
Fruit—particularly bananas, cubes or slices threaded on skewers, in their skins or skinned and wrapped in foil

POT ROASTING

This is a one-pot method of cooking larger pieces of meat, whole birds and fish. It involves the minimum of preparation and long, slow cooking. Simply brown the meat all over in hot fat in a heavy pan, remove from the pan while browning vegetables in the fat. Place the meat on top of the vegetables; add a little liquid, cover and cook in a moderate oven.

For an even quicker pot roast use the cold start method and simply put all the ingredients in the pot at once and place in the oven. The cooking time will be longer.

Good foods to pot roast
Brisket or topside of beef; boned, stuffed and rolled breast of lamb or veal; stuffed hearts; rolled shoulder of venison and chicken.

CASSEROLING

With very little preparation and long, slow cooking you have a dish that can be prepared in advance and then reheated as required. Casseroles freeze very well and can be brought to the table in their casserole dish. In short, they save you a great deal of time.

There are two types of casseroles—brown (fry start) and white (cold start). To make a brown casserole, fry small chunks of meat in fat until browned all over. Remove and drain on absorbent kitchen paper. Add vegetables to the pan and fry until well coated. Add seasoning, stir in some flour, put back the meat and add some liquid. Cover tightly and simmer either on top of the cooker or in a slow to medium oven until tender. A white casserole is

quicker to prepare. Simply layer the same ingredients as for a brown casserole into your dish and place in a slow to moderate oven, cooking until tender.

GOOD FOODS FOR CASSEROLING

Beef—leg, shin, chuck, flank, blade, skirt, joints of topside, top rump, brisket, silverside
Lamb—breast, scrag, middle or best end of neck, loin. Shoulder and leg may be cooked as joints or boned and cubed
Pork—hand, spare rib, belly (trimmed of fat). Also, loin chops, spare rib chops and fillet. Gammon steaks and joints and cooked, cubed ham
Veal—breast, neck, shoulder, shin, leg, knuckle
Offal—ox and sheep's kidneys; calves' and sheep hearts; lambs' and sheep's tongues; oxtail
Poultry—joints
Game—grouse, rabbit
Pulses

BOILING

Boiling is an easy technique that involves covering the food in a liquid, heating it until it comes to boiling point and then, more often than not, lowering the heat and simmering it. The cooking time will depend on what type of food is being cooked as well as its size. You can boil meat, fish, grains, pulses and vegetables.

Boiling meat and poultry
Tie or truss joints and poultry carefully with string, so that they retain their shape during cooking. Smoked and salty gammon and ham should be soaked in cold water before hand and the soaking water should be discarded. This gets rid of some of the saltiness. Place the meat or poultry in a large pan with enough cold water to cover. Bring to the boil. Lower the heat and remove any surface scum with a slotted spoon. Add chopped onion, some chopped peeled root vegetables, a bay leaf, a small bunch of parsley, a few

Removing surface scum

peppercorns and a blade of mace. (Add salt at the end of the cooking time or the meat will toughen. Don't add it to pickled or cured meat.) Cover the pan tightly and simmer very gently. The exact time depends on the type of meat; with boiling fowl it depends on age. As an approximate guide, allow 30 minutes for every 450 g (1 lb), plus an extra 30 minutes.

Suitable meats for boiling
Beef—brisket or silverside
Lamb—leg of mutton
Pork—belly
Gammon and bacon—corner gammon, middle gammon, gammon slipper, boned and rolled hock
Poultry—boiling fowl
Grains
Pulses
Vegetables

Freezing and Other Handy Tricks

Owning a freezer is rather like having a second pair of hands in the kitchen. You need a pastry case: don't bake one, take it out of the freezer! You want some real stock for a special dish; don't make some, thaw some! If you have a culinary disaster—never mind—here's how to turn it into a success. Plus some tricks of the trade to make the simplest dishes look and taste superb.

FREEZING

Careful and thoughtful use of your freezer not only speeds up your cooking, but it makes it a lot easier. Never be tempted to freeze food for the sake of filling the freezer; you should only freeze food that you and your family like and that you will enjoy serving to guests.

Your freezer should be a great help when it comes to planning menus, especially for parties and other large functions. Food from your freezer should always be complemented by seasonal fresh foods, both to give you satisfaction as the cook, and to offer variety. No one is going to be particularly impressed by eating frozen raspberries when fresh ones are in season. Watch this overlap carefully when planning menus.

Apart from freezing made-up dishes, freezers are immensely useful for storing odd bits and pieces which will speed up food preparation. Things like, for example, breadcrumbs, grated cheese, chopped fresh herbs and leftover wine. All these can be added to the freezer in a spare moment and are indispensable when cooking in a hurry.

Do not be tempted to put food in your freezer and forget about it. Always label foods clearly. Although food that is kept past its recommended storage time is perfectly edible and safe to eat, it will deteriorate somewhat in flavour, texture and appearance.

Always use very fresh ingredients; the food that you take out of the freezer is only as good as the food that you put in. Freeze foods in amounts that you know you will use in one go; it is usually impossible to separate out small quantities from a larger pack. People tend to disagree on which foods can be frozen and which cannot. In fact *all* foods *can* be frozen, but the thawed result is often far from acceptable. It is the water content in food which

freezes first; if the water content of a food is very high, the food will collapse on thawing. Two very good examples are raw lettuce and cucumber; it would be an absolute disaster to try and freeze either. However, they can be frozen in the form of soup.

WHAT TO FREEZE

SOUPS

It is a very practical proposition to freeze soups. Always make them in large quantities as they freeze particularly well. Soups based on vegetable purées freeze best of all. Homemade stocks give a better flavour to soup that is to be frozen; any excess stock can always be frozen separately. Cool soup very quickly after making it, pack it in suitable sized containers, and freeze it as soon as possible. If a soup needs cream, it is advisable to add it on reheating, otherwise it may separate.

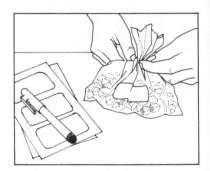

Packing croûtons for freezing

Croûtons are handy soup garnishes and can be frozen, already fried, in freezer bags. They can be 'freshened up' from frozen in a moderately hot oven.

GOOD SOUPS FOR FREEZING

Carrot and orange soup; cauliflower soup; French onion soup and potato and watercress soup.

Recommended storage life: 3 months.

FISH

Fish is a highly perishable food, and even more care has to be taken when you are buying it for the freezer, than when buying it to be eaten fresh. Make a good friend of your fishmonger, so that you can rely on him choosing really good quality fish for you. Always freeze fish the day it is bought. If you are freezing uncooked fresh fish pack it in such a way that you will be able to take out just the quantity that you need; interleave fillets

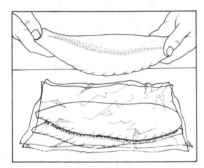

Interleaving fillets with freezer wrap

and steaks with freezer wrap. White fish stands up to freezing far better than shellfish and smoked fish.

GOOD FISH DISHES FOR FREEZING

Cod provençale; fish loaf; homemade fish cakes; smoked fish mousses; smoked haddock croquettes and salmon quiche.

Recommended storage life: 2 months for dishes containing white fish; 1 month for dishes using smoked or shellfish.

CHEESE

Cheese does not freeze very well in its raw state as it tends to lose texture and become crumbly. Bags of grated cheese are useful to have in the freezer—frozen grated cheese is free-flowing and useful when in a hurry. Made up dishes containing cheese freeze most successfully. Some cheese dishes are best frozen uncooked or only partly cooked.

GOOD CHEESE DISHES FOR FREEZING

Croquettes; cheese and ham flan and pizza.

Recommended storage life: 2 months.

MEAT AND POULTRY

Most varieties of meat and poultry freeze extremely well, both raw and made up into complete dishes. Dishes that take time and effort to prepare are the ones to freeze. They are invariably the sort of dishes that are perfect for unexpected dinner guests or for family meals. Pasta-based dishes; cooked meat or poultry in a gravy or sauce; homemade beefburgers or meatballs are all excellent from the freezer. When making casseroles for the freezer, reduce the initial cooking time by about 30 minutes. Casseroles are best thawed before reheating; it is safer, and the texture of the ingredients is much better.

GOOD MEAT AND POULTRY DISHES FOR FREEZING

Meat and chicken casseroles; chicken Kiev; meat loaves; pâtés and terrines; meat fillings (to use for pies); pasta dishes such as lasagne; mince based dishes such as moussaka; beefburgers and meatballs; beef olives.

Recommended storage life: 3 months.

TO FREEZE A CASSEROLE

Line a casserole dish with freezer foil and fill with the cooled,

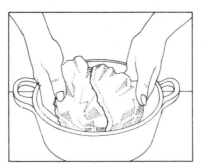

Lifting out parcel of frozen casserole

cooked casserole. Pinch the foil over to seal, and freeze until solid. Lift out the foil parcel with the frozen casserole in it, and overwrap. Return to the freezer. (In this way you are not minus a casserole dish.) When you want to use the frozen casserole: take it out of the freezer, remove the wrapping and place the solid casserole back into the casserole dish in which it was originally cooked Allow it to thaw and then reheat. No messy freezer containers, and the casserole looks as if it has been cooked in the dish in which you serve it.

SAUCES AND STOCKS

Sweet and savoury sauces are both very worthwhile items to have in the freezer; they save a lot of time and last-minute effort. Choose sauces that are versatile. Basic white or brown sauces are both good; they are useful in their own right but can also be used as the base for many other simple sauces. Thickened sauces stand up to freezing far better if they are thickened with cornflour rather than with wheat flour. For sweet sauces, freeze those based on a fruit purée or pulp, and smooth sauces like those made from chocolate. Sauces are best frozen in quite small quantities (even in ice cube trays); amounts that you can use in one go. The most convenient way of packing sauces which are to be served hot, is to use 'boil-in-the-bag' bags; they can quickly be thawed and heated be lowering them into a pan of boiling water.

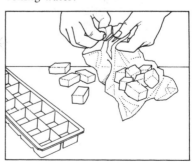

Packing frozen stock cubes

GOOD SAUCES FOR FREEZING

Basic brown sauce; basic white sauce; Bolognese sauce; curry sauce; fresh tomato sauce and onion sauce.

Apple; butterscotch; chocolate and cranberry.

Recommended storage life: 6 months for most, but 2 months for those containing strong flavours such as curry, or perishable ingredients such as meat.

DESSERTS AND PUDDINGS

The perfect puddings to have in your freezer are those which can be taken out and are ready to serve as soon as they have thawed. Dessert 'bases' are also very useful to have on hand in the freezer, such as, pastry cases, sponge cases and choux buns.

Homemade ice creams are easy to prepare when you have a freezer, and are far superior to the bought varieties. Cooked fruit purées are very useful; once thawed they can be topped with pastry lids or crumble mixtures. Pies can be baked before freezing, or left uncooked, in which case they can be cooked from frozen; if you use foil pie plates, make sure that the fruit does not come in contact with the foil as the fruit acid reacts on foil.

GOOD DESSERTS AND PUDDINGS FOR FREEZING

Flans; flan cases; fruit pies and purées; ice creams, homemade and profiteroles (freeze choux buns and chocolate sauce separately); mousses and soufflés.

Recommended storage life: up to 6 months for most puddings and desserts.

DESSERT AND PUDDING GARNISHES

CRUNCHY BISCUIT CRUMBS

Crumble stale biscuits into crumbs; fry in butter with a little demerara sugar. Cool and freeze in a freezer bag. Use frozen to crumble over ice creams or as a cheat crumble topping.

LEMON SLICES

Open freeze thin slices, or half slices, of lemon. Pack into freezer bags. Once thawed they can be used for decorating puddings and desserts, or for adding to drinks.

WHIPPED CREAM ROSETTES

Pipe rosettes of whipped cream

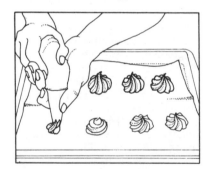

Piping rosettes of whipped cream

onto waxed paper and open freeze. Pack into rigid containers, separating layers and return to the freezer. Thaw on absorbent kitchen paper, before placing on top of the pudding or dessert.

BAKING

Nearly all baked foods, such as cakes, breads and biscuits, freeze extremely well. Many of them are also quite time-consuming to make, so it is a great advantage to be able to freeze them. Baked foods also tend to go stale quite quickly; the freezer keeps them beautifully fresh until required. All baked goods should be really cold before they are packed for the freezer. Thin icings can go very runny on thawing so it is better to

stick to the thicker types such as buttercreams and frostings. Cakes or gâteaux which have a piped or elaborate decoration on top should always be 'open-frozen' before being packed.

GOOD BAKED ITEMS FOR FREEZING

Brandy snaps; bread, all types; cheesecakes; chocolate cake; éclairs (unfilled); scones (sweet or savoury); sponge cake layers (ready for assembly).

Recommended storage time: about 2 months.

Breadcrumbs: When you have some slightly stale bread, make it into breadcrumbs, and freeze in freezer bags. (They are very useful in savoury cooking as well as in sweet recipes.

VEGETABLES AND FRUIT

If there is a glut of any particular fruit, or you happen to have it growing in the garden, then it is always worth freezing some down for using later in the year. Raspberries and blackberries are both good choices.

The same really applies to vegetables, as far as freezing them in their natural state is concerned. Some made up vegetable dishes also freeze very well; two good examples are stuffed peppers and stuffed aubergines.

GOOD VEGETABLES AND FRUITS FOR FREEZING

Asparagus, broad beans, broccoli, Brussels sprouts, calabrese, carrots, cauliflower, courgettes, fennel, leeks, mangetout, peas, peppers, runner beans and sweetcorn.

Apples, blackberries, blackcurrants, damsons, gooseberries, greengages, lemons (in slices), peaches, pears, raspberries and rhubarb.

Recommended storage time: 12 months for most vegetables, if blanched, and 12 months for most firm fruits; 4 months for soft fruits.

TRICKS OF THE TRADE

Food should look as good as it tastes, and vice versa. Presentation is very much part of the art of cooking, and it is eye appeal which first sets the taste buds working. Some garnishes and decorations are very time-consuming to prepare, but many are both quick and easy. Ideally the garnish or decoration on any dish should be edible, and echo the ingredients in that particular dish. Garnishes and decorations can also help to balance texture and colour; you would use crisp garnishes with smooth, otherwise soft foods, and rich greens or reds to offset cream-coloured sauces. Keep these 'finishing touches' as simple and uncluttered as possible; the food should never look fussy or contrived.

FINISHING TOUCHES

- If a colourful ingredient is used in a dish, keep a little back before cooking to use as a garnish—a ring or two of green or red pepper, a few peas, feathery tops from fresh carrots, celery leaves or fennel
- Leave the small fresh green leaves on cauliflower when cooking it; it looks much more attractive
- Browned flaked almonds add a crunch to cooked white fish, and a pleasing contrast to grilled whole fish, such as trout

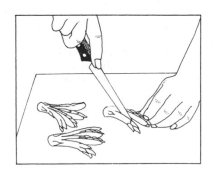

Fanning out asparagus tips

- Use asparagus tips fanned out on top of a cooked chicken breast or lamb cutlet
- Finely snipped crisp bacon adds a pleasing savoury crunch on top of creamed potato
- Sprinkle a mixture of oven-dried breadcrumbs and finely grated lemon rind over cooked green vegetables, such as broccoli
- Give a mimosa garnish to pale vegetables such as cauliflower or Jerusalem artichokes. Chop the whites of hard-boiled eggs finely and sieve the yolks. Sprinkle the white over first of all, and then the sieved yolk
- Black lumpfish roe looks stunning on yellow or cream-coloured dishes, such as egg mayonnaise, or noodles in a cream sauce
- Chop set aspic jelly with a wet knife; use to garnish joints of cold meat or cold fish such as salmon
- If a dish is to be served with a side-serving of mayonnaise or hollandaise sauce; fill a large hollowed out tomato or half a lemon with the chosen sauce

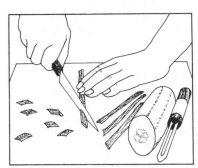

Cutting leaves from cucumber peel

- Cut leaves from cucumber peel to garnish fish mousses and pâtés
- Peel carrots. Using a potato peeler, cut thin spirals of carrot; plunge into a bowl of iced water. Use to garnish portions of pâté and terrines
- Put orange and lemon rind into the liquidiser with granulated sugar; blend until smooth. Use

for sprinkling over the top of fruit pies and crumbles

Cutting angelica with dampened scissors

- When using angelica and glacé cherries for decoration, you will obtain a neater finish if you chop both of them with dampened kitchen scissors
- Use mint sprigs for garnishing portions of melon or grapefruit. For a truly sparkling finish, dip the mint sprigs in beaten egg white and then in caster sugar
- A brandy snap filled with a whirl of cream makes a pretty garnish for a fruit mousse or fool
- Try a curl of plain chocolate for a special ice cream or mousse;

Cutting curls of plain chocolate

use chocolate that is firm but not chilled, and form the curls using a potato peeler
- Sandwich ratafia biscuits together with plain chocolate and leave until set. Use to decorate trifles and large mousses

● Clever doiley-dusting looks most effective on plain sponge cakes. Use icing sugar to dust

Dusting icing sugar over a doiley

over a doiley; and then dust cocoa or chocolate powder over another doiley.

ADD A DASH OF FLAVOUR

● For a strong orange flavour, use frozen concentrated orange rather than freshly squeezed orange juice
● Add an extra piquant flavour to canned soups: a dash of white wine to fish or chicken soups, and a dash of sherry to oxtail and other rich brown soups
● If you are making up a salad which contains quite a sizeable quantity of fruit, use orange juice in the dressing rather than white wine vinegar—it is less harsh
● Use chopped fresh coriander as a garnish for soups which respond to a spicy addition; it is good with carrot, mushroom and Jerusalem artichoke
● For potato salad, pour the pre-pared dressing over the potatoes while they are still warm—for an unusual flavour add a dash of Pernod
● Cook vegetables in real chicken stock for a really rich flavour

PRESENTATION

Here are some garnishes and decorations which have that extra panache; they are simple to make but ultra effective.

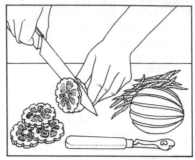

Slicing oranges into cartwheels

Orange or lemon cartwheels

Using a canapé cutter, cut down the length of the lemon or orange, taking strips out of the rind. Cut the fruit into slices. Use to decorate desserts or drinks.

Stuffed cucumber rings

Cut thickish slices of cucumber, and hollow out the centres. Fill with cream cheese, finely chopped red pepper and chopped spring onion. Chill and then cut into thinner slices. An attractive garnish for Parma ham and salami.

CRAFTY TRICKS

● Not enough cream to go round? Fold whisked egg whites into whipped cream.
● If a soup is too salty, add a peeled potato or a good slice of French bread; simmer for a few minutes to allow some of the salt to be absorbed.
● To mend a cracked pastry flan case, brush all over the cracks with beaten egg white. Return to the oven for a few minutes until the egg white has sealed the cracks.
● If you want to make mayon-naise or white sauce to further, thin it with top of the milk, single cream, natural yogurt or soured cream.

Dipping fruit in frosting mixture

Frosted fruits

They can be used as a most attractive garnish for both sweet and savoury dishes. You simply dip the fruits in a mixture of egg white and icing sugar. Grapes and strawberries look particularly attractive frosted. Use them on platters of cold meat or as a border garnish for elaborate gâteaux.

Pastry crescents

Roll out puff pastry trimmings and cut out small crescent shapes. Glaze with beaten egg and bake until golden. Use to garnish fish dishes.

Gherkin fans

Hold the gherkin firmly on a chopping board at one end. Using a small sharp knife cut a series of tongue-shaped slices along the length of the gherkin; do not cut right through the stem end. Fan out each cucumber fan. Use to garnish platters of cold meat and savoury mousses.

Cutting out pastry crescents

QUICK MEALS

With a well-stocked store cupboard, last-minute dishes can be fun to put together, and very satisfying for the cook.

The following ideas are based on store cupboard ingredients, with a few fresh foods as well.

SOUPS

PRAWN AND ASPARAGUS BISQUE
Mix canned asparagus soup with a little white wine; add peeled prawns (frozen or canned). Heat through and swirl in cream.

QUICK VICHYSSOISE
Blend drained canned celery with drained canned new potatoes; add chicken stock and cream to give a smooth soup-like consistency.

STARTERS

MARINATED ARTICHOKES WITH MUSHROOMS
Make a dressing with orange juice, olive oil, chopped mint (fresh or dried) and seasoning. Add drained canned artichoke hearts and button mushrooms and chill. Serve with bread.

MAIN DISHES

MEAT

CHINESE CHICKEN
Cook chicken drumsticks until tender. Add canned sweet and sour sauce and sliced canned water chestnuts. Heat through.

SAUSAGE CASSEROLE
Mix cooked sausages with canned red cabbage, canned red wine sauce, sliced green peppers, dill seeds and seasoning. Heat through in the oven.

FISH

FISHERMAN'S PIE
Mix a can of flaked salmon with a can of mushroom soup and some fried sliced onion; top with made up instant mashed potato mixed with egg yolk and grated cheese. Bake until golden.

SMOKED SALMON FONDUE
Heat canned smoked salmon soup with a little white wine, cream and chopped fresh herbs.

EGG

EGG RISOTTO
Heat ready cooked canned rice in butter with chopped spring onion; add chopped hard-boiled egg, chopped parsley and a little cream and heat through.

PASTA

NOODLE BAKE
Mix cooked green noodles with soured cream, thawed frozen peas, chopped ham, grated Parmesan cheese and seasoning. Place in a gratin dish, sprinkle with extra cheese and bake until golden.

SUPPERS AND SNACKS

CHICKEN AND POTATO GRATIN
Mix canned chicken soup with chopped canned chicken breast and finely chopped red pepper. Put into a gratin dish and top with frozen potato balls. Sprinkle with grated cheese and a few dried breadcrumbs. Bake until golden.

PIZZA-STYLE FRENCH BREAD
Cut lengths of bread and split in half; brush with or dip in oil. Top with drained canned tomatoes, slivers of cheese and/or salami, anchovy fillets and black olives. Brush with oil and bake.

VEGETABLES

Wrap *frozen potato croquettes* in rashers of streaky bacon, and bake until crisp.
Mix thawed and drained *frozen spinach* purée with bottled tartare sauce; heat through in the oven in a covered dish.
Toss blanched almonds in melted butter until lightly golden; add frozen *brussels sprouts*, and heat through.
Lightly cook *button mushrooms* and stir in sufficient canned curry sauce to bind lightly. Delicious with steak and other grilled meats.

PUDDINGS AND DESSERTS

BUTTERED PINEAPPLE PASTRY
Roll out thawed frozen puff pastry to a rectangle; brush with beaten egg white. Top with canned pineapple slices, well drained (or slices of fresh pineapple) and knobs of butter. Scatter with demerara sugar and bake until well puffed and golden. Serve hot with cream.

PEACHES WITH MELBA SAUCE
Use canned whole peaches or skinned fresh ones. Blend raspberry jam with orange juice and a little brandy until smooth. Put peaches into glass dishes and spoon over the sauce.

RASPBERRY ROMANOFF
Crush packet meringues coarsely or, alternatively, use sponge finger biscuits. Mix with lightly whipped cream and well drained canned raspberries. Spoon into stemmed glasses and garnish with a twist of orange.

Basic Sauces and Dressings

These are the essential recipes that are the basis of quick and easy cooking. They provide those vital shortcuts which save precious time in the kitchen without sacrificing flavour or goodness.

BASIC SAUCES AND DRESSINGS

WHITE SAUCE (POURING)

One-stage method

Makes 300 ml (½ pint)

15 g (½ oz) butter or margarine

15 g (½ oz) flour

300 ml (½ pint) milk

salt and freshly ground pepper

1 Place the butter or margarine, flour and milk in a saucepan. Heat, whisking continuously, until the sauce thickens. Season with salt and pepper.

WHITE SAUCE (COATING)

1 Follow the recipe for Pouring Sauce (above), but use **25 g (1 oz)** each of **butter** and **flour**.

Blender or food processor method

1 Use the ingredients in the same proportions as for Pouring or Coating Sauce (above).

2 Put the butter, flour, milk and seasoning in the machine and blend until smooth.

3 Pour into a saucepan and bring to the boil, stirring, until the sauce thickens.

Roux method

1 Use the ingredients in the same quantities as for Pouring Sauce or Coating Sauce (above).

2 Melt the butter in a saucepan. Add the flour and cook over a low heat, stirring with a wooden spoon, for 2 minutes. Do not allow the mixture (roux) to brown.

3 Remove the pan from the heat and gradually blend in the milk, stirring after each addition to prevent lumps from forming. Bring to the boil slowly and continue to cook, stirring all the time, until the sauce comes to the boil and thickens.

4 Simmer very gently for a further 2–3 minutes. Season with salt and freshly ground pepper.

————— VARIATIONS —————

Parsley Sauce
A traditional sauce for bacon, ham and fish dishes.

1 Follow the recipe for the Pouring Sauce or Coating Sauce (above).

2 After seasoning with salt and pepper, stir in 15–30 ml (1–2 tbsp) **finely chopped fresh parsley**.

Onion Sauce
For grilled and roast lamb.

1 **Add 1 large onion**, skinned and finely chopped, to the ingredients for Pouring or Coating Sauce (above) and use the roux method.

2 Soften the onion in the butter before adding the flour.

3 Reheat gently before serving.

Cheese Sauce
For fish, poultry, ham, bacon, egg and vegetable dishes.

1 Follow the recipe for Pouring or Coating Sauce (above).

2 Before seasoning with salt and pepper, stir in **50 g (2 oz)** of **finely grated Cheddar cheese** or any other hard cheese, 2.5–5 ml (½–1 tsp) **prepared mustard and a pinch of cayenne pepper.** Cook gently until the cheese melts.

Lemon Sauce
For fish, poultry, egg and veal dishes.

1 Follow the recipe for Pouring or Coating Sauce (page 566).

2 Before seasoning with salt and pepper stir in the **finely grated rind of 1 small lemon** and **15 ml (1 tbsp) lemon juice**. Reheat gently before serving.

BASIC VINAIGRETTE

Makes 135 ml (9 tbsp)

90 ml (6 tbsp) olive oil

45 ml (3 tbsp) wine vinegar, cider vinegar or lemon juice

2.5 ml ($\frac{1}{2}$ tsp) sugar

2.5 ml ($\frac{1}{2}$ tsp) wholegrain, Dijon or French mustard

salt and freshly ground pepper

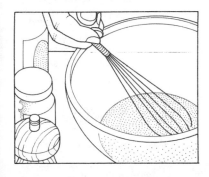

1 Place all the ingredients in a bowl or screw-topped jar and whisk or shake together.

2 Before use, whisk or shake dressing again, as the oil separates out on standing. Taste and adjust seasoning.

Note: If a recipe calls for 150 ml ($\frac{1}{4}$ pint) of dressing, add an extra 15 ml (1 tbsp) oil.

MAYONNAISE MADE IN A BLENDER OR FOOD PROCESSOR

Most blenders and food processors need at least a two-egg quantity in order to ensure that the blades are covered. Remember to have all the ingredients at room temperature.

Makes 300 ml ($\frac{1}{2}$ pint)

2 egg yolks

5 ml (1 tsp) mustard powder or 5 ml (1 tsp) Dijon mustard

5 ml (1 tsp) salt

2.5 ml ($\frac{1}{2}$ tsp) freshly ground pepper

5 ml (1 tsp) sugar (optional)

30 ml (2 tbsp) white wine vinegar lemon juice

about 300 ml ($\frac{1}{2}$ pint) vegetable oil

1 Put the egg yolks, mustard, salt, freshly ground pepper, sugar, if using, and 15 ml (1 tbsp) of the vinegar or lemon juice into the blender goblet or food processor bowl fitted with the metal blade. Blend well together.

2 If your machine has a variable speed control, run it at a slow speed. Add the oil drop by drop through the top of the blender goblet or the feed tube of the processor while the machine is running, until the egg and oil emulsify and become thick. Continue adding the oil gradually in a thin, steady stream. If the mayonnaise becomes too thick, add a little more of the vinegar or of the lemon juice.

3 When all the oil has been added, gradually add the remaining vinegar or lemon juice with the machine still running and blend thoroughly. Taste and adjust seasoning before serving.

STORING MAYONNAISE
Homemade mayonnaise does not keep as long as bought varieties as it is free from added emulsifiers, stabilisers and preservatives. The freshness of the eggs and oil used and the temperature at which it is stored also affect how long it will keep. Mayonnaise keeps for 1 week in the refrigerator in a screw-topped glass jar.

RESCUE REMEDIES
If the mayonnaise separates while you are making it, don't worry there are ways to save it. All these ways involve beating the curdled mixture into a fresh base.

This base can be any one of the following: 5 ml (1 tsp) hot water; 5 ml (1 tsp) vinegar or lemon juice; 5 ml (1 tsp) Dijon mustard or 2.5 ml ($\frac{1}{2}$ tsp) mustard powder (the mayonnaise will taste more strongly of mustard than usual); or a fresh egg yolk to every 300 ml ($\frac{1}{2}$ pint) of mayonnaise. Add the curdled mixture to the base, beating hard. When the mixture is smooth, continue adding the oil as above. (If you use an extra egg yolk you may find that you need to add extra oil.)

——— VARIATIONS ———

These variations are made by adding the ingredients to 300 ml ($\frac{1}{2}$ pint) mayonnaise.

Caper mayonnaise Add **60 ml (4 tsp) chopped capers, 10 ml (2 tsp) chopped pimento** and **5 ml (1 tsp) tarragon vinegar.** Caper mayonnaise makes an ideal accompaniment for fish.

Celery mayonnaise Add **30 ml (2 tbsp) chopped celery** and **30 ml (2 tbsp) snipped fresh chives.**

Cucumber mayonnaise Add **60 ml (4 tbsp) finely chopped cucumber.** This mayonnaise goes well with fish salads, especially crab, lobster or salmon.

Herb mayonnaise Add **60 ml (4 tbsp) snipped fresh chives** and **30 ml (2 tbsp) chopped fresh parsley.** This mayonnaise goes well with hard-boiled eggs.

Horseradish mayonnaise Add **30 ml (2 tbsp) horseradish sauce.**

Piquant mayonnaise Add **10 ml (2 tsp) tomato ketchup, 10 ml (2 tsp) chopped stuffed olives** and **a pinch of paprika.**

HOLLANDAISE SAUCE MADE IN A BLENDER OR FOOD PROCESSOR

Makes about 150 ml ($\frac{1}{4}$ pint)

2 egg yolks

salt and freshly ground pepper

30 ml (2 tbsp) wine or tarragon vinegar or lemon juice

15 ml (1 tbsp) water

75–100 g (3–4 oz) butter

1 Put the egg yolks and seasoning into the blender goblet or food processor bowl fitted with the metal blade. Blend well together.

2 Put the vinegar or lemon juice and water in a small pan and boil until reduced to about 15 ml (1 tbsp). At the same time, melt the butter in another pan and bring to the boil.

3 With the machine running, add the boiling vinegar then the butter in a slow, steady stream through the top of the machine or through the feeder tube, then mix well.

4 Taste the sauce—if it is too sharp, add a little more butter—it should be slightly piquant, almost thick enough to hold its shape.

5 Turn into a warmed serving jug. Serve warm rather than hot. It is excellent with fish in particular but it is also good with asparagus, broccoli or poached eggs.

——————— VARIATION ———————

Mousseline Sauce
Stir 15–30 ml (1–2 tbsp) whipped double cream into the sauce before serving.

QUICK TOMATO SAUCE

Makes about 450 ml ($\frac{3}{4}$ pint)

397 g (14 oz) can tomatoes

5 ml (1 tsp) tomato purée

1 small onion, skinned and chopped

1 clove garlic, skinned and crushed (optional)

pinch of dried basil

pinch of sugar

freshly ground pepper

15 ml (1 tbsp) vegetable oil

1 Put all the ingredients in a blender or food processor and blend until smooth.

2 Heat in a saucepan for 10–15 minutes until slightly thickened. Serve on pasta or use in made-up dishes.

BARBECUE SAUCE

Makes about 450 ml ($\frac{3}{4}$ pint)

1 medium onion, skinned and chopped or 30 ml (2 tbsp) dried onions

60 ml (4 tbsp) malt vinegar

75 g (3 oz) soft brown sugar

5 ml (1 tsp) mustard powder

30 ml (2 tbsp) Worcestershire sauce

150 ml ($\frac{1}{4}$ pint) tomato ketchup

300 ml ($\frac{1}{2}$ pint) water

salt and freshly ground pepper

5 ml (1 tsp) lemon juice

1 Put all ingredients in a pan. Bring to the boil and simmer gently for 15 minutes, stirring occasionally, until slightly thickened.

2 Strain through a sieve. Heat in a saucepan before serving with sausages, hamburgers or chops.

PIMENTO AND PAPRIKA SAUCE

Makes 450 ml ($\frac{3}{4}$ pint)

40 g (1$\frac{1}{2}$ oz) butter

15 ml (1 tbsp) paprika

45 ml (3 tbsp) flour

450 ml ($\frac{3}{4}$ pint) stock

salt and freshly ground pepper

5 ml (1 tsp) lemon juice

30 ml (2 tbsp) red wine

115 g (4 oz) can pimento, drained and thinly sliced

1 Melt the butter in a saucepan, stir in the paprika and flour and cook gently for 2 minutes.

2 Remove the pan from the heat and gradually stir in the stock, beating well after each addition.

3 Bring to the boil and continue to cook, stirring until the sauce thickens. Simmer for 5 minutes.

4 Season. Add lemon juice, red wine and pimentos. Reheat, and check for seasoning. Serve with cauliflower, celeriac and marrow.

SWEET AND SOUR SAUCE

Makes about 450 ml ($\frac{3}{4}$ pint)

75 g (3 oz) sugar

60 ml (4 tbsp) cider vinegar

45 ml (3 tbsp) soy sauce

30 ml (2 tbsp) cornflour

300 ml ($\frac{1}{2}$ pint) water

1 green pepper, blanched and cut into thin strips

225 g ($\frac{1}{2}$ lb) tomatoes, skinned and quartered

312 g (11 oz) can crushed pineapple

1 Put the sugar, vinegar and soy sauce in a saucepan. Blend the cornflour with the water and add to the pan. Bring to the boil, stirring; simmer gently for 5 minutes. Add the remaining ingredients and simmer for a further 5 minutes.

SATÉ SAUCE (PEANUT SAUCE)

Makes about 450 ml (¾ pint)

100 g (4 oz) crunchy peanut butter

100 g (4 oz) creamed coconut, crumbled

300 ml (½ pint) boiling water

20 ml (4 tsp) lemon juice

15 ml (1 tbsp) soy sauce

15 ml (1 tbsp) soft brown sugar

2.5–5 ml (½–1 tsp) chilli powder

1 Put the peanut butter, coconut, water, lemon juice, soy sauce, sugar and chilli powder in a pan and bring slowly to the boil, stirring constantly. Lower the heat and simmer gently for about 5 minutes until the coconut has dissolved and the sauce thickens. Taste and adjust seasoning, to taste.

CHOCOLATE SAUCE

Makes 300 ml (½ pint)

15 ml (1 tbsp) cornflour

15 ml (1 tbsp) cocoa powder

30 ml (2 tbsp) sugar

300 ml (½ pint) milk

knob of butter

1 Blend the cornflour, cocoa and the sugar with enough of the milk to give a smooth paste.

2 Heat the remaining milk with the butter until boiling and pour on to the blended mixture, stirring all the time to prevent lumps forming.

3 Return the mixture to the pan and bring to the boil, stirring until it thickens. Cook for a further 1–2 minutes. Serve on steamed or baked sponge puddings.

EGG CUSTARD SAUCE

Curdling can be a problem with egg custards. It occurs if the custard is boiled, so as soon as the mixture coats the back of a wooden spoon it must be removed from the heat. To help prevent curdling, add 2.5 ml (½ tsp) cornflour to every 300 ml (½ pint) milk.

Makes 300 ml (½ pint)

2 eggs

10 ml (2 tsp) caster sugar

300 ml (½ pint) milk

5 ml (1 tsp) vanilla flavouring (optional)

1 In a bowl, beat the eggs with the sugar and 45 ml (3 tbsp) of the milk. Heat the remaining milk to lukewarm and beat into the eggs.

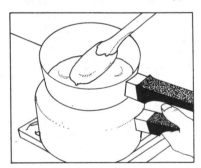

2 Pour into a double saucepan or bowl standing over a pan of simmering water. Cook, stirring continuously, until the custard is thick enough to thinly coat the back of a spoon. Do not boil.

3 Pour into a cold jug and stir in vanilla flavouring, if liked. Serve hot or cold. The sauce thickens slightly on cooling.

BUTTERSCOTCH SAUCE

Makes about 200 ml (8 fl oz)

50 g (2 oz) butter

60 ml (4 tbsp) soft brown sugar

30 ml (2 tbsp) golden syrup

90 ml (6 tbsp) chopped nuts

squeeze of lemon juice (optional)

1 Warm the butter, sugar and syrup in a saucepan until well blended.

2 Boil for 1 minute and stir in the nuts and lemon juice. Serve at once over ice cream.

QUICK APRICOT SAUCE

Makes 200 ml (7 fl oz)

425 g (15 oz) can apricots

10 ml (2 tsp) brandy

1 Drain the apricots, reserving the juice. Put the apricots in a blender or food processor with 60 ml (4 tbsp) of the juice and blend until smooth.

2 Pour the purée into a saucepan and add the brandy. Heat gently for 2–3 minutes. Serve over ice cream.

SABAYON SAUCE

50 g (2 oz) caster sugar

60 ml (4 tbsp) water

2 egg yolks

grated rind of ½ lemon

juice of 1 lemon

30 ml (2 tbsp) rum or sherry

30 ml (2 tbsp) single cream

1 Put the sugar and water in a heavy-based saucepan and heat gently, stirring, until the sugar has dissolved. Bring to the boil and boil for 2–3 minutes.

2 Beat the egg yolks in a basin and slowly pour on the hot syrup, whisking until pale and thick.

3 Add the lemon rind, lemon juice and rum and whisk for a further 2–3 minutes, cool for 30 minutes. Fold in the cream and leave to cool. Chill thoroughly for at least 1 hour.

Guide to Cuts, Cooking Methods and Techniques for Lamb and Pork

In this chapter you will find information on all the different cuts of lamb and pork, with tips for buying and storage. The best methods of cooking are also explained, with a useful roasting chart giving cooking times and temperatures for the most common cuts. Plus techniques of meat preparation, such as boning, and information on the best equipment for the job.

LAMB

Leg An excellent roasting joint comprising lean meat with a thin covering of fat and skin. Can be cooked on the bone, or boned, rolled and stuffed. Often divided in half to form the fillet end and the knuckle half leg or shank end. Leg slices approximately 1 cm ($\frac{1}{2}$ inch) thick are also available; these can be used for grilling or braising or cubed for kebabs.

Shoulder A succulent, tender roasting joint containing a fair proportion of bone and fat. Sold whole or halved into blade and knuckle. Shoulder can be a difficult cut to carve, so for convenience it is often boned, stuffed and rolled. The meat can also be cubed for kebabs and casseroles. The blade half of the shoulder makes a good small roasting joint, while the knuckle half has more bone and is more useful for braising.

Loin A prime lean joint either for roasting in the piece, or for boning and stuffing. Loin is usually divided into loin end and chump end, and cut into chops for grilling and frying. Chump chops are recognisable by the small round bone in the centre. Loin chump ends are the end pieces of chump which tend to be bony but make an economical cut for braising with vegetables.

Best End of Neck Can be purchased as a roasting joint with a row of 6 or 8 rib bones. The butcher will chine or chop the back bone if requested, to make carving easier. Can be roasted on the bone or boned, stuffed and rolled. Two best end necks joined together and curved, bones outwards, make a Crown Roast. Facing each other, fat side outwards, they make a Guard of Honour. Both these special occasion dishes can be stuffed before roasting. Best end of neck chops are small chops cut between the rib bones.

Scrag and Middle Neck Usually sold as chops on the bone and used for stewing and braising. Traditional cuts for Lancashire Hot Pot and Irish Stew.

Neck Fillet Tender, boneless strip of meat taken from the neck of large lambs. Use for kebabs, curries, casseroles, grilling and frying.

Breast Long thin cut, streaked with fat and lean. When boned, rolled and stuffed, it makes an economical cut for roasting and braising. Cut into riblets, can be cooked in a barbecue sauce as for pork spareribs, after simmering in stock to tenderise.

Minced Lamb Lean minced lamb for use in moussaka, pies, burgers, patties, etc.

OFFAL

Lamb's Liver Has a good flavour, fine texture and is very tender. Can be grilled, fried or casseroled. Avoid overcooking, which toughens the meat.

Lamb's Kidneys Are small, about 50–75 g (2–3 oz) each, and are ideal for grills and quick frying. Need careful cooking as easily become tough when cooked for too long. Allow 2–3 kidneys per portion.

Lamb's Hearts Need to be cooked long and slow, and make flavoursome, economical meals. The meat is very lean and is best stewed or braised to prevent it becoming dry. Serve 1 lamb's heart per portion.

Lamb's Tongues A little fiddly to prepare, but very good hot or cold. Should be soaked in salted water for 2–3 hours before cooking, then simmered for $2\frac{1}{2}$–3 hours. The tongues should then be skinned before serving.

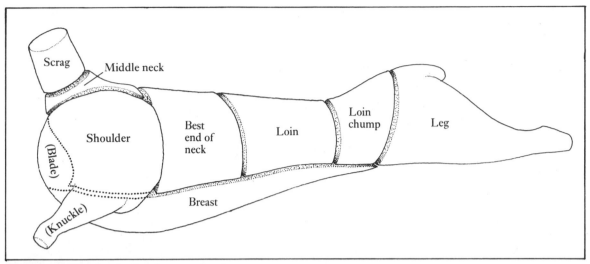

Major cuts of lamb to be found at your butcher

Lamb's Sweetbreads Have a delicate texture and flavour and must always be sold very fresh or frozen. After soaking for several hours, changing the salted water occasionally, they are simmered in flavoured milk or stock for 8–10 minutes. The cooking liquid can then be made into a sauce to accompany the sweetbreads. Alternatively, they can be braised or coated in egg and crumbs before frying.

CHOOSING AND BUYING LAMB
Look for fine-grained, lean meat with a bright red colour tinged with brown. The fat should be creamy white, and not brittle. The bones should be moist and white at the joints. Legs and shoulders should have a thin covering of fat. The fat of some cuts is covered with a thin papery skin. This should be pliable, not hard and wrinkled. Remove from chops before cooking, but leave on roasting joints as it helps the meat to retain moisture. English new season's lamb is available between March and November, although supplies are at their peak between August and November. All joints, except those from the neck, can be roasted, and the individual cuts from them grilled or fried.

STORING LAMB
Freshly cut meat should be stored in a cool place, preferably in the refrigerator. Minced lamb should be used within 24 hours. If no

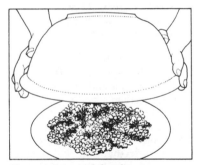

Cover mince with bowl to store

refrigerator is available, place the meat on a plate in a cool place and cover with an upturned large bowl. In a refrigerator, wrap the meat in foil or cling film. Never leave fresh meat in the sealed polythene bag in which it was bought. It should be placed on the shelf below the frozen food compartment. Lamb can be stored for up to 4 days in the refrigerator.

PORK

Neck End A large, economical roasting joint, particularly good when boned, stuffed and rolled. Often divided into blade and sparerib. These 2 smaller cuts can also be roasted, braised or stewed. Boned sparerib makes the best filling for pies. Sparerib chops are suitable for braising, and for slow grilling and frying.

Hand and Spring A large roasting joint, often divided into smaller cuts, hand and shank. As well as being suitable for roasting, hand and shank can be used for casseroles and stews.

Belly A long thin cut with streaks of fat and lean. Stuffed thick end of belly makes an economical roast. Belly is sometimes rather fat, and is better used sliced for grilling and frying rather than braising and stewing.

Leg Can be cut into 4 or more succulent roasting joints, often divided into fillet end and knuckle end. Fillet end is the prime roasting joint, which can be boned and stuffed. Sometimes sliced into steaks for grilling and frying.

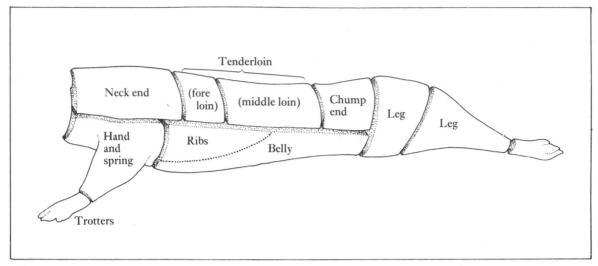

Major cuts of pork to be found at your butcher

Loin A popular roast on the bone, or boned and rolled. Often divided into loin chops, with or without kidney, and large chump chops. Both these chops are very good grilled, fried or baked. Loin of pork produces good crackling.

Tenderloin A tender, lean cut from underneath the back bone of the loin. Sometimes called pork fillet. Can be stuffed and rolled for roasting, cubed for kebabs or grilled. Can also be cut into slices or cubes for frying.

Trotters (feet) Usually salted and boiled and used to make brawn. They are also used to make a flavoursome gelatinous stock.

Ribs Rib bones with a thin covering of lean and fat. Use for barbecued spareribs. Sometimes also called Chinese spareribs.

Knuckle A large bone, covered with meat and rind. Used mainly for enriching slow-cooking casseroles, and as an addition to braised meats.

OFFAL

Pig's Liver Darker in colour and stronger in flavour than lamb's liver. Can be soaked for 1–2 hours in salted water or milk, to reduce the strong taste. Cook as for lamb's liver, or use in pâtés, terrines, faggots, etc.

Pig's Kidneys Similar to lamb's, but slightly larger and with a stronger flavour and firmer texture. Soak in salted water for several hours to reduce the strong taste. Grill, fry or slice and add to casseroles and hot pots. When grilling or frying, time the cooking carefully to avoid overcooking.

Pig's Hearts Larger than lamb's, weighing 8 oz–1 lb (225 g–450 g) each. Best stuffed and braised, or pot roasted, for 2–3 hours until tender. Serve $\frac{1}{2}$–1 pig's heart per portion.

CHOOSING AND BUYING PORK

Good-quality pork is available all year round. Look for firm, dry lean meat with a good pinkish colour. The fat should be firm and creamy white. The rind should be smooth and supple. When deeply scored, the rind forms crackling on roast pork. Ask the butcher to score the meat if you want crackling.

STORING PORK

Pork is highly perishable, and should be eaten as soon after buying as possible. If no refrigerator is available, cook on the day of purchase. To store in a refrigerator, wrap in foil or cling film, to prevent the meat drying out. Never leave fresh meat in the sealed polythene bag in which it was bought. Cook within 2 days of purchase.

SALTING PORK

All cuts of pork, with the exception of loin, can be salted. If salt pork is not available from your butcher, it is very simple to prepare at home.

SALT PORK

1.8 kg (4 lb) piece pork
175 g (6 oz) coarse salt
30 ml (2 tbsp) brown sugar
15 ml (1 tbsp) juniper berries
4 cloves
3 bay leaves
1 blade mace
2 sprigs thyme

1 Wipe the meat with absorbent kitchen paper. Pour 1 litre (1¾ pints) water into a pan, add the salt and sugar and bring to the boil.

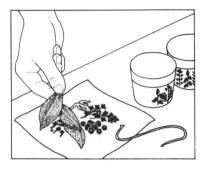

2 Wrap the spices and herbs in muslin and tie with string. Add to the liquid and boil for 2 minutes. Remove from heat and allow the brine to cool completely.

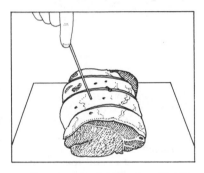

3 Remove the muslin bag. Prick the meat several times with a trussing needle. Place in a deep stoneware or earthenware crock. Pour the cold brine over the meat. Place a plate on top and weight down to keep the meat submerged. Cover the pot with a clean tea towel.

4 Stand the pot in a cool dark place, stirring every 2 days. Remove when sufficiently salted to your taste, from 3–7 days.

5 Before cooking, soak the meat in cold water for at least 3 hours, preferably overnight.

COOKING METHODS FOR LAMB AND PORK

There are no hard and fast rules for cooking meat, as each cut lends itself to a variety of treatments. However, the tender, leaner cuts are generally roasted or grilled, whereas the more economical, fattier cuts, which have more connective tissue, are usually more suitable for pot-roasting, braising or stewing. Before you start to cook, wipe the surface of the meat with damp absorbent kitchen paper. Trim off any excess fat, but do not remove it all as this helps with the flavour and moistness.

ROASTING

This is the most popular method of cooking large prime cuts of meat. It is only really suitable for cuts which have little connective tissue. Very lean meat will need added fat to prevent it from drying out. Lamb and pork are best roasted slowly to keep shrinkage to a minimum.

BASIC ROASTING METHOD

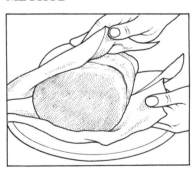

1 Wipe the meat with damp absorbent kitchen paper. Stand the meat on a rack if possible, in a roasting tin. Insert a meat thermometer, if available, into the centre of the thickest part of the joint, making sure the tip of the thermometer is clear of the bone.

2 Spread lamb joints that are particularly lean with a little lard, oil or butter. To make crackling, brush the scored rind of a joint of pork with oil, then rub in salt. Do not baste during cooking.

3 Cook in the oven at 180°C (350°F) mark 4 for the recommended time (see chart below). When ready, lift on to a warmed dish and leave to stand for 10–15 minutes. This makes carving easier and more economical. Meanwhile, make the gravy in the roasting tin.

ROASTING CUTS, TEMPERATURES AND TIMES

PORK

Suitable cuts: loin; leg; shoulder; fore-end of hand; stuffed tenderloin; belly
Cooking temperature
180°C (350°F) mark 4. For crackling, increase temperature to 200°C (400°F) mark 6 for the last 20 minutes.
Cooking time
30 minutes per 450 g (1 lb) plus 30 minutes
Meat thermometer reading
80°C (180°F)
Classic Accompaniments
Sage and onion stuffing; apple sauce; gravy

LAMB

Suitable cuts: leg; shoulder; best end neck; loin; boned and rolled breast
Cooking temperature
180°C (350°F) mark 4
Cooking time
Medium: 25 minutes per 450 g (1 lb) plus 25 minutes
Well done: 30 minutes per 450 g (1 lb) plus 30 minutes
Meat thermometer reading
Medium: 70°C (160°F)
Well done: 80°C (180°F)
Classic Accompaniments
Mint sauce; mint jelly; redcurrant jelly; onion sauce; gravy

SPIT ROASTING

The meat is placed on a revolving spit or skewers and cooked under a direct heat source, either in the oven or as a grill attachment. This method is suitable for any roasting joint, providing it is a uniform shape, well trussed and securely fastened to the spit. Normally, spit-roasted meats need no extra fat as they are self basting. Check your cooker instructions for cooking times.

BRAISING

Braising can be on top of the cooker, or in the oven. After browning in hot fat to seal the meat, it is placed on a bed of aromatic vegetables such as onion, carrot and celery, with just enough liquid to cover them. The pot is tightly covered and the meat cooks in the steam created by the liquid. After cooking, the meat is removed and the liquid boiled until reduced, then used to glaze the meat. The vegetables can be puréed to thicken the sauce.
Cooking temperature: 180°C (350°F) mark 4
Cooking time: 45 minutes per 450 g (1 lb)

The following cuts are suitable for braising:
Pork: neck end; sparerib chops; liver; heart; kidney.
Lamb: middle neck; breast; shoulder; scrag; sweetbreads; heart; liver; kidney.

CASSEROLING AND STEWING

Less tender cuts of meat which are not suitable for grilling or roasting are best cooked slowly in liquid which can be water, stock, wine, cider or beer. Flavourings such as vegetables, herbs and spices, are added to give character to the dish. The meat should be cooked in no more than 300 ml (½ pint) liquid for each 450 g (1 lb) of meat and the liquid should be kept at a gentle simmer, never boiled. The casserole can be prepared either by the fry start method, where the meat and then the vegetables are browned in fat before adding the liquid, or by the cold start method in which the frying process is omitted and all the ingredients are brought slowly the boil.
Cooking temperature: 170°C (325°F) mark 3.

The following cuts are suitable for stewing and casseroling:
Pork: hand and spring; shoulder; kidney.
Lamb: scrag; shoulder; middle neck; neck fillet; heart; liver; kidney; tongue.

FRYING

Only small pieces of tender, quick-cooking meats should be fried. It is therefore a good cooking method for chops, steaks, sausages and bacon, offal such as liver and kidney. Ideally, the meat to be fried should be no more than 2.5 cm (1 inch) thick. Use a large, heavy-based frying pan to ensure the meat cooks evenly. Have the fat preheated before adding the meat to seal in the juices quickly, then reduce the temperature to cook the meat through.

Meat can be coated before frying to give a crisp surface and to protect the meat from drying in the hot fat. The cooking time varies according to the thickness of the meat, so the following is simply a rough guide:
2.5 cm (1 inch) thickness: 7–10 minutes
1 cm (½ inch) thickness: 4–5 minutes.

The following cuts are suitable for frying:
Pork: loin chops; chump chops; sparerib chops; sliced belly; leg steaks; kidney; liver; tenderloin.
Lamb: best end neck cutlets; loin chops; chump chops; neck fillet; kidney; liver.

GRILLING

A quick-cooking method for tender cuts such as steaks, chops, sausages and bacon. As the heat is fierce, the meat often needs to be moistened with melted butter or oil before cooking. Grilling times vary according to the thickness of the meat and the preferred degree of cooking. Pork should always be thoroughly cooked through. Grilling always begins under high heat to help seal in the meat juices. The heat is then lowered to cook the meat further if necessary. Prepare the meat by wiping with

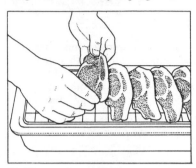

Grilling rashers of bacon

damp absorbent kitchen paper. Trim off any excess fat, or cut through the fat at regular intervals to prevent the meat from curling up during cooking. Brush with oil or melted butter and sprinkle with pepper. It is best to salt the meat when cooking is under way as salt draws out the natural meat juices.

The following cuts are suitable for grilling:
Pork: loin chops; chump chops; sparerib chops; sliced belly; leg steaks; tenderloin; kidney; liver.
Lamb: best end neck cutlets; loin chops; chump chops; neck fillet; kidney; liver.

BOILING

This is a useful method of cooking less tender cuts, salted and cured meats and tongues. The meat is not really boiled, but gently simmered in water with root vegetables and sometimes herbs. The stock left over from cooking the meat makes an excellent base for soups and sauces. Salted meat for boiling should be soaked overnight or for at least 3 hours. If there is no time, place the meat in the pan with cold water to cover, bring slowly to the boil, skimming if necessary. Drain the meat and return it to a clean pan with water and root vegetables and proceed as usual.

Cooking times: Large salted joints should be cooked for 30 minutes per 450 g (1 lb) plus an extra 30 minutes. Small joints should be given a minimum of 1½ hours. Calculate the cooking time from the moment when the water reaches a simmer.

The following cuts of meat are suitable for boiling:

Pork: belly; hand and spring; tongue; head; cheek; trotters.
Lamb: tongue.

TECHNIQUES WITH LAMB AND PORK

Boning a piece of meat makes it easier to carve, and creates a useful cavity for the stuffing. Once you know how, it is not as complicated as you may think, and this section takes you through all the stages to ensure success. Other techniques of meat preparation are also covered.

EQUIPMENT

Choppers have heavy rectangular blades with strong edges. A heavy meat chopper will go through most bones and joints, but you may need a little practice to ensure you hit the right spot each time.

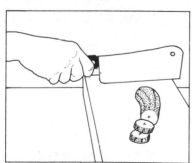

A heavy chopper has many uses

The technique is to use your fore arm and not your wrist and to look at the target, not the chopper. A chopper is also useful for flattening steaks and escalopes.

Butcher's knives are usually fairly heavy, with long, firm blades. They are useful for slicing raw meat and for trimming and finishing joints before cooking.

Saws are used for cutting a carcass and are the only tool which will cut through any bone. A hacksaw will cut through most smaller bones, but with a butcher's bow saw you would be able to cut up a carcass yourself, although this is rarely necessary. When sawing through bone, remove any dust from the meat immediately.

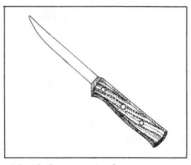

A knife for removing bones

Boning knives are used for removing bones from raw meat and poultry. They are smallish knives, with small sharp pointed blades. The knife should be kept very sharp for maximum efficiency.

Skewers hold meat firmly in shape during cooking. Both wooden and metal skewers are available in various sizes. Kebab

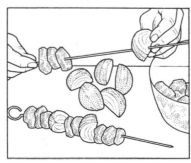

Steel skewers are used for kebabs

skewers are made of flat strips of steel to prevent the food from swinging round while being barbecued or grilled.

Larding needles have sharp points and long hollow bodies for threading small strips of fat through very lean meat. These are rarely used these days as modern cooking techniques prevent meat from drying out during cooking.

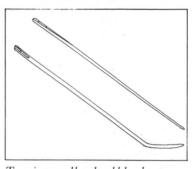

Trussing needles should be sharp

Trussing needles are like very large darning needles. The eye must be large enough to take fine string and the point should be very sharp. They are useful for tying up meat and sewing up stuffed joints. Check you thread enough string on to the needle to complete the job.

HOW TO TIE UP A JOINT

1 Gather or roll the meat to a neat shape. Cut a piece of fine string to a suitable length.

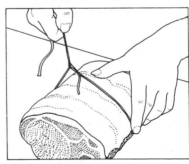

2 Slide the string under the joint and make a loop in one end. Thread other end through the loop and pull ends to tighten.

3 Tie a knot and cut off the ends of the string. Repeat at 2.5–5 cm (1–2 inch) intervals.

HOW TO BONE A LEG OF LAMB OR PORK

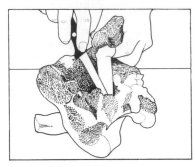

1 Starting from the fillet end, cut around the bone. Scrape the meat from the bone, rolling back the flesh as you go. Continue until the joint is reached.

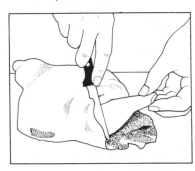

2 Turn the meat round and cut around the shank end to release the meat from the bone. Continue working down the meat, rolling back the flesh from the joint, then pull out the bone.

3 Fill the cavity with chosen stuffing, if used. Skewer the joint or tie into a neat shape with string or trussing thread.

HOW TO BONE A SHOULDER OF LAMB

1 Follow the same method as for boning a leg of lamb, starting by freeing the meat from the flat blade bone. Scrape the meat away from the bone, rolling it back until you reach the joint.

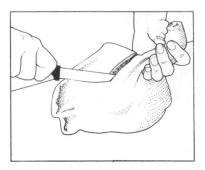

2 Turn the joint around and free the meat from around the shank bone. If necessary, split the flesh up to the bone a little to make it easier. Scrape the flesh away from the shank end until the joint is reached.

3 Pull the bone out from the cavity and add the stuffing. Tie or skewer into a neat shape.

HOW TO BONE A BREAST OF LAMB

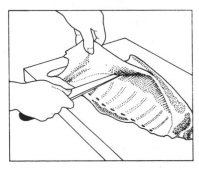

1 Place the breast skin side down on a board. Cut along the flap of meat over the bones and pull back to reveal the bones. Carefully cut around each bone using a small sharp pointed knife.

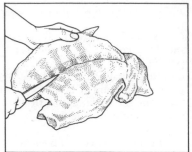

2 Working from one end, scrape away the meat from each bone. Lift the bones from the meat. Trim off excess fat and skin.

3 Turn the meat over and remove the skin by cutting between the skin and fat, pulling the skin away with the other hand.

4 Turn the meat over again and spread evenly with stuffing. Roll up from one long edge. Tie neatly at intervals with trussing string into an even shape.

HOW TO BONE A LOIN OF PORK

1 Remove the kidney if necessary. Place the loin on a board with the skin side down. Trim away any loose fat.

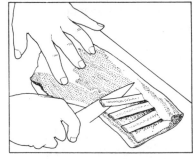

2 Cut along both sides of one rib at a time. Gently pull the rib upwards away from the meat and insert the knife under the bone. Work down the bone to free it from the meat.

3 Twist the bone sharply to break it away from the spine. Repeat with each rib.

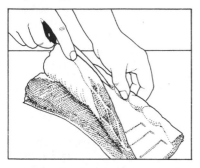

4 Remove the fillet from the spine through the strip of connective tissue. Keep the knife close to the spine as you go.

5 Work down the spine with the point of the knife to free it from the meat. Stuff the joint, roll it up firmly and tie into a neat shape with trussing string.

HOW TO MAKE A GUARD OF HONOUR

1 You will need 2 best end necks of lamb (sometimes called racks of lamb). Place them skin side up on a board. With the point of a sharp knife, remove the thin piece of bone from one end of each rack of lamb.

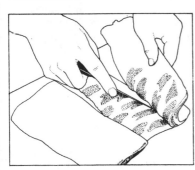

2 Score a straight line across each rack, about 7.5 cm (3 inches) from the tips of the bones. Remove the layer of fat and meat between the scored line and the bone tips. Cut out the meat from between each bone. Scrape the bones clean of meat and fat.

3 Place the bones flat on the board. Using a heavy knife, cut each tip diagonally.

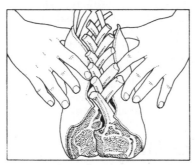

4 Place the 2 racks up, concave sides facing each other. Press them together, interlacing the bone ends. Tie in 3 places.

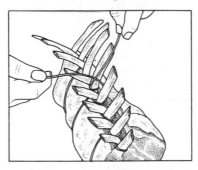

5 With a long piece of string, interlace the bone ends, tying them firmly at the end. The cavity may be filled with stuffing.

HOW TO PREPARE NOISETTES OF LAMB

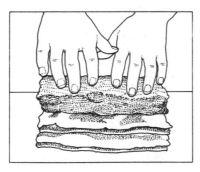

1 Bone out a best end of neck, following the instructions given for boning a loin of pork. Roll the meat up tightly, starting from the eye of meat.

2 Tie the lamb roll neatly at 2.5 cm (1 inch) intervals, using fine string. Cut between each piece of string to make noisettes.

HOW TO PREPARE KIDNEYS

1 Remove fat (suet) if still attached. Remove fine membrane around the kidney.

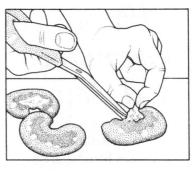

2 Cut each kidney almost in half from rounded side to core. Snip out white core with scissors.

3 Wash the kidneys well. Soak in salted water for 15 minutes, then drain and pat dry.

HOW TO PREPARE A HEART

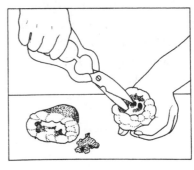

1 Wash heart in water to remove any blood. Snip out the arteries and tendons. Soak in salted water for 15 minutes, then drain and pat dry. Stuff heart if liked, then sew up.

Guide to Bacon, Gammon and Ham

Meat was originally cured to provide food during the long winters when little fresh meat was available. It was discovered that pork was easier to salt than beef, as the flesh of the smaller animal was penetrated more easily by the curing salts. Nowadays we eat bacon, gammon and ham purely for the good flavour and to give variety.

BACON

Bacon is cured from the sides and back of a pig, bred specially for its lean meat. All bacon is preserved in salt and it can then be smoked, or left unsmoked. Unsmoked, or green, bacon has a pale rind and pink flesh. Smoked bacon has a golden-brown rind and a darker pink flesh than unsmoked.

GAMMON AND HAM

Gammon is the name given to the entire hind leg of a bacon pig after curing. When cooked and served cold, it is usually called ham. Speciality hams, such as York Ham, are produced from whole legs separated from the carcass before being cured and cooked by traditional methods. Cooked ham is sold freshly sliced or as vacuum-packed slices. Uncooked gammon is usually sold as joints or steaks.

CUTS OF BACON

Back Prime back is sliced into rashers or thicker chops. It can be grilled, fried or baked. It can also be bought as one piece for boiling or braising. Long back is usually sliced into rashers and can be used for grilling and frying.

Collar A more economical joint which is best boiled or braised. It is also sliced into rashers.

Forehock A good joint for casseroling, or the meat can be removed from the bone and used in stews and casseroles.

Middle or Through Cut Back and streaky together, giving a double piece with a good proportion of fat and lean. Cut into rashers, it is grilled and fried. As a joint, it is good stuffed and rolled for baking.

Streaky A good mixture of lean and fat. It can be bought in the piece for boiling and is delicious cold. Thinly sliced streaky rashers can be grilled or fried.

Gammon Is the prime cut of bacon. As it is a large piece it is generally cut into 3 joints. The middle gammon is lean and meaty; gammon rashers and steaks are cut from this piece. It can be boiled, braised or roasted. Corner gammon is a small, triangular-shaped piece. It is best boiled for serving hot or cold. Gammon hock is a large piece with a large bone, but also plenty of lean meat. It can be boiled, baked or braised.

BUYING BACON
Bacon should have a pleasant smell, with no stickiness. The rind should be thin and smooth, and the fat smooth and white. Bacon can be bought ready boned and rolled into convenient-sized joints, or it can be cling film wrapped or vacuum packed. Some joints are also sold in convenient boilable bags.

STORING BACON
Wrap bacon joints in foil and store in the refrigerator for up to 3 days. Green, or unsmoked, bacon rashers can be stored for up to 7 days, smoked for up to 10 days. Wrap in foil or place in a covered plastic food container. Cooked bacon joints can be stored in the refrigerator for up to 4 days.

PREPARING BACON FOR COOKING
Mild-cured bacon needs little preparation. It is not over salty and it is usually not necessary to soak it. Other joints should be soaked for 3 hours for unsmoked, and 6 hours or overnight for smoked. To soak: place the joint in a large bowl or saucepan and cover it with cold water. After soaking for the correct time, drain off and discard the water. Use fresh water for boiling the joint.

To prepare rashers, steaks and

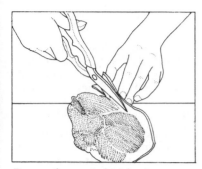

Remove bacon rind with scissors

chops: remove the rind with scissors, or snip through the rind and fat around thick rashers, steaks and bacon chops to prevent curling. Remove any small bones.

COOKING METHODS FOR BACON

Joints of bacon can be boiled, baked or braised. Rashers, chops and steaks are grilled or fried.

BOILING

1 Soak the joint if necessary for the correct time. Discard the soaking liquid.

2 Weigh the joint and calculate the cooking time. Allow 30 minutes per 450 g (1 lb) for joints up to 4.5 kg (10 lb) and 25 minutes per 450 g (1 lb) if larger.

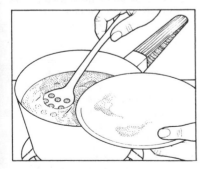

3 Place in a saucepan and add water to cover. Bring slowly to the boil. Remove any scum with a slotted spoon.

4 Time the cooking from the moment when the water reaches boiling point. Cover and simmer for the calculated time.

5 Remove the bacon from the pan and rest for 10 minutes before slicing.

BAKING

1 Prepare the joint as above and calculate the cooking time as for boiling. Put in a pan, cover with water and simmer for half the calculated cooking time. Drain.

2 Wrap the drained joint in foil and place in a roasting tin. Bake in the oven at 180°C (350°F) mark 4 for the remainder of the calculated cooking time.

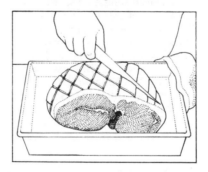

3 If you wish to glaze the joint, remove the foil 30 minutes before the end of the cooking time. Strip off the rind and score the fat into diamonds with a sharp knife.

4 Glaze with any of the following and return to the oven for the remaining cooking time: 30 ml (2 tbsp) brown sugar and 10 ml (2 tsp) mustard powder mixed together; honey; marmalade (orange, lemon, lemon and lime, ginger); pieces of canned apricots or pineapple, basting with the juices from the can.

BRAISING

1 Melt a little fat in a flameproof casserole large enough to take the joint comfortably. Lightly fry a selection of root vegetables.

2 Cover the vegetables with stock or cider and bring to the boil. Place the bacon joint on top and cover the pan tightly. Braise in the oven at 180°C (350°F) mark 4 for 30 minutes per 450 g (1 lb) for joints up to 4.5 kg (10 lb), and 25 minutes per 450 g (1 lb) if the joint is larger.

3 Thirty minutes before the end of the calculated cooking time, remove the rind from the joint and return the casserole to the oven, uncovered.

4 Thicken the cooking liquid with a little blended cornflour before serving with the bacon.

GRILLING RASHERS

1 Preheat the grill to hot. Arrange the rashers on the grill rack, with the fat over the lean.

2 Put under the preheated hot grill for 3–5 minutes, depending on the thickness of the rashers and crispness required. Turn halfway through the cooking time. Drain on absorbent kitchen paper before serving.

GRILLING STEAKS AND CHOPS

1 Preheat the grill to hot. Place the steaks or chops on the grill pan rack.

2 Brush the lean with melted fat or oil. Put under the preheated hot grill and cook for 12–15 minutes for chops, 10–12 minutes for steaks. Reduce the heat and turn the bacon over halfway through the cooking time.

FRYING RASHERS

1 Place the rashers in a cold frying pan. Overlap back rashers with the fat under the lean.

2 Heat the pan gently. To crisp the rashers, increase the heat. Cook for 3–5 minutes, turning the rashers over halfway.

Guide to Cuts and Techniques for Beef and Veal

In this chapter you will find all the cuts of beef and veal carefully explained, with the most appropriate ways of cooking them. Techniques of meat preparation, including boning and larding, are explained in detail to assist both the beginner and the experienced cook.

BUYING BEEF

Beef is available all year round, and offers a variety of cuts to suit all cooking methods and occasions, from large roasting joints to economical braising and stewing cuts. When buying fresh beef look for a fresh, slightly moist appearance. The redness of the meat will vary after cutting and exposure to air, but this need not effect your choice. The lean of roasting joints should be smooth and velvety in texture. Coarse-textured lean beef is usually an indication that the meat is suitable only for braising and stewing. Beef that is very coarse will almost certainly need slow cooking to tenderise it.

The lean should be surrounded by a layer of creamy-white fat. The colour of the fat may vary for a number of reasons, none of which will affect the taste. The fat should, however, always be firm and dry. Marbling, or flecks of fat in the meat, will help to keep the meat moist during the cooking and often gives it a better flavour. Very

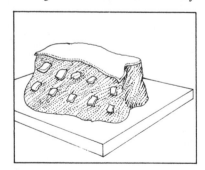

A lean larded roasting joint

lean roasting joints are sometimes sold larded with fat to help keep them moist.

CUTS OF BEEF

1 Top Rump Also called thick flank, bed of beef or first cutting. This is a lean cut that is often sold sliced ready for frying or braising. Joints need a slow moist cooking method such as pot roasting.

2 Brisket An economical and tasty joint sold on the bone or boned and rolled. It has a high percentage of fat and needs a slow moist cooking method, such as pot roasting or braising, to prevent shrinkage and to tenderise it. If roasting, wrap the joint in foil to seal in the juices. It is often salted or pickled, in which case it should be boiled.

3 Silverside The traditional joint used for boiled beef and carrots. It contains no bone and is very lean. This joint is also pickled ready for boiling. In Scotland, silverside is usually roasted.

4 Shin An excellent cut for stews and soups. Meat and bone are cooked together to give a jellied stock. Shin of beef is very nutritious and makes richly flavoured stews and casseroles. The traditional cut for making beef tea.

5 Leg Similar to shin; makes excellent soups and stews. Cubed, shin and leg are often sold together as 'stewing steak'.

6, 7 Neck and Clod Two economical cuts, and a good choice for hot-pots and stews as the rich juices make superb gravy.

8 Flank An inexpensive cut which deserves wider recognition. It is ideal for pot roasting on the bone, and for stews and hot-pots. This cut is sometimes salted or pickled to boil with spices for pressed beef. Not suitable for dry heat cooking methods.

9, 10 Chuck and Blade Lean meat from the shoulder which is removed from the bone and used for braising, stewing and pies. Also called shoulder.

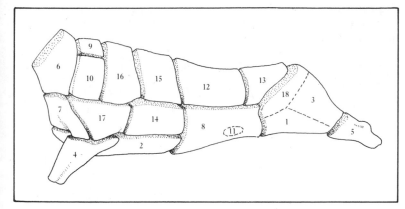

Major cuts of beef to be found at your butcher

BUYING VEAL

The colour and quality of veal depends greatly on the age at the time of slaughter, and the method of rearing. Milk-fed calves have very pale flesh that is highly valued. The best veal comes from calves that are fed on a rich milk diet and, as this method of rearing is expensive, the price of veal is high. As the calf is weaned from milk and starts to eat grass, the flesh tends to become darker. When buying veal the flesh should be pinkish beige, with no dark or discoloured particles. It should be very lean and moist with no juice running from it.

11 Skirt A tasty economical stewing meat which comes from inside the ribs and the flank.

12 Sirloin A tender and delicious prime cut. Can be roasted in the piece or grilled as steaks. The fillet is found on the inside of the sirloin bone, and the fillet and sirloin together provide an ideal roasting joint. The sirloins from both sides of the carcass when undivided, are known as baron of beef. T-bone, sirloin and porterhouse steaks come from the sirloin. The joints for roasting can be bone-in or boneless. The fillet can also be separated from the sirloin for roasting in the piece or sliced into fillet steaks—the most tender for grilling or frying.

13 Rump Steak The perfect steak for grilling or frying. Although not as tender as fillet, it is preferred by many as it has a fuller flavour. The lean should be velvety, close-grained and bright red in colour, with a moderate amount of fat.
Ribs May be bone-in or boned and rolled. Rib joints should have a layer of firm dry fat and marbling in the lean.

14 Wing Ribs A popular roast, but also cut into steaks for grilling and frying. Also called standing rib or chine.

15 Fore Ribs Similar to wing ribs. The traditional cut for English roast beef.

16, 17 Back and Top Ribs Less expensive than fore ribs and ideal for pot roasting and braising. The rib eye is a boneless piece.

18 Topside A lean cut, usually sold with a layer of fat wrapped around it. Roast slowly and keep well basted. Usually more tender when served slightly underdone. Makes a perfect pot roast. In Scotland, topside is braised.

CUTS OF VEAL

1 Shoulder A large joint, usually boned, rolled and tied, then cut into various sized joints. It can be stuffed, then pot roasted or braised. The meat can be cubed for casseroles and pies.

2 Fillet Thin slices cut from the leg. They are very lean and usually flattened before cooking. Can be fried or stuffed as for beef olives.

3 Schnitzel Thin slices cut across the grain from the topside. They are very lean and usually flattened before cooking. Shallow frying is the best cooking method.

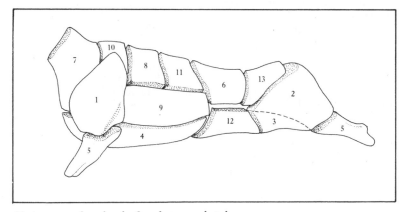

Major cuts of veal to be found at your butcher

4 Breast Usually sold boned, this cheaper cut can be rolled and tied, and stuffed if desired. It can be pot roasted or braised.

Pie Veal Shin, leg and neck cut into small pieces for use in pies, blanquettes and casseroles.

5 Knuckle Cut into rounds, with the marrow bone in the centre. Traditional cut for Osso Bucco.

6 Loin A succulent roasting joint. Veal chops are cut from the loin.

Fricandeau, Leg, Shoulder or Breast Small boneless joints wrapped in a thin covering of pork fat for slow, or pot roasting.

7 Neck A stewing cut which needs slow moist cooking. It can be cut into small pieces for pies.

Minced Veal Very lean meat, useful for patties, particularly when mixed with ground pork to keep the mixture succulent.

8 Best Neck A good value cut. It can be chined and roasted on the bone, or boned, stuffed and rolled for roasting. Also suitable for braising and stewing. Cutlets can be cut if the 'eye' muscle is large.

9 Ribs when boned are sliced and braised or casseroled.

10 Middle Neck is usually sliced into cutlets for braising.

11 Cutlets are trimmed neatly of most fat and used for grilling or frying.

12 Flank is a tough cut that can be stewed or minced and cooked slowly for a long time.

13 Rump is a tender cut usually sliced into escalopes or medallions to be fried or grilled.

HOW MUCH MEAT TO BUY
Although servings vary according to the age, taste and appetite of the people being served, as a guide allow 100–175 g (4–6 oz) raw meat without bone and 175–350 g (6–12 oz) with bone, per person.

STORING FRESH BEEF AND VEAL
Freshly cut meat should be stored in a cool place, preferably a refrigerator. Unwrap the meat and

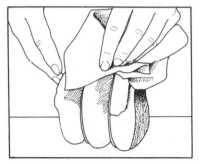

Wiping meat with absorbent paper

wipe the surface with absorbent kitchen paper, then wrap in foil or cling film to prevent the surface drying out. Place the meat in the coldest part of the refrigerator, at the top if you have a larder refrigerator, otherwise on the shelf immediately below the frozen food storage compartment, away from cooked meats and other foods. Fresh meat can be kept for 3–5 days in the refrigerator, although it is advisable to cook smaller cuts within 1–2 days.

STORING COOKED BEEF AND VEAL
Cooked meats should be wrapped or covered to prevent them drying out before they are put in the refrigerator. Leftover stews and casseroles should first be allowed to cool and then put in the refrigerator or a cool place in a covered dish. They should be used within 2 days and reheated thoroughly before they are eaten. Bring the dish to boiling point and simmer for at least 10 minutes.

TECHNIQUES WITH BEEF AND VEAL

HOW TO BONE A BREAST OF VEAL

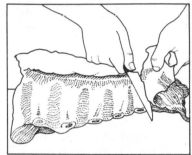

1 Place the breast of veal, skin side down, on a board. Cut along the flap of the meat over the bones and pull back to reveal the bones.

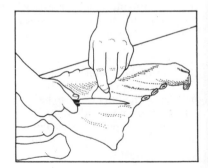

2 Carefully cut round each bone with a small sharp knife. Working from one end, scrape each bone away from the meat, then lift the bones from the meat. Any meat left on the bones can be scraped off and placed on the boned meat.

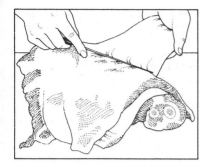

3 Trim off excess fat and skin. Turn the meat over and remove the skin by cutting between the skin and the fat, pulling skin away with other hand.

4 Turn the meat over and spread stuffing evenly over it. Roll up from one long edge. Tie neatly at regular intervals.

HOW TO ROLL UP BEEF OR VEAL OLIVES

1 Place slices of beef or veal between 2 sheets of dampened greaseproof paper. Bat out with a meat mallet or rolling pin.

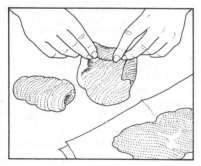

2 Place a small pile of the stuffing of your choice near one end of each slice of meat. Roll up the meat from this end, tucking in the sides as you work, to form a neat parcel. Tie the parcel into a firm shape with fine string.

HOW TO TIE UP A JOINT

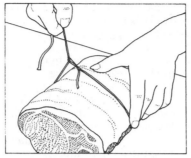

1 Gather or roll the meat to the required shape. Slide a piece of uncoloured string under the joint and make a loop with one end.

2 Thread the other end of the string through the loop, then pull the end to tighten. Tie a knot and cut off the ends of the string.

3 Repeat at 2.5–5 cm (1–2 inch) intervals, depending on how firm the joint is.

HOW TO BARD A LEAN JOINT

If you are roasting a particularly lean cut of meat with little fat, a sheet of extra fat will help to keep it moist.

1 Trim the bard to the size and shape of your joint, overlapping the pieces slightly.

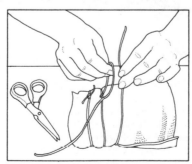

2 Tie the meat and fat securely into a neat shape, using fine string. Loop it firmly around the length and width of the joint at 2.5–5 cm (1–2 inch) intervals.

3 Tie each piece of string in a double knot and cut off the ends of the string to make a neat joint.

HOW TO LARD A JOINT

Strips of fresh pork fat, called lardons, are threaded through the meat before cooking to help keep the meat moist and baste it from within. The easiest way to thread the lardons into the meat is with a special larding needle.

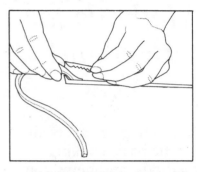

1 Cut the pork fat into long strips about 5 mm ($\frac{1}{4}$ inch) wide. You will need 25–40 g (1–1$\frac{1}{2}$ oz) fat per 450 g (1 lb) of meat.

2 Using a hinged larding needle, close the toothed clip securely over the end of a strip of pork fat.

3 Push the point of the needle under the surface of the meat and draw it through the meat. Release the clip and trim off excess fat, leaving a short length.

4 Repeat at 2.5–5 cm (1–2 inch) intervals until the surface of the meat is evenly larded.

Cooking Methods for Beef and Veal

This chapter covers all the basic cooking methods, and helps you to choose the best one for the different cuts of meat. At-a-glance roasting, braising and grilling charts help you to time your cooking to perfection.

All varieties and cuts of beef and veal are available throughout the year, although beef tends to be more plentiful in the autumn. It is particularly important to choose cuts of beef appropriate to the chosen method of cooking. As a rough guide, cuts with more connective tissue need long moist cooking in liquid at low temperatures, e.g. stewing, boiling, braising or pot roasting. Cuts with little connective tissue can be cooked for a shorter time at higher temperatures and by drier methods, e.g. frying, grilling and roasting.

Before you start to cook, wipe the surface of the meat with damp absorbent kitchen paper. Trim off

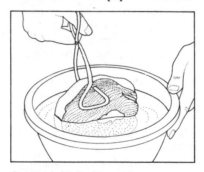

Soaking salt beef in cold water

any excess fat, but do not remove it all as this helps with the flavour and keeps the meat moist. Soak salt beef in cold water for at least 3 hours, preferably overnight, before cooking.

ROASTING

The process known as oven roasting is in fact baking. It is a popular way of cooking prime cuts of meat. It is only really suitable for cuts which have little connective tissue. Very lean meat will need added fat to prevent it from drying out. Low temperature roasting is best, as it produces succulent meat with the minimum shrinkage. The traditional high temperature cooking is only really suitable for top-quality meat. Use

a meat thermometer if possible to determine accurately whether the meat is cooked.

SPIT ROASTING

The meat is placed on a revolving spit or skewers, and cooked under or over a direct heat source, either in the oven or as a grill attachment or over a barbecue. This method is suitable for any roasting joint, provided it is a uniform shape, well trussed and securely fastened to the spit. Generally speaking, spit-roasted meats need no extra fat as they are self basting. Allow 15 minutes per 450 g (1 lb) plus 15 minutes extra.

BASIC ROASTING METHOD

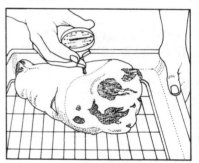

1 Wipe the meat with damp absorbent kitchen paper. Stand the meat on a rack, if possible, in a roasting tin. Insert a meat thermometer, if using, into the centre of the thickest part of the joint, making sure that the tip of the thermometer is well clear of any bone.

2 Spread joints that are particularly lean with a little dripping, oil or butter. Sprinkle with pepper, but do not add salt at this stage as it extracts moisture from the meat. Salt the meat towards the end of cooking time.

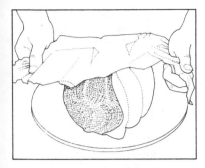

3 Cook in the oven at 180°C (350°F) mark 4 for the recommended time (see right). When the joint is cooked, lift on to a warmed dish and cover with foil. Leave to stand in a warm place for 10–15 minutes to allow the meat to firm. This makes carving easier and more economical. Make the gravy or sauce while the meat is standing.

BRAISING

Braising is a combination of stewing, steaming and roasting. It can be done on top of the cooker or in the oven. The meat is cooked in a saucepan or casserole over a bed of vegetables, with just sufficient liquid for the steam to keep it moist. The pot is tightly covered and the meat cooks in the steam created by the liquid. After cooking the liquid is often boiled until reduced and concentrated in flavour, then used to glaze the meat. The cooking vegetables can be puréed to thicken the sauce.

RECOMMENDED ROASTING CUTS, TEMPERATURES AND TIMES

BEEF
Suitable cuts: top rump; fresh silverside; fore rib; wing rib; sirloin; topside
Cooking temperature
180°C (350°F) mark 4
*Cooking time**
Rare: 15 minutes per 450 g (1 lb) plus 15 minutes
Medium Rare: 20 minutes per 450 g (1 lb) plus 20 minutes
Well Done: 25 minutes per 450 g (1 lb) plus 25 minutes
Meat thermometer reading
Rare: 60°C (140°F)
Medium Rare: 70°C (160°F)
Well Done: 80°C (180°F)
Classic accompaniments
Yorkshire pudding; horseradish sauce; mustard

VEAL
Suitable cuts: loin; fillet; leg; shoulder; breast
Cooking temperature
180°C (350°F) mark 4
*Cooking time**
25 minutes per 450 g (1 lb) plus 25 minutes
Meat thermometer reading
80°C (180°F)
Classic accompaniments
Lemon and herb stuffing; bacon rolls
* These roasting times are intended only as a guide, as a large joint will take proportionally longer to cook than a very small joint. Similarly, a long thin piece of meat will take proportionally less time to cook than a thick, rolled joint of the same weight.

BRAISING CUTS AND TIMES

BEEF
Suitable cuts: brisket; flank; topside; fresh silverside; thick slices of buttock or braising steak; thick rib; oxtail
Cooking temperature
180°C (350°F) mark 4
Cooking time
45 minutes per 450 g (1 lb)

VEAL
Suitable cuts: all cuts
Cooking temperature
180°C (350°F) mark 4
Cooking time
40 minutes per 450 g (1 lb)

BASIC BRAISING METHOD

1 Heat oil or dripping to thinly cover the base of pan. Add the meat and fry lightly to seal the surfaces. Remove.

2 Add chopped aromatic vegetables such as carrot, turnip, onion and celery and fry until lightly browned. Drain off excess fat.

3 Add sufficient stock, wine, cider, beer or water to just cover vegetables. Add herbs and seasonings.

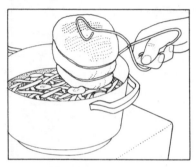

4 Return the meat to the pan. Cover tightly and simmer either on top of cooker or in the oven for calculated cooking time. Check occasionally, adding more liquid if necessary.

5 Remove the meat from the pan and keep warm. Boil the cooking juices hard to reduce by half. Skim off any surface fat, then strain the stock. Purée the vegetables and add to stock if desired. Serve with the meat, cut into thick slices.

CASSEROLING AND STEWING

Less tender cuts of meat are best cooked slowly in water, stock, wine, cider or beer. Vegetables, herbs and spices are added to give character to the dish. The meat should be cooked in no more than 300 ml ($\frac{1}{2}$ pint) liquid for each 450 g (1 lb) meat and the liquid kept at a gentle simmer, never boiled. Stews are cooked on top of the cooker, casseroles cooked in the oven.

Suitable cuts: beef (thin flank; shin; leg; neck and clod; chuck and blade; skirt; cheek; oxtail; liver; kidney); veal (shoulder; pie veal; knuckle; neck; best neck)
Cooking temperature
170°C (325°F) mark 3

TIPS FOR SUCCESSFUL CASSEROLING AND STEWING

1 Cook the meat slowly and for a long time to tenderise it. Keep the liquid at a gentle simmer, never boil it.

2 Use a small amount of liquid for a rich concentrated sauce. Use stock, water, wine, cider, stout or beer.

3 Cut the meat into small evenly sized cubes to expose the maximum surface area to the cooking liquid.

4 Use plenty of seasonings, adding salt towards the end of the cooking time.

5 Use a pan or casserole with a tightly fitting lid to prevent steam escaping. Make a flour and water paste seal for maximum efficiency.

FRYING

Only small pieces of tender, quick-cooking meats should be fried. It is therefore a good cooking

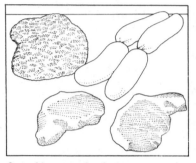

Suitable meats for frying

method for chops, steaks and sausages. Ideally, the meat to be fried should not be more than 2.5 cm (1 inch) thick. Use a large, heavy-based pan which will ensure even cooking. Preheat the fat before adding the meat to seal in the juices quickly, then reduce the temperature to cook the meat to your liking.

Meat can be coated before frying to give a crisp surface and to protect the meat from the drying effects of the hot fat.

Covered frying is a slower, gentler and moister method of cooking. After browning the meat, the pan is covered with a tightly fitting lid and the trapped steam helps to tenderise the meat by breaking down the fibres. A little liquid can be added to the pan, along with tender vegetables such as mushrooms and tomatoes.

PREPARING MEAT FOR FRYING

1 Wipe the meat with damp absorbent kitchen paper. Beat escalopes with a rolling pin or meat mallet to tenderise them.

2 Coat as required. Pat un-coated meat dry with absorbent kitchen paper before frying.

Suitable cuts: beef (rump steak; fillet steak; sirloin steak); veal (loin chops; schnitzel; fillet)
Cooking times
Times vary according to the thickness of the meat and how you like it cooked, so the following is a rough guide only.
2.5 cm (1 inch) thick steak —
7–10 minutes
1 cm ($\frac{1}{2}$ inch) thick steak —
4–5 minutes

GRILLING

A quick method of cooking by radiant heat from a preheated grill. As the heat is fierce, the meat must be moistened with melted butter or oil before cooking. Grilling always begins under high heat to help seal the meat juices. The heat is then lowered to cook the meat further if necessary.

PREPARING MEAT FOR GRILLING

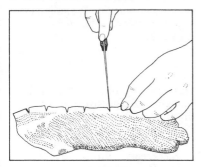

1 Wipe the meat with damp absorbent kitchen paper and trim off any excess fat. Cut through fat with a sharp knife to prevent the meat from curling up.

GRILLING CUTS AND TIMES

These times are for medium rare. Adjust the cooking times to suit your preference. Most cuts of veal are unsuitable for grilling as they dry out easily under the fierce heat. Baste with butter or oil several times during the cooking time.

BEEF
Fillet Steak

2.5 cm (1 inch) thick	5–6 minutes
1 cm ($\frac{1}{2}$ inch) thick	4–5 minutes

Rump Steak

2.5 cm (1 inch) thick	6–7 minutes
1 cm ($\frac{1}{2}$ inch) thick	5–6 minutes

Sirloin Steak

2.5 cm (1 inch) thick	6–7 minutes
1 cm ($\frac{1}{2}$ inch) thick	5–6 minutes

Homemade hamburgers

2.5 cm (1 inch) thick	8–10 minutes

VEAL
Loin Chop

2.5 cm (1 inch) thick	12–15 minutes (well done)

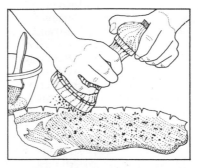

2 Brush both sides of the meat with oil or melted butter and grind pepper over the top. Leave the salt until later as it tends to draw out the meat juices.

BOILING

This is a useful method of cooking less tender cuts, salted and cured meat and tongues. The meat is not truly boiled, but gently simmered in water with root vegetables and seasonings. Dumplings are sometimes added towards the end of the cooking time.

The stock left over from the cooking time makes an excellent base for soups and sauces. Salted meat for boiling should be soaked in cold water overnight or for at least 3 hours. If time is short, place the meat in a pan with cold water to cover, bring slowly to the boil, skimming if necessary. Drain the meat and return it to a clean pan with water and root vegetables, then proceed as usual.

BOILING CUTS AND TIMES

SALT BEEF
30 minutes per 450 g (1 lb) plus 30 minutes. Small joints should be given a minimum of 1$\frac{1}{2}$ hours. Calculate the cooking time from when simmering point is reached

CURED OX TONGUE
3$\frac{1}{2}$–4$\frac{1}{2}$ hours, depending on size

FRESH CALF TONGUE
3–3$\frac{1}{2}$ hours

Choosing Poultry

With the different types of bird available — ranging from economical frozen chicken to luxurious fresh goose — and the many different ways they are sold, poultry is a popular choice for every sort of occasion. Use the information in this chapter to help you make exactly the right selection for the meals you cook.

BUYING POULTRY

By far the tastiest poultry to buy is that which has been farmyard reared and is freshly killed. But as with most things, the best is also the most expensive. For a more economical product, factory-reared chilled and frozen birds are generally of an acceptable quality.

Chicken and turkey are the most popular poultry and are readily available all year round. When buying a fresh chicken or turkey look for a plump, well-rounded breast, and skin that is free from blemishes and bruising.

When buying by weight, particularly a chicken, remember to check whether the giblets are with the bird; these weigh approximately 175 g (6 oz), which is a significant proportion of a bird weighing, say, 1.4 kg (3 lb) and will affect the number of portions you get after cooking. Don't reject the giblets, though, if available, as they make superb stock for gravy.

Other points to look for when buying frozen chicken and turkeys are whether the bird is already stuffed, 'butter-basted' or otherwise different from a straightforward dressed bird. All these pre-treated birds have their uses, but make sure they are what you want at that particular moment — if you need a bird for casseroling, you will not want it pre-stuffed.

The smallest chickens available are *poussins*, which are baby chickens weighing 350–450 g (12 oz–1 lb). One serves 1–2 people. Double poussins weigh 550–900 g ($1\frac{1}{4}$–2 lb) and will serve 3–4 people.

Most of the birds available are *broilers* weighing 1.1–1.6 kg ($2\frac{1}{2}$–$3\frac{1}{2}$ lb); these are suitable for all methods of cooking and serve 3–4 people. A *spring chicken* is a small broiler weighing 900 g–1.1 kg (2–$2\frac{1}{2}$ lb); one serves 2–3 people. Larger *roasting chickens* and *capons* (young cockerels that have been castrated and specially fattened) are available up to about 4.6 kg (10 lb), and will serve 6–10 people. *Boiling fowl*, not usually sold in supermarkets but available from traditional butchers and poulterers, are older, tougher birds weighing 1.8–3.2 kg (4–7 lb), and are excellent if poached or slowly casseroled.

Turkeys range in weight from about 2.6–14 kg (6–30 lb). A 4 kg (9 lb) oven-ready turkey is equivalent to one of about 5.4 kg (12 lb) undressed weight. Allow 275–350 g (10–12 oz) dressed weight per portion when estimating what size to buy.

When a whole bird is too large for your requirements, buy *chicken and turkey portions*. These range from boned and rolled joints ready for roasting and easy slicing, through halved and quartered birds, down to individual serving portions. You can also buy chicken livers, turkey sausages, burgers and packs of meat for casseroles, soups and stews.

Duck is widely available frozen or chilled and occasionally in portions. It is more difficult to buy a fresh farmyard duck than a chicken, as the demand is much less, but the flavour will be good if you can find one. Don't buy ducks weighing less than 1.4 kg (3 lb) as the proportion of bone to meat is excessively high in a small bird. Allow about 450 g (1 lb) dressed weight per portion. Again, look for a well-rounded, unblemished breast, but don't buy a duck that has noticeably large amounts of fat as the meat is very rich anyway.

Goose is largely a seasonal bird, though frozen geese can be bought throughout the year. It is advisable to order a goose in advance as butchers, poulterers and supermarkets tend not to keep large stocks. Birds range in size from about 3 kg (7 lb) to as much as 6.75 kg (15 lb). Allow 350–400 g (12–14 oz) dressed weight per portion.

Guinea fowl are available all the year round, and are obtainable both fresh and frozen. An average guinea fowl will serve 4 people. When buying, look out for a plump breast and smooth-skinned feet.

Quail are sold plucked but not drawn, as they are eaten whole. Allow one per person.

STORING POULTRY

To store fresh poultry remove the giblets from inside the bird (except quail) as soon as you get it home. Remove any tight packaging, cover the bird loosely with a bag, and store in the refrigerator for a maximum of 3 days. The giblets should preferably be cooked straight away as they deteriorate more quickly than the rest of the bird. If storing, keep separate from the rest of the bird.

Frozen poultry

Frozen chicken will keep in good condition in the freezer for up to a year, but the giblets will start to deteriorate after about 2 months. Commercially frozen chickens packed with the giblets in the cavity should therefore be cooked within 1–2 months of purchase. Frozen stuffed poultry should also be stored for up to 2 months.

Turkey with the giblets removed stores well for about 6 months, duck or goose (which are much fattier) store for 4–5 months.

To freeze fresh poultry, remove the giblets and pack them separately. Wrap the bird in heavy-duty

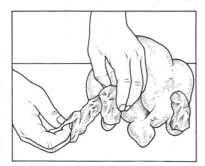
Padding poultry legs with foil

polythene, padding the legs with foil first so that they can't spike their way through the bag. Exclude as much air as possible before sealing and labelling.

To save space and provide you with individual portions when it comes to cooking, you may prefer to cut the bird into portions before

Cutting the bird into portions

freezing. Cut a chicken or turkey into quarters or into eight portions, halve ducks or guinea fowl. Wrap each joint individually in foil or polythene bags and then combine them in a larger package.

Freeze at the lowest temperature available in your freezer (ideally −32°C/−26°F); higher temperatures can give disappointing results. Remember to turn the temperature control down 24 hours before you intend to freeze the bird to give the cabinet time to get really cold. Once the bird is frozen return the control to the normal storage temperature.

Thawing poultry

Frozen poultry must be thawed completely before cooking. Poultry cooked from frozen, or even with a few ice crystals remaining, is a serious health risk.

Birds up to 2.7 kg (6 lb) should be thawed in the refrigerator. Larger birds should be thawed at room temperature (16–17°C/65–70°F). Do not thaw in the refrigerator as the process is too slow. Thaw the bird in its wrappings but open the bag and take any giblets from the cavity as soon as they can be moved. Once thawed, cook as soon as possible.

Approximate thawing times in the refrigerator
1.4 kg (3 lb) oven-ready	9 hours
2.3 kg (5 lb) oven-ready	15 hours

At room temperature
4.5 kg (10 lb) oven-ready	9 hours
6.8 kg (15 lb) oven-ready	24 hours
9 kg (20 lb) oven-ready	30 hours

Joints: Allow 6 hours.

Thawing in a microwave oven

Leave polythene wrappings in place but remove foil or wire ties.

Placing bird in microwave-safe dish

Place whole package in a microwave-safe dish. Open end and remove the giblets as soon as they can be moved.

Whole chickens, ducks, geese, guinea fowl: 6–8 minutes per 450 g (1 lb) on low setting. Then close the wrappings and place the bird in cold water for 30 minutes. **Whole turkeys:** 10–12 minutes per 450 g (1 lb) on low setting. **Joints:** 4–7 minutes per 450 g (1 lb) on low setting. Then remove wrappings and place in cold water for 15 minutes.

Storing cooked poultry

Leftover roast poultry should be cooled as quickly as possible. Remove stuffing and wrap meat in polythene or foil before storing in the refrigerator. Eat within 3 days. Use cooked dishes within 1 day.

To freeze cooked poultry, cool quickly and remove any stuffing. Large joints are best removed from the bone. Pack portions in foil and overwrap with heavy-duty polythene. Store for 2 months.

Poultry Techniques

The way a bird is presented can transform the appearance of the finished dish. By mastering the basic skills which can be employed in preparing and serving poultry, you will be able to cope with a variety of exciting dishes and your guests will always be impressed. It's easy when you know how!

PREPARING POULTRY

To get the best out of poultry prepare it carefully before cooking. If any quills have been left behind after plucking (this is most likely with the large birds such as goose and turkey) remove them carefully with tweezers. If there are hairs left on the skin, singe them off with a lighted taper. Rinse all birds well, inside and out, in cold water and dry thoroughly with kitchen paper.

TRUSSING

Trussing keeps poultry in a good shape for roasting, making it more attractive on the table and easier to carve. Always remove the butcher's or packager's trussing so that you can wash and dry the bird, then truss it again yourself. A *trussing needle* (a long needle with a large eye) is useful, but failing this, use a skewer and fine string to truss the bird.

First fold the neck skin under the body and fold the tips of the wings back towards the backbone so that they hold the skin in position; set the bird on its back and press the legs well into the sides, raising and plumping the breast. Make a slit in the skin above the vent and put the tail (the 'parson's nose') through this.

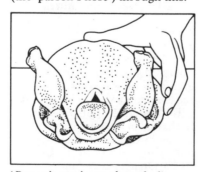

'Parson's nose' seen through slit

Thread the needle with fine string and insert it close to the second joint of the right wing; push it right through the body, passing it out so as to catch the

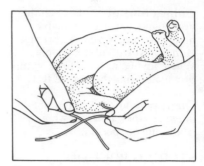

Tying the ends of string

corresponding joint on the left side. Insert the needle again in the first joint of the left wing, pass it through the flesh at the back of the body, catching the tips of the wings and the neck skin, and pass it out through the first joint of the wing on the right side. Tie the ends of the string in a bow.

To truss the legs, re-thread the needle and insert it through the gristle at the right side of the parson's nose. Pass the string over the right leg, under the back and over the left leg, through the gristle at the left side of the

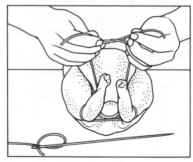

Trussing the legs

parson's nose. Carry it behind the parson's nose and tie the ends firmly together.

If using a skewer, insert it right through the body of the bird just below the thigh bone and turn the bird over on its breast. First,

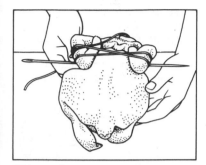

Using a skewer to truss

catching in the wing tips, pass the string under the ends of the skewer and cross it over the back. Turn the bird over and tie the ends of the string together round the tail, securing the drumsticks.

JOINTING

Although poultry portions are readily available, jointing a bird yourself is cheaper and leaves you with bones and giblets for stock. Joint a chicken several hours before starting to cook a casserole so that you can make stock first. Or, if you have to use water for cooking, add the backbone to it.

Use a sharp, heavy knife or *poultry shears*. Start by trimming off the excess skin at the neck end and removing any chunks of fat from inside the body cavity. Cut off the knuckle ends from the legs, and the wing tips; use for stock.

With the bird breast side up, neck towards you, cut straight along one side of the breast bone from the vent to the neck. Spread open and cut along one side of the backbone to divide it in half. If your knife is not sharp enough, lay

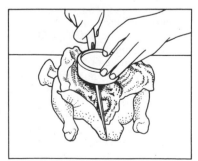

Breaking the bones with a weight

it along the cutting line and give the back of the knife a firm bang with a heavy weight to break the bones first. Then cut along the other side of the backbone and remove to use in the stock.

To quarter a chicken or guinea fowl cut each half in half again crossways between the breast and

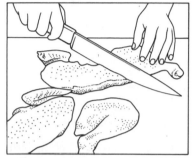

Quartering poultry

the leg. To quarter a duck, leave plenty of breast meat with the leg portion as there is very little meat on the leg. For duck recipes using breast only, use all the breast and save the thin legs for pâté.

Large birds may require dividing again. The leg can be divided in two through the centre of the joint to give a thigh and a drumstick portion. The wing quarter can be divided to give a wing and a breast portion.

Alternative method

If you prefer to take the meat off the carcass rather than cutting right through the bones you will need a small sharp knife, sometimes known as a *filleting knife*.

Start with the chicken breast side up with the neck end towards you. Gently pull the leg away from the body and cut through the skin between the thigh and the breast; repeat on the other side of the bird. Turn the bird over and continue cutting through the skin around the legs, following the natural line of the thighs down towards the backbone. You will find a tiny succulent portion of meat where the backbone joins the thigh—the oyster. Loosen the oysters but don't detach yet. With

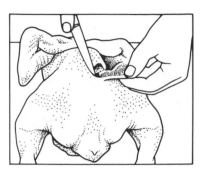

Loosening the oyster

bird on its back, push the legs outwards until the joints release. Turn the bird over, slip knife into joint and ease the legs away from the backbone, making sure oyster is still attached. Set aside.

Turn bird over, wings towards you. Cut through the skin and

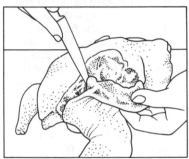

Working breast meat from bones

flesh along one side of the breast bone. With knife flat against rib cage, work breast from the bones, keeping the meat in one piece.

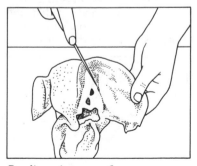

Bending wing away from carcass

Then grasp the wing firmly and bend it away from the carcass until

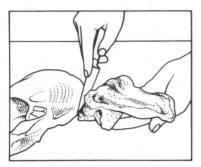

Cutting through sinews and tendons

the joint releases. Cut through any sinews and tendons and set the joint aside. Repeat on the other side. You are now left with a bare carcass that can be used for stock.

To make a *chicken 'suprème'* take the breast portion only, with no wing attached and remove the skin. With a sharp knife, cut and scrape the meat from the bones, gently pulling back the meat in one piece as you cut. Underneath the main breast meat is a thin fillet of meat only loosely attached to the rest; try not to separate this. Discard bones and cut out the white tendon that remains.

SPATCHCOCKING

Spatchcocking is a way of preparing a small whole bird for grilling. The bones are left in but the body is opened flat. Use for poussins, spring chickens and guinea fowl. You will need poultry shears or a sharp, heavy knife.

The easiest method is to lay the bird on its breast and cut along the centre of the backbone with shears. With a knife, work from inside

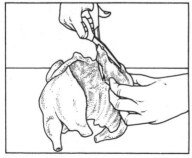

Cutting along the backbone

the cavity; insert the knife through the vent, put as much weight on it as you can and press down to break your way through the bone. The skin should remain attached to the bone on either side.

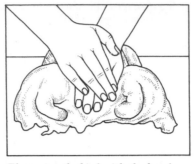

Flattening the bird with the hands

Force the two halves of the bird open with your hands, turn it over and lay it as flat as you can on a board. Then, with the heel of your hand, bang the centre of the bird firmly to break the breast bone, collar bones and wishbone. With a slightly bigger bird you may find this easier with the flat of a meat mallet or a rolling pin.

Although the body now seems quite flat, it will start to curl back into its natural shape as soon as the heat gets to it. To prevent this happening thread skewers across the body to hold it flat during cooking. Use two long skewers, one from leg to leg, the other from wing to wing and remove them before serving.

SKINNING

One of the joys of roast poultry is the crisp brown skin. But for recipes in which the skin is not crisped it is often nicer to remove the skin before cooking. Slimmers particularly will want to remove the skin as this is where most of the fat lies.

For a breast portion with no wing attached this is a simple matter, the skin will peel away easily. But wing and leg portions are not so easy as the skin is very firmly attached at the thin ends of the joints.

To help you keep a grip on the meat use a clean damp cloth and grasp the joint firmly. For a leg portion, first slip your fingers under the skin at the thigh end and loosen it all round. Grasp the

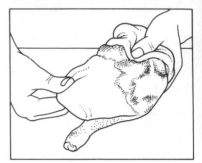

Peeling the skin off the joint

meaty part firmly with a cloth in one hand and peel the skin off the joint so that it is inside out. When you reach the point where it is bonded to the bone take a small sharp knife and slip it between skin and bone to cut the skin away cleanly.

On a wing portion, lift the skin away from the breast where it is loose and gently peel it away along the first wing bone as far as it will go. Then hold the meaty part firmly with a cloth in one hand, take your small sharp knife and, working with the tip, ease the skin away from the joint. There is very little meat on the second wing bone so the skin clings tightly. Slit the skin on the inside of the wing and gently peel it away all round. Cut off the wing tip just above the joint, taking all the skin with it.

BONING

With the bones removed, a chicken or duck makes a lovely meaty casing for stuffing and the resulting joint is easy to carve. A classic galantine or ballotine is made this way. The stuffed bird is shaped into a neat roll, stitched up securely with fine string and either roasted or poached. After cooking it is chilled and usually finished with a glaze of aspic or a creamy chaudfroid sauce.

Sometimes a ballotine is served hot with a rich accompanying sauce—very impressive for a party dish and much easier to carve in front of guests than a whole bird. Usually the stuffing is rich so that one bird will serve up to twice as many prepared this way rather than simply roasted.

Even more dramatic is the traditional quail inside a chicken, inside a goose—rarely served these days but a delight to imagine.

Another approach is to bone only the breast, leaving the leg and wing bones intact. This way the cavity can be generously filled with stuffing and the breast re-formed to its natural shape. This gives a finished dish that looks like the conventional roast poultry, but with an amount of stuffing that makes it go much further. The savoury flavours of the stuffing will permeate right through the breast flesh as it cooks.

Individual portions with the bones removed also make attractive casings for savoury fillings. *Chicken Kiev* is the example most people know—a boneless chicken breast with the wing bone attached; the breast meat is wrapped round a portion of garlic butter, and the whole thing is dipped in egg and bread-crumbs and deep-fried.

A leg portion with the bone removed can be filled in the same way; the end of the knuckle bone is usually left in place to give the joint shape and keep the end firmly closed.

Boning a whole bird

The secret of success is a sharp knife; a boning knife with a blade about 12.5–15 cm (5–6 inches) long would be a good one to choose. The procedure is the same for all birds even though the carcass shapes differ somewhat.

Lay the bird on a board breast side up. Cut off the wings at the second joint and the legs at the first. Turn the bird breast down.

Cut cleanly through the skin and flesh down the centre of the

back from vent to neck. Keeping the knife close to the carcass and slightly flattened to avoid damaging the flesh, carefully work

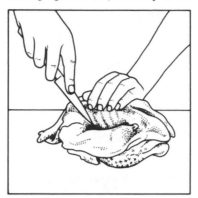

Exposing the wing joint

the flesh off the rib cage on one side of the bird until the wing joint is exposed; repeat on the other side to expose the other wing joint.

Take hold of the severed end of one wing joint. Scrape the knife over the bone backwards and forwards, working the flesh from the bone; try not to damage the

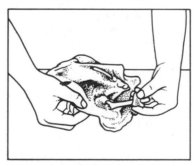

Drawing out the bone

skin. When the wing and socket are exposed, sever the ligaments with the point of the knife and draw out the bone. Repeat with the second wing.

Continue working the flesh off the main frame until the leg joint is exposed. Sever the ligaments attaching the bone to the body

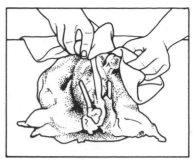

Breaking the leg joint

flesh and break the leg joint by twisting it firmly (use a cloth to get a good grip). Working from the body end of the leg, hold the end of the bone firmly and scrape away all the flesh from the thigh. Cut carefully round the joint with the point of the knife and scrape the drumstick clean in the same way. Pull the bone free. Repeat with the other leg.

Now go on to work the flesh from the rest of the main frame. Take care not to cut the skin over the breast bone, where the flesh becomes very thin, as the two halves of the breast must remain attached to each other.

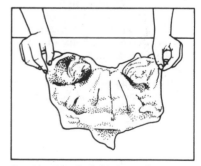

Laying the whole bird out flat

You can now lay the whole bird out flat ready to spread the stuffing over the cut surface.

Leaving the limbs on

If you want to leave the bones in the wings and legs, sever the appropriate joints with a knife as you reach them and continue round the carcass as before.

Boning a leg

With the point of a sharp knife cut round the end of the bone at the thigh end of the leg to free the

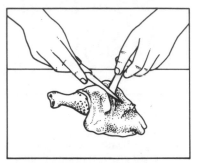

Scraping the flesh off the bone

flesh. Then grasp the end firmly and scrape the flesh carefully off the bone, taking care that you do not cut through the flesh. When you reach the joint use the point again to sever the ligaments all round. Scrape and work your way down the drumstick until you reach the knuckle. Cut off the bone joint above the knuckle and remove it.

CARVING

For perfect carving you need a long, sharp knife and a long-handled fork with two long prongs and a finger-guard. Place the bird on a flat carving dish or board— sides higher than about 1 cm (½ inch) will get in your way. Some carving dishes have spikes to hold the meat in place, some have a channel round the edge to drain the juices away from the standing bird or joint.

If you garnish the bird with vegetables or other trimmings to take it to the table, remove these before you start to carve so that you have room to work. If you have a large carving dish you can arrange the carved meat along the edge of the dish ready for serving; if using a smaller dish have another hot dish ready to take the slices as they are prepared. Carving on to individual plates is not ideal as you will not be able to mix dark and light meats in each serving.

Carving chicken and turkey

Place the bird on the dish so that one wing is towards your left hand with the breast diagonally towards

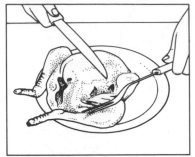

Prising the leg outwards with fork

you. Steadying the bird with the flat of the knife, prise the leg out-wards with the fork, exposing the thigh joint. Cut through the joint to sever the leg. On a turkey or large chicken hold the end of the drumstick in one hand and cut slices from the leg in a downward slant away from you, turning the leg to get slices from all round the joint. When the bone is bare set it to one end of the dish. For a medium-sized chicken the leg will not have enough meat for carving but can be divided into two at the joint, giving a thigh and a drum-stick portion. If the chicken is small the leg may be served as a single portion.

Next remove the wing that is facing you. Hold the wing with the fork and cut through the outer layer of the breast into the joint. Ease the wing from the body and cut through the gristle. A turkey wing may be divided again; a chicken wing is too small and is served in one piece.

Carve the breast in thin slices parallel with the breast bone. If the bird is stuffed, the outer slices of meat and stuffing will carve together; the rest of the stuffing will have to be scooped out with a spoon. Carve one side of the carcass clean before turning the dish round and starting the pro-cess again on the other side of the bird.

Carving duck and goose

Duck and goose have particularly tough leg and wing ligaments and a shorter, heavier knife is needed to cut through these. Place bird on carving dish with legs diagonally

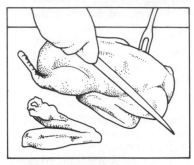

Cutting through wing joint

towards you. Hold the body firmly with the fork and cut down through the wing joint. Move fork closer to leg end and cut firmly through the joint. Leave a duck leg whole; separate a goose leg into two. With a long carving knife carve thin breast slices.

Jointing small cooked chickens and guinea fowl

Halve or quarter small chickens such as poussins, or guinea fowl. Use a strong, heavy knife and cut the bird in two straight through the breast and backbone. Halve each piece crossways for quarters.

Jointing a duckling

Place the bird on a board with the legs facing you. With poultry shears, cut along the top, keeping the blades just to one side of the breast bone. When you reach the wishbone, cut firmly through it and open up the bird. Next cut through the back, just to one side of the backbone. Cut down the other side and discard it.

Lay the two duckling halves skin side up on the board and with a sharp knife cut through the skin and flesh between the wing and leg sections. Leave plenty of breast meat with the leg portion. Use the shears to cut through the bone to divide the portions.

ACCOMPANIMENTS TO POULTRY

STUFFINGS

Stuffing, or forcemeat as it is sometimes known, serves a triple purpose. It fills the neck cavity of the bird, helping to keep the breast looking plump and well-rounded; it adds flavour to the meat and it extends the meat to give more servings.

Assemble the ingredients for a stuffing well ahead if you wish but don't mix in the liquid or egg as it tends to make the stuffing stodgy.

Don't put a meat stuffing in the bird until you are ready to cook. It is not safe to leave uncooked meat-based stuffing around, even if it is in the refrigerator, for more than 2–3 hours.

Most stuffings are made from a base of fresh breadcrumbs, sausagemeat or other minced meat, rice or suet. Breadcrumbs are best made from a loaf that is 2–3 days old—new bread makes crumbs which are rather too moist. Rice should be cooked and left to cool before adding to a stuffing; it is particularly good in stuffings containing fruit or nuts.

Most stuffings need a little fat, and suet is the one most commonly used. Fresh suet from the butcher has the best flavour, but packet shredded suet is more

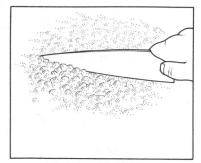

Chopping fresh suet finely

convenient. Chop fresh suet very finely, dusting it with flour to stop it sticking to the knife. Butter is used in some recipes in place of suet, and many people prefer the flavour of a stuffing made with butter if it is to be served cold.

Forcemeat balls

To make forcemeat balls, use any finely minced stuffing mixture. Instead of putting it inside the bird, roll the mixture into small balls. To cook, either roast them round the bird, or fry them separately. Use as a garnish and serve 2–3 balls per person.

CHESTNUT STUFFING

Makes enough for a 4.5 kg (10 lb) turkey

50 g (2 oz) bacon, rinded and chopped
225 g (8 oz) unsweetened chestnut purée
100 g (4 oz) fresh white breadcrumbs
5 ml (1 tsp) chopped parsley
25 g (1 oz) butter or margarine, melted
grated rind of 1 lemon
salt and freshly ground pepper
1 egg, beaten

Fry the bacon gently in its own fat until crisp and drain well on absorbent kitchen paper. Then mix with all the remaining ingredients.

HERB STUFFING

Makes enough for a 1.8 kg (4 lb) chicken

50 g (2 oz) bacon, rinded and chopped
45 ml (3 tbsp) shredded suet
100 g (4 oz) fresh white breadcrumbs
15 ml (1 tbsp) chopped parsley
10 ml (2 tsp) dried mixed herbs or 30 ml (2 tbsp) chopped fresh mixed herbs
grated rind of $\frac{1}{2}$ a lemon
1 small (size 6) egg, beaten
salt and freshly ground pepper
milk or stock, to bind

Fry the bacon in its own fat without browning and drain it on absorbent kitchen paper. Then mix it with the remaining ingredients, moistening with enough milk or stock to bind the mixture.

SAGE AND ONION STUFFING

Makes enough for a 1.8 kg (4 lb) duck. Double the quantities for a goose

2 large onions, skinned and chopped
25 g (1 oz) butter or margarine
salt and freshly ground pepper
100 g (4 oz) fresh white breadcrumbs
10 ml (2 tsp) dried sage

Put the onions in a saucepan and cover with water. Bring to the boil and cook for 10 minutes. Drain and mix with the other ingredients.

SAUSAGE AND APPLE STUFFING

Makes enough for a 4.5 kg (10 lb) turkey

450 g (1 lb) sausagemeat
3 cooking apples, peeled, cored and chopped
1 medium onion, skinned and chopped
2 sticks of celery, trimmed and chopped
225 g (8 oz) fresh white breadcrumbs
2 eggs, beaten
salt and freshly ground pepper

1 Brown the sausagemeat and remove from the pan. Pour off all but 60 ml (4 tbsp) fat.

2 Add the apples, onion and celery and cook for 5–10 minutes until soft. Stir in the sausagemeat and remaining ingredients. Cool before using.

SULTANA AND LEMON STUFFING

Makes enough for a 1.8 kg (4 lb) duck.
Double the quantities for a goose

1 medium onion, skinned and finely chopped
50 g (2 oz) sultanas
150 ml (¼ pint) dry cider
100 g (4 oz) fresh white breadcrumbs
5 ml (1 tsp) grated lemon rind
15 ml (1 tbsp) chopped parsley
salt and freshly ground pepper
1 egg, beaten

1 Put the onion, sultanas and cider into a small saucepan and simmer for 20 minutes, or until the liquid is almost absorbed.

2 Mix with the breadcrumbs, grated lemon rind and parsley and season well with salt and pepper. Bind with the beaten egg.

POTATOES

Various types of potato are traditionally served with poultry, notably roast potatoes, creamed potatoes, game chips and matchstick potatoes. Fried crumbs are served with quail.

Roast potatoes: Using old potatoes, peel in the usual way and cut into even-sized pieces. Cook in salted water for 5–10 minutes—depending on the size—and drain well. Transfer them to a roasting tin containing 100 g (4 oz) of hot lard or chicken fat, baste well and cook in the oven at 220°C (425°F) mark 7 for about 20 minutes; turn them and continue cooking for another 20 minutes, or until soft inside and crisp and brown outside. Drain well on absorbent kitchen paper and serve in an uncovered serving dish, sprinkled with salt.

If preferred, do not parboil the potatoes to begin with—in this case they will take about 50–60 minutes to cook.

They can also be cooked in the tin around the bird, when little or no extra fat will be needed.

Creamed potatoes: Mash boiled potatoes with a knob of butter, salt and pepper to taste and a little milk. Beat them well over a gentle heat with a wooden spoon until fluffy. Serve in a heated dish, mark with a fork and sprinkle with chopped parsley.

Slicing potatoes for game chips

Game chips: Scrub and peel the potatoes and slice very thinly into rounds. Soak them in cold water, dry and fry in deep fat at 190°C (375°F) for about 3 minutes. Remove and drain on absorbent kitchen paper. Just before serving, reheat the fat and fry the chips again rapidly until crisp and browned. Drain well on absorbent kitchen paper and serve in an uncovered dish, sprinkled with salt.

Matchstick potatoes: Cut potatoes into very small chips of matchstick size. Follow the method for game chips.

Fried crumbs: Fry 50–100 g (2–4 oz) fresh white breadcrumbs in 25 g (1 oz) butter until golden

Making fried breadcrumbs

brown. Stir from time to time to ensure even browning.

TRADITIONAL ACCOMPANIMENTS FOR ROAST POULTRY

Chicken	forcemeat balls chipolata sausages bacon rolls thin gravy roast potatoes
Duck	sage and onion stuffing fruit stuffing apple sauce thin gravy
Turkey	forcemeat balls chipolata sausages bacon rolls bread sauce cranberry sauce watercress giblet gravy
Goose	sage and onion stuffing apple sauce giblet gravy
Guinea Fowl	watercress bread sauce thin gravy
Quail	croûtes thin gravy fried crumbs matchstick or chipped potatoes

GRAVIES FOR POULTRY

The best gravies are made with stock based on the giblets, with any bones that are available. After cooking your poultry, never throw away the bones but use them to make a stock for next time; either freeze it or store in the refrigerator, boiling every 2–3 days.

The lighter meats, such as chicken and guinea fowl, are usually served with a thin gravy, turkey and goose are served with a richer version (see Giblet gravy).

Thin gravy
Pour the fat very slowly from the roasting tin, draining it off carefully from one corner and leaving the sediment behind. Season well

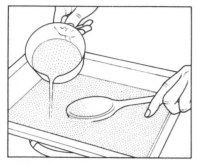

Adding hot stock to roasting tin

and add 300 ml ($\frac{1}{2}$ pint) hot stock. Stir thoroughly with a wooden spoon until all the sediment is scraped from the tin and the gravy is a rich brown; return the tin to the heat and boil for 2–3 minutes. Serve very hot.

POULTRY STOCK
Makes about 1.1–1.4 litres (2–2$\frac{1}{2}$ pints)

1 carcass, fresh or cooked, with giblets (except liver)
1.4–1.7 litres (2$\frac{1}{2}$–3 pints) cold water
1 small onion, skinned and sliced
2 carrots, peeled and sliced
1 stick of celery, sliced
1 bouquet garni
5 ml (1 tsp) salt

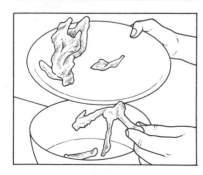

1 Break down the carcass and put it in a large saucepan with the giblets. Add the water and the remaining ingredients.

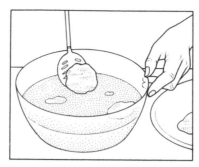

2 Bring to the boil uncovered and remove the scum. Cover and simmer for 3 hours. Strain, and when cold remove all traces of fat from the surface.

Pressure Cooker Method

1 Follow step 1 (see left), using the pressure cooker instead of a saucepan, but reduce the amount of cold water to 1.1 litres (2 pints).

2 Bring to high (15 lb) pressure and cook for 45 minutes if using a cooked carcass, 1 hour if using a fresh carcass. Reduce pressure at room temperature. After cooking finish as above.

GIBLET GRAVY
Makes 600 ml (1 pint)

poultry giblets
1 small onion
1 small carrot, peeled
1 stick of celery, trimmed and cut into chunks
bacon rinds
salt and freshly ground pepper
1.1 litres (2 pints) water
15 ml (1 tbsp) flour
butter

1 Put the gizzard, heart and neck (not the liver) in a saucepan with the vegetables, a few bacon rinds, seasoning and the water. Bring to the boil, cover and simmer for about 2 hours.

2 Strain the giblet stock into a basin. Discard the vegetables and bacon rinds and, if you wish, set aside the cooked giblets for use in another dish.

3 When cooked, remove the bird to a warm plate and pour off most of the fat from the tin, leaving behind sediment and about 30 ml (2 tbsp) fat.

4 Blend the flour into the fat in the roasting tin. Cook until it turns brown, stirring continuously and scraping any sediment from the bottom of the tin. Slowly stir in 600 ml (1 pint) giblet stock. Bring to the boil, stirring.

5 Meanwhile, sauté the liver in a knob of butter until just cooked. Remove from the pan, drain and chop it into small pieces.

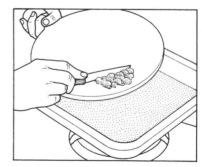

6 Add the chopped liver to the gravy and simmer for 2–3 minutes to heat. Check the seasoning. Pour into a gravy boat and keep hot until needed.

Cooking Poultry

It is the versatility of poultry which makes it such a favourite with both the cook and her family and friends. Each of the basic cooking methods can be used — choose your recipe depending on the type, size and age of the bird and on whether you are cooking joints or a whole bird.

GRILLING

Grilling is a quick method of cooking, searing the meat with a dry heat. It is therefore suitable only for the tenderest meats. Portions of young chicken such as poussins, spring chickens or small roasting birds are ideal. The outside will be crisp and brown, the inside moist and juicy.

Whole birds are not suitable for grilling and large portions on the bone, such as turkey legs, are too uneven to grill well. But boneless steaks of light or dark turkey meat grill well and the boneless meat can also be cut into chunks for kebabs. Grilled duck breasts are good but don't grill the legs as they tend to burn on the outside before they are cooked through to the bone. For a special occasion, grill a spatchcocked guinea fowl.

To prevent the meat from drying in the heat of the grill, brush it well with melted butter or oil before and during cooking, or marinate it first to add extra juiciness and flavour.

Always preheat the grill to give the skin a good crisp outside and cook under a steady, moderate heat. Try to select portions of a similar thickness—chicken legs for example take longer to cook than the breast portions, so add breasts to the grill pan about 5 minutes after the legs.

Poultry must be cooked through to the bone, so pierce the thickest part of the flesh with a skewer to check. The meat is cooked when the juices run clear.

BARBECUING

When grilling on a barbecue, be sure to light the fire well ahead. It will take at least 30 minutes for the charcoal to reach the correct heat for cooking; there should be no flames or red coals but the heat should be steady and even.

There is a tendency for poultry to cook too fast over charcoal; if this happens, raise the grid further from the fire or move the centre portions to the outside of the grid,

Wrapping meat in foil

which will be cooler. If necessary, brown the outside then continue cooking wrapped in foil.

TURKEY AND SAUSAGE KEBABS

Serves 6

1.1–1.4 kg (2½–3 lb) turkey meat
75 ml (5 tbsp) soy sauce
75 ml (5 tbsp) dry sherry
15 ml (1 tbsp) sugar
45 ml (3 tbsp) vegetable oil
225 g (8 oz) sausages
8 large spring onions, trimmed
226-g (8-oz) can pineapple, drained

1 Cut the turkey into 2.5-cm (1-inch) chunks. Mix the soy sauce, sherry, sugar and oil.

2 Add the turkey pieces and coat with the marinade. Cover and refrigerate for 30 minutes.

3 Meanwhile, halve the sausages crossways and cut the spring onions into 4-cm (1½-inch) pieces.

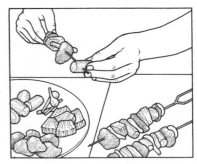

4 Thread chunks of turkey, sausage, pineapple and spring onion alternately on to skewers.

5 Cook under a hot grill for 20–25 minutes until the meat is tender, turning the kebabs and basting with the marinade.

TANDOORI CHICKEN

Serves 8

8 chicken joints

salt and freshly ground pepper

lemon wedges and chopped fresh coriander leaves, to garnish

For the marinade

225 ml (8 fl oz) natural yogurt

5 ml (1 tsp) freshly ground pepper

10 ml (2 tsp) salt

7.5 ml (1½ tsp) chilli powder

pinch of ground ginger

pinch of ground coriander

1 large garlic clove, skinned and crushed

juice of 1½ lemons

1 Wipe the chicken joints, prick skin with a fork and season. Combine the yogurt with all of the remaining marinade ingredients.

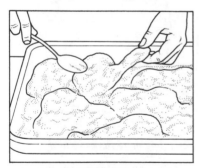

2 Add the chicken pieces, turning to coat well. Cover and leave to stand for 3–4 hours, turning occasionally.

3 Place the chicken, skin side down, in a grill pan and baste with some of the marinade. Grill for 25 minutes under medium heat; turn and baste again. Grill for a further 15 minutes or until the chicken is tender.

4 Transfer the chicken to a heated serving dish and garnish with lemon and coriander.

SAVOURY CHICKEN

Serves 4

1.4–1.6 kg (3–3½ lb) chicken, quartered

For the marinade

10 medium garlic cloves, skinned

175 ml (6 fl oz) tarragon vinegar

25 g (1 oz) sugar

15 ml (1 tbsp) vegetable oil

15 ml (1 tbsp) Worcestershire sauce

10 ml (2 tsp) mustard powder

5 ml (1 tsp) salt

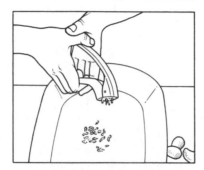

1 Crush the garlic cloves and put into a large, shallow dish. Add the remaining ingredients for the marinade and mix well.

2 Prick the skin of the chicken pieces with a fork and add to marinade, turning to coat. Cover and refrigerate for at least 2 hours.

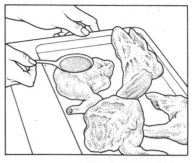

3 Place the chicken, skin side down, in a grill pan and baste with the marinade. Grill under medium heat for 40 minutes, or until the chicken is tender, turning once and basting with the marinade during cooking.

VARIATION

BARBECUED CHICKEN

Marinate the chicken as above. Prepare an outdoor grill; pour a little melted butter on each chicken joint and place on the barbecue grid over very hot coals. Brown quickly on all sides then remove from the grid and place each joint on a 38-cm (15-inch) square piece of foil. Wrap round the chicken and seal the edges securely. Place each packet on the grid and cook for a further 20 minutes, turning once. Heat the marinade in a small saucepan and serve separately as a sauce. Serve

the chicken in the foil packets so that none of the buttery juices are lost.

GRILLED DUCK BREASTS

Serves 4

4 duck breasts, with skin on

salt

For the marinade

200 ml (7 fl oz) vegetable oil

100 ml (4 fl oz) red wine

5 ml (1 tsp) salt

freshly ground pepper

1 large onion, skinned and thinly sliced

3 large garlic cloves, skinned and thinly sliced

2 bay leaves, roughly crumbled

1 In a shallow dish large enough to hold the duck breasts in one layer, mix all the marinade ingredients together.

2 Lay the duck breasts in the marinade, baste thoroughly, cover, and marinate for at least 3 hours, turning the pieces from time to time.

3 Remove the breasts from the marinade. Strain the marinade through a fine sieve and discard the flavourings.

4 Arrange the duck breasts, skin side down, on the grill rack, sprinkle lightly with salt and grill 10 cm (4 inches) from high heat for about 15 minutes, lowering the heat or the rack so that the duck browns slowly without burning. Baste every 5 minutes or so with the strained marinade.

5 Turn the breasts over, sprinkle with salt again, and grill for a further 10–15 minutes, basting two or three times with the strained marinade.

6 When the duck is tender and a deep golden-brown, arrange the pieces on a heated serving dish, and serve immediately.

POUSSINS IN A BASKET

Serves 4

4 poussins

100 g (4 oz) butter or margarine, melted

salt and freshly ground pepper

2 medium onions, skinned and sliced, and watercress, to garnish

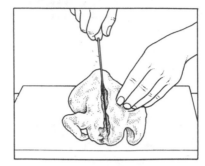

1 With a heavy knife, split the poussins down the back. Trim off the legs and the wings at the first joints, open out the birds and flatten them as much as possible. Run a long skewer through from leg to leg on each bird to hold flat.

2 Brush each bird all over with melted fat and season lightly. Grill under medium heat for about 20 minutes, turning the birds once or twice, or until the poussins are cooked through and are tender.

3 Serve each bird on a napkin in a basket, garnished with onion rings and sprigs of watercress.

SPIT ROASTING

Spit roasting achieves a similar effect to grilling for whole birds or large joints. Many gas and electric cookers can be fitted with a rotisserie for the purpose, or you can buy a separate, electrically operated model. A charcoal barbecue may be fitted with a battery-operated spit.

For the best results choose a small bird, up to about 1.6 kg (3½ lb). Remove the giblets and rinse and dry the bird inside and out. Fold the neck skin over the

back and skewer it in position. Tie the wings close to the body. Insert

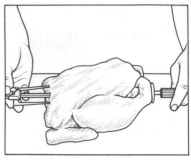

Inserting spit through the bird

the spit through the body from end to end and tighten the holding prongs. Make sure the bird is balanced on the spit.

Using fine string, tie the parson's nose and drumsticks securely on to the spit. Check that the spit will revolve freely and evenly.

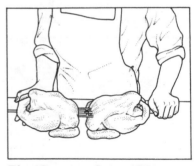

Threading more than one bird

If you are cooking more than one bird at a time, thread them on to the spit in opposite directions to make sure they balance properly.

Preheat the grill, barbecue or rotisserie and place the loaded spit in position. Place a drip tray under the bird to catch the melting fat, and use the fat to baste the bird occasionally as it cooks. Cook for about 1½ hours. If you are using a basting sauce, use it only during the last 20 minutes or so of cooking time.

MARINATING

A marinade is a convenient, trouble-free way of flavouring and tenderising poultry. It is ideal to use in conjunction with quick cooking methods like grilling and barbecuing. Soak the poultry for a few hours beforehand in the flavoursome liquid, then use any remaining marinade in a sauce.

A marinade is generally based on a fat or oil to give dry meat extra moisture. Olive oil is a good choice, but other more or less highly flavoured oils are also suitable. A liquid such as yogurt will serve the same purpose for a special recipe. As well as the oil you need an acid ingredient to break down the fibres in the meat—wine, vinegar or lemon juice are the usual choices for this. Add spices or herbs for flavour.

Vary a basic marinade and add extra zing by using bottled relishes. These frequently contain vinegar as the preservative and the blend of spices included will save you making up your own recipe.

For marinating you can use fresh or frozen poultry—this is an excellent way of adding flavour to a factory-bred bird. But thaw a frozen bird completely and dry it well before you put it in the marinade, or the liquid will be diluted with water from the bird.

To marinate a whole bird, put the flavouring liquid in a large polythene bag, add the bird and place it in a deep dish. Turn the

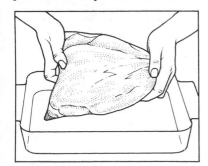

Soaking the whole of the bird.

bag and bird from time to time to soak the whole of the bird.

For poultry portions, choose a large shallow dish that will take all the pieces in a single layer; don't use an aluminium or enamelled iron pan as these could be damaged by the acid. Mix the marinade ingredients thoroughly.

Dry the poultry well on absorbent kitchen paper and prick the skin all over with a fork, to help the flavour penetrate. Place the pieces in the dish in a single layer and spoon or brush the liquid all over them. Cover with

Covering with cling film

cling film and leave for at least 2 hours, turning the pieces occasionally. If the room is warm or if you are leaving it for longer than 2 hours, place the dish in the refrigerator until required.

When you are ready to cook, drain the marinade off each portion but save the remaining liquid for basting during cooking and for making a sauce to serve with the finished dish.

SPRING ONION AND SOY MARINADE

| 100 ml (4 fl oz) soy sauce |
| 30 ml (2 tbsp) dry sherry |
| 50 g (2 oz) spring onions, thinly sliced |
| 30 ml (2 tbsp) soft light brown sugar |
| 2.5 ml ($\frac{1}{2}$ tsp) salt |
| 2.5 ml ($\frac{1}{2}$ tsp) ground ginger |

Mix the ingredients in a shallow dish and blend well. Spoon over the chicken and marinate for at least 2 hours.

CHICKEN WITH CHILLI MARINADE

Serves 4

| 1.4 kg (3 lb) chicken, quartered or jointed |
| *For the marinade* |
| 350-g (12-oz) bottle mild chilli relish |
| 5 ml (1 tsp) salt |
| 10 ml (2 tsp) dried horseradish |
| 1 garlic clove, skinned and quartered |
| 100 ml (4 fl oz) wine vinegar |

1 Prick the chicken skin all over with a fork. Mix all the marinade ingredients in a large dish. Add the chicken pieces and coat well. Cover and refrigerate for at least 2 hours, turning from time to time.

2 Arrange the chicken in a single layer in the grill pan. Grill for 35–45 minutes under medium heat, until tender, turning frequently and basting with the chilli marinade.

ORANGE HERB MARINADE

| 150 ml ($\frac{1}{4}$ pint) white wine or dry vermouth |
| 45 ml (3 tbsp) olive oil |
| juice of 2 oranges |
| 5 ml (1 tsp) each chopped fresh rosemary, thyme and marjoram |
| 1 garlic clove, skinned and crushed |

Mix the ingredients in a shallow dish and stir until well blended. Spoon over the chicken and marinate for at least 2 hours.

LIME MARINADE

| 100 ml (4 fl oz) lime juice |
| 45 ml (3 tbsp) vegetable oil |
| 15 ml (1 tbsp) grated lime rind |
| 20 ml (4 tsp) salt |
| 1.25 ml ($\frac{1}{4}$ tsp) crushed peppercorns |

Mix the ingredients in a shallow dish and stir until well blended. Spoon over the chicken and marinate for at least 2 hours.

PAN FRYING AND SAUTÉS

Individual portions of poultry are ideal for frying and sautés. The secret is to sear the surface quickly first, to seal in the juices and give a good brown colour, then reduce the heat and cook slowly until the meat is cooked right through and tender.

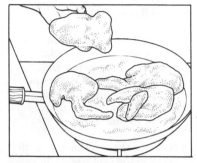

Frying poultry in single layer

When frying poultry, choose a wide, heavy-based, shallow pan that will take the pieces in a single layer; or use two pans. If you layer one piece on top of another they will stew rather than fry. For sautés in which the cooking is finished in a sauce you will need a tightly fitting lid, or a sheet of foil.

Choose oil, butter, margarine or rendered chicken fat for frying. In many dishes, particularly those finished with a delicate or creamy sauce, butter gives the best flavour. Use clarified butter if possible as the high temperature can cause ordinary butter to burn, leaving black specks on the meat and spoiling the flavour. Or use part oil and part butter, which will help prevent the butter burning. Oil alone will give you a good crisp outside, with less flavour but also with less risk of burning.

If the poultry is to be cooked without a coating, it must be completely dry when it goes into the hot fat. A coating of flour or breadcrumbs will help contain the juices and prevent the outer meat from hardening in the hot fat.

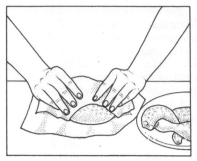

Drying meat well

If using flour alone, dry the meat well and roll it in seasoned flour just before cooking; if left to stand after coating, the flour will turn to paste with the moisture from the meat.

If coating with breadcrumbs, on the other hand, it is best to chill the coated pieces briefly before cooking to help the coating adhere. Roll the portions in flour first to absorb any moisture, then dip in beaten egg and roll in

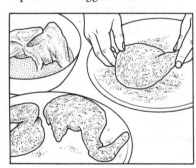

Rolling portions in breadcrumbs

breadcrumbs. Pat the crumbs on firmly and chill for about 15 minutes for the best results. The moisture will be absorbed by the flour and will not soak through to the crumbs.

To cook, heat the fat to frying temperature and add the poultry pieces in a single layer. Remember that the side that goes into the fat first will look the best, so portions with bone should go in fleshy side down. Cook briskly until golden,

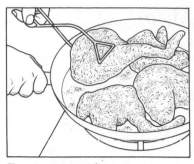

Turning meat with tongs

then turn the meat with tongs or two spoons to avoid piercing the flesh. Cook until the second side is golden then reduce the heat, cover the pan if the recipe calls for it, and continue cooking until the meat is tender and cooked.

Depending on the recipe you can then either add a little liquid to the poultry in the pan and make a small amount of sauce, or remove the cooked poultry to keep hot while you make a sauce.

STIR-FRIED POULTRY

Stir-frying is the traditional Chinese way of cooking high-quality meats. Very thin slices of

Stir-frying thinly sliced meat

meat are cooked and stirred over high heat in a small amount of oil. Cooking is very quick and the result should be crisp and tender. Fine-fleshed, lean poultry is an ideal meat for stir-fried dishes.

Stir-fried recipes invariably include a variety of vegetables, which serve both to extend a small quantity of poultry and to give the blend of many flavours that is typical of Chinese foods.

FRIED CHICKEN WITH PARSLEY SAUCE

Serves 4

1.1–1.4 kg (2½–3 lb) chicken, jointed
salt and freshly ground pepper
flour
vegetable oil
For the sauce
15 ml (1 tbsp) flour
150 ml (¼ pint) milk
150 ml (¼ pint) chicken stock
salt and freshly ground pepper
15–30 ml (1–2 tbsp) chopped parsley

1 Season the chicken pieces with salt and pepper and roll them in the flour to completely coat.

2 Using a large frying pan, pour in enough oil to cover the bottom of the pan. Heat the oil and fry the chicken, turning the pieces, until brown.

3 Reduce the heat and cook the chicken for 15 minutes on each side until tender. Remove from the pan with kitchen tongs, arrange the chicken pieces on a warmed serving dish and keep hot.

4 Drain off all but 30 ml (2 tbsp) oil and sprinkle in 15 ml (1 tbsp) flour. Cook over medium heat, stirring until well browned.

5 Blend in the liquids. Bring the sauce to the boil, stirring all the time, and boil for 2–3 minutes or until thickened. Adjust the seasoning, then add the parsley and pour sauce over the chicken.

CURRIED TURKEY WITH AVOCADO

Serves 4

350 g (12 oz) turkey fillet
30 ml (2 tbsp) flour
15 ml (1 tbsp) ground cumin
15 ml (1 tbsp) ground ginger
salt and freshly ground pepper
1 egg, beaten
1 ripe but still firm avocado
15 ml (1 tbsp) lemon juice
about 45 ml (3 tbsp) peanut oil
1 garlic clove, crushed
225-g (8-oz) can bamboo shoots, drained and thinly sliced
1 bunch spring onions, chopped

1 Slice the turkey into strips. Toss in the flour, cumin, ginger and seasonings. Stir in the egg.

2 Peel and slice the avocado. Coat in lemon juice.

3 Heat the oil, with the garlic, in a large frying pan. Add the turkey strips, fry over a high heat, stirring all the time, until golden, adding more oil if necessary.

4 Reduce heat, stir in the bamboo shoots and spring onions. Cook, stirring, for 1–2 minutes. Off heat fold in avocado.

CHINESE CHICKEN WITH VEGETABLES

Serves 4

450 g (1 lb) chicken meat
45 ml (3 tbsp) vegetable oil
5 ml (1 tsp) salt
30 ml (2 tbsp) soy sauce
2–3 sticks of celery, trimmed
½ green pepper, seeded
270-g (9½-oz) can beansprouts
100-g (4-oz) can water chestnuts
50 g (2 oz) mushrooms
150 ml (¼ pint) chicken stock
15 ml (1 tbsp) cornflour
salt and freshly ground pepper
50 g (2 oz) flaked almonds, toasted

1 Carefully slice the uncooked chicken into thin strips, about 0.5 cm (¼ inch) wide.

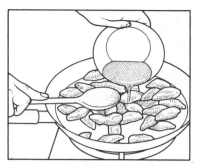

2 Heat the oil in a large frying pan and add the chicken and salt. Stir-fry for 3–5 minutes. Add the soy sauce and blend well.

3 Slice the celery and green pepper into thin strips. Add with the drained beansprouts and chestnuts, mushrooms and stock. Cover and simmer for 15 minutes.

4 Blend the cornflour with a little water and add to the pan. Bring slowly to the boil, stirring. Season and sprinkle with almonds.

SAUTÉ OF DUCKLING WITH PEAS

Serves 4

1.8 kg (4 lb) duckling, jointed
15 ml (1 tbsp) flour
300 ml (½ pint) jellied chicken stock
150 ml (¼ pint) red wine
15 ml (1 tbsp) fresh chopped sage
salt and freshly ground pepper
450 g (1 lb) fresh peas, podded

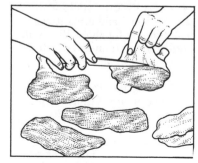

1 Ease the skin and fat off the duckling joints and halve the leg joints. Snip the skin into small pieces and brown in a large sauté pan until crisp. Set aside.

2 Drain off all but 45 ml (3 tbsp) fat from the sauté pan and brown the duckling joints. Sprinkle in the flour, stir to combine with the fat and cook gently for 1 minute. Stir in the stock, wine, sage and seasoning and bring to the boil. Cover the pan and simmer for 25 minutes, then turn the duckling pieces over.

3 Add the peas to the sauté pan, submerging them as far as possible. Cover and continue simmering for 25 minutes, or until duckling and peas are tender.

4 Adjust the seasoning and garnish with the reserved pieces of crisp duck skin.

LEMON SESAME CHICKEN

Serves 4

8 small chicken drumsticks, about 75 g (3 oz) each
30 ml (2 tbsp) cornflour
1 egg, beaten
225 g (8 oz) leeks, trimmed
1 lemon
15 ml (1 tbsp) soy sauce
15 ml (1 tbsp) cider vinegar
15 ml (1 tbsp) demerara sugar
60 ml (4 tbsp) dry sherry
about 15 ml (1 tbsp) sesame oil
about 30 ml (2 tbsp) peanut oil
salt and freshly ground pepper

1 Cover the drumsticks with cold water and bring to the boil. Simmer for about 30 minutes until tender. Drain and pat dry with absorbent kitchen paper.

2 Mix together the cornflour and egg; use to thoroughly coat the chicken drumsticks.

3 Cut the leeks into 1-cm (½-inch) slices. Grate the rind from the lemon. Whisk together the grated lemon rind, soy sauce, cider vinegar, sugar and sherry.

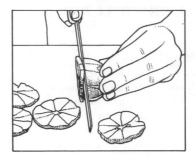

4 Peel and thinly slice the lemon. Heat the oils together in a wok or large frying pan until smoky hot. Brown the drumsticks a few at a time. Remove.

5 Over a medium heat, fry the leeks and sesame seeds for 1–2 minutes, adding more oil if necessary. Return all the drumsticks with the sauce mixture to the pan. Raise heat, bring to the boil and simmer for 3–4 minutes, stirring occasionally. Season.

6 Transfer to a warmed serving dish. Lightly sauté the lemon slices in the wok or frying pan. Garnish the drumsticks with the lemon and serve immediately.

ROASTING POULTRY

Roast poultry is the traditional dinner for Christmas and many other celebrations. It is also popular as an alternative to a roast joint for Sunday lunch. The presentation of the bird may be as elaborate or simple as you like, but the technique remains the same.

Roasting was originally a method of cooking by the fierce dry heat in front of an open fire. The term is now used almost universally to mean 'oven-roasting', or baking. The heat is still fierce but the confines of the oven keep the air moist and the flesh of the bird retains its juices.

Good roast poultry has a well-browned, crisp and tasty skin without losing the succulence of the flesh beneath. Achieving this is perhaps easiest with a chicken. This smallish bird has a fairly even distribution of flesh and fat over the bones and will cook evenly with a minimum of effort.

A duck is more difficult. The skin is very fatty indeed and it is a skilled job to crisp the skin without cooking the inner flesh to a frazzle. A goose gives similar problems, compounded by the larger size of the bird. With both these birds, prick the skin all over with a fork before you start to cook, to allow the fat to run out freely. Then stand the bird on a

Standing the bird on a rack

rack in the roasting tin, clear of the fat which collects. Very little basting is required. A turkey is lean by comparison but there is a marked contrast in textures between the light meat of the breast and the dark meat of legs and wings; the difficulty with turkey is to cook the dark meat sufficiently without overcooking the breast.

Covering the bird with foil protects the breast, but you must remember to remove it 30 minutes before the end of cooking to allow the skin to brown. It also helps if you start the bird cooking breast side down, turning it the 'right way up' after the dark meat is partially cooked.

Guinea fowl is generally smaller than chicken and has very little fat. Take care, therefore, to add plenty of extra fat while cooking, to baste well and never overcook. A quail is equally sensitive—a tiny bird that could be ruined by 5 minutes too long in the oven . To make the best of a quail cover the breast with a little fat bacon and place the bird on a round of fried bread to cook. The bread soaks up the juices as the bird cooks, and is served as part of the finished dish.

To achieve best results with each type of bird, vary the oven temperature according to the chart. Baste where recommended, add extra fat to those birds that are exceptionally lean. Cover or partially cover with foil according to the recipe, for even cooking.

Preparing Poultry for Roasting
If the bird is frozen allow it to thaw completely before cooking (see page 589).

Wash the bird inside and out, and dry on absorbent kitchen paper. If it is to be stuffed, put the

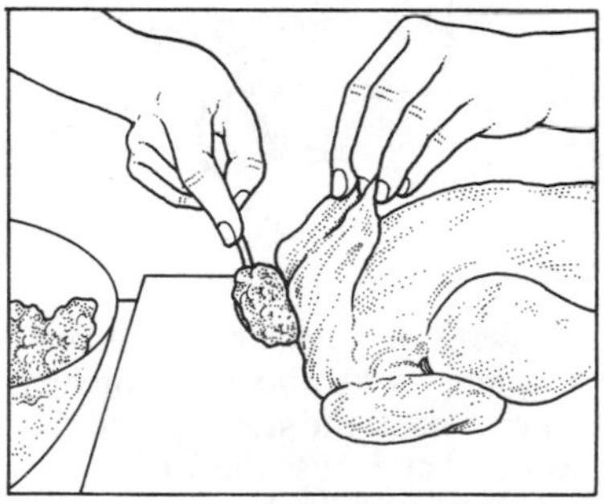

Stuffing the neck end of the bird

stuffing in the neck end only. If placed in the body cavity, stuffing can prevent the bird cooking through thoroughly, which is a health risk. Pull the skin lightly over the stuffing and truss the bird neatly to keep it a good shape. If you are not using stuffing, you can add extra flavour by putting half an onion or an apple inside the body cavity (this will not slow the cooking) and seasoning the inside well. Lean birds such as young chickens might benefit from a little butter flavoured with lemon rind or herbs inside the cavity.

Add any extra fat to the breast—softened butter or chicken fat are ideal, or rashers of streaky bacon—and cover if you wish. Or you can cover towards the end of the cooking time if the breast is browning too quickly. Preheat the oven and have the bird at room temperature before it goes in. Time the cooking according to the chart. For French-roasted birds add a little stock or wine to the roasting tin for basting.

To test when poultry is cooked: Insert a meat thermometer into the thickest part of the meat. When cooked the thermometer reading should be 88°C (190°F). Or, insert a skewer into the thickest part; on withdrawing it the juices should be clear.

POULTRY ROASTING CHART

Chicken and Capon	190°C (375°F) mark 5	20 minutes per 450 g (1 lb) plus 20 minutes
Duck	190°C (375°F) mark 5	20 minutes per 450 g (1 lb)
Guinea fowl	190°C (375°F) mark 5	45–60 minutes
Goose	220°C (425°F) mark 7 Then reduce to 180°C (350°F) mark 4 and cover breast	20 minutes 13–15 minutes per 450 g (1 lb)
Quail	180°C (350°F) mark 4	20 minutes

TURKEY

Oven-ready weight (including stuffing if used)	Hours at 170°C (325°F) mark 3	Hours at 230°C (450°F) mark 8
2.7–3.6 kg (6–8 lb)	3–3½	2¼–2½
3.6–4.5 kg (8–10 lb)	3½–3¾	2½–2¾
4.5–5.4 kg (10–12 lb)	3¾–4	2¾
5.4–6.3 kg (12–14 lb)	4–4¼	3
6.3–7.3 kg (14–16 lb)	4¼–4½	3–3¼
7.3–8.2 kg (16–18 lb)	4½–4¾	3¼–3½
8.2–9 kg (18–20 lb)	4¾–5	3½–3¾
9–10 kg (20–22 lb)	5–5¼	3¾–4

ROAST CHICKEN

Serves 4

1.6–1.8 kg (3½–4 lb) chicken
herb stuffing (see page 593)
1 onion, skinned (optional)
1 thick lemon wedge (optional)
knob of butter (optional)
oil or melted butter
salt and freshly ground pepper
streaky bacon rashers, rinded

1 Wash the inside of the bird and stuff it at the neck end with the herb stuffing. To add flavour put an onion, lemon wedge or knob of butter in the body of the chicken.

2 Brush the bird with oil or melted butter, sprinkle it with salt and pepper and put it in a shallow roasting tin. Lay streaky bacon over the breast to prevent it becoming too dry.

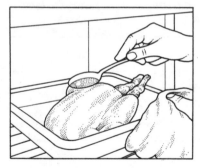

3 Cook in the oven at 190°C (375°F) mark 5, basting from time to time and allowing 20 minutes per 450 g (1 lb), plus 20 minutes. Put a piece of grease-proof paper over the breast if the skin becomes too brown. Alternatively, wrap the chicken in foil before roasting; allow the same cooking time but open the foil for the final 15–20 minutes to allow the chicken to brown.

4 Serve with bacon rolls, force-meat balls, small sausages, bread sauce and thin gravy.

FRENCH ROAST CAPON

Serves 8

75 g (3 oz) butter
salt and freshly ground pepper
3.6 kg (8 lb) capon
5–6 sprigs tarragon or parsley
melted butter
2 bacon rashers, rinded
300 ml (½ pint) chicken stock

1 Cream the butter with salt and pepper and put inside capon with the herbs. Truss firmly.

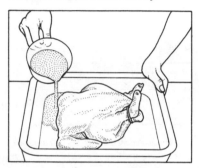

2 Brush the breast with melted butter and cover with bacon. Put in roasting tin, add the stock.

3 Roast at 190°C (375°F) mark 5 for 3 hours, basting often. Remove bacon for last 15 minutes.

ROAST QUAIL

Serves 4

4 rounds of fried bread
4 quail
2 bacon rashers, cut into strips

1 Put fried bread in a roasting tin. Place quail on bread and cover breasts with the bacon.

2 Roast in the oven at 180°C (350°F) mark 4 for about 20 minutes, basting with butter.

3 Serve on the bread with the bacon; thin gravy, fried crumbs and chipped potatoes are usual accompaniments.

ROAST DUCK

Serves 4

1.8 kg (4 lb) duck
sage and onion stuffing (see page 593)
salt and freshly ground pepper
15 ml (1 tbsp) flour
600 ml (1 pint) duck stock

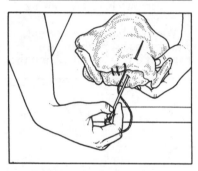

1 Wash the duck and dry it completely with absorbent kitchen paper. Spoon the stuffing into the neck end and truss the duck. Weigh it and calculate cooking time, allowing 20 minutes per 450 g (1 lb).

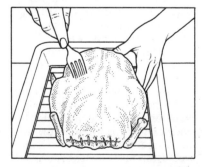

2 Put the duck on a wire rack in a roasting tin and sprinkle the breast liberally with a mixture of salt and pepper. Rub the seasoning thoroughly into the skin. Prick the skin all over with a sharp fork or skewer to allow fat to escape.

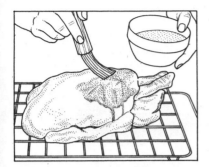

3 Roast at 190°C (375°F) mark 5 for the calculated cooking time, basting occasionally with the fat in the tin.

4 While the duck is cooking, strain the stock into a pan and bring to the boil. Boil rapidly until reduced to about 300 ml (½ pint). Cool and skim the fat off the surface of the liquid.

5 When the duck is cooked, a skewer pushed into the meat should release clear, not pink, juices. Transfer to a warm plate, remove the trussing string and keep hot.

6 Drain the fat from the roasting tin and stir the flour into the remaining juices. Cook over moderate heat until it bubbles, stirring all the time to prevent it sticking.

7 Gradually stir in the reduced stock. Cook the gravy for about 10 minutes, stirring until smooth and thickened. Season to taste and serve with the duck.

ROAST GOOSE

Serves 6

1 goose
salt
1 sour apple (optional)
1 apple, cored and cut into rings, lemon juice and oil, to garnish (optional)

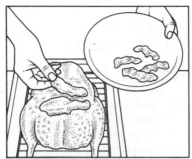

1 Wash and dry the goose. Prick the skin all over with a fork. Sprinkle the bird with salt and put it on a rack in a roasting tin. Cover the goose with the fat taken from inside. Place a sour apple in the roasting tin if you wish.

2 Roast the goose at 220°C (425°F) mark 7 for 20 minutes. Then reduce the temperature to 180°C (350°F) mark 4, cover the breast with greaseproof paper and roast for 13–15 minutes per 450 g (1 lb). Remove the paper during the last 30 minutes to allow the bird to brown.

3 Spoon off the fat from the tin and make giblet gravy (see page 157) with the remaining juices. Serve the goose with gravy and, if you wish, with apple rings that have been dipped in lemon juice, brushed with oil and lightly grilled. The goose may also be served with apple sauce.

BOHEMIAN ROAST GOOSE

Serves 8–10

two 566-g (1¼-lb) cans sauerkraut
4–5 kg (9–11 lb) goose
225 g (8 oz) apples, peeled, cored and cut into cubes
5 ml (1 tsp) salt
2.5 ml (½ tsp) caraway seeds

1 Put the sauerkraut with its liquid in a large saucepan and bring to the boil. Reduce the heat, cover and simmer for 30 minutes. Drain and rinse with cold water; drain again.

2 Wash and dry the goose. Prick the skin with a fork in several places. Add the apples, salt and caraway seeds to the sauerkraut and spoon into the neck end of the goose. Skewer the neck skin to the back of the goose and truss.

3 Put the goose breast side up on a rack in a roasting tin and roast in the oven at 220°C (425°F) mark 7 for 20 minutes, then reduce the temperature to 180°C (350°F) mark 4, cover the breast with greaseproof paper and roast for 4 hours or until tender. Remove the paper during the last 30 minutes to allow the bird to brown. Let the goose stand at room temperature for 15 minutes, so that it is easier to carve.

ROAST STUFFED TURKEY

Serves 8–10

4.5–5.5 kg (10–12 lb) turkey
chestnut stuffing (see page 595)
melted dripping or butter
salt and freshly ground pepper

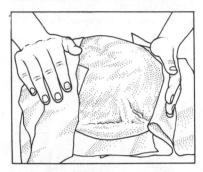

1 Remove the giblets and wash the bird. Drain well and dry with absorbent kitchen paper. Stuff the neck end of the turkey with chestnut stuffing taking care not to pack it too tightly. Cover the stuffing smoothly with the neck skin.

2 With the bird breast side up, fold the wing tips neatly under the body, catching in the neck skin. Truss the bird and tie the legs together. Make the body as plump and even in shape as possible. Weigh it and calculate the cooking time according to the chart on page 605.

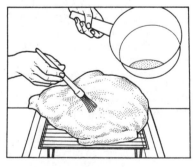

3 Put the bird breast side up on a rack in a roasting tin. Brush with the melted fat and season well with salt and pepper.

4 Cover the bird loosely with foil; roast at 230°C (450°F) mark 8 for the calculated cooking time until tender.

5 Remove the foil and baste 30 minutes before the end of cooking time. Serve with giblet gravy (see page 597) and cranberry sauce.

BONED AND STUFFED ROAST TURKEY

Serves 16

4.5 kg (10 lb) turkey, boned (see page 593)
100 g (4 oz) butter or margarine, softened
salt and freshly ground pepper
watercress sprigs, to garnish
For the apricot and ginger stuffing
700-g (1½-lb) can apricot halves, drained, or 300 g (12 oz) dried apricots, soaked overnight
12 pieces of stem ginger
350 g (12 oz) fresh white breadcrumbs
175 g (6 oz) shredded suet
3 large eggs (size 2), beaten
salt and freshly ground pepper

1 Make the stuffing. Chop the apricots and ginger finely and mix with the breadcrumbs and suet. Bind with the egg and season to taste.

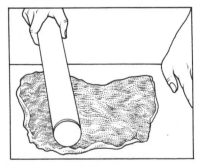

2 Lay the boned turkey skin side down on a board and pound to even thickness with a meat mallet or rolling pin.

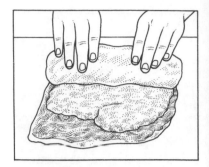

3 Cover the surface of the meat with the apricot and ginger stuffing and carefully roll it up. Do not roll too tightly or the stuffing will burst out during cooking.

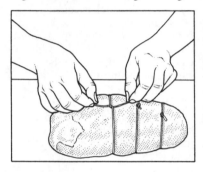

4 Tie the roll at intervals with fine string, or sew it up using a trussing needle. Weigh the stuffed roll and calculate the cooking time, allowing 35–40 minutes per 450 g (1 lb) prepared weight.

5 Put the roll skin side up in a roasting tin and spread with the softened fat. Cover with foil and roast in the oven at 170°C (325°F) mark 3 until 30 minutes before the end of the calculated cooking time.

6 Remove the foil and baste the turkey well with the juices in the tin. Increase the oven temperature to 220°C (425°F) mark 7. Pour off the excess fat and return the tin to the oven to roast for a further 30 minutes.

7 To serve, place the turkey roll on a serving dish and remove the strings. Garnish with watercress. Serve hot or cold.

ROAST DUCK WITH CRANBERRY GLAZE

Serves 4

two 1.6 kg (3½ lb) ducks

175 ml (6 fl oz) water

salt

flour for dredging

30 ml (2 tbsp) cornflour

30 ml (2 tbsp) lemon juice

60 ml (4 tbsp) red wine

396-g (14-oz) jar whole berry cranberry sauce

watercress sprigs, to garnish

1 Put the duck giblets and water in a saucepan. Cover, and simmer for 1 hour.

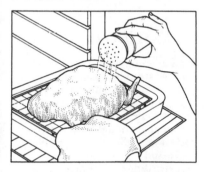

2 Wash and dry the ducks. Prick the skin and rub well with salt. Place on a rack in a roasting tin and roast at 190°C (375°F) mark 5 for 20 minutes per 450 g (1 lb), basting occasionally. About 15 minutes before the end of cooking time, baste, dredge with flour and finish at 220°C (425°F) mark 7.

3 Meanwhile, blend the cornflour, lemon juice and wine and stir in the strained giblet stock. Heat the cranberry sauce until softened, add the cornflour mixture and bring to the boil, stirring. Simmer for 3–4 minutes. Pour two thirds into a sauceboat and keep warm. Strain remaining sauce into a clean saucepan.

4 Spoon the fat from the roasting juices and add the juices to the strained sauce; boil rapidly until reduced to a rich glaze. Brush over the ducks in the tin.

5 Halve the ducks, arrange them on a serving dish and pour any remaining glaze over them. Garnish with watercress and serve with the cranberry sauce.

'BRICK' COOKERY

One of the favourite ways of cooking in the days of open fires was by encasing the meat in a coating of wet clay and baking the whole package in the embers. When baked the hard clay could be cracked off and the meat was revealed, moist, tender and full of flavour. The modern equivalent of this is cooking in a 'chicken brick'.

A chicken brick is made of unglazed clay and shaped more or less to the contours of a chicken. The porous clay absorbs steam from the chicken as it cooks, so that the effect is to roast it rather than to steam or boil. But because the food is covered, the juices are plentiful and the meat moist. There is no spitting and there is less evaporation than from an uncovered tin.

To prepare your brick the first time you use it, soak it in cold water for 30 minutes. After that a 10-minute soak is needed each time. This water soaked into the porous clay is what stops the chicken drying during cooking.

To prepare the chicken, rub the breast lightly with oil and a little salt. Put an onion or a lemon wedge in the body cavity for extra flavour if you wish. Then put the

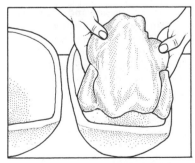

Putting chicken into soaked brick

chicken into the soaked brick and put the top on. Put the brick into a *cold* oven and set the temperature at 250°C (450°F) mark 8. Don't put the brick into a hot oven or it will crack; it must heat up gradually. Likewise, when you take it out of the oven put it on a board, not on metal or laminate.

Bake a 1.8 kg (4 lb) chicken for 1½ hours. Bake chicken portions

Pouring off the juices

for 1 hour. For extra crispness, pour off the juices and return the brick to the oven uncovered for 10 minutes at the end of the cooking time. Serve the chicken with gravy made from the juices.

Poultry casseroles can also be cooked in the brick, but the results are little different from cooking in a conventional casserole, and cleaning the brick after cooking with a sauce is rather difficult.

After cooking, don't leave the empty brick to cool and dry. When the chicken is removed, immerse the brick at once in *hot* water with no soap (clay may retain the soapy taste) and leave it to soak until convenient. Then scrub with a brush to remove stuck-on food and marks. The brick will never look really clean again, because of its unglazed surface, but if it is well scrubbed it is quite hygienic. If you find the smell or flavour of the cooked food lingers on, soak it in salt or vinegar solution for a few hours.

POACHING

Gentle simmering in plenty of water, with vegetables and herbs for flavour, is the perfect way to cook a chicken that is not tender enough to roast. 'Boiled chicken' is the term traditionally used, but the water must never boil, as this would toughen the connective tissues and dry out the meat.

For the best flavour in a poached dish, choose a 'boiling fowl'; this will be an older, tougher chicken than a roaster, with a more pronounced flavour. A roasting chicken can be poached, but reduce the cooking time.

Turkey can also be poached, though usually in joints because the size of the whole bird demands such a large pot. Duck and goose are not usually poached.

For tender, succulent meat, bring the water just to the boil, then reduce the heat and maintain it at no more than a gentle, bubbling simmer. After cooking, strain the stock and use it for a sauce to serve with the meat, or save it for soup. If you are cooking joints, include the backbone for extra flavour, straining it out afterwards.

BOILED CHICKEN WITH PARSLEY SAUCE

Serves 6

1.8 kg (4 lb) boiling fowl
½ lemon
salt
1 onion, skinned and stuck with 3–4 cloves
1 carrot, peeled
1 bouquet garni
For the sauce
20 g (¾ oz) butter or margarine
30 ml (2 tbsp) flour
150 ml (¼ pint) milk
15–30 ml (1–2 tbsp) chopped parsley
salt and freshly ground pepper

1 Clean the chicken and truss firmly. Rub skin with a lemon half to preserve the white colour.

2 Put the chicken into a large saucepan with some salt, the onion, carrot and bouquet garni and add water to cover. Bring to the boil, cover and simmer for about 3 hours for a boiling fowl, 1 hour for a younger bird.

3 Drain the chicken, remove the strings and keep it hot while making the sauce. Strain the cooking stock and reserve.

4 For the sauce, melt the fat in a small saucepan and blend in the flour. Cook over a gentle heat, stirring, until the mixture begins to bubble. Gradually stir in the milk and 150 ml (¼ pint) of the chicken stock. Bring to the boil, stirring, and cook for 1–2 minutes until smooth and thickened. Add the parsley but do not re-boil or the sauce may turn green. Adjust the seasoning and serve with the boiled chicken.

CHICKEN FRICASSEE

Serves 4

1.1 kg (2½ lb) boiling fowl, jointed
2 onions, skinned and chopped
2 carrots, peeled and sliced
100 g (4 oz) mushrooms, sliced
1 bouquet garni
salt and freshly ground pepper
50 g (2 oz) butter or margarine
50 g (2 oz) flour
1 egg yolk
45 ml (3 tbsp) double cream
juice of ½ a lemon
4 bacon rolls, grilled, and parsley sprigs, to garnish

1 Put the chicken and vegetables into a large saucepan with enough water to cover. Add the bouquet garni, salt and pepper. Bring to the boil, cover and simmer gently for 1½ hours, or until the chicken is tender.

2 Strain the stock; reserve the vegetables and stock separately. If you wish, remove the skin from the chicken. Carve the meat and cut it into cubes.

3 Melt the fat, stir in the flour and cook for 2–3 minutes. Remove from the heat and gradually add 600 ml (1 pint) stock. Bring to the boil and cook until the sauce thickens, stirring constantly. Add the meat and vegetables; remove from the heat.

4 Beat the egg yolk and cream together, add a little sauce and blend well. Return the mixture to the sauce and heat through without boiling. Add the lemon juice.

5 Pour into a serving dish and garnish with the grilled bacon rolls and parsley sprigs.

CASSEROLING

Casseroles of chicken and other poultry are amongst the tastiest dishes invented. Long slow cooking in a good stock or other flavoursome liquid will make any bird tender enough to cut with a fork. The addition of vegetables, herbs and other ingredients gives an extra dimension of flavour that can be varied endlessly.

Poultry can be casseroled whole, if small, or in portions. The meat from a very large bird such as a turkey is often removed from the bones and cut into cubes for more convenient cooking. The skin may be left on or removed, as you prefer. All types of poultry are good casseroled, though expensive quail and tender baby poussins are generally reserved for plainer methods. The joy of casseroling is that it can turn a bird of doubtful quality into a dish that will satisfy the most demanding gourmet.

To prepare poultry for casseroling, rinse and dry it as usual. Joint it if appropriate. In many recipes for casseroles the meat is first fried in a little oil, butter or margarine to seal in the juices and give a good golden colour. If you use reduced chicken or duck fat, it will give the dish even more flavour. Frying can be done either in the casserole, if it is flameproof, or in

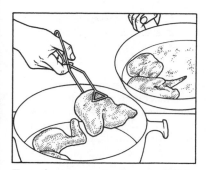

Transferring meat to ovenproof dish

a frying pan and the meat transferred to an ovenproof dish for cooking. The vegetables may also be browned or softened in the hot fat before adding to the meat.

Then, with all the ingredients in the pot, liquid is added; the amount varies from a few spoonfuls if the meat is likely to be tender and juicy itself, to much larger quantities for tougher meats that will require longer cooking. In addition to stock, wine or cider are popular cooking liquids, adding a luxurious flavour.

The oven temperature should be low so that the liquid in the pot never boils, but maintains a gentle simmer. If you have a heavy pot with a tightly fitting lid you can also cook a casserole very gently on top of the stove.

Once the poultry is tender the casserole may be ready to serve just as it is. With some dishes the sauce will need thickening, or the meat can be removed and the sauce boiled to reduce it and concentrate the flavour. If the bird is portioned or the meat cut in cubes, serve straight from the cooking pot. For a whole bird you will need to transfer it to a carving dish for serving, with the sauce in a separate bowl; or you may carve the bird in the kitchen, returning it to the original pot for serving.

CHICKEN IN A POT

Serves 6

25 g (1 oz) butter or margarine
225 g (8 oz) carrots, peeled and sliced
225 g (8 oz) small onions, skinned
100 g (4 oz) streaky bacon, rinded and cut in small pieces
1 lemon
large pinch of thyme
1 garlic clove, skinned
1.8 kg (4 lb) chicken
salt and freshly ground pepper
450 g (1 lb) Jerusalem artichokes
chopped parsley, to garnish

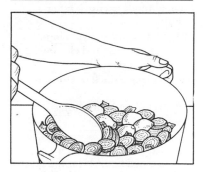

1 Using a flameproof casserole a little larger than the chicken, melt the fat and sauté the carrots, onions and bacon for 10 minutes until browned.

2 Pare the lemon and add the rind to the pan. Stir in the thyme and garlic. Remove the mixture from the pan.

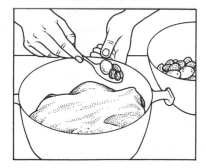

3 Put the chicken in the casserole, spoon the vegetables around it and season lightly. Cover and cook in the oven at 150°C (300°F) mark 2 for 2 hours.

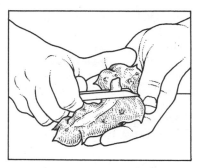

4 Just before the 2 hours are up, peel the artichokes, putting them in salted water to prevent discoloration. When all the artichokes are peeled, drain them and add to the casserole, mixing them gently with the other vegetables.

5 Return the casserole to the oven without its lid, and cook for a further 30 minutes, until the chicken is tender.

6 Remove from the oven; transfer the chicken to a warmed serving dish and spoon the vegetables around it. Keep hot while you reduce the juices.

7 Discard the garlic and lemon rind from the casserole; skim the fat from the juices and boil the juices until reduced by half.

8 Spoon the reduced cooking juices over the chicken and vegetables on the serving dish and sprinkle chopped parsley generously over the top.

TURKEY IN CIDER

Serves 4–6

15 ml (1 tbsp) vegetable oil

1.1–1.4 kg (2½–3 lb) turkey legs

450 ml (¾ pint) chicken stock

1 large onion, skinned and thinly sliced

7.5 ml (1½ tsp) salt

1.25 ml (¼ tsp) freshly ground pepper

40 g (1½ oz) flour

150 ml (5 fl oz) single cream

25 g (1 oz) butter or margarine

175 g (6 oz) mushrooms, sliced

75 ml (5 tbsp) finely chopped parsley

300 ml (½ pint) dry cider

1 Heat the oil in a large sauce-pan and fry the turkey legs until well browned all over. Add the stock, onion, salt and pepper and bring to the boil. Reduce the heat, cover and simmer for 1½–2 hours, or until the meat is tender.

2 Remove the turkey legs from the pan and allow to cool slightly. Discard the skin, carve the meat off the bones and cut into 2.5-cm (1-inch) pieces. Mean-while, boil the cooking stock rapidly until it is reduced to 175 ml (6 fl oz).

3 Blend the flour with half the cream and gradually add to the turkey stock, stirring all the time until smooth. Stir in the remaining cream and cook the sauce over a gentle heat until it boils and thickens, stirring well all the time.

4 Melt the fat in a small pan and sauté the sliced mushrooms until tender. Add them to the sauce with the turkey meat and 60 ml (4 tbsp) of the parsley. Stir in the cider and heat through.

5 Spoon the turkey mixture into a warmed serving dish and garnish with remaining parsley.

DUCK AND ORANGE CASSEROLE

Serves 4

1.8–2.6 kg (4–6 lb) duck, jointed

seasoned flour

knob of rendered duck fat or butter

100 g (4 oz) mushrooms, sliced

2 onions, skinned and chopped

25 g (1 oz) flour

450 ml (¾ pint) duck or chicken stock

150 ml (¼ pint) orange juice

1 orange

1 Coat the duck joints with seasoned flour. Heat the fat in a frying pan and fry the duck joints for 8–10 minutes, until brown, then transfer to a casserole.

2 Fry the mushrooms and onions lightly in the fat in the pan, then add to the casserole.

3 Stir the flour into the fat in the pan and brown it over low heat, stirring all the time. Off heat, stir in stock and juice.

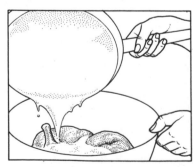

4 Return the pan to the heat and bring the sauce to the boil, stirring; continue to stir until it thickens then pour over the duck.

5 Cover the casserole and cook in the oven at 180°C (350°F) mark 4 for 1 hour, or until the duck is tender.

6 Pare off the coloured part of the orange rind with a vege-table peeler and cut it into very thin strips. Divide the orange it-self into segments, removing any pith or pips.

7 Simmer the strips of rind in water until tender—about 5 minutes; drain well and sprinkle over the cooked duck joints. Garnish with the orange segments.

CHICKEN WITH MINT

Serves 4

25 g (1 oz) butter

4 chicken quarters, halved and skinned, 900 g (2 lb) total weight

900 g (2 lb) potatoes, peeled and thinly sliced

225 g (8 oz) leeks, roughly chopped

30 ml (2 tbsp) chopped fresh mint or 10 ml (2 tsp) dried

15 ml (1 tbsp) flour

salt and freshly ground pepper

60 ml (4 tbsp) chicken stock

chopped fresh mint or parsley, to garnish

1 Heat the butter in a large fry-ing pan, add the chicken quarters, two at a time, and fry until well browned.

2 In a deep, buttered 1.7-litre (3-pint) casserole, layer the potato, chicken and leeks with the mint and flour. Season well between each layer. Finish with a layer of potato. Pour over the chicken stock.

3 Cover the casserole tightly and bake in the oven at 170°C (325°F) mark 3 for 1 hour. Uncover and cook for about a further 30 minutes until the chicken is tender and the top brown. Serve garnished with chopped fresh mint or parsley.

CROCKPOT COOKING

Cooking in a crockpot or electric casserole is a modern extension of the principle of casseroling. By cooking at a low, even temperature for long periods, the foods become tender and flavours blend to give tasty meals with the minimum of trouble and attention.

When cooking poultry in an electric casserole, cut it into small joints and remove all the skin. Be sure frozen poultry is completely thawed before cooking starts.

Some manufacturers state that pre-frying the meat and vegetables is not necessary, but results are much better if you do take the trouble to do this. Fry the poultry pieces and vegetables in a separate pan for 5–10 minutes before putting them in the slow cooker, to give them a good golden colour and seal in the juices and flavour. Stir the stock or cooking liquid into the frying pan, scraping any sediment from the base, and bring that to the boil before you pour it over the poultry.

Once you have done this, you should generally not lift the lid of the casserole until cooking is complete. If you need to add extra ingredients towards the end of the time, allow for the heat loss and increase the cooking time; keep the lid off the casserole for as short a time as possible by adding the fresh ingredients quickly. Don't add frozen vegetables to the slow cooker as they bring down the temperature too much.

Test if the poultry is cooked by piercing with a sharp knife. If more cooking is required replace the lid and cook for at least another hour.

Thickening: To thicken the sauce, either toss the poultry pieces in seasoned flour before pre-frying or blend a little cornflour or flour to a smooth paste with cold water and stir it into the electric casserole at the end of the cooking process. If the dish has been cooked on a high setting the sauce will thicken immediately; on low setting you will need to replace the lid and cook for a further 10–15 minutes.

Adapting recipes

You can cook all your favourite poultry casserole recipes in the electric casserole, but remember to remove all skin and use only about two thirds of the normal quantity of liquid unless rice, pasta or dried beans are to be added at the end.

CREAMED CHICKEN WITH GINGER AND CELERY

Serves 4

40 g (1½ oz) flour
15 ml (1 tbsp) paprika
salt and freshly ground pepper
2.5 ml (½ tsp) ground ginger
4 chicken portions, skinned
50 g (2 oz) butter
15 ml (1 tbsp) vegetable oil
1 medium onion, skinned and chopped
4 sticks of celery, trimmed
225 g (8 oz) button mushrooms
225 g (8 oz) tomatoes, skinned and chopped
450 ml (¾ pint) chicken stock
150 ml (¼ pint) white wine
175 g (6 oz) spaghetti, broken up
142 ml (5 fl oz) soured cream
chopped chives, to garnish

1 Stir the flour, paprika, seasoning and ginger together and coat the chicken portions with the mixture.

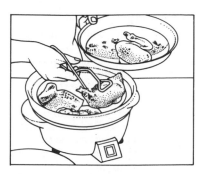

2 Heat the butter and oil in a large frying pan and fry the chicken for 10 minutes until golden brown all over. Remove and place in the casserole.

3 Fry the onion, celery, mushrooms and tomatoes for 2–3 minutes, add the stock and wine and bring to the boil. Pour into the electric casserole.

4 Place the lid in position and cook on high for 3–4 hours or low for 6–8 hours.

5 About 45 minutes before the end of cooking time, turn the electric casserole to high, add the pieces of spaghetti, replace lid and cook until chicken is tender. Stir in cream, garnish and serve.

PRESSURE COOKING

Small birds and poultry joints can be cooked very quickly in a pressure cooker. Use any casserole or poaching recipe.

When cooking a casserole, brown the bird or pieces in hot fat in the pressure cooker, without the trivet. Remove and brown or soften any vegetables. Return the poultry to the cooker, using the vegetables as a bed to keep the bird off the base of the cooker. Add the liquid, according to the weight and cooking time (see chart).

Then put on the lid and bring the cooker to high (15 lb) pressure. Cook for the required time and reduce pressure quickly by placing cooker in a bowl of cold water and running cold water over it.

If the sauce needs thickening, use a little flour mixed with an equal quantity of softened butter. Place the open cooker over the heat and whisk the paste a little at a time into the sauce.

For poaching, stand poultry on the trivet and add vegetables and water. Cook according to the chart. Reduce pressure as above and strain the stock for use in a sauce if wished.

Adding liquid: Calculate the cooking time by the chart. Allow 300 ml ($\frac{1}{2}$ pint) liquid for up to 900 g (2 lb) poultry for the first 15 minutes cooking, then add 150 ml ($\frac{1}{4}$ pint) for every 450 g (1 lb) weight.

GUIDE TO COOKING TIMES IN A PRESSURE COOKER

Chicken	spring and poussin	4–6 minutes per 450 g (1 lb)
	roasting 1.1–1.3 kg ($2\frac{1}{2}$–$3\frac{1}{2}$ lb)	6–8 minutes per 450 g (1 lb)
	boiling fowl 2.2 kg (5 lb)	10–12 minutes per 450 g (1 lb)
	3.1 kg (7 lb) halved	10–12 minutes per 450 g (1 lb)
	joints or pieces	4–6 minutes
Turkey	joints or pieces	10–15 minutes
Duck	whole 1.3 kg ($3\frac{1}{2}$ lb)	6–8 minutes per 450 g (1 lb)
	halved 2–2.7 kg ($4\frac{1}{4}$–6 lb)	4–5 minutes per 450 g (1 lb)
Guinea fowl	whole 700 g ($1\frac{1}{2}$ lb)	6–8 minutes per 450 g (1 lb)
	halved or jointed	4–5 minutes per 450 g (1 lb)

CHICKEN WITH TARRAGON SAUCE

Serves 4

5 ml (1 tsp) salt
freshly ground pepper
25 g (1 oz) butter
a few fresh tarragon leaves, chopped (stalks reserved)
1.4 kg (3 lb) chicken, with giblets
15 ml (1 tbsp) lemon juice
1 medium onion, skinned
1 bay leaf
600 ml (1 pint) water
3 egg yolks
150 ml (5 fl oz) double cream
30 ml (2 tbsp) dry white wine
lemon wedges and extra tarragon leaves, to garnish

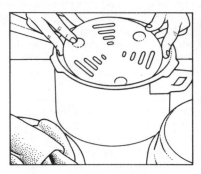

2 Put the trivet in the pressure cooker and stand the chicken and giblets on it. Add the onion, bay leaf and tarragon stalks. Pour on the water and put on the lid.

3 Bring to high (15 lb) pressure. Cook for about 20 minutes.

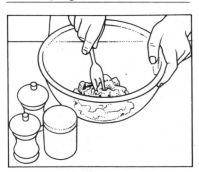

1 Mash the salt and pepper with the butter and tarragon. Rub chicken with the lemon juice and put butter mixture in body cavity.

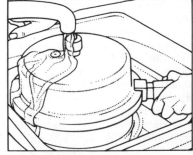

4 Place the cooker in a bowl of cold water and run cold water over it to reduce pressure. Lift out the bird on to a plate.

5 Strain the stock, measure 450 ml (¾ pint) into a saucepan and heat. Whisk together the egg yolks, cream and wine. Remove the stock from the heat, stir in the egg and cream mixture and continue to heat gently, stirring constantly until it thickens. Do not allow to boil. Adjust seasoning.

6 Pour the sauce over the whole chicken and leave to get cold. Carve the chicken and serve on a flat dish garnished with lemon wedges and tarragon leaves.

SPRING CHICKEN CASSEROLE

Serves 4

1.1 kg (2½ lb) chicken
25 g (1 oz) butter or margarine
2 medium onions, skinned and sliced
350 g (12 oz) small carrots, pared
396-g (14-oz) can of tomatoes
600 ml (1 pint) chicken stock
salt and freshly ground pepper
30 ml (2 tbsp) flour

For the parsley dumplings

100 g (4 oz) self raising flour
50 g (2 oz) shredded suet
1.25 ml (¼ tsp) salt
pinch of freshly ground pepper
15 ml (1 tbsp) chopped parsley
about 75 ml (5 tbsp) cold water

1 Cut the chicken into eight pieces and remove the skin. Melt the fat in the uncovered pressure cooker and fry the chicken pieces for 5–10 minutes until they are well browned. Remove the chicken and fry the onions until they are just golden.

2 Return the chicken to the cooker with the carrots, drained tomatoes (reserving the juice), stock and seasoning. Put on the lid and bring to high (15 lb) pressure. Cook for 4–6 minutes.

3 Mix the dumpling ingredients to a soft dough with the water. Divide into eight balls.

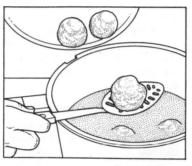

4 Reduce pressure quickly. Bring to boiling point, uncovered, and add the dumplings. Put on the lid and lower the heat to allow the cooker to steam gently for 3 minutes. Increase the heat to bring to low (5 lb) pressure and cook a further 4 minutes. Reduce pressure quickly.

5 Put chicken, vegetables and dumplings in a casserole. Blend the flour to a smooth cream with some of the tomato juice and stir in some of the cooking liquid. Add to the cooker and bring to the boil uncovered, stirring until thick. Pour over the chicken.

BRAISED TURKEY LEGS

Serves 4

4 streaky bacon rashers, rinded
4 turkey drumsticks
30 ml (2 tbsp) vegetable oil
2 medium onions, skinned and quartered
2 carrots, peeled and sliced
2 sticks of celery, trimmed and chopped
100 g (4 oz) mushrooms, sliced
450 ml (¾ pint) chicken or turkey stock
salt and freshly ground pepper
1 bouquet garni
15 ml (1 tbsp) tomato purée
30 ml (2 tbsp) cornflour

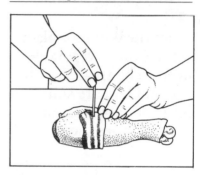

1 Wrap the bacon round the turkey and secure with cocktail sticks. Heat the oil in the uncovered cooker and fry until brown.

2 Remove, and brown the vegetables. Drain off the excess fat, stir in the stock, seasoning, bouquet garni and tomato purée. Put the turkey legs on the vegetables. Cover with the lid and bring to high (15 lb) pressure. Cook for 15 minutes.

3 Reduce pressure quickly. Discard bouquet garni and sticks. Put turkey and vegetables in a serving dish. Mix cornflour to a smooth cream with a little water and add a little cooking liquid.

4 Add the mixture to the cooker and bring to the boil uncovered, stirring until the gravy thickens. Pour over the turkey.

Know your Vegetables

From the commonplace to the exotic, vegetables need to be treated with care. Here are some hints on how to choose and store them.

BUYING AND STORING VEGETABLES

When buying vegetables always choose them carefully and make sure that they are not already old or wilted. Buy little and often to ensure freshness.

Vegetables, like fruits, can be grouped in families and each family needs to be treated in a certain way.

Brassicas and leafy vegetables, which include broccoli, sprouts, cauliflower, cabbages and spinach, don't keep well; 1–2 days in a cool, airy place, 3 days if wrapped in paper and refrigerated.

The **onion** family, which comprises leeks, garlic, shallots and spring onions, need to be chosen carefully. Make sure onions are firm, dry and not sprouting; check that the base of leeks is firm. Onions and garlic can sometimes be bought in strings. They are best stored in a cool, airy place, whereas leeks and spring onions should be wrapped in paper and refrigerated.

Pods and seeds—these are all the beans, peas, okra and sweetcorn. For the best flavour buy peas and beans as young as possible. Okra should be bought with an unmarked skin. Sweetcorn should be clean and green with silky, yellow tassels and plump, tightly packed kernels. Store peas and beans in a cool place or wrap in paper and refrigerate for 1–2 days. (If you shell peas keep them covered in the refrigerator.)

Roots and tubers, like potatoes, swedes, carrots and celeriac, should be bought firm and unwrinkled. If you buy potatoes ready washed in polythene bags it is best to transfer them to a paper bag so that they do not become soft and spongy. Store all these vegetables in a cool, airy place, such as a vegetable rack, so that air can circulate round them.

Stalks and shoots, like celery, artichokes, asparagus and fennel, should be crisp and fresh and any leaf tops should be fresh and

Celery keeps fresh if kept in water

green. Keep them wrapped in paper in the refrigerator or upright in a jug of water.

Nowadays many different types of **mushrooms** are available — button, flat cap and oyster are a few of them. Dried ones like porcini can be bought at delicatessens. Fresh ones should have unblemished skins and should be stored in paper in the refrigerator. As they deteriorate they darken in colour, so make sure they are fresh looking.

Salad leaves, like lettuce, chicory and watercress, should be bought as fresh as possible and unwrinkled. Inspect inner as well as outer leaves as the inner ones can sometimes be slimy. Apart from Iceberg lettuces, which are crisp and firm, most salad leaves do not keep well. Always refrigerate lettuce. You can wash it and dry it well and store it for 1–2 days in the refrigerator in a polythene bag.

Some vegetables are known as vegetable fruits; these include: tomatoes, courgettes, aubergines, avocados, cucumber, peppers and olives. All should be bought with unblemished skins. Tomatoes and avocados can be bought under-ripe and left to ripen.

UNUSUAL VEGETABLES

You may have come across vegetables that you would love to buy but simply don't know what to do with them. Here are some guidelines on how to treat the more unusual ones.

Artichokes, globe: to serve whole, cut off the stalk to make base level, and pull off tough, outer leaves. Tips of leaves may be

Trim the leaf tips off artichokes

trimmed off: cut off about 2.5 cm (1 inch) from the top and snip off the points of the remaining leaves round the sides. To prevent browning, cover in acidulated water. Chokes can be removed before or after cooking: spread the top leaves apart and pull out the central cone of small leaves. Scrape out the hairy choke with a teaspoon and discard, leaving the heart exposed. The heart is considered a delicacy and may be served on its own.

After preparation, globe artichokes take 20–40 minutes to cook in a large pan of boiling salted water until a leaf pulls away easily, then drain upside down. They can also be braised whole, or cut into quarters and the choke removed.

Artichokes, Jerusalem: peel the skin like potatoes, and cover immediately in acidulated water to prevent discoloration. If they are very knobbly and difficult to peel,

scrub them well in water and cook until tender. The skins should then peel away more easily.

Asparagus: wash carefully and trim off woody ends of stalks so that they are all the same length. If the stems are very woody, they can be scraped from tip to base with a sharp knife. Tie the spears in bundles with all the heads together. The bundles can be cooked upright in a special asparagus steamer or tall saucepan or, alternatively, lying down in a wide pan. Pour over boiling water and simmer for 10–15 minutes until tender.

Cardoon: similar to the globe artichoke plant, but cultivated for its leaf stalk which looks like overgrown, greyish-green celery. Trim off the fibrous skin, which is prickly at the ridges. Use raw like celery, or cook like artichokes in acidulated water.

Celeriac: peel, then cut into dice or julienne strips (see under Techniques—page 133). Immerse immediately in acidulated water to prevent browning. Large roots can be quite tough to peel, so it may be easier to cut into slices before peeling. Celeriac can also be eaten grated raw, dressed with lemon juice or vinaigrette dressing.

Fennel: trim off stalks and feathery leaves and reserve for garnish. Wash and trim away any brown bits. Cut into wedges lengthways, or slice crossways. Serve cooked or raw.

Kale: separate leaves from stems, cutting out coarse mid-ribs at base of leaves. Wash well and cut into pieces. Cook as for cabbage.

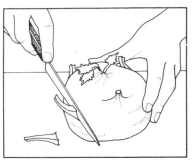

Trim sprouting stalks off the bulb

Kohlrabi/Cabbage Turnip: cut off sprouting stalks around the bulb and trim off the base. Peel, then slice or dice as required, or leave small ones whole. May also be peeled after cooking if preferred. Cook and eat as for turnips.

Okra: wash well, then trim but do not remove the stems (if the seeds inside are exposed, okra lose their shape during cooking and the sticky juices run out). Okra can be sliced into rings (seeds, too) before cooking, or for adding to stews.

Pumpkin and Squash: cut in half and then into wedges. Scoop out the seeds and cut the flesh into cubes for cooking. Small squash can be halved and baked.

Salsify/Scorzonera/Black Salsify: scrub well and trim off the root end. Peel or scrape off the skin, cut into pieces and immediately immerse in acidulated water to prevent browning. If the skin is difficult to peel, wash before cooking, then peel after cooking.

Seakale: trim the roots and wash the stalks. They can be tied in bundles and cooked like asparagus to serve hot or cold.

Seakale Beet/Swiss Chard is prepared and cooked like spinach, although the stalks can be cooked separately like asparagus.

Sweet Potatoes/Yams/Taro Cassava: peel, chop and cook like potatoes. They can also be baked in their jackets.

Preparation Techniques and Equipment for Vegetables

Vegetables are versatile and can be prepared in a number of different ways to add flavour, texture and colour to dishes. Here are some hints on how to prepare a range of vegetables to get the most out of them.

PREPARATION TECHNIQUES

Whether they are to be served raw or cooked, most vegetables need very simple preparation: after thorough cleaning they can be cut to the desired shape and size. However, some vegetables need special attention or a special technique for a particular effect.

CHOPPING
To chop an onion, cut in half lengthways and place on a board with the cut side down. With a very sharp, pointed knife, make horizontal cuts not quite through the length of the onion. Cut down

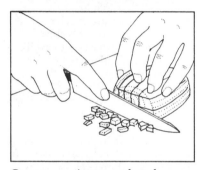

Cut across onions to make cubes

the length of the onion, then follow with downwards cuts across the onion to make cubes. The number of cuts made each way will determine how coarsely or finely chopped the onion will be.

Large, firm vegetables such as cabbages are easier to chop if they

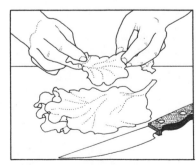

Chop leafy vegetables in layers

are first cut in halves or wedges before cutting lengthways and then across.

Large leafy vegetables can be chopped by placing several leaves on top of each other before cutting.

To chop small leafy vegetables and herbs very finely, first chop or shred the leaves on a large board. With a large, sharp knife, hold down the point with your other hand while chopping quickly with a pivotal action across the

Chopping fresh herbs finely

vegetable. Turn the board at right angles and chop in the same way, repeating until the leaves are finely chopped.

DÉGORGEING
This technique removes the juices from watery vegetables which may be bitter, e.g. aubergines and cucumbers.

1 Cut the vegetables into slices about 5 mm ($\frac{1}{4}$ inch) thick, or according to the recipe. Place in a colander, sprinkling each layer with salt.

2 Cover the slices with a plate, place heavy weights on top and leave to drain for 30 minutes, until the juices have seeped out of the vegetable. Rinse well to remove the salt and bitter juices, then dry with absorbent kitchen paper.

DICING

1 Cut slices either lengthways or across the vegetable to the same thickness as the desired cube, which may be large or small. Cut each slice into sticks.

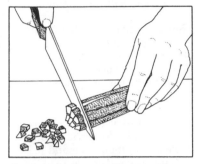

Cutting sliced vegetable into cubes

2 Cut across the sticks to make cubes (some smaller vegetables may be kept whole by careful handling until the final cuts into cubes).

GRATING

Vegetables can be grated finely or coarsely, depending on the grating blade used. Usually used for salads and in some oriental dishes.

JULIENNE

These are strips of vegetable that are matchstick shape and size. Cut the vegetable into thin slices the size of a matchstick. Cut the slices

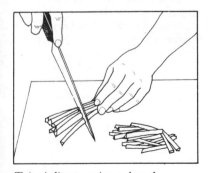

Trim julienne strips to length

into thin sticks, then trim to the desired length.

PREVENTING DISCOLORATION

Some vegetables such as avocado pears and Jerusalem artichokes turn an unpleasant brown colour on contact with the air once they have been peeled or prepared. Acid in the form of lemon juice will prevent them from browning if sprinkled or brushed over the cut surfaces immediately after cutting.

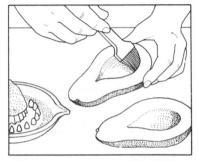

Brush lemon juice over cut avocados

Covering the cut vegetable immediately with cling film will also help prevent browning. If the vegetable is to be served in a salad it may be tossed in a dressing made with lemon juice or vinegar. Vegetables that are going to be cooked may be immersed in water that has been acidulated with a little lemon juice or vinegar.

SHREDDING

A large, firm vegetable like a cabbage should first be cut in half, quarters or wedges. Slice across or lengthways down the vegetable to shave off thin slivers.

For leafy vegetables, place several on top of each other and roll up lengthways. Hold firmly and cut across the roll into very thin slices which will unfurl into long, thin shreds.

SKINNING

Some vegetables can be very difficult to skin, but there are several 'tricks' to make it easy.

To skin tomatoes: place in a bowl or saucepan and pour over boiling water. Leave for a few seconds, then drain and plunge into cold water. The skin should peel off easily. Alternatively, pierce the tomato on a fork and hold over the gas flame until the skin is slightly charred. Leave until cool enough to handle, then peel off.

To skin peppers: place whole or half peppers (skin side up) under a hot grill until all the skin is black and charred. Rub the skins off under cold running water. The pepper underneath will have a deliciously smoky flavour.

EQUIPMENT

For preparing vegetables, the only absolute essentials are a chopping board and selection of sharp knives. However, there are several pieces of equipment and useful gadgets that will save time and energy.

Blender/Liquidiser: will purée vegetables containing liquid and some soft pâté mixtures. Also useful for making soups, drinks, sauces, mayonnaise and dips.

Electric Mixer: useful for mixing large quantities together, e.g. pâtés and stuffings, etc. May have attachments, e.g. liquidiser.

Food Processor: it will chop, shred, slice or grate, or mix different ingredients together; it will also process raw or cooked vegetables. Very useful when preparing large quantities.

Cooking Methods for Vegetables

Cooking vegetables in the correct way is very important to preserve the nutrients as well as the flavour, colour and texture. There are many different methods of cooking, so choose the most appropriate method for the type of vegetable and the time and facilities available. In general, vegetables should be cooked as little ·as possible so that they are still crisp, and never soggy, and they should be served immediately.

HOW TO COOK

BAKING
Vegetables should be baked in a moderate oven without fat or liquid until tender. They can be cooked in their skins such as jacket potatoes, or halved and stuffed (e.g. marrows and peppers), covered or uncovered.
Suitable vegetables for baking Tubers, onions, vegetable fruits and cabbages.

BOILING
Vegetables are cooked in boiling water in a saucepan.
Suitable vegetables for boiling Root vegetables, tubers, onions, brassicas and leaves, vegetable fruits, pods and seeds, pulses and mushrooms.

Root vegetables are prepared and placed in a saucepan and covered with cold water. Cover the pan, bring to the boil and simmer until just tender.

All other vegetables should be added to boiling water; or place the prepared vegetables in a saucepan and pour over boiling water from a kettle. Return to the boil, cover and simmer until just tender but crisp and a bright colour.

Drain off the water and use it for sauces, stocks, soups, etc; or reduce by boiling rapidly and use to glaze the vegetables.

Steam-boiling: use the minimum amount of water and a saucepan with a tight-fitting lid so that the stalks or tougher parts of the vegetable cook in the boiling water and the more delicate tops will cook more gently in the steam. This method is especially suitable for asparagus, cauliflower and broccoli, etc.

Vegetable Purées: can be made from boiled vegetables which have been cooked until tender (but not soggy) so that they are soft enough to purée. Drain off but reserve the cooking water and purée the vegetables in a mouli-légumes or food processor, or work them through a sieve.

BRAISING
Braising is a combination of frying and stewing (boiling). The prepared vegetables are fried in a little oil or fat, then liquid such as stock, water or wine is added to come about half way up the vegetables. Cover the pan and simmer until just tender and most of the liquid has evaporated. Towards the end of the cooking time it may be necessary to uncover the pan and boil the liquid to reduce it.

An alternative method of braising is to place the vegetables in a casserole after frying, add a little liquid, then cover and bake in a moderate oven until tender. This method is suitable for vegetables which are firmer and take longer to cook, and are eaten with their liquid.
Suitable vegetables for braising
Root vegetables, tubers, stalks and shoots.

FRYING
Shallow Frying: vegetables are cooked in an uncovered frying pan in a small amount of hot oil or butter (or a combination of the two). They are turned until golden brown and cooked through. If liked, they can be dusted in seasoned flour before cooking.

Sauté: firm vegetables such as potatoes are par-boiled then thoroughly drained and dried before frying to a crisp, golden brown.

Stir frying: an excellent method for cooking vegetables

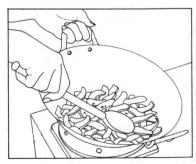

Stir-frying thinly sliced vegetables

quickly so that they retain their colour, flavour and crisp texture. The vegetables are cooked in a little oil over high heat in a wok or large heavy pan, turning all the time until just tender and crisp. Often used in oriental cooking, but preparation is time-consuming as vegetables should be thinly and evenly sliced to cook quickly.

Suitable vegetables for shallow frying

Onions, courgettes, aubergines, Chinese leaf, root vegetables and tubers, pods.

Deep Frying: vegetables are cooked in oil in a deep-fat frier or heavy saucepan. The temperature of the oil varies according to individual vegetables and recipes, but is usually 180°C (350°F) or until a cube of stale bread browns in 1 minute. Except for chips, vegetables are usually coated in flour or batter or egg and bread-crumbs. Place the vegetables in a

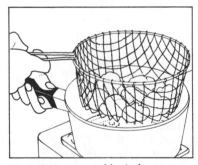

Deep frying vegetables in batter

frying basket or slotted spoon and lower into the hot oil. Cook until golden brown and crisp on the outside and just tender in the middle.

Suitable vegetables for deep frying

Onions, potatoes, aubergines, courgettes, cauliflower and mushrooms.

GRILLING

Vegetables may be cooked under a moderate grill or on a barbecue until browned and crisp on the outside, tender in the centre. They may be brushed with oil or topped with a knob of butter and

Grilling vegetables and kebabs

sprinkled with herbs, spices and seasonings first. Firmer vegetables may need to be par-boiled before grilling. Skewer on to kebab sticks to turn over easily.

Suitable vegetables for grilling

Vegetable fruits, but not avocados or small mushrooms.

PRESSURE COOKING

Very useful for reducing the cooking time and therefore more economical on fuel. With the increased pressure, the water boils at a higher temperature and there-fore cooks the food more quickly. An ideal cooking method for vegetables that normally take a long time to cook, e.g. potatoes, old root vegetables, pulses, etc. but care must be taken with other vegetables as it is very easy to overcook them. Follow manufacturer's instructions carefully for individual vegetables.

Suitable vegetables for pressure cooking

Old root vegetables, tubers, pulses.

ROASTING

Vegetables may be roasted in fat in a hot oven, or placed round a roast joint of meat until golden brown and crisp on the outside and tender inside. Firm vegetables such as potatoes may be par-boiled, then drained and dried before roasting.

Suitable vegetables for roasting

Root vegetables, tubers.

STEAMING

All vegetables which are suitable for boiling can also be cooked in steam over rapidly boiling water. This method takes a little longer than boiling, but preserves the nutrients and texture of the vegetables better. Special steamers

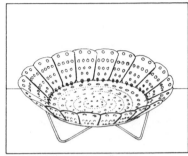

Collapsible steamers fit any pan

are available, otherwise use a saucepan with a tight-fitting lid and fit a collapsible steamer inside, or improvise with a sieve or colander to hold the vegetables. A pressure cooker without the weights is also ideal. Several vegetables may be steamed at once. Layer them up, placing the vegetables that take the longest to cook at the bottom of the steamer, or in the boiling water.

EQUIPMENT FOR COOKING VEGETABLES

Selection of saucepans and frying
  pans
Steamer
Pressure cooker
Deep-fat frier
Wok
Casseroles
Terrines and pâté dishes
Moulds for mousses
Baking dishes: pie, gratin, soufflé,
  tartlet and quiche tins
Roasting tins
Baking trays
Kebab skewers
Colander and sieves
Slices, spatulas, draining spoons
Wooden spoons

Pulses, Grains, Nuts and Seeds

Apart from vegetables, pulses, grains, nuts and seeds form the basis of a vegetarian diet. Nowadays, they are readily available from supermarkets as well as from health shops. Here are some of the ingredients you may not as yet know but which all contribute to a nutritionally balanced diet.

PULSES

Pulse is a collective term for the dried seeds of leguminous plants (peas and beans). Pulses are extremely useful in vegetable and vegetarian cookery as they have a high nutritional content; they are especially rich in protein. Pulses are not primary proteins like meat, fish and dairy produce and do not contain all the necessary amino-acids. However, if eaten in combination with grains, a perfect protein is achieved and they make an excellent cheap and fatless substitute for meat. They are extremely versatile and can be used for making soups, salads, stews or curries.

BUYING PULSES
As they are dried, pulses make a useful store cupboard ingredient. However, although they will keep for a long time, they are best eaten within about 1 year, after which time they become tough even after lengthy cooking. It is, therefore, important to find a shop where the dried pulses are relatively fresh and stock is regularly renewed.

They are often sold loose in health-food shops and delicatessens, and prepacked in supermarkets and grocers.

As well as in their dried form, pulses can be bought already cooked in cans, which saves considerable time in soaking and cooking, but is more expensive.

STORAGE
Pulses should be stored in a cool, dry place. They look attractive if

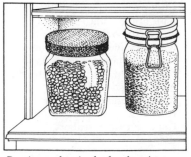
Storing pulses in dark, glass jars

stored in glass jars, but the colours tend to fade if stored in bright light. Ideally, you should store them in dark, glass jars.

Storage time depends on the quality and age of the beans, but as a general rule should not be kept more than a year for the best results.

PREPARATION
Pulses that are sold loose should be carefully picked over and any stones and grit removed; they should then be washed in several changes of cold water to remove dust. Pre-packed varieties should not need such thorough going over but should also be washed carefully.

SOAKING
Most pulses need to be soaked before cooking so that they soften and reconstitute to their original shape and size. The exceptions are split peas and lentils which can be cooked without soaking, but will cook more quickly if they have been pre-soaked.

Always soak pulses in plenty of water as they double in size and weight on soaking. Depending on the time available, they may be soaked in several ways:
Long soaking—soak in a bowl of cold water for 8–12 hours.
Short soaking—(a) place in a bowl, pour over boiling water and soak for 2 hours; (b) place in a large saucepan and pour over cold water. Bring to the boil, cook for 2 minutes, then remove from the heat, cover the pan and leave the beans to soak for 1 hour.

The soaking water should be thrown away. Place the pulses in a sieve or colander and run cold water through the pulse to wash away the impurities that can make pulses indigestible.

COOKING
Place the soaked beans in a saucepan and pour over plenty of water (add salt towards the end of cooking as this can toughen the beans). Bring to the boil and boil

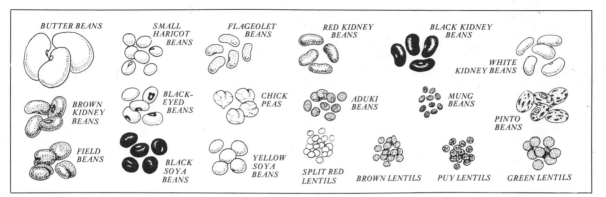

Pulses are an important source of protein in a vegetarian diet

for 10 minutes, then simmer for the required cooking time until tender. (Red kidney beans must always be boiled rapidly for 10 minutes before simmering, since they contain a toxin which can cause intestinal disturbances. This toxicity is destroyed by rapid cooking.) The cooking time will depend on the type and quality of the bean, as well as the length of soaking, and will vary from 30 minutes to 3 hours (soaked lentils will only take 10–15 minutes to cook).

Some beans will produce a scum which should be skimmed off after a few minutes boiling. Once boiled, the beans may be cooked slowly in the oven or in a slow cooker. They may also be cooked in a pressure cooker, but instructions should be followed carefully.

GRAINS

Grains are a valuable addition to vegetable dishes and a vegetarian diet in that they provide variety as well as nutritional content. Eaten in combination with pulses, grains provide the ideally balanced protein meal.

Some grains, like rice, may be familiar, but there are others, like for example, buckwheat, which are less familiar and equally delicious.

BARLEY

Barley is now more widely used for brewing than eating, but is still popular in certain parts of the world, including Scotland.

Pot barley is the whole grain with only the outer husk removed. It needs to be soaked before several hours of cooking to make it tender. It is served like rice as an accompaniment to savoury dishes or added to stews.

Pearl barley is the polished grain with the hull removed. This reduces the nutritional content but makes it easier to cook.

Barley meal/Barley flour are ground from pot and pearl barley, respectively. They contain no gluten, but can be added to wheat flour for making bread.

CORN

'Corn' is sometimes used as a generic term for all grains, but is more specifically applied to maize. There are numerous varieties of corn and it comes in various forms:

Hominy is hulled, dried corn. It can be bought dried, or ready cooked in cans, or ground into 'grits', which are served as a breakfast cereal. The whole grain can be served as an accompaniment or in savoury dishes.

Cornmeal is ground from white or yellow corn, and is available in coarse and medium grinds. There are many cornmeal dishes from the United States, and the Italian dish polenta is made from it. Finely ground white cornmeal is made into Mexican tortilla.

Cornflour/Cornstarch is the white kernel of the corn finely ground into a smooth powder. It is used for thickening, in some cakes and biscuits.

OATS

Oats are a very nutritious cereal, most popular in Scottish cookery. They are rich in fats but lacking in gluten, so they cannot be made into breads.

Oatmeal comes in 3 grades: coarse (pin-head), medium and fine. Medium oatmeal is traditionally made into porridge. Coarse oatmeal is added to soups and stews, and the fine is used for baking cakes and biscuits. The coarser the meal, the longer it will take to cook.

Rolled oats/oatflakes/porridge oats have been steamed and flattened between rollers which makes them quicker to cook than whole oats. Good for savoury crumbles or in a quiche-type pastry.

RICE

Rice is the staple diet of many countries in the world. There are thousands of varieties, but they can be divided into 3 main groups: long, medium and short grains.

Long grain rice is fluffy and separate when cooked, and is best for serving as plain boiled rice and for use in savoury rice dishes. Patna and Basmati are 2 of the best varieties to buy.

Medium and short grain rice produces a stickier, moist rice on cooking and is used for rice puddings, stuffings and risottos. Look for Carolina, Java and Italian varieties.

Brown rice is the whole grain with only the husk removed and is therefore much more nutritious than the processed white or polished rice. As a general rule, brown rice takes twice as long to cook as white rice.

Converted/Easy cook rice has been steam treated so that it cooks quickly and separates well. It is also more nutritious than white rice as the steaming is done before milling and the nutrients from the bran are included.

Ground Rice from polished rice is used for desserts and baked products.

Rice flour is finely ground to a powder, and is used for thickening as well as baking.

Wild Rice is prized for its flavour, colour and texture. Not, strictly speaking, a rice at all but a rare reed. Grown mostly in the United States, it is very expensive.

RYE

A strong-flavoured grain with a high gluten content, rye is often made into bread, particularly in Scandinavia, Germany and Russia.

Whole rye kernels need to be cracked and soaked before cooking until tender. They can be added to many savoury dishes.

Rye flour makes a heavy, brown or black loaf with a distinctive flavour. It can be mixed with wheat flour to give a lighter colour and texture. It is also used to make crispbreads.

BUCKWHEAT

Buckwheat, which is really a seed rather than a grain, has a nutty flavour and is popular in Russia and North East Europe, where it is cooked as a whole grain and also ground into flour for blinis and pancakes. In France, buckwheat is used in crêpe batter.

WHEAT

Wheat is the most common food grain to be cultivated throughout the world and is the staple food in

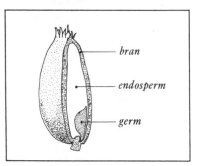

Wholewheat grain

many countries. It comes in many different forms, from the whole wheat grain to finely milled and sifted. Wholewheat flour can be made into pastry for pizzas, quiches, pies and used in bread.

Wholewheat grain must be soaked and then boiled in water for a couple of hours. It can then be eaten in the same way as rice to accompany meat, fish or vegetables, or made into a salad. It can also be boiled into a porridge like the old-fashioned 'frumenty' and served with spices and honey.

Sprinkle cracked wheat over salads

Cracked/Kibbled wheat is the whole grain cracked between rollers so that it takes less time to cook. It is eaten in the same way as wholewheat, or can be sprinkled on top of breads and salads as a crunchy topping.

Burghul/Bulgar is cracked wheat that has been hulled and par-boiled, which makes it easier to cook with a lighter texture and flavour. It can be eaten like rice or in salads. It is used in the Middle Eastern dish, tabbouleh.

Bran is the thin outer covering of the wheat grain which is removed during the refining process. It is valuable for providing extra roughage, and can be eaten raw, sprinkled on to cereals and salads or added to bread, and cake mixtures.

Wheat germ is the heart of the wheat grain and is rich in nutrients. Use like bran.

Semolina is produced during milling from the starchy part of the grain. It is often used to make milk puddings and cakes, and also for couscous and gnocchi.

Wheat flours can be divided into 2 basic types:

Hard wheat/high gluten flour grows in hot dry areas of the world and is used for making bread and pasta.

Soft wheat/low gluten flour grows in temperate climates and is used for cakes, biscuits and general use.

BUYING GRAINS

Grain products are usually bought dried and are therefore a useful store cupboard food. They do not keep indefinitely, however, and should be bought from a shop where you know there is a high turnover and the goods will be as fresh as possible and not infested by insects. They may be bought loose or prepacked.

STORAGE

Grains should be stored in a cool, dry place as they will deteriorate quickly in a warm, damp atmosphere. Prepacked grains can be stored in their packets if unopened, but once opened or if bought loose should be transferred to airtight containers such as glass or polythene.

Grains that contain fats such as oats do not keep very well as they turn rancid; they should only be kept for 1 month.

PREPARATION

Grains that are sold loose should be picked over to remove any grit, then washed. Prepacked grains should not need cleaning.

Whole grains usually need soaking in water for a few hours or overnight to soften them so that the cooking time will be reduced. Soaking varies from one type of grain to another: follow instructions on individual packets or recipes.

COOKING

The amount of cooking required depends on the type of grain and the degree of processing it has undergone, so follow individual packet or recipe instructions. The more it has been processed the less cooking it will need, and some grain products such as flakes can be eaten raw as cereals, salads or toppings.

Grains can, therefore, be served in numerous ways to provide an economical and wholesome contribution to the diet.

NUTS AND SEEDS

Nuts and seeds are a valuable food in their own right and are particularly useful in a vegetarian diet as they provide vegetable protein, fat, vitamins and minerals. They also add variety with their range of flavours and textures.

Nuts and seeds are extremely versatile and can be used raw in appetisers, snacks, salads, toppings, garnishes and cold desserts. Nuts can also be cooked into many savoury and sweet dishes such as nut pâtés and roasts for vegetarian meals, or added to vegetable, meat and fish dishes, and baked into pastries, cakes, biscuits and hot puddings. Ground nuts can also be used as a thickening agent for sauces or instead of flour in some cakes.

BUYING NUTS AND SEEDS

Fresh nuts in their shells are usually sold in greengrocers and vegetable departments of supermarkets. Buy them as fresh as possible when they are new in season and still sweet and moist and heavy for their size. As they get older they will dry out and rattle in their shells.

Shelled nuts may be sold loose or already prepacked, and may be plain or roasted. They can be bought whole, halved or split, flaked, chopped or ground. Bought from grocers and supermarkets they are usually blanched with the inner skins removed, but in healthfood shops they are often sold in their skins.

Some nuts such as chestnuts are preserved in cans or jars either whole or as a purée. Sesame seeds are made into a paste such as tahini, and peanut butter is made by grinding peanuts. Nuts should be bought in small quantities as their high oil content makes them deteriorate quickly.

Pumpkin, sesame and sunflower seeds are the most commonly available. They are very nutritious, being rich in minerals and vitamins. Buy in small quantities and use raw in salads or roast them.

STORAGE

Nuts and seeds should be stored in a cool, dry place to preserve the oil content as long as possible. Shelled nuts should be stored in airtight containers.

PREPARATION

Nuts in shells need to be cracked open using nut crackers, or a hammer against a hard surface.

The thin, brown, inner skin surrounding the nut kernel can be left on or removed by blanching. To blanch, pour boiling water over the nuts and leave for a few seconds or minutes (depending on the type of nut). While still warm, the skins will peel off easily, or, in

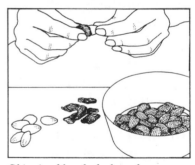

Skinning blanched almonds

the case of almonds, chestnuts and pistachios, they can be pinched between thumb and forefinger and the nuts will slip out. Hazelnuts need to be toasted until lightly browned before the skins will loosen, then they can be rubbed against each other in a bag or clean tea towel to remove the skins. Nuts such as almonds, cashews, peanuts can also be fried, toasted, roasted or grilled until golden.

Nuts can be halved, chopped or ground using a sharp knife on a chopping board. For large quantities it is quicker to use a nut mill, blender or food processor. Do not store ground nuts for they tend to go rancid quickly.

Herbs, Spices and Other Flavourings

The term herb applies when leaves, flowers and sometimes the stem of a non-woody plant are used, either fresh or dried. A spice, on the other hand, refers to parts of an aromatic, often woody plant and may include the seeds, bark or roots. It is usually dried and then used either whole or ground. Herbs and spices can be used either individually or in combinations.

A–Z OF HERBS

ANGELICA
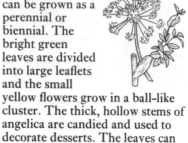
A tall plant that can be grown as a perennial or biennial. The bright green leaves are divided into large leaflets and the small yellow flowers grow in a ball-like cluster. The thick, hollow stems of angelica are candied and used to decorate desserts. The leaves can be used fresh in savoury dishes and both stems and leaves are used for herb teas.

BASIL
Basil is a delicate annual plant that survives only during the summer months. It has small, soft, oval leaves and tiny white flowers. It can be used fresh or dried, in most savoury dishes and is particularly good in those that contain tomatoes. It is also an essential ingredient in the famous Italian pesto sauce. Try it in soups, sauces and dressings, stuffings and casseroles.

BAY
Bay leaves come from an evergreen tree that can be kept small in pots or allowed to grow to full height in the open. The leaves are large, flat, oval and glossy. Used fresh but most often dried (the fresh leaves can sometimes taste rather bitter), bay leaves are tied into bouquets garnis, they can also be used alone (both whole and crumbled) to flavour sauces, soups and casserole dishes, as well as milk puddings, creams and custards. Always discard the whole bay leaves before serving.

BERGAMOT
Bergamot is a perennial plant, bushy and about 30 cm (12 inches) high. The leaves are broad and oval and the flowers large, red and shaggy. Bergamot is mostly used to make a herbal tea known as oswego tea, but it can also add a fresh flavour to summer drinks. Use sparingly in salads.

BORAGE
Borage is an annual plant with large, fleshy, hairy leaves and small blue flowers. The leaves have a delicate, cucumber like flavour and, when young, can be added to summer salads. They can also be candied. Both flowers and leaves can be added to summer drinks such as Pimm's, and the flowers are used to decorate fruit salads.

CHAMOMILE
Chamomile is an annual plant with feathery leaves and white, daisy-like flowers. It should not be confused with the low-growing lawn chamomile. Rarely used in cooking, chamomile's chief use is in making a delicate-flavoured, soothing tea (for which the dried flower-heads are used).

CHERVIL
Chervil is an annual plant, closely related to parsley. It has very delicate, lacy leaves with a hint of liquorice about their flavour. Because they are so delicate, large amounts of the fresh herb must be

used. Chervil can be used in fish dishes and herb butters, and is particularly good with eggs and with vegetables such as carrots. It also brings out the flavour of other herbs, and is used in *fines herbes* mixtures (see page 156).

CHIVES

Chives are a perennial member of the onion family. The thin, almost grass-like leaves grow in clumps and have a delicate, onion flavour. Snip them away with scissors and more will grow. Chives are often added to egg salads and omelettes and they are good with oily fish, in green summer salads and in herb butters. The tufted purple flowers are edible and make a pretty garnish.

COMFREY

Comfrey is a tall, perennial plant with clusters of purple, bell-like flowers and large, fleshy, hairy leaves. It is often used medicinally, but the fresh leaves can be cooked in butter or deep-fried and eaten as a vegetable. They can also be used (dried and powdered) in herbal teas and, when young, can be added to salads. In addition, the dried root is sometimes used to flavour country wines.

CORIANDER

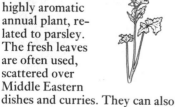

Coriander is a highly aromatic annual plant, related to parsley. The fresh leaves are often used, scattered over Middle Eastern dishes and curries. They can also be used sparingly in salads and stuffings, and look good sprinkled over summer soups.

CURRY PLANT

The curry plant is a shrubby perennial plant that grows into a low spreading bush with green, spiky leaves. Although it is not used in authentic Indian curries, the leaves do have a strong curry-like flavour. Add them sparingly to winter soups and stews, to stuffings for game and to veal dishes. They can be used fresh or dried.

DILL WEED

Dill is an annual plant, related to parsley and growing quite tall with feathery leaves. These are referred to as dill weed so as to distinguish them from the seed (see spices). Dill is often used in cucumber salads and pickles. It is good with fish and summer vegetables, and in Scandinavia is an essential ingredient in the dish of salted raw salmon known as Gravlax. It is also macerated in wine vinegar to make dill vinegar.

FENNEL

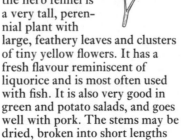

Not to be confused with the bulbous stem vegetable, Florence fennel, the herb fennel is a very tall, perennial plant with large, feathery leaves and clusters of tiny yellow flowers. It has a fresh flavour reminiscent of liquorice and is most often used with fish. It is also very good in green and potato salads, and goes well with pork. The stems may be dried, broken into short lengths and placed under meat which is to be barbecued.

LAVENDER

Lavender is a well-loved, sweetly scented perennial plant with long, spearlike, grey-green leaves and spikes of purple flowers. Lavender is usually grown for its aromatic properties, but it can be added to mixtures of herbs for stews, casseroles and marinades for game. The flowers can be crystallised, used to make conserves or made into jelly.

LEMON BALM

This perennial plant is also known as balm or bee-balm. It has pale green, heart-shaped leaves which have a distinct lemony flavour. Use them in fish and poultry dishes, in sauces, marinades and stuffings. They can be added to salads, cream cheese, fruit salads and milk puddings, and will make a refreshing addition to summer fruit cups as well as a soothing tea.

LEMON VERBENA

Lemon verbena is a perennial plant that likes a warm, sunny situation. It is a tall shrub with long, pale green, pointed, lemon-scented leaves, which can be used in stuffings (sparingly) and to flavour fish and poultry. Add them to fruit salads and sweet puddings, or use them to flavour wine cups and to make a refreshing tea.

LOVAGE

A medicinal as well as a culinary herb, lovage grows very tall, with dark, shiny leaves and clusters of yellow flowers. It has a celery-like flavour, which adds a sharp spiciness to casseroles and soups, as well as green salads and omelettes.

MARJORAM

Although there are two varieties of marjoram (sweet and wild), the name marjoram is usually applied to the sweet—the wild being more commonly referred to as oregano (see right). Sweet marjoram is a low-growing perennial plant with small, oval leaves. It has a spicy, slightly sweet flavour that will enhance rather than mask delicate flavours. Marjoram is often tied into bouquets garnis, and is used to flavour soups and stews. It is good with pork, veal and poultry, eggs and vegetables; and also in milk drinks and puddings.

MINT

There are many different varieties of this perennial, oval-leaved plant. The one most used is *spearmint*. It is a favourite accompaniment to lamb, and is made into mint jelly and a mint sauce with vinegar. Add a sprig to new potatoes and green peas as they cook and scatter chopped fresh mint over them for serving. Add chopped mint to salads (both sweet and savoury) and to Middle Eastern tabbouleh. *Applemint* has rounded slightly furry leaves. As its name implies, it has a slight apple flavour. It makes delicious mint sauce and jelly and a sprig added to apple jelly as it cooks will improve the flavour. Chopped applemint leaves can be added to fresh fruit salads or sprinkled over cut grapefruit. *Peppermint* has dark green, shiny leaves with a hint of purple. Oil distilled from them contains menthol and is used to flavour confectionery, liqueurs and toothpaste. The chopped leaves can be added to fruit salads and made jellies, sauces and peppermint tea.

OREGANO

Also known as wild marjoram, oregano is a perennial plant. It has a more pungent, spicy flavour than sweet marjoram (see left) and it is much used in Italian cooking, adding interest to pasta dishes and pizzas. It also makes a good addition to vegetable dishes, particularly those containing tomatoes, aubergines, courgettes and sweet peppers. It is nearly always used dried.

PARSLEY

Parsley is probably the most used of all herbs. It is a biennial plant with bright green leaves which can either be curled (English parsley) or flat (Continental parsley). It is always included in bouquets garnis and *fines herbes*. It can be used too as a garnish for all savoury dishes and can be chopped into salads and herb butters. It can also be used to make parsley sauce, and tartare and Ravigote sauce and is excellent with fish and seafood, with veal, poultry, eggs and vegetables.

ROSEMARY

Rosemary is a perennial, shrubby bush, the leaves of which can be picked all through the year. They are small and spiked, dark green on one side and grey-green on the other. Rosemary has a strong, pungent flavour. It may overpower other herbs, so is best used on its own to flavour lamb, pork and poultry, root vegetables and fish. In small quantities it can also be used to flavour bread rolls and scones. It is available fresh, as dried leaves or in powder form.

RUE

Rue is a perennial herb with a woody stem and small, blue-green, irregularly cut leaves. It has a slightly bitter flavour so should be used sparingly. Add tiny amounts of the chopped leaves to salads and a small pinch to cream or cottage cheese or egg for sandwiches. It is dangerous to use rue in large quantities as some people are allergic to it.

SAGE

Sage is a perennial herb with grey-green, oval leaves. It has been used for centuries to flavour and counteract the richness of fatty meats such as pork, goose and duck. It has also been used to flavour cheese and can be put into cheese dishes. It is often included in a bouquet garni and can be added to casseroles, stews, stuffings and sausages.

SALAD BURNET

Salad burnet is a perennial herb, its leaves grow in a fountain-shaped clump. Each has a red stem with six or more pairs of round leaflets on either side. Salad burnet has a slightly bitter, cucumber-like flavour and the young leaves can be added to salads and used to flavour vinegar. It can also be added to vegetable dishes and soups and stuffings.

SAVORY

There are two types of savory, the perennial winter and the annual summer savory. They look similar with small, spiky dull-green leaves. Both have a peppery flavour, but that of summer savory is fresher. Both types are good with pork and can be added to beef casseroles, egg dishes, tomato-flavoured sauces and veal pies. Summer savory is known as 'the bean herb'. Add it to both broad and runner beans.

SORREL

For flavour and delicacy of texture, choose French sorrel with its shiny, large, spear-shaped leaves. It is a perennial plant and can be picked for most of the year. It can be used to make the delicately-flavoured sorrel soup and also in omelettes, sauces and stuffings (particularly with fish). The raw leaves can be chopped and added to salads and can also be cooked alone as a vegetable.

SWEET CICELY

Sweet cicely is a tall, attractive perennial plant with ferny leaves and clusters of tiny white flowers. The leaves have a sweet, aniseed-like flavour. Add them to green salads and salad dressings, omelettes and pancakes. They are also delicious sprinkled into fruit salads, and act as both sweetener and flavouring when cooked with tart fruits. Sweet cicely is often used as a flavouring for liqueurs.

TANSY

A tall perennial plant with ferny, dark-green leaves and button-like yellow flowers. Use the youngest leaves as they are the most tender. Traditionally, chopped tansy has been added to omelettes, but it can also be put into stuffings, casseroles and sausages. With the chopped leaves of sage and mint, it makes a delicious herb butter.

TARRAGON

The best culinary variety is French tarragon. It is a perennial which dies down in autumn and has narrow, green shiny leaves and a spicy flavour. Russian tarragon is less spicy. Tarragon is often used in chicken dishes and is an essential ingredient in Béarnaise, Tartare and Hollandaise sauces and in *fines herbes*. It can also be used to make herb butter and added to salads.

THYME

The low-growing, perennial thyme with its tiny, dull green leaves is a favourite in most herb gardens. Tie it into bouquets garnis and use it in soups, stuffings, casseroles and sauces. It goes well with all meats and can be added to a court bouillon for poaching fish. Use the chopped leaves to make herb butter, add them to bread and scone doughs and use them to make a jelly to serve with roast meats.

Lemon thyme is a variety of thyme. A low-growing perennial with tiny, shiny leaves on woody stems, its flavour is that of lemon with strong undertones of thyme. Use it with fish dishes, and also with lamb and veal. Add the leaves to fruit salads and put a sprig into the pan when scalding milk or cream for sweet dishes.

WOODRUFF

Woodruff is a delicate, perennial plant with small, spiked leaves growing in whirls around the delicate stems. The white star-like flowers grow on the top ruff of leaves. Woodruff has a vanilla-like scent and can be used like a vanilla pod. Steep the leaves in milk before making custard or pastry cream, or add it to the saucepan while you are scalding cream to make ice-cream.

A–Z OF SPICES

AJOWAN

Small, light brown, slightly elongated seeds which have a rather coarse flavour of thyme, ajowan is a spice related to caraway and cumin. It is used most often in Indian cookery, both to flavour food and to counteract the effect of ingredients such as pulses which can cause flatulence. It is also used medicinally to relieve stomach upsets.

ALLSPICE

Also known as Jamaica pepper, the seeds of allspice are just slightly larger than peppercorns and dark brown in colour. Despite its alternative name it is not peppery in flavour, but delicately spicy with a tinge of cloves, cinnamon and nutmeg. Allspice can be bought whole or ground and it can be added to both sweet and savoury dishes. Add ground allspice to ginger cakes and scald whole seeds in milk for making puddings and custards. It is also an ingredient in pickling spice and is used in salting meats.

ANISEED

The tiny, purse-shaped seeds of anise have a warm, sweet, pungent flavour and can be used in sweet and savoury dishes.
Add them to cakes, biscuits and confectionery, to the syrups of fruit salads and to syllabubs and custards. Their flavour also goes well with fish and pork, vegetables and cream cheese.

ANISE PEPPER

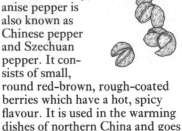

Used mainly in Chinese cookery, anise pepper is also known as Chinese pepper and Szechuan pepper. It consists of small, round red-brown, rough-coated berries which have a hot, spicy flavour. It is used in the warming dishes of northern China and goes with fish, chicken and lamb. When ground and dry-fried with salt it is used as a condiment for seafood. Anise pepper is one of the ingredients of five-spice powder (see page 635).

CARAWAY

The small, elongated, dark brown seeds of caraway have a warming but slightly sharp flavour. Their valuable digestive properties make them particularly suitable for eating with rich, fatty foods such as pork, but they are also excellent added to cabbage dishes and sauerkraut. Most often, however, they are added to cakes and pastries and baked apples. In Germany they are used to flavour cheese and are an ingredient in some liqueurs.

CARDAMOM

Available as pods and seeds, cardamom comes from a perennial plant related to ginger. The pods (which contain the seeds) can be either green or black. Cardamom seeds should always be bought inside their pods, removed by crushing and discarding the pods, and ground at home as, once ground, their light, sweet, sherbety flavour is quickly lost. Green cardamom has the finer flavour and is added to both sweet and savoury dishes,

particularly in Indian cooking. Use it with meat, poultry and rice; add it to Turkish coffee and hot punches. Black cardamom has a slightly coarser flavour but may be used in the same ways.

CASSIA

Related to cinnamon. The dried bark, the dried unripe seeds and the dried leaves are all used in cookery. The bark has a similar flavour to cinnamon but is not as strong; it may be used in the same way as cinnamon sticks. The seeds, sometimes known as Chinese cassia buds, are used in drinks and confectionery and are added to pots pourris.

CAYENNE PEPPER

Derived from a hot, red variety of the capsicum family. The pods are small, long and narrow and, when picked and dried, both pods and seeds are ground together. Cayenne pepper has a clean, sharp flavour and is used for flavouring seafood in many parts of the world. It is also added to Indian curries and the spiced stews of the Middle East, as well as the classic brown and Hollandaise sauces in Western cooking.

CELERY SEEDS

The tiny, light brown, slightly elongated seeds of celery have a bitter, celery flavour and therefore should be used sparingly in soups and casseroles. Add them to a court bouillon for poaching fish and to pickle mixtures for vegetables and seafood. A small pinch will enliven a salad dressing; they can also be added to bread rolls.

CHILLIES

Small varieties of capsicum with a specially hot flavour. *Whole dried chillies* are added to pickling spice and are used for flavouring spiced vinegars. They can be finely chopped and added to hot spiced dishes when fresh chillies are not available. The seeds are the hottest part, so if you want a less fiery flavouring, omit these. Always wash your hands thoroughly after handling chillies. *Chilli powder* is made by grinding dried red chillies and has a clean, fresh, hot taste. It is added to Indian curries, spiced Middle Eastern dishes and used in Caribbean and Creole cookery. It is good with seafood and in sauces. *Chili Seasoning* consists of chilli powder that has been mixed with oregano, chocolate, cumin and other flavourings. It is often used in Mexican dishes and is popular in the United States. *Fresh chillies* are small and tapering and should look smooth and shiny. They are sold either unripe (green) or ripe (red). They have a hot flavour and are used in curries and other hot dishes; they can also be added very sparingly to salads made from dried pulses. Core and seed them before use, although a few seeds can be left in if a very hot, pungent effect is needed for a particular recipe.

CINNAMON

Native to Ceylon, cinnamon is the bark of a tree which is a member of the laurel family. The bark is peeled from the young shoots of the tree, then left to dry in the sun so that it curls into quills, known as cinnamon sticks. The bark of the cassia tree is often sold as cinnamon, which it resembles closely, both in flavour and appearance. Known for centuries for its fragrant and therapeutic qualities, cinnamon has many uses in cooking. Use the sticks to infuse flavour into drinks, pickles, fruit compotes, milk puddings and casseroles. Ground cinnamon is best for cakes and puddings—it has a special affinity with chocolate.

CLOVES

The name clove comes from the Latin word for nail, *clavus*, which the spice resembles in appearance. Cloves are in fact the flower buds of an evergreen shrub native to the Moluccas or Spice Islands, but nowadays the majority are imported from Zanzibar and Madagascar. The volatile oil of cloves is a powerful antiseptic (it is a standard remedy for toothache) and cloves are also used in the making of pomanders. In cooking, cloves are used both in their whole and ground form. Whole cloves are most often used in marinades for meat and fish, and for infusing pickles and hot drinks; they are also used for studding whole onions and hams. Use ground cloves in baking and puddings, particularly with apples.

CORIANDER

Round, light brown seeds with a fresh, spicy flavour. They can be bought whole or ground and are used in many Indian and Pakistani dishes. Their flavour is improved if they are gently dry-roasted before grinding. Use coriander in curries and put the whole seeds into vegetables à la grecque. Ground coriander can be added to bread and cakes. The spice is an ingredient in liqueurs and vermouths.

CUMIN

Small, dark brown, elongated seeds with a rich, dry flavour. Cumin is frequently used in Indian and Middle Eastern dishes. In European cooking the whole seeds are sometimes used in pickling. A sweet, spicy drink is made with cumin, ginger and tamarind, but apart from this cumin is not used in sweet dishes.

DILL

The oval, flattened seeds of the dill plant are dried and used whole as a spice. Use them in pickles and sprinkle them sparingly into salads. They can be added to cabbage and to dishes of braised root vegetables. Like caraway seeds, they can be added to cake mixtures, buns and confectionery.

FENNEL SEEDS

The tiny, purse-like seeds of fennel have a warm, slightly bitter, aniseed flavour. They have strong digestive qualities and so are often used with rich meats and oily fish. Sprinkle them over mackerel or herrings before grilling. Add them to pork and creamy sauces. They can also be used to flavour pickles and added to bread and cakes. Fennel is also used occasionally to flavour curries.

FENUGREEK

Small, hard, yellow-brown seeds. To remove their slightly bitter taste, fry them in hot oil before using until they brown. Whole or ground fenugreek is used in the cooking of Mediterranean countries, but is most often used in Indian curries. The whole, untreated seeds can be used to flavour pickles; they can also be sprouted and used in salads, providing an excellent source of vitamin E.

GINGER

Dried ginger root can be bought whole, taking the form of small, fibrous, light-coloured pieces about 2.5–5 cm (1–2 inches) long; or ground in the form of a light, beige-coloured powder. The whole pieces should be bruised before being used in pickling. *Ground ginger* is often used to flavour cakes, biscuits, puddings, wines and cordials. *Fresh ginger root* has a warm, citrus-like flavour. It is usually peeled and grated or finely chopped and used to flavour fish, poultry, soups and casseroles. It is also added to curries and other oriental and South-east Asian dishes. Try it in marinades for chicken and fish.

JUNIPER

Round, purple-brown berries, about twice the size of pepper-corns with smooth skins. They are always bought whole and are easy to grind as they are soft. Juniper berries are often included in spice mixtures for meat and are excellent with pork and game. They can be added to casseroles and pâtés, and are also good with cabbage. Juniper berries are an important flavouring ingredient in gin.

LAOS POWDER

Closely related to ginger and is similar in that the root is the part used. It has a peppery ginger taste and is used in the hot dishes of Southeast Asia. In Europe it is used to flavour liqueurs and bitters. It is also known as galangal or galingale.

MACE

Mace blades form the outer casing of the nutmeg (see right). They are bright red when harvested and dry to a deep orange. Mace can be bought whole in the form of small lacy orange pieces or blades, or ground to an orange powder. The flavour is similiar to nutmeg, but more delicate. Blades of mace are often used to flavour sauces. Ground mace is added to stuffings, pâtés, soups, stews, cheese sauces and cakes.

MUSTARD SEED

There are three types of mustard seed, black, brown and white. *Black mustard* is grown in only a few areas in Europe. *Brown mustard* has a similar flavour and is used in most English mustard mixes. *White mustard* is used mostly in American mixed mustards. Whole mustard seeds are used in pickling and can also be used in stuffings, sausages and certain curried dishes—particularly those containing spinach. They are increasingly being used in spiced grainy mustards.

English Mustard Powder was once made from ground black mustard seeds, but since these have become more scarce it is made from brown mustard with a little white mustard added. Also added are ground turmeric and wheat flour. To mix, add warm water to make a fine paste and leave for 10 minutes. Mustard powder has numerous uses in cooking, wherever a hot flavour is called for.

NUTMEG

Bought whole, as a small, oval, shiny nut, or ground. If bought whole, grate it only as you need it using a special nutmeg grater or other fine grater.

Nutmeg can be used in sweet and savoury dishes. Add it to puddings, cakes and biscuits and grate it over milk puddings. Use it with vegetables (particularly spinach); in sausages and stuffings and Middle Eastern spiced dishes; and in punches and night-time drinks.

PEPPER

Available whole or ground. Black and white peppercorns come from a tropical vine. To produce *black pepper* the berries are picked when green and dried whole. For *white pepper*, they are allowed to ripen and turn red and the skin is removed before drying. White pepper has a milder flavour than black. It is used in delicately flavoured dishes and light-coloured sauces and mayonnaise. Black pepper is used in most savoury dishes and can also be used in desserts. *Green peppercorns*: Some peppercorns are picked when still green and pickled in brine or vinegar or in their own juices.

These can be used whole or

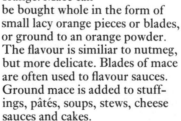
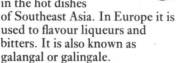

coarsely crushed, and give a hot 'pickle' taste to recipes. They are used to flavour most meats and game (but particularly steak and duck) pâtés and sausages and savoury butters. Green pepper-corns also go well with fresh strawberries.

Pink peppercorns are totally un-related to the black peppercorn family, but come from a com-pletely different plant, sometimes known as Brazilian pepper. Al-though they enjoyed some popu-larity a few years ago, this was short-lived as it was discovered that they can cause an allergic reaction.

POPPY SEED

Sometimes called maw seeds, these are derived from the opium poppy. The most common type in Europe is called black poppy seed, although in colour the tiny round seeds are blue-grey. The type used in India has a smaller, creamy-yellow seed. Both have a distinct nutty flavour.

Poppy seed is used in curries, but most often is sprinkled over breads and used as a filling in cakes and pastries.

SAFFRON

The tiny dried stigmas of the saffron crocus, this is the most expensive spice in the world. The stigmas or strands of saffron should be a brilliant orange colour and have a pungent, bitter taste.

Ground saffron is usually cheaper, but does not have such a good flavour and varies enor-mously in quality.

Saffron is used extensively in Indian and Mediterranean cooking and to flavour many rice dishes such as pilafs and paella, soups and fish dishes.

SESAME

Tiny, flat, oval seeds which may be red, light brown or black. They have a rich, nutty flavour and are often sprinkled over breads. They can also be toasted and used in salads and sprinkled over hot spiced dishes. A nutty flavoured edible oil is derived from sesame seeds. They are also ground to produce a rich grey paste known as tahini, which is used for dips, a dip of chick peas called hummus.

STAR ANISE

The star-shaped fruit of an ever-green tree native to southwest China. When dried it is a red-brown colour and the flavour is one of pungent aniseed.

In China, star anise is used to flavour stewed and simmered dishes, particularly those of duck, beef, chicken and lamb. It is also placed under whole fish for steam-ing. It is used whole and one star is quite sufficient to flavour a large dish. Star anise is one of the in-gredients of five-spice powder (see page 635).

TURMERIC

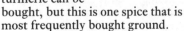

Related to ginger and the part used is the knobbly rhizome, which is bright orange in-side the peel. Whole pieces of turmeric can be bought, but this is one spice that is most frequently bought ground.

Use it quickly as its flavour de-teriorates on keeping. Turmeric is used in curries and curry powder and is added to mustards and pickles. Its bright colour makes it useful for colouring rice and sweet Indian dishes.

VANILLA

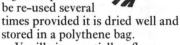

The pod of a type of orchid, yellow-green when picked and dark brown after curing and dry-ing. The pod can be re-used several times provided it is dried well and stored in a polythene bag.

Vanilla is essentially a flavour-ing for sweet dishes particularly ice creams, custards and pastry cream. Use it to flavour hot choc-olate or coffee drinks and infuse it in wine cups. Keep it permanently in a jar of caster sugar to make your own vanilla sugar.

GRINDING YOUR OWN SPICES

Spices taste better when freshly ground. Peppercorns and allspice berries can have their own peppermills. Small amounts of spice can be crushed with a pestle and mortar or with a rolling pin. Grind large amounts in an electric or hand grinder, remembering to wipe it out well each time with kitchen paper, so that no cross flavouring occurs. Most spices benefit from being gently dry-fried for a few minu-tes before being ground. This releases extra flavour, especially with spices such as cumin and coriander. To dry-fry spices, see page 635.

OTHER FLAVOURINGS

ASAFOETIDA

This is not a true spice but is derived from the resin of a plant native to Afghanistan and Iran. It can be bought in solid form but as it is very hard is best bought ground, in powder form. The flavour is pungent, a little like spicy garlic. Like ajowan, it is used to counteract flatulence. Asafoetida is used in very small quantities, mainly in Indian cooking for pickles, fish and vegetables. In India, it is often used as a substitute for salt.

CAPERS

The pickled buds of the caper bush that grows wild around the Mediterranean. Capers are dull green, pointed at one end and with a pungent pickle flavour. They are used with fish and in sauces such as Tartare, Remoulade and Ravigote. They can also be used to flavour butter and as a garnish, sprinkled over salads and seafood.

COCONUT MILK

The coconut milk referred to in many recipes has nothing to do with the natural 'milk' or juice in the centre of the coconut, but is actually made using either fresh coconut or creamed coconut (sold in compressed block form in supermarkets and delicatessens). In Indian and Southeast Asian dishes, it gives a subtle, creamy flavour and takes the harsh 'edge' off hot, fiery spices.

GARLIC

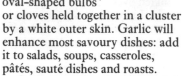

Garlic is a perennial plant that is more often grown as an annual. It is a member of the onion family and has small, white, oval-shaped bulbs or cloves held together in a cluster by a white outer skin. Garlic will enhance most savoury dishes: add it to salads, soups, casseroles, pâtés, sauté dishes and roasts.

Garlic is readily available dried and powdered, and is a convenient substitute for fresh garlic in soups and savoury dishes.

GERANIUM

The geraniums most used for culinary purposes are the rose-scented, mint-scented and lemon-scented varieties. Put leaves into the base of a cake tin when making a sponge cake and remove them when the cake is cooked. When making custard add them to the pan when scalding the milk. They can also be used to flavour milk puddings, sweet sauces, sorbets, jellies, jams and herb teas.

HORSERADISH

The grated root of the horseradish plant is available dried in jars. Use it as for fresh. Horseradish, related to mustard, is a perennial plant, of which the long tapering, creamy coloured root is used. Lift the roots in Autumn, scrub and grate them and preserve them in jars, covered with wine vinegar. Use horseradish to make a creamy sauce for roast beef. Add it to beetroot or cucumber salads and to vinaigrette dressings. Sprinkle it over mackerel fillets before grilling.

LEMON GRASS

Lemon grass is grown mostly in tropical and sub-tropical countries but is imported to the West, in fresh and dried forms and as a powder (sereh powder). It has thick, grass-like leaves which smell and taste strongly of lemon. It is most often used in the cooking of Sri Lanka and Southeast Asia to flavour curry and meat dishes. It can also be used with fish and to flavour sweet puddings.

ROSE

Both the petals and hips of sweet scented roses can be used for culinary purposes. The petals can be crystallised and made into jam. Rose vinegar (made from rose petals infused in wine vinegar) adds a delicate flavour to salads and you can make rose petal wine. Rose hips are an excellent source of vitamin C. Make them into syrup or rose hip jelly. Probably the most common use of roses in cooking, however, is in rosewater, used to flavour and perfume many Middle Eastern sweets and confections.

TAMARIND

Tamarind is the large pod that grows on the Indian tamarind tree. After picking, it is seeded, peeled and pressed into a dark-brown pulp.

It is used to add a sour flavour to chutneys, sauces and curries, to which it is added in the form of tamarind juice.

VIOLET

Sweet violets grow wild and can also be cultivated. The violet is a tiny perennial plant with heart-shaped leaves and sweet-scented mauve or white flowers. The petals can be crystallised and used to decorate confectionery. They can also be used to make an unusual vinegar to flavour all kinds of sauces and stews. The petals are placed in a glass bottle to about one-third full and then topped up with red or white wine vinegar. The bottle is sealed and left in a warm place for two to three weeks before straining for use. The petals are also steeped in white wine cups.

DRY-FRYING SPICES

Dry-frying will mellow the flavour of spices. They can be dried singly or in mixtures. If mixing the spices, put the hardest ones such as fenugreek into the pan first and add softer ones such as coriander and cumin after a few minutes.

Heat a heavy frying pan over moderate heat. Put in the spices and stir them constantly until they are an even brown (do not allow them to burn). Tip the spices out to cool and then grind them in an electric grinder.

In China, a mixture of anise pepper and salt is roasted in this way to be used as a condiment for seafood and poultry.

HERB AND SPICE MIXTURES

BOUQUET GARNI

This is a small bunch of herbs, tied together with string so it can be suspended in soups, casseroles and sauté dishes and removed before serving. The classic ingredients are bay, parsley and thyme, but other herbs can be added to suit a particular dish. When dried herbs are used for a bouquet garni they are tied in a small muslin bag.

CURRY POWDER

The flavourings for authentic Indian curries are made up of different mixtures of ground spices which include cumin, coriander, chilli powder and other aromatics.

You can mix your own but for speed, bought curry powders are available. Besides using it in ethnic dishes, curry powder can add spice to many other types of dishes.

Add it to salad dressings, sprinkle it into sauces and casseroles, and rub it into chicken skin before poaching.

FINES HERBES

This is a mixture of the finely chopped or dried leaves of parsley, chervil, chives and tarragon.

FIVE-SPICE POWDER

A ground mixture of star anise, anise pepper, fennel seed, cloves and cinnamon or cassia. Five-spice powder is used in authentic Chinese cookery. It is cocoa coloured and very pungent and should be used sparingly. Five-spice powder is used to season Chinese red-cooked meats (meats simmered in soy sauce) and roast meats and poultry. It can also be added to marinades and sprinkled over whole steamed fish and vegetable dishes.

GARAM MASALA

A mixture of spices used in Indian cookery. It most frequently contains black pepper, cumin, cinnamon, black or green cardamoms, cloves and bay leaves.

HARISSA

Harissa is a hot mixture of chilli and other spices that is used in Middle Eastern cooking. It can be bought in powder and paste form and may contain up to twenty spices. It is often served with couscous and other North African dishes: it is put into a separate bowl, stock from the main dish is poured in to dilute it and it is spooned back over the dish to taste.

MIXED SPICE

This is a mixture of sweet-flavoured ground spices. The main ingredient is nutmeg and included in smaller amounts are cinnamon, cloves, ginger, cardamom, vanilla, allspice and sometimes fennel seed.

Mixed spice is most often used in sweet dishes, cakes, biscuits and confectionery, but it can be added sparingly to curries and spiced Middle Eastern dishes.

PICKLING SPICE

Pickling spice is a pungent mixture of varying spices, usually based on black peppercorns, red chillis and varying proportions of mustard seed, allspice, cloves, ginger, mace and coriander seed.

Cooking with Fruit

There is now a wide variety of fresh fruits available all year round and each fruit offers its own distinctive flavour and texture.

GLOSSARY OF FRESH FRUIT

APPLES

Apples are available all year round and are at their best in the late autumn months. Cooking apples tend to be larger than eating apples. They are too tart to eat on their own but when cooked with sugar they have a wonderful sweet and sharp flavour. Cooking apples are juicy and will cook to a fluffy purée. When making purées add the sugar towards the end of cooking time. To help apples keep their shape add the sugar at the start of cooking. Look for Bramley's Seedling, Lord Derby and Grenadier.

Eating apples often have more flavour than cooking apples. Cox's Orange Pippin, Newton Wonder, Laxton Superb, Worcester Pearmain and Granny Smith all have distinctive flavours, making them good additions to raw fruit salads and to pies, tarts and puddings. These apples also hold their shape more easily during cooking. Avoid mealy tasteless apples. Less sugar is needed when cooking eating apples.

Look for firm apples with un-blemished skins. Keep apples cool and dry. Apples kept at room temperature should be eaten within 2 weeks. Simply wipe and wash before eating.

To prepare them for cooking, apples are usually peeled and then quartered and cored. An apple corer is a handy gadget which

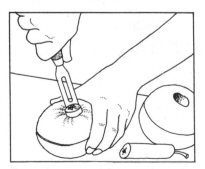

Removing cores with an apple corer

makes coring easy and neat. Apple slices should be brushed with lemon juice to prevent browning.

APRICOTS

Unripe apricots are hard and sour; overripe ones will be mealy and tasteless. Leave apricots to ripen at room temperature. Once ripe, they should be eaten within 2–3 days. Apricots are available for a relatively short period in spring and summer.

Cracking apricot kernels

Prepare apricots by washing, cutting them in half and removing the stone. To peel apricots, blanch in boiling water for 30 seconds to loosen the skins, then peel. Sliced apricots should be brushed with lemon juice to prevent browning. Apricot stones have a subtle almond flavour. Crack the kernels and use to flavour sugar syrups when poaching apricots.

BANANAS

Bananas for eating are picked hard and green. When buying look for evenly coloured skins. They are ready to eat when yellow and slightly flecked brown. They will ripen if kept in the dark at room temperature. Once peeled bananas should be brushed with lemon juice to prevent discolouring.

BLACKBERRIES

Blackberries ripen in late summer and early autumn. When buying avoid stained containers as this may indicate crushed fruit below. Once picked blackberries lose their flavour rapidly and if bought should be eaten on the same day.

To prepare blackberries, wash them and remove the stalks. Remove any damaged fruit. Blackberries are especially good cooked with other fruit such as apples. They can be baked, bottled, eaten raw or frozen. Freeze only fully ripe undamaged fruit, without washing. Damaged or wet fruit can be cooked before freezing but will only keep for about 6 months.

CHERRIES

Cherries are a summer fruit. A number of different types are available as the different varieties have a very short picking time. Cherries are sold mainly on the stalk. Avoid split, diseased or immature fruit. For raw eating cherries look for large soft berries either white, red or black. Smaller hard varieties are better for cooking.

Prepare cherries by rinsing them in a colander and removing the stalks. Cherry stoners are available for the purpose or you can cut into them with the point of a knife and prise out the stone.

Stringing currants with a fork

CURRANTS

Currants are ripe in midsummer. Blackcurrants are more common than red or white. They are normally on a strip or stalk and are more expensive when not. Avoid withered or dusty currants; choose firm ones with a distinct gloss. To remove the currants from their stalks use a fork to rake them off. Currants can be frozen raw, cooked or pulped. If storing in the refrigerator keep covered for up to 10 days, removing damaged fruit.

DAMSONS

Damsons are available in September to early October. Select ripe but firm fruit showing no bird or insect damage. Store them in a cool place and cook soon after purchase as ripe damsons do not keep. Prepare damsons by washing and halving them. The

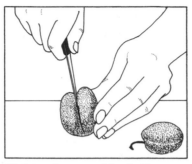

Halving damsons with a knife

stones can be taken out with a sharp knife. Damsons need to be cooked with a sweetener as they are very sour. They are best frozen in sugar syrup but the skin will toughen.

GOOSEBERRIES

Unripe gooseberries are always green. As they ripen they turn gold, red or even white; some of them bear whiskers. Buy evenly coloured fruit, keep it refrigerated and eat within 3 days. Wash the gooseberries and snip off the stem and flower ends (top and tail); discard damaged fruit. Gooseberries are sour and will always need sweetening. For puddings, slightly immature fruits are better.

Snipping off gooseberry stems

Ripe gooseberries do not freeze well but barely or under ripe fruit can be frozen. Cooked gooseberries stewed or pulped will keep frozen for up to 1 year.

GRAPEFRUIT

These large citrus fruits are always available. Select evenly coloured glossy fruit. They will keep for 4 days at room temperature and 2 weeks refrigerated.

Prepare grapefruit by cutting in half and separating the flesh from the skin with a serrated knife. Then divide the segments. Or, peel the skin off cutting just below the pith, then hold the fruit in one

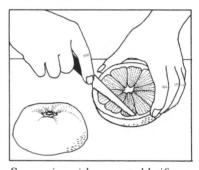

Segmenting with a serrated knife

hand and cut out the segments with the other leaving the protective membrane behind.

GRAPES

Grapes can range from pale amber to a deep blue colour. Buy plump unbruised grapes still attached to their stems. Keep grapes refrigerated and use within 3 days. Grapes should be left unwashed until ready to serve. Pips can be removed by halving the fruit with a knife and flicking out the pips with a knife. To leave the fruit whole, push a sterilised hair pin into the grape and push out the pips. Remove the skins by placing grapes in boiling water for 20 seconds; the skins can then be peeled off with a knife. Black grapes are not usually peeled.

KIWI FRUIT (Chinese gooseberries)

Available from midsummer to late winter, kiwi fruit are egg shaped with a brown furry skin. Ripeness is tested by gentle pressure and a slight yielding of the flesh. Kiwi fruit should be kept at room temperature until ripe and then used within 2 days. Preparation simply consists of peeling the fruit with a small sharp knife and slicing the bright green flesh crossways. There is a pleasant pattern of edible black seeds in the flesh.

KUMQUATS

Kumquats are very small members of the orange family, about the size of a plum. They are available all the year round. They should have smooth shiny skins; avoid those with shrivelled skins. They can be stored at room temperature for up to 2 days and refrigerated for up to 1 week. Prepare kumquats by rinsing them (in a colander) and removing the stems. Halve lengthways or leave whole, and slice thinly for dessert decoration. Both the skin and flesh are eaten and they are best when poached.

Slicing kumquats thinly

LEMONS AND LIMES

Lemons and limes are available all year round, though limes are not sold as widely as lemons. Limes are greener than lemons (the darker the colour the better) and slightly smaller but for preparation limes may be treated the same way as lemons. Look for lemons which are a strong 'lemon yellow'

colour and have a moist-looking skin; they should feel heavy for their size. A shrivelled skin will indicate that some of the juice has evaporated. Lemons will be at their best for only a few days if kept at room temperature and up to 2 weeks in the refrigerator.

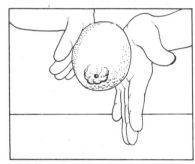

Softening lemon for maximum juice

To extract the maximum amount of juice from a lemon or lime, it should be at room temperature. Roll the fruit back and forth in your hands, pressing gently with the palm to help soften the fruit. Then slice the fruit in half crossways and either squeeze hard or use a lemon squeezer. *One large lemon contains about 30 ml (2 tbsp) juice.*

The skins of limes are tougher and much thinner than those of lemons and so release much less zest. When grating lemon zest make sure that none of the bitter tasting white pith is grated. To thinly pare lemons, peel the rind with a vegetable peeler, again avoiding any of the bitter white pith.

LOGANBERRIES AND TAYBERRIES

Both these fruits can be treated the same as raspberries and are available in the summer months. They do not keep well. Very ripe fruit should be eaten right away. Only freeze dry fruit which is just ripe. For eating raw, make sure the fruits are firm, dry and fully ripe. Second-quality fruit can be puréed and frozen.

MANGOES

Mangoes are available most of the year except in early winter. Ripe mangoes are very juicy and have a yellow or orange skin; they should give to a gentle squeeze. Avoid soft or shrivelled mangoes. Ripe mangoes should be kept and used within 3 days.

To prepare mangoes, cut a large slice from one side of the fruit, cutting close to the stone. Cut another slice from the opposite side. The flesh in the cut segments can be scooped out into squares lengthways and crossways without breaking the skin. Push the skin inside out to expose the cubes of flesh. Use a sharp knife to peel the remaining centre section and cut the flesh away from the stone in chunks or slices.

MELONS

Melons are available all year round except for watermelons which are only available in summer, the time of year when melons are most abundantly available. Depending on the variety, melons can be smooth skinned or have a light or heavy netting. Many have a light or heavy ridging—conveniently the ridges can be used as guides for serving portions. Ogen, charentais and galias are round melons and can be small or large. Honeydews are usually large round shapes or they can be oval. All melons have a highly perfumed sweet juicy flesh. Usually, the more fragrant the melon the sweeter and juicier its flesh will be.

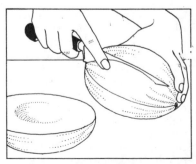

Cutting melon into wedges

Melons should be stored tightly wrapped in the refrigerator as they can easily pick up the flavours of other foods. Ripe melons are firm but have a slight give when pressed at the ends. Use within 2–3 days. Soft patches on the rind indicate bruising rather than ripeness. Buy slices or wedges only if they have been kept with the cut surface covered with cling film.

TO SERVE ROUND MELONS

Cut melons in half crossways and scoop out the seeds with a spoon. They will look more attractive if the edges are cut in a zig-zag pattern. To use the halves as *melon bowls*, cut a small slice off the bottom of each half so they stand upright. Keep the bowls tightly wrapped in the refrigerator until ready to serve.

TO MAKE MELON WEDGES

Halve fruit lengthways, scoop out seeds and cut into wedges. Cut the flesh free from the rind, but leave in place; divide it into cubes.

TO MAKE MELON BALLS

Scoop out the melon flesh with a melon baller.

NECTARINES

Nectarines can be bought from midsummer to early autumn and from early winter into the spring. Shop for plump rich-coloured fruit softening along the indent. Hard, extremely soft or shrivelled fruit should be avoided. Nectarines will ripen at room temperature but once ripened should be refrigerated and used within a period of 5 days.

Preparation is simply washing. They may be peeled with a sharp knife if desired then halved and stoned. Brush the exposed flesh with lemon juice to stop discolouring.

ORANGES

Oranges are at their best in the early months of the year. Choose firm fruit that feel heavy and have a glossy skin. Avoid those with dry or hard looking skins. Thick-skinned navel oranges are easy to peel and are seedless; thinner-skinned oranges are more difficult to peel but are usually more juicy and have a more pronounced orange flavour.

Oranges will keep for 4 days at room temperature and if wrapped

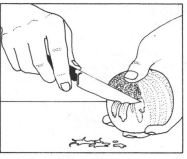

Scraping off the white pith

and stored in the refrigerator they will keep for at least 2 weeks.

When serving sliced oranges the white pith should be scraped off with a knife after the orange is peeled. When dividing the oranges into segments hold the fruit over a bowl to catch all the juices. The pith is more easily removed from warm oranges than cold ones. Pour over boiling water to cover and leave the oranges for several minutes before peeling.

To use orange peel in cooking, peel the rind with a vegetable peeler avoiding any of the bitter white pith, then blanch the peel for 3 minutes, rinse under cold water and then shred before using.

PEACHES

Peaches are available all the year round, but are at their best in summer. Ripe peaches are slightly soft and have a yellow to orange skin. Avoid green, bruised or 'sale' fruit. Eat peaches within 2 days if kept at room temperature or if wrapped and chilled within 5 days. Peaches can be peeled by immersing them in boiling water for about 15 seconds, then cooling in cold water. Use a sharp knife to separate the loosened skin from the flesh. Very ripe peaches are best if skinned and stoned under running water, as scalding them will soften and slightly discolour the flesh. Cut lengthways along the indentation in the fruit and twist the fruit in half, then remove the stone. Brush cut fruit with lemon juice to prevent browning.

TO MAKE A MELON BASKET

Honeydews and watermelons can be used to make large baskets and small round melons such as ogens can be used to make individual baskets. Cut a thin slice off the bottom of the melon so it will stand upright. Make 2 cuts each about 1 cm ($\frac{1}{2}$ inch) from the top stem of the melon and cut straight down to the centre of the melon.

Then slice horizontally to make 2 wedges; remove the wedges. Remove the seeds from the centre of the melon and evenly cut away the flesh from the piece that is forming the basket handle. Scoop out the melon flesh with a large spoon or melon baller, discarding seeds if using a watermelon. Chill, tightly wrapped, until required.

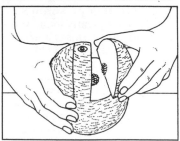

Removing wedges to make handle

Scooping out flesh with a spoon

UNUSUAL FRUIT

The variety of fruits available seems to be ever increasing as we see more and more unusual looking fruits in markets bearing prickly wrinkled skins, odd shapes and often giving off exotically perfumed aromas. These fruits are often very expensive but can be bought in very small quantities and used to liven up fruit salads or to make unusual decorations for puddings. In a moment of extravagance they can be used to make very special sorbets. Many of them are available canned. Preparing them need not be a mystery.

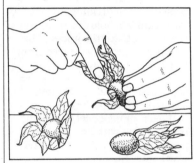

Bending calyx on cape gooseberries

Cape gooseberry or Chinese lantern. When ripe the berries are enclosed in a lantern-shaped case or calyx, and are orange yellow in colour. If the case or calyx is bent back to form a petal around the central berry, they can be used as a decoration for cakes. They can also be eaten raw or added to fruit salads.

Custard apples. The flesh has a flavour reminiscent of custard and is soft and pulpy in texture. Cut the fruit in half and scoop out the flesh with a spoon.

Dates. The stones of fresh dates can be easily removed by cutting off the stem end and gently squeezing the date—the stone should slip out. Fresh dates are plump with a slightly mealy texture. Slice and add to fruit salads.

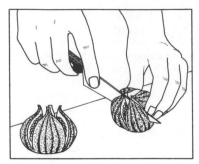

Slicing and opening figs for serving

Figs. These can be simply sliced or partially sliced and opened like a flower. They are juicy and have a more delicate flavour than their more frequently used dried counterpart.

Guavas. A juicy fruit full of seeds, guavas can be pear-shaped, or round looking like tomatoes. They should be peeled then puréed or baked.

Breaking and peeling lychee skin

Lychees. The hard, red-brown scaly skin should be broken and then peeled. The white pulpy flesh surrounds a soft brown stone. Remove the stone and serve the lychees chilled. They have a distinctive flavour—slightly acid yet sweet.

Papaya. A large smooth-skinned fruit which ripens from green to yellow to orange. Slice the fruit in half and remove the black seeds in the centre. Cut into slices and add to fruit salads—papayas have a smooth soft texture and a distinctive rich flavour.

Passion fruit. Most varieties we see have a hard brown wrinkled skin. Slice the fruit in half and scoop out the flesh with a tea-spoon; the seeds can be eaten and when passion fruit is used in fruit creams and sorbets the seeds should be included in the purée.

Scrubbing prickles off prickly pear

Prickly pear or Indian Fig. A prickly pear has a greenish-orange skin covered with tiny prickles. The sweet juicy pink flesh has edible seeds. Wash and scrub off the prickles, cut off each end, slit downwards and peel back the skin. Slice the flesh and serve with a squeeze of lemon juice.

Halving sharon fruit with a knife

Sharon fruit or persimmon. The most frequently found variety of persimmon in this country is the sharon fruit. It looks like a large plump tomato and has a sweet, slightly sour tasting flesh. Unlike other persimmons it is seedless and both skin and flesh are eaten. The flesh can be puréed and used in many types of ice-creams and mousses.

PEARS

Pears are available all the year round. Buy well formed firm pears with no oozing or softness. Ripe pears give a little at the stem end. They do not remain ripe for long and so should be checked often. They will ripen indoors but then should be refrigerated and used within 3 days. For eating raw, Williams, Conference, Comice or Lacton's are good. Use firm pears for cooking.

Prepare pears by washing and peeling; scoop out the core with a teaspoon. A pear wedger will core

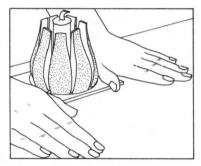

Slicing and coring with a wedger

and cut a pear quickly. Lemon juice will prevent slow deterioration of peeled pears.

PINEAPPLES

Pineapples are available all year round. Ripe pineapples give off a sweet aroma and in addition a leaf will pull easily from the crown. Avoid pineapples that are bruised or discoloured or have wilting leaves. These fruits continue to ripen after picking and are often sold slightly unripe. However a really unripe pineapple with no aroma will not ripen properly. The most common method of preparation is to cut off the leaf crown and cut the pineapple into thick slices crossways. Use the tip of the blade to trim off the outer skin and remove the tiny brown spots from the flesh. Use either a small knife or an apple corer to remove the central core. Pineapples can also be served in wedges. Cut the fruit in half and

Separating pineapple flesh

then quarters lengthways, cutting through but not removing the leaf crown. Use a small knife to cut out the exposed central core. Use a curved knife to separate the flesh from the skin and cut it downwards in order to make wedge-shaped slices.

PLUMS

The different varieties of this fruit are available from the late spring to early autumn. The colour may vary from yellow or green to red or almost black. Hard, shrivelled or split plums should be avoided. Sweet plums can be eaten raw and all varieties can be cooked. Sweet or dessert plums will ripen at home in a few days. Greengages are sweet, amber-coloured plums; deep purple Victorias are good all-rounders.

Prepare plums by washing and halving them. Stones can be removed with the tip of a knife.

Plums freeze well, preferably top-quality just ripe fruit. The stones if left in during the cooking will produce an almond-like flavour. Some varieties of plum skin hardens in freezing. If freezing in sugar syrup add ascorbic acid or lemon juice.

POMEGRANATES

Pomegranates are available in the autumn. Buy fruit with hard russet coloured skin. Keep pomegranates refrigerated and use within 7 days. Prepare by cutting a slice off the stem end with a sharp knife. Then slice the skin sections lengthways and draw the sections

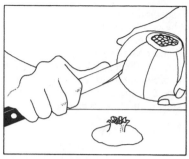

Slicing pomegranate skin

apart. Push in the skin and push out the seeds from the inside. Seeds can be eaten or juiced. Pomegranates should not be frozen.

QUINCES

Quinces are available in October to November. Avoid scabby, split or small fruit. The apple-shaped quinces stew well and the pear-shaped ones keep well. Store them in a cool dry place away from absorbent foods likely to be affected by the strong aroma of quinces. A few quinces are eaten raw but most are cooked with other fruit, especially apples. To prepare quinces simply peel and slice or chop.

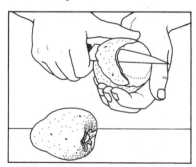

Peeling quinces with a sharp knife

RASPBERRIES

The main season for raspberries is from late June to mid August although some varieties are sold into early autumn. Raspberries are sold hulled which makes them liable to crushing. When shopping avoid stained containers and wet fruit especially. After damp weather they are likely to mould quickly; any deteriorating fruit should be discarded as soon as possible. Use only the best dry fruit at the point of ripening when freezing. Over-ripe or damaged fruit may be sieved and frozen as pulp.

RHUBARB

Forced rhubarb can be bought in winter and early spring; maincrop rhubarb comes in spring and early summer. Forced rhubarb is pink and tender looking and sweet tasting. Maincrop variety has a stronger colour and a thicker stem and is more acid to taste. Rhubarb should be kept cool or refrigerated and used within 4 days. If maincrop rhubarb looks a little limp it can be stood, leaf up, in cold water, like flowers, to crispen. To prepare rhubarb, chop off and discard the leaves and root ends and wash the stems. Some maincrop rhubarbs have a tougher stem which may need peeling. Chop the

Cutting rhubarb into chunks

stems into chunks for cooking. For short term freezing trim the ends, wash, drain and freeze. For longer freezing blanch it in boiling water for 1 minute.

SATSUMAS AND TANGERINES

Look for these fruits in the winter months. Choose small loose-skinned varieties with a bright orange colour. Avoid dry ones or those with patches of soft skin. They will keep at room temperature for a few days or if kept

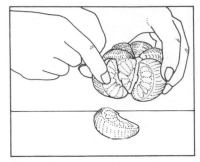

Segmenting satsumas/tangerines

refrigerated up to 10 days. The skin does not cling to the flesh and can be peeled off by hand. Pick off remaining bits of white pith. Divide the fruit into segments, eat raw or in salads.

STRAWBERRIES

A true summer fruit, the majority available during the summer season are British grown. As with most berries check the base of the punnet for staining as this will indicate squashed fruit. Strawberries are probably most famous for being eaten raw, with cream but are also delicious puréed and chilled. Be sure to buy plump glossy berries with their green frills still attached. Only wash berries just before hulling. Sugared, hulled strawberries yield the juice readily. Besides eating raw strawberries can be stewed and put into flans, tarts and pies. Freeze only the best just ripe fruit. Damaged or over-ripe fruit can be frozen as pulp with a little lemon juice or citric acid added.

Puréeing strawberries with a sieve

FRUIT SAUCES

The distinctive flavours of fruit sauces will add enormously to the enjoyment of desserts and puddings. Because fruit sauces are often sharp and tangy as well as quite sweet, they can be the perfect complement to bland desserts such as meringues, cold soufflés, pancakes or simple steamed puddings and they come into their own when simply poured over vanilla ice-cream.

Fruit sauces are very simple to make. Usually a purée of fruit is sweetened and lightly thickened. *Cornflour* is always first dissolved in a cold liquid before it is added to a hot one, otherwise it will be lumpy. Cornflour thickened sauces need to be cooked to remove the raw taste of the starch; during this time the sauce thickens. A sauce thickened with *arrowroot* will be clear and shiny but it should be served soon after making as arrowroot soon loses its thickening properties.

FRUIT SAUCE

Makes 300 ml ($\frac{1}{2}$ pint)

425 g (15 oz) can fruit in syrup
10 ml (2 tsp) arrowroot or cornflour
squeeze of lemon juice (optional)

1 Strain the juice from the fruit. Sieve the fruit, make up to 300 ml ($\frac{1}{2}$ pint) with juice and heat until boiling.

2 Blend the arrowroot with a little of the unused fruit juice until it is a smooth cream and stir in the puréed fruit. Return the mixture to the pan and heat gently, continuing to stir, until the sauce thickens and clears. Stir in the lemon juice if using.

——— VARIATION ———

Omit the lemon juice. Add 15 ml (1 tbsp) rum, sherry or fruit liqueur to the sauce immediately before serving.

BILBERRY SAUCE

Makes 600 ml (1 pint)

450 g (1 lb) bilberries, washed
225 ml (8 fl oz) water
15 ml (1 tbsp) cornflour
175 g (6 oz) caster sugar
pinch of salt
5 ml (1 tsp) lemon juice

1 Trim the bilberries. Bring the water to the boil, add the berries and bring back to the boil.

2 Meanwhile, mix the cornflour to a smooth paste with a little cold water. Stir it into the bilberries with the sugar and salt and cook until the mixture has thickened, stirring constantly, then add the lemon juice.

GOOSEBERRY SAUCE

Makes 400 ml (¾ pint)

225 g (8 oz) gooseberries, washed
50 g (2 oz) sugar
300 ml (½ pint) water
juice of 1 orange
15 ml (1 tbsp) cornflour

1 Trim the gooseberries. Put the sugar and water into a large saucepan and heat gently until the sugar has completely dissolved. Add the gooseberries and simmer until they are tender.

2 Mix the orange juice with the cornflour, stir in a little of the gooseberry juice and pour the mixture into the sauce, stirring well. Bring to the boil and simmer for 1–2 minutes until the sauce has thickened.

CREAMY PLUM SAUCE

Makes 400 ml (¾ pint)

4 eating plums, washed
100 g (4 oz) icing sugar
225 g (8 oz) cream cheese, softened

1 Halve and stone the plums. Put them in a blender with the sugar and blend until smooth, or rub through sieve to remove skins.

2 Add the cream cheese and beat until well blended. Cover and chill until required.

BRANDIED CHERRY SAUCE

Makes 400 ml (¾ pint)

450 g (1 lb) cherries, washed and stoned
100 ml (4 fl oz) brandy
100 g (4 oz) sugar
10 ml (2 tsp) cornflour
5 ml (1 tsp) almond flavouring

Put the cherries into a large saucepan with the brandy, sugar and cornflour and cook, stirring all the time, until the mixture has thickened and just begins to boil. Remove from the heat and stir in the almond essence.

MELBA SAUCE

Makes 400 ml (¾ pint)

450 g (1 lb) raspberries
60 ml (4 tbsp) redcurrant jelly
15 ml (1 tbsp) icing sugar
30 ml (2 tbsp) arrowroot
15 ml (1 tbsp) water

1 Rub the raspberries through a sieve into a saucepan. Add the jelly and sugar and bring to boil.

2 Blend the arrowroot with the cold water to a smooth cream and stir in a little of the raspberry mixture. Return the sauce to the pan and bring to the boil, stirring with a wooden spoon, until it thickens and clears. Strain and leave to cool.

FRUIT PURÉES

Many fruit sauces are based on purées. Usually the fruit is first cooked with sugar until softened. Soft berry fruits however are sometimes not cooked before puréeing. The softened fruit is rubbed through a sieve which should be nylon as metal can sometimes react with the acid in the fruit and taint the flavour. Although it is much simpler to purée the fruit in a blender or food processor it may still be necessary to sieve the fruit in order to remove any small pips. A fruit purée can make a simple dessert on its own served with cream.

FRUIT GLAZES

Glazes not only give fruit flans and tarts a shiny covering but they also help protect the fruits from discolouring or drying out.

When making fruit glazes use a jam which complements the colour of the fruit to be covered. About 150 ml (¼ pint) glaze is enough to cover two 20-cm (8-inch) flans.

APRICOT GLAZE

Makes 150 ml (¼ pint)

100 g (4 oz) apricot jam
30 ml (2 tbsp) water

Glazing a fruit flan

Sieve the jam into a small saucepan and add the water. Heat gently, stirring, until the jam softens. Bring to the boil and simmer for 1 minute. Allow to cool until warm then spoon over the flan or tart.

——— VARIATION ———

Redcurrant Use redcurrant jelly instead of apricot jam; there is no need to sieve the jelly, just stir until completely blended.

Perfect Pastry

There is no doubt that making your own pastry does take time, but the end results are usually worth it. There are many different types of pastry and each has its own distinctive texture, flavour and use. The art of producing good pastry lies in understanding the basic rules by which each one is made and sticking to them.

PASTRY

For successful pastry, work in a cool kitchen with cool utensils and ingredients. As you work, handle the pastry as little as possible and use just your finger and thumb tips for rubbing in fat.

For most pastries, use plain flour. For puff pastry use strong flour, to help give it a light, open structure. Butter and block margarine are interchangeable in short pastries, and give good results when mixed with lard. Proprietary vegetable shortenings and pure vegetable oils can also be used, but follow the manufacturer's directions as the quantities required may be less. In richer pastries stick to butter. Add liquid to a pastry mixture gradually, using just enough to bind it.

Pâte sucrée is a really rich shortcrust that keeps its shape well; use it for continental pâtisseries. *Shortcrust* is probably the most widely used pastry, and is quick and easy to prepare. *Flan pastry* is a slightly richer pastry made by the same method. It is usually sweetened, and it is ideal for flans.

Puff pastry is the richest of all and rises to layer upon layer of crisp, delicate flakes. Because it takes so long to make most people make it only occasionally, making up a large batch and freezing it in small quantities for future use.

Flaky pastry is used where a rich pastry is required but when the rise is not so important. *Rough puff* is quicker and easier to make and similar in appearance to flaky, but the texture is not so even.

Choux pastry is made by melting the fat and beating in the flour and the resulting paste is piped to shape. The result is a light, crisp shell, almost hollow inside.

* When a recipe states 225 g (8 oz) pastry, use pastry made with 225 g (8 oz) flour. If using bought pastry, buy a packet weighing twice that amount.

PÂTE SUCRÉE

100 g (4 oz) plain flour
pinch of salt
50 g (2 oz) caster sugar
50 g (2 oz) butter, at room temperature
2 egg yolks

1 Sift the flour and salt together on to a working surface or, preferably, a marble slab.

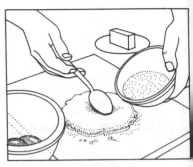

2 Make a well in the centre of the mixture and add the sugar, butter and egg yolks.

3 Using the fingertips of one hand, pinch and work the sugar, butter and egg yolks together until well blended. Gradually work in all the flour, adding a little water if necessary to bind it together.

4 Knead lightly until smooth, then wrap the pastry in foil or cling film and leave to 'rest' in the refrigerator or a cool place for about 1 hour.

5 Roll out the pastry on a lightly floured surface and use as required. *Pâte sucrée* is usually cooked at 190°C (375°F) mark 5.

SHORTCRUST PASTRY

175 g (6 oz) plain flour
pinch of salt
75 g (3 oz) butter or block margarine and lard
about 30 ml (2 tbsp) cold water

1 Mix the flour and salt together in a bowl. Cut the fat into small pieces and add it to the flour.

2 Using both hands, rub the fat into the flour between finger and thumb tips until the mixture resembles fine breadcrumbs.

3 Add the water, sprinkling it evenly over the surface. Stir it in with a round-bladed knife until the mixture begins to stick together in large lumps.

4 With one hand, collect the mixture together and knead lightly for a few seconds to give a firm, smooth dough. The pastry can be used straight away, but is better allowed to 'rest' for about 30 minutes. It can also be wrapped in cling film and kept in the refrigerator for a day or two.

5 *To roll out:* sprinkle a very little flour on a working surface and the rolling pin, not on the pastry, and roll out the dough evenly in one direction only, turning it occasionally. The ideal thickness is usually about 0.3 cm ($\frac{1}{8}$ inch). Do not pull or stretch the pastry. When cooking shortcrust pastry, the usual oven temperature is 200–220°C (400–425°F) mark 6–7.

FLAN PASTRY

100 g (4 oz) plain flour
pinch of salt
75 g (3 oz) butter or block margarine and lard
5 ml (1 tsp) caster sugar
1 egg, beaten

1 Mix the flour and salt together in a bowl. Cut the fat into small pieces, add it to the flour and rub it in as for shortcrust pastry until the mixture resembles fine breadcrumbs. Stir in the sugar.

2 Add the egg, stirring with a round-bladed knife until the ingredients begin to stick together in large lumps.

3 With one hand, collect the mixture together and knead lightly for a few seconds to give a firm, smooth dough.

4 Roll out as for shortcrust pastry and use as required. When cooking flan pastry the usual oven temperature is 200°C (400°F) mark 6.

BAKING BLIND

Baking blind is the process of baking a pastry case without the filling—essential if the filling is to be uncooked or if it only requires a short cooking time. First shape the pastry into the baking tin. Prick the pastry base with a fork. For large cases, cut a round of greaseproof paper rather larger

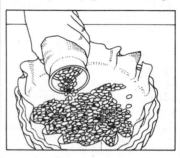

than the tin. Use this to line the pastry and weight it down with some dried beans, pasta or rice. Alternatively, screw up a piece of foil and use that to line the base of the pastry case. Bake the pastry at the temperature given in the recipe for 10–15 minutes, then remove the baking beans and paper or foil lining and return the tin to the oven for a further 5 minutes to crisp the pastry. Leave the baked case to cool and shrink slightly before removing it from the tin. (The baking beans can be kept for use again.)

For small cases, it is usually sufficient to prick the pastry well with a fork before baking.

Baked unfilled pastry cases can be kept for a few days in an airtight container.

ROUGH PUFF PASTRY

225 g (8 oz) plain flour

pinch of salt

75 g (3 oz) butter or block
    margarine

75 g (3 oz) lard

about 150 ml ($\frac{1}{4}$ pint) cold water

a squeeze of lemon juice

beaten egg, to glaze

1 Mix the flour and salt together
in a bowl. Cut the fat (which
should be quite firm) into cubes
about 2 cm ($\frac{3}{4}$ inch) across.

2 Stir the fat into the flour without breaking up the pieces.
Add enough water and lemon juice
to mix to a fairly stiff dough.

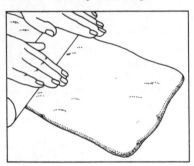

3 On a lightly floured surface,
roll out into an oblong three
times as long as it is wide.

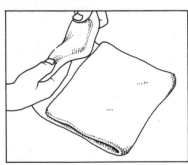

4 Fold the bottom third up and
the top third down, then turn
the pastry so that the folded edges
are at the sides. Seal the ends of
the pastry by pressing lightly with
a rolling pin.

5 Repeat this rolling and folding
process three more times,
turning the dough so that the
folded edge is on the left hand side
each time.

6 Wrap the pastry in greaseproof
paper and leave to rest in the
refrigerator or a cool place for
about 30 minutes before using.

7 Roll out the pastry on a lightly
floured surface to 0.3 cm ($\frac{1}{8}$
inch) thick and use as required.
Brush with beaten egg before
baking. The usual oven temperature is 220°C (425°F) mark 7.

PUFF PASTRY

450 g (1 lb) strong white flour

pinch of salt

450 g (1 lb) butter

about 300 ml ($\frac{1}{2}$ pint) cold water

15 ml (1 tbsp) lemon juice

beaten egg, to glaze

1 Mix the strong plain flour
and a pinch of salt together
in a large mixing bowl.

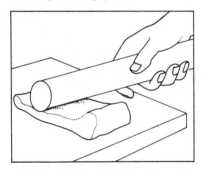

2 Cut off 50 g (2 oz) butter and
pat the remaining butter with
a rolling pin to a slab 2 cm ($\frac{3}{4}$ inch)
thick.

3 Rub the 50 g (2 oz) butter into
the flour with the finger and
thumb tips. Stir in enough water
and lemon juice to make a soft,
elastic dough.

4 Knead dough until smooth and
shape into a round. Cut through
half the depth in a cross shape.

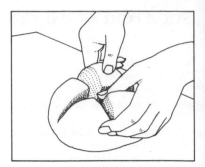

5 Open out the flaps to form a
star. Roll out, keeping the
centre four times as thick as the
flaps.

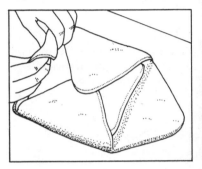

6 Place the slab of butter in the
centre of the dough and fold
over the flaps, envelope-style.
Press gently with a rolling pin.

7 Roll out into a rectangle
measuring about 40 × 20 cm
(16 × 8 inches). Fold the bottom
third up and the top third down,
keeping the edges straight. Seal
the edges by pressing with the
rolling pin.

8 Wrap the pastry in greaseproof
paper and leave in the refrigerator to rest for 30 minutes.

9 Put the pastry on a lightly
floured working surface with
the folded edges to the sides and
repeat the rolling, folding and
resting sequence five times.

10 After the final resting, roll
out the pastry on a lightly
floured surface and shape as required. Brush with beaten egg.
The usual oven temperature is
230°C (450°F) mark 8.

FLAKY PASTRY

225 g (8 oz) plain flour
pinch of salt
75 g (3 oz) butter or block margarine
75 g (3 oz) lard
about 150 ml (¼ pint) cold water
a squeeze of lemon juice
beaten egg, to glaze

1 Mix the flour and salt together in a bowl. Soften the fat by working it with a knife on a plate, then divide it into four equal portions.

2 Add one quarter of the fat to the flour and rub it in between finger and thumb tips until the mixture resembles fine bread-crumbs.

3 Add enough water and lemon juice to make a soft elastic dough, stirring it in with a round-bladed knife.

4 Turn the dough on to a lightly floured surface and roll out in to an oblong three times as long as it is wide.

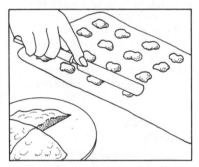

5 Using a round-bladed knife, dot another quarter of the fat over the top two-thirds of the pastry in flakes, so that it looks like buttons on a card.

6 Fold the bottom third of the pastry up and the top third down and turn it so that the folded edges are at the side. Seal the edges of the pastry by pressing with a rolling pin.

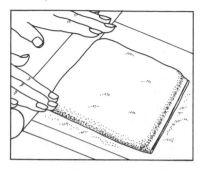

7 Re-roll as before and repeat the process twice more until the remaining portions of fat have been used up.

8 Wrap the pastry loosely in greaseproof paper and leave it to rest in the refrigerator or a cool place for at least 30 minutes before using.

9 Roll out the pastry on a lightly floured working surface to 0.3 cm (⅛ inch) thick and use as required. Brush with beaten egg before baking to give the characteristic glaze. When cooking flaky pastry, the usual oven temperature is 220°C (425°) mark 7.

CHOUX PASTRY

50 g (2 oz) butter or block margarine
150 ml (¼ pint) water
65 g (2½ oz) plain flour, sifted
2 eggs, lightly beaten

BEATING CHOUX PASTRY

Add the beaten egg gradually to choux pastry, taking care to add only just enough to give a piping consistency. When beating by hand with a wooden spoon the arm tends to tire, the beating speed is reduced and the final consistency is often too slack to retain its shape. In this case a little less egg should be added. Use size 4 eggs if beating by hand and size 2 eggs when using an electric mixer.

1 Put the fat and water together in a pan, heat gently until the fat has melted, then bring to the boil. Remove pan from heat.

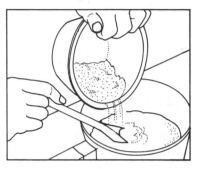

2 Tip all the flour at once into the hot liquid. Beat thoroughly with a wooden spoon, then return the pan to the heat.

3 Continue beating the mixture until it is smooth and forms a ball in the centre of the pan. (Take care not to over-beat or the mixture will become fatty.) Remove from the heat and leave the mixture to cool for a minute or two.

4 Beat in the egg, a little at a time, adding only just enough to give a piping consistency. Beat the mixture vigorously at this stage to trap in as much air as possible. Continue beating until the mixture develops an obvious sheen, then use as required. When cooking choux pastry the usual oven temperature is 200–220°C (400–425°F) mark 6–7.

Cake-making Techniques

Plain or rich, fruity, spicy or laden with cream, cakes are pure fun. Wholly superfluous to our nutritional needs, they represent all that is sociable and pleasing about food. If you can master the techniques to produce a really beautiful cake you will give your family and friends a real treat—and yourself a lot of creative pleasure into the bargain.

RUBBED-IN CAKES

For plain cakes, in which the proportion of fat to flour is half or less, the fat is literally rubbed into the flour with the fingertips and thumbs. Cakes made like this have a soft, light texture, they are easy to make and economical too. Just because they are called 'plain' doesn't mean these cakes can't be varied with fruits and spices, but icings and fillings are generally kept to a minimum as these are the cakes that naturally form everyday tea-time fare for the family.

To make cakes by the 'rubbing in' method, first sift the dry ingredients into a bowl. Cut the firm fat into pieces and add to the bowl. Then rub the fat lightly into the flour between the fingertips and

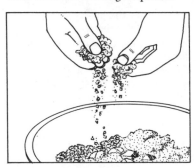

thumbs. Lift your hands well up over the bowl and work lightly to incorporate air into the mixture; this helps to make the cake light, though the main raising agents are chemical. Shake the bowl occasionally to bring any large lumps to the surface and rub in until the mixture resembles fine breadcrumbs.

Sugar and flavourings go in next, then the liquid. Adding the liquid is a crucial stage in the making of a rubbed-in mixture. Too much liquid can cause a heavy, doughy texture, while insufficient gives a dry cake. Beaten egg and milk are the commonest liquids; add them cautiously, using just enough to bring the mixture to the right consistency. For cakes baked in a tin, the mixture should have a soft dropping consistency.

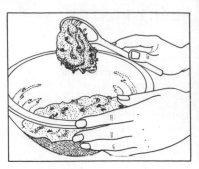

That is, it should drop easily from the spoon when the handle is tapped against the side of the bowl. For small cakes and buns that are baked flat on a baking sheet (such as rock buns or scones), the mixture should be stiff enough to hold

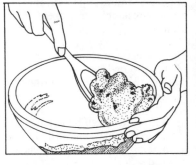

its shape without spreading too much during the baking time. A stiff consistency describes a mixture which clings to the spoon.

Because they are low in fat, these cakes do not keep well. They are best eaten the day they are made.

ALTERNATIVE RAISING AGENTS

If plain flour and baking powder are used instead of self-raising flour, allow 15 ml (1 tbsp) baking powder to 225 g (8 oz) flour and sift them together twice before using. If you use cream of tartar and bicarbonate of soda in place of baking powder, allow 5 ml (1 tsp) cream of tartar and 2.5 ml ($\frac{1}{2}$ tsp) bicarbonate of soda to 225 g (8 oz) plain flour with ordinary milk, or 2.5 ml ($\frac{1}{2}$ tsp) bicarbonate of soda and 2.5 ml ($\frac{1}{2}$ tsp) cream of tartar with soured milk.

SCONES

Makes 10–12

225 g (8 oz) self-raising flour
2.5 ml ($\frac{1}{2}$ tsp) salt
5 ml (1 tsp) baking powder
25–50 g (1–2 oz) butter or block
  margarine
150 ml ($\frac{1}{4}$ pint) milk
beaten egg or milk, to glaze
  (optional)

1 Preheat a baking sheet in the oven. Sift together the flour, salt and baking powder into a bowl. Cut the butter into small pieces and add to the flour.

2 Rub in the fat until the mixture resembles fine breadcrumbs. Make a well in the centre and stir in enough milk to give a fairly soft dough. Turn it on to a floured working surface, and knead very lightly if necessary to remove any cracks.

3 Roll out the dough lightly to about 2 cm ($\frac{3}{4}$ inch) thick, or pat it out with the hand. Cut into rounds with a 5-cm (2-inch) cutter dipped in flour, or cut into triangles with a sharp knife.

4 Place on the baking sheet, brush if you wish with beaten egg or milk to glaze and bake in the hottest part of the oven at 230°C (450°F) mark 8 for 8–10 minutes until well risen and brown. Cool on a wire rack and serve split and buttered.

ROCK BUNS

Makes 12

225 g (8 oz) plain flour
pinch of salt
10 ml (2 tsp) baking powder
50 g (2 oz) butter or block
  margarine
50 g (2 oz) lard
75 g (3 oz) demerara sugar
75 g (3 oz) mixed dried fruit
grated rind of $\frac{1}{2}$ a lemon
1 egg, beaten
a little milk

1 Lightly grease two baking sheets. Sift together the flour, salt and baking powder into a mixing bowl. Cut the butter and lard into small pieces and add it to the plain flour.

2 Rub the fat lightly into the flour between thumb and fingertips, holding the hands high above the bowl to keep the mixture cool and light. Shake the bowl occasionally to bring any large lumps to the surface. Rub in thoroughly until the mixture resembles fine breadcrumbs.

3 Add the sugar, fruit and lemon rind to the mixture and mix in thoroughly. Make a well in the centre, gradually pour in the beaten egg and mix with a fork. Add just enough milk to mix to a moist but stiff dough.

4 Using two forks, shape small quantities of mixture into rocky heaps on the prepared baking sheets.

5 Bake in the oven at 200°C (400°F) mark 6 for about 20 minutes until golden brown. Leave to cool on a wire rack and serve while still fresh.

FARMHOUSE SULTANA CAKE

Serves 8

225 g (8 oz) plain flour
10 ml (2 tsp) mixed spice
5 ml (1 tsp) bicarbonate of soda
225 g (8 oz) plain wholemeal flour
175 g (6 oz) butter or block
  margarine
225 g (8 oz) soft dark brown sugar
225 g (8 oz) sultanas
1 egg, beaten
about 300 ml ($\frac{1}{2}$ pint) milk
10 sugar cubes

1 Grease and line a 20.5-cm (8-inch) square, loose bottomed cake tin.

2 Sift the plain flour, spice and bicarbonate of soda into a large bowl and stir in the wholemeal flour. Rub in the fat until the mixture resembles fine breadcrumbs and stir in the sugar and sultanas.

3 Make a well in the centre and gradually pour in the egg and milk. Beat gently until well mixed and of a soft dropping consistency, adding more milk if necessary.

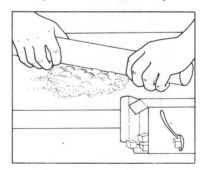

4 Turn the mixture into the prepared tin and level the surface. Roughly crush the sugar cubes with the end of a rolling pin and scatter over the cake.

5 Bake in the oven at 170°C (325°F) mark 3 for about 1 hour 40 minutes or until a fine, warmed skewer inserted into the centre comes out clean. Turn out to cool on a wire rack.

CREAMED CAKES

Cakes that contain half as much fat as flour, or more, are made by creaming the fat and sugar at the start. These cakes are rich and moist, firm to touch and they are excellent iced. They cut easily into fancy shapes, so make good children's party cakes.

Use butter or block margarine and take it out of the refrigerator a while before you want to use it. Choose a large mixing bowl, to give you room for vigorous beating and warm it a little to make creaming easier. Beat the fat and sugar together with a wooden spoon until they are as pale and fluffy as whipped cream. If the fat is a little hard to start with, beat it alone until well softened before adding the sugar. An electric mixer makes creaming easier.

Next beat in the eggs. These too should be at room temperature, and add them a little at a time to prevent curdling. If the mixture starts to curdle, add a little sifted flour with each portion of egg and beat in. Fold in the remaining flour with a large metal spoon.

Quicker to make than creamed cakes are those made by the 'all-in-one' method. For these you need soft 'tub' margarine, which is soft enough to beat straight from the refrigerator and which has been developed to give the best results with the 'all-in-one' method. You can use butter or block margarine but they must be soft; leave them at room temperature for at least 1 hour first.

For all-in-one cakes simply beat all the ingredients together with a wooden spoon for 2–3 minutes, or with a mixer for even less time. Use self-raising flour, to give the cake an extra boost, and caster or soft brown sugar, which dissolve quicker than other sugars.

The result of this method is a cake that is similar to one made by creaming, but it won't keep as well. Put it in an airtight container or wrap tightly in foil as soon as it is cold to prevent it going stale.

VICTORIA SANDWICH

Serves 6–8

100 g (4 oz) butter or block margarine
100 g (4 oz) caster sugar
2 eggs, beaten
100 g (4 oz) self-raising flour
caster sugar, to dredge
60 ml (4 tbsp) jam or 150 ml (5 fl oz) double cream, whipped or ½ quantity butter cream (see page 662), to fill

1 Grease two 18-cm (7-inch) sandwich tins and line the base of each with greased greaseproof paper.

2 Put the fat and sugar into a warmed mixing bowl and cream together with a wooden spoon until pale and fluffy. Scrape mixture down from sides of bowl from time to time to ensure that no sugar crystals are left.

3 Add the egg a little at a time; beat well after each addition. Gradually sift the flour on to the mixture and fold it in as quickly and lightly as possible.

4 Place half the mixture in each of the prepared sandwich tins. Lightly smooth the surface of the mixture with a palette knife. Bake both cakes on the same shelf of the oven at 190°C (375°F) mark 5 for about 20 minutes until they are well risen and begin to shrink away from sides of tins.

5 Turn out and leave the cakes to cool on a wire rack, then sandwich them together with jam.

VARIATIONS

Chocolate sandwich Replace 45 ml (3 tbsp) flour with 45 ml (3 tbsp) cocoa powder. For a more moist cake, blend the cocoa with a little water to give a thick paste and beat it into the creamed ingredients with the eggs. Use chocolate butter cream as filling.
Coffee sandwich Dissolve 10 ml (2 tsp) instant coffee in a little water and add it to the creamed mixture with the egg, or use 10 ml (2 tsp) coffee essence. Use coffee butter cream as filling.
Orange or lemon sandwich Add the finely grated rind of one orange or lemon to the mixture and use orange or lemon curd or orange or lemon butter cream as filling. Use some of the juice from the orange or lemon to make glacé icing (see page 662).

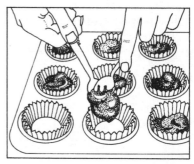

Cup cakes Divide the mixture between 18 paper cases and bake as above. If liked, fold 50 g (2 oz) chocolate polka dots, sultanas, raisins, chopped walnuts or glacé cherries into the mixture with the

flour. When cold, top each cup cake with glacé icing (see page 660).

MADEIRA CAKE

Serves 6–8

100 g (4 oz) plain flour
100 g (4 oz) self-raising flour
175 g (6 oz) butter or block margarine
175 g (6 oz) caster sugar
5 ml (1 tsp) vanilla flavouring
3 eggs, beaten
15–30 ml (1–2 tbsp) milk (optional)
2–3 thin slices citron peel

1 Grease and line an 18-cm (7-inch) round cake tin. Sift the flours together.

2 Cream the butter or margarine and the sugar together until pale and fluffy, then beat in the vanilla flavouring.

3 Add the egg a little at a time, beating well after each addition.

4 Fold in the sifted flour with a metal spoon, adding a little milk if necessary to give a dropping consistency.

5 Turn the mixture into the prepared tin and bake in the oven at 180°C (350°F) mark 4 for 20 minutes.

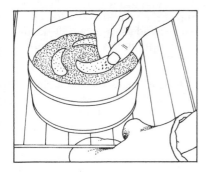

6 Lay the citron peel on top of the cake, return it to the oven and bake for a further 40 minutes until firm to the touch. Turn out and leave to cool on a wire rack.

CHOCOLATE BATTENBERG CAKE

Serves 10

175 g (6 oz) butter or margarine
175 g (6 oz) caster sugar
a few drops of vanilla flavouring
3 eggs, beaten
175 g (6 oz) self-raising flour
30 ml (2 tbsp) cocoa powder
a little milk, to mix (optional)
225 g (8 oz) almond paste
caster sugar, to dredge
225 g (8 oz) apricot jam, melted

1 Grease and line a 30 × 20.5-cm (12 × 8-inch) Swiss roll tin and divide it lengthways with a 'wall' of greaseproof paper.

2 Cream fat and sugar together until pale and fluffy, then beat in vanilla flavouring. Add the egg a little at a time, beating well.

3 Gradually sift the flour over the mixture and fold it in lightly. Turn half the mixture into one side of the tin and level the surface. Sift the cocoa over the other half and fold in, adding a little milk if necessary to give a dropping consistency.

4 Turn the chocolate mixture into the tin and level surface. Bake in the oven at 190°C (375°F) mark 5 for 40–45 minutes until well risen and firm. Turn out and leave to cool on a wire rack.

5 When cold, trim cakes to an equal size and cut each in half lengthways. On a working surface sprinkled with caster sugar, roll out the almond paste to a 30-cm (12-inch) square.

6 Place one strip of cake on the almond paste so that it lies up against the edge of paste. Place an alternate coloured strip next to it.

7 Brush top and sides of cake with melted jam and layer up with alternate coloured strips.

8 Bring almond paste up and over cake to cover it. Press paste firmly on to cake, then seal and trim join. Place cake seam-side down and trim both ends with a sharp knife. Crimp top edges of paste with the thumb and fore-finger and mark the top in a criss-cross pattern with a knife. Dredge lightly with caster sugar.

APPLE CAKE

Serves 8

350 g (12 oz) self-raising flour
2.5 ml (½ tsp) salt
5 ml (1 tsp) ground cinnamon
2.5 ml (½ tsp) ground nutmeg
2.5 ml (½ tsp) ground cloves
5 ml (1 tsp) bicarbonate of soda
450 ml (¾ pint) apple purée
100 g (4 oz) butter or block margarine
175 g (6 oz) light brown soft sugar
1 egg, separated
100 g (4 oz) seedless raisins

1 Grease and line with greased greaseproof paper a 20.5-cm (8-inch) round cake tin. Sift together the flour, salt and spices.

2 Add the bicarbonate of soda to the apple purée and stir until dissolved.

3 Cream the butter or margarine and the sugar together until pale and fluffy, then beat in the egg yolk.

4 Fold in the flour and apple purée alternately, then stir in the seedless raisins.

5 Whisk the egg white until stiff, and fold in with a large metal spoon.

6 Turn the mixture into the prepared tin. Bake in the oven at 180°C (350°F) mark 4 for about 1–1½ hours until firm to the touch. Turn out and leave to cool on a wire rack.

RICH FRUIT CAKES

A rich fruit cake is traditional for family celebrations. At weddings and Christenings, anniversaries and Christmas, the centrepiece will most often be a beautiful cake decorated with royal icing; beneath the sugar coating will be a dark, glossy cake loaded with fruit, candied peel, nuts and spices and deliciously soaked with brandy.

Like other rich cakes, fruit cakes are made by the creaming method (see page 136), but the mixture is slightly stiffer to support the weight of the fruit. If the mixture is too wet fruit is inclined to sink to the bottom. Remember that all dried fruit should be thoroughly cleaned and dried before use; glacé cherries should be rinsed to remove excess syrup, then dried. Toss all fruit in a little of the measured flour.

You will find that creaming and mixing a rich fruit cake is quite hard work, especially if it is a large cake, and the baking times are long. So it is useful to know that you can mix one day and bake the next if it is more convenient. Put the prepared mixture in the tin, cover it loosely with a clean cloth and leave it in a cool place until you are ready to bake.

Protect the outside of a rich fruit cake from overbrowning during the long cooking by wrapping a double thickness of brown paper round the outside of the tin. Stand the tin on several thicknesses of brown paper or newspaper in the oven and cover the top of the cake towards the end of cooking if necessary.

All fruit cakes keep well, but the richest actually improve if kept for two or three months before you cut them. When the cake is cold, wrap it in greaseproof paper and put it in an airtight container or wrap in foil; every two or three weeks, get it out, prick the surface with a fine skewer and spoon over a little brandy or other spirit.

RICH FRUIT CAKE
(see quantity chart, opposite)

1 Grease and line the cake tin for the size of cake you wish to make, using a double thickness of greaseproof paper. Tie a double band of brown paper round the outside.

2 Prepare the ingredients for the appropriate size of cake according to the chart opposite. Wash and dry all the fruit, if necessary chopping any over-large pieces, and mix well together in a large bowl. Add the flaked almonds. Sift flour and spices into another bowl with a pinch of salt.

3 Put the butter, sugar and lemon rind into a warmed mixing bowl and cream together with a wooden spoon until pale and fluffy. Add the beaten eggs, a little at a time, beating well after each addition.

4 Gradually fold the flour lightly into the mixture with a metal spoon, then fold in the brandy. Finally fold in the fruit and nuts.

5 Turn the mixture into the prepared tin, spreading it evenly and making sure there are no air pockets. Make a hollow in the centre to ensure an even surface when cooked.

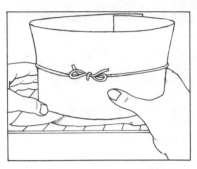

6 Stand the tin on newspaper or brown paper in the oven and bake at 150°C (300°F) mark 2 for the required time (see chart), until a fine skewer inserted in the centre comes out clean. To prevent the cake from overbrowning, cover it with greaseproof paper after about 1½ hours.

7 When cooked, leave the cake to cool in the tin before turning out on to a wire rack. Prick the top of the cake all over with a fine skewer and slowly pour 30–45 ml (2–3 tbsp) brandy over it before storing.

8 Wrap the cake in a double thickness of greaseproof paper and place upside down in an airtight tin. Cover with foil to store.

QUANTITIES AND SIZES FOR RICH FRUIT CAKES

To make a formal cake for a birthday, wedding or anniversary, the following chart will show you the amount of ingredients required to fill the chosen cake tin or tins, whether round or square.

Note   When baking large cakes, 25 cm (10 inches) and upwards, it is advisable to reduce the oven heat to 130°C (250°F) mark $\frac{1}{2}$ after two-thirds of the cooking time.

Square tin size		15 cm (6 inches) square	18 cm (7 inches) square	20.5 cm (8 inches) square
Round tin size	15 cm (6 inches) diameter	18 cm (7 inches) diameter	20.5 cm (8 inches) diameter	23 cm (9 inches) diameter
Currants	225 g (8 oz)	350 g (12 oz)	450 g (1 lb)	625 g (1 lb 6 oz)
Sultanas	100 g (4 oz)	125 g (4½ oz)	200 g (7 oz)	225 g (8 oz)
Raisins	100 g (4 oz)	125 g (4½ oz)	200 g (7 oz)	225 g (8 oz)
Glacé cherries	50 g (2 oz)	75 g (3 oz)	150 g (5 oz)	175 g (6 oz)
Mixed peel	25 g (1 oz)	50 g (2 oz)	75 g (3 oz)	100 g (4 oz)
Flaked almonds	25 g (1 oz)	50 g (2 oz)	75 g (3 oz)	100 g (4 oz)
Lemon rind	a little	a little	a little	¼ lemon
Plain flour	175 g (6 oz)	215 g (7½ oz)	350 g (12 oz)	400 g (14 oz)
Mixed spice	1.25 ml (¼ tsp)	2.5 ml (½ tsp)	2.5 ml (½ tsp)	5 ml (1 tsp)
Cinnamon	1.25 ml (¼ tsp)	2.5 ml (½ tsp)	2.5 ml (½ tsp)	5 ml (1 tsp)
Butter	150 g (5 oz)	175 g (6 oz)	275 g (10 oz)	350 g (12 oz)
Sugar	150 g (5 oz)	175 g (6 oz)	275 g (10 oz)	350 g (12 oz)
Eggs, beaten	2½	3	5	6
Brandy	15 ml (1 tbsp)	15 ml (1 tbsp)	15–30 ml (1–2 tbsp)	30 ml (2 tbsp)
Time (approx.)	2½–3 hours	3 hours	3½ hours	4 hours
Weight when cooked	1.1 kg (2½ lb)	1.6 kg (3¼ lb)	2.2 kg (4¾ lb)	2.7 kg (6 lb)

Square tin size	23 cm (9 inches) square	25.5 cm (10 inches) square	28 cm (11 inches) square	30.5 cm (12 inches) square
Round tin size	25.5 cm (10 inches) diameter	28 cm (11 inches) diameter	30.5 cm (12 inches) diameter	
Currants	775 g (1 lb 12 oz)	1.1 kg (2 lb 8 oz)	1.5 kg (3 lb 2 oz)	1.7 kg (3 lb 12 oz)
Sultanas	375 g (13 oz)	400 g (14 oz)	525 g (1 lb 3 oz)	625 g (1 lb 6 oz)
Raisins	375 g (13 oz)	400 g (14 oz)	525 g (1 lb 3 oz)	625 g (1 lb 6 oz)
Glacé cherries	250 g (9 oz)	275 g (10 oz)	350 g (12 oz)	425 g (15 oz)
Mixed peel	150 g (5 oz)	200 g (7 oz)	250 g (9 oz)	275 g (10 oz)
Flaked almonds	150 g (5 oz)	200 g (7 oz)	250 g (9 oz)	275 g (10 oz)
Lemon rind	¼ lemon	½ lemon	½ lemon	1 lemon
Plain flour	600 g (1 lb 5 oz)	700 g (1 lb 8 oz)	825 g (1 lb 13 oz)	1 kg (2 lb 6 oz)
Mixed spice	5 ml (1 tsp)	10 ml (2 tsp)	12.5 ml (2½ tsp)	12.5 ml (2½ tsp)
Cinnamon	5 ml (1 tsp)	10 ml (2 tsp)	12.5 ml (2½ tsp)	12.5 ml (2½ tsp)
Butter	500 g (1 lb 2 oz)	600 g (1 lb 5 oz)	800 g (1 lb 12 oz)	950 g (2 lb 2 oz)
Sugar	500 g (1 lb 2 oz)	600 g (1 lb 5 oz)	800 g (1 lb 12 oz)	950 g (2 lb 2 oz)
Eggs, beaten	9	11	14	17
Brandy	30–45 ml (2–3 tbsp)	45 ml (3 tbsp)	60 ml (4 tbsp)	90 ml (6 tbsp)
Time (approx.)	6 hours	7 hours	8 hours	8½ hours
Weight when cooked	4 kg (9 lb)	5.2 kg (11½ lb)	6.7 kg (14¾ lb)	7.7 kg (17 lb)

MERINGUES

If you want the simplest possible cake for a special tea or dessert, a meringue is a good choice. Light as air and sweet as sugar, they are easy to make and few people can refuse them.

All meringues are based on stiffly whisked egg whites. The most common type is made by folding in caster sugar; when baked this gives a crisp, off-white meringue with a very slightly soft inside. It can be formed into rounds or mounds or piped—either in the traditional 'shell' shape or in nests to hold fruit or cream fillings. Using the same method but substituting icing sugar gives a much drier, whiter meringue. For a firm meringue for elaborate baskets, the sugar is added in the form of a hot syrup. Finally, a really soft meringue can be made by adding a little vinegar and cornflour. This is used to make a pavlova.

Meringues are best made with eggs that are 2–3 days old. Separate the whites from the yolks carefully, making sure that no trace of yolk gets into the whites. If possible, keep the separated whites in a covered container in the refrigerator for up to 24 hours before use—this makes them more gelatinous and whisk more quickly to a greater volume. Otherwise use them straight after separating, but the colder the better; a pinch of salt or cream of tartar can be added to help them hold their shape.

Whisk until the whites are stiff enough to stand in peaks, then add the sugar. For a basic meringue, whisk in half the sugar first, then fold the rest in lightly with a large metal spoon. Shape the meringue quickly, before the mixture separates, on a baking sheet lined with non-stick paper. Dry out or bake in a low oven for several hours until crisp. When cool, store in an airtight container; meringues keep well unfilled for 2–3 weeks; they also freeze very successfully in rigid polythene containers.

SMALL MERINGUES

2 egg whites
100 g (4 oz) caster sugar
150 ml (5 fl oz) double cream

1 Line a large baking sheet with non-stick paper. Whisk the egg whites until very stiff.

2 Add half the sugar and whisk again until the mixture regains its former stiffness. Fold the remaining sugar into the mixture very lightly with a metal spoon.

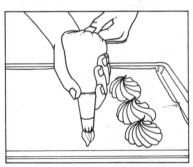

3 Spoon the mixture into a piping bag fitted with a large star nozzle and pipe small mounds on to the prepared baking sheet.

4 Dry out in the oven at 130°C (250°F) mark ½ for 2–3 hours until the meringues are firm and crisp but still white. If they begin to colour, prop the oven door open slightly. Ease the meringues off the paper and leave to cool on a wire rack. Whip cream until stiff and use to sandwich meringues in pairs.

MOCHA MERINGUE

3 egg whites
175 g (6 oz) caster sugar
15 ml (1 tbsp) instant coffee powder
For the filling
300 ml (10 fl oz) double cream
2 egg whites
5 ml (1 tsp) instant coffee powder
25 g (1 oz) chocolate, grated
25 g (1 oz) almonds, finely chopped
chopped almonds and grated chocolate, to decorate

1 Draw two 20.5-cm (8-inch) circles on non-stick paper and place on two baking sheets.

2 Whisk the egg whites until very stiff. Whisk in half the sugar, add the instant coffee and whisk until the mixture is really stiff and no longer speckled with coffee. Carefully fold in the remaining sugar with a metal spoon.

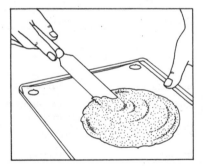

3 Divide the mixture between the baking sheets and spread evenly to fill the circles. Bake in the oven at 150°C (300°F) mark 2 for about 2 hours until dry. Leave to cool on the baking sheets before carefully lifting them off.

4 To make up the filling, whip the cream until thick. Whisk the egg whites until stiff, then carefully fold into the cream. Fold in the coffee, chocolate and nuts.

5 Sandwich the meringue layers together with half the cream mixture. Spread remainder on top; decorate with nuts and chocolate 30 minutes before serving.

MELTED CAKES

If honey, treacle, syrup or chocolate are included in a recipe, the cake is made by melting these ingredients with the sugar and fat before mixing with the flour. This ensures that they blend in evenly. The result is a cake with a moist and irresistibly sticky texture. The method is a very easy one, traditionally used for gingerbreads and American brownies.

The raising agent in cakes made by this method is usually bicarbonate of soda, which reacts with the natural acids present in liquid sweeteners, and spices are often added to enhance the flavour and counteract any soda taste.

Measure treacle, syrup and honey carefully, as too much of these products can cause a heavy, sunken cake. Warm the fat, sugar and liquid sweetener gently, just until the sugar is dissolved and the fat melted. Do not let the mixture boil or it will be unusable.

Let the mixture cool slightly and add any other liquids such as milk and eggs before adding to the flour. If a hot liquid is added to the flour, it will begin to cook and the cake will be hard.

If the recipe includes chocolate, break the chocolate into a bowl and add the fat, cut into pieces. Place the bowl over a saucepan of hot, but not boiling, water and heat it gently until melted. The chocolate and butter should blend to a smooth cream when stirred together. Let it cool a little before adding to the flour.

The final mixture will be a thick, heavy batter that can be poured into the tin. It will not need smoothing, as it will find its own level. Cakes made by this method are generally baked at a low to moderate temperature until just risen and firm to the touch. They are best left for a day or two before cutting, to allow the crust to soften and the flavour to mellow, and they keep well if stored in an airtight container.

GINGERBREAD

Serves 8–10

450 g (1 lb) plain flour
5 ml (1 tsp) salt
15 ml (1 tbsp) ground ginger
15 ml (1 tbsp) baking powder
5 ml (1 tsp) bicarbonate of soda
225 g (8 oz) demerara sugar
175 g (6 oz) butter or block margarine
175 g (6 oz) black treacle
175 g (6 oz) golden syrup
300 ml ($\frac{1}{2}$ pint) milk
1 egg, beaten

1 Grease and line a 23-cm (9-inch) square cake tin. Sift together the flour, salt, ginger, baking powder and bicarbonate of soda into a large mixing bowl.

2 Put the sugar, fat, treacle and syrup in a saucepan and warm gently over a low heat until melted and well blended. Do not allow the mixture to boil. Then remove the pan from the heat and leave to cool slightly, until you can hold your hand comfortably against the side of the pan.

3 Mix in the milk and beaten egg. Make a well in the centre of the dry ingredients, pour in the liquid and mix very thoroughly.

4 Pour the mixture into the prepared tin and bake in the oven at 170°C (325°F) mark 3 for about $1\frac{1}{2}$ hours until firm but springy to the touch.

5 Leave the gingerbread in the tin for about 10 minutes after baking, then turn out on to a wire rack, remove the lining paper and leave to cool.

BOSTON BROWNIES

Makes about 16

50 g (2 oz) plain chocolate
65 g (2$\frac{1}{2}$ oz) butter or block margarine
175 g (6 oz) caster sugar
65 g (2$\frac{1}{2}$ oz) self-raising flour
1.25 ml ($\frac{1}{4}$ tsp) salt
2 eggs, beaten
2.5 ml ($\frac{1}{2}$ tsp) vanilla flavouring
50 g (2 oz) walnuts, roughly chopped

1 Grease and line a shallow 20.5-cm (8-inch) square cake tin. Then break up the chocolate and put it in a bowl with the butter, cut into pieces. Stand the bowl over a pan of hot water and heat gently, stirring occasionally, until melted. Add the caster sugar.

2 Sift together the flour and salt into a bowl. Add the chocolate mixture, eggs, vanilla flavouring and walnuts. Mix thoroughly.

3 Pour the mixture into the prepared tin and bake in the oven at 180°C (350°F) mark 4 for 35–40 minutes until the mixture is risen and just beginning to leave the sides of the cake tin.

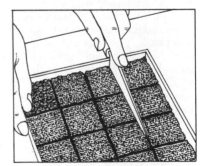

4 Leave in the tin to cool, then cut the Boston brownies into squares with a sharp knife.

SPONGE CAKES

The classic sponge cake is light and feathery, made by whisking together eggs and caster sugar, then folding in the flour. There is no fat in the mixture, and the cake rises simply because of the air incorporated during whisking. For an even lighter cake the egg yolks and sugar can be whisked together, with the whites whisked separately and folded in afterwards.

The whisking method produces the lightest of all cakes. Sponges are perfect for filling with whipped cream and fruit and are used for many gâteaux, dessert cakes and for Swiss rolls. Because they have no fat they always need a filling, and they do not keep well. Bake a sponge the day you wish to eat it.

A moister version of a whisked sponge is a Genoese sponge. This is also made by the whisking method, but melted butter is added with the flour. This gives a delicate sponge, lighter than a Victoria sandwich, but with a moister texture than the plain whisked sponge, and a delicious buttery taste. Don't try to substitute margarine for butter in this recipe or the flavour and texture will be lost. A Genoese sponge keeps better than a plain whisked sponge.

To make a really good sponge, don't rush. The eggs and sugar must be whisked until thick enough to leave a trail when the whisk is lifted from the surface. If you use a rotary whisk or a hand-held electric mixer, place the bowl over a saucepan of hot water to speed the thickening process and make it less hard work. Do not let the bottom of the bowl touch the water or the mixture will become too hot. When the mixture is really thick and double in volume, take the bowl off the heat and continue to whisk until it is cool.

Add the flour carefully. Sift it first, then add a little at a time to the whisked mixture and fold it in until evenly blended. Do not stir or you will break the air bubbles and the cake will not rise.

WHISKED SPONGE CAKE

Serves 6–8

3 eggs, size 2
100 g (4 oz) caster sugar
75 g (3 oz) plain flour

1 Grease and line two 18-cm (7-inch) sandwich tins and dust with a little flour or with a mixture of flour and caster sugar.

2 Put the eggs and sugar in a large deep bowl and stand it over a pan of hot water. The bowl should fit snugly over the pan and the bottom of the bowl should not touch the bottom of the pan.

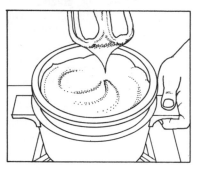

Whisk the eggs and sugar together until doubled in volume and thick enough to leave a trail on the surface when the whisk is lifted. If whisking by hand, this will take 15–20 minutes; if a hand-held electric mixer is used, 7–10 minutes will be enough.

3 Remove the bowl from the heat and continue whisking for a further 5 minutes until the mixture is cooler and creamy looking.

4 Sift half the flour over the mixture and fold it in very lightly, using a large metal spoon. Sift and fold in the remaining flour in the same way.

5 Pour the mixture into the prepared tins, tilting the tins to spread the mixture evenly. Do not use a palette knife or spatula to smooth the mixture as this will crush out the air bubbles.

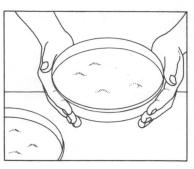

6 Bake the cakes in the oven at 190°C (375°F) mark 5 for 20–25 minutes until firm but springy to the touch. Turn out and leave to cool on a wire rack for 30 minutes.

7 When the cakes are cold, sandwich them together with strawberry or apricot jam, whipped cream or butter cream and dredge with caster sugar or cover the top with glacé icing (see page 662).

SWISS ROLL

Serves 6–8

3 eggs, size 2
100 g (4 oz) caster sugar
100 g (4 oz) plain flour
15 ml (1 tbsp) hot water
caster sugar, to dredge
100 g (4 oz) jam, warmed

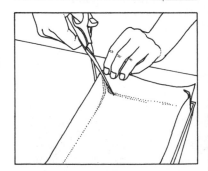

1 Grease a 33 × 23 cm (13 × 9 inch) Swiss roll tin. Cut a piece of greaseproof paper about 5 cm (2 inches) larger all round than the tin. Place it on the tin, creasing it to fit, and make cuts from corners of paper to corners of creases. Put in tin and grease.

2 Put the eggs and sugar in a large bowl, stand this over a pan of hot water and whisk until thick, creamy and pale in colour. The mixture should be stiff enough to leave a trail on the surface when the whisk is lifted.

3 Remove the bowl from the heat and whisk until cool. Sift half the flour over the mixture and fold in very lightly with a metal spoon. Sift and fold in the remaining flour, then lightly stir in the hot water.

4 Pour the mixture into the prepared tin and tilt the tin backwards and forwards to spread the mixture in an even layer. Bake in the oven at 220°C (425°F) mark 7 for 7–9 minutes until golden brown, well risen and firm to the touch.

5 Meanwhile, place a sheet of greaseproof paper over a tea towel lightly wrung out in hot water. Dredge the paper thickly with caster sugar.

6 Quickly turn out the cake on to the paper, trim off the crusty edges; spread with warmed jam.

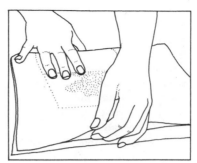

7 Roll up the cake with the aid of the paper. Make the first turn firmly so that the whole cake will roll evenly and have a good shape when finished, but roll more lightly after this turn.

8 Place seam-side down on a wire rack and dredge with sugar. Leave to cool for 30 minutes before serving.

——————— VARIATION ———————

Chocolate Swiss roll Replace 15 ml (1 tbsp) flour with 15 ml (1 tbsp) cocoa powder. Turn out the cooked sponge and trim as above, then cover with a sheet of greaseproof paper and roll with the paper inside. When the cake is cold, unroll and remove the paper. Spread with whipped cream or butter cream and re-roll. Dust with icing sugar.

GENOESE SPONGE

Serves 6–8

40 g (1½ oz) butter
3 eggs, size 2
75 g (3 oz) caster sugar
65 g (2½ oz) plain flour
15 ml (1 tbsp) cornflour

1 Grease and line two 18-cm (7-inch) sandwich tins or one 18-cm (7-inch) deeper cake tin.

2 Put the butter into a saucepan and heat gently until melted, then remove from the heat and leave to stand for a few minutes to cool slightly.

3 Put the eggs and sugar in a bowl, stand it over a pan of hot water and whisk until thick, creamy and pale in colour. The mixture should be stiff enough to leave a trail on the surface when the whisk is lifted. Remove from the heat and continue whisking until cool.

4 Sift the flours together into a bowl. Fold half the flour into the egg mixture with a metal spoon.

5 Pour half the cooled butter round the edge of the mixture. Gradually fold in the remaining butter and flour alternately. Be sure to fold in very lightly or the fat will sink to the bottom and cause a heavy cake.

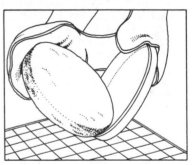

6 Pour the mixture into the prepared tins. Bake sandwich cakes in the oven at 180°C (350°F) mark 4 for 25–30 minutes, or a deep cake for 35–40 minutes, until golden brown and firm to the touch. Turn out and leave to cool on a wire rack for 30 minutes before serving.

——————— VARIATION ———————

Chocolate Genoese For either cake, replace 15 g (½ oz) plain flour with 15 g (½ oz) cocoa powder.

YEAST CAKES

Cakes baked with yeast have a magic of their own. The lively rising of the dough before it is cooked and the characteristic yeasty smell during baking make this type of baking a special pleasure.

Fresh and dried yeast give equally good flavour and texture to the finished cake; only the method of using them is different. Fresh yeast is rather like putty in colour and texture and should crumble easily when broken. Although it will store for up to 1 week wrapped in foil in the refrigerator or for up to 3 months in the freezer, it will give best results when absolutely fresh, so buy it in small quantities when required. Dried yeast keeps well in an airtight container in a cool dry place for at least 6 months.

Yeast needs warmth in which to grow, so all the cake ingredients should be at warm room temperature. When using fresh yeast, blend it with tepid liquid (which feels warm when tested with a little finger) before adding to the flour. Dried yeast must be activated in advance by mixing with a proportion of the recipe liquid (usually a third) and a little sugar; leave for 15 minutes before use.

In plain mixtures the yeast liquid can be blended straight into the flour and fat, kneaded and left to rise. Rich mixtures containing larger proportions of fat and eggs retard the growth of the yeast, so to help it you start it off with a 'sponge batter'. This is made with about a third of the flour and all the liquid; the yeast is blended into the batter and it is left until frothy before blending with remaining ingredients. With the sponge batter method there is no need to activate dried yeast ahead.

Always use strong flour for recipes made with yeast; the extra gluten helps give the cake a light, open texture. With a plain mixture, kneading will help develop the gluten and give a better rise.

DOUGHNUTS

Makes 10–12

15 g (½ oz) fresh yeast or 10 ml (2 tsp) dried yeast
about 60 ml (4 tbsp) tepid milk
pinch of sugar (optional)
225 g (8 oz) strong white flour
2.5 ml (½ tsp) salt
knob of butter or block margarine
1 egg, beaten
jam
fat, for deep frying
sugar and ground cinnamon

1 If using dried yeast sprinkle it on the milk and add the sugar; leave for about 15 minutes until frothy. If using fresh yeast, just blend it with the milk.

2 Sift the flour and salt into a bowl and rub in the fat. Add the yeast liquid and egg and mix to a soft dough, adding a little more milk if necessary. Beat well until smooth. Cover with a clean cloth and leave to rise in a warm place until doubled in size.

3 Knead lightly on a lightly floured working surface and divide into ten–twelve pieces.

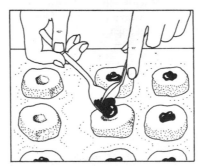

4 Shape each piece into a round, with a small hole in the middle. Put 5 ml (1 tsp) jam in the centre and draw up edges to form a ball.

5 Heat the fat to 180°C (360°F) or until it will brown a 2.5-cm (1-inch) cube of bread in 1 minute. Fry the doughnuts for 5–10 minutes until golden. Drain and toss in sugar mixed with cinnamon.

RUM BABAS

Makes 16

25 g (1 oz) fresh yeast or 15 ml (1 tbsp) dried
90 ml (6 tbsp) tepid milk
225 g (8 oz) strong white flour
2.5 ml (½ tsp) salt
30 ml (2 tbsp) caster sugar
4 eggs, beaten
100 g (4 oz) butter, softened
100 g (4 oz) currants
300 ml (10 fl oz) double cream
120 ml (8 tbsp) clear honey
120 ml (8 tbsp) water
a little rum

1 Lightly grease sixteen 9-cm (3½-inch) ring tins with lard and place them on baking sheets.

2 Put the yeast, milk and 50 g (2 oz) flour into a bowl and blend until smooth. Cover with a clean cloth and leave in a warm place for 15 minutes until frothy.

3 Add the remaining flour, the salt, sugar, eggs, butter and currants and beat well with a wooden spoon for 3–4 minutes.

4 Half-fill the prepared tins with the dough, cover with a cloth and leave to rise in a warm place until tins are two-thirds full.

5 Bake in the oven at 200°C (400°C) mark 6 for 15–20 minutes until well risen, golden and just beginning to shrink away from the sides of the tins. Leave to cool in the tins for a few minutes.

6 Meanwhile, make the rum syrup. Put the honey and water together in a pan and warm gently. Add rum to taste.

7 Turn the rum babas out on to a wire rack and put a tray underneath. While the babas are still hot, spoon rum syrup over each one until well soaked. Cool. To serve, whip the cream until thick and spoon or pipe some in to the centre of each baba.

WHAT WENT WRONG

Too close a texture
1 Too much liquid.
2 Too little raising agent.
3 Insufficient creaming of the fat and sugar–air should be well incorporated at this stage.
4 Curdling of the creamed mixture when the eggs are added (a curdled mixture holds less air than one of the correct consistency).
5 Over-stirring or beating the flour into a creamed mixture when little or no raising agent is present.

Uneven texture with holes
1 Over-stirring or uneven mixing in of the flour.
2 Putting the mixture into the cake tin in small amounts— pockets of air trapped in the mixture.

Dry and crumbly texture
1 Too much raising agent.
2 Too long a cooking time in too cool an oven.

Fruit cakes dry and crumbly
1 Cooking at too high a temperature.
2 Too stiff a mixture.
3 Not lining the tin thoroughly —for a large cake, double greaseproof paper should be used.

Fruit sinking to the bottom of the cake
1 Damp fruit.
2 Sticky glacé cherries.
3 Too soft a mixture: a rich fruit cake mixture should be fairly stiff, so that it can support the weight of the fruit.
4 Opening or banging the oven door while the cake is rising.
5 Using self-raising flour where the recipe requires plain, or using too much baking powder —the cake over-rises and cannot carry the fruit with it.

'Peaking' and 'cracking'
1 Too hot an oven.
2 The cake being placed too near top of the oven.
3 Too stiff a mixture.
4 Too small a cake tin.

Close, heavy-textured whisked sponge
1 The eggs and sugar being insufficiently beaten, so that not enough air is enclosed.
2 The flour being stirred in too heavily or for too long—very light folding movements are required and a metal spoon should be used.

Cakes sinking in the middle
1 Too soft a mixture.
2 Too much raising agent.
3 Too cool an oven, which means that the centre of the cake does not rise.
4 Too hot an oven, which makes the cake appear to be done on the outside before it is cooked through, so that it is taken from the oven too soon.
5 Insufficient baking.

Burnt fruit on the outside of a fruit cake
1 Too high a temperature.
2 Lack of protection: as soon as the cake begins to colour, a piece of brown paper or a double thickness of greaseproof paper should be placed over the top for the remainder of the cooking time to prevent further browning.

A heavy layer at the base of a Genoese sponge
1 The melted fat being too hot —it should be only lukewarm and just flowing.
2 Uneven or insufficient folding in of fat or flour.
3 Pouring the fat into the centre of the mixture instead of round the edge.

DISGUISING THE DAMAGE

If a cake goes wrong in the baking, there is no way of going back and putting it right without baking a new cake. But there are ways of disguising the damage so that only you will know.

- If a chocolate cake turns out rather too moist, call it a pudding and serve it with a fluffy sauce.

- If homemade biscuits crumble badly, use them to make a biscuit crumb flan case.

- If the top of a fruit cake gets burnt, cut it off and use a well flavoured almond paste to disguise it.

- If meringues break as you lift them off the baking sheet, serve large pieces on top of fruit and cream.

- If a sponge cake turns out a thin, flat layer, cut into fancy shapes with a biscuit cutter and sandwich together with jam and cream.

- If your cake rises unevenly, level the top, turn it over and ice the bottom.

- If a cake breaks as you take it out of the tin, disguise it as a pudding with custard sauce or fruit.

- If a cake sinks in the middle, cut out the centre and turn it into a ring cake. Ice it with butter cream or almond paste and royal icing, according to type, or decorate with whipped cream and fill the centre with fruit for a dessert.

- If a sponge or plain cake is dry, crumbly or heavy, use it as the base for a trifle and soak it in plenty of booze!

Decorating Cakes

'The icing on the cake' is the finishing touch that turns a workaday cake into a loving creation. Decorations for informal cakes may be anything from a light dusting of caster sugar or a smooth coat of glacé icing to whirls of butter cream interspersed with nuts or coloured sweets. For formal cakes you need to master piping techniques and the method of flat icing with royal icing.

EQUIPMENT

Simple decorations need no special equipment, but the right tools do help when you start to attempt more elaborate work.

An icing comb helps with icing the sides of a deep cake.

An icing nail is a small metal or polythene nail with a large head that is designed to hold decorations such as icing roses, while you make them. It enables you to hold the rose securely, and turn it without damaging it.

An icing ruler is useful for flat icing a large cake. You can substitute anything with a fine straight edge, long enough to extend both sides of the cake.

An icing turntable gives you clearance from the working surface and enables you to turn the cake freely. If you do not have a turntable, place the cake board on an upturned plate, to give it a little lift from the working surface.

Nozzles can be used with paper or fabric piping bags. A fine plain nozzle for writing and piping straight lines and simple designs, plus a star or shell nozzle, are the basics; more advanced piping work demands a whole range of different shapes and sizes. For use with paper piping bags, choose nozzles without a screw band; the band is useful with a fabric bag.

Piping bags can be made from greaseproof paper, or bought ready-made in fabric. Special icing pumps are also available.

A silver cake board or 'drum' sets off any iced cake. Some are made from thin card, or stronger ones are about 1 cm ($\frac{1}{2}$ inch) thick. Choose a board that is 5 cm (2 inches) larger than the cake, so that a border shows all round.

Apart from the above, the only tools you will need are everyday kitchen equipment: a palette knife, a table fork and a wire rack; for flat icing with royal icing you will need some fine sandpaper.

ICING

The cake must be completely cold before you start icing. The surface must be level; if necessary, turn the cake upside down and ice the flat bottom.

If making a sandwich or layer cake, put the filling in first. Then apply any decorations to the sides. Ice the top last.

For simple icings, place the cake on a wire rack to decorate it. Lifting it from one plate to another may crack the icing, and you are sure to make drips on the plate.

To use glacé icing, if coating both the top and sides of the cake, stand it on a wire rack with a tray underneath to catch the drips. As soon as the icing reaches a coating consistency and looks smooth and glossy, pour it from the bowl on to the centre of the cake. Allow the icing to run down the sides, guiding it with a palette knife. Keep a little icing back to fill the gaps.

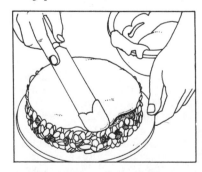

If the sides are decorated and only the top is to have glacé icing, pour the icing on to the centre of the cake and spread it with a palette knife, stopping just inside the edges to prevent it dripping down the sides. If the top is to be iced and the sides left plain, protect them with a band of greaseproof paper tied round the cake and projecting a little above it. Pour on the icing and let it find its own level. Peel off the paper when the icing is hard.

Arrange any ready-made decorations such as nuts, cherries, sweets, silver balls etc in position as soon as the icing has thickened and formed a skin. Except for feather icing, leave the icing until quite dry before applying piped decorations.

To feather ice, make a quantity of glacé icing (see page 662) and mix to a coating consistency. Make up a second batch of icing using half the quantity of sugar and enough warm water to mix it to a thick piping consistency; tint the second batch with food colouring. Spoon the coloured icing into a greaseproof paper piping bag.

Coat the top of the cake with the larger quantity of icing. Working quickly, before it has time to form a skin, snip the end off the piping bag and pipe parallel lines of coloured icing about 1–2 cm ($\frac{1}{2}$–$\frac{3}{4}$ inch) apart, over the surface. Then quickly draw the point of a skewer or a sharp knife across the piped lines, first in one direction then in the other, spacing them evenly apart.

Butter cream can be used as a filling or icing. Spread it over the top only, or over the top and sides. Decorate by making swirl marks

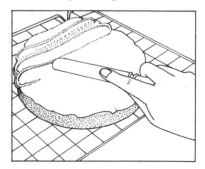

with the flat of a knife blade, or spread it evenly with a palette knife

and mark with the prongs of a fork. Add any extra decorations before it sets. For more elaborate decoration, butter cream pipes well.

Crème au beurre is a richer form of butter cream suitable for more elaborate cakes.

American frosting is a fluffy, soft icing. You need a sugar thermometer to make it. *Seven-minute frosting* is similar, but can be made without the help of a thermometer.

Almond paste is used on fruit cakes, either as a decoration in its own right, when it may be shaped and coloured as you wish, or as a firm base for royal icing.

Royal icing is the hard icing used on fruit cakes for formal occasions.

CAKE DECORATIONS

Add ready-made decorations before the icing hardens completely, or stick them in place with a little dab of fresh icing.

Nuts of all sorts, but particularly walnuts, hazelnuts, almonds and pistachios, are popular. Buy crystallised violets and roses in small quantities and keep them in a dark place to avoid bleaching. When buying angelica, look for a really good colour and a small amount of sugar. To remove sugar, soak briefly in hot water, then drain and dry well.

Chocolate and coloured vermicelli stale quickly and become speckled, so buy in small quantities as needed. Silver dragees (balls) keep well in a dry place; use tweezers for handling. They come in other colours than silver. Hundreds and thousands are useful for children's cakes, as are all sorts of coloured sweets, and for more sophisticated decorations, look for sugar coffee beans.

When decorating with chocolate, choose plain eating chocolate for chopping and grating. Chocolate-flavour cake covering is useful for scrolls and curls and also for melting, but the flavour is not so good. Crumbled chocolate flake makes a useful last minute decoration.

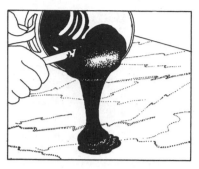

Chocolate caraque Melt 100 g (4 oz) chocolate in a bowl over a pan of hot water. Pour it in a thin layer on to a marble slab or cold baking tray and leave to set until it no longer sticks to your hand when you touch it. Holding a large knife with both hands, push the blade

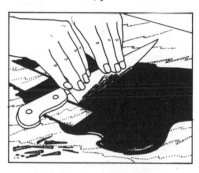

across the surface of the chocolate to roll pieces off in long curls. Adjust the angle of the blade to get the best curls.

Chocolate shapes Make a sheet of chocolate as above and cut into neat triangles or squares with a sharp knife, or stamp out circles with a small round cutter.

Chocolate curls Using a potato peeler, pare thin layers from the edge of a block of chocolate.

GLACÉ ICING

Makes about 100 g (4 oz)

100 g (4 oz) icing sugar

a few drops of vanilla or almond flavouring (optional)

15 ml (1 tbsp) warm water

colouring (optional)

1 Sift the icing sugar into a bowl. If you wish, add a few drops of vanilla or almond flavouring.

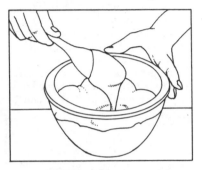

2 Gradually add the warm water. The icing should be thick enough to coat the back of a spoon. If necessary add more water or sugar to adjust consistency. Add colouring, if liked, and use at once.

———— VARIATIONS ————

Orange or lemon Replace the water with 15 ml (1 tbsp) strained orange or lemon juice.
Chocolate Dissolve 10 ml (2 tsp) cocoa powder in a little hot water and use instead of the same amount of water.
Coffee Flavour with 5 ml (1 tsp) coffee essence or dissolve 10 ml (2 tsp) instant coffee in a little hot water and use instead of the same amount of water.
Mocha Dissolve 5 ml (1 tsp) cocoa powder and 10 ml (2 tsp) instant coffee in a little hot water and use instead of the same amount of water.
Liqueur Replace 10–15 ml (2–3 tsp) of the water with the same amount of any liqueur.

BUTTER CREAM

Makes 250 g (9 oz)

75 g (3 oz) butter

175 g (6 oz) icing sugar

a few drops of vanilla flavouring

15–30 ml (1–2 tbsp) milk or warm water

Put the butter in a bowl and cream until soft. Gradually sift and beat in the sugar, adding the vanilla flavouring and milk or water.

———— VARIATIONS ————

Orange or lemon Replace the vanilla flavouring with a little finely grated orange or lemon rind. Add a little juice from the fruit, beating well to avoid curdling the mixture.
Almond Add 30 ml (2 tbsp) finely chopped toasted almonds and mix.
Coffee Replace the vanilla flavouring with 10 ml (2 tsp) instant coffee blended with some of the liquid, or replace 15 ml (1 tbsp) of the liquid with the same amount of coffee essence.
Chocolate Dissolve 15 ml (1 tbsp) cocoa powder in a little hot water and cool before adding to the mixture.
Mocha Dissolve 5 ml (1 tsp) cocoa powder and 10 ml (2 tsp) instant coffee in a little warm water taken from the measured amount. Cool before adding to the mixture.

APRICOT GLAZE

Makes 150 ml (¼ pint)

100 g (4 oz) apricot jam

30 ml (2 tbsp) water

Put the jam and water in a saucepan and heat gently, stirring, until the jam softens. Bring to the boil and simmer for 1 minute. Sieve the glaze and use while still warm.

CRÈME AU BEURRE
(Rich Butter Cream)

Makes about 275 g (10 oz)

75 g (3 oz) caster sugar

60 ml (4 tbsp) water

2 egg yolks, beaten

175 g (6 oz) butter

1 Place the sugar in a heavy based saucepan, add the water and heat very gently to dissolve the sugar, without boiling.

2 When completely dissolved, bring to boiling point and boil steadily for 2–3 minutes, to reach a temperature of 107°C (225°F).

3 Pour the syrup in a thin stream on to the egg yolks in a deep bowl, whisking all the time. Continue to whisk until the mixture is thick and cold.

4 In another bowl, cream the butter until very soft and gradually beat in the egg yolk mixture.

———— VARIATIONS ————

Chocolate Melt 50 g (2 oz) plain chocolate with 15 ml (1 tbsp) water. Cool slightly and beat in.
Coffee Beat in 15–30 ml (1–2 tbsp) coffee essence.
Fruit Crush 225 g (8 oz) fresh strawberries, raspberries etc, or thaw, drain and crush frozen fruit. Beat into the basic mixture.
Orange or lemon Add freshly grated rind and juice to taste.

CRÈME PATISSIÈRE

Makes 300 ml (½ pint)

2 eggs
50 g (2 oz) caster sugar
30 ml (2 tbsp) plain flour
30 ml (2 tbsp) cornflour
300 ml (½ pint) milk
a few drops of vanilla flavouring

1 Cream the eggs and sugar together until really pale and thick. Sift the flour and cornflour in to the bowl and beat in with a little cold milk until smooth.

2 Heat the rest of the milk until almost boiling and pour on to the egg mixture, stirring well all the time.

3 Return the custard to the saucepan and stir over a low heat until the mixture boils. Add vanilla flavouring to taste and cook for a further 2–3 minutes. Cover and allow to cool before using.

SEVEN-MINUTE FROSTING

Makes about 175 g (6 oz)

1 egg white
175 g (6 oz) caster sugar
pinch of salt
pinch of cream of tartar
30 ml (2 tbsp) water

1 Put all the ingredients into a bowl and whisk lightly. Then place the bowl over a pan of hot water and heat, whisking continuously, until the mixture thickens sufficiently to stand in peaks. This will take about 7 minutes depending on the whisk used and the heat of the water.

2 Pour the frosting over the top of the cake and spread with a palette knife.

——— VARIATIONS ———

Use the same flavourings as for American frosting.

ROYAL ICING

Makes about 900 g (2 lb)

4 egg whites
900 g (2 lb) icing sugar
15 ml (1 tbsp) lemon juice
10 ml (2 tsp) glycerine

1 Whisk the egg whites in a bowl until slightly frothy. Then sift and stir in about a quarter of the icing sugar with a wooden spoon. Continue adding more sugar gradually, beating well after each addition, until about three quarters of the sugar has been added.

2 Beat in the lemon juice and continue beating for about 10 minutes until the icing is smooth.

3 Beat in the remaining sugar until the required consistency is achieved, depending on how the icing will be used.

4 Finally, stir in the glycerine to prevent the icing hardening. Cover and keep for 24 hours to allow air bubbles to rise to the surface.

ALMOND PASTE

Makes 900 g (2 lb)

225 g (8 oz) icing sugar
225 g (8 oz) caster sugar
450 g (1 lb) ground almonds
5 ml (1 tsp) vanilla flavouring
2 eggs, lightly beaten
10 ml (2 tsp) lemon juice

1 Sift the icing sugar into a bowl and mix in the caster sugar and ground almonds.

2 Add the vanilla flavouring, egg and lemon juice and mix to a stiff dough. Knead lightly and into a ball.

AMERICAN FROSTING

Makes about 225 g (8 oz)

1 egg white
225 g (8 oz) caster or granulated sugar
60 ml (4 tbsp) water
pinch of cream of tartar

1 Whisk the egg white until stiff. Then gently heat the sugar with the water and cream of tartar, stirring until dissolved. Then, without stirring, boil to 120°C (240°F).

2 Remove the syrup from the heat and, immediately the bubbles subside, pour it on to the egg white in a thin stream, beating the mixture continuously.

3 When it thickens, shows signs of going dull round the edges and is almost cold, pour the frosting quickly over the cake and spread evenly with a palette knife.

——— VARIATIONS ———

Orange Beat in a few drops of orange essence and a little orange food colouring before it thickens.
Lemon Beat in a little lemon juice before the mixture thickens.
Caramel Substitute demerara sugar for the white sugar.
Coffee Beat in 5 ml (1 tsp) coffee essence before mixture thickens.

CHOCOLATE FROSTING

Makes about 200 g (7 oz)

25 g (1 oz) plain chocolate
150 g (5 oz) icing sugar
1 egg
2.5 ml (½ tsp) vanilla flavouring
25 g (1 oz) butter

1 Break the chocolate into pieces and put in a bowl over a pan of hot water. Heat gently, stirring, until the chocolate has melted.

2 Sift in the icing sugar, add the egg, vanilla flavouring and butter and beat until smooth.

APPLYING ALMOND PASTE

Measure round the cake with a piece of string. Dust the working surface with icing sugar and roll out two-thirds of the paste to a rectangle, half the length of the string by twice the depth of the

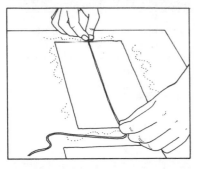

cake. Trim the edges, then cut in half lengthways with a sharp knife.

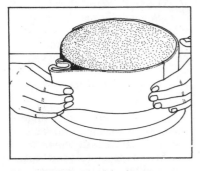

Place the cake upside down on a board and brush the sides with apricot glaze. Gently lift the almond paste and place it firmly in position round the cake.

Smooth the joins with a palette knife and keep the top and bottom edges square. Roll a jam jar lightly round the cake to help the paste stick more firmly.

Brush the top of the cake with apricot glaze and roll out the remaining almond paste to fit. With the help of the rolling pin, lift it

carefully on to the cake. Lightly roll with the rolling pin, then smooth the join and leave to dry for 2–5 days before starting to ice.

FLAT ICING WITH ROYAL ICING

Always apply royal icing over a layer of almond paste rather than directly on to the cake. Spoon almost half the icing on to the top of the cake and spread it evenly with a palette knife, using a paddling action to remove any air bubbles that may remain. Using an icing ruler or palette knife longer than the width of the cake, without

applying any pressure, draw it steadily across the top of the cake at an angle of 30°. Neaten the edges with a palette knife. Leave to dry for 24 hours before icing the sides.

To ice the sides, place the board on an icing turntable or on an upturned plate. Spread the remaining icing on the side of the cake and smooth it roughly with a small palette knife. Hold the palette knife or an icing comb upright and at an angle of 45° to the cake.

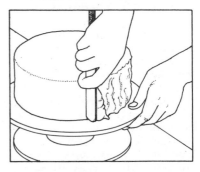

Draw the knife or comb towards you to smooth the surface. For a square cake, apply icing to each side separately. Reserve the surplus icing for decorating.

For a really smooth finish, allow to dry for 1–2 days then apply a second thinner coat of icing. Use fine sandpaper to sand down any imperfections in the first coat. Allow to dry thoroughly before adding piped decorations.

ICING AND ALMOND PASTE QUANTITIES

The amounts of almond paste quoted in this chart will give a thin covering. The quantities of royal icing should be enough for two coats.

Square tin size		15 cm (6 inches) square	18 cm (7 inches) square	20.5 cm (8 inches) square	23 cm (9 inches) square	25.5 cm (10 inches) square	28 cm (11 inches) square	30.5 cm (12 inches) square
Round tin size	15 cm (6 inches) round	18 cm (7 inches) round	20.5 cm (8 inches) round	23 cm (9 inches) round	25.5 cm (10 inches) round	28 cm (11 inches) round	30.5 cm (12 inches) round	
Almond paste	350 g (12 oz)	450 g (1 lb)	550 g (1¼ lb)	800 g (1¾ lb)	900 g (2 lb)	1 kg (2¼ lb)	1.1 kg (2½ lb)	1.4 kg (3 lb)
Royal icing	450 g (1 lb)	550 g (1¼ lb)	700 g (1½ lb)	900 g (2 lb)	1 kg (2¼ lb)	1.1 kg (2½ lb)	1.4 kg (3 lb)	1.6 kg (3½ lb)

PIPING

Butter cream, *crème au beurre*, stiff glacé icing and royal icing can all be piped. It is usual to pipe on to a base of the same kind of icing, though butter cream is sometimes piped on to glacé icing.

The icing used for piping must be completely free of lumps, or it will block the nozzle. It must also be exactly the right consistency to force easily through the nozzle, but still retain its shape.

Work with a small quantity at a time, refilling the piping bag frequently if necessary. If you are a beginner, practise on an upturned plate first. The practice icing can be scraped up while still soft and reused. Even on the real cake, if the base icing is hard mistakes can be scraped off and corrected.

Making a piping bag Fold a 25.5-cm (10-inch) square of greaseproof paper diagonally in half, then roll into a cone. Fold the points inwards to secure them. To insert a nozzle, snip off the tip of the bag and drop in the nozzle before adding the icing. For a very fine line, just snip off the end of the bag and use without a nozzle.

USING A PIPING BAG

Never more than half-fill the bag. When using a paper piping bag, fold the top flap down, enclosing the front edge, until the bag is sealed and quite firm; twist a fabric bag firmly closed. To hold the bag, lay it across the palm of one hand; with a paper bag, place your thumb firmly over the top of the bag, grasp the rest with the other four fingers and apply a steady even pressure until icing starts to come out of the nozzle. With a fabric bag grasp the bag where it is twisted with thumb and first finger and apply pressure with the remaining fingers.

To pipe a straight line: Place the tip of the nozzle where the line is to start. Apply slight pressure to the bag; as the icing starts to come out of the nozzle, lift the bag about 2.5 cm (1 inch) from the surface. This allows even the shakiest of hands to pipe a straight line. Move your hand in the direction of the line, guiding it with the other hand if you want, allowing the icing to flow evenly. About 1 cm ($\frac{1}{2}$ inch) before the end of the line, stop squeezing the bag and gently lower the tip of the nozzle to the surface.

To pipe dots: Only a slight pressure on the piping bag is required. Place the tip of the nozzle on the surface and hold the bag almost upright. Squeeze the bag gently and at the same time lift the nozzle slightly. Stop squeezing, move the nozzle slightly in a gentle shaking action to avoid a 'tail', and lift the nozzle. Larger dots can be made by moving the nozzle in a small circle or by using a larger nozzle.

To pipe stars: Fit the bag with a star nozzle. Hold the bag upright and just above the surface of the cake. Squeeze the icing out. As soon as the star is formed, stop squeezing and lift the bag away sharply.

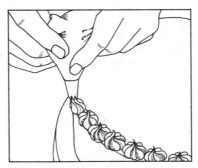

To pipe rosettes: Fit the bag with a star nozzle. Hold the icing bag upright, just above the surface of the cake. Squeeze gently and move the nozzle in a complete circle, filling in the centre. Pull the nozzle away sharply to avoid forming a point on the iced surface which would spoil the appearance of the piped rosette.

To pipe a shell border: Use either a star nozzle or a special shell nozzle; a shell nozzle will give a flatter, fuller shell with more ridges. In either case the movement is the same. Hold the bag at an angle to the surface and just above it. Squeeze until the icing begins to come from the nozzle and forms a head. Pull the bag gently and at the same time release

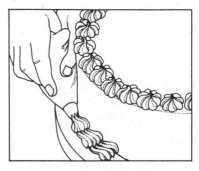

pressure to form the tail. Pipe the next shell just touching, and remember to release pressure each time to form the tail of the shell.

Writing: Use a plain writing nozzle and pipe as for a straight line (see left). Practise with simple capital letters at first. Before attempting to write on the cake, draw the letters on greaseproof paper and prick them on to the base icing with a pin; use the pin pricks as a guide. For fancier writing, magazines provide a useful source of stylised lettering.

To pipe a rose: Place a little icing on the top of an icing nail and stick a small square of non-stick paper on top. Fit the piping bag with a petal nozzle. Hold the bag with the thin part of the nozzle uppermost. Pipe a cone of icing, twisting the nail between thumb and finger, to form the centre of the rose. Pipe 5 or 6 petals around the centre, overlapping each petal and piping the outer ones so that they are more open, and lie flatter. Lift the square of paper from the nail and leave the rose uncovered for about 24 hours to dry. Attach it to the cake with a dab of icing.

DECORATING A CHRISTMAS CAKE

Christmas is a family occasion, so there's no need for an elaborate cake—keep it as simple as possible. Make the cake itself well in advance to give the flavour time to mature, and dose it with brandy from time to time.

Rough icing, to give the effect of snow, is a favourite choice for Christmas cakes, and the technique is simple enough even for a beginner—see the instructions for Festive Christmas Cake (right). Ready-made decorations such as Christmas trees and snowmen traditionally complete the picture, or you could make your own decorations: mould them from coloured almond paste, or shape them in tinted royal icing.

If you want something just a little more stylish try our Christmas Rosette Cake (right), decorated with ribbons and a candle.

Aim to complete the decorating about a week before Christmas. Once iced, the cake will keep fresh without an airtight tin, but protect it by covering it with a cake dome or an upturned box.

FESTIVE CHRISTMAS CAKE

Christmas cake (see page 652)

apricot glaze (see page 662)

550 g (1¼ lb) almond paste (see page 663)

700 g (1½ lb) royal icing (see page 663)

ribbon and Christmas cake decorations such as Santa Claus, snowmen, robins, reindeer or Christmas trees, to finish

1 14–20 days before required, place the cake on a 23-cm (9-inch) cake board. Brush with apricot glaze and cover with almond paste (see page 664). Loosely cover the cake and store in a cool dry place for 4–5 days.

2 Using the royal icing, roughly flat ice the top sides of the cake (see page 664). Leave to dry for 24 hours.

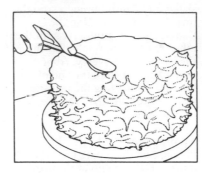

3 Spoon the remaining icing on top of the flat icing and roughly smooth it over with a palette knife. Using the palette knife or the back of a teaspoon, pull the icing in to well formed peaks.

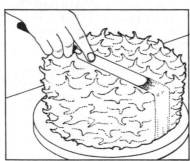

4 Using a palette knife, smooth a path down the centre of the top and side of the cake. Leave to dry for about 24 hours.

5 Place a piece of ribbon along the pathway, securing the ends with pins. Arrange the decorations on top, securing them if necessary with little dabs of fresh icing.

CHRISTMAS ROSETTE CAKE

Christmas cake (see page 652)

apricot glaze (see page 662)

550 g (1¼ lb) almond paste (see page 663)

700 g (1½ lb) royal icing (see page 663)

narrow red and green ribbons, a red candle and wide red ribbon, to finish

1 14–20 days before required, place the cake on a 23-cm (9-inch) cake board. Brush with apricot glaze and cover with almond paste (see page 664). Loosely cover the cake and store in a cool dry place for 4–5 days.

2 Using the royal icing, flat ice the top and sides of the cake. Leave to dry for about 24 hours.

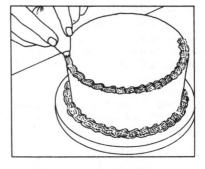

3 Using a piping bag fitted with an eight point star nozzle, pipe a shell border round the top edge. Pipe a shell border around the bottom edge.

4 Make a ribbon rosette with the narrow ribbons. Cut 3 longer pieces of green ribbon and 3 of red and arrange on top of the cake to form a star shape. Fix the ribbons and rosette in place with a little icing. Stand the candle firmly in the centre of the rosette. Place the wide ribbon round the cake and secure with a pin. Lay the narrow green ribbon over the wide ribbon, making sure it is central, then secure.

INDEX